EASY PIANO

THE BEST HYMNS EVER

ISBN 0-634-08063-6

7777 W. Bluemound Rd. P.O. Box 13819 Milwaukee, WI 53213

Visit Hal Leonard Online at
www.halleonard.com

CONTENTS

ABIDE WITH ME

Words by HENRY F. LYTE
Music by WILLIAM H. MONK

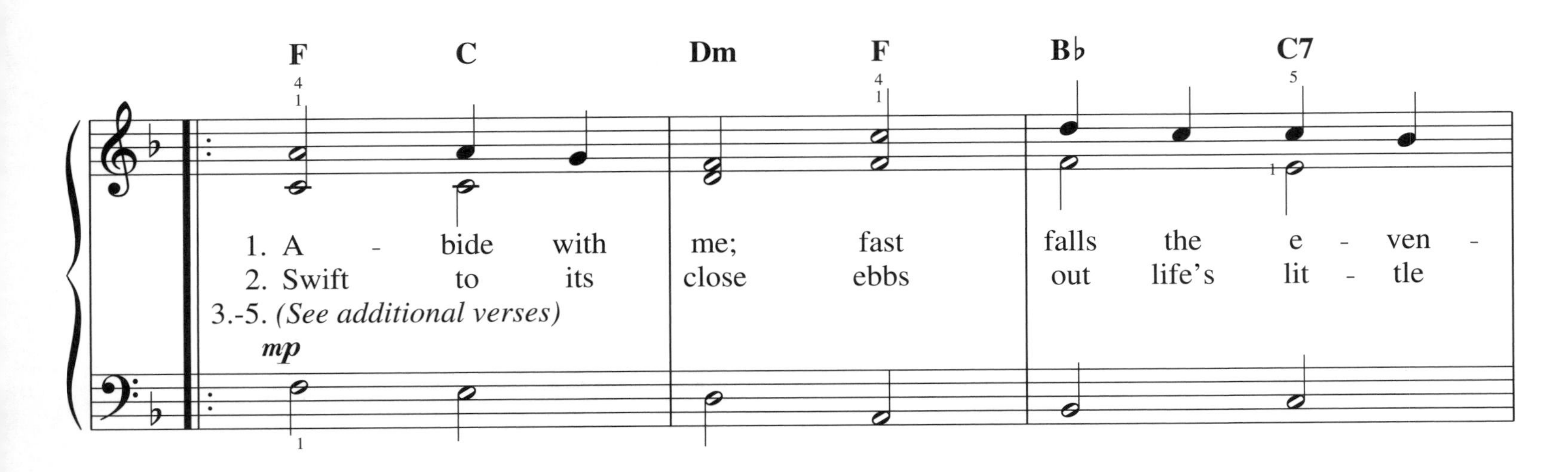

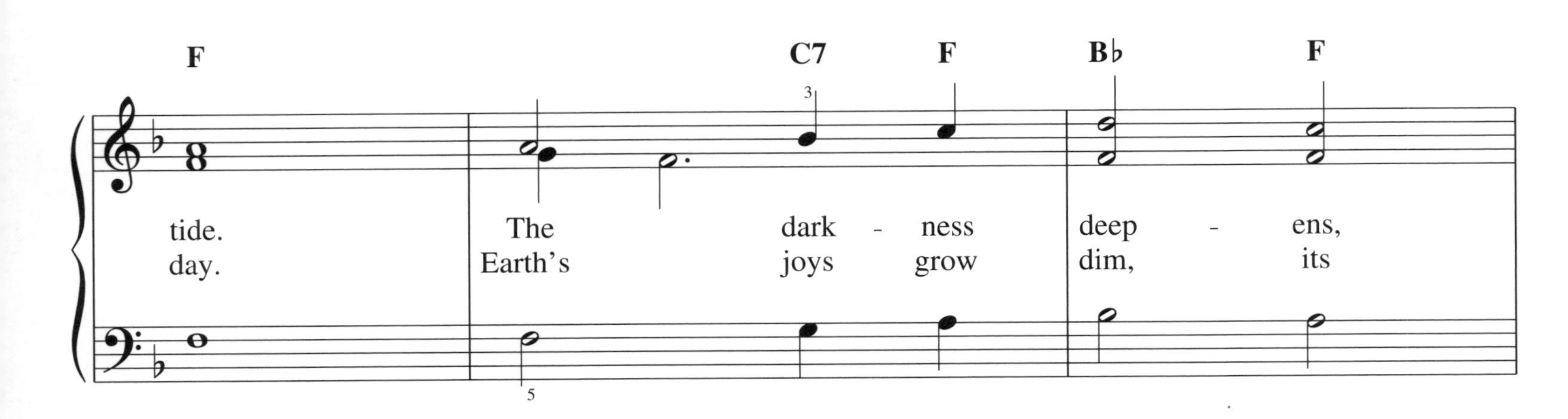

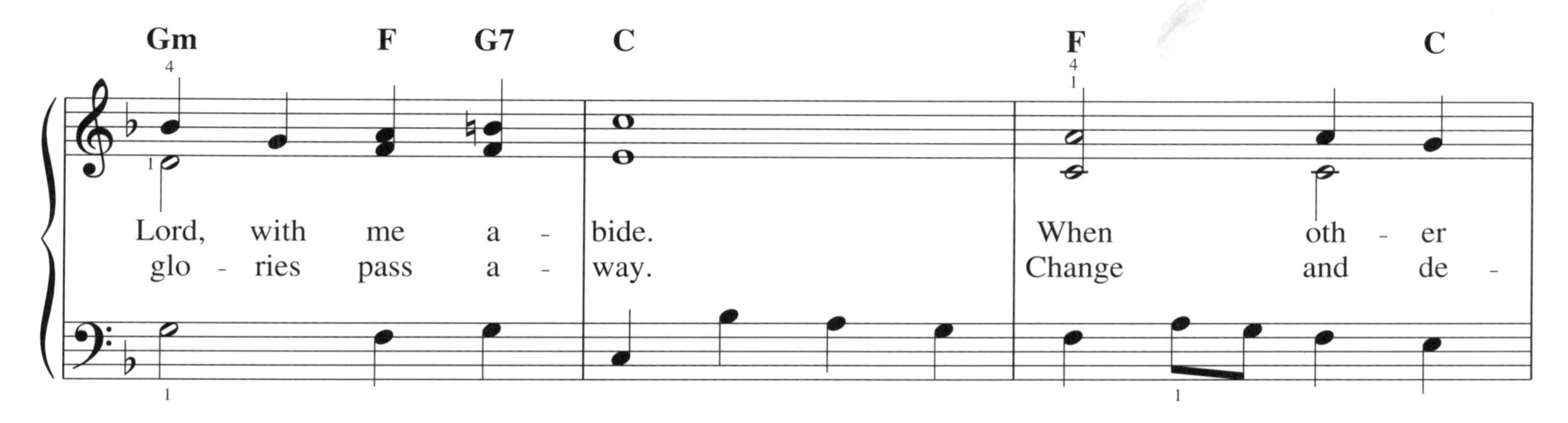

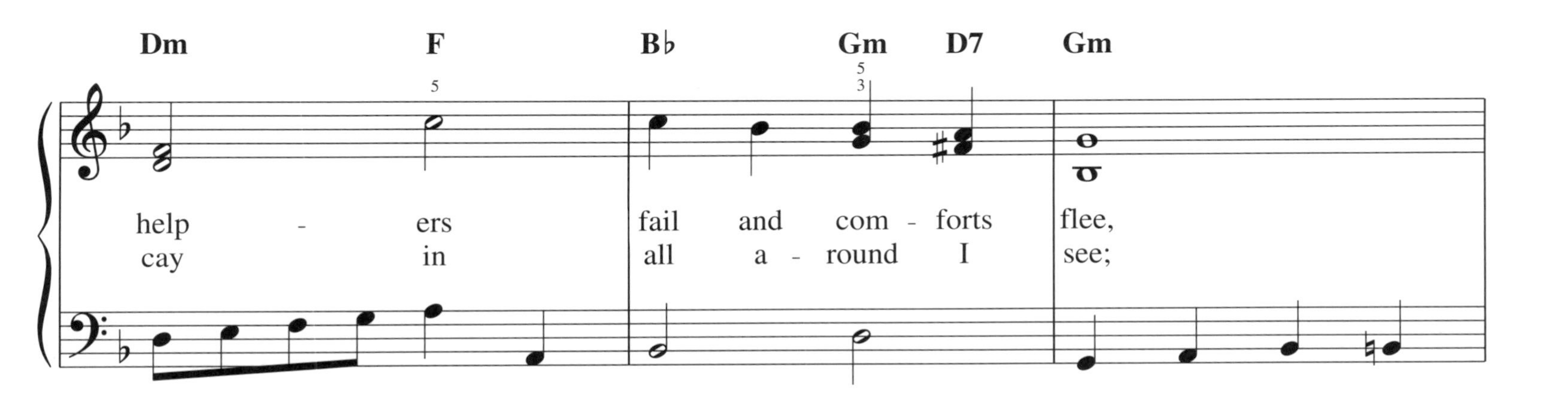

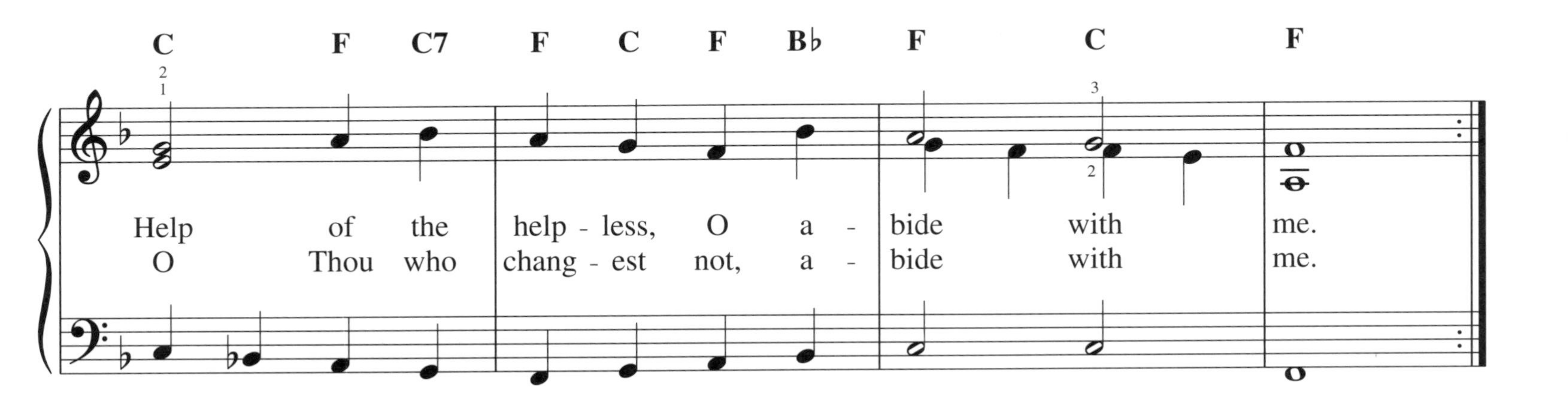

Additional Verses

3. I need Thy presence every passing hour.
   What but Thy grace can foil the tempter's power?
   Who, like Thyself, my guide and stay can be?
   Through cloud and sunshine, Lord, abide with me.

4. I fear no foe, with Thee at hand to bless;
   Ills have no weight, and tears no bitterness.
   Where is death's sting? Where, grave, thy victory?
   I triumph still, if Thou abide with me.

5. Hold Thou Thy cross before my closing eyes;
   Shine through the gloom and point me to the skies.
   Heaven's morning breaks, and earth's vain shadows flee;
   In life, in death, O Lord, abide with me.

ALAS, AND DID MY SAVIOR BLEED

Words by ISAAC WATTS
Music by HUGH WILSON

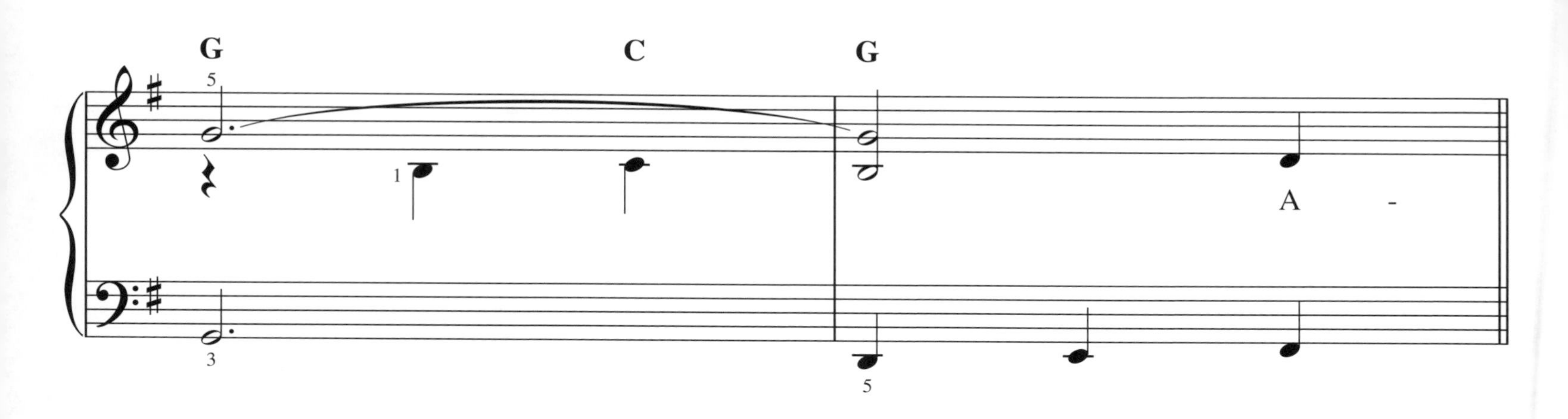

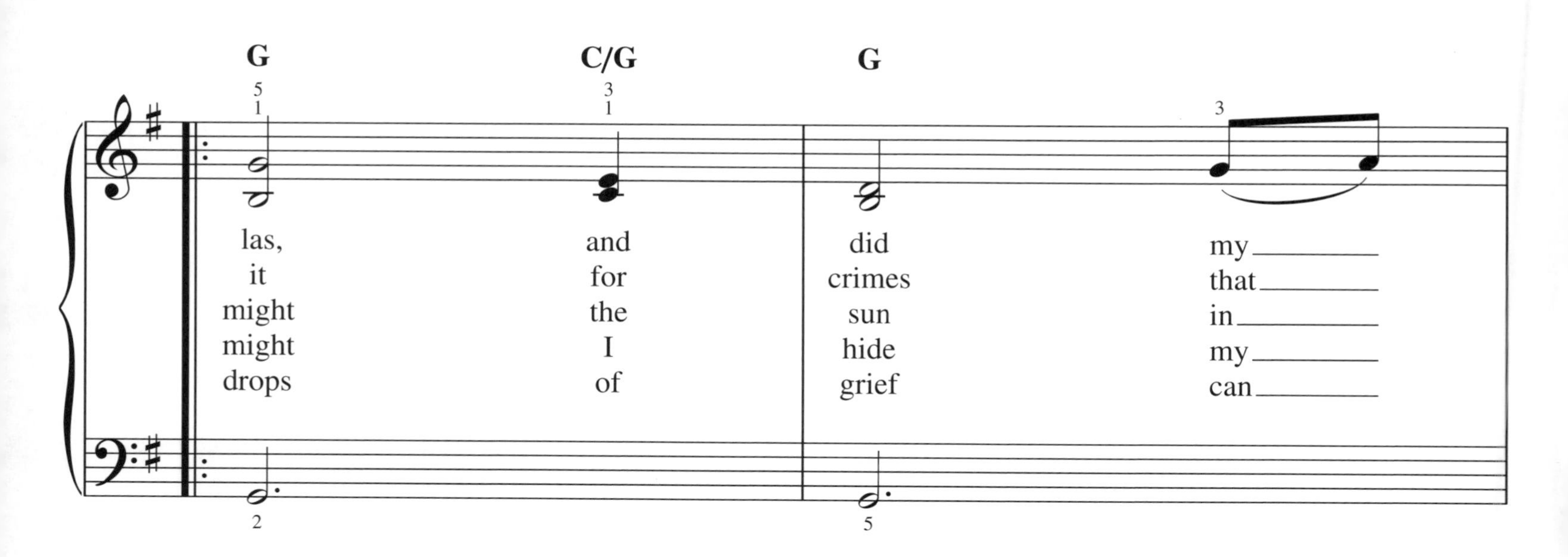

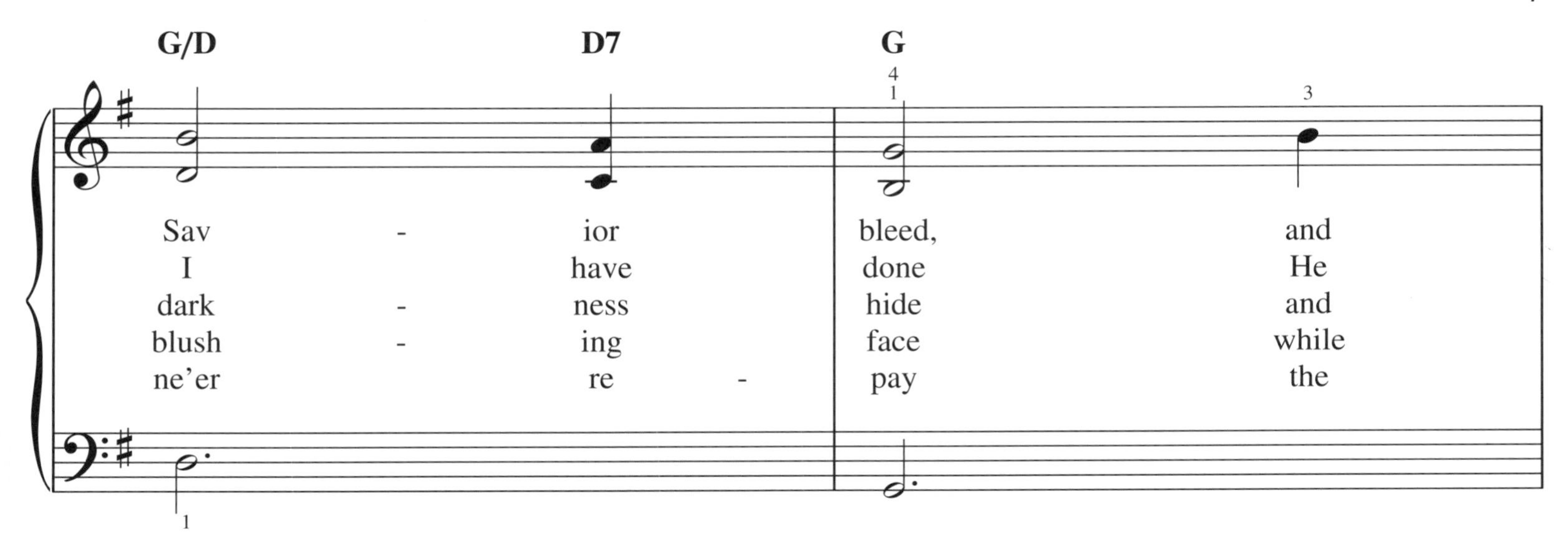
G/D
D7
G
Sav - ior bleed, and
I have done He
dark - ness hide and
blush - ing face while
ne'er re - pay the

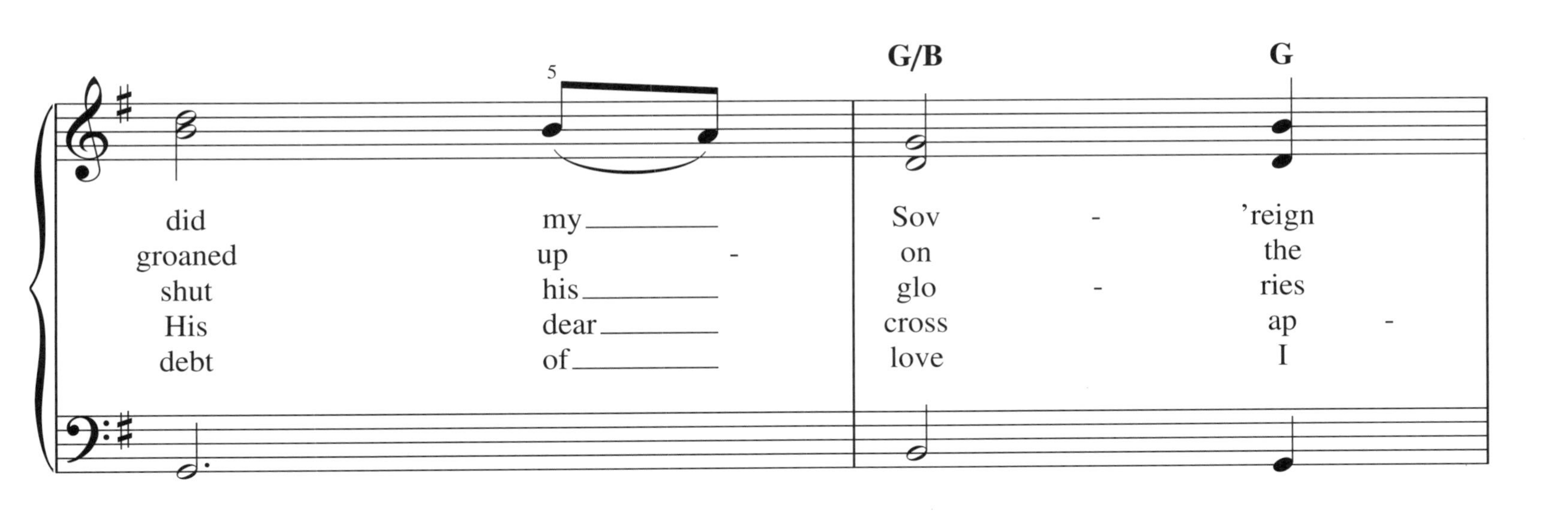
G/B
G
did my Sov - 'reign
groaned up - on the
shut his glo - ries
His dear cross ap -
debt of love I

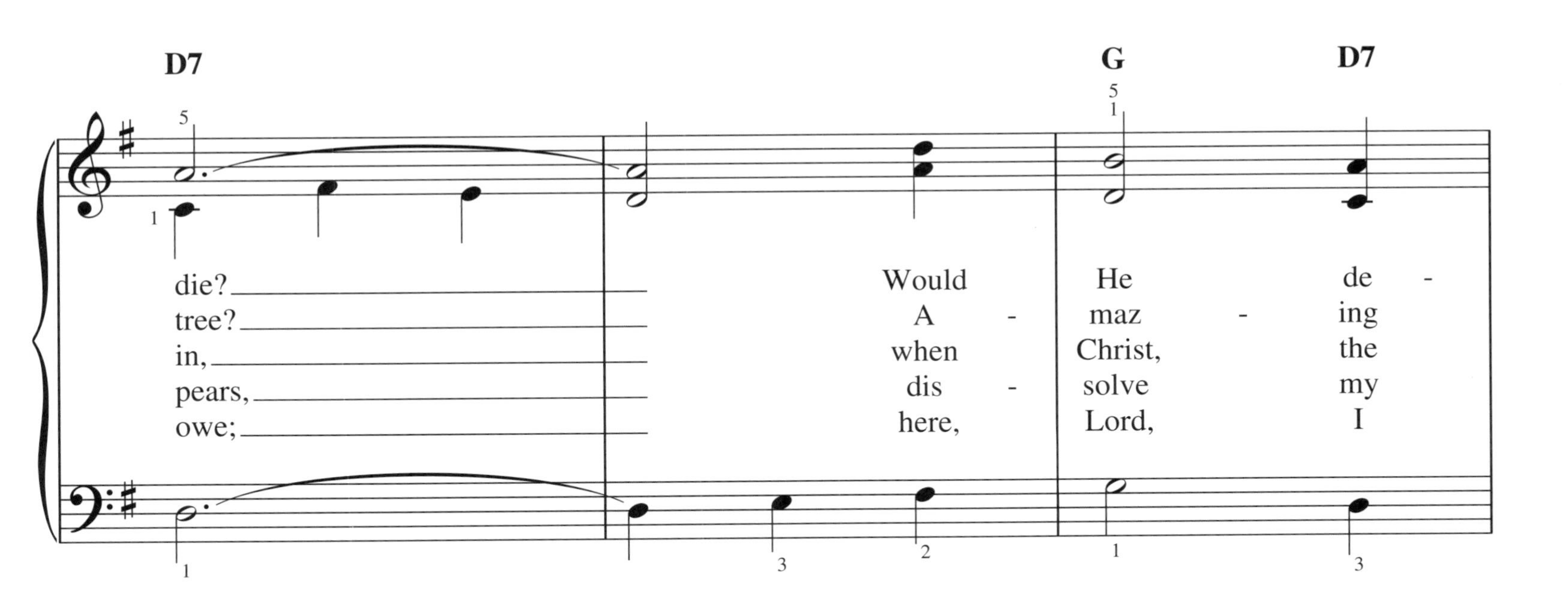
D7
G
D7
die? Would He de -
tree? A - maz - ing
in, when Christ, the
pears, dis - solve my
owe; here, Lord, I

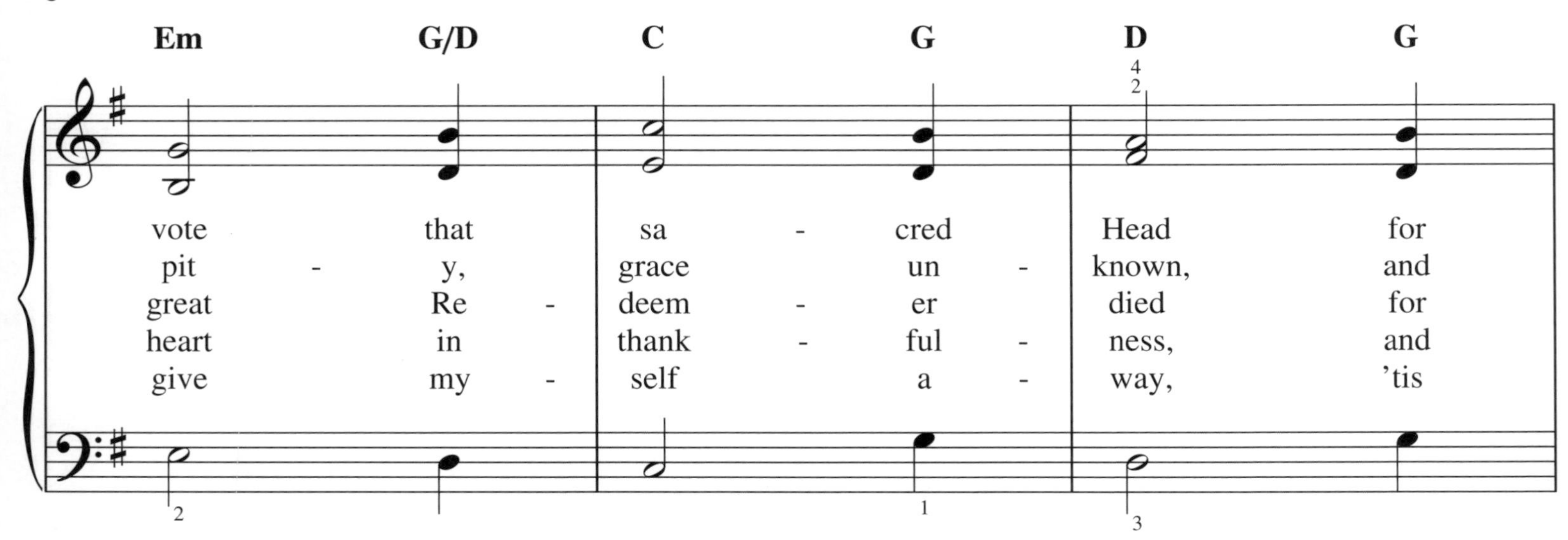
Em G/D C G D G
vote that sa - cred Head for
pit - y, grace un - known, and
great Re - deem - er died for
heart in thank - ful - ness, and
give my - self a - way, 'tis

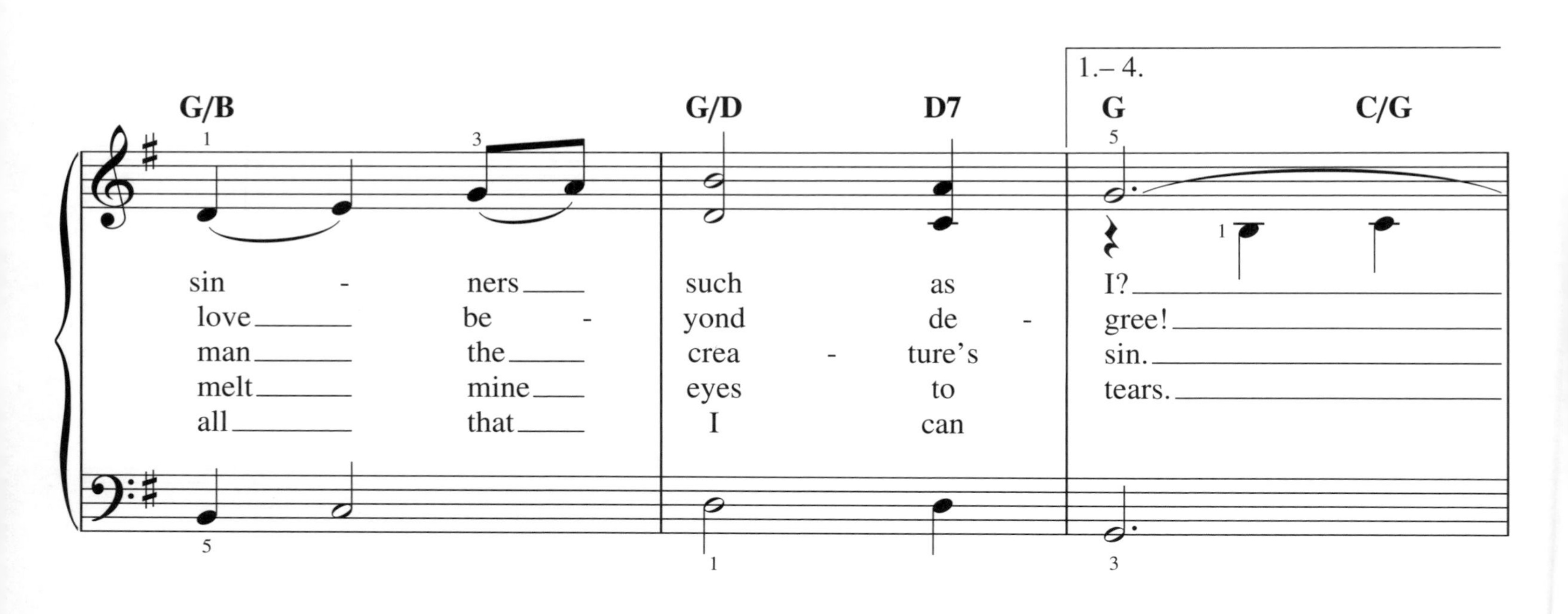
G/B G/D D7
1.– 4.
G C/G
sin - ners such as I?
love be - yond de - gree!
man the crea - ture's sin.
melt mine eyes to tears.
all that I can

G
5.
G C/G G
Was
Well
Thus
But
do.

AMAZING GRACE

Words by JOHN NEWTON
Traditional American Melody

Gsus G Em G/D D7 G C
found, was blind, but now I see.
far, and grace will lead me home.
G G7 C
'Twas grace that taught my heart to
The Lord has prom - ised good to
G
fear and grace my fears re -
me, His word my hope se -
D G G7
lieved. How pre - cious did that
cures. He will my shield and

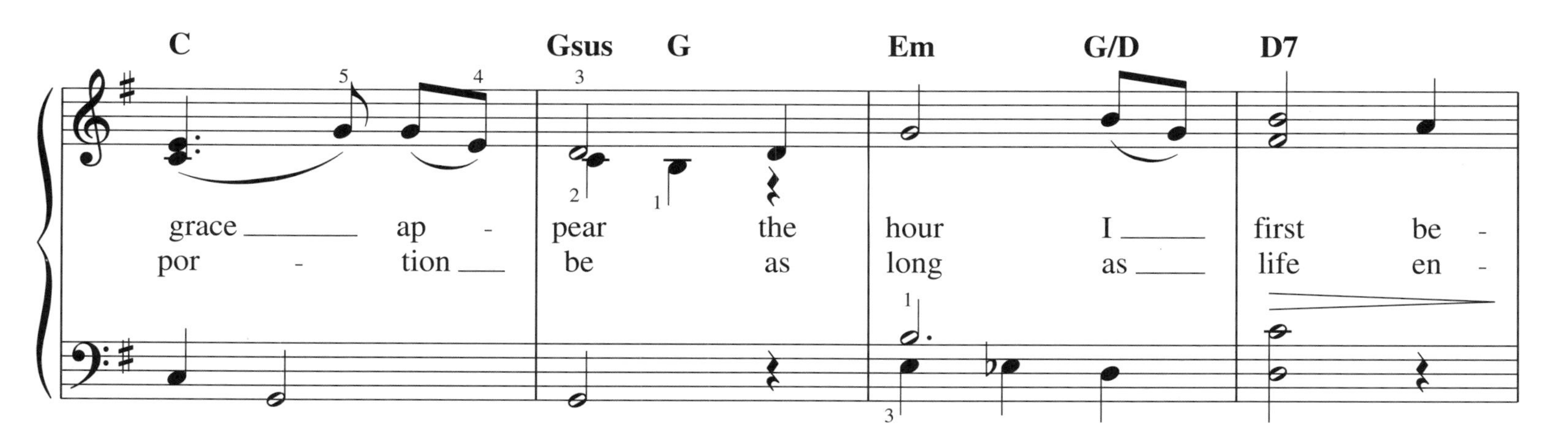

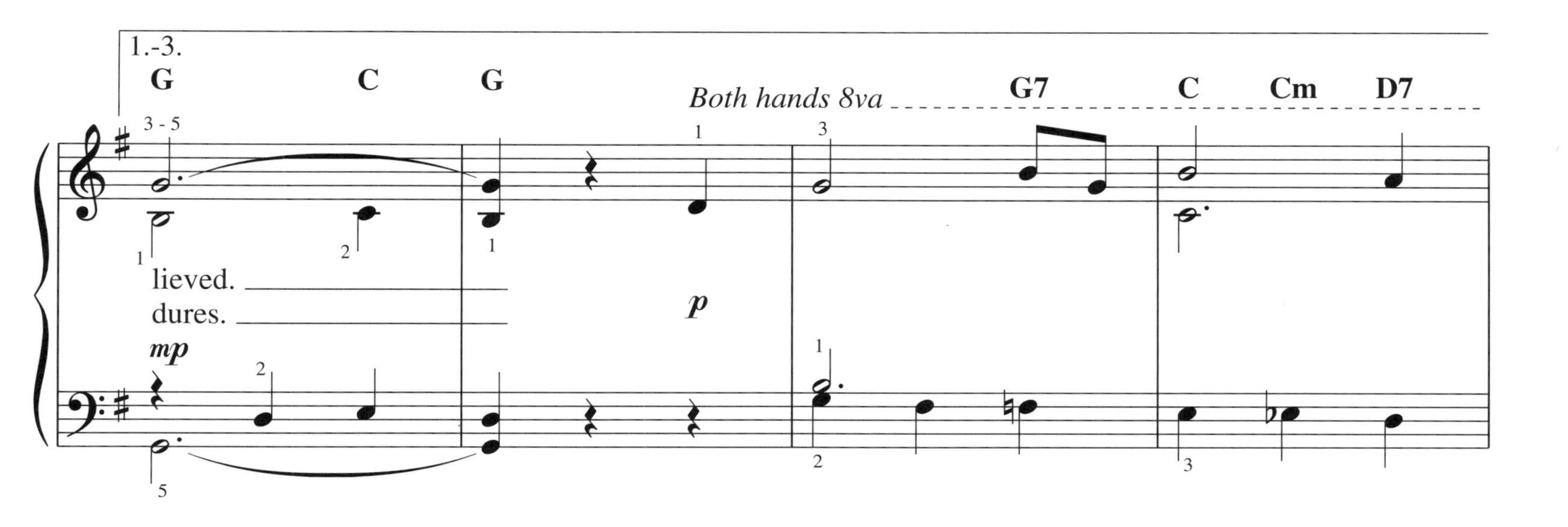

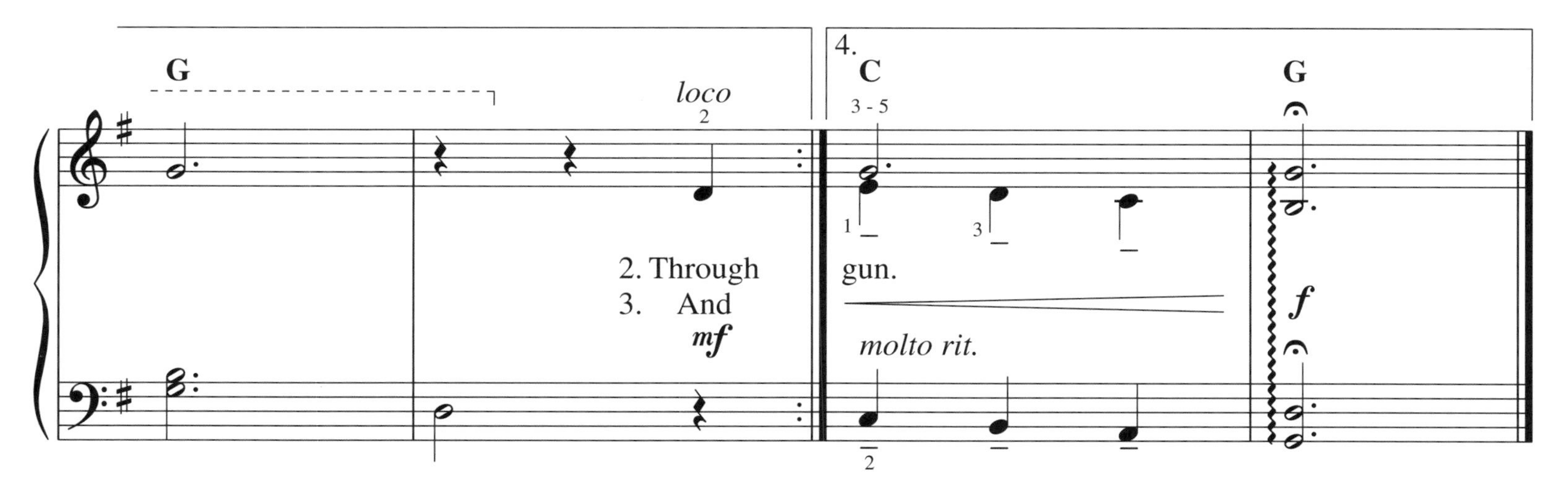

Additional Verses

3. And when this flesh and heart shall fail
   And mortal life shall cease,
   I shall possess within the veil
   A life of joy and peace.

4. When we've been there ten thousand years,
   Bright shining as the sun,
   We've no less days to sing God's praise
   Than when we first begun.

ALL CREATURES OF OUR GOD AND KING

Words by FRANCIS OF ASSISI
Translated by WILLIAM HENRY DRAPER
Music from *Geistliche Kirchengesang*

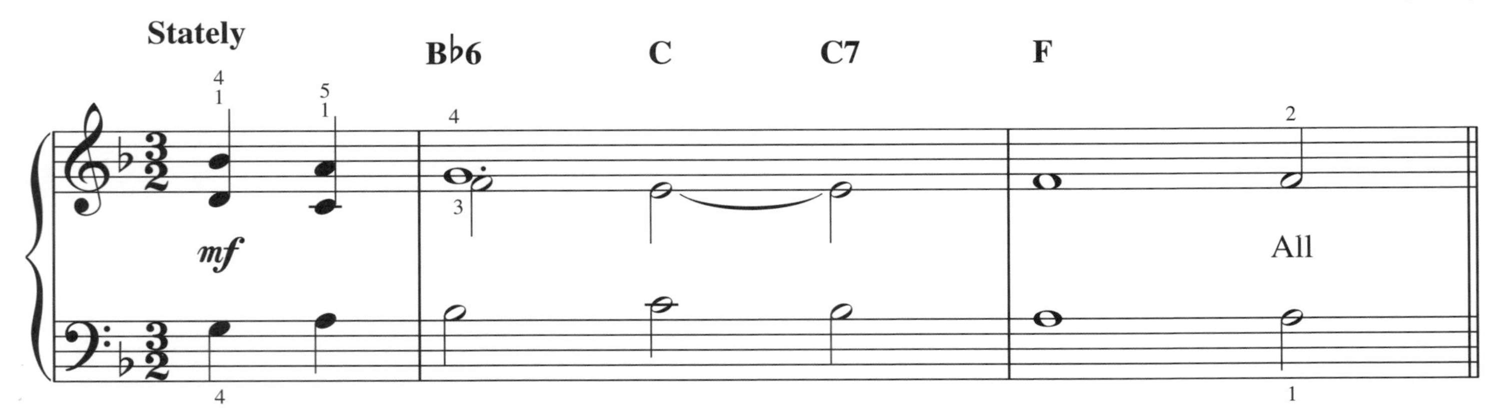

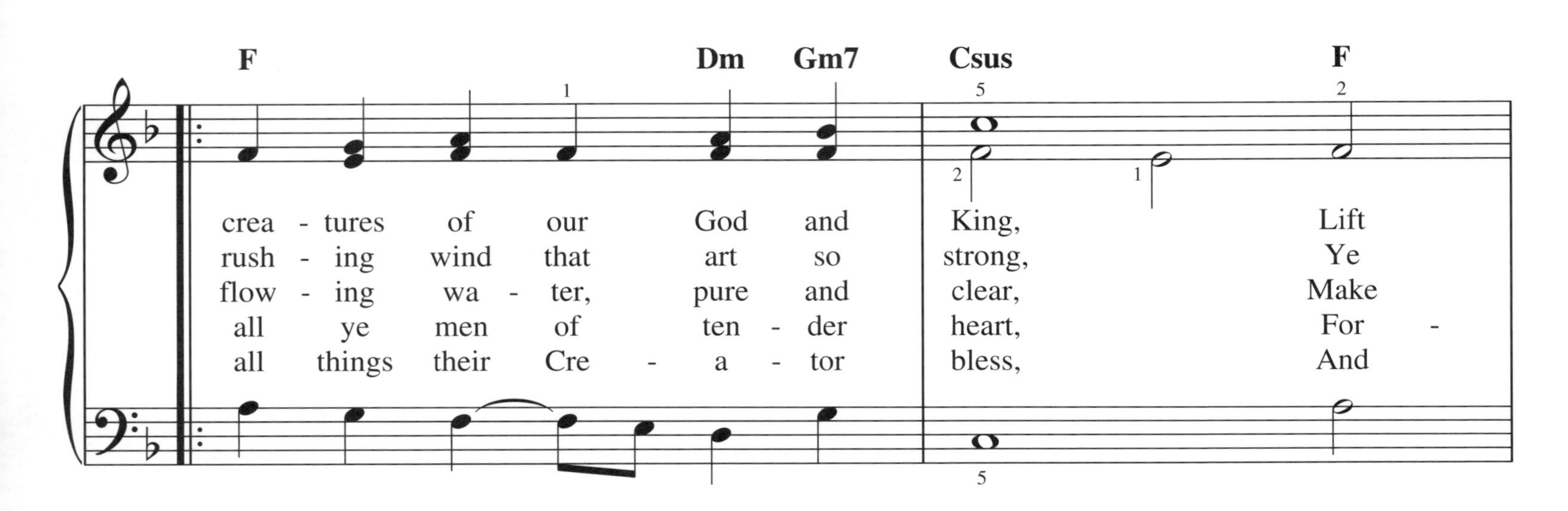

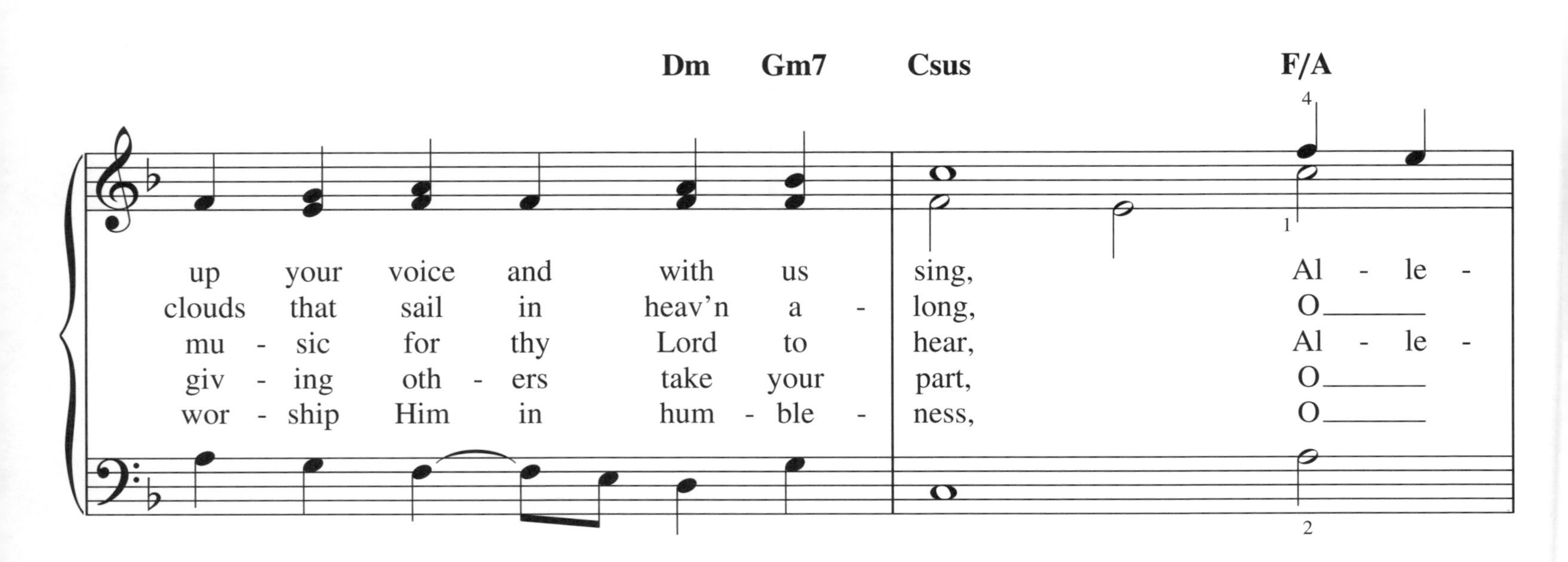

B♭ F Dm C/E F G C F/A F B♭/D
lu - ia! Al - le - lu - ia! Thou burn - ing sun with gold - en
praise Him! Al - le - lu - ia! Thou ris - ing morn, in praise re -
lu - ia! Al - le - lu - ia! Thou fire so mas - ter - ful and
sing ye! Al - le - lu - ia! Ye who long pain and sor - row
sing ye! Al - le - lu - ia! Praise, praise the Fa - ther, praise the
Csus F/A F B♭/D F B♭
beam, Thou sil - ver moon with soft - er gleam,
joice; Ye lights of eve - ning, find a voice!
bright, That giv - est man both warmth and light, O
bear, Praise God and on Him cast your care!
Son, And praise the Spir - it, Three in One!
Csus/B♭ F/A Gm F/A Csus/B♭ Dm C/E F G C Dm C/E
praise Him! O praise Him! Al - le - lu - ia! Al - le -
F Gm C/E D/F♯ Gm F/A B♭6 C C7
1.– 4. F
5. F
lu - ia! Al - le - lu - ia!
Thou
Thou
And
Let
ia!

ALL GLORY, LAUD AND HONOR

Words by THEODULPH OF ORLEANS
Translated by JOHN MASON NEALE
Music by MELCHIOR TESCHNER

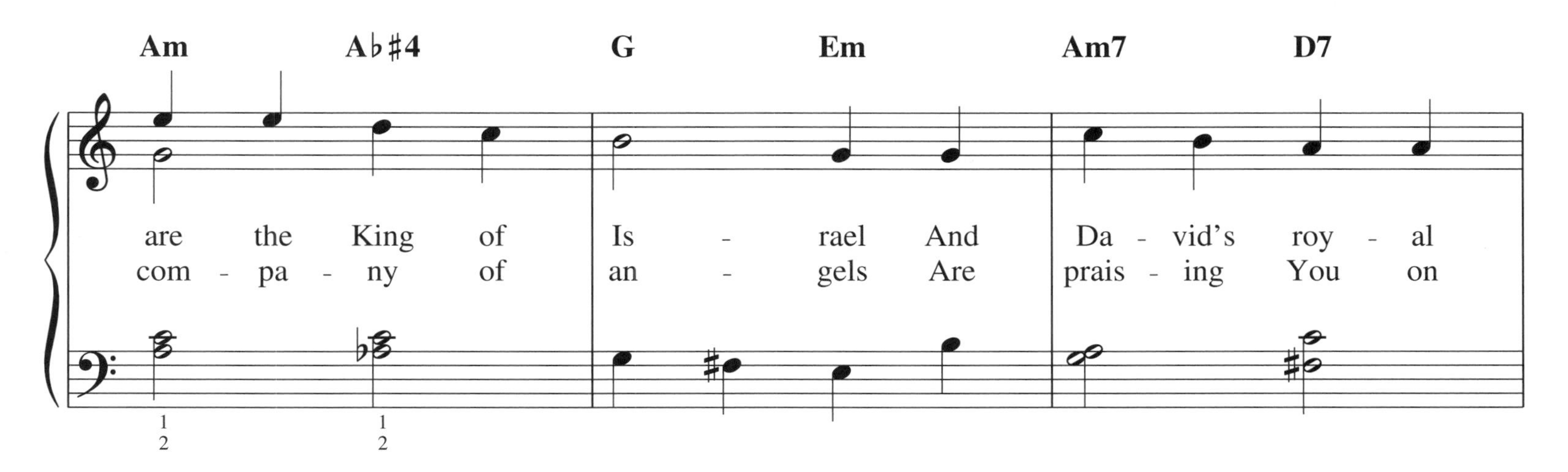

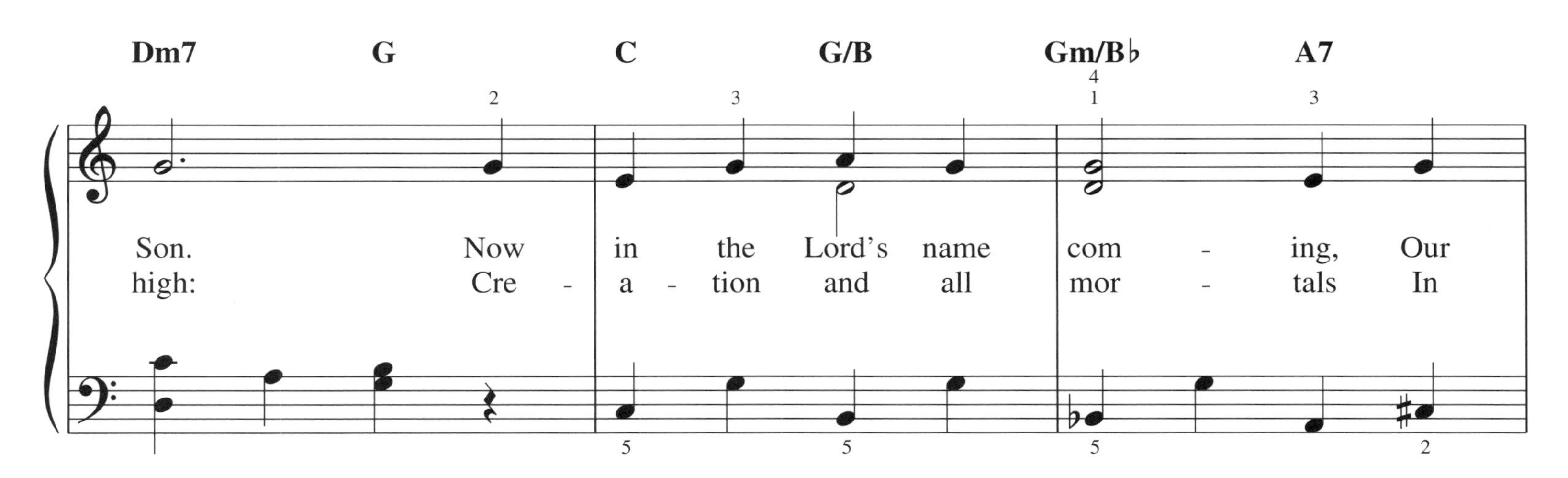

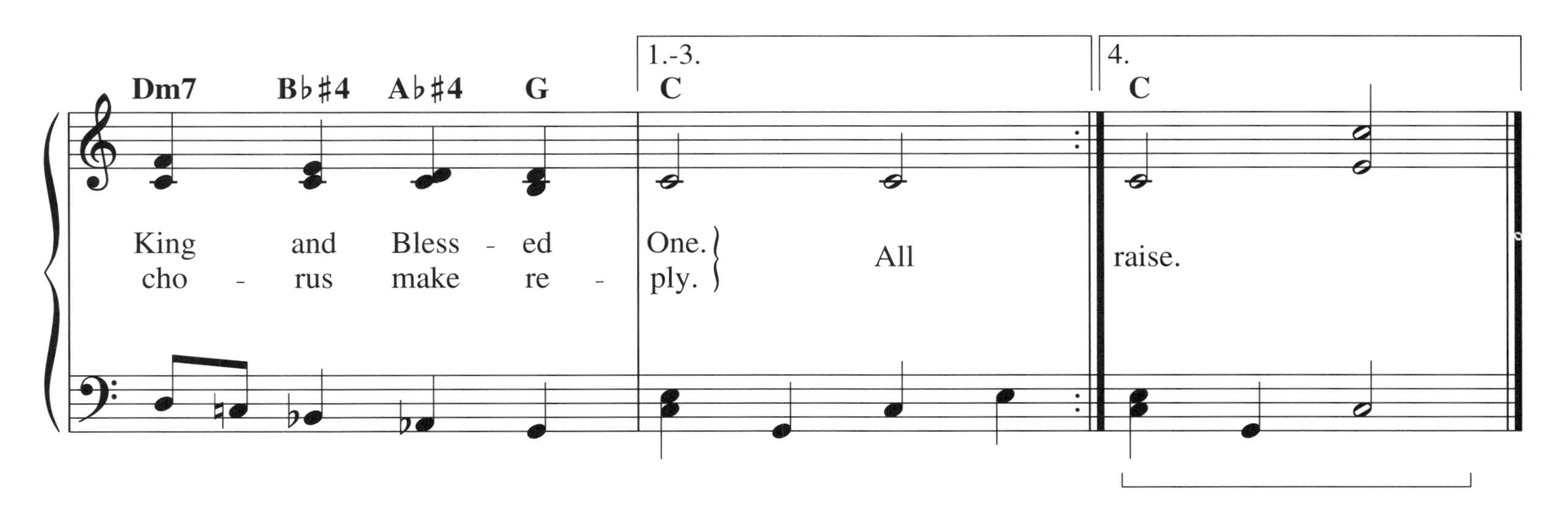

Additional Verses

3. The multitude of pilgrims
   With palms before You went.
   Our praise and prayer and anthems
   Before You we present.
   Refrain:

4. To You, before Your Passion,
   They sang their hymns of praise.
   To You, now high exalted,
   Our melody we raise.

AMERICA, THE BEAUTIFUL

Words by KATHERINE LEE BATES
Music by SAMUEL A. WARD

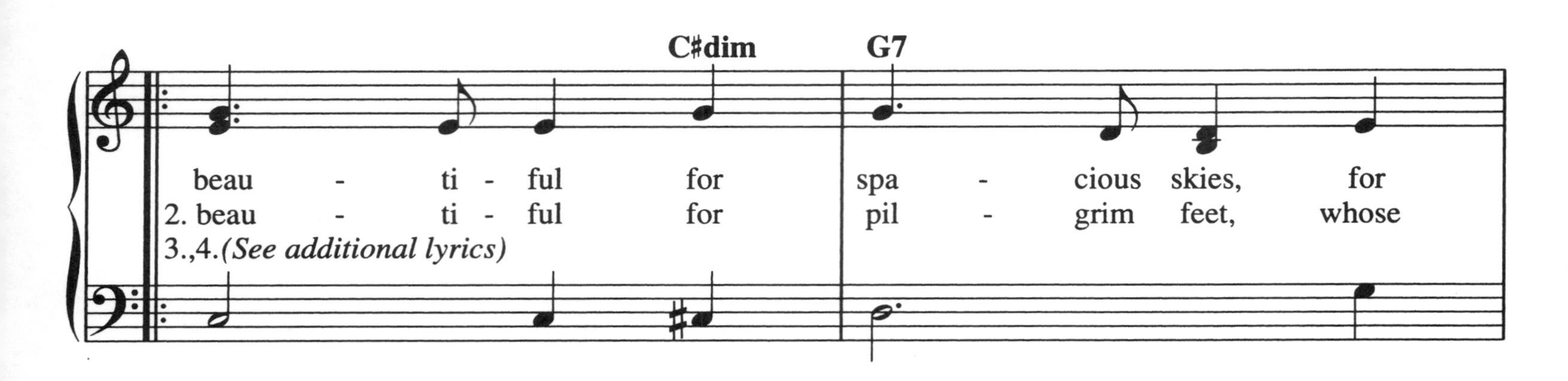

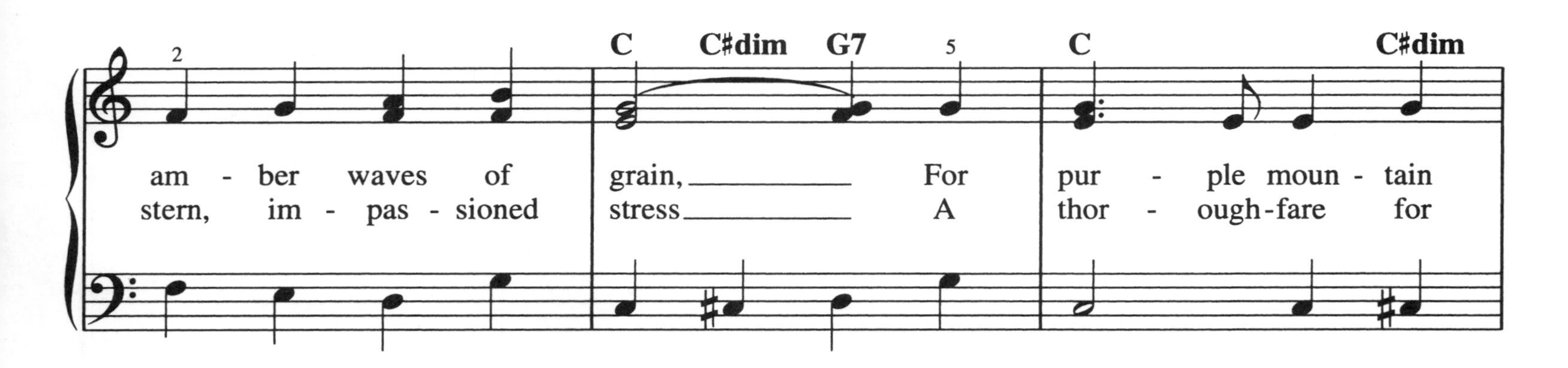

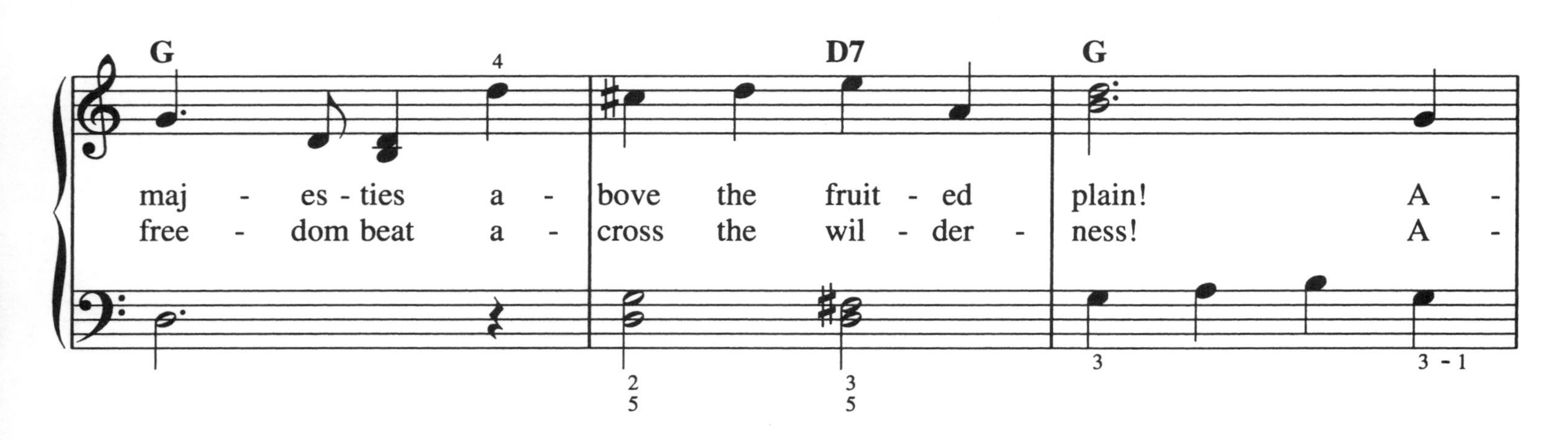

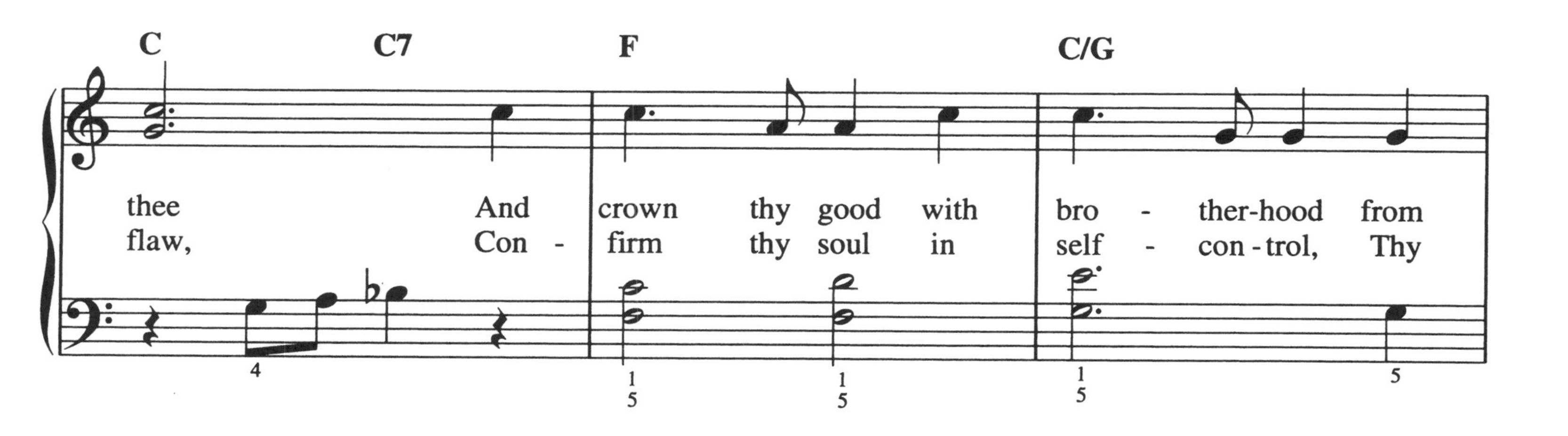

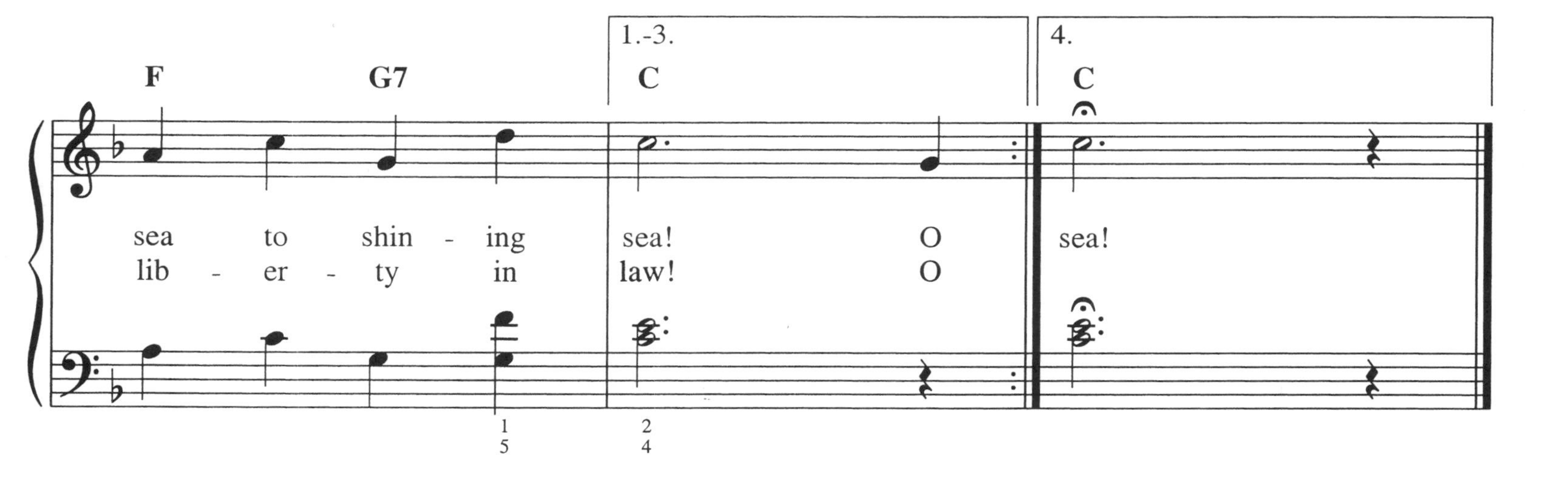

Additional Lyrics

3. O beautiful for heroes proved in liberating strife,
   Who more than self their country loved, and mercy more than life!
   America! America! May God thy gold refine,
   Till all success be nobleness and every gain divine!

4. O beautiful for patriot dream that sees beyond the years
   Thine alabaster cities gleam undimmed by human tears!
   America! America! God shed His grace on thee,
   And crown thy good with brotherhood from sea to shining sea!

AND CAN IT BE THAT I SHOULD GAIN

Words by CHARLES WESLEY
Music by THOMAS CAMPBELL

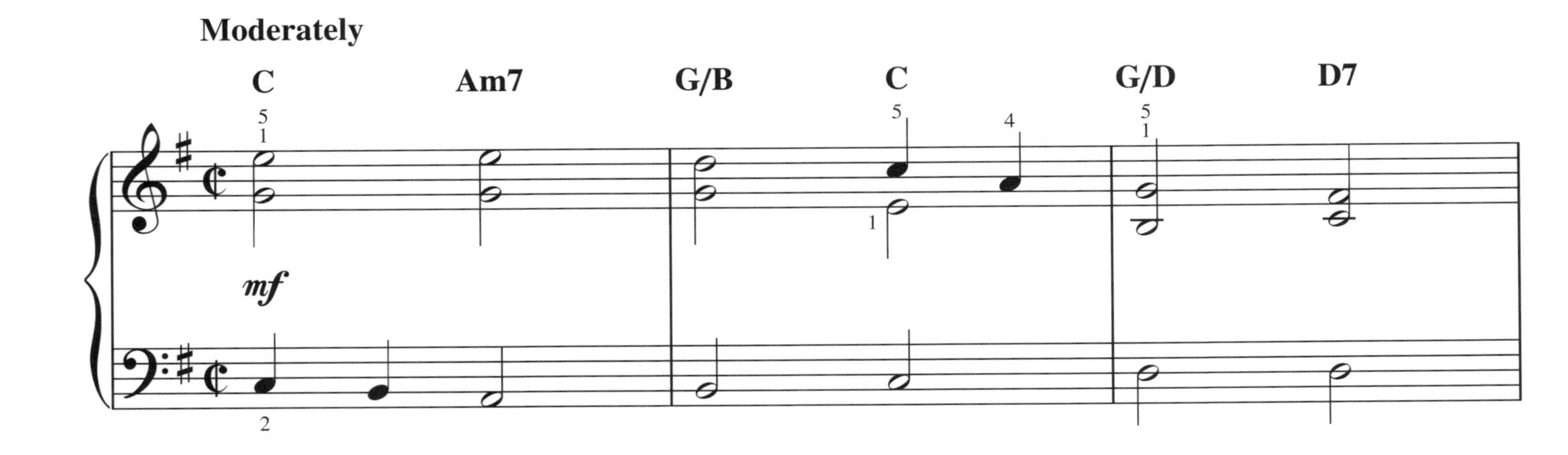

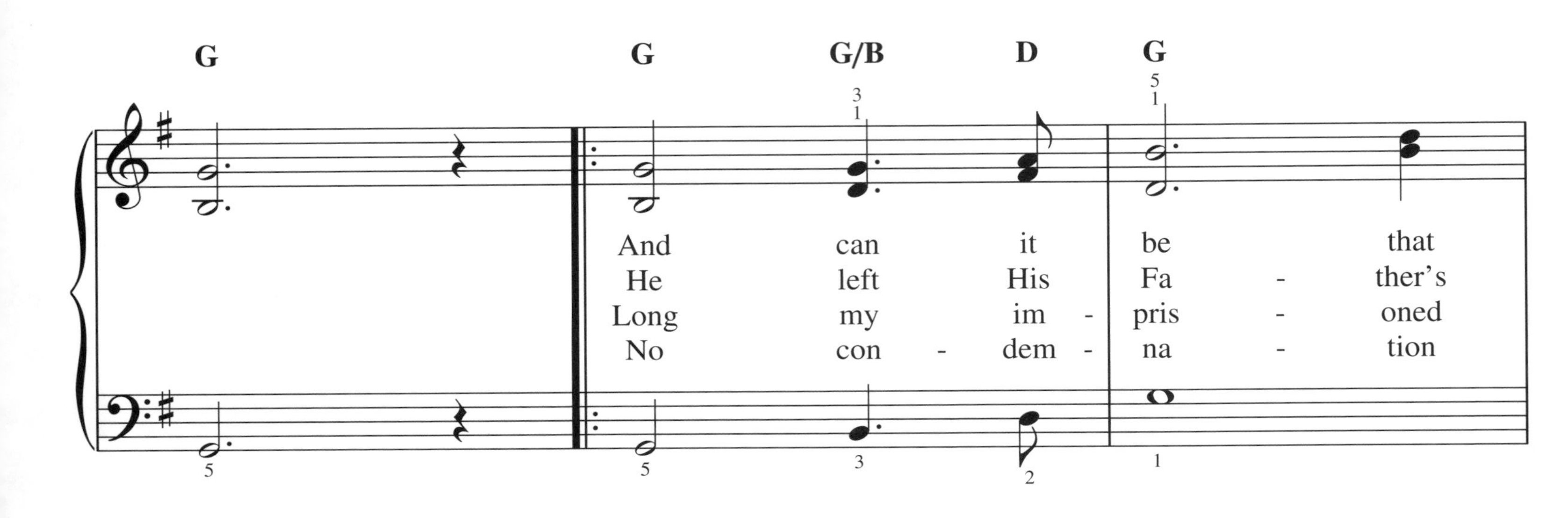

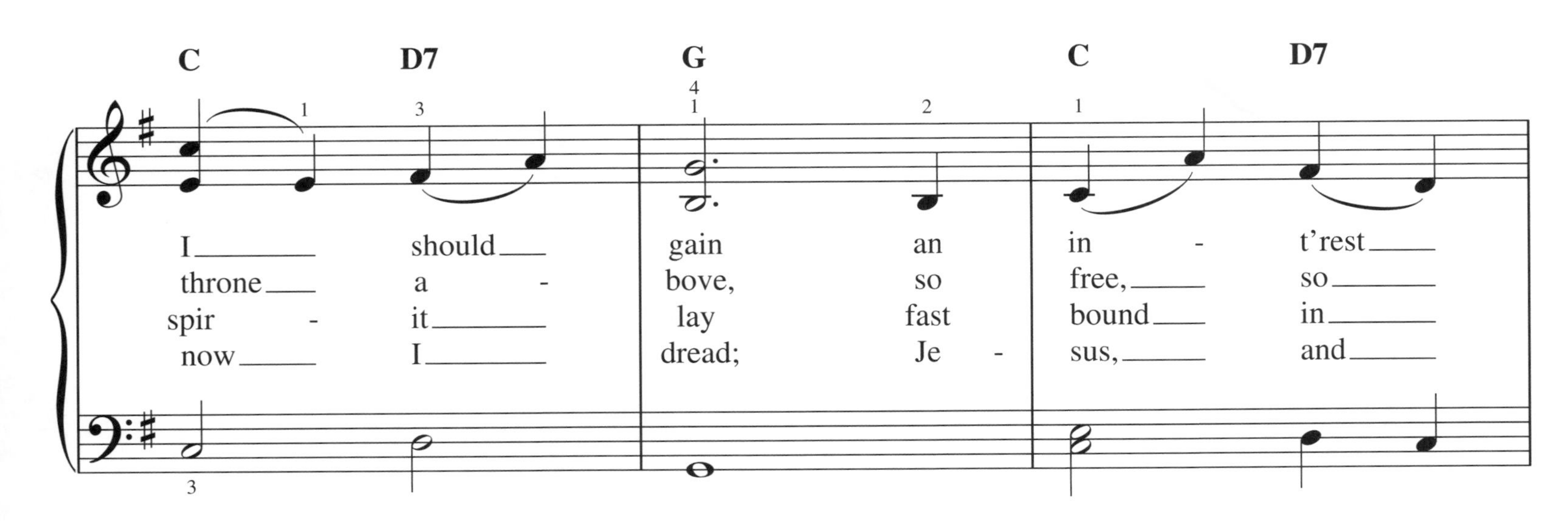

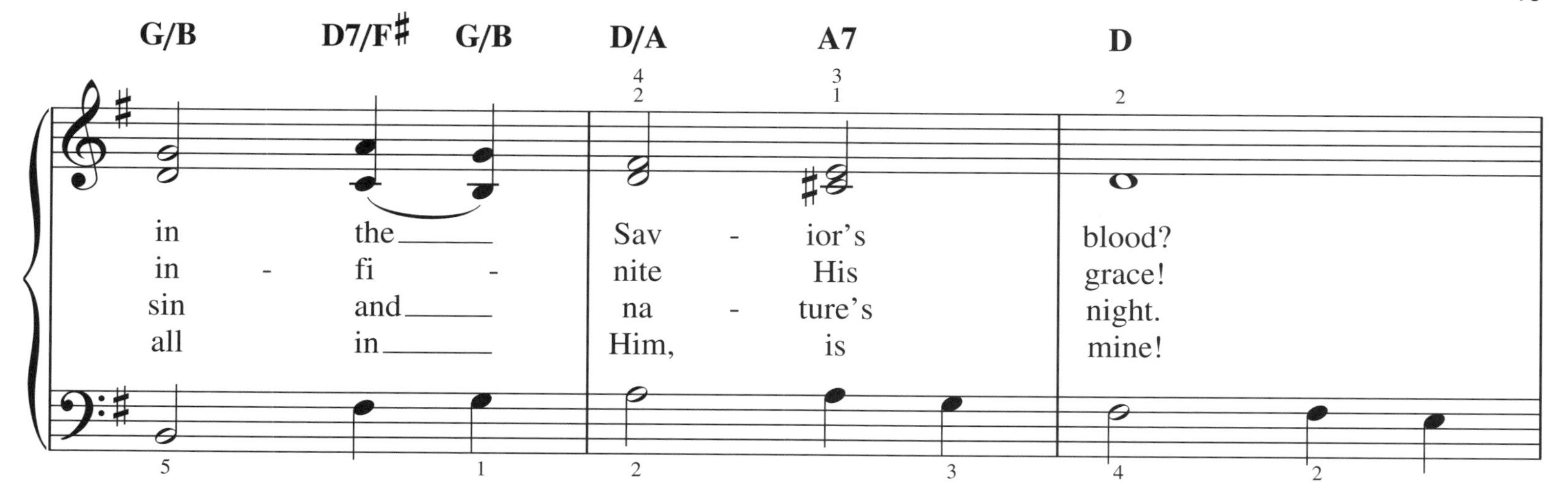
G/B D7/F♯ G/B D/A A7 D
in the Sav - ior's blood?
in - fi - nite His grace!
sin and na - ture's night.
all in Him, is mine!

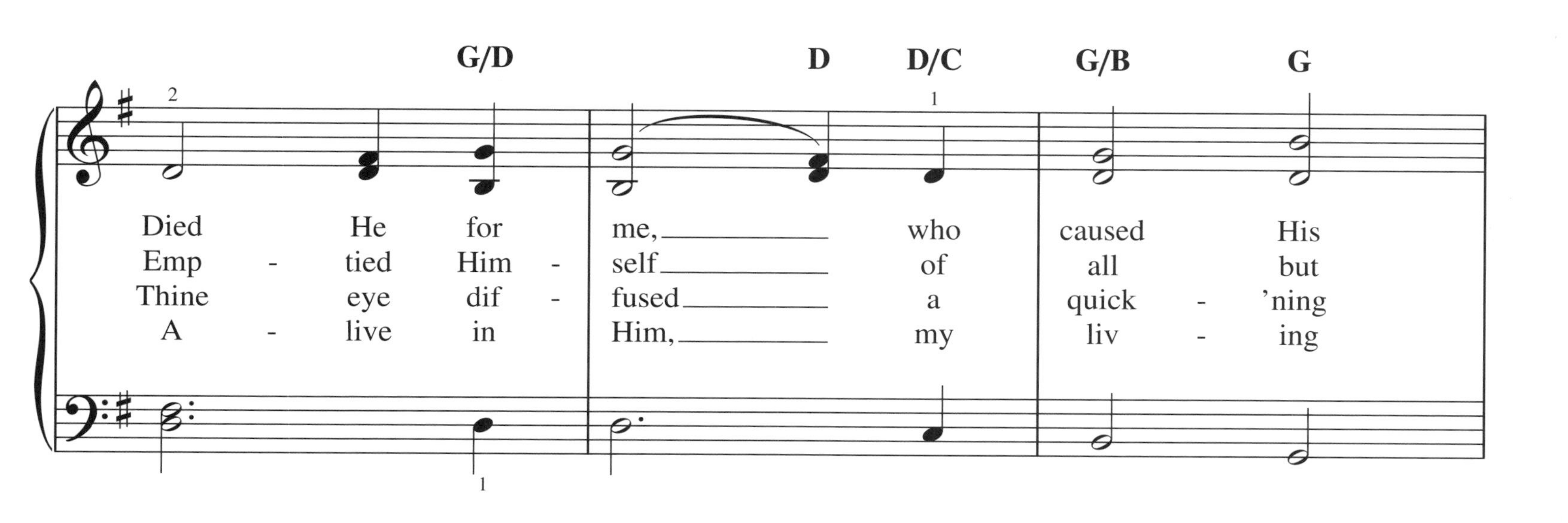
G/D D D/C G/B G
Died He for me, who caused His
Emp - tied Him - self of all but
Thine eye dif - fused a quick - 'ning
A - live in Him, my liv - ing

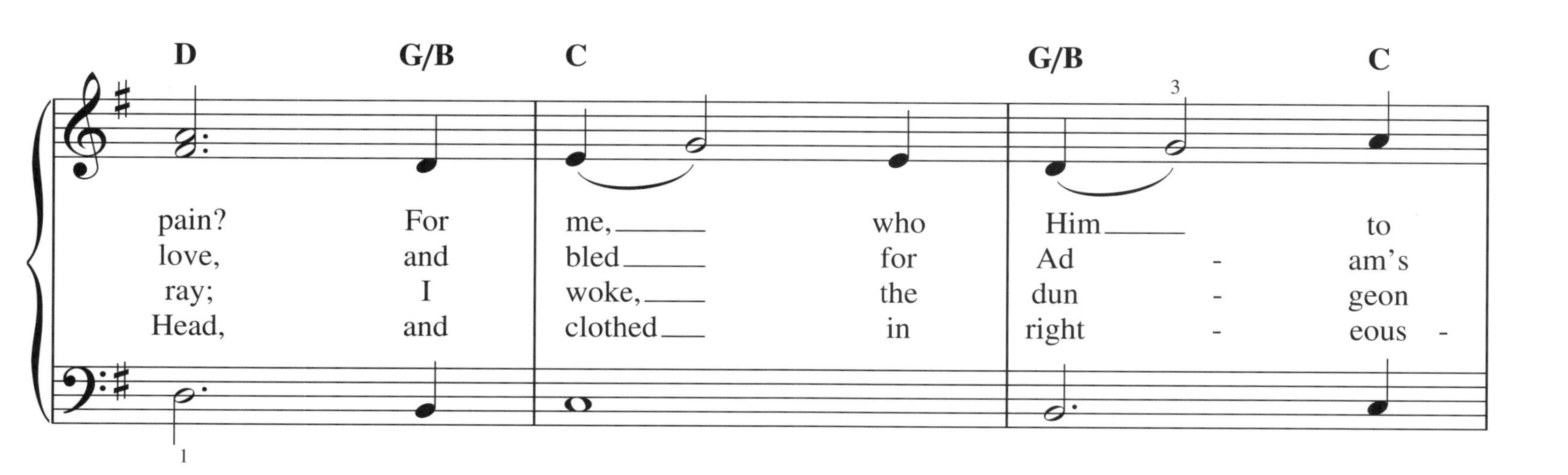
D G/B C G/B C
pain? For me, who Him to
love, and bled for Ad - am's
ray; I woke, the dun - geon
Head, and clothed in right - eous -

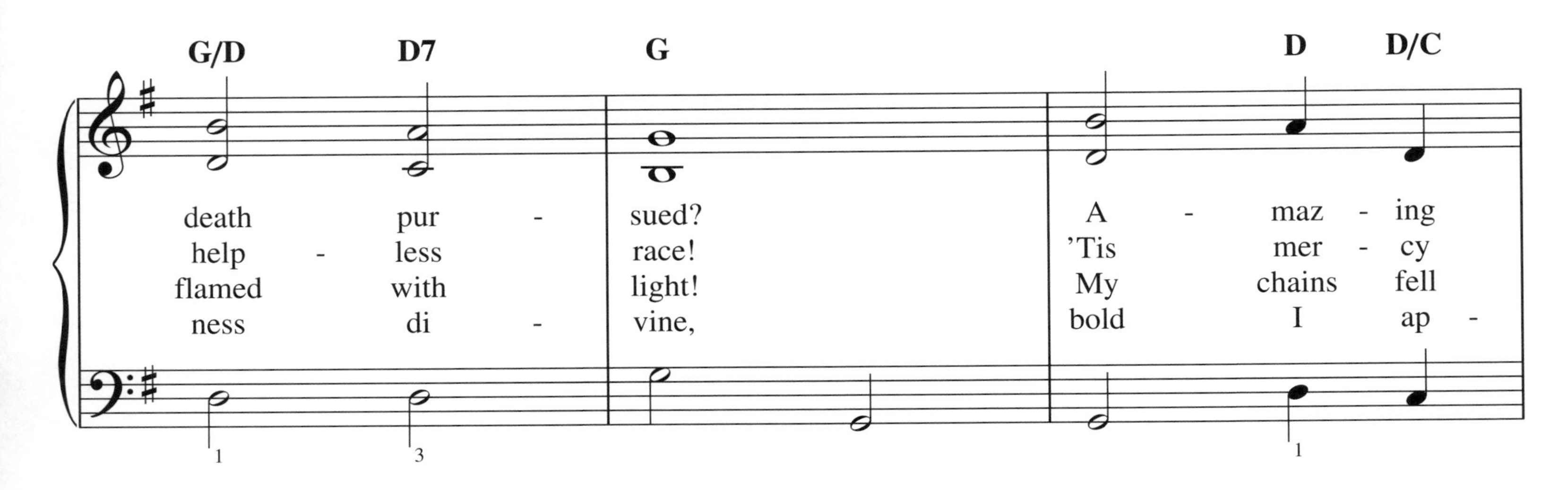
G/D D7 G D D/C
death pur - sued? A - maz - ing
help - less race! 'Tis mer - cy
flamed with light! My chains fell
ness di - vine, bold I ap -

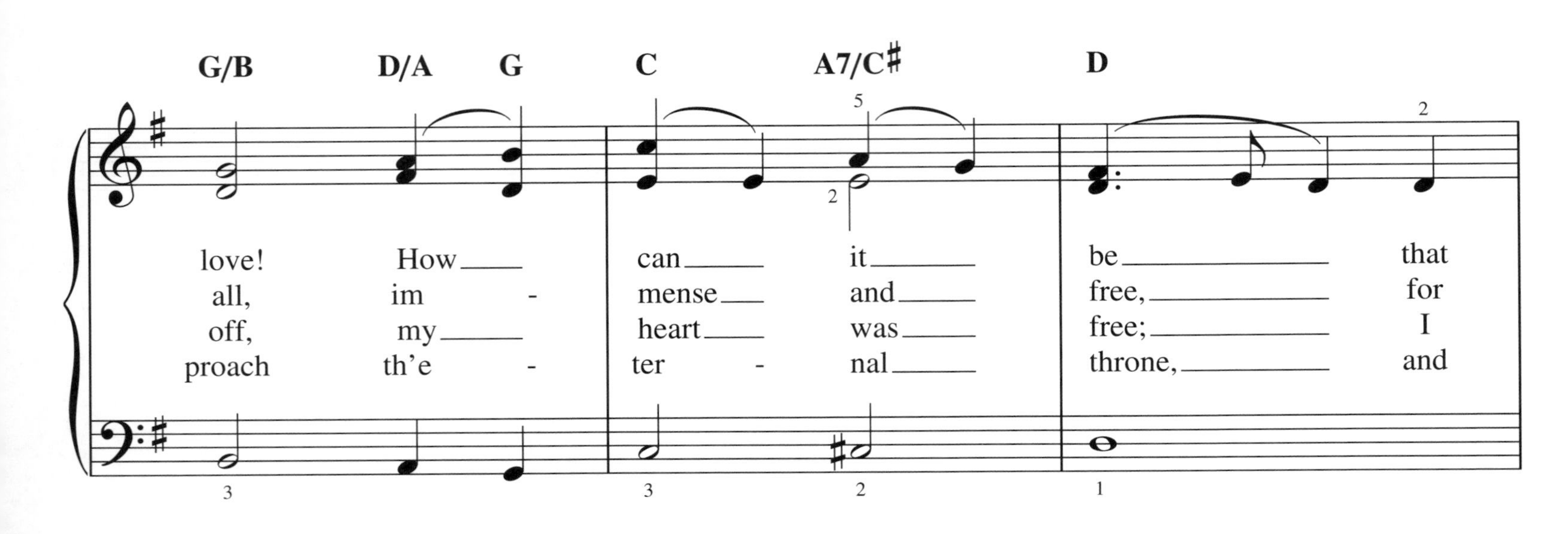
G/B D/A G C A7/C♯ D
love! How can it be that
all, im - mense and free, for
off, my heart was free; I
proach th'e - ter - nal throne, and

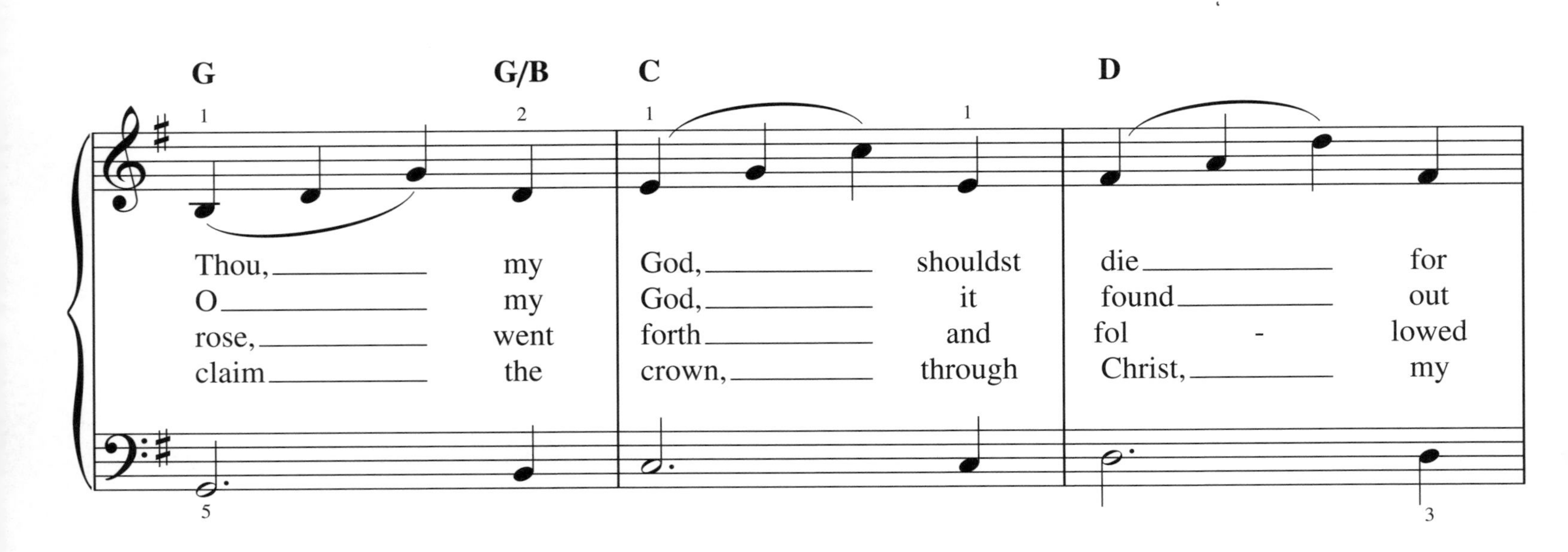
G G/B C D
Thou, my God, shouldst die for
O my God, it found out
rose, went forth and fol - lowed
claim the crown, through Christ, my

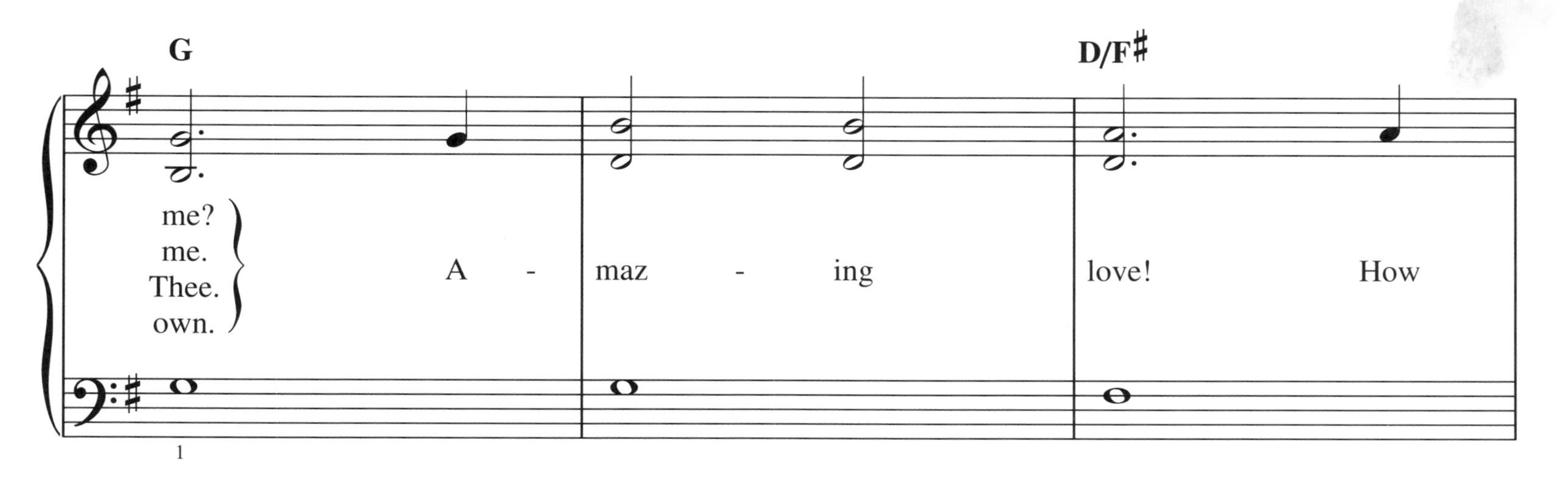
G
D/F♯
me?
me.
Thee.
own.
A - maz - ing love! How
1

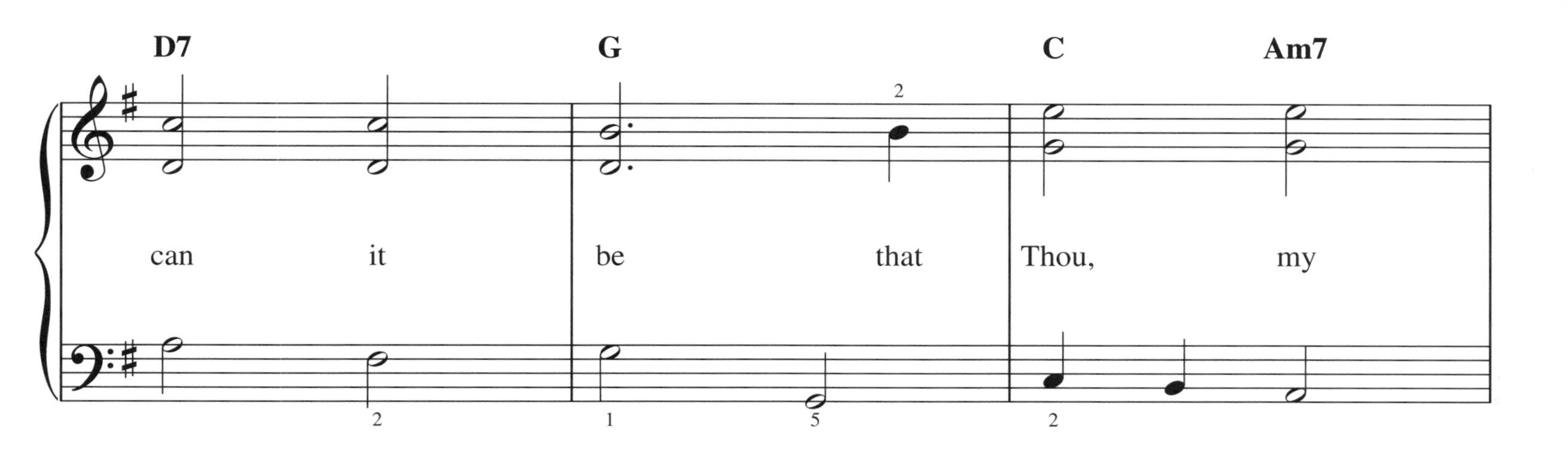
D7
G
C
Am7
can it be that Thou, my

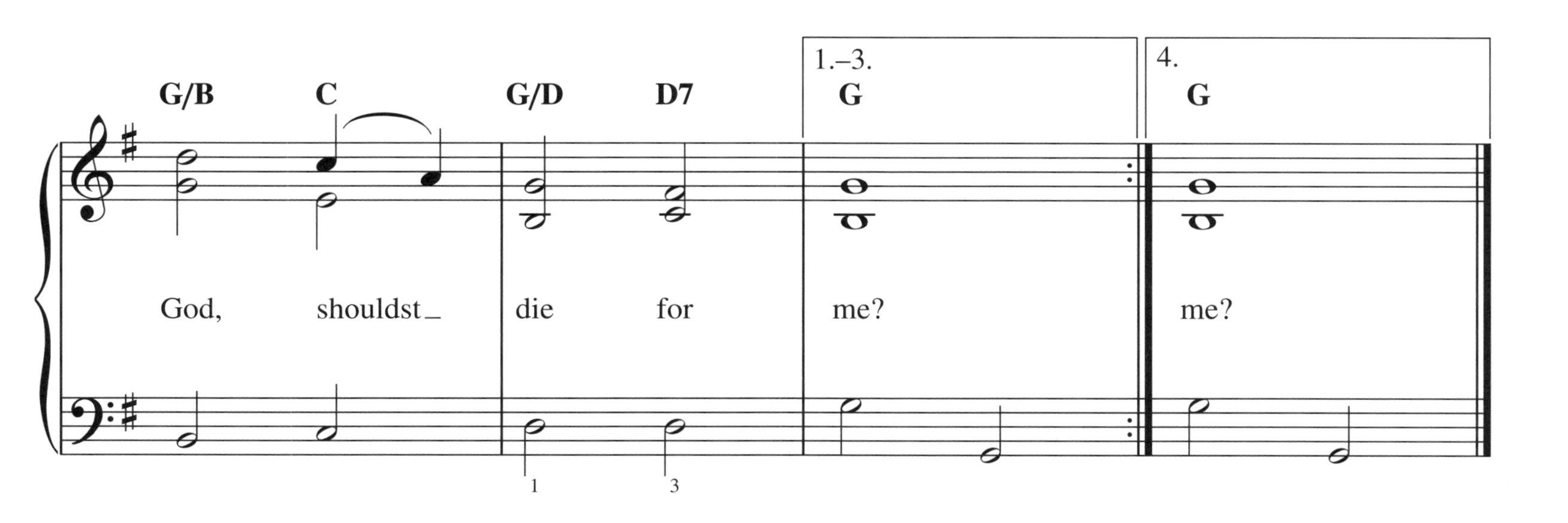
G/B
C
G/D
D7
1.–3.
G
4.
G
God, shouldst die for me?
me?

AT CALVARY

Words by WILLIAM R. NEWELL
Music by DANIEL B. TOWNER

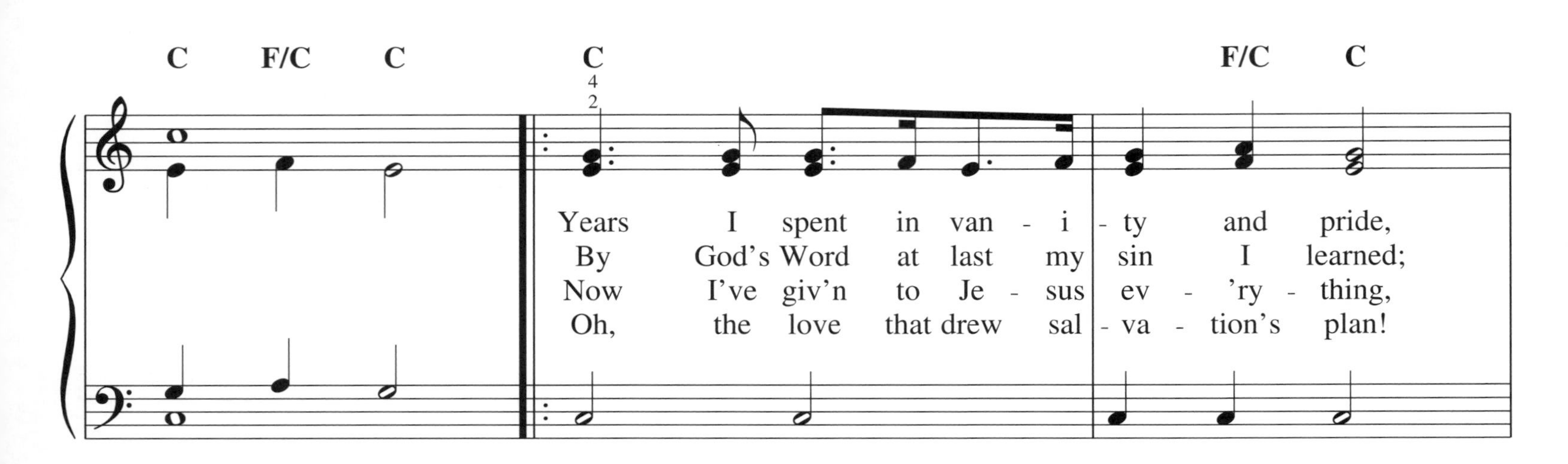

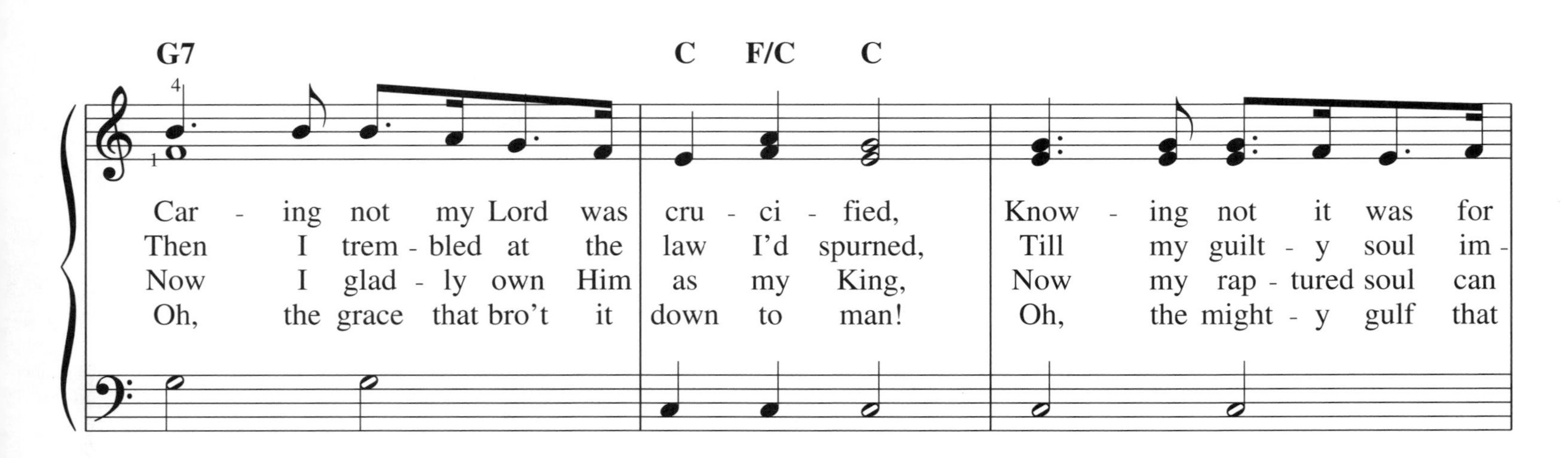

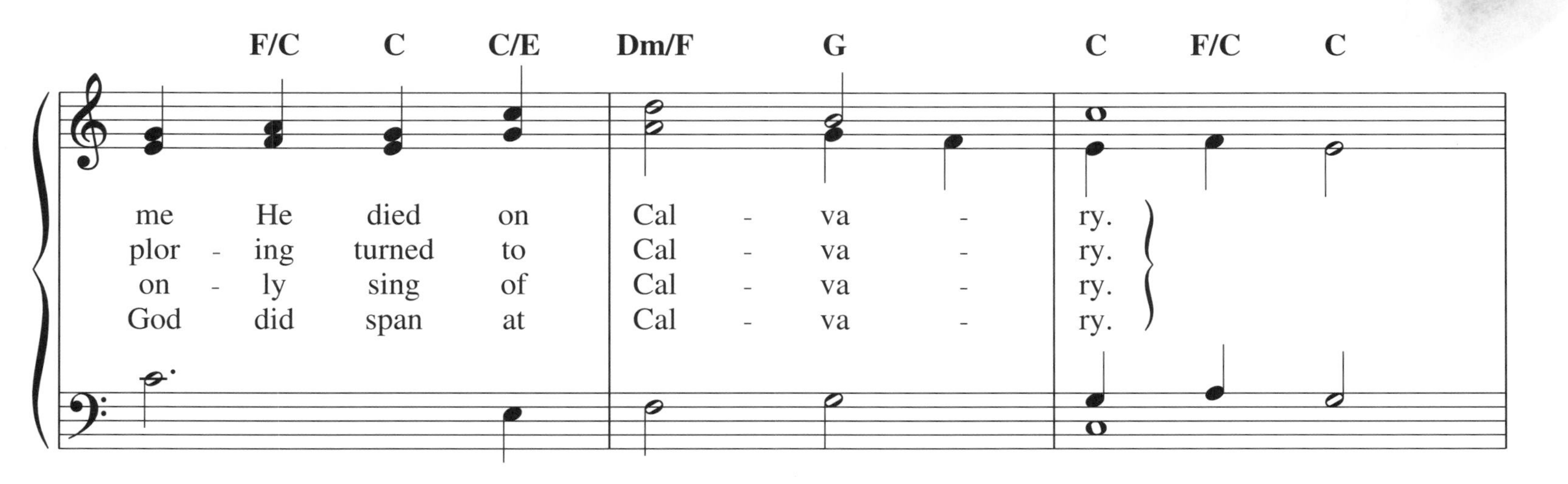
F/C C C/E Dm/F G C F/C C
me He died on Cal - va - ry.
plor - ing turned to Cal - va - ry.
on - ly sing of Cal - va - ry.
God did span at Cal - va - ry.

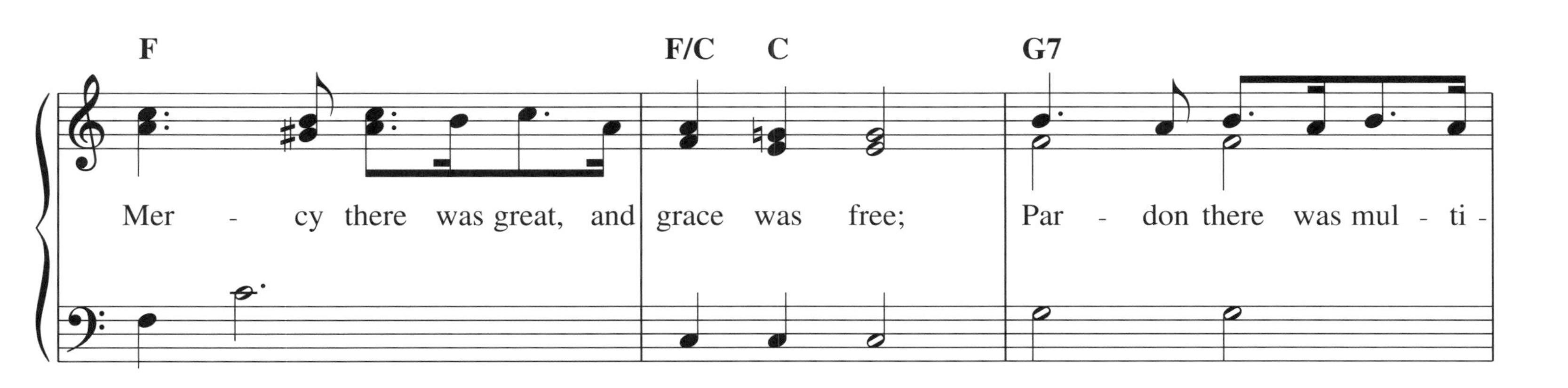
F F/C C G7
Mer - cy there was great, and grace was free; Par - don there was mul - ti -

C F F/C C C/E
plied to me; There my bur - dened soul found lib - er - ty At

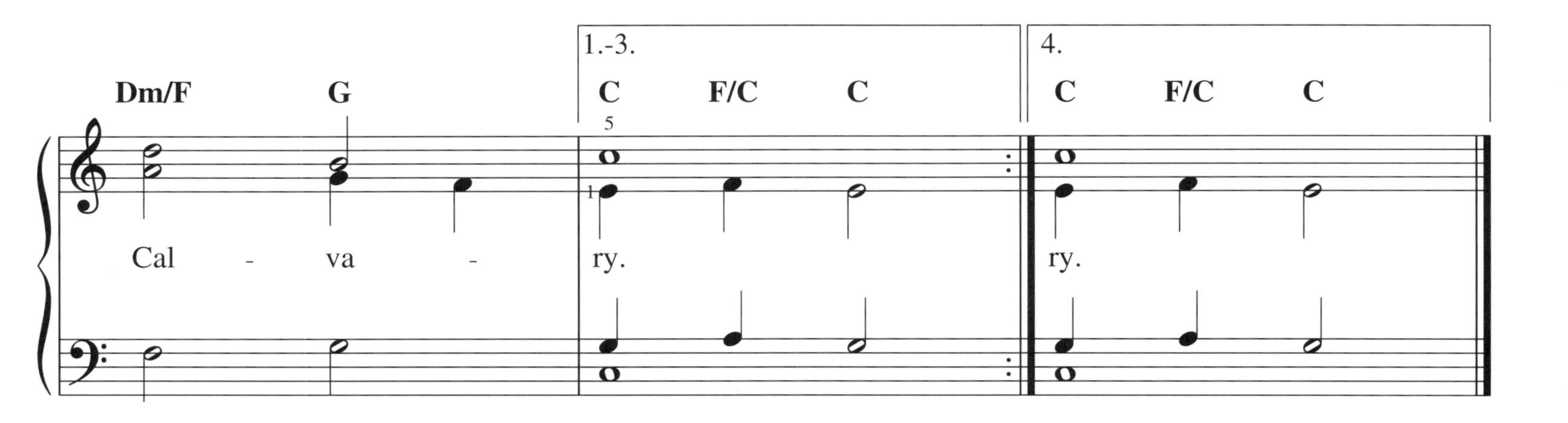
1.-3.
4.
Dm/F G C F/C C C F/C C
Cal - va - ry. ry.

BATTLE HYMN OF THE REPUBLIC

Additional Lyrics

3. I have read a fiery gospel writ in burnished rows of steel:
   "As ye deal with my condemners, so with you my grace shall deal;
   Let the Hero, born of woman, crush the serpent with his heel,
   Since God is marching on."
   To Chorus:

4. He has sounded forth the trumpet that shall never call retreat;
   He is sifting out the hearts of men before His judgement seat:
   Oh, be swift, my soul, to answer Him! be jubilant, my feet!
   Our God is marching on.
   To Chorus:

5. In the beauty of the lilies, Christ was born across the sea,
   With a glory in His bosom that transfigures you and me:
   As He died to make men holy, let us die to make men free,
   While God is marching on.
   To Chorus:

BE PRESENT AT OUR TABLE, LORD

Words by JOHN CENNICK
Music attributed to LOUIS BOURGEOIS

BENEATH THE CROSS OF JESUS

BE THOU MY VISION

Traditional Irish
Translated by MARY E. BYRNE

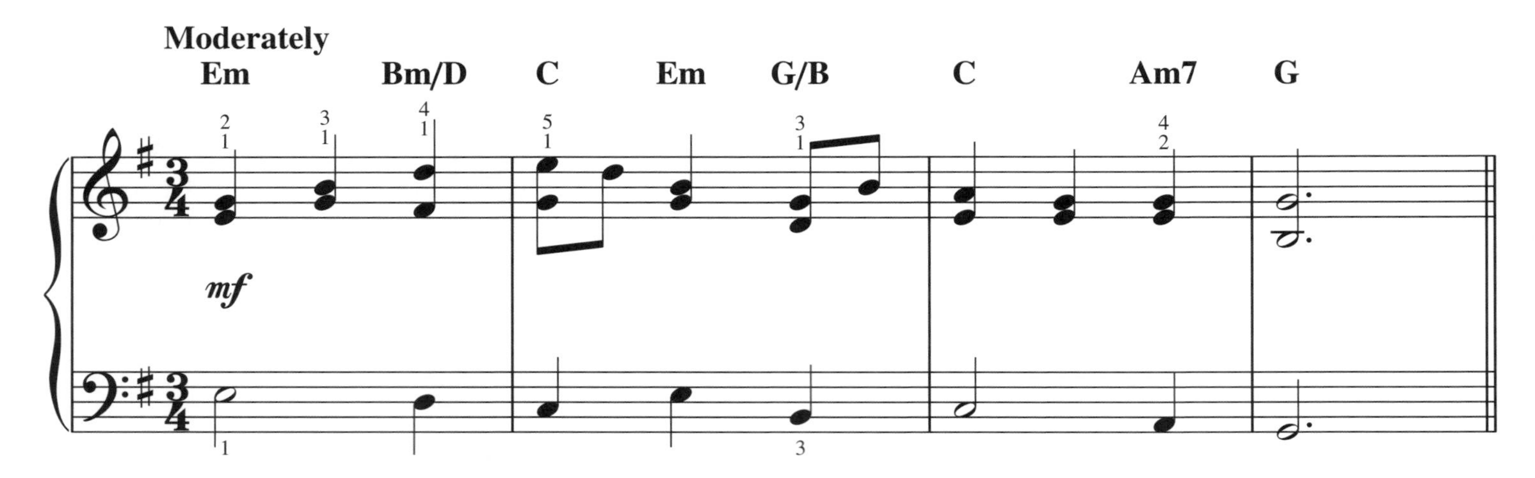

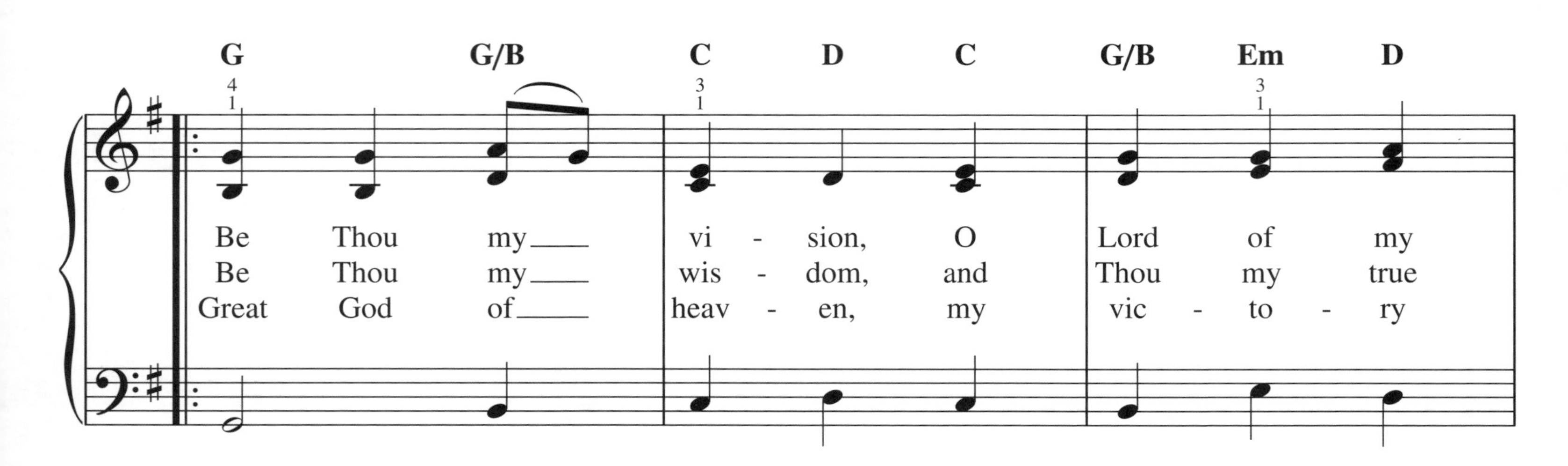

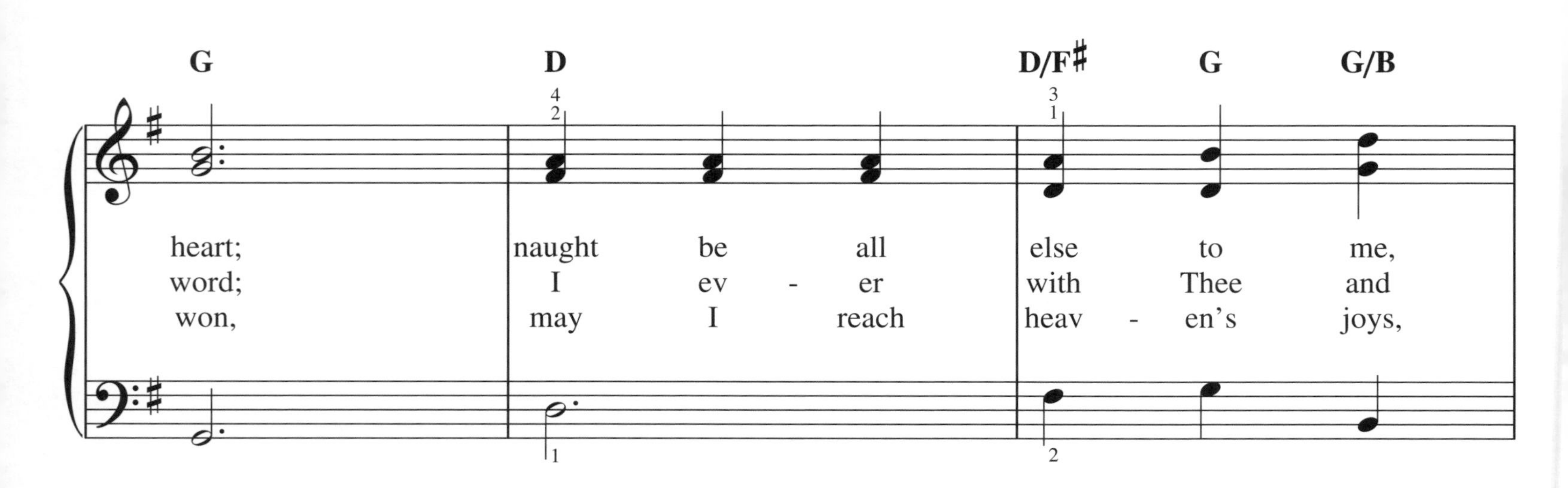

C G/B Em Dsus D C
save that Thou art. Thou my best
Thou with me, Lord; Thou and Thou
O bright heav'n's Sun! Heart of my

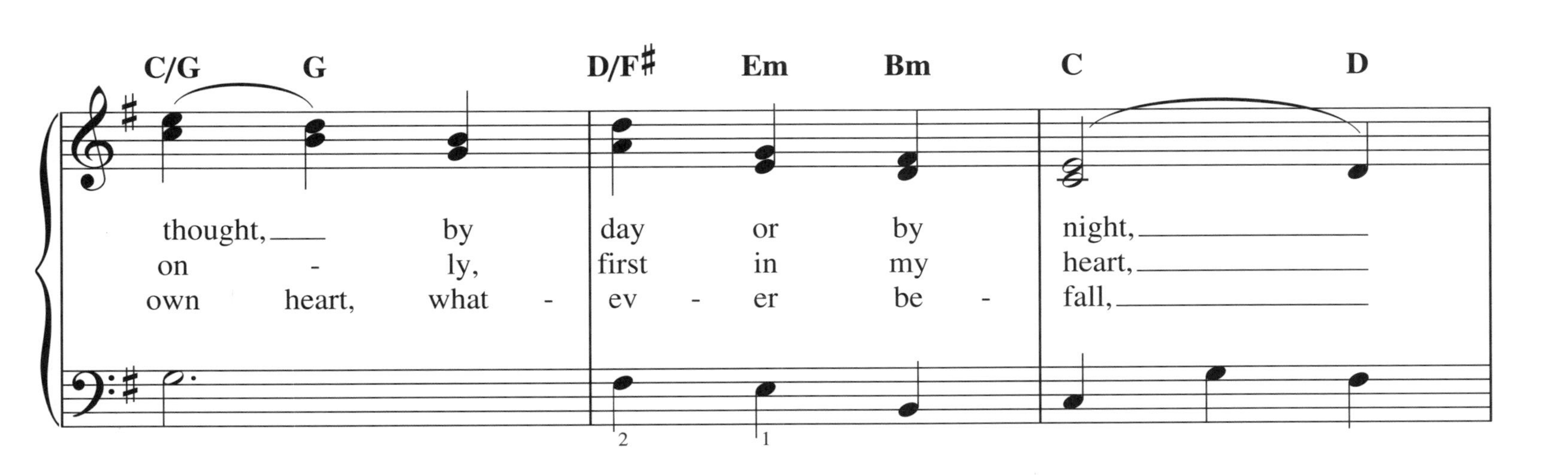
C/G G D/F# Em Bm C D
thought, by day or by night,
on - ly, first in my heart,
own heart, what - ev - er be - fall,

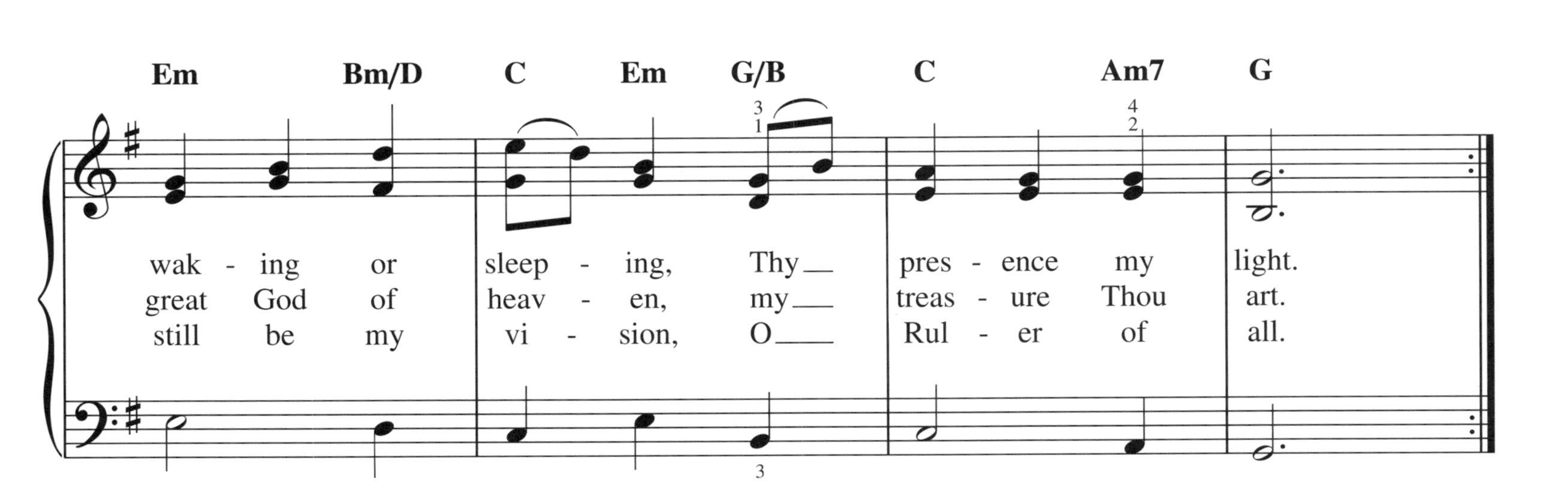
Em Bm/D C Em G/B C Am7 G
wak - ing or sleep - ing, Thy pres - ence my light.
great God of heav - en, my treas - ure Thou art.
still be my vi - sion, O Rul - er of all.

BEAUTIFUL SAVIOR

Words from *Munsterisch Gesangbuch*
Translated by JOSEPH A. SEISS
Music adapted from Silesian Folk Tune

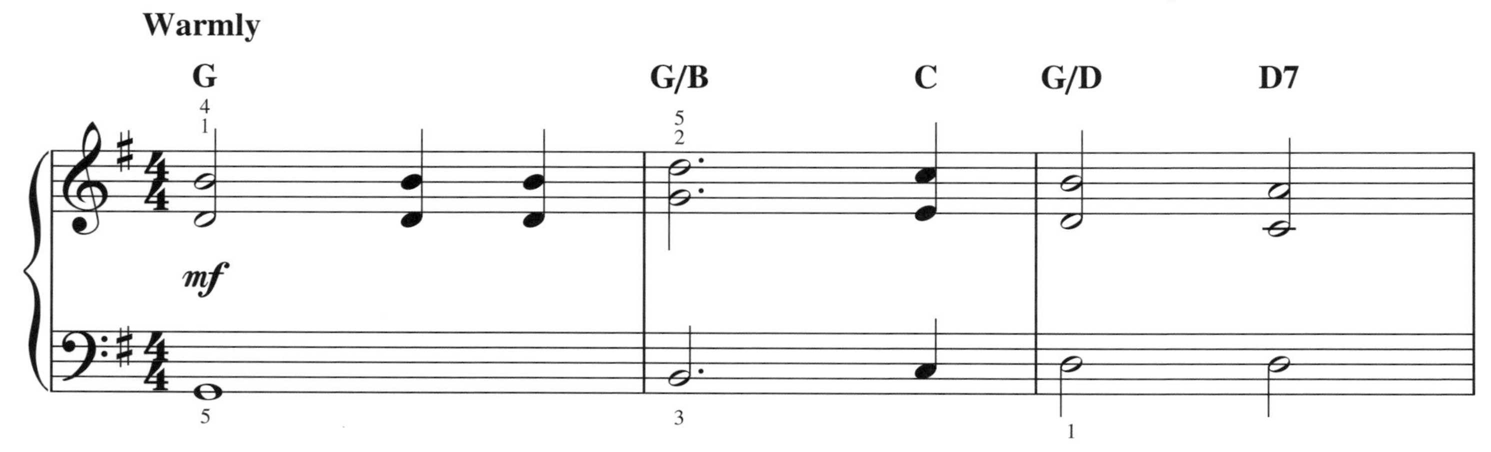

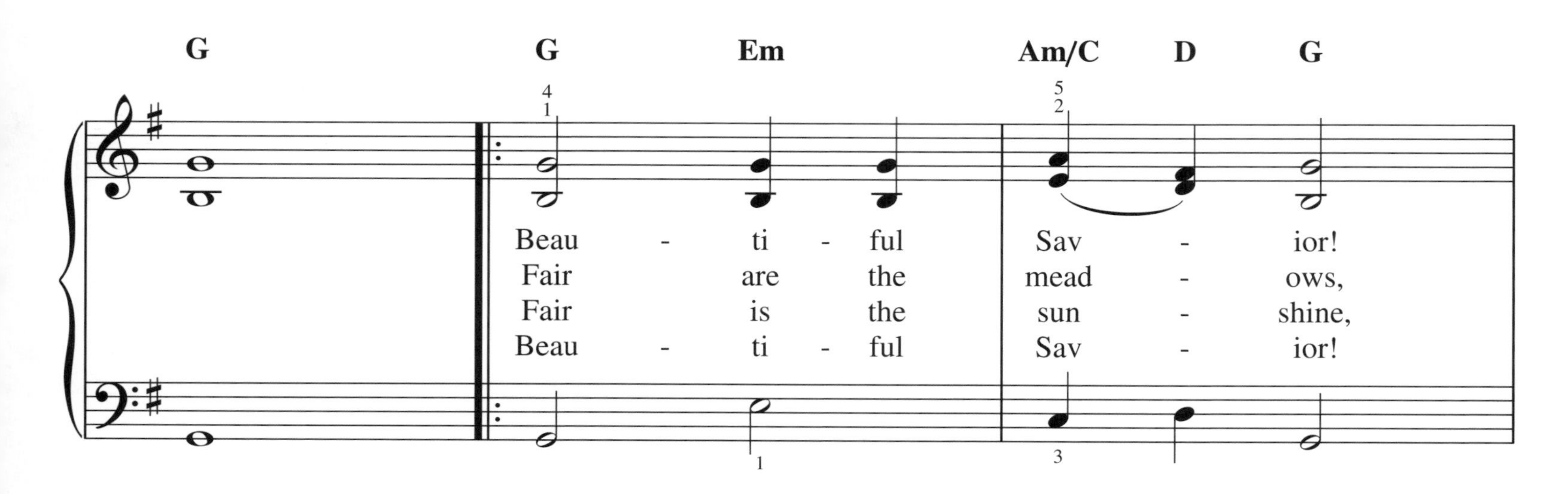

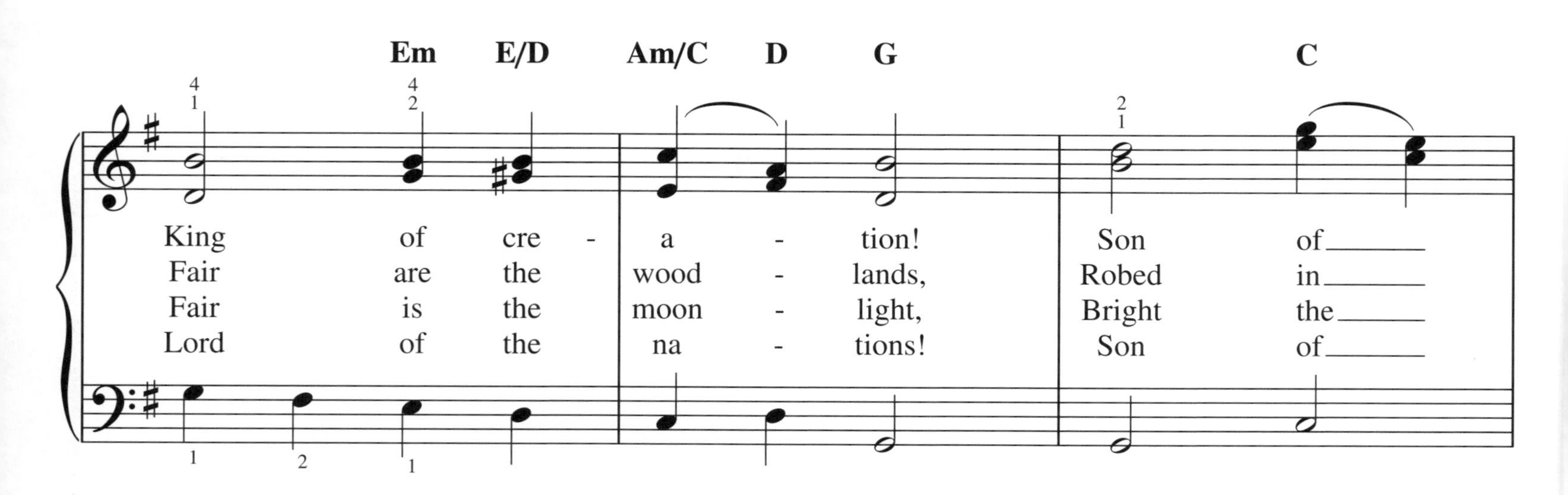

G D7/A G Dsus D
God and Son of Man!
flow'rs of bloom - ing spring:
spar - kling stars on high:
God and Son of Man!
G/B C G/D E7 Am E7/B Am/C
Tru - ly I'd love Thee, Tru - ly I'd
Je - sus is fair - er, Je - sus is
Je - sus shines bright - er, Je - sus shines
Glo - ry and hon - or, Praise, ad - o -
D7 G G/B C
serve Thee, Light of my soul, my
pur - er; He makes our sor - r'wing
pur - er Than all the an - gels
ra - tion, Now and for - ev - er -
G/D D7 1.–3. G 4. G
joy, my crown.
spir - it sing.
in the sky.
more be Thine!

BLESSED ASSURANCE

Lyrics by FANNY J. CROSBY
Music by PHOEBE PALMER KNAPP

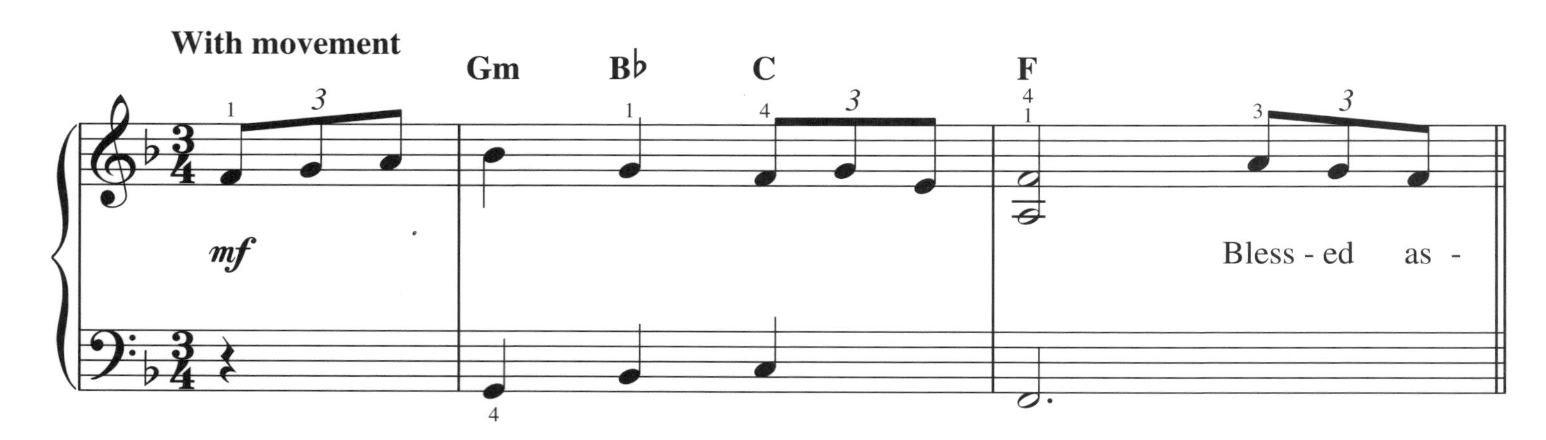

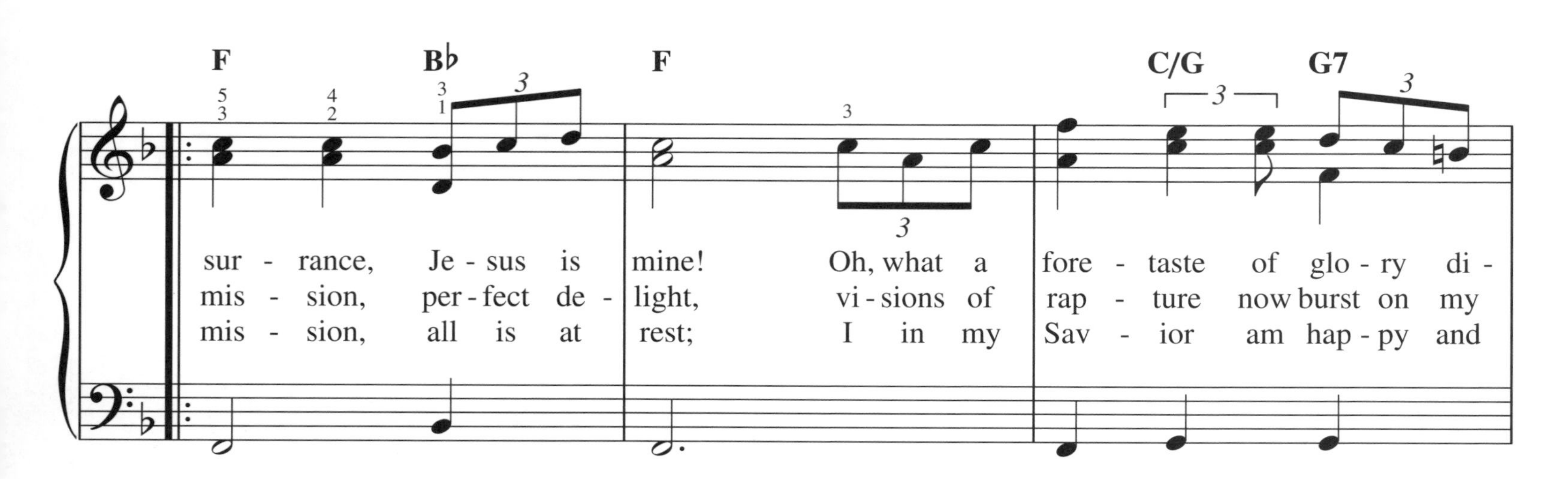

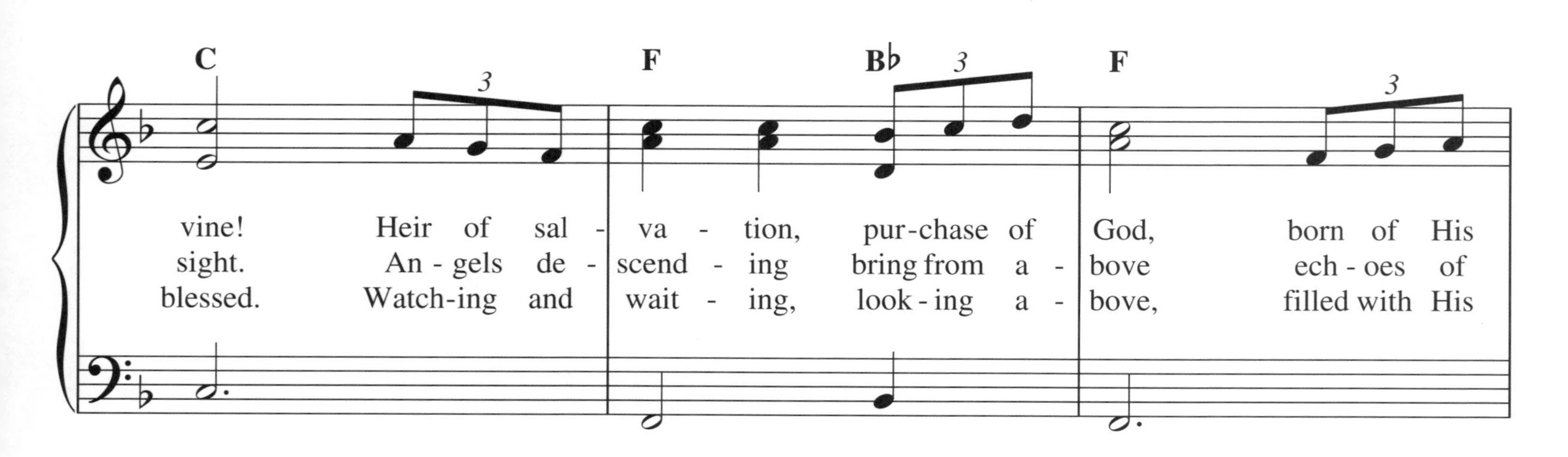

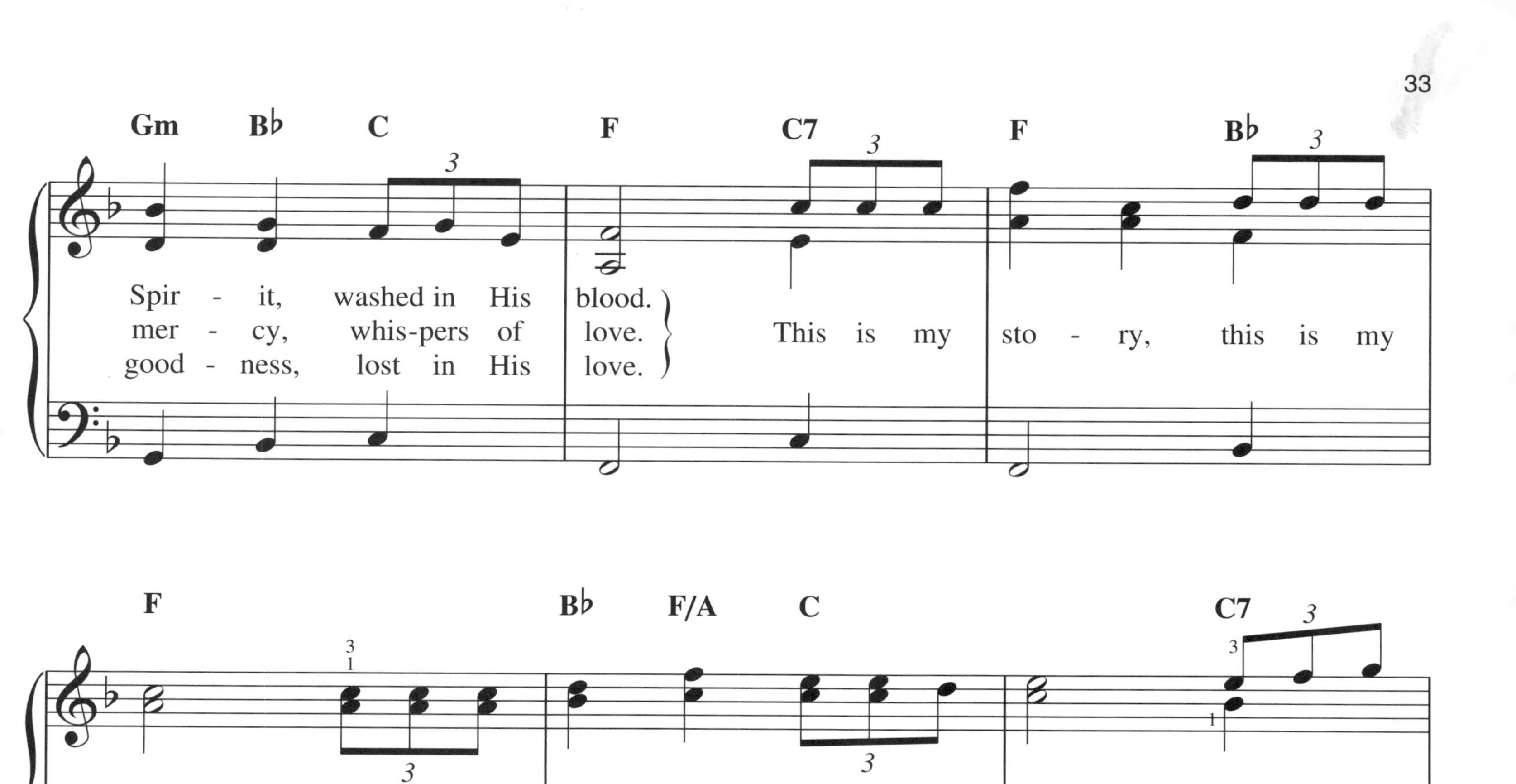
Gm Bb C F C7 F Bb
Spir - it, washed in His blood.
mer - cy, whis-pers of love.
good - ness, lost in His love.
This is my sto - ry, this is my
F Bb F/A C C7
song, prais - ing my Sav - ior all the day long. This is my

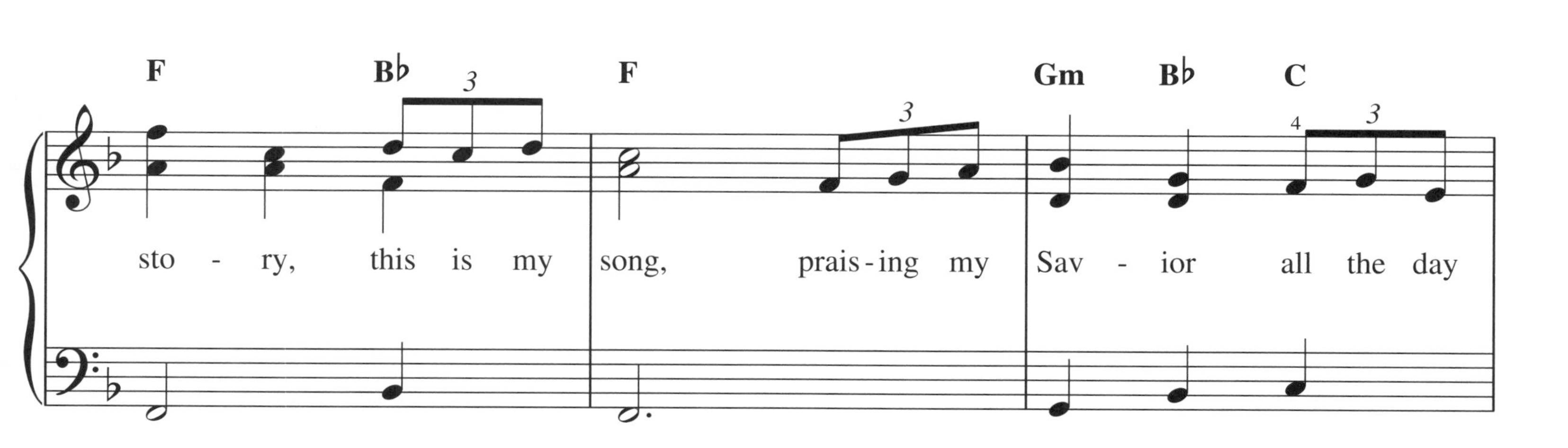
F Bb F Gm Bb C
sto - ry, this is my song, prais - ing my Sav - ior all the day

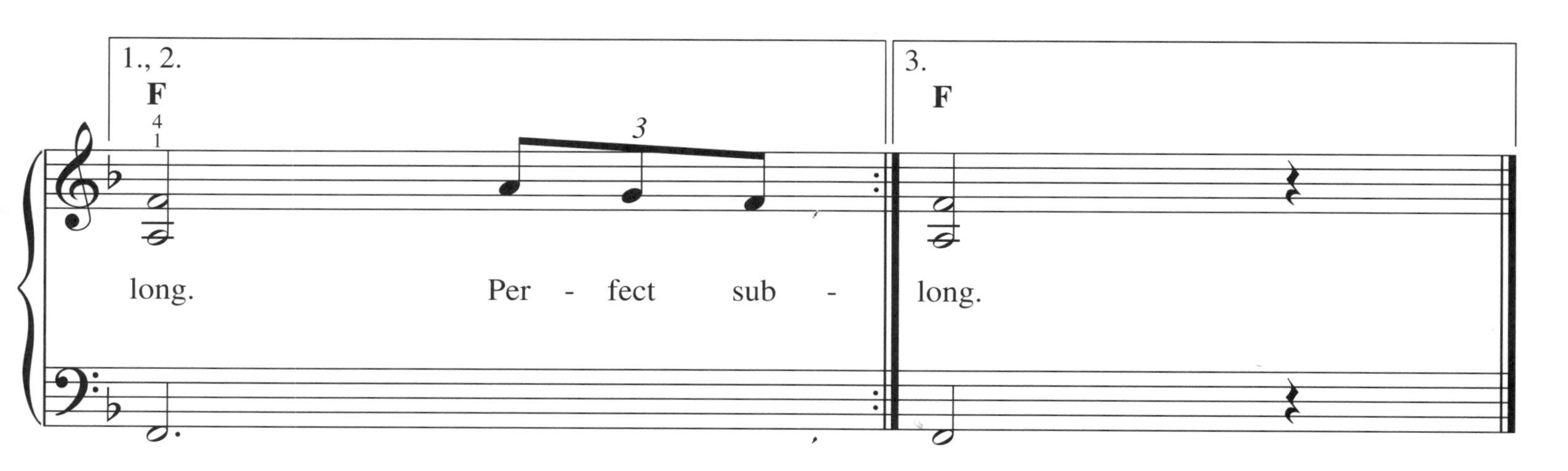
1., 2.
F
long. Per - fect sub -
3.
F
long.

BREAK THOU THE BREAD OF LIFE

Words by Mary ARTEMESIA LATHBURY
Music by WILLIAM FISKE SHERWIN

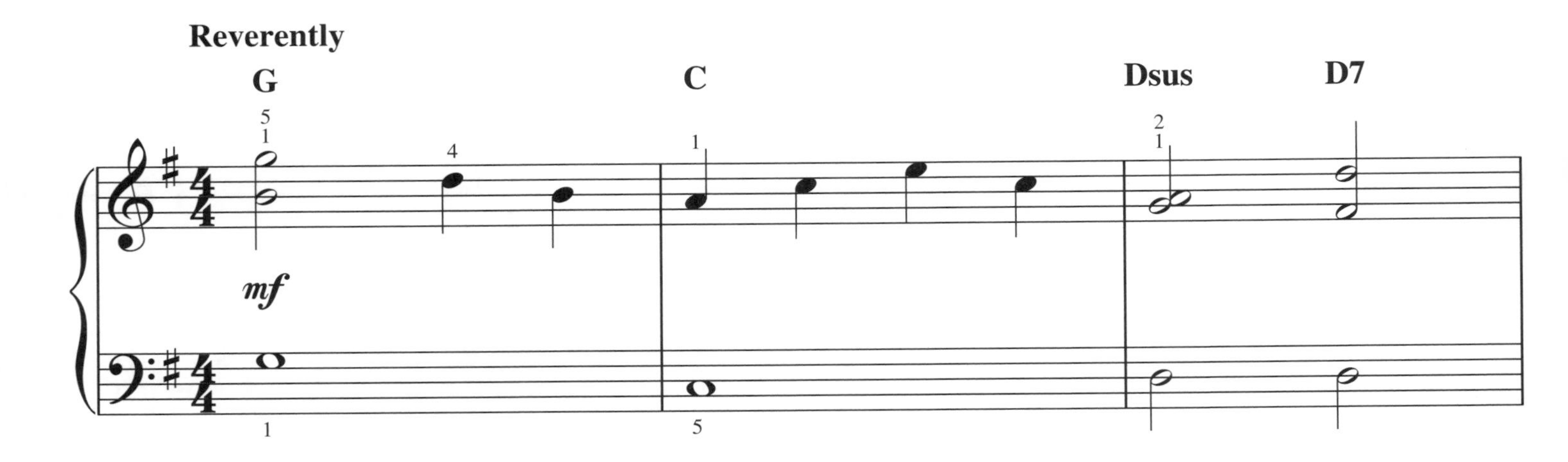

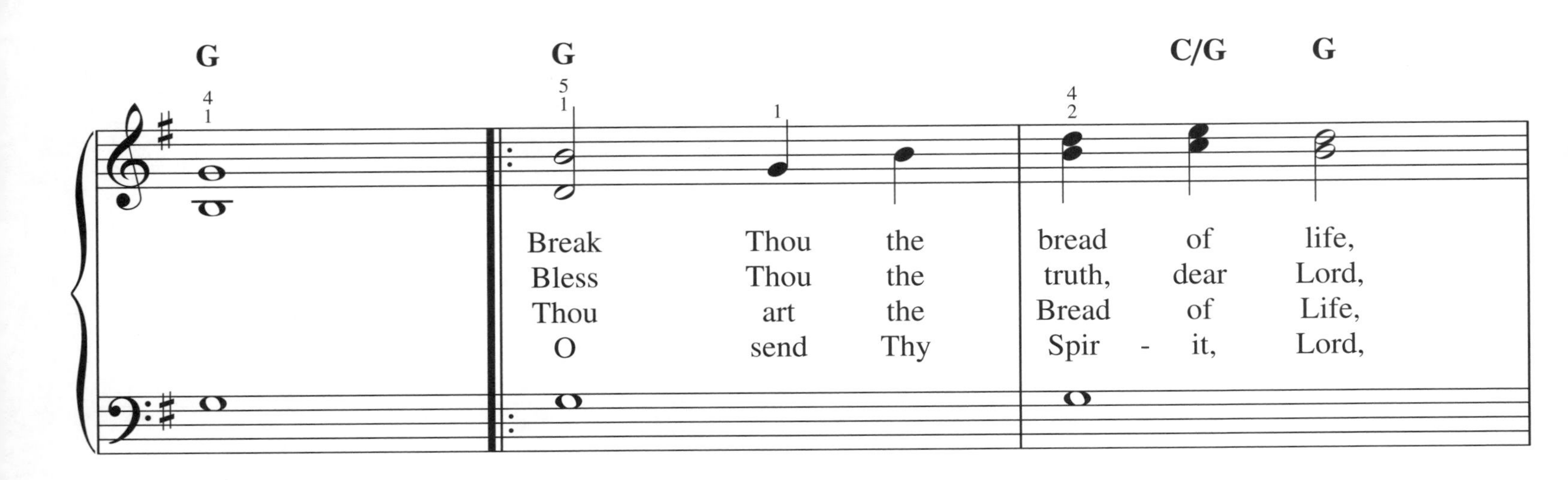

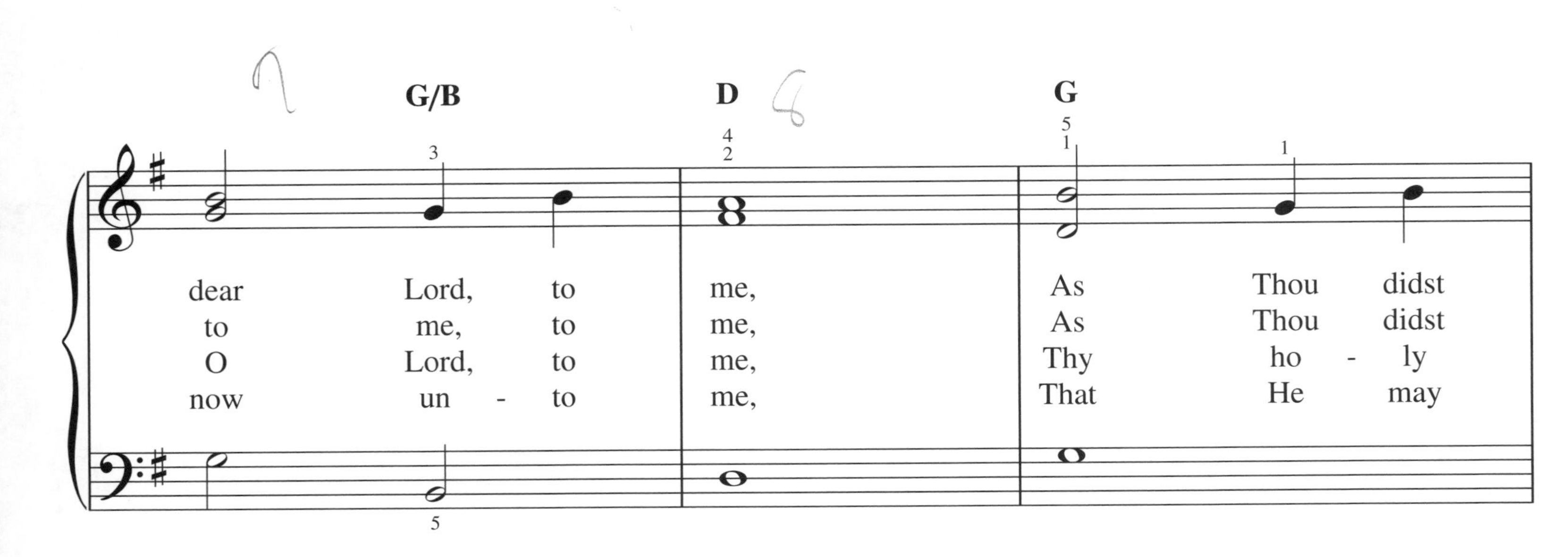

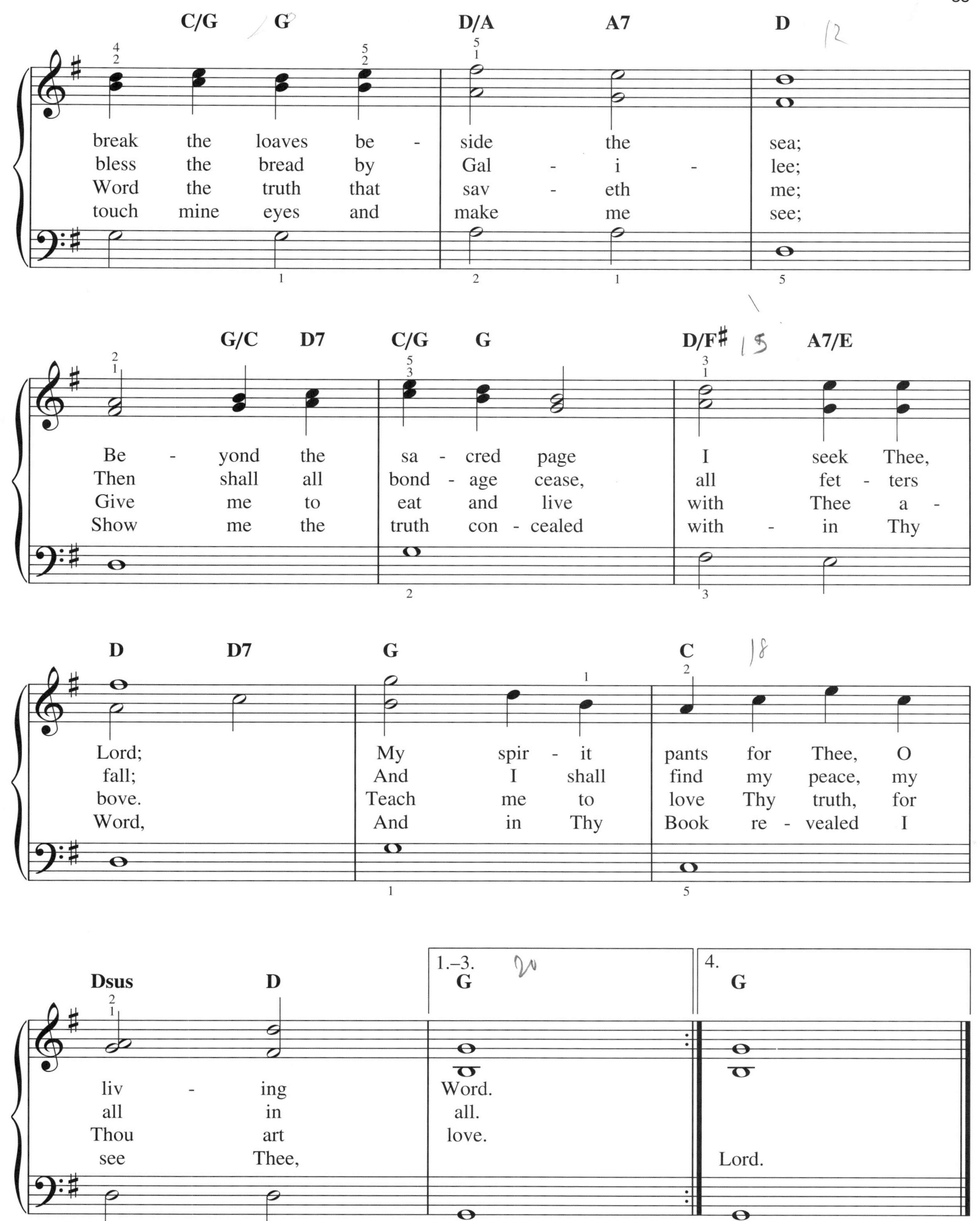
C/G G D/A A7 D
break the loaves be - side the sea;
bless the bread by Gal - i - lee;
Word the truth that sav - eth me;
touch mine eyes and make me see;
G/C D7 C/G G D/F♯ A7/E
Be - yond the sa - cred page I seek Thee,
Then shall all bond - age cease, all fet - ters
Give me to eat and live with Thee a -
Show me the truth con - cealed with - in Thy
D D7 G C
Lord; My spir - it pants for Thee, O
fall; And I shall find my peace, my
bove. Teach me to love Thy truth, for
Word, And in Thy Book re - vealed I
Dsus D
1.–3.
G
4.
G
liv - ing Word.
all in all.
Thou art love.
see Thee, Lord.

BREATHE ON ME, BREATH OF GOD

Words by EDWIN HATCH
Music by ROBERT JACKSON

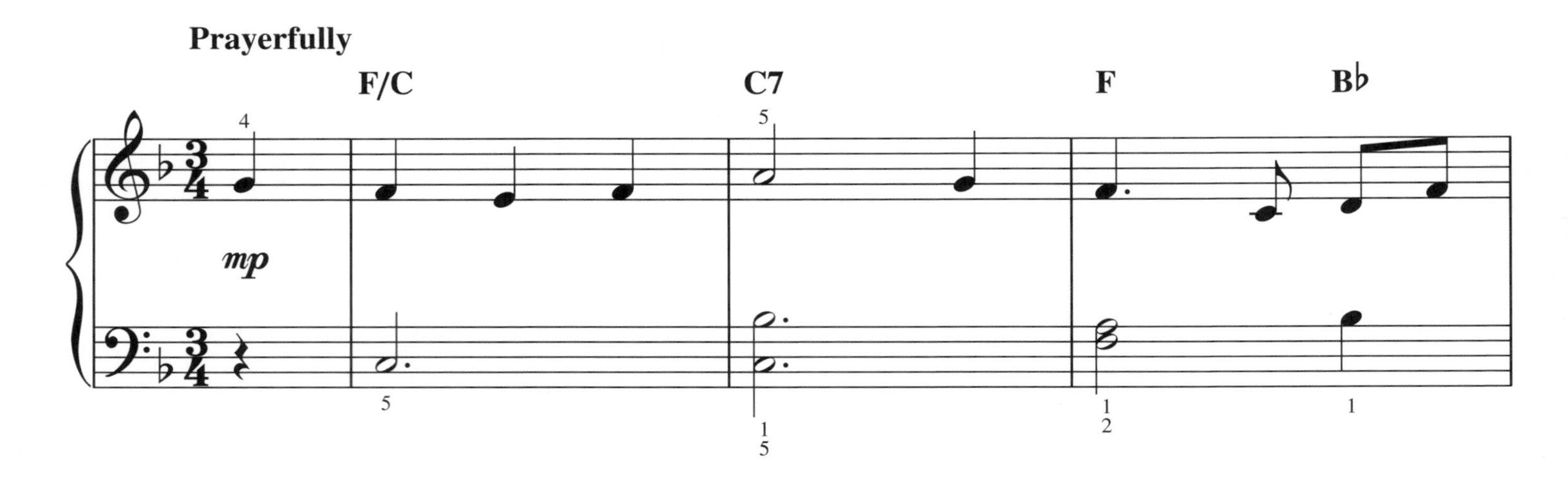

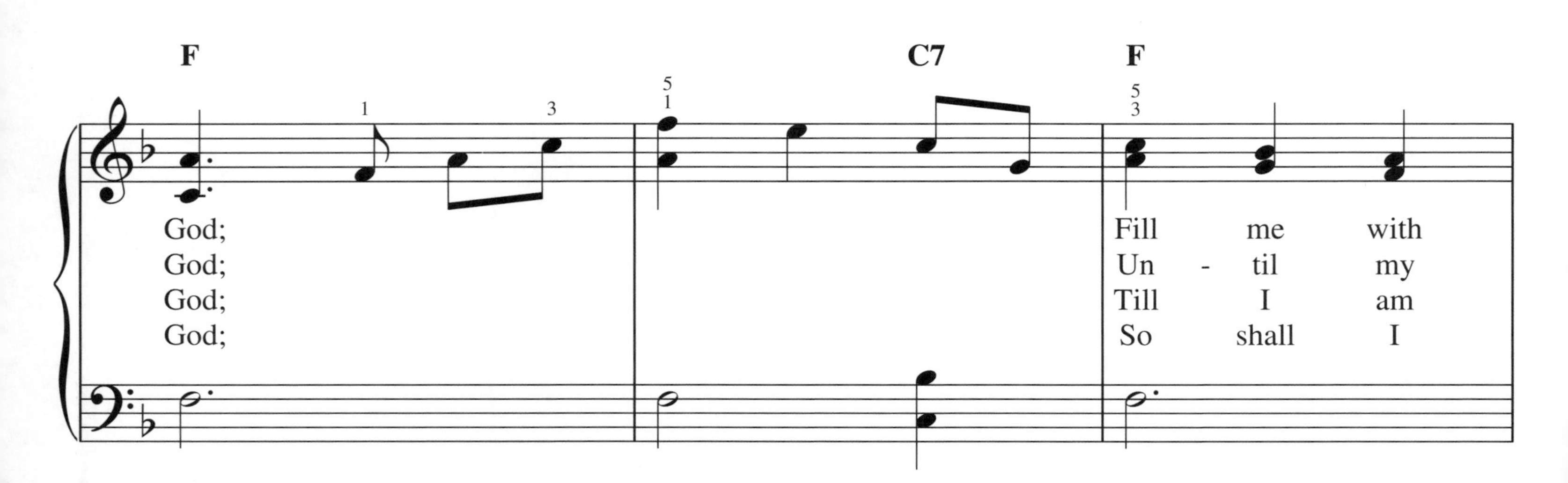

B♭6 Bm7♭5 C7sus C7
life a - new,
heart is pure,
whol - ly Thine,
nev - er die,

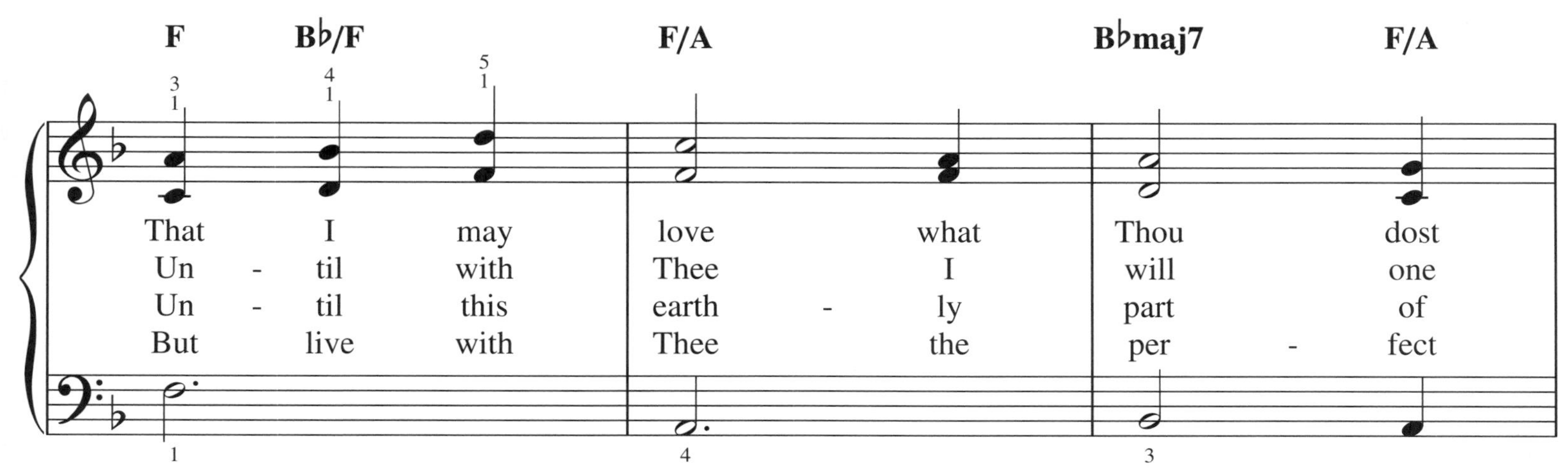
F B♭/F F/A B♭maj7 F/A
That I may love what Thou dost
Un - til with Thee I will one
Un - til this earth - ly part of
But live with Thee the per - fect

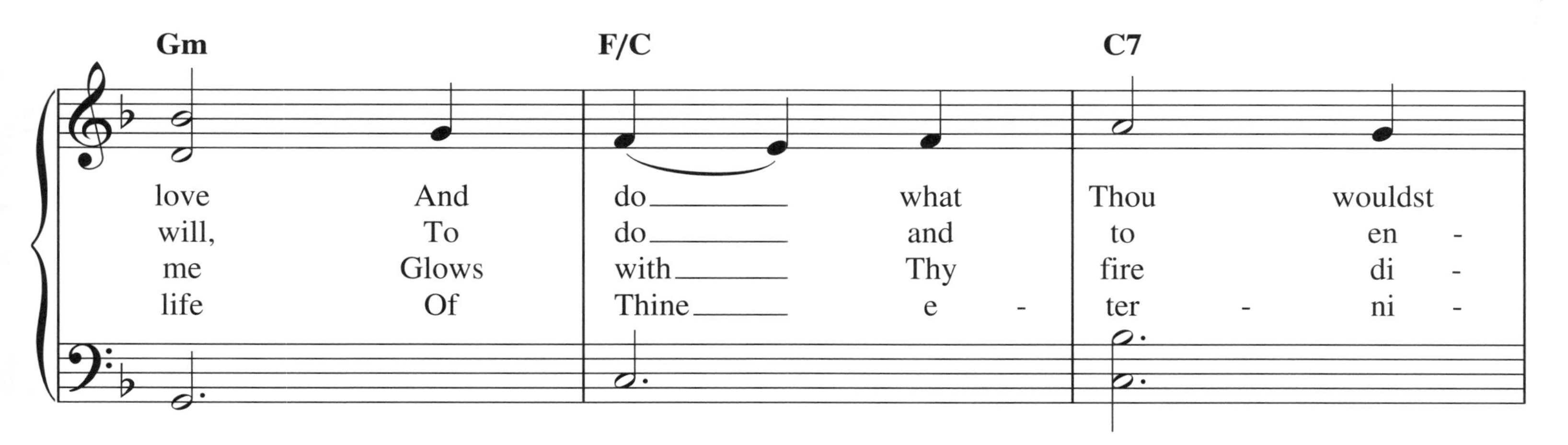
Gm F/C C7
love And do what Thou wouldst
will, To do and to en -
me Glows with Thy fire di -
life Of Thine e - ter - ni -

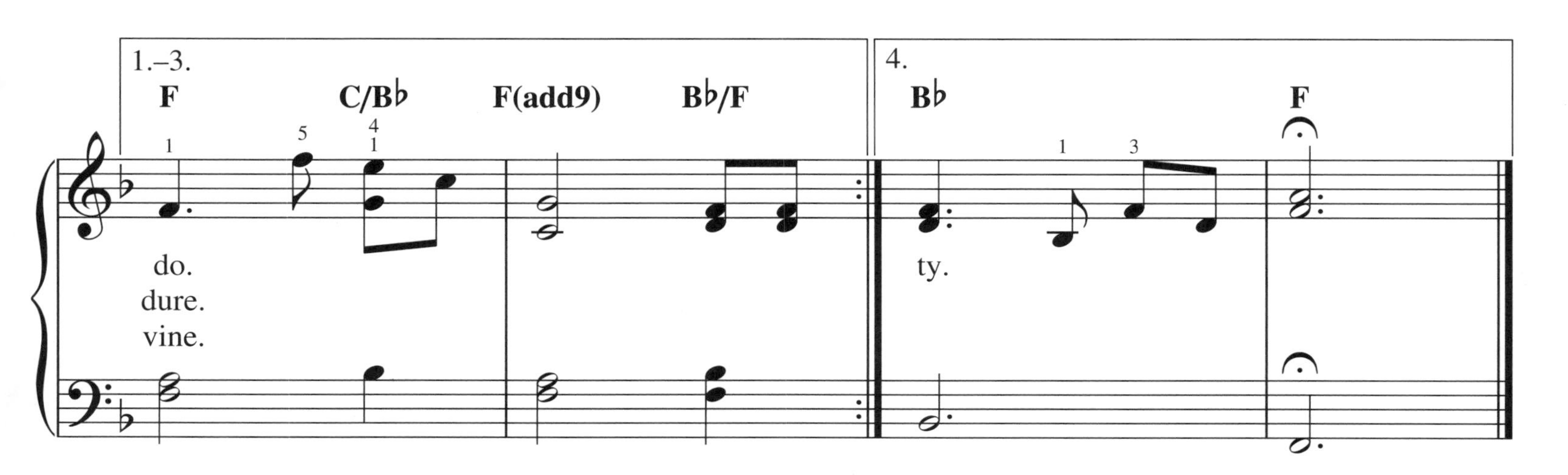
1.–3.
F C/B♭ F(add9) B♭/F
do.
dure.
vine.
4.
B♭ F
ty.

CHRIST AROSE
(Low in the Grave He Lay)

Words and Music by
ROBERT LOWRY

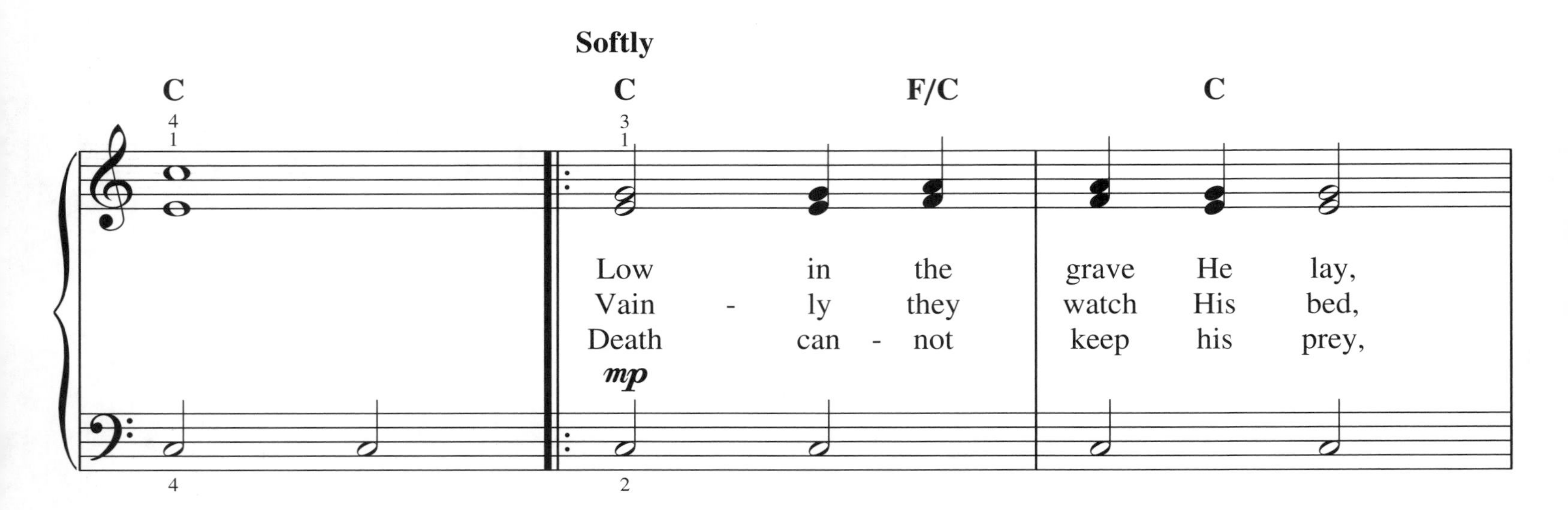

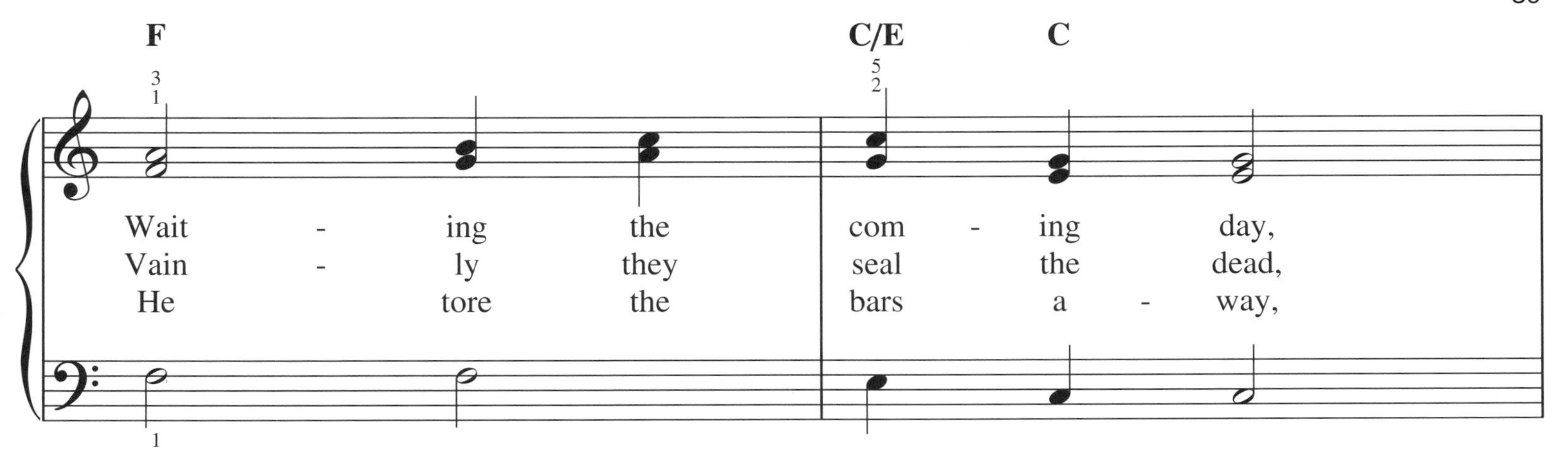
F
C/E
C
Wait - ing the com - ing day,
Vain - ly they seal the dead,
He tore the bars a - way,

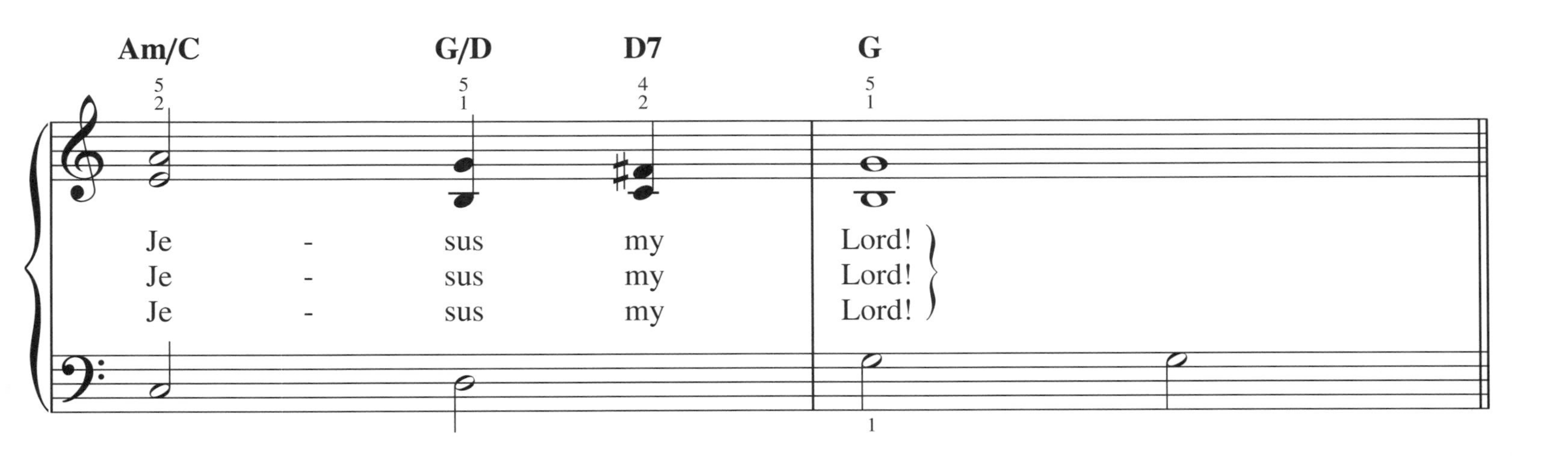
Am/C
G/D
D7
G
Je - sus my Lord!
Je - sus my Lord!
Je - sus my Lord!

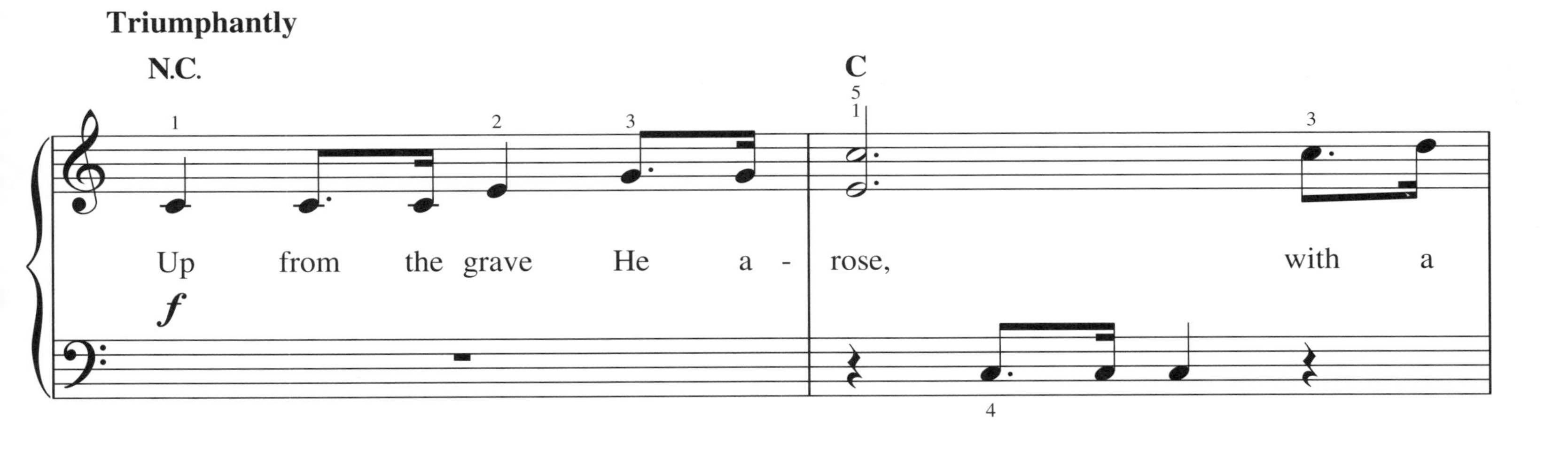
Triumphantly
N.C.
C
Up from the grave He a - rose, with a
f

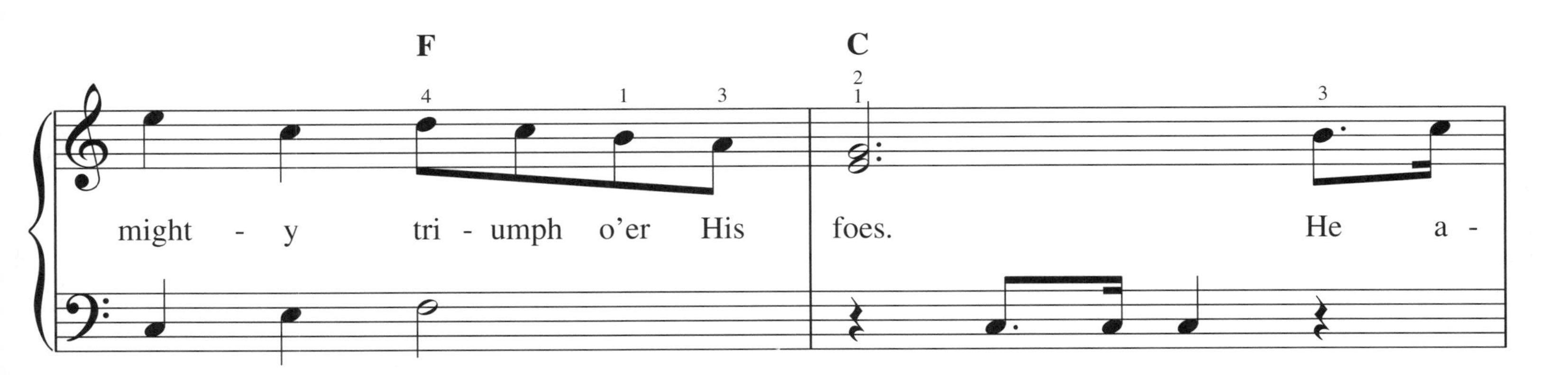
F
C
might - y tri - umph o'er His foes. He a -

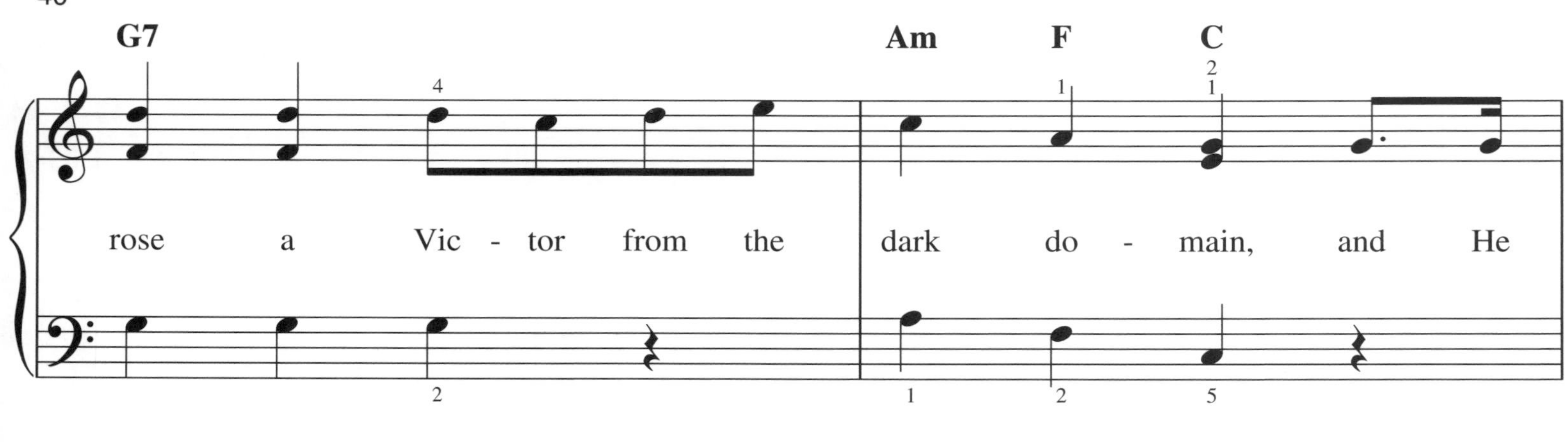
G7
Am F C
rose a Vic - tor from the dark do - main, and He

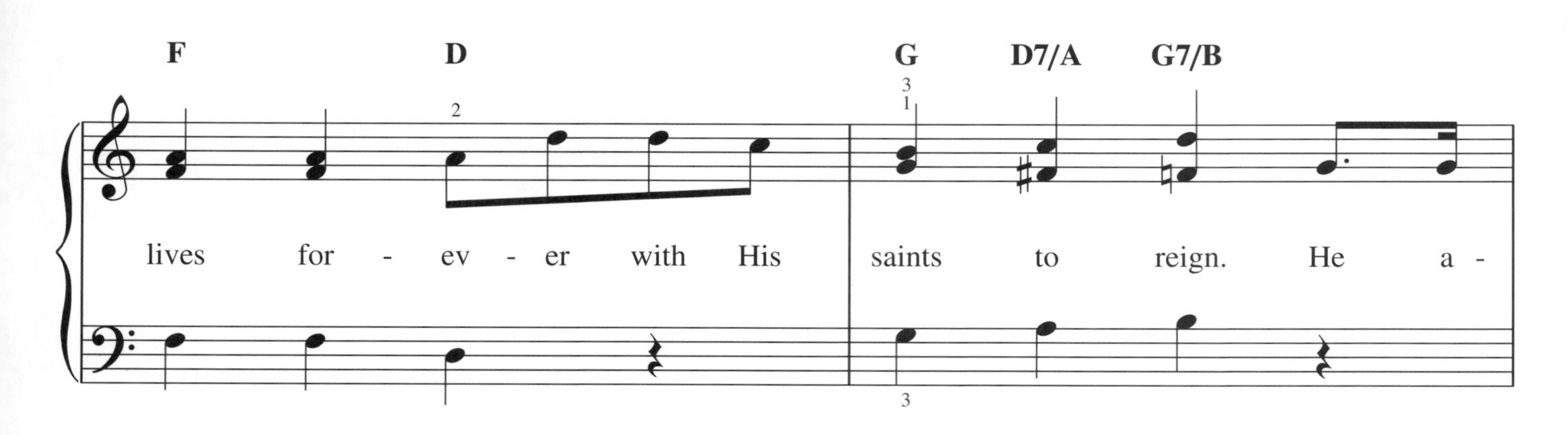
F D G D7/A G7/B
lives for - ev - er with His saints to reign. He a -

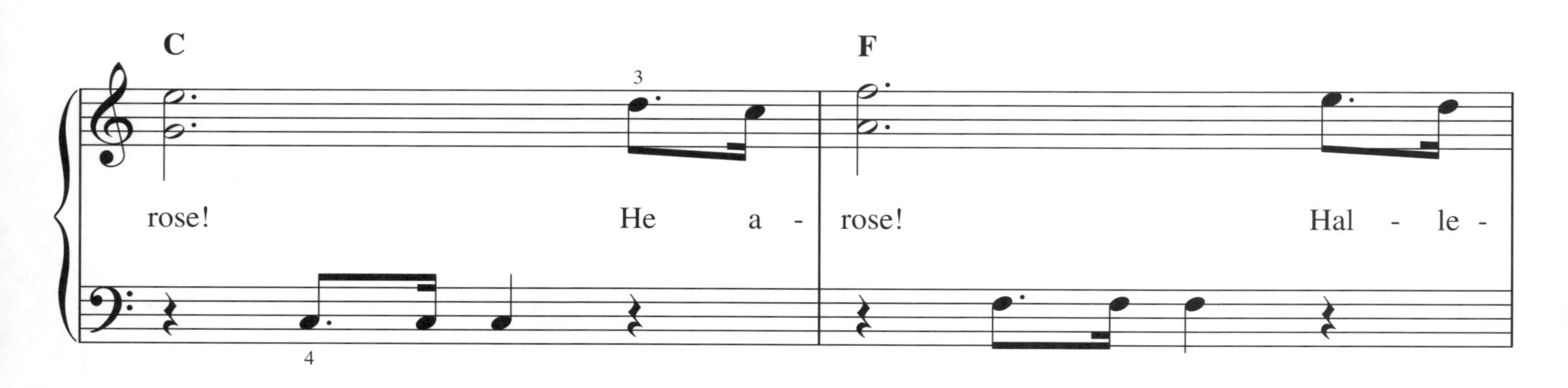
C F
rose! He a - rose! Hal - le -

C/G G7 C C
1., 2.
3.
lu - jah, Christ a - rose! rose!

THE CHURCH'S ONE FOUNDATION

Words by SAMUEL JOHN STONE
Music by SAMUEL SEBASTIAN WESLEY

CHRIST THE LORD IS RISEN TODAY

Words by CHARLES WESLEY
Music adapted from *Lyra Davidica*

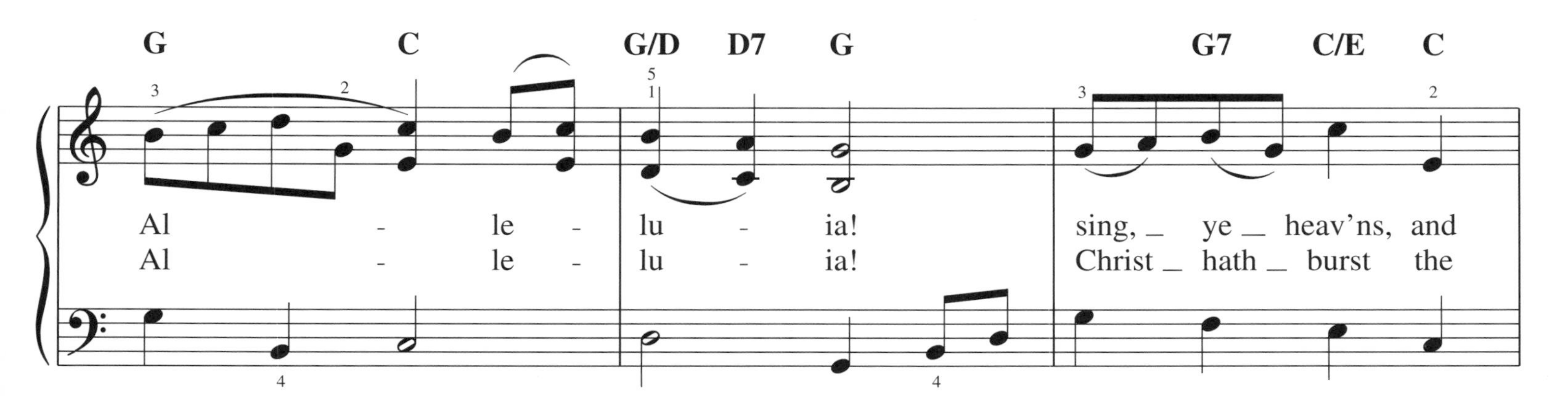

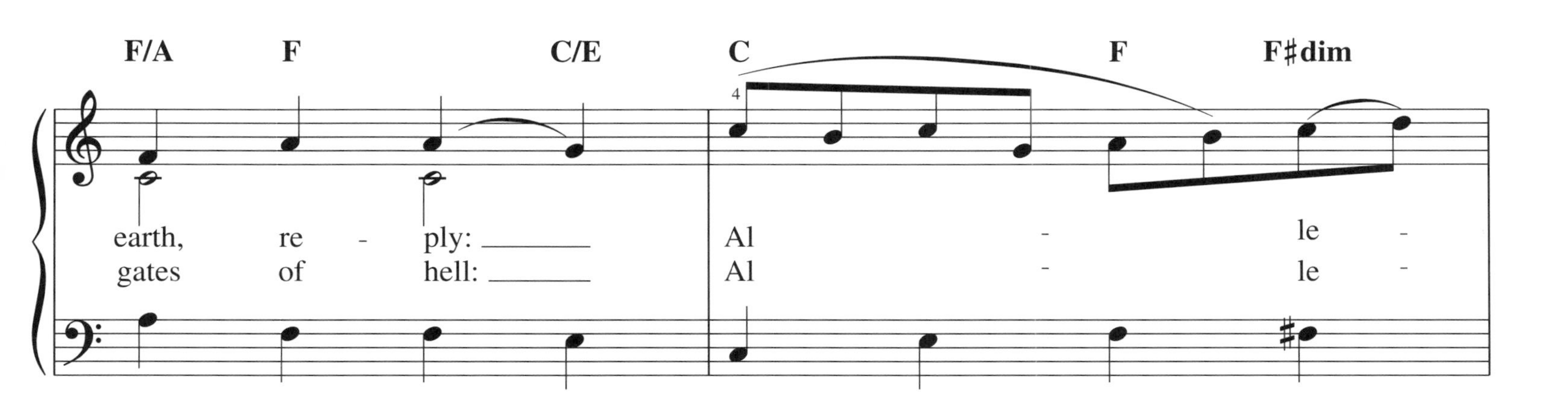

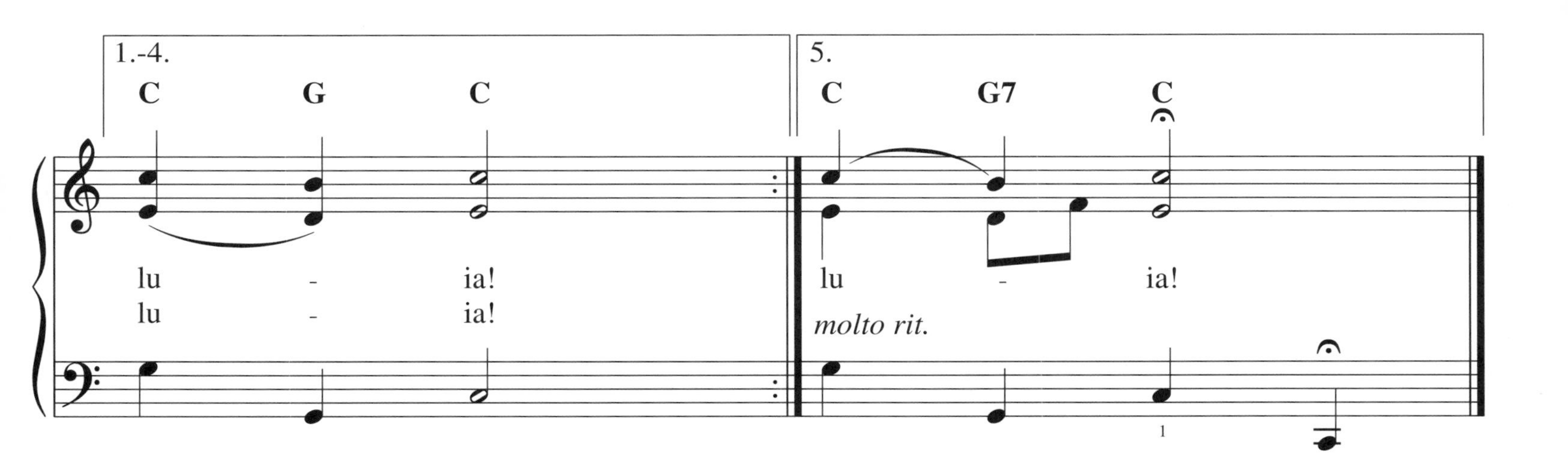

Additional Verses

3. Lives again our glorious King; Alleluia,
   Where, O death, is now thy sting? Alleluia.
   Once he died our souls to save; Alleluia,
   Where's thy victory, boasting grave? Alleluia.

4. Soar we now where Christ hath led, Alleluia,
   Following our exalted Head: Alleluia.
   Made like Him, like Him we rise; Alleluia,
   Ours the cross, the grave, the skies: Alleluia.

5. King of glory! Soul of bliss! Alleluia,
   Everlasting life is this, Alleluia.
   Thee to know, Thy power to prove, Alleluia,
   Thus to sing, and thus to love: Alleluia.

CHURCH IN THE WILDWOOD

Words and Music by
DR. WILLIAM S. PITTS

Moderate steady beat

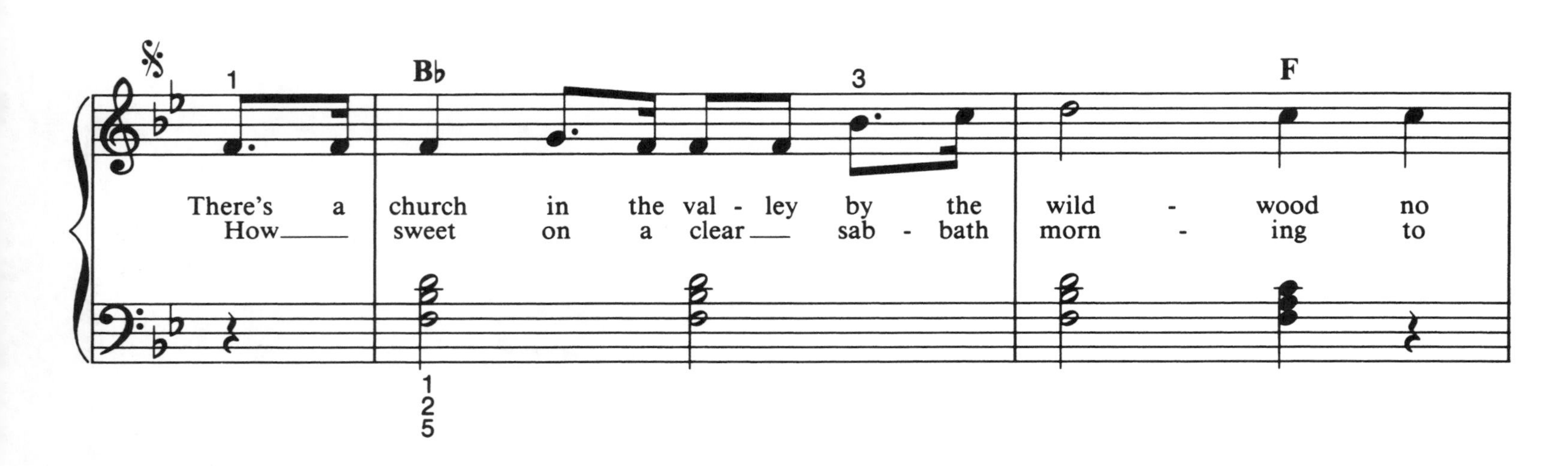

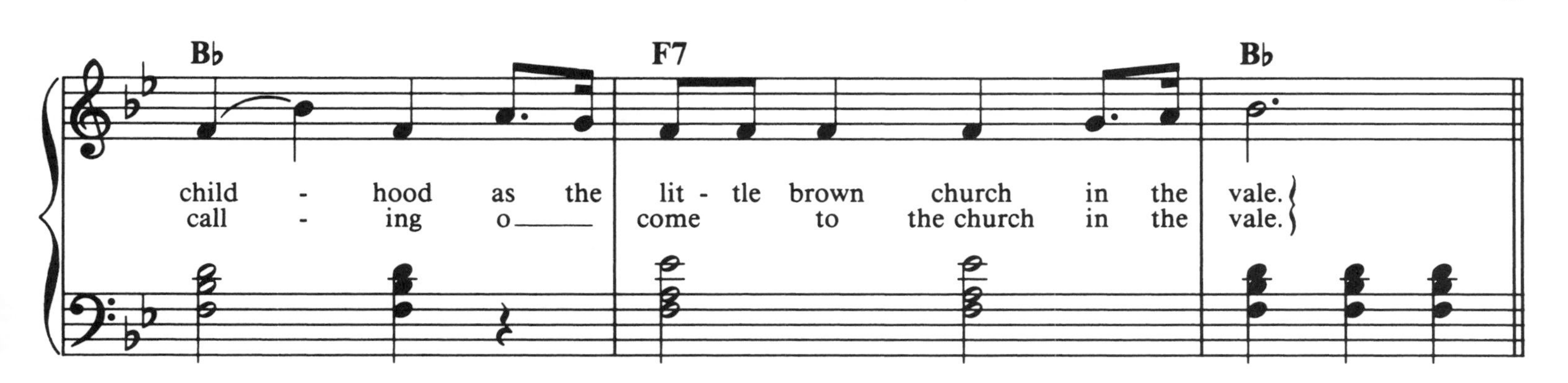
B♭
F7
B♭
child - hood as the lit - tle brown church in the vale.
call - ing o come to the church in the vale.

B♭
F
(Oh come come come come) Come to the church in the wild - wood oh

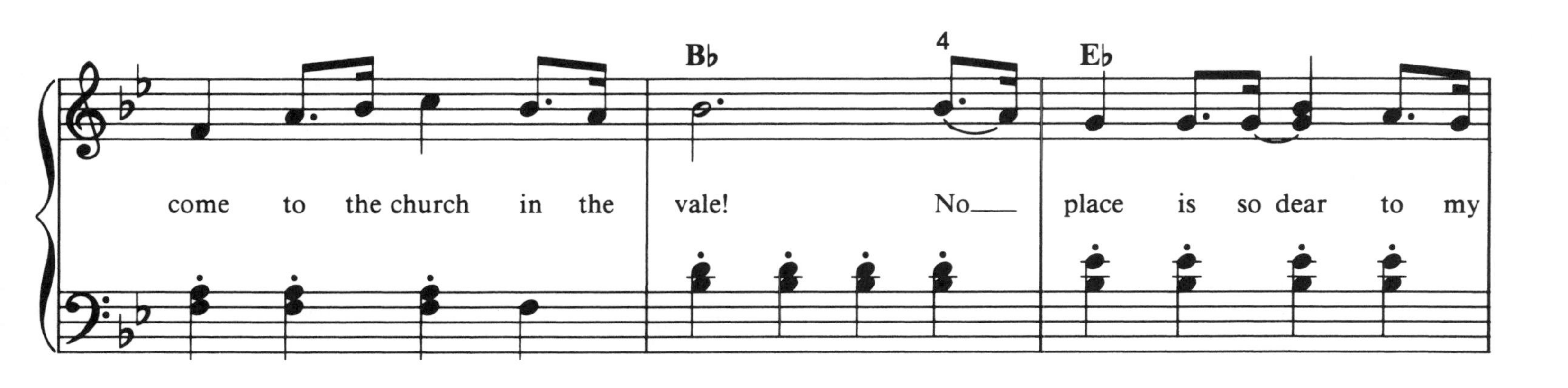
B♭
E♭
come to the church in the vale! No place is so dear to my

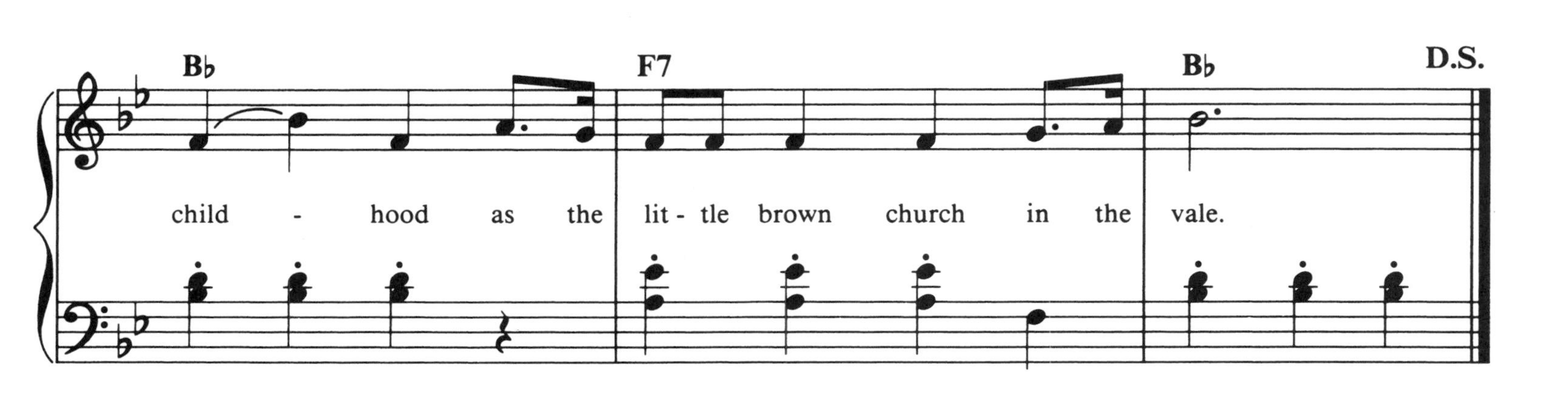
B♭
F7
B♭
D.S.
child - hood as the lit - tle brown church in the vale.

COME, THOU ALMIGHTY KING

DOWN BY THE RIVERSIDE

African-American Spiritual

lay down my sword and shield_ down by the
join hands with ev - 'ry - one___ down by the

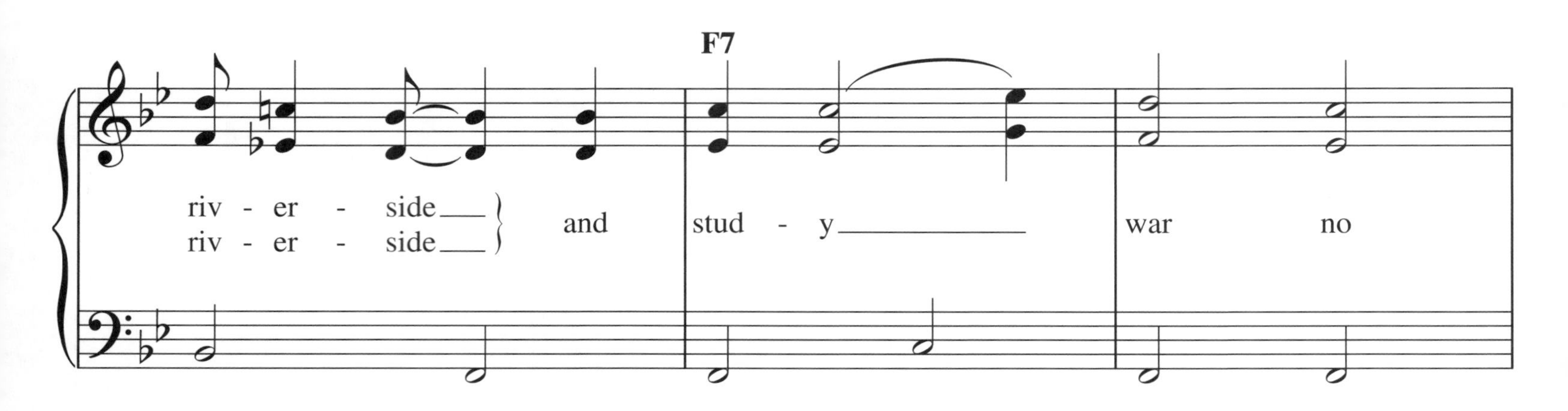
F7
riv - er - side___ and stud - y_______ war no
riv - er - side___

B♭
1.
2.
B♭7
more. Gon - na I ain't gon - na

E♭
B♭
stud - y war no more,___ I ain't gon - na stud - y war no more,_

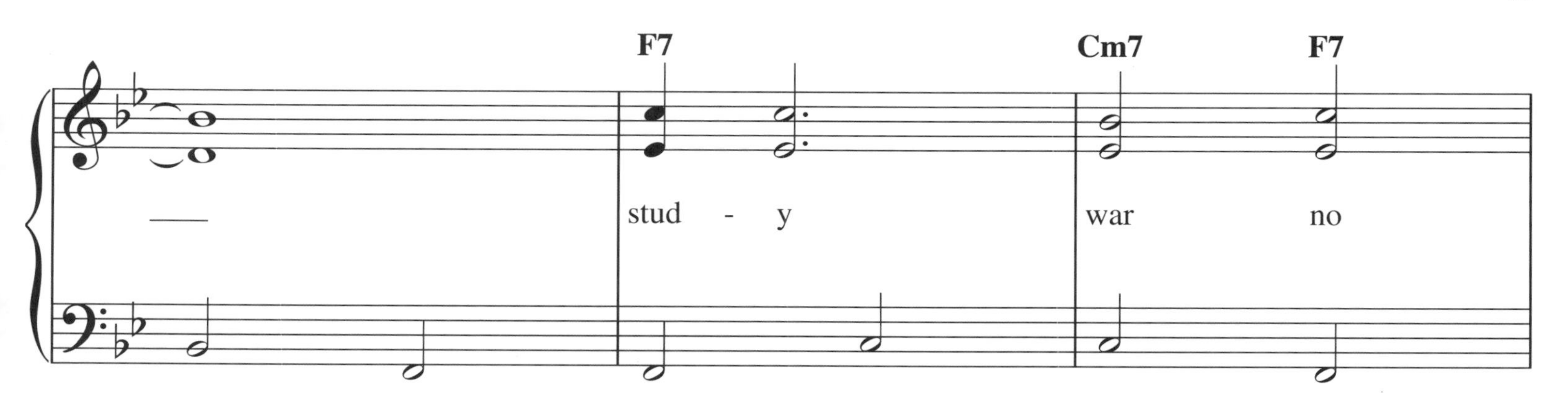
F7
Cm7
F7
stud - y
war
no

B♭
B♭7
E♭
more.
I ain't gon - na
stud - y war no more,

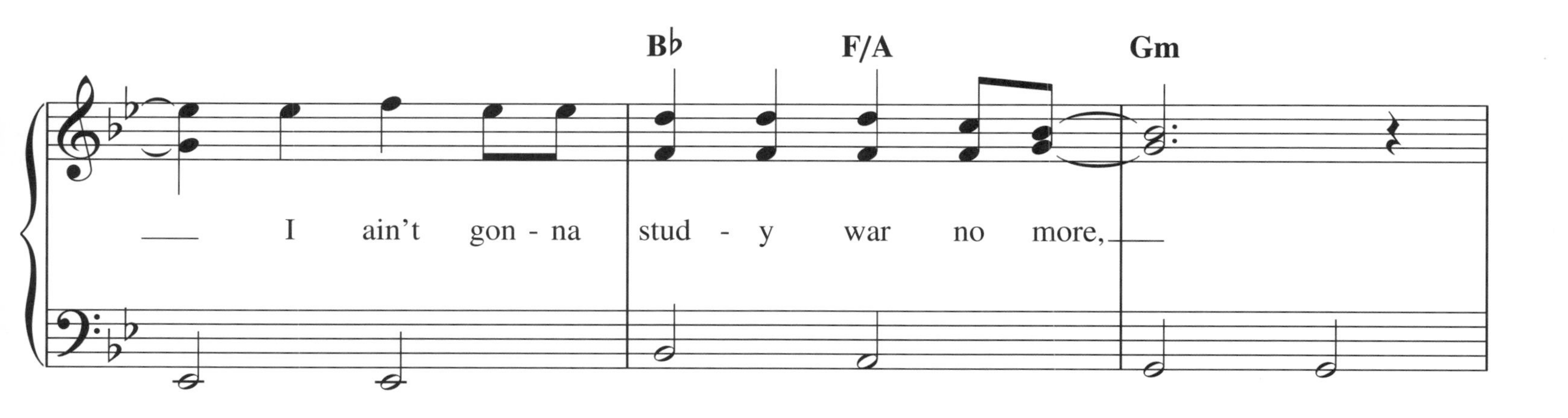
B♭
F/A
Gm
I ain't gon - na
stud - y war no more,

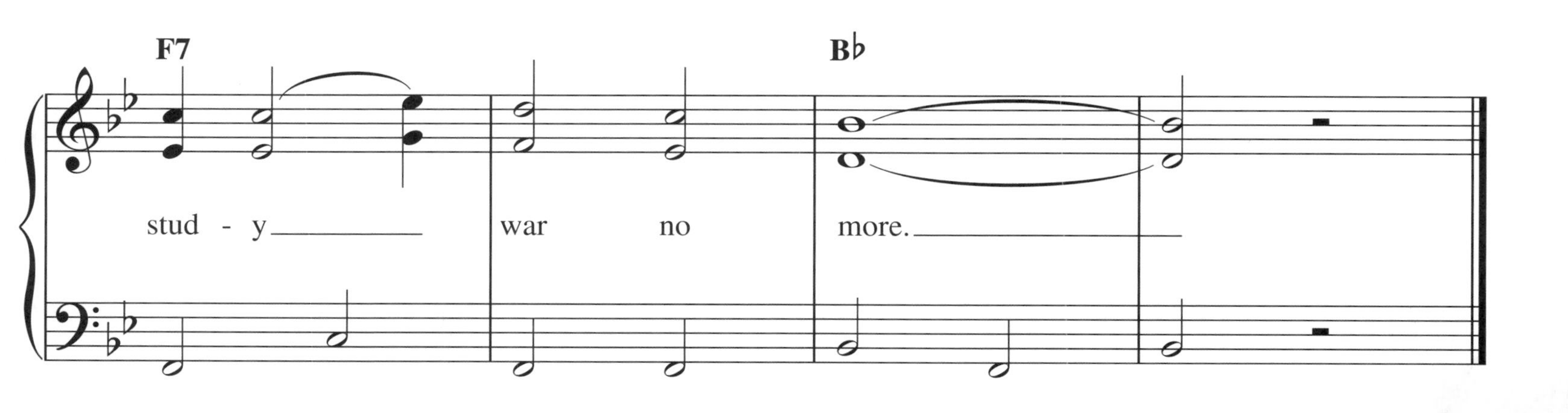
F7
B♭
stud - y
war no
more.

COME, THOU FOUNT OF EVERY BLESSING

Words by ROBERT ROBINSON
Music from JOHN WYETH's *Repository of Sacred Music*

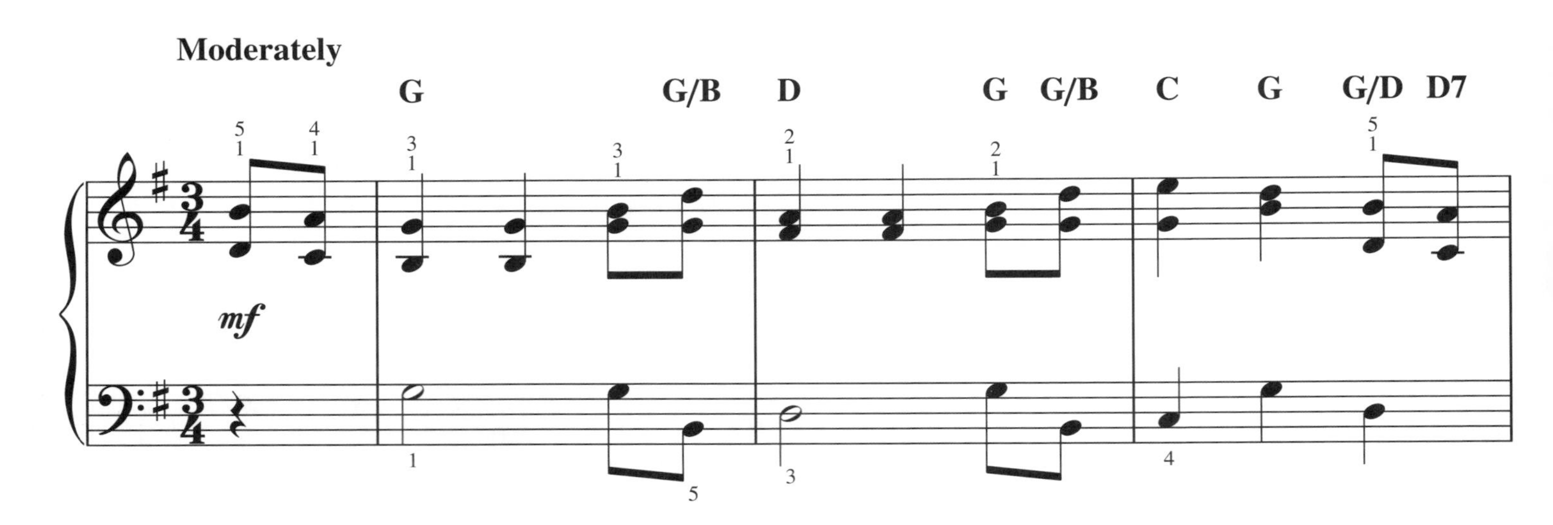

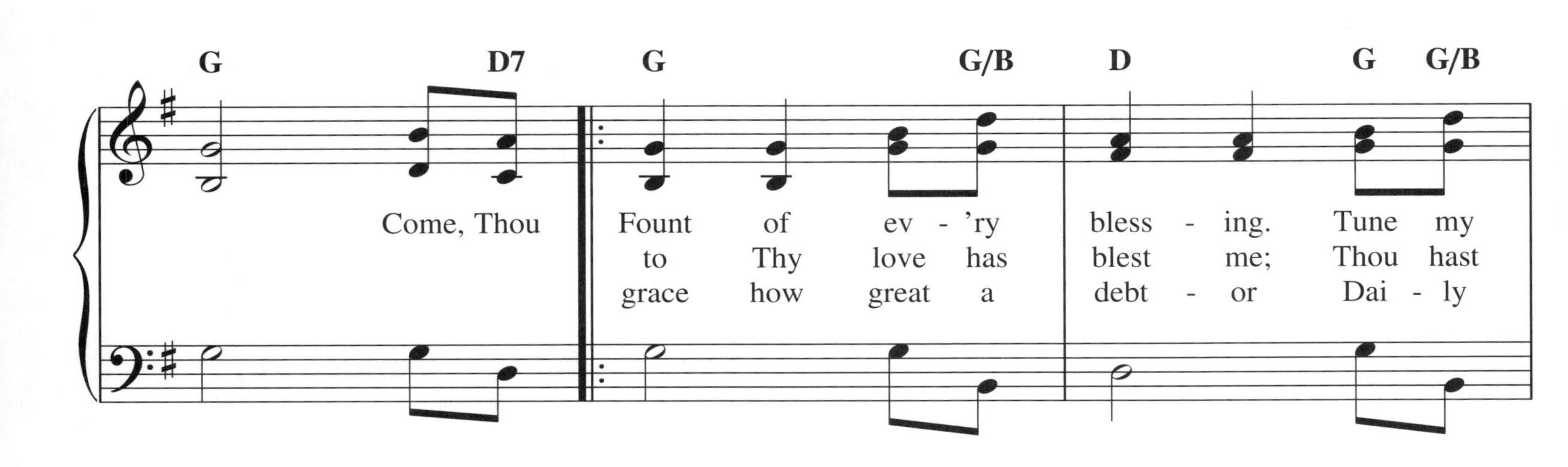

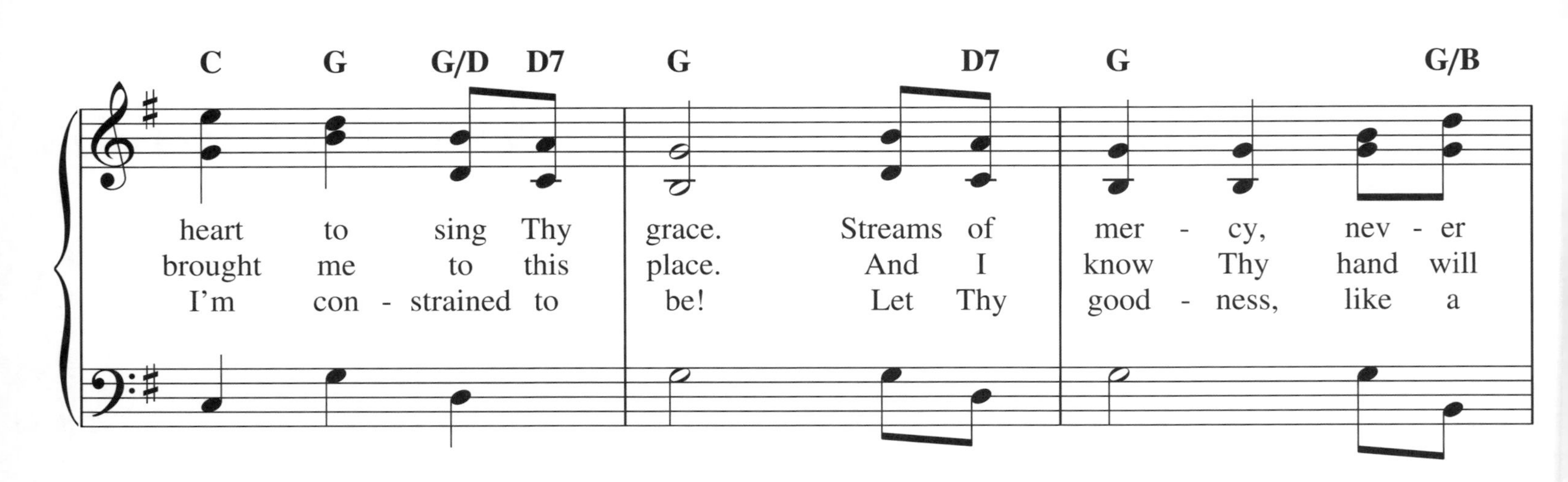

D G G/B C G G/D D7 G G/B D7/A
ceas - ing, Call for songs of loud - est praise. Teach me
bring me Safe - ly home by Thy good grace. Je - sus
fet - ter, Bind my wan - d'ring heart to Thee. Prone to
G Bm C G C/G G G/B D7/A G Bm C G
some me - lo - dious son - net, Sung by flam - ing tongues a -
sought me when a stran - ger, Wan - d'ring from the fold of
wan - der, Lord, I feel it, Prone to leave the God I
D7 G G/B D G G/B
bove. Praise His name, I'm fixed up - on it, Name of
God. He, to res - cue me from dan - ger, Bought me
love. Here's my heart, O take and seal it; Seal it
1., 2. 3.
C G G/D D7 G D7 G
God's re - deem - ing love. Hith - er -
with His pre - cious blood. O to
for Thy courts a - bove.

COME, YE FAITHFUL, RAISE THE STRAIN

Words by JOHN OF DAMASCUS
Translated by JOHN MASON NEALE
Music by ARTHUR SEYMOUR SULLIVAN

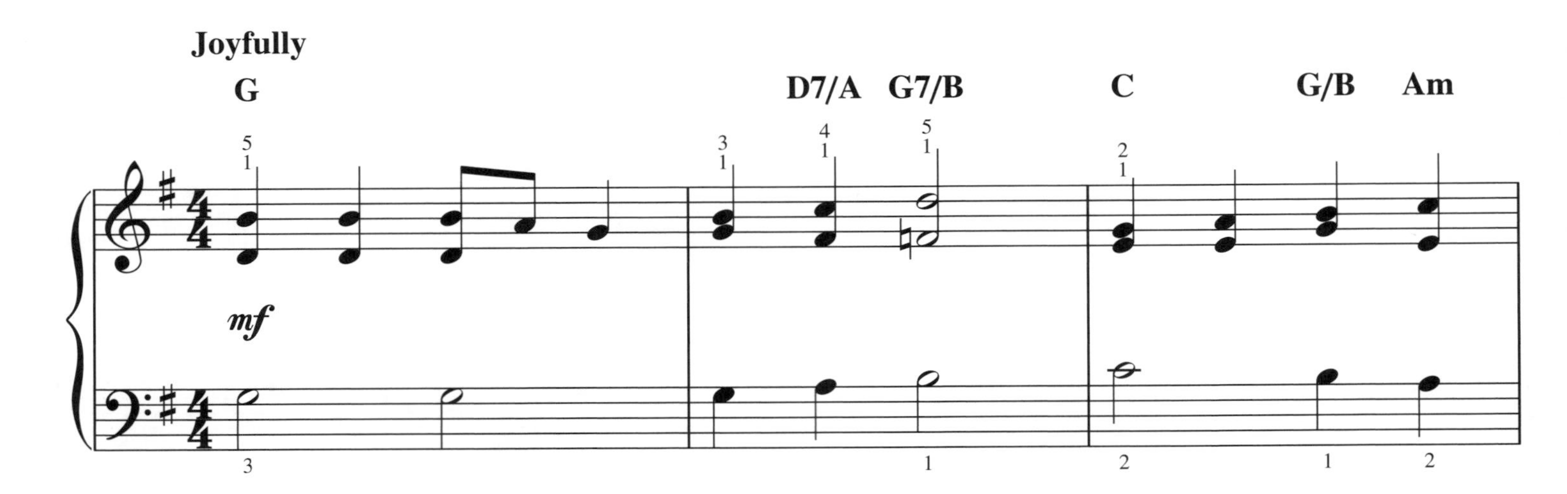

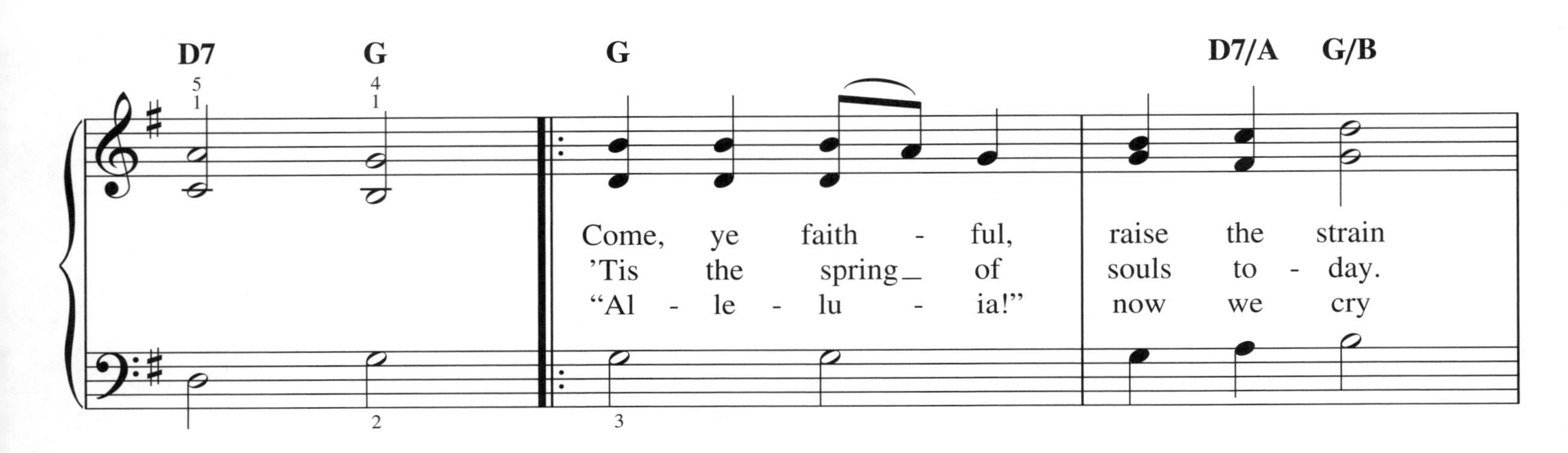

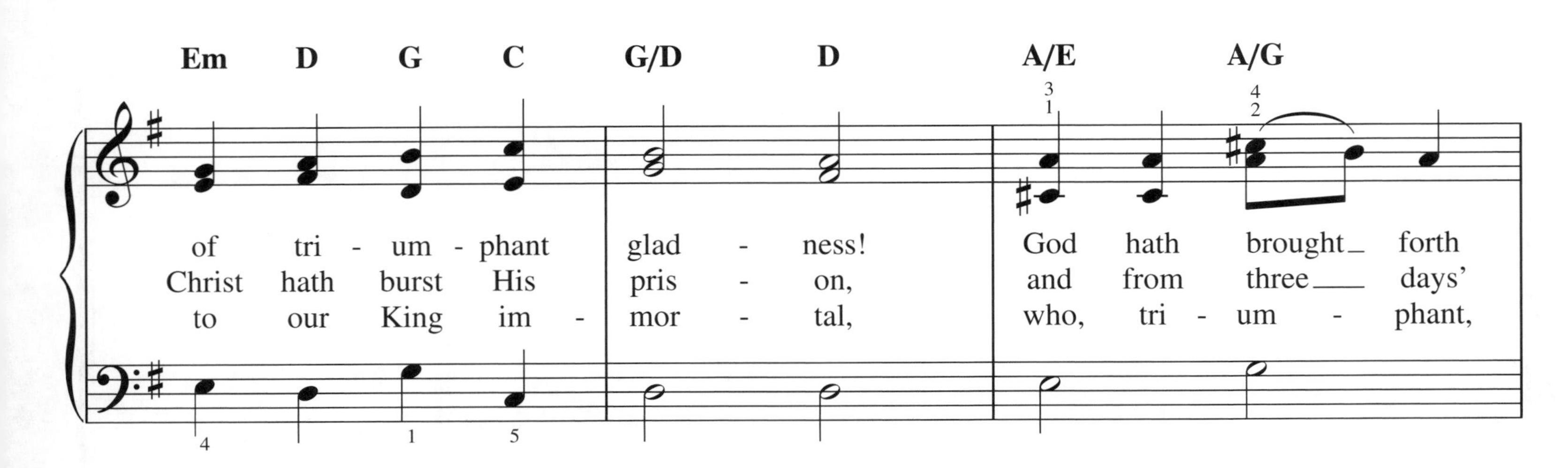

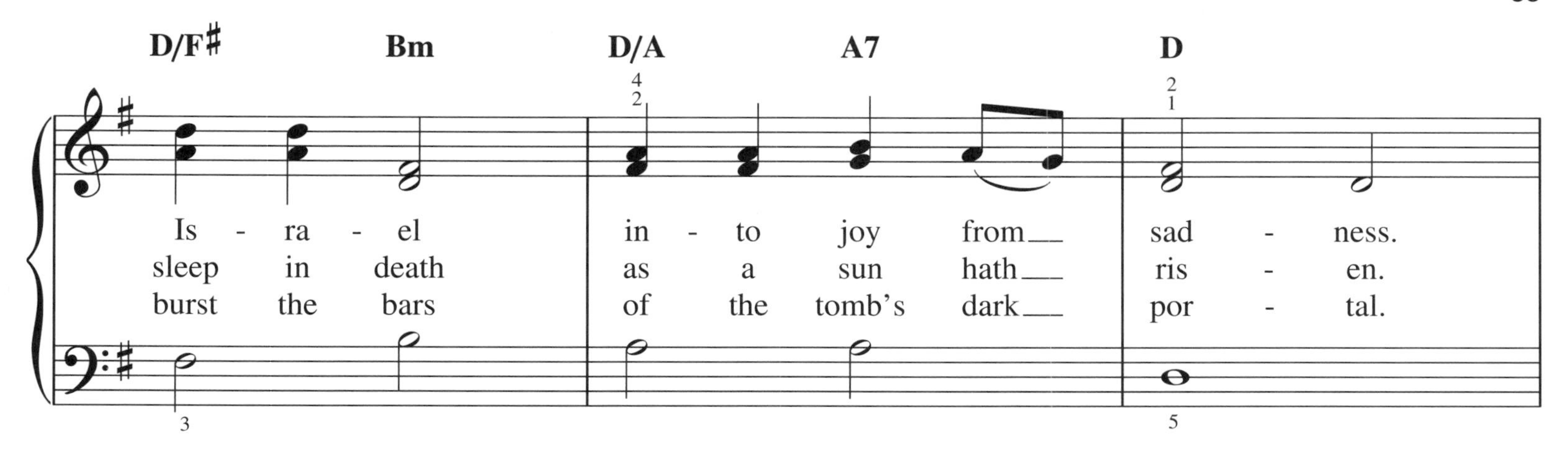
D/F♯ Bm D/A A7 D
Is - ra - el in - to joy from sad - ness.
sleep in death as a sun hath ris - en.
burst the bars of the tomb's dark por - tal.

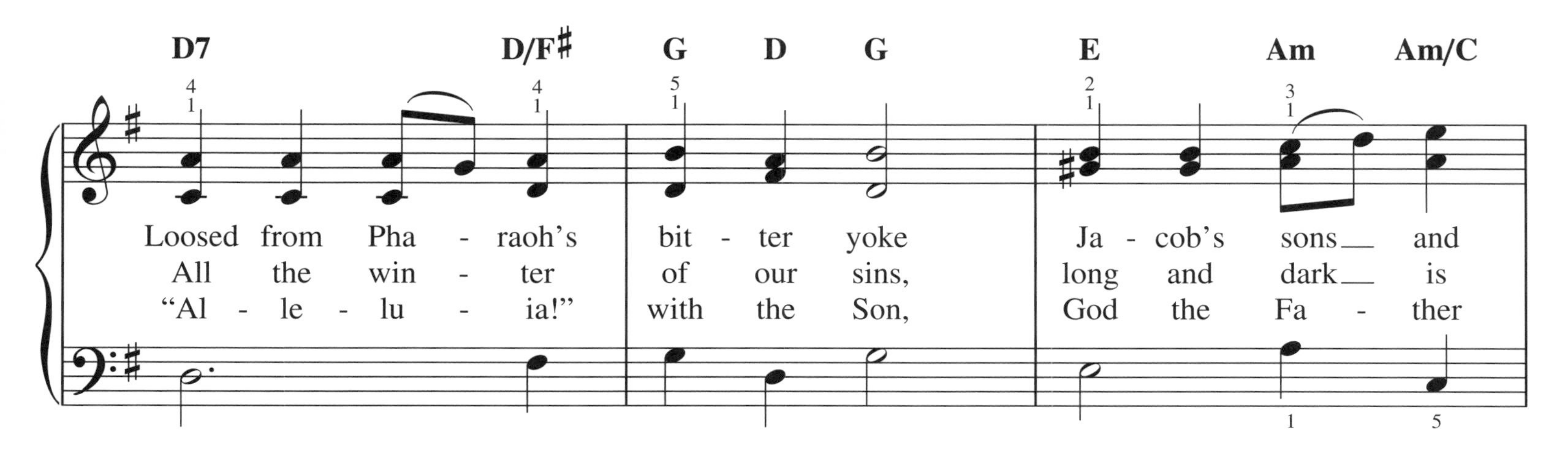
D7 D/F♯ G D G E Am Am/C
Loosed from Pha - raoh's bit - ter yoke Ja - cob's sons and
All the win - ter of our sins, long and dark is
"Al - le - lu - ia!" with the Son, God the Fa - ther

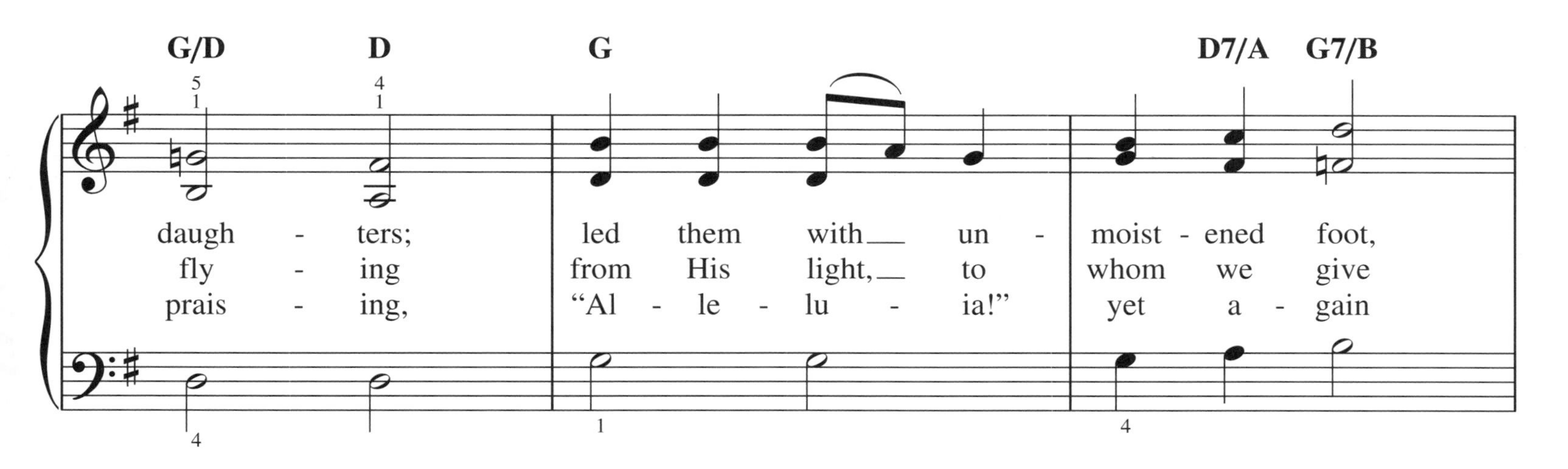
G/D D G D7/A G7/B
daugh - ters; led them with un - moist - ened foot,
fly - ing from His light, to whom we give
prais - ing, "Al - le - lu - ia!" yet a - gain

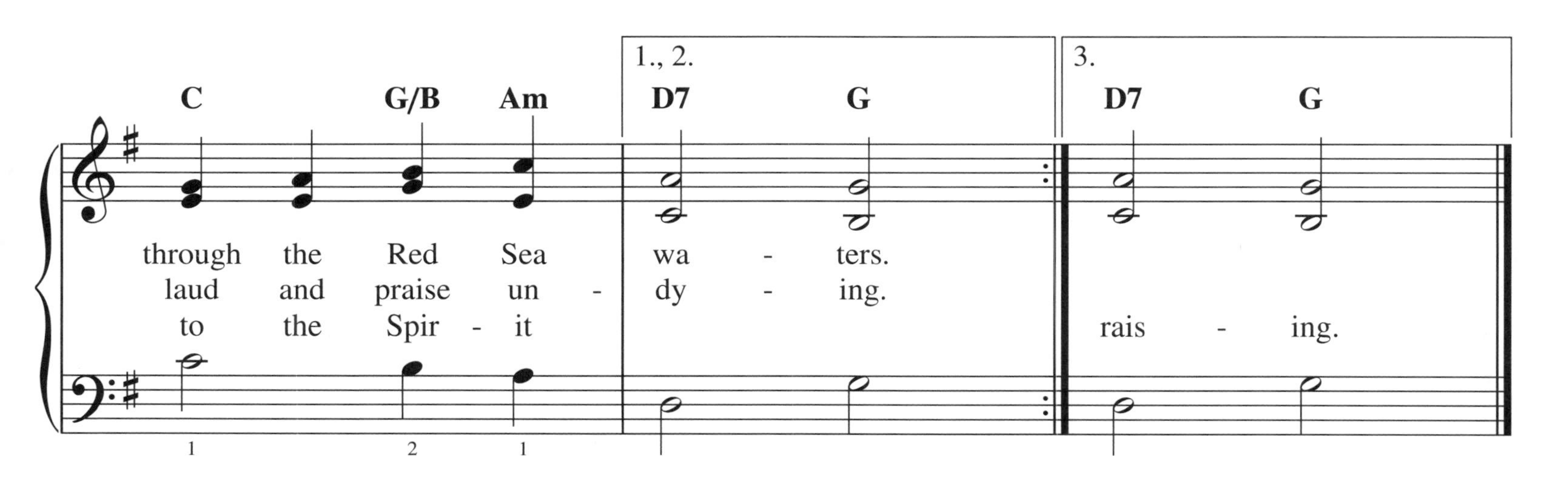
1., 2.
3.
C G/B Am D7 G D7 G
through the Red Sea wa - ters.
laud and praise un - dy - ing.
to the Spir - it rais - ing.

COME, YE THANKFUL PEOPLE, COME

Words by HENRY ALFORD
Music by GEORGE JOB ELVEY

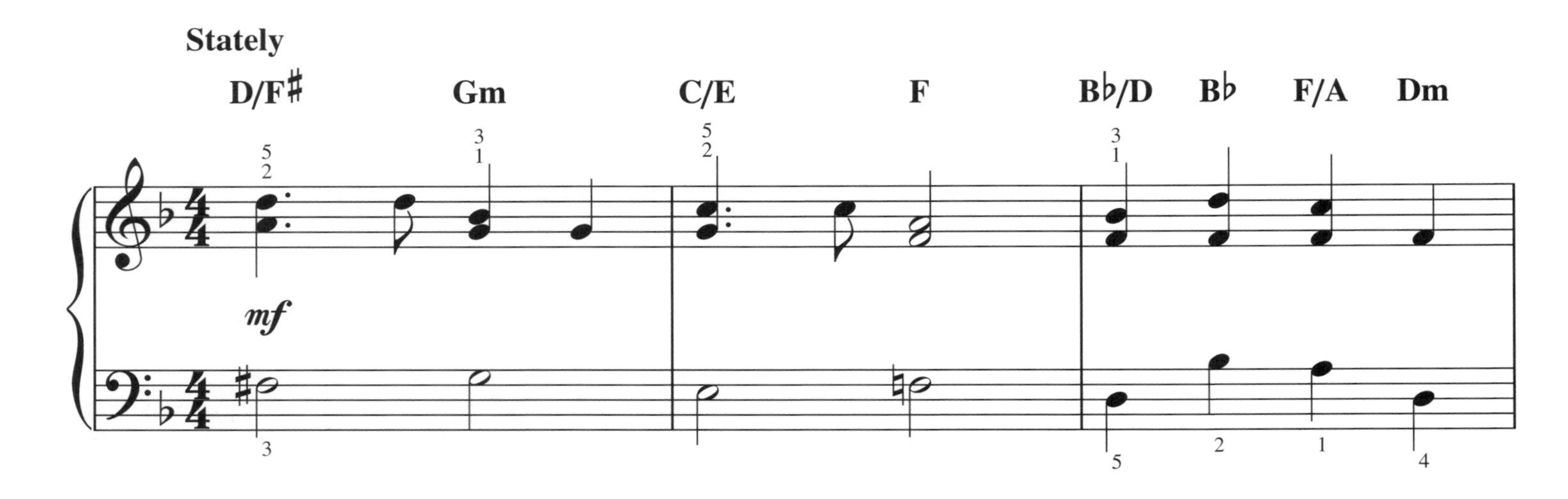

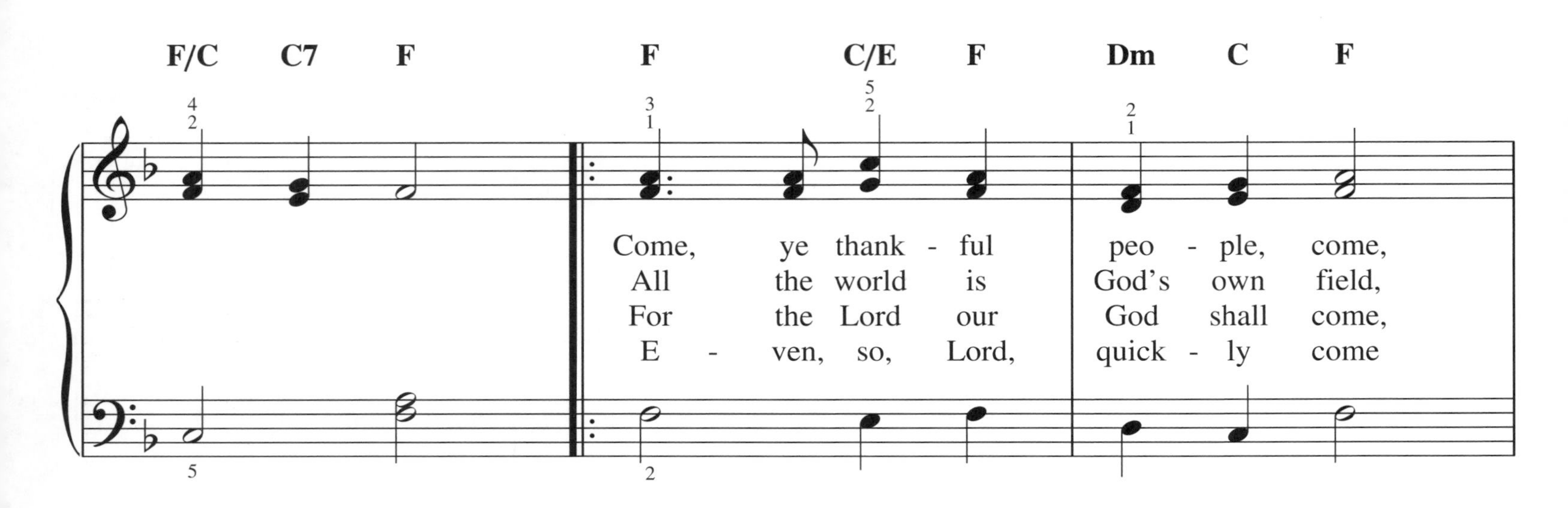

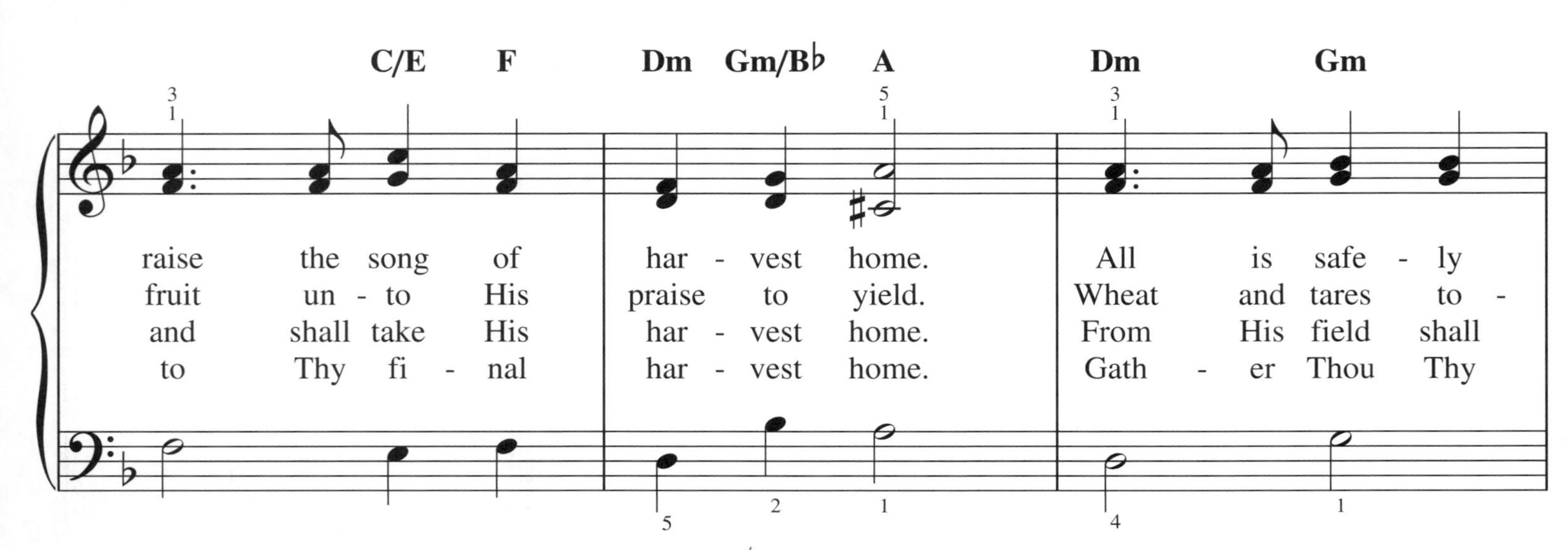

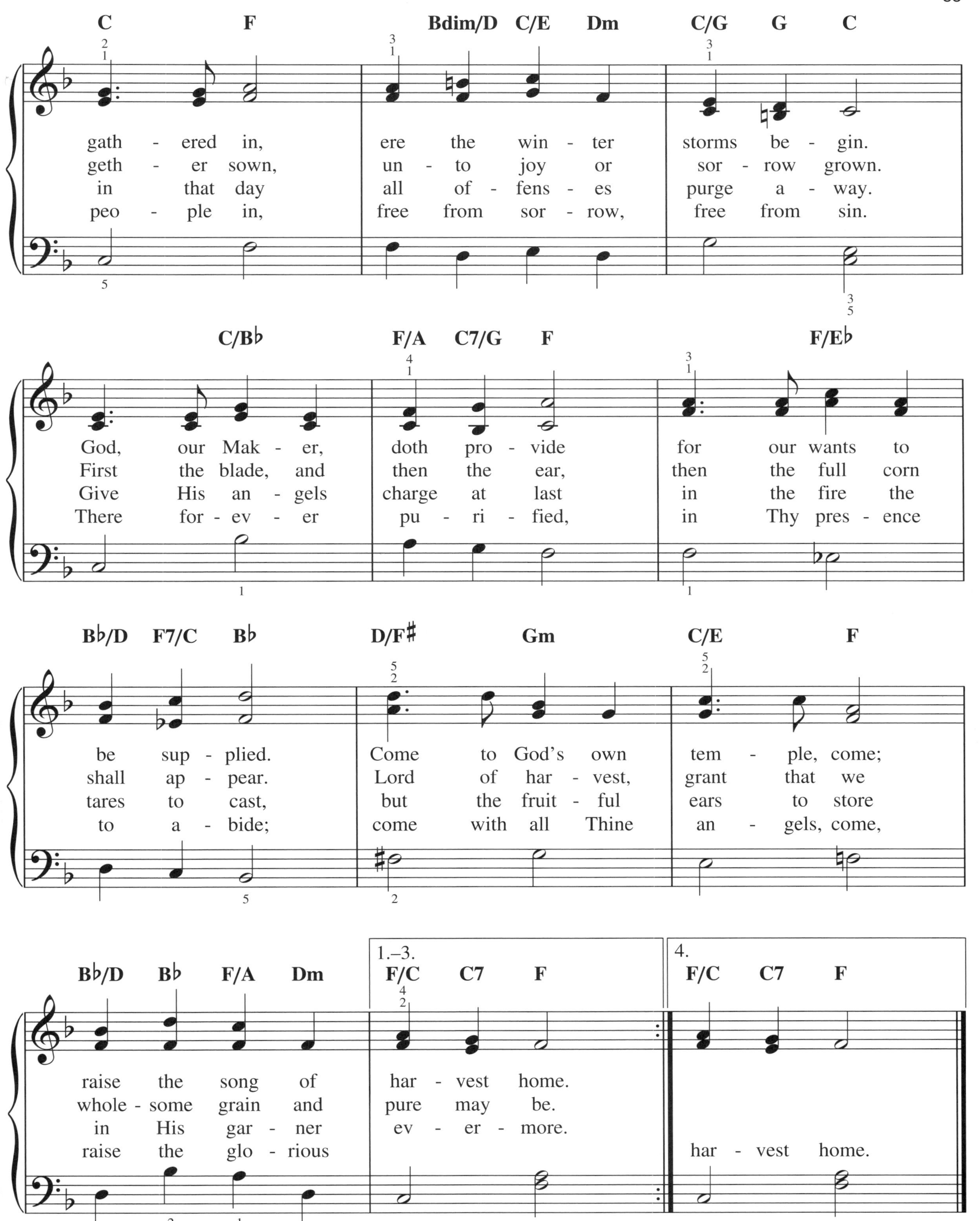
C F Bdim/D C/E Dm C/G G C
gath - ered in, ere the win - ter storms be - gin.
geth - er sown, un - to joy or sor - row grown.
in that day all of - fens - es purge a - way.
peo - ple in, free from sor - row, free from sin.
C/B♭ F/A C7/G F F/E♭
God, our Mak - er, doth pro - vide for our wants to
First the blade, and then the ear, then the full corn
Give His an - gels charge at last in the fire the
There for - ev - er pu - ri - fied, in Thy pres - ence
B♭/D F7/C B♭ D/F♯ Gm C/E F
be sup - plied. Come to God's own tem - ple, come;
shall ap - pear. Lord of har - vest, grant that we
tares to cast, but the fruit - ful ears to store
to a - bide; come with all Thine an - gels, come,
B♭/D B♭ F/A Dm
1.–3.
F/C C7 F
4.
F/C C7 F
raise the song of har - vest home.
whole - some grain and pure may be.
in His gar - ner ev - er - more.
raise the glo - rious har - vest home.

COUNT YOUR BLESSINGS

Words by JOHNSON OATMAN, JR.
Music by EDWIN O. EXCELL

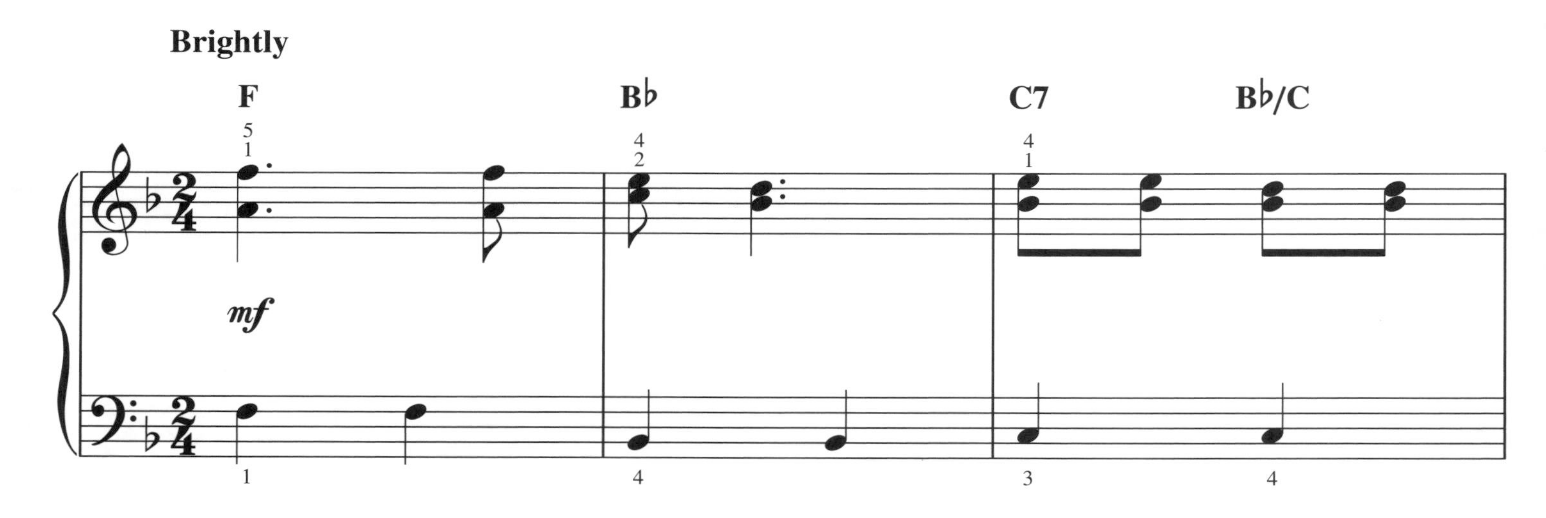

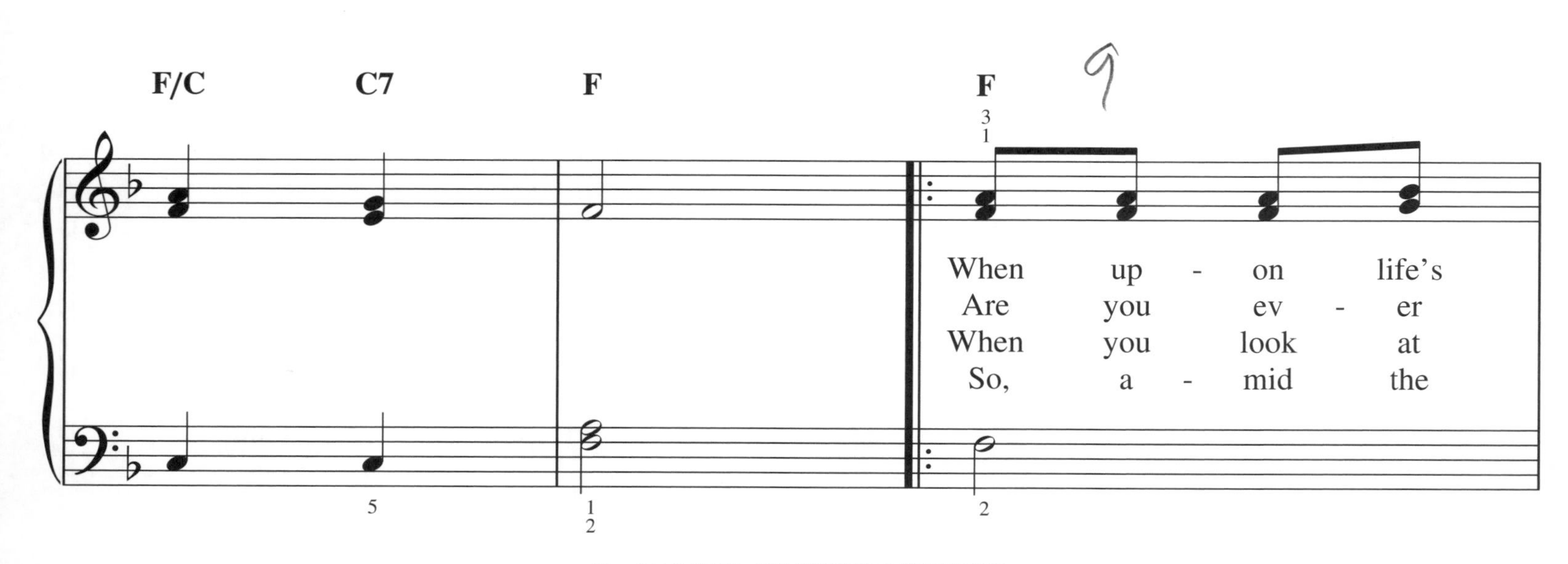

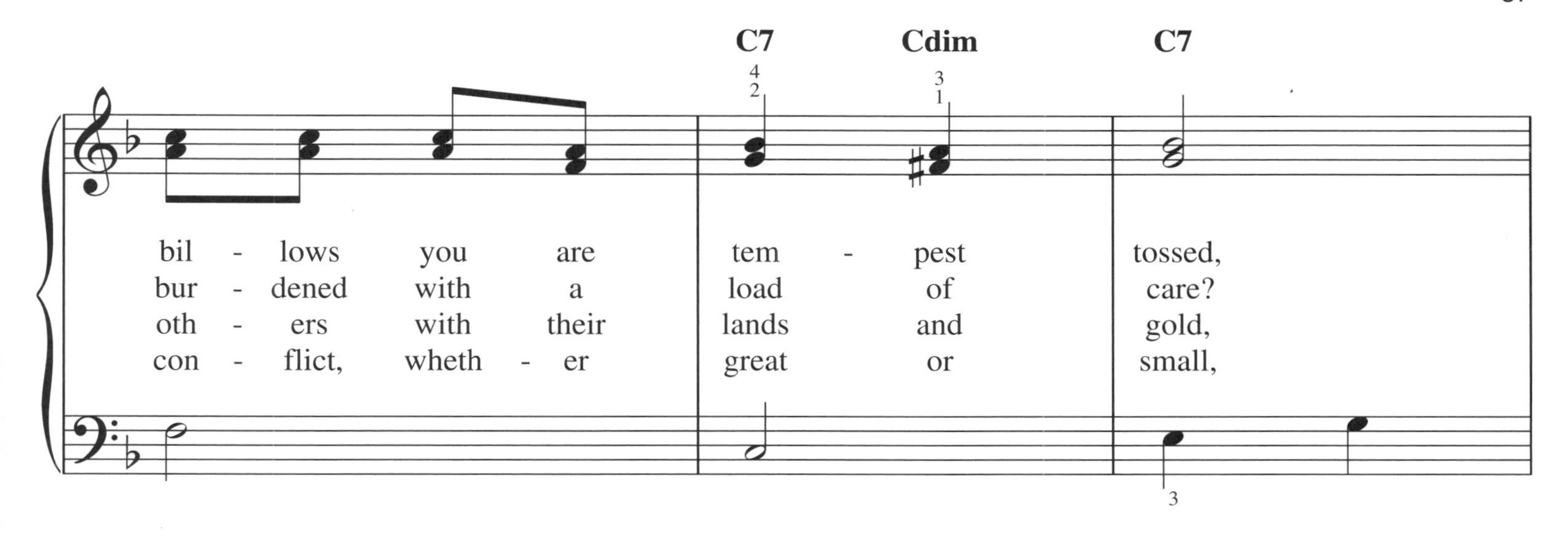
C7 Cdim C7
bil - lows you are tem - pest tossed,
bur - dened with a load of care?
oth - ers with their lands and gold,
con - flict, wheth - er great or small,

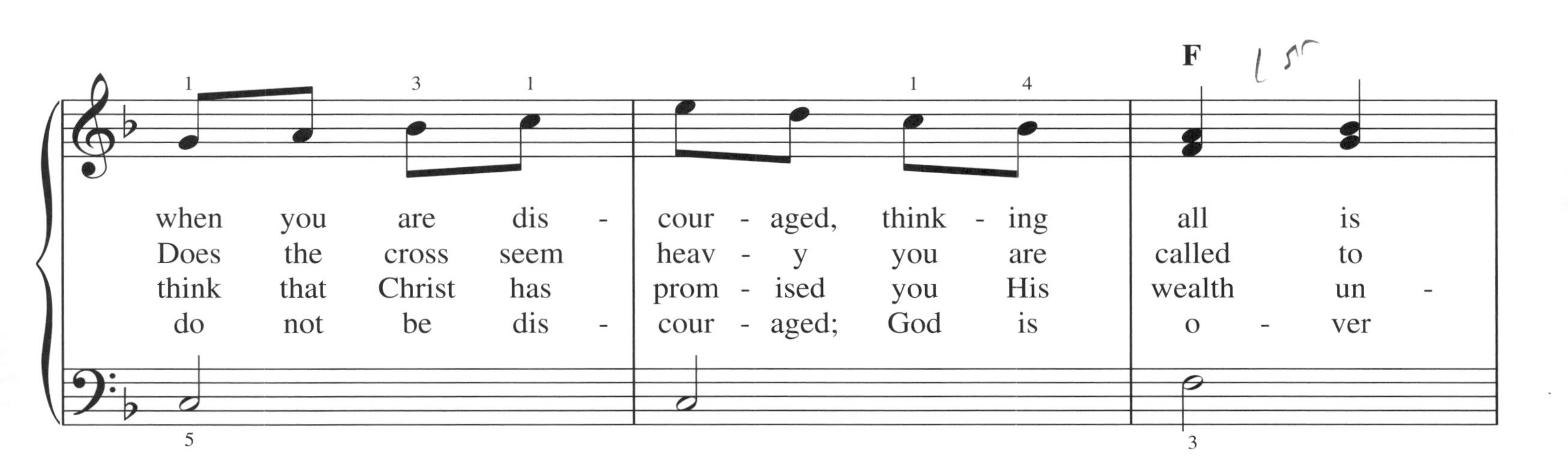
F
when you are dis - cour - aged, think - ing all is
Does the cross seem heav - y you are called to
think that Christ has prom - ised you His wealth un -
do not be dis - cour - aged; God is o - ver

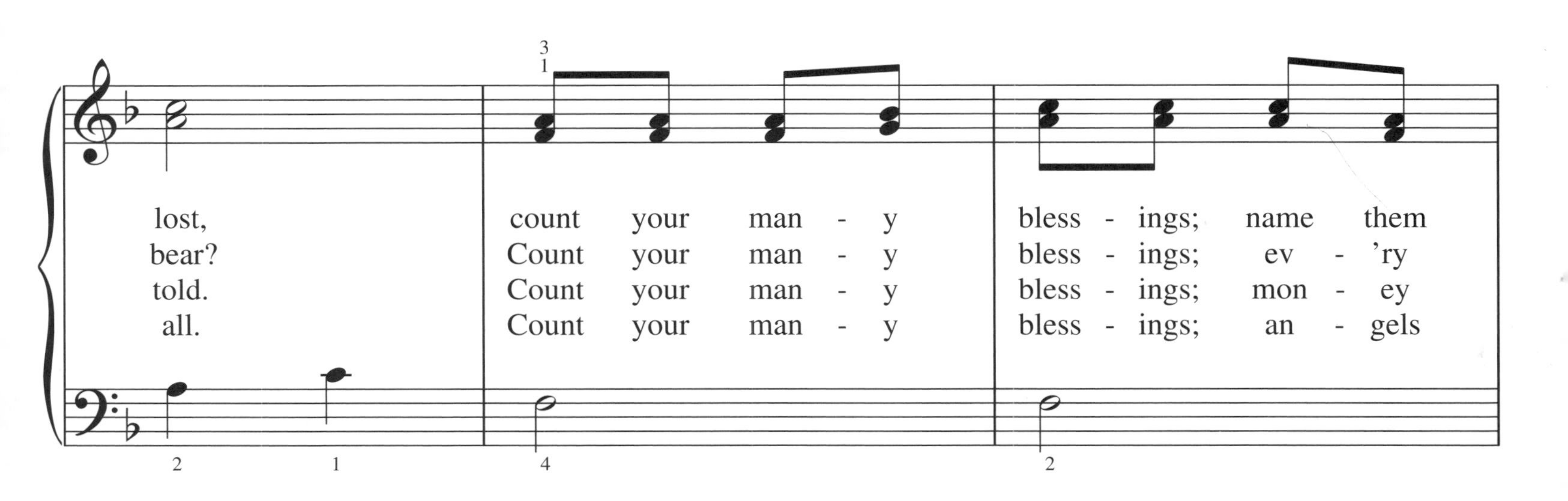
lost, count your man - y bless - ings; name them
bear? Count your man - y bless - ings; ev - 'ry
told. Count your man - y bless - ings; mon - ey
all. Count your man - y bless - ings; an - gels

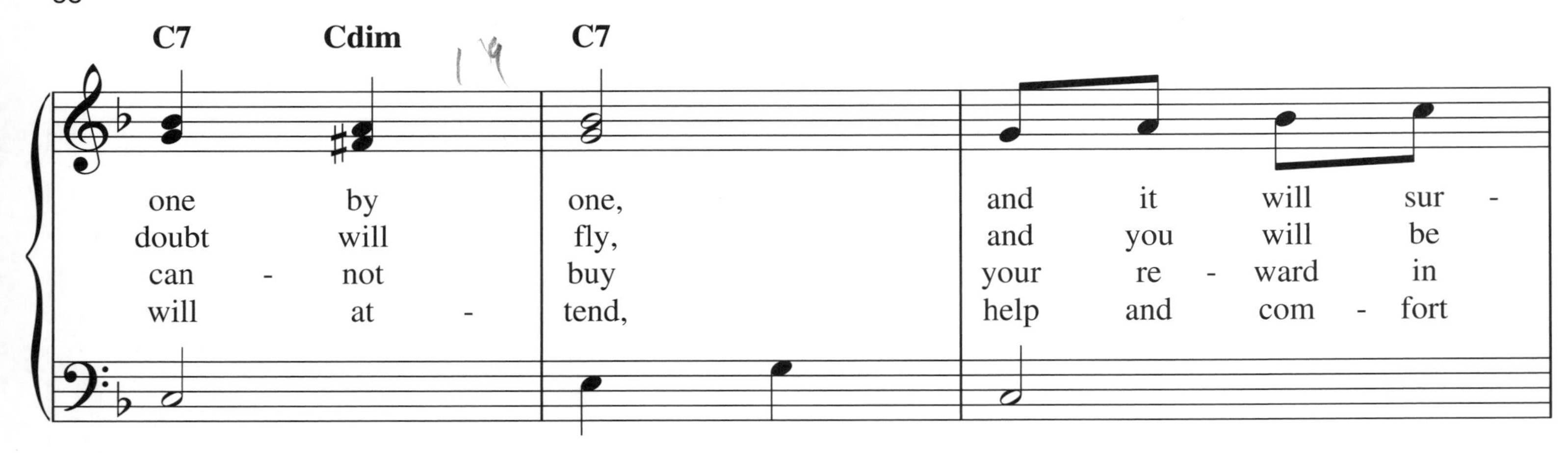
C7 Cdim C7
one by one, and it will sur -
doubt will fly, and you will be
can - not buy your re - ward in
will at - tend, help and com - fort

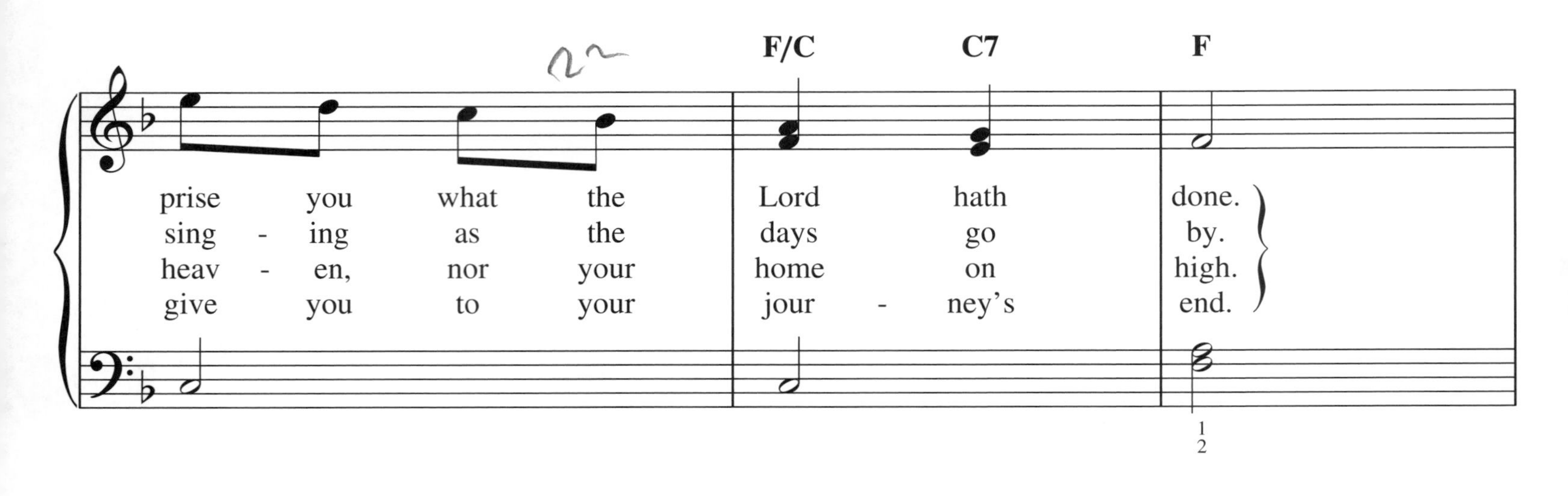
F/C C7 F
prise you what the Lord hath done.
sing - ing as the days go by.
heav - en, nor your home on high.
give you to your jour - ney's end.

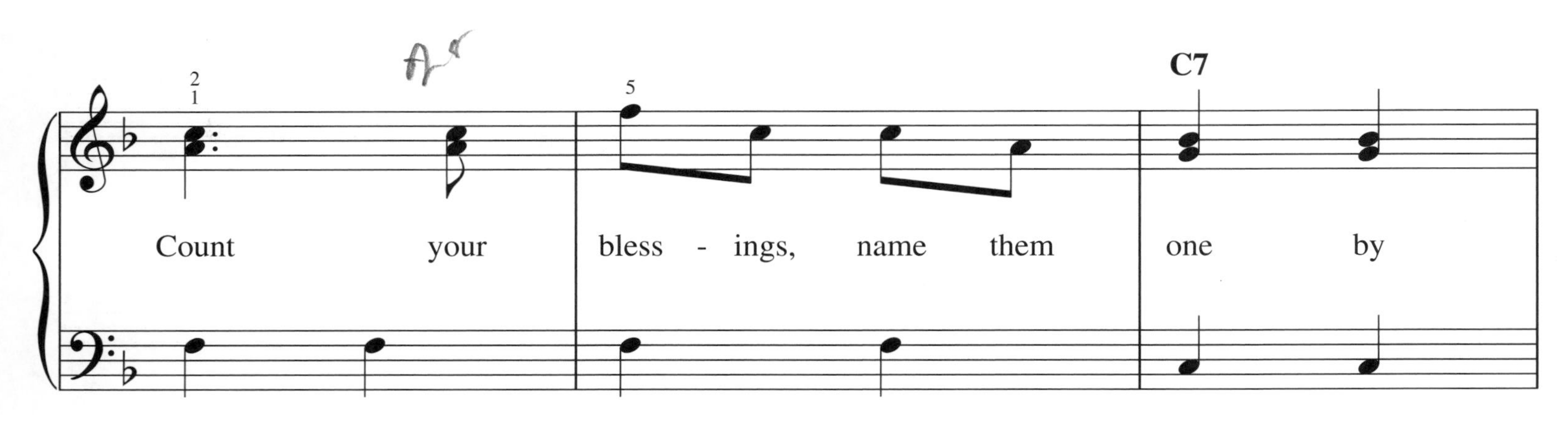
C7
Count your bless - ings, name them one by

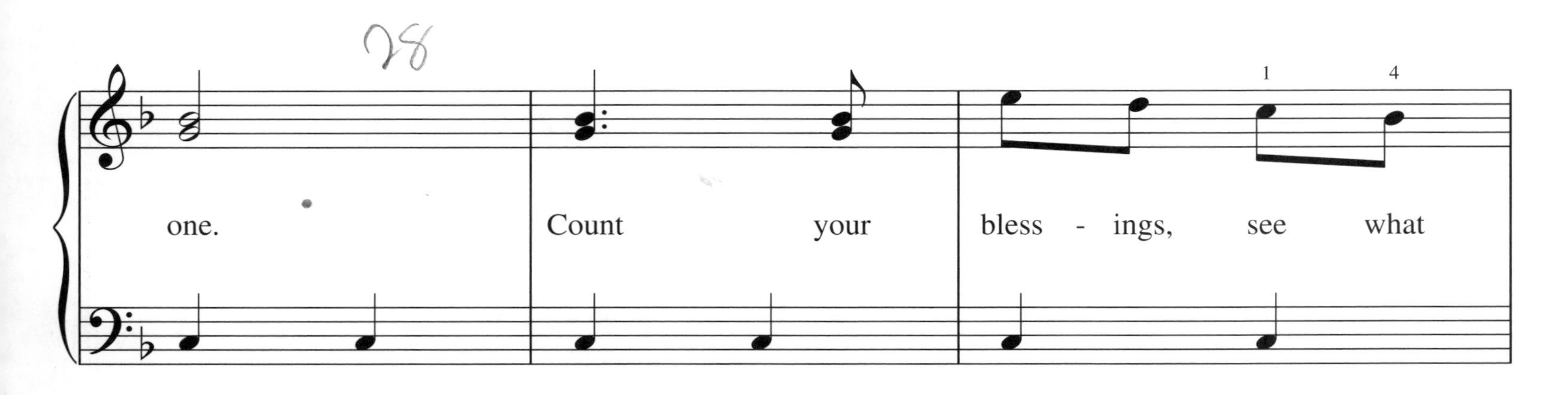
one. Count your bless - ings, see what

F
God hath
done.
Count your

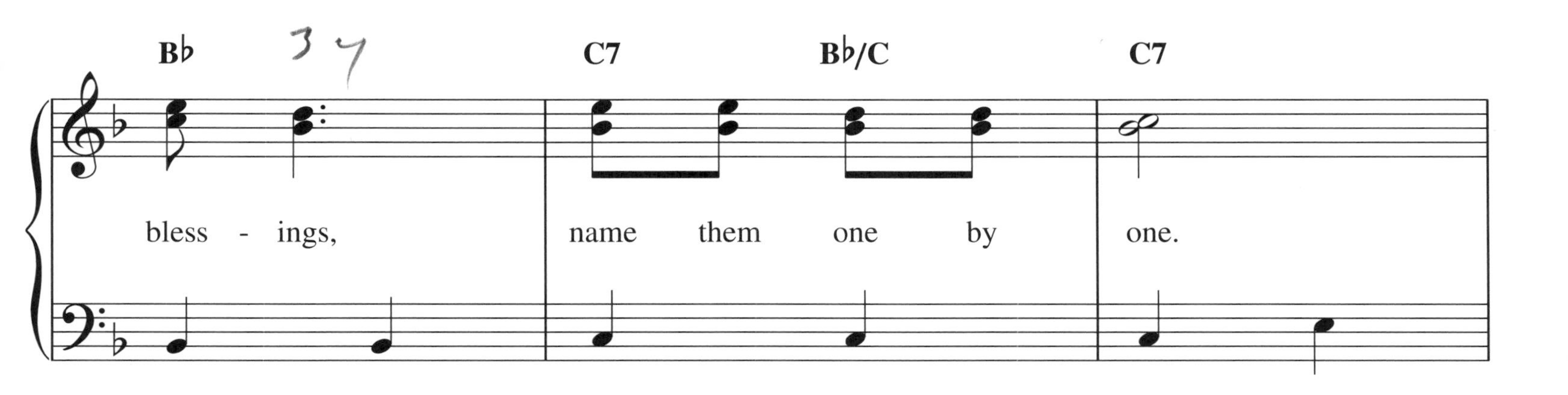
B♭
C7
B♭/C
C7
bless - ings,
name them one by
one.

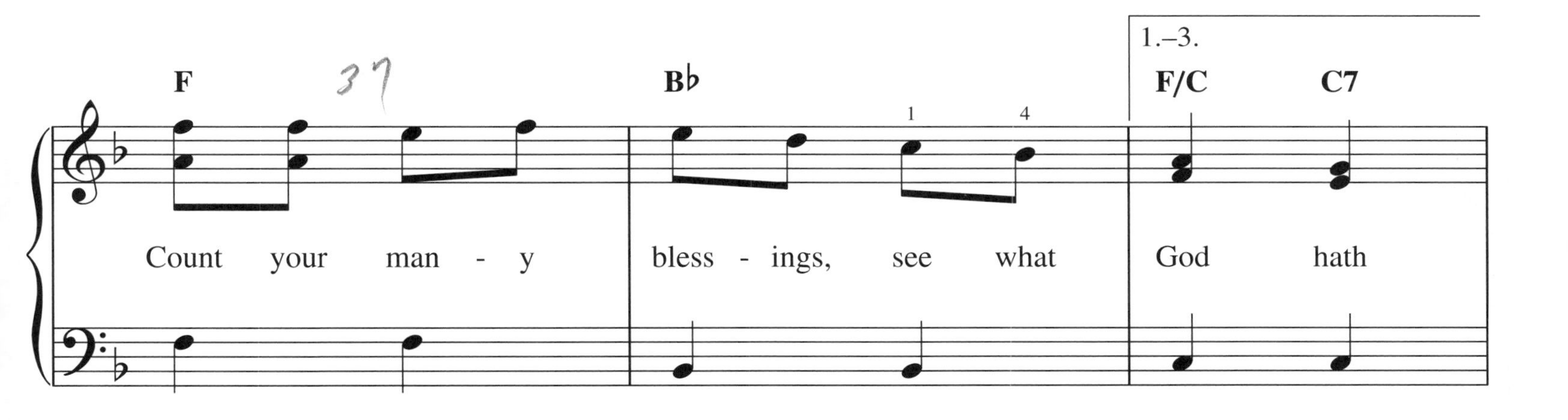
F
B♭
1.–3.
F/C
C7
Count your man - y
bless - ings, see what
God hath

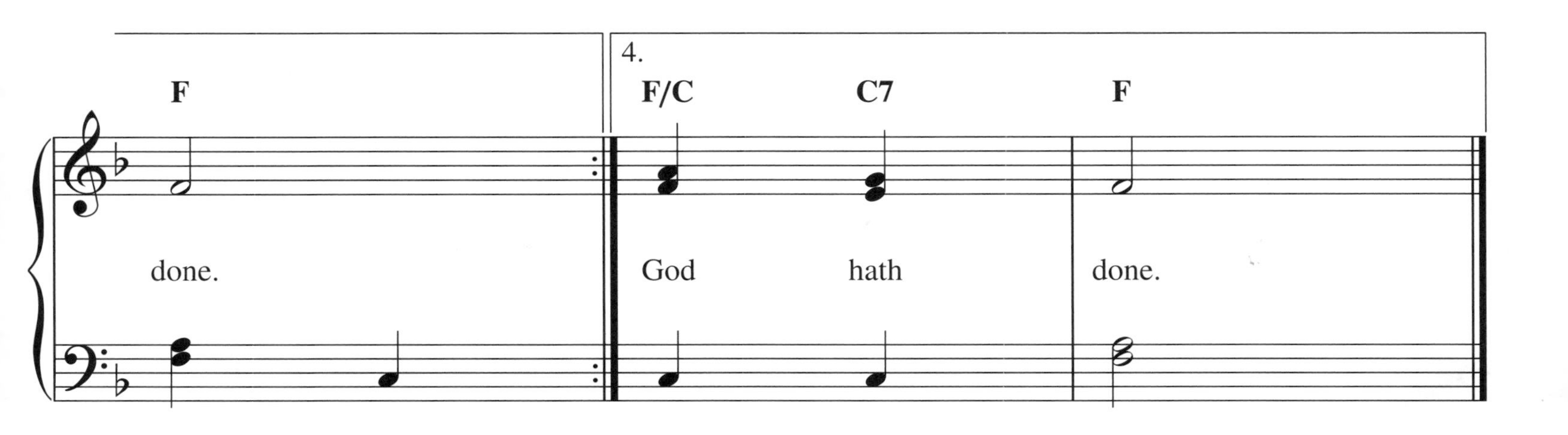
F
4.
F/C
C7
F
done.
God hath
done.

CROWN HIM WITH MANY CROWNS

Words by MATTHEW BRIDGES and GODFREY THRING
Music by GEORGE JOB ELVEY

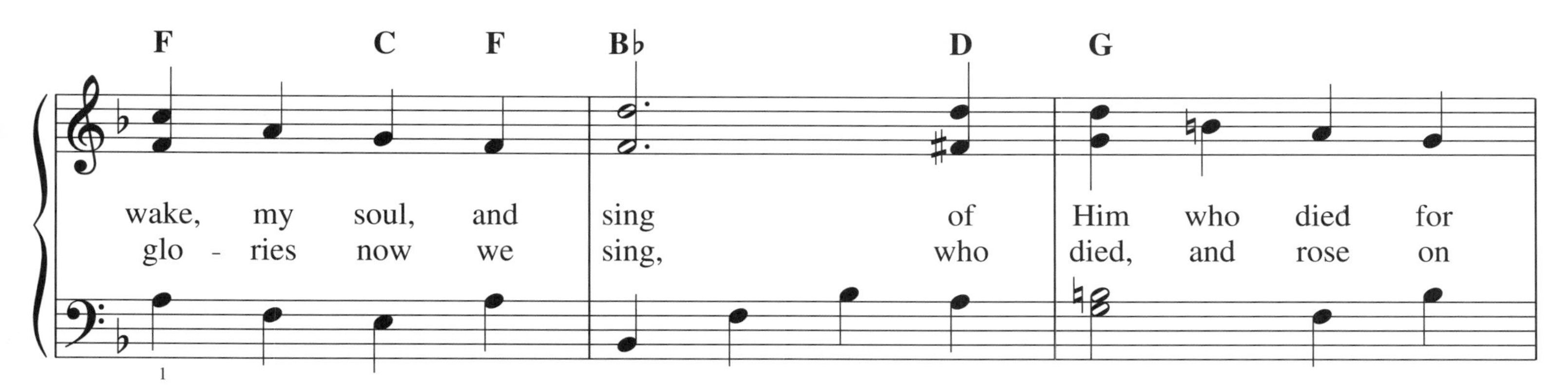

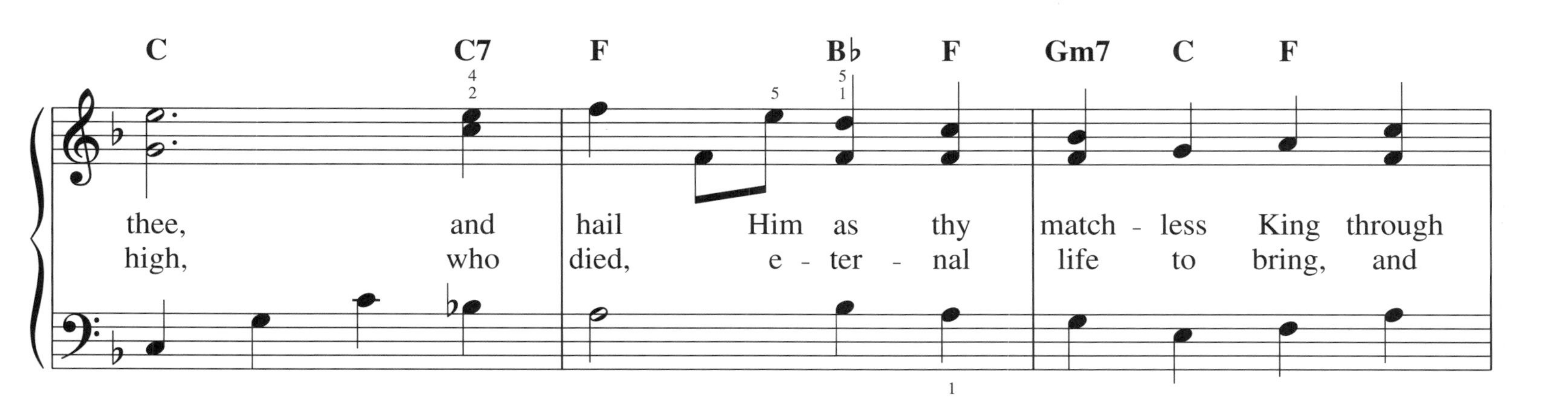

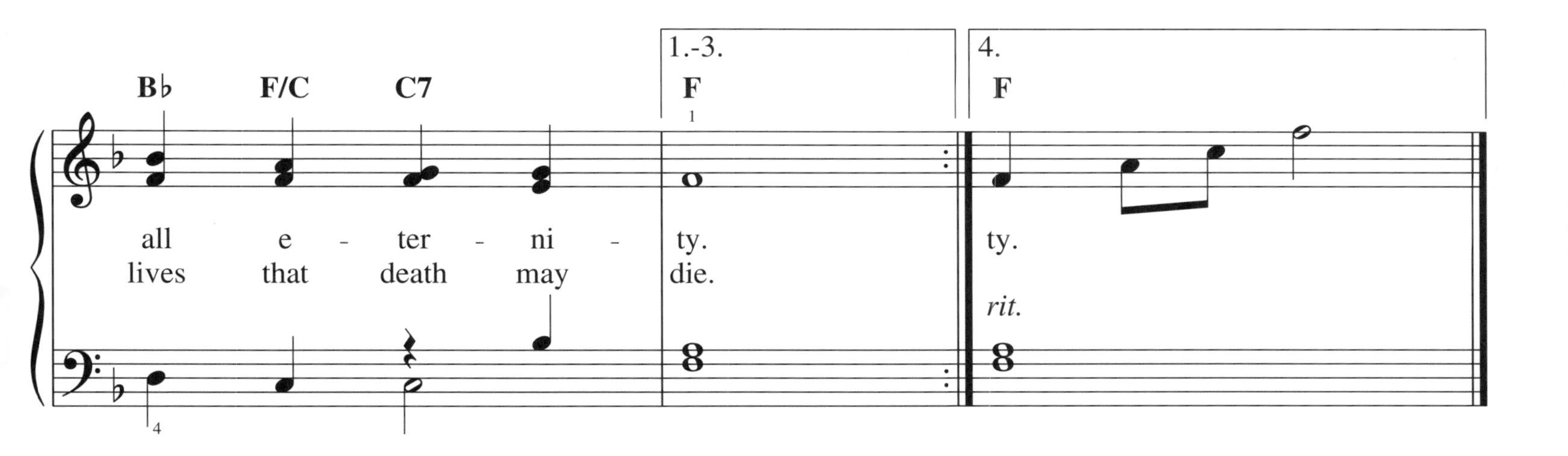

Additional Verses

3. Crown Him the Lord of peace, whose power a scepter sways
   From pole to pole, that wars may cease, and all be prayer and praise.
   His reign shall know no end, and round His pierced feet
   Fair flowers of paradise extend their fragrance ever sweet.

4. Crown Him the Lord of love; behold His hands and side,
   Those wounds, yet visible above, in beauty glorified.
   All hail, Redeemer, hail! For Thou hast died for me;
   Thy praise and glory shall not fail throughout eternity.

DAY IS DYING IN THE WEST

Words by MARY A. LATHBURY
Music by WILLIAM F. SHERWIN

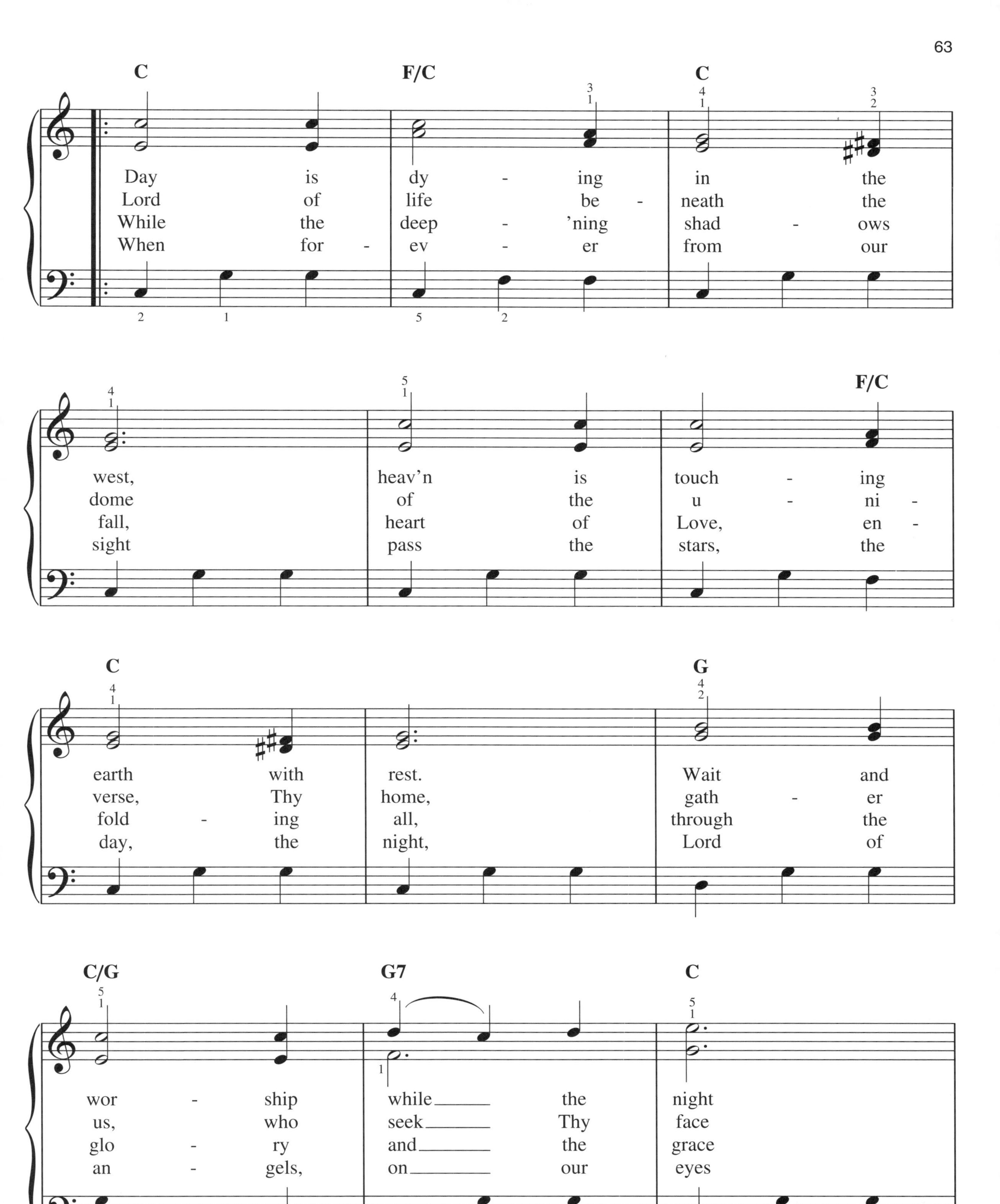
C
F/C
C
Day is dy - ing in the
Lord of life be - neath the
While the deep - 'ning shad - ows
When for - ev - er from our
west, heav'n is touch - ing
dome of the u - ni -
fall, heart of Love, en -
sight pass the stars, the
F/C
C
G
earth with rest. Wait and
verse, Thy home, gath - er
fold - ing all, through the
day, the night, Lord of
C/G
G7
C
wor - ship while the night
us, who seek Thy face
glo - ry and the grace
an - gels, on our eyes

G7/B
C
D7
sets her eve - ning lamps a -
to the fold of Thy em -
of the stars that veil Thy
let e - ter - nal morn - ing
G
C
G/D
D7
light through all the
brace, for Thou art
face, our hearts as -
rise, and shad - ows

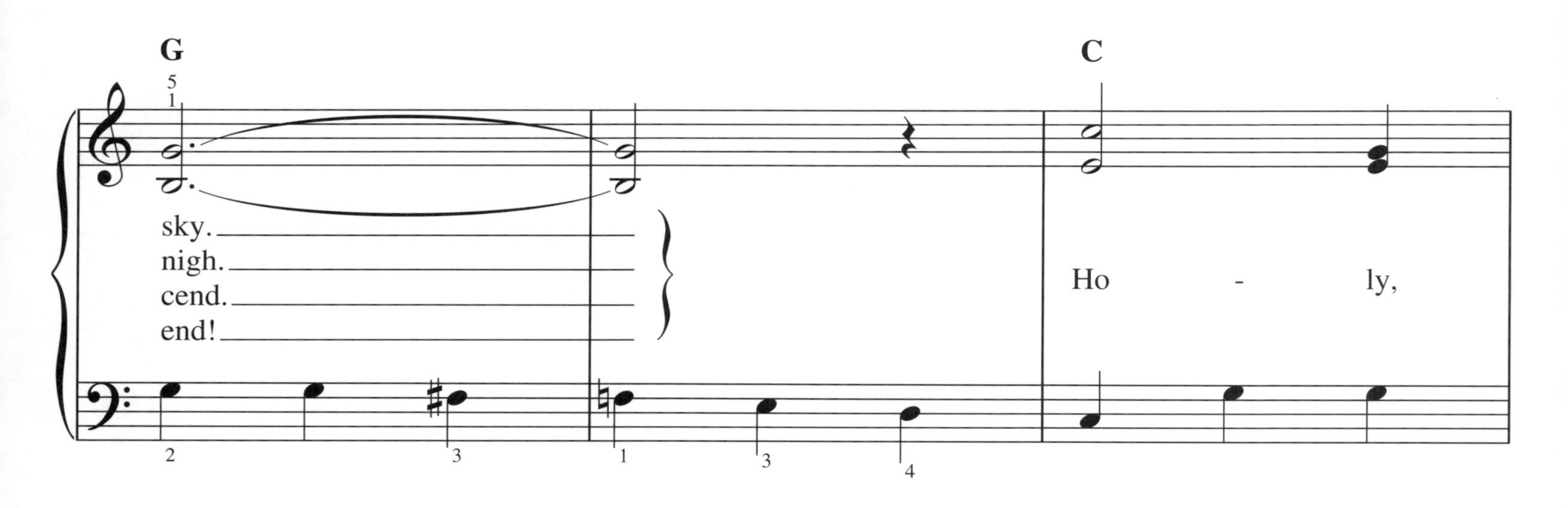
G
C
sky.
nigh.
cend.
end!
Ho - ly,

ho - ly, ho - ly, Lord

G7
C
F
God of Hosts!
Heav'n and
C
G7
earth are full of Thee!
Heav'n and
C
F
C/G
earth are prais - ing Thee, O Lord
G7
1.–3.
C
4.
C
Most High!
High!
*second time

DEAR LORD AND FATHER OF MANKIND

Words by JOHN GREENLEAF WHITTIER
Music by FREDERICK CHARLES MAKER

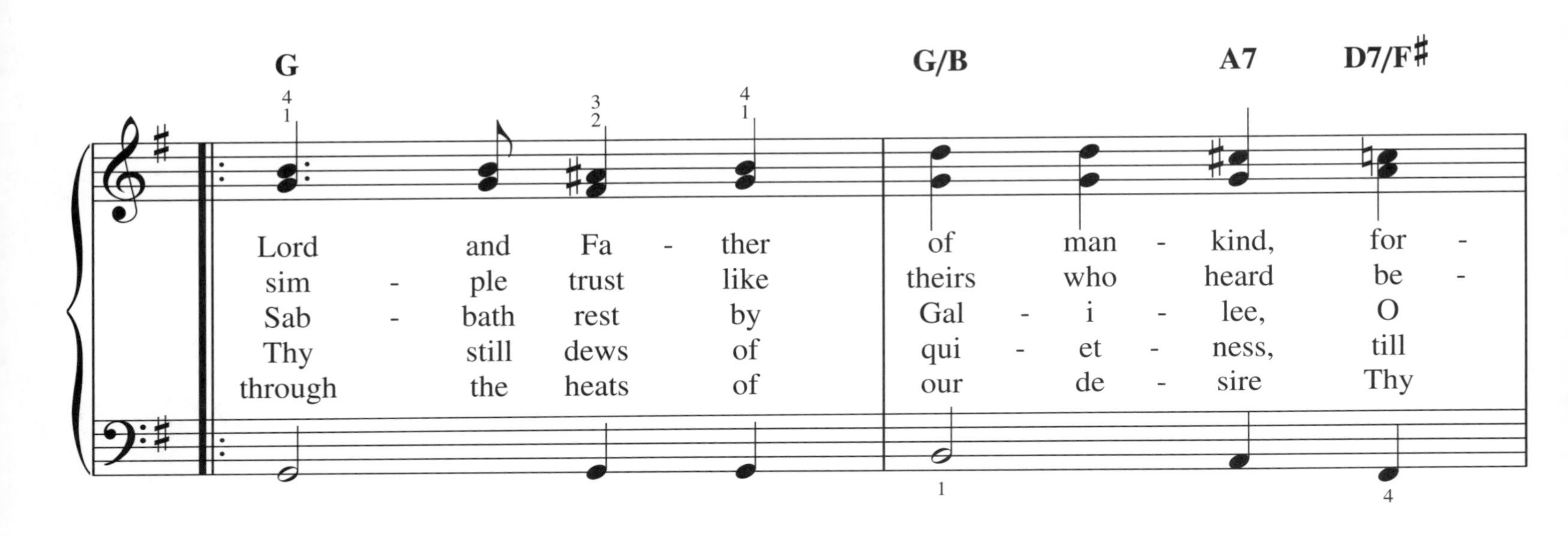

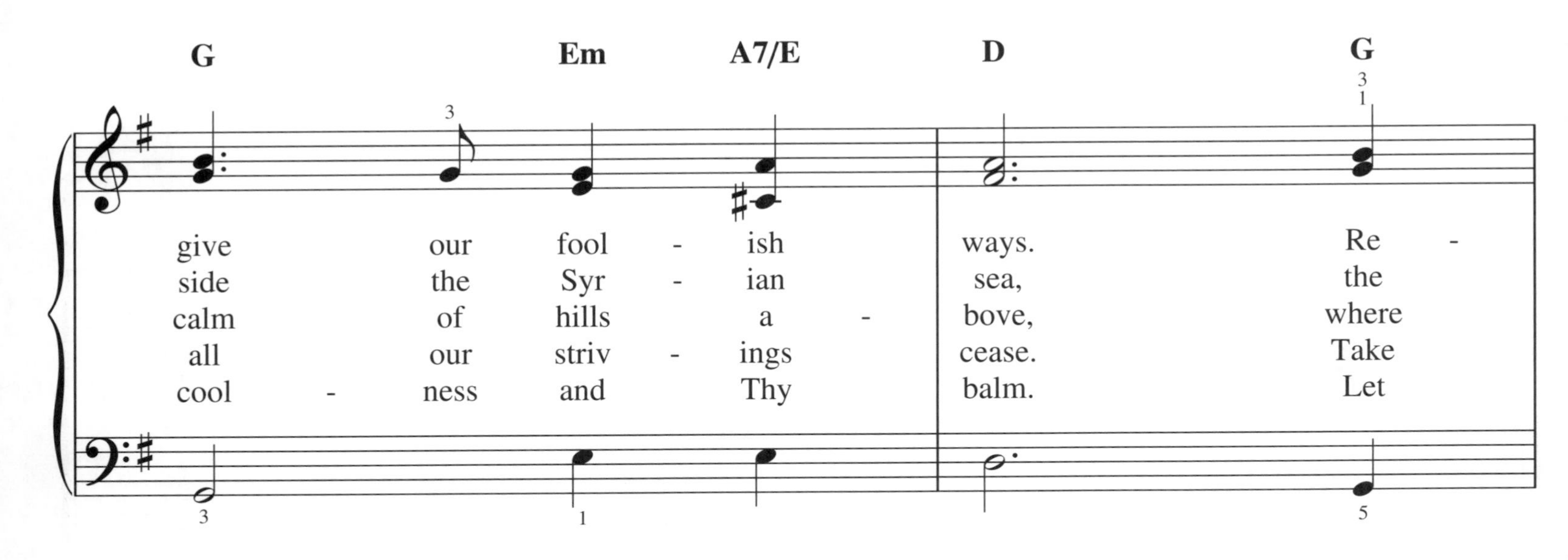

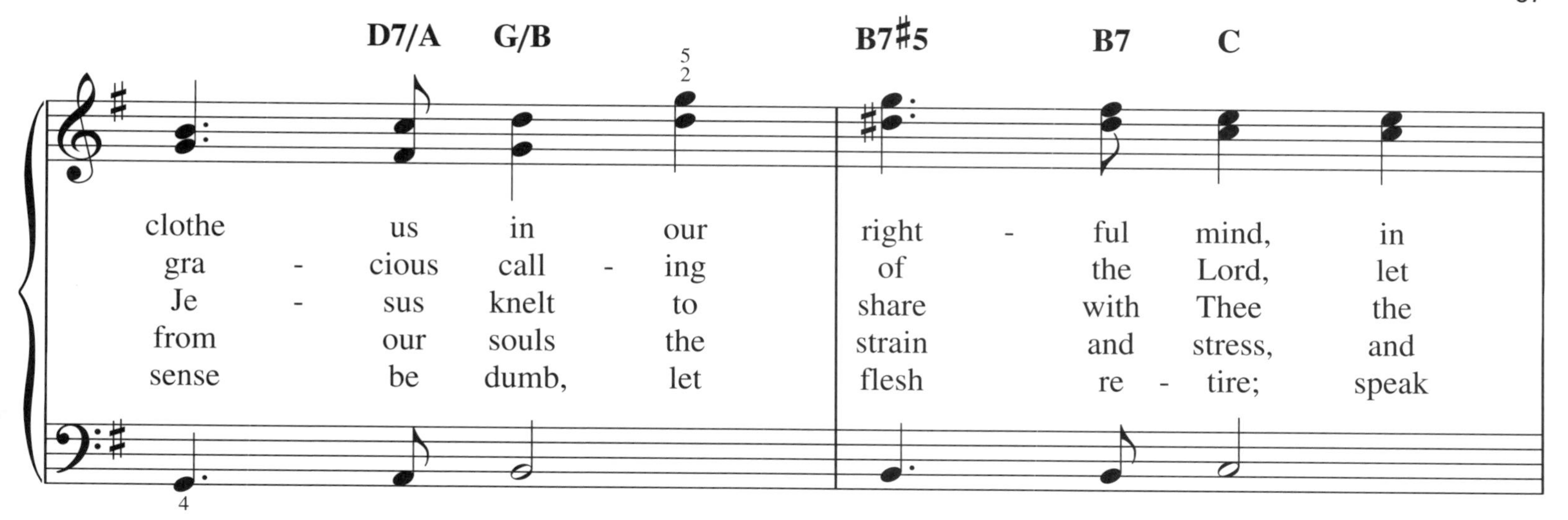
D7/A G/B B7♯5 B7 C
clothe us in our right - ful mind, in
gra - cious call - ing of the Lord, let
Je - sus knelt to share with Thee the
from our souls the strain and stress, and
sense be dumb, let flesh re - tire; speak

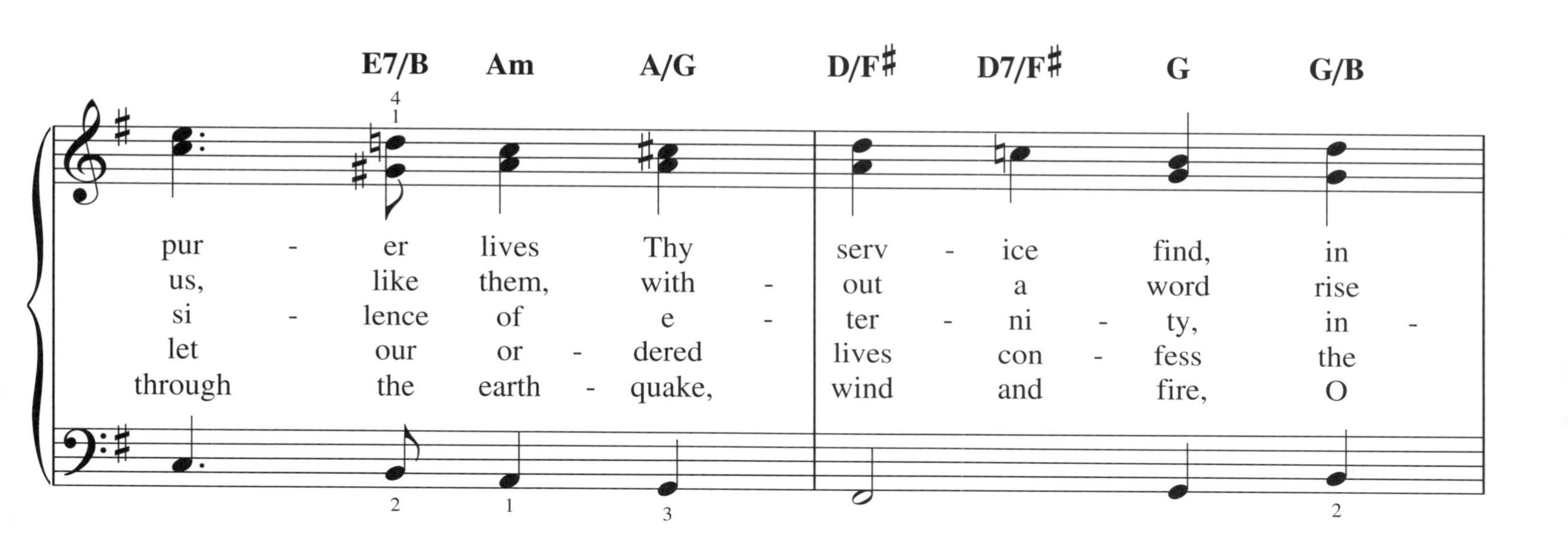
E7/B Am A/G D/F♯ D7/F♯ G G/B
pur - er lives Thy serv - ice find, in
us, like them, with - out a word rise
si - lence of e - ter - ni - ty, in -
let our or - dered lives con - fess the
through the earth - quake, wind and fire, O

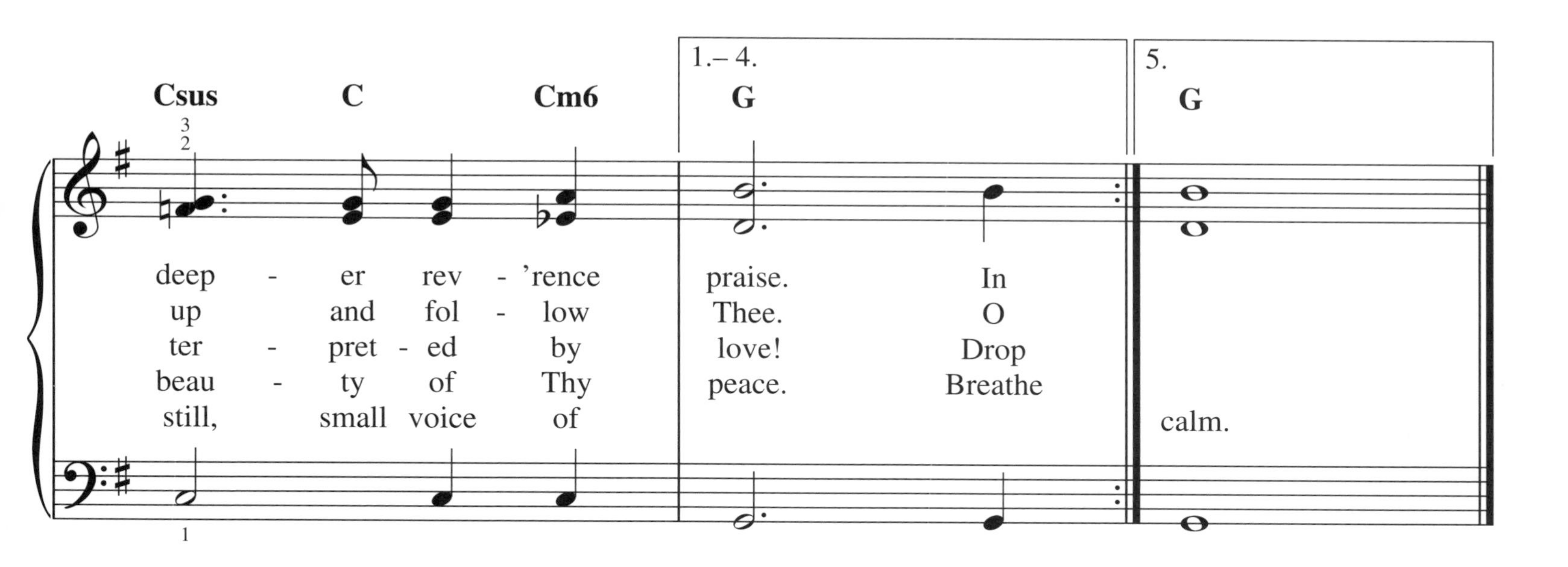
1.– 4.
5.
Csus C Cm6 G G
deep - er rev - 'rence praise. In
up and fol - low Thee. O
ter - pret - ed by love! Drop
beau - ty of Thy peace. Breathe
still, small voice of calm.

ETERNAL FATHER, STRONG TO SAVE

Words by WILLIAM WHITING
Music by JOHN BACCHUS DYKES

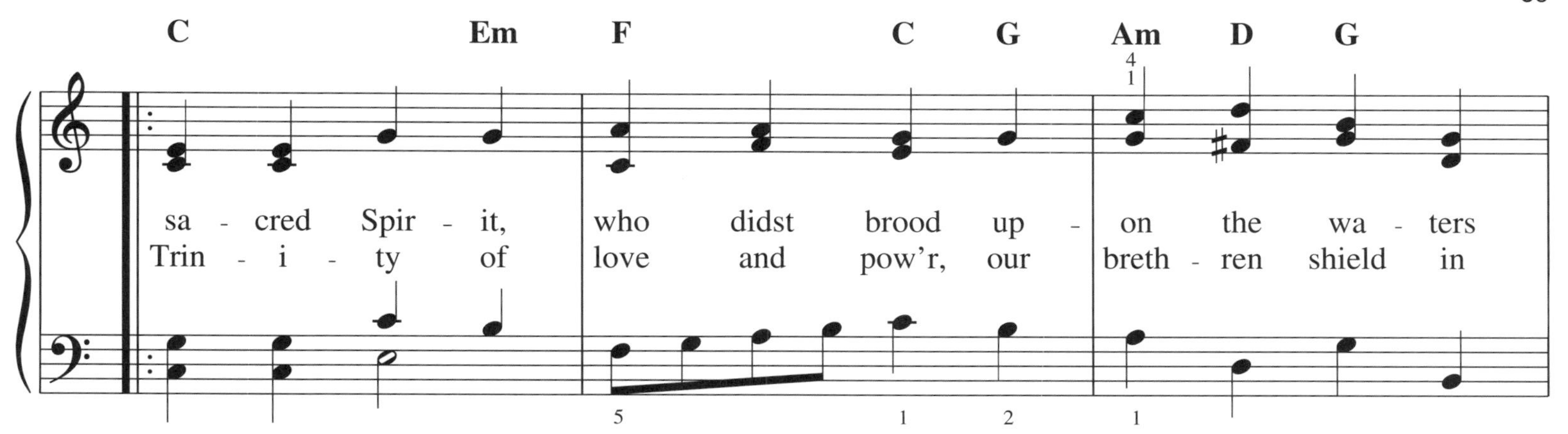
C Em F C G Am D G
4
1
sa - cred Spir - it, who didst brood up - on the wa - ters
Trin - i - ty of love and pow'r, our breth - ren shield in
5 1 2 1

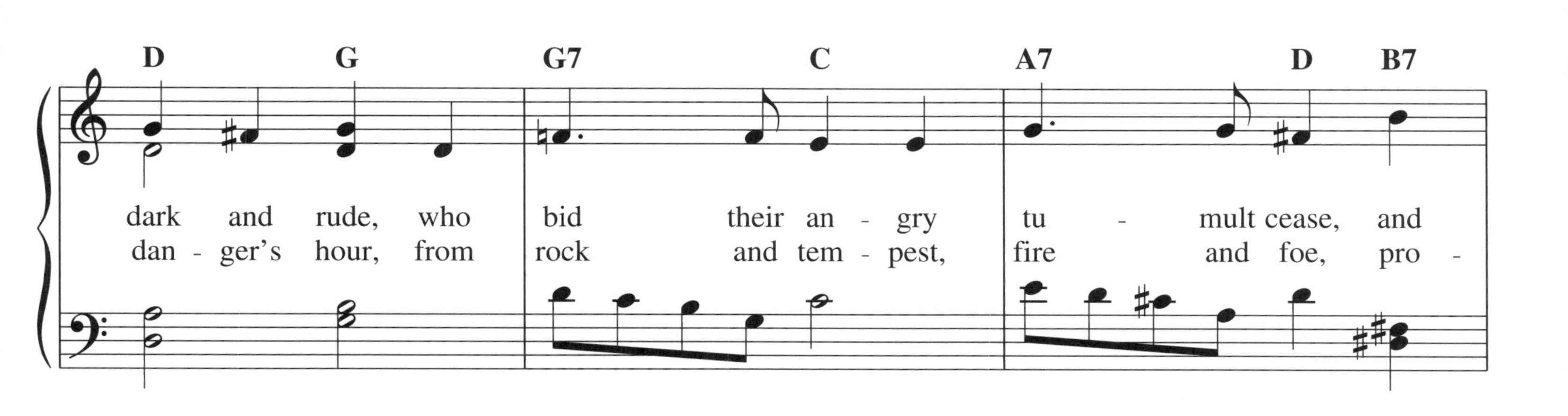
D G G7 C A7 D B7
dark and rude, who bid their an - gry tu - mult cease, and
dan - ger's hour, from rock and tem - pest, fire and foe, pro -

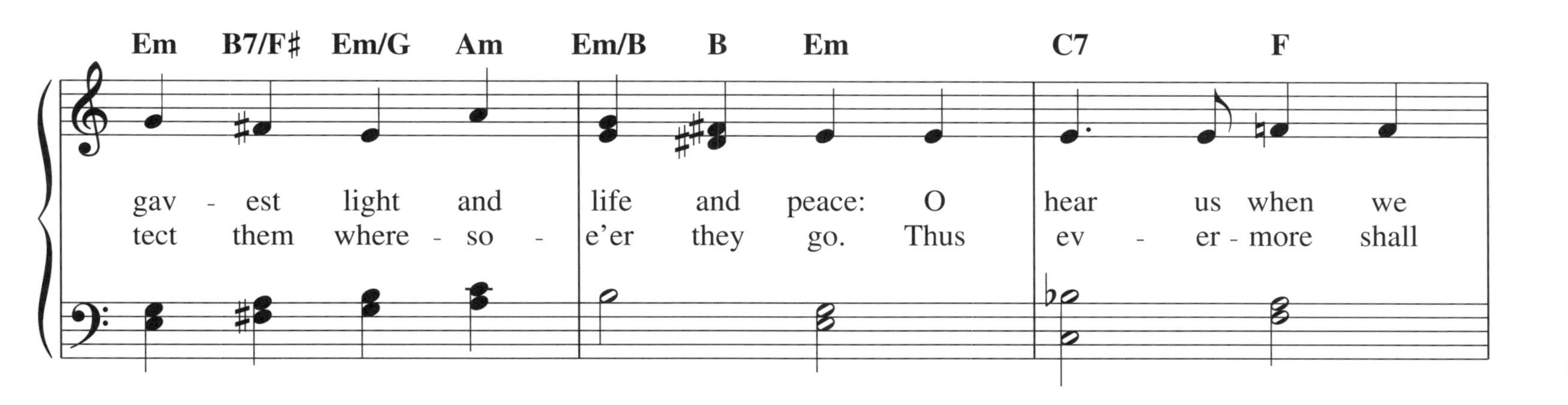
Em B7/F♯ Em/G Am Em/B B Em C7 F
gav - est light and life and peace: O hear us when we
tect them where - so - e'er they go. Thus ev - er - more shall

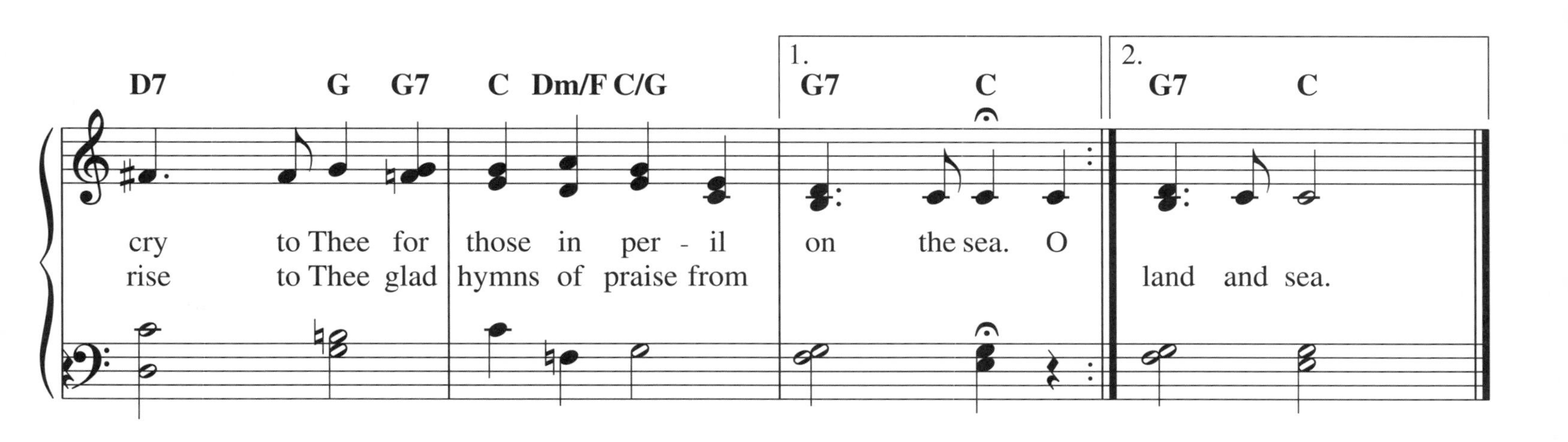
1. 2.
D7 G G7 C Dm/F C/G G7 C G7 C
cry to Thee for those in per - il on the sea. O
rise to Thee glad hymns of praise from land and sea.

FAIREST LORD JESUS

Words from *Münster Gesangbuch*
Music from *Schlesische Volkslieder*

HAVE THINE OWN WAY, LORD

Words by ADELAIDE A. POLLARD
Music by GEORGE C. STEBBINS

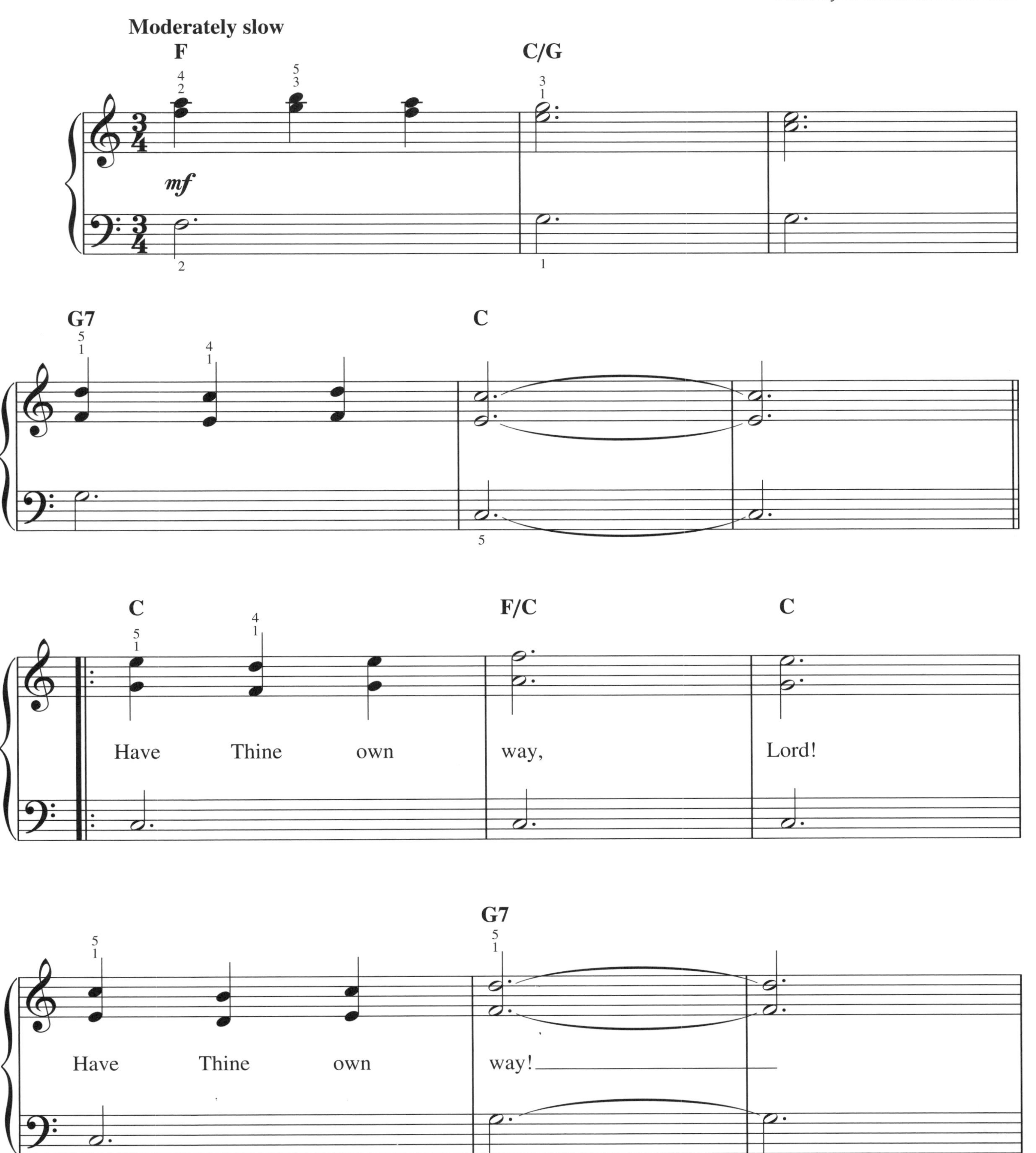

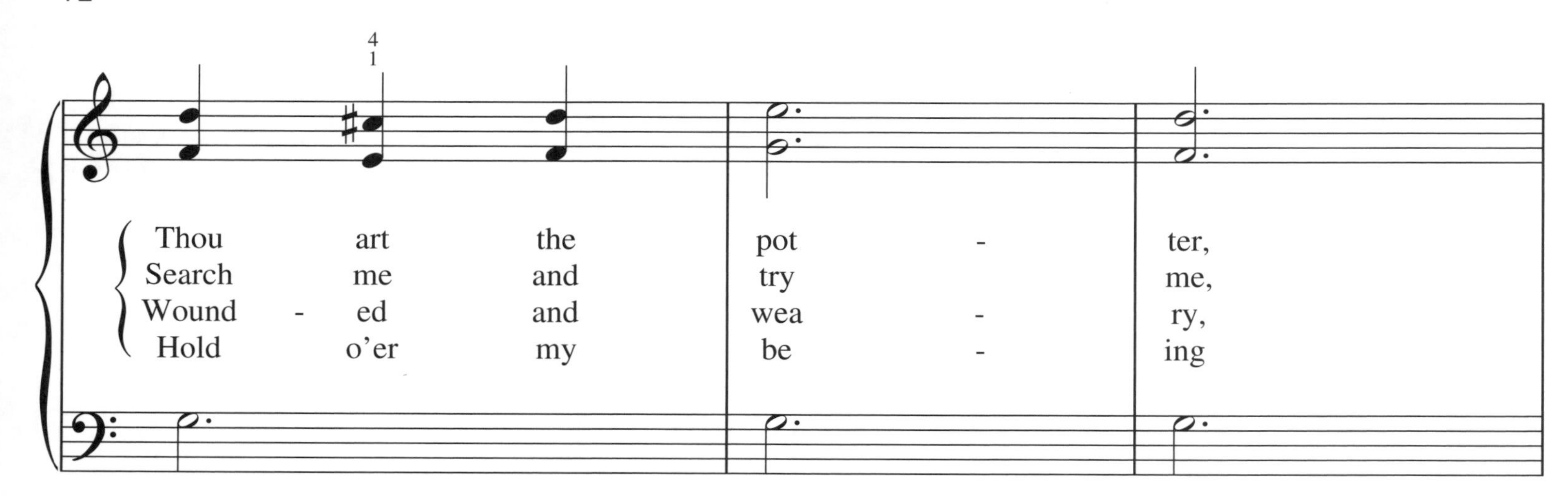
4
1
Thou art the pot - ter,
Search me and try me,
Wound - ed and wea - ry,
Hold o'er my be - ing

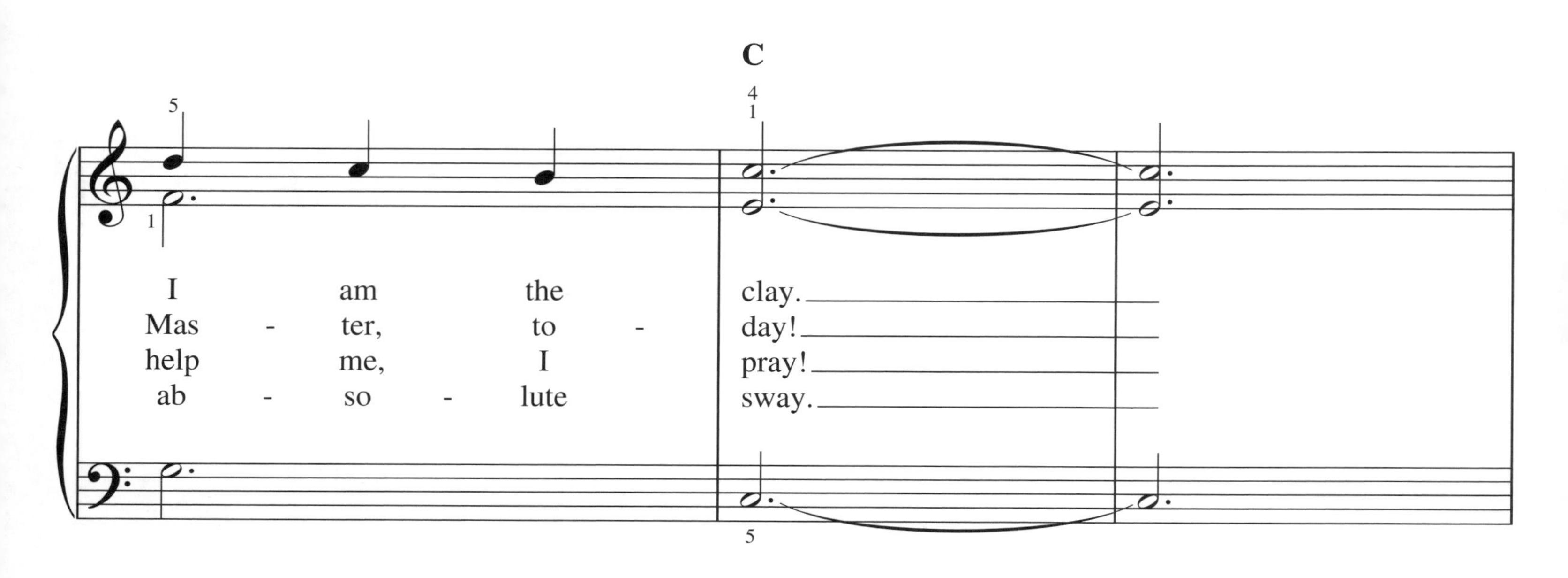
C
5
1
4
1
I am the clay.
Mas - ter, to - day!
help me, I pray!
ab - so - lute sway.
5

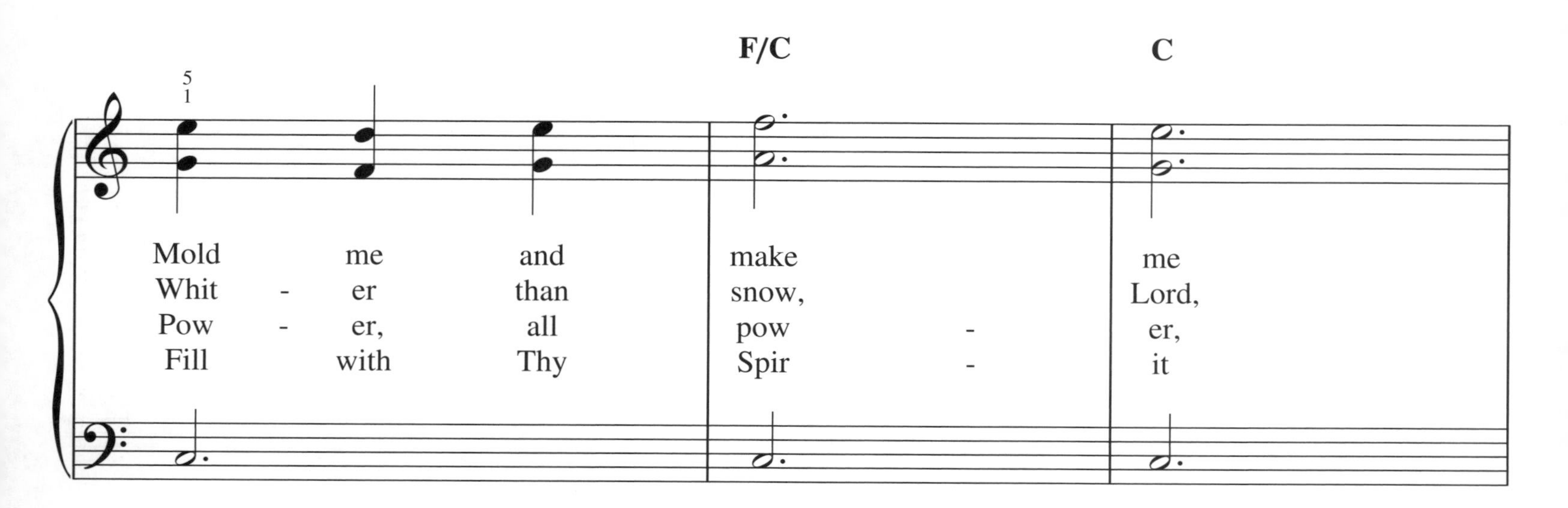
F/C
C
5
1
Mold me and make me
Whit - er than snow, Lord,
Pow - er, all pow - er,
Fill with Thy Spir - it

C7
F
af - ter Thy will,
wash me just now,
sure - ly is Thine!
till all shall see

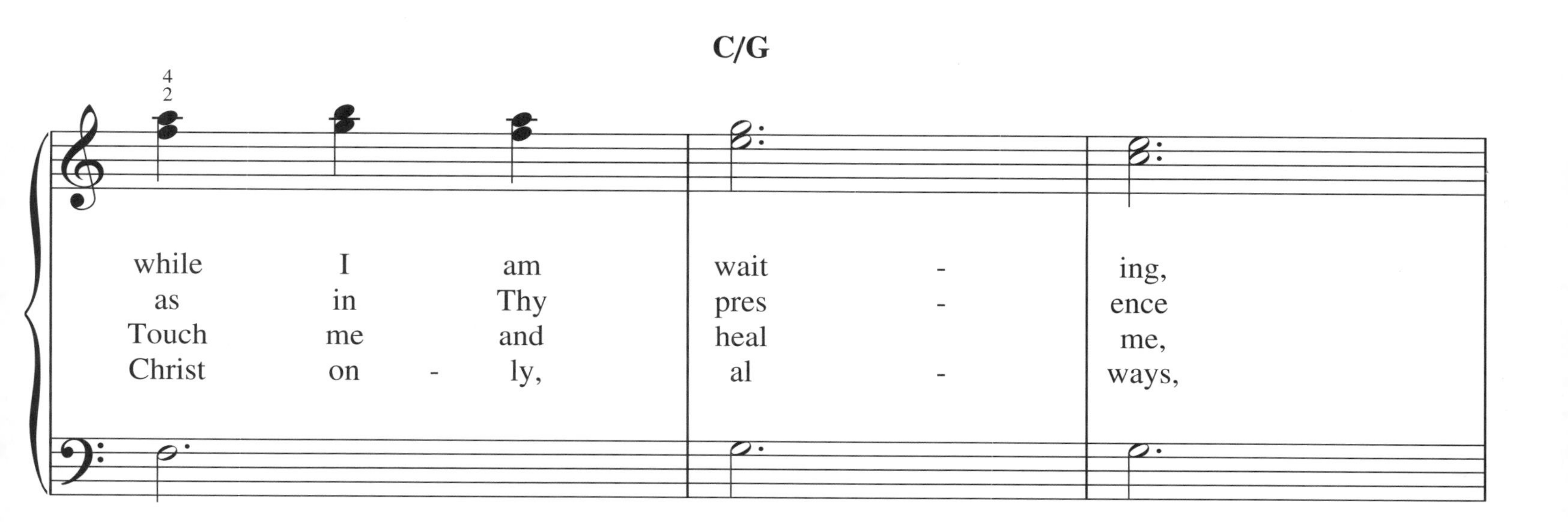
C/G
while I am wait - ing,
as in Thy pres - ence
Touch me and heal me,
Christ on - ly, al - ways,

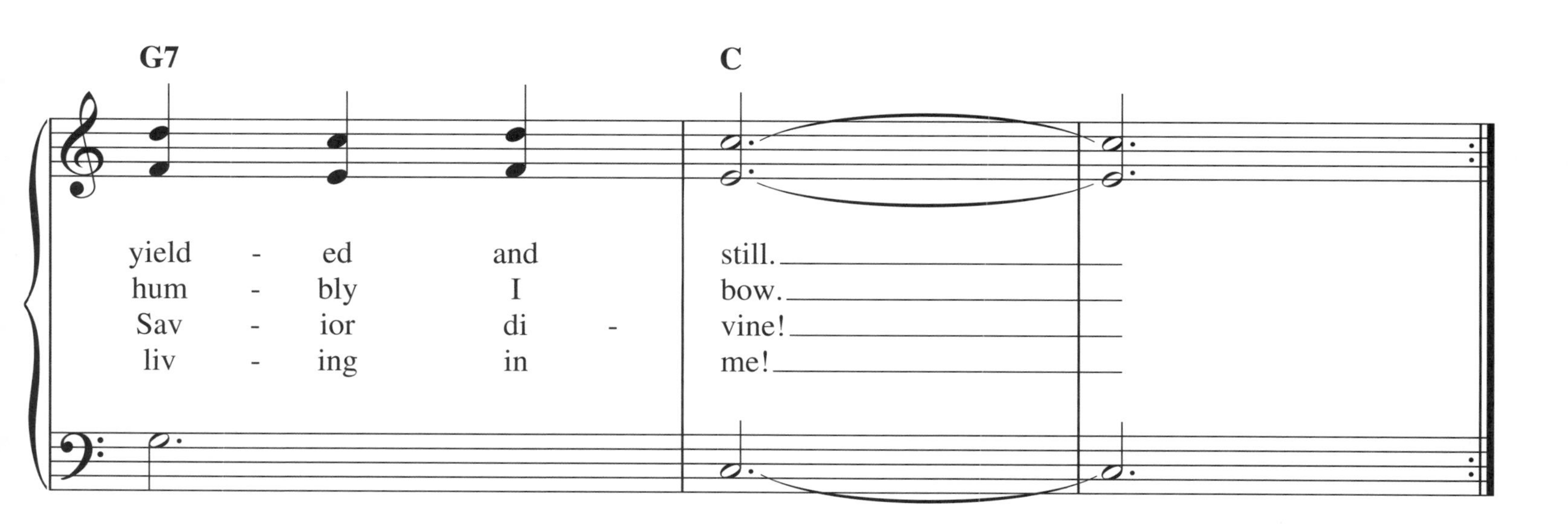
G7
C
yield - ed and still.
hum - bly I bow.
Sav - ior di - vine!
liv - ing in me!

FAITH OF OUR FATHERS

Words by FREDERICK WILLIAM FABER
Music by HENRI F. HEMY and JAMES G. WALTON

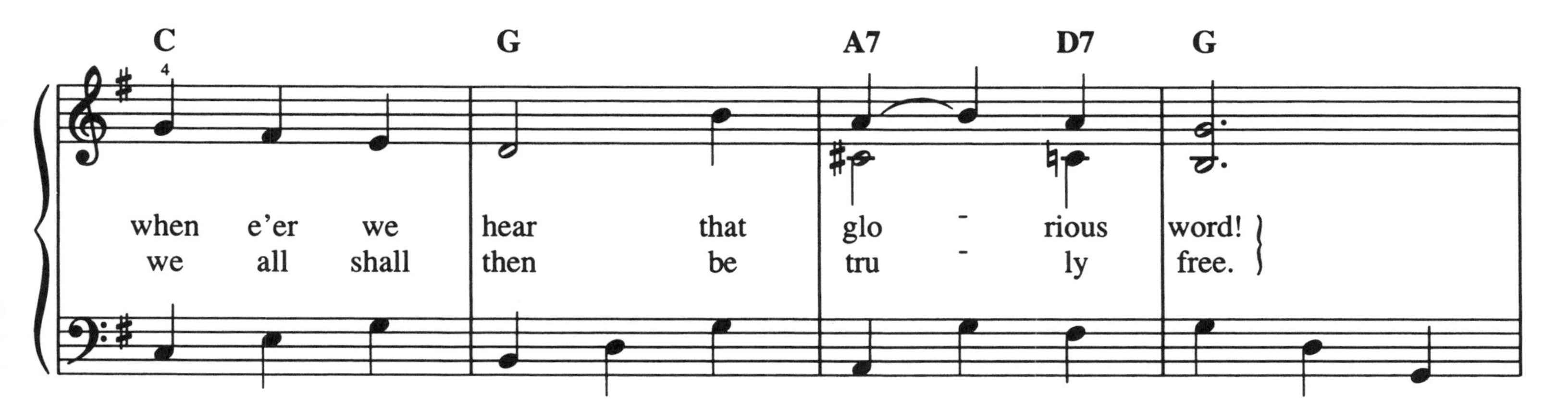

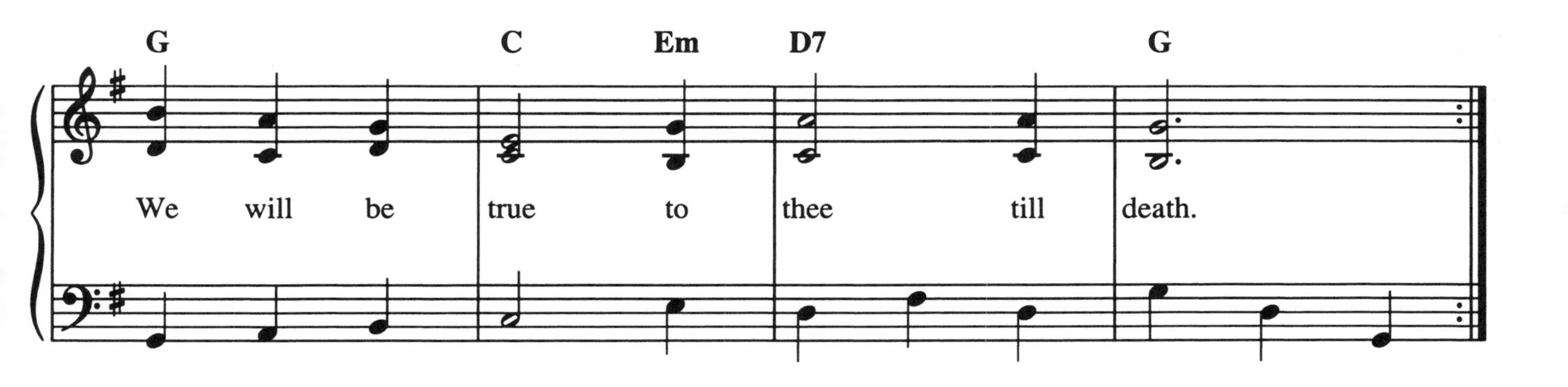

Additional Verse

Faith of our fathers, we will love
both friend and foe in all our strife;
and preach thee, too, as love knows how
by kindly words and virtuous life.
To Chorus

FOOTSTEPS OF JESUS

Words by MARY B.C. SLADE
Music by ASA B. EVERETT

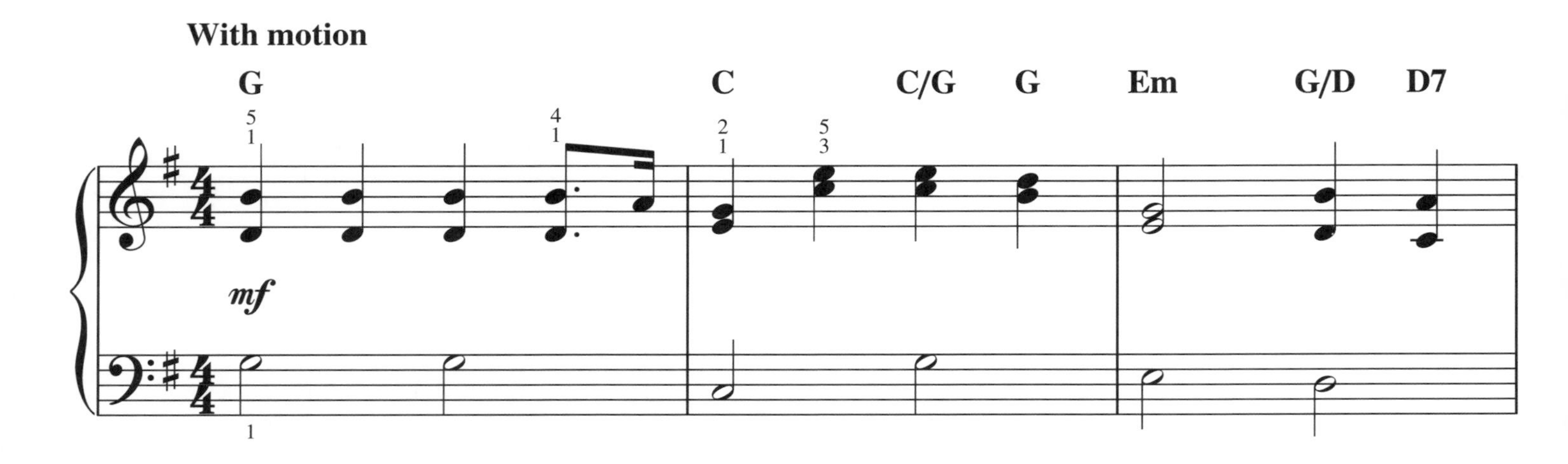

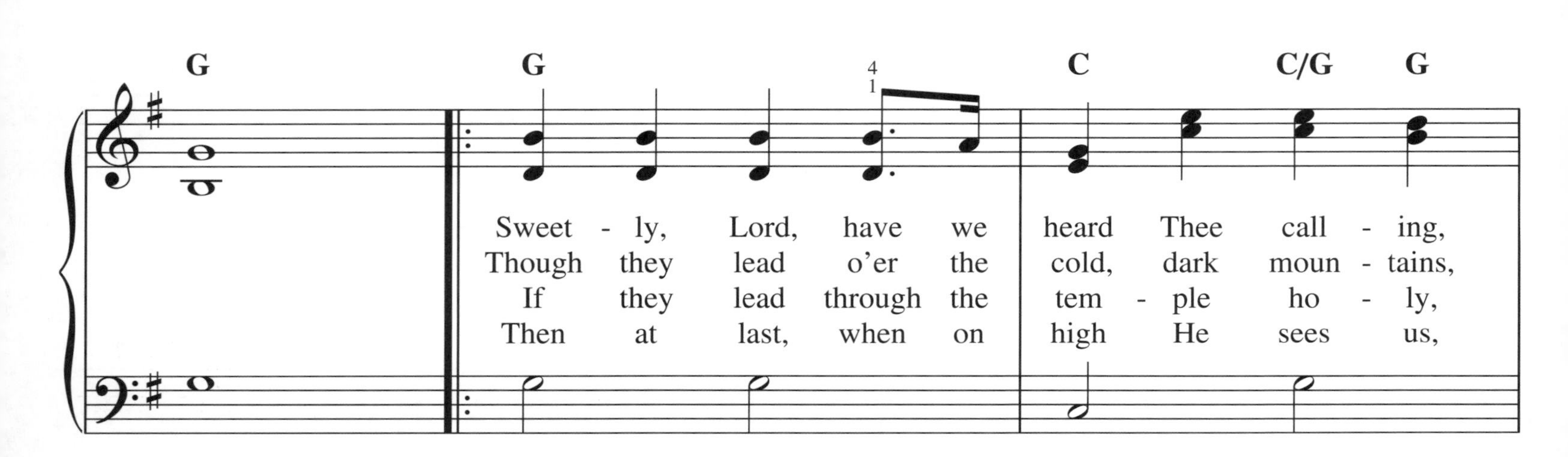

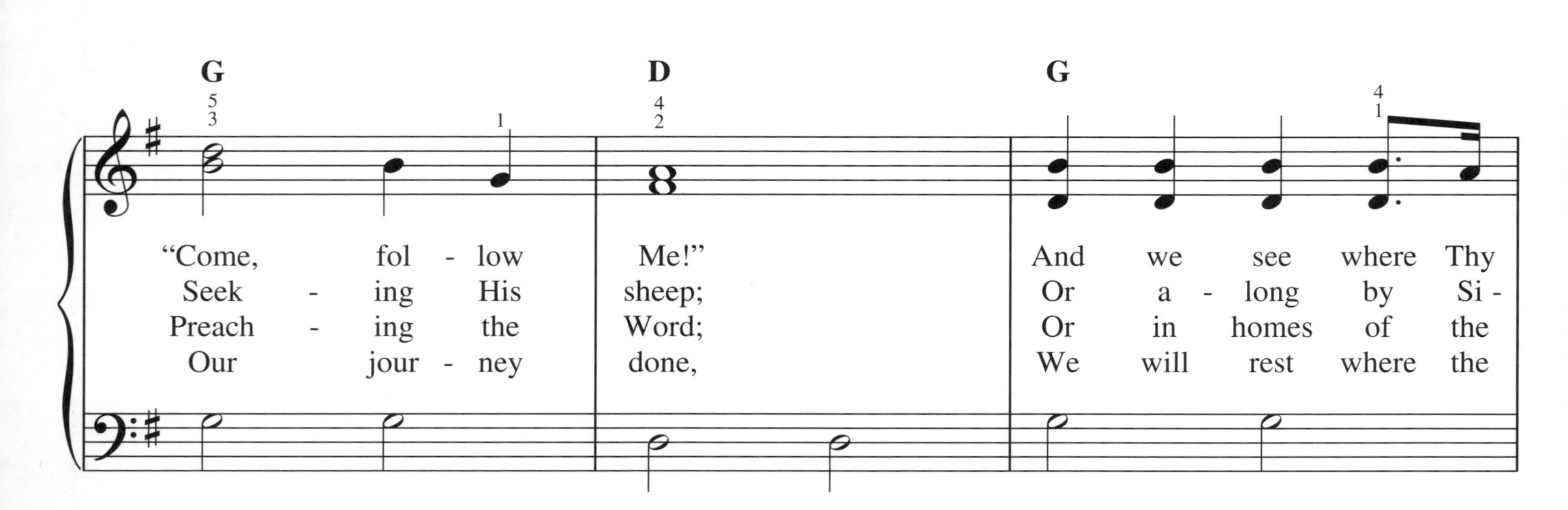

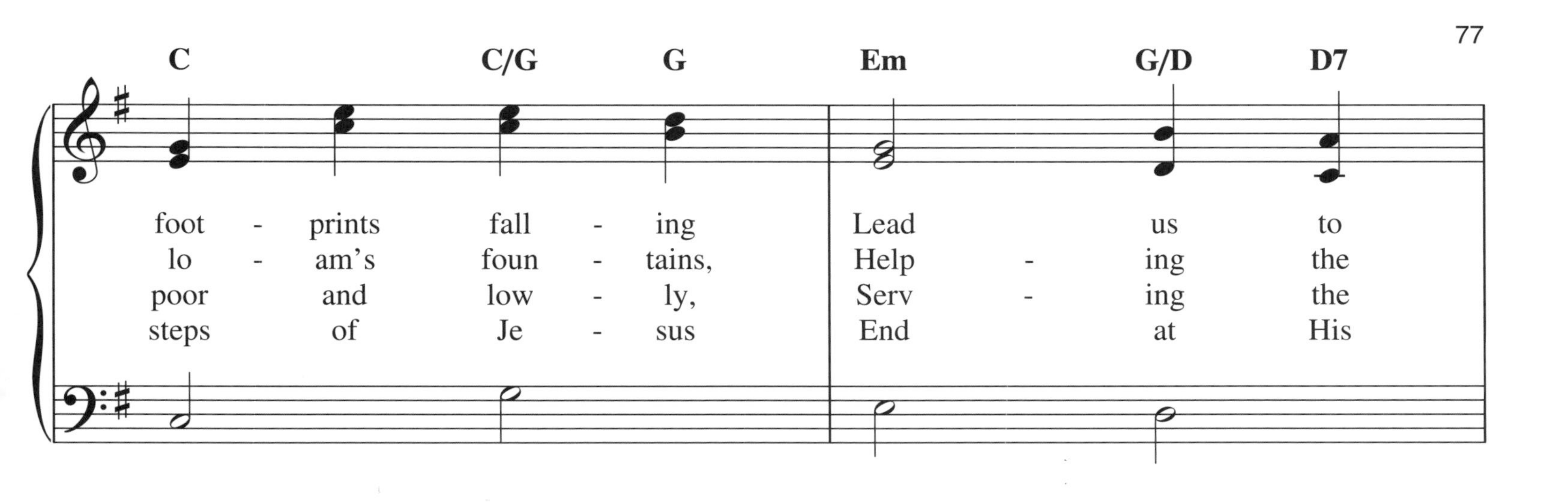
C
C/G
G
Em
G/D
D7
foot - prints fall - ing
Lead us to
lo - am's foun - tains,
Help - ing the
poor and low - ly,
Serv - ing the
steps of Je - sus
End at His

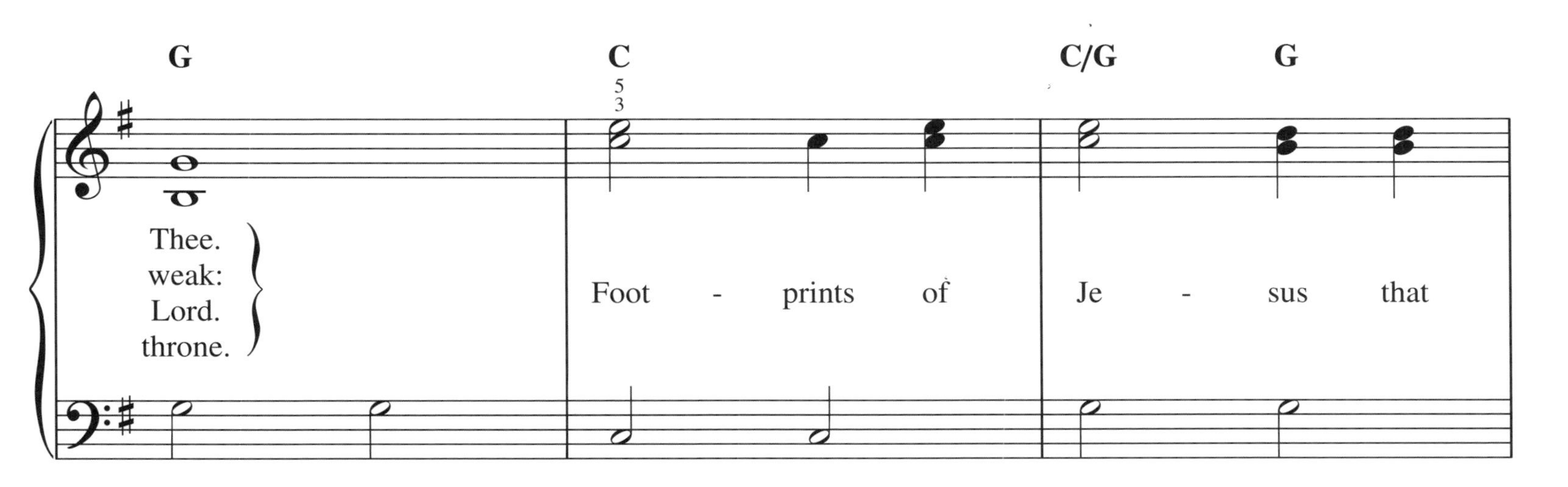
G
C
C/G
G
Thee.
weak:
Lord.
throne.
Foot - prints of Je - sus that

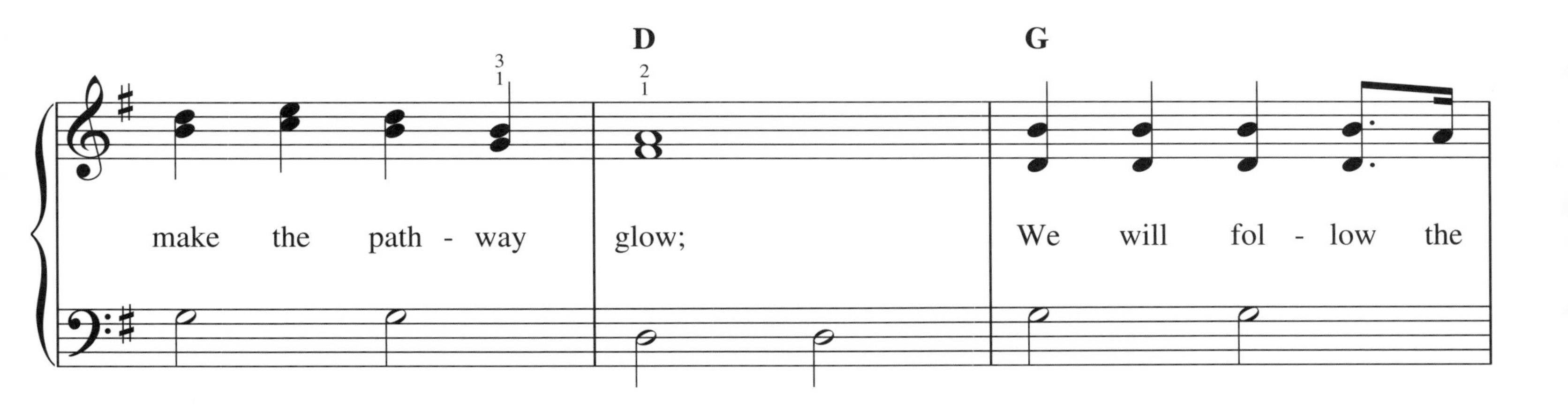
D
G
make the path - way glow;
We will fol - low the

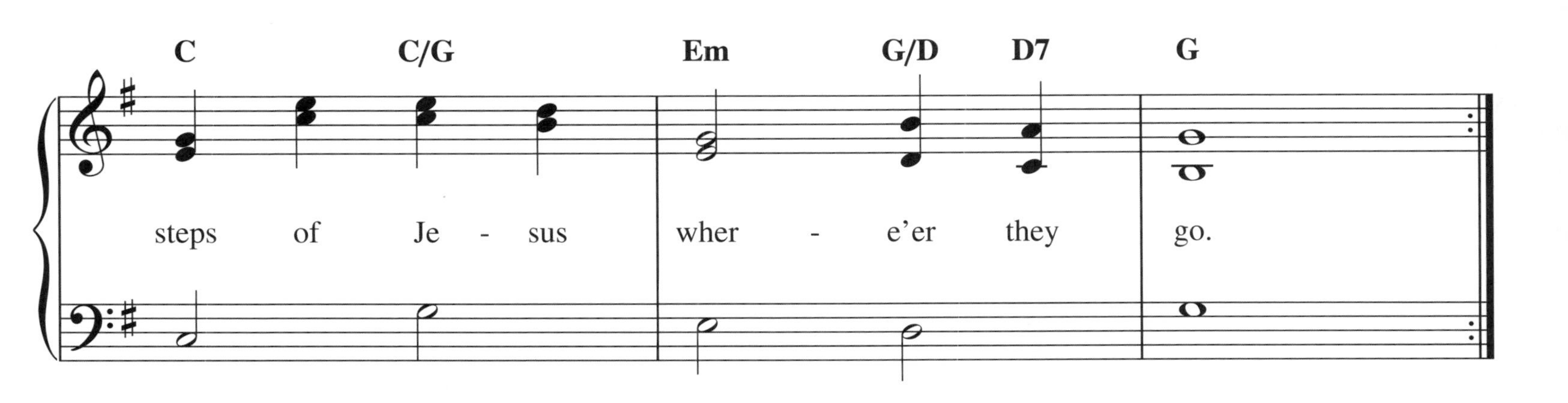
C
C/G
Em
G/D
D7
G
steps of Je - sus wher - e'er they go.

FOR ALL THE SAINTS

Words by WILLIAM W. HOW
Music by RALPH VAUGHAN WILLIAMS

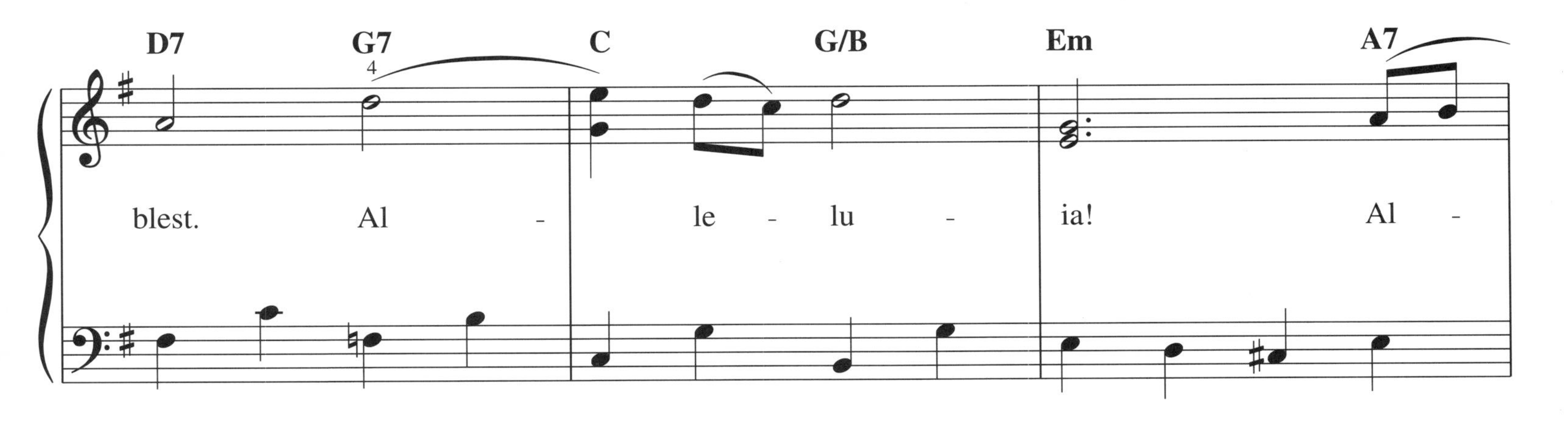

Additional Verses

2. You were their rock, their fortress, and their might;
You, Lord, their captain in the well-fought fight;
You, in the darkness drear, their one true light.
Alleluia! Alleluia!

3. Oh, blest communion, fellowship divine,
We feebly struggle, they in glory shine;
Yet all are one within your great design.
Alleluia! Alleluia!

4. And when the strife is fierce, the warfare long.
Steals on the ear the distant triumph song,
And hearts are brave again and arms are strong.
Alleluia! Alleluia!

5. Oh, may your soldiers, faithful, true and bold,
Fight as the saints who nobly fought of old
And win with them the victor's crown of gold.
Alleluia! Alleluia!

6. The golden evening brightens in the west;
Soon, soon to faithful warriors comes their rest;
Sweet is the calm of paradise the blest.
Alleluia! Alleluia!

FOR THE BEAUTY OF THE EARTH

Words by FOLLIOT S. PIERPOINT
Music by CONRAD KOCHER

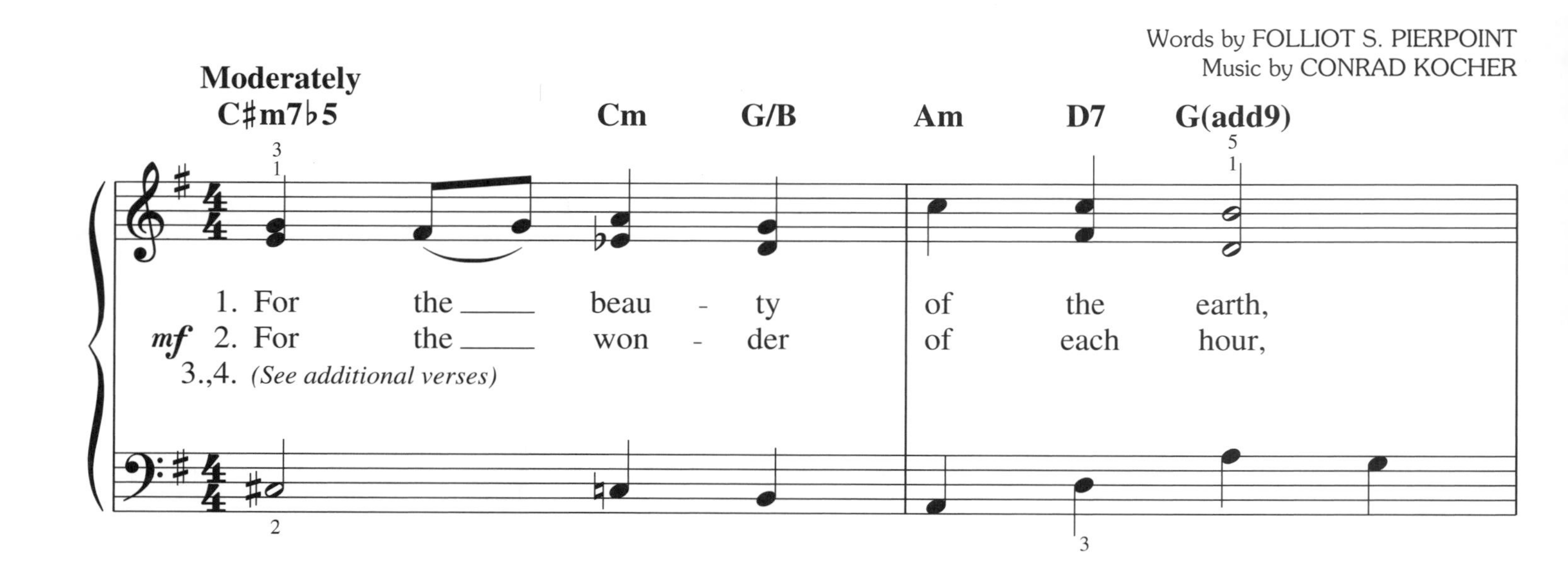

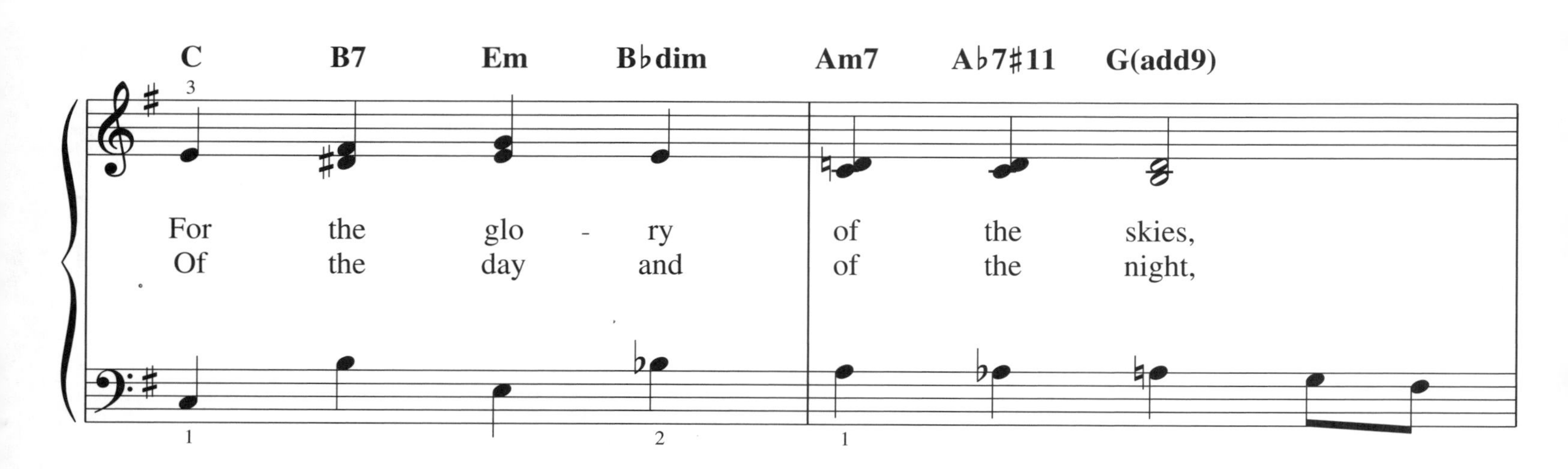

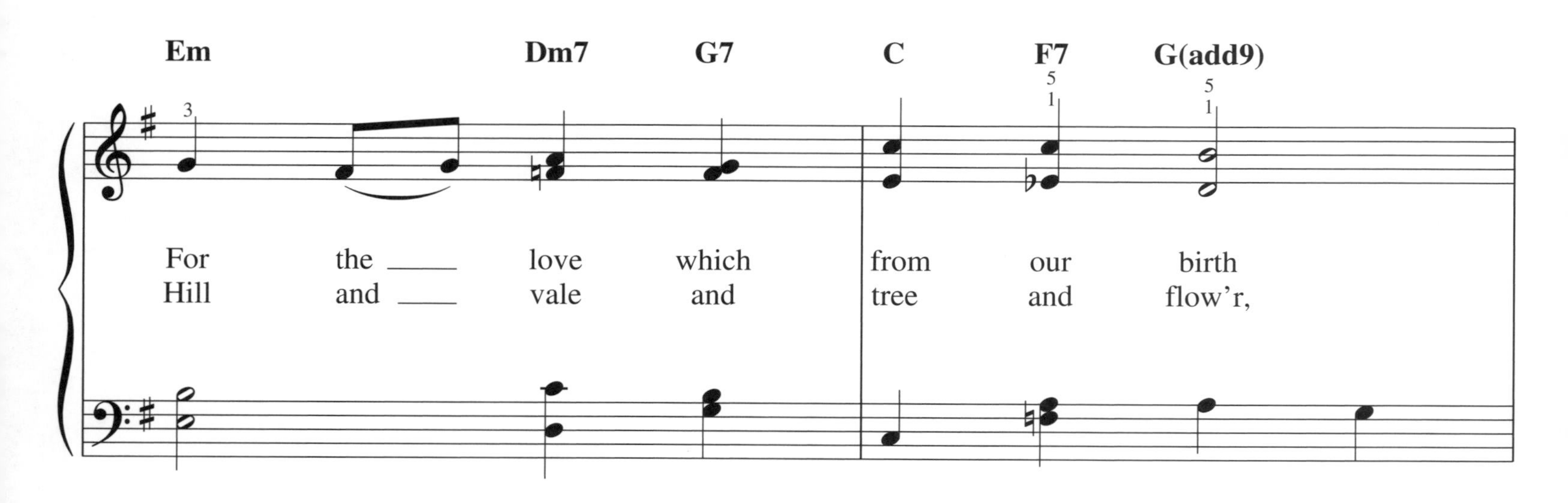

Additional Verses

3. For the joy of ear and eye,
   For the heart and mind's delight,
   For the mystic harmony
   Linking sense to sound and sight:
   Refrain:

4. For the joy of human love,
   Brother, sister, parent, child,
   Friends on earth and friends above;
   For all gentle thoughts and mild;
   Refrain:

GOD BE WITH YOU TILL WE MEET AGAIN

Words by JEREMIAH E. RANKIN
Music by WILLIAM G. TOMER

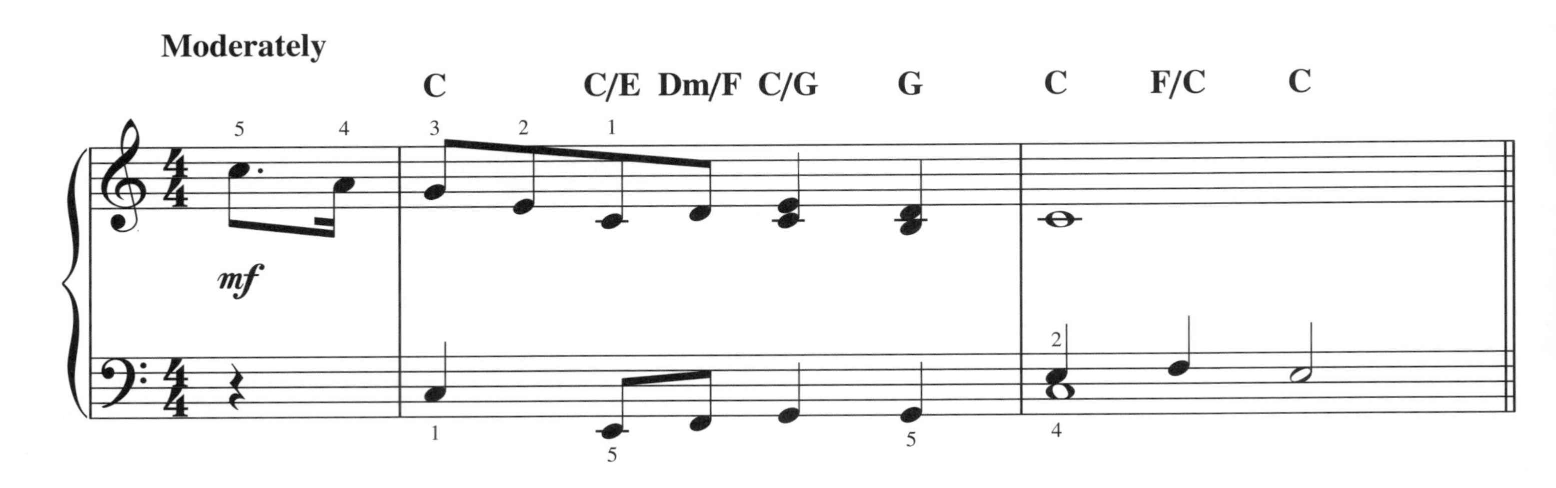

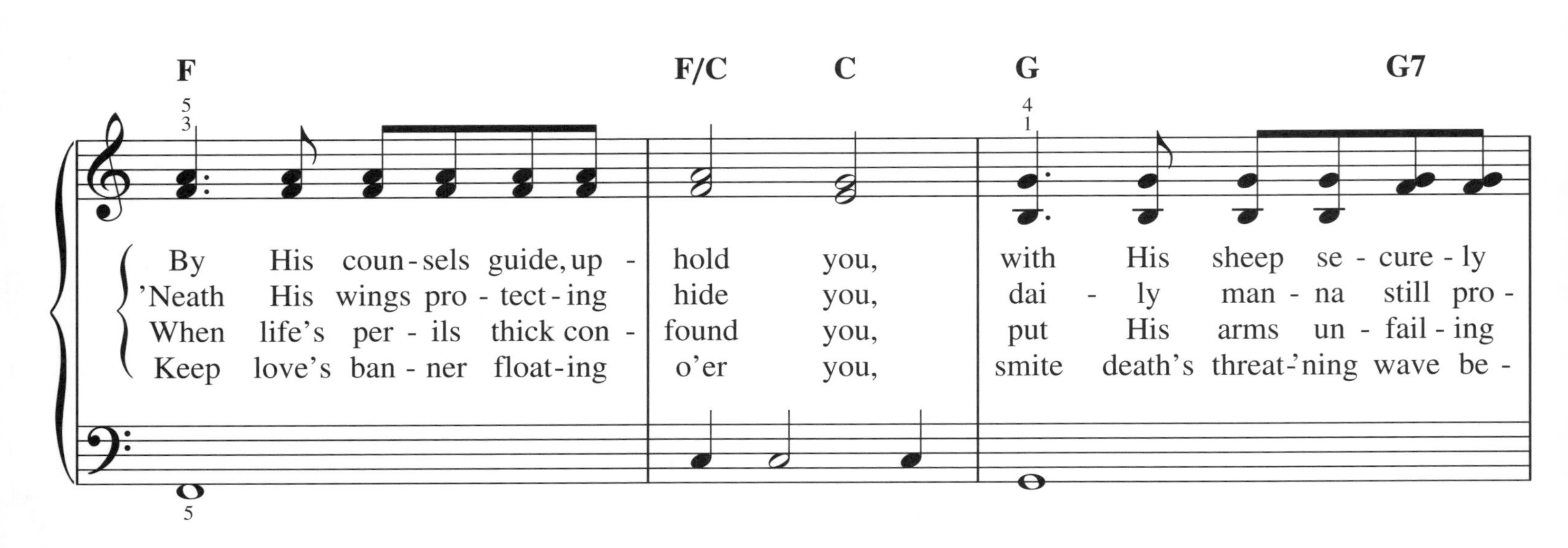

C
F
C/G G7 C
fold you.
vide you.
'round you.
fore you.
God be with you till we meet a - gain. Till we
F
C
meet, till we meet, till we meet at Je - sus'
G
C
F
feet, till we meet, till we meet, God be
C C/E Dm/F C/G G7
1.–3.
C F/G G
4.
C F/C C
with you till we meet a - gain.
gain.

GOD WILL TAKE CARE OF YOU

Words by CIVILLA D. MARTIN
Music by W. STILLMAN MARTIN

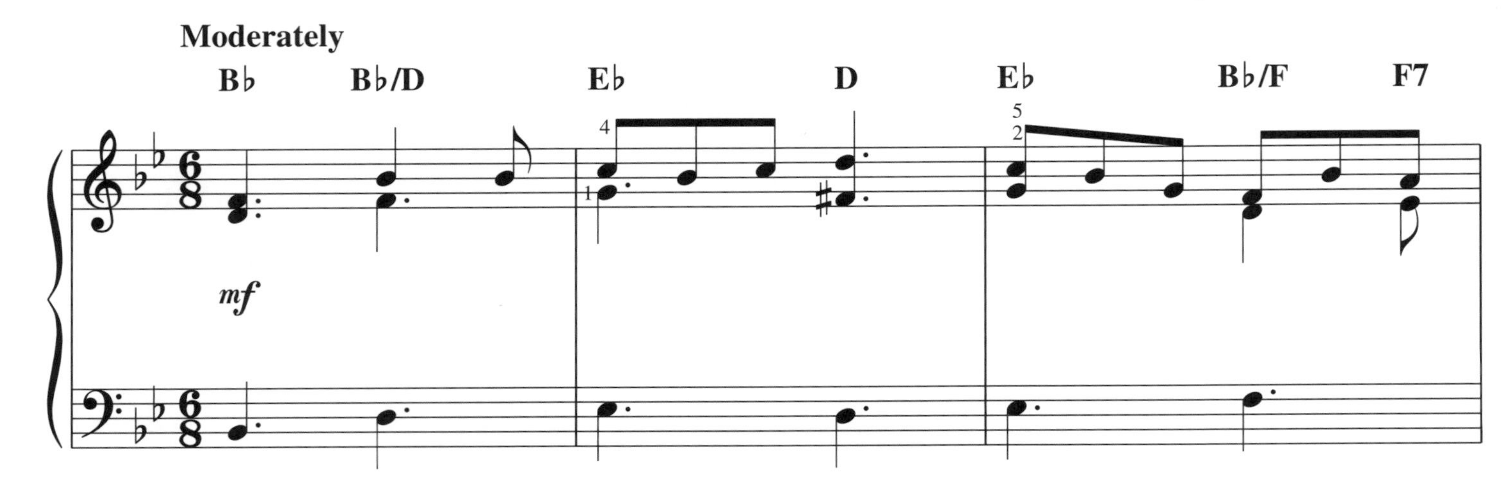

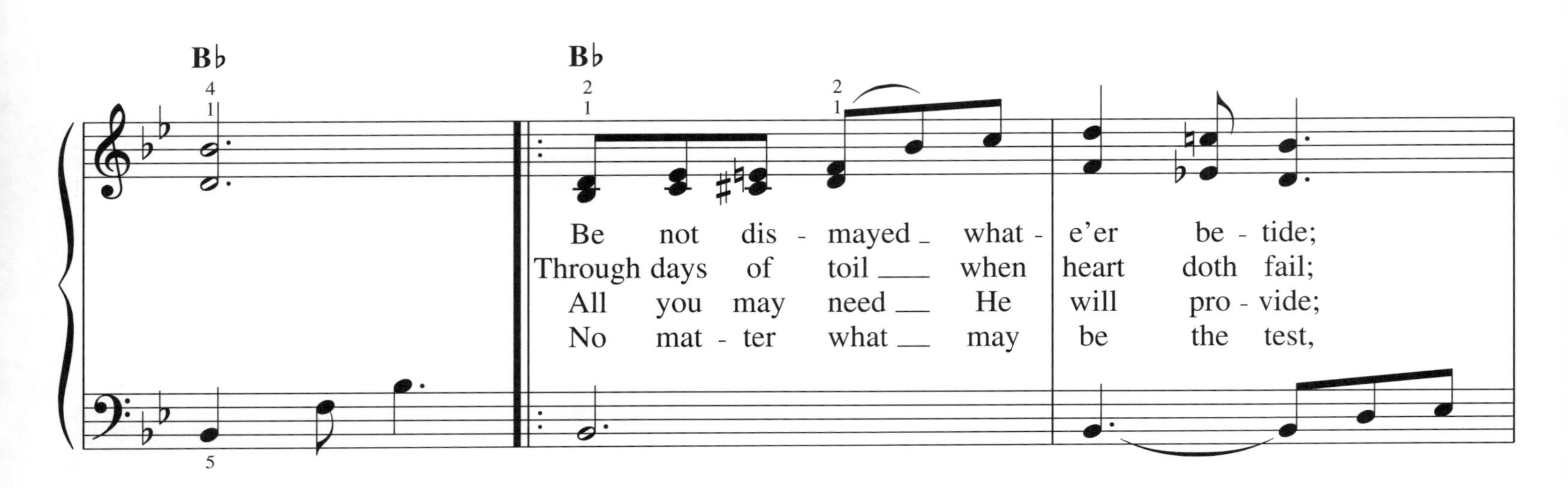

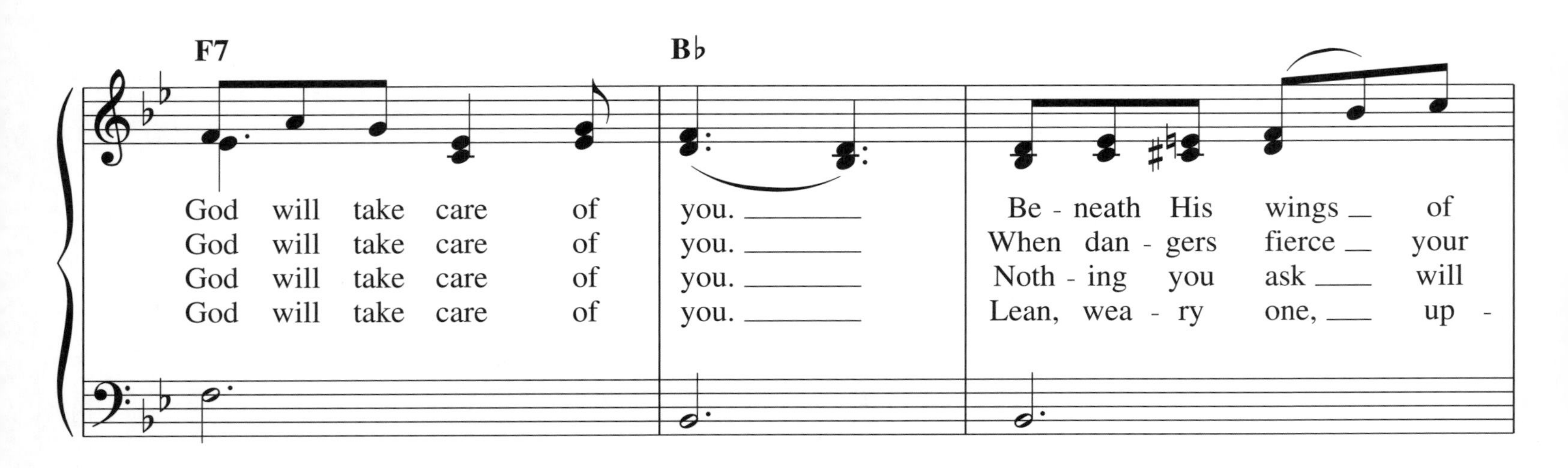

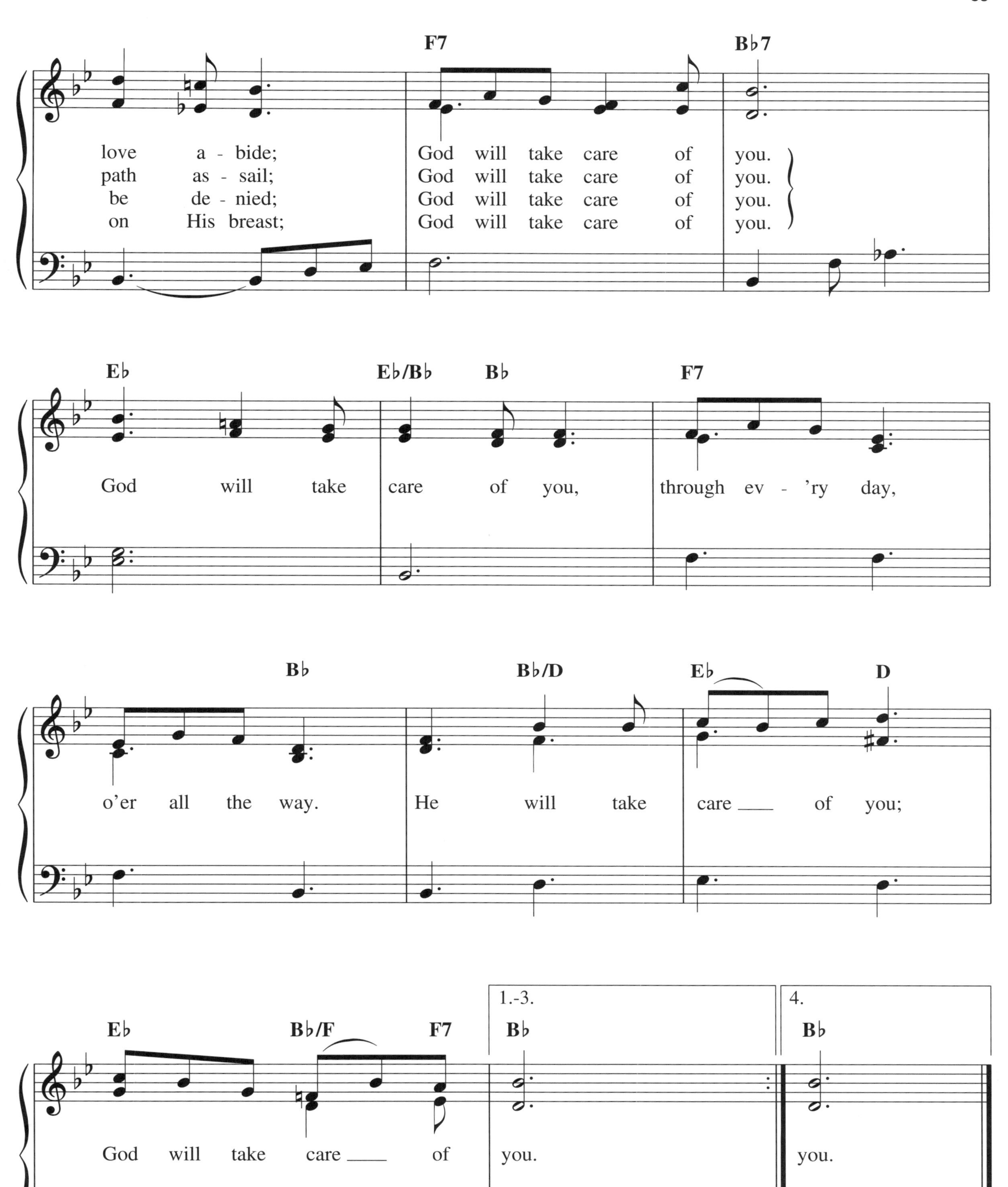
F7
B♭7
love a - bide; God will take care of you.
path as - sail; God will take care of you.
be de - nied; God will take care of you.
on His breast; God will take care of you.
E♭
E♭/B♭
B♭
F7
God will take care of you, through ev - 'ry day,
B♭
B♭/D
E♭
D
o'er all the way. He will take care of you;
E♭
B♭/F
F7
1.-3.
B♭
4.
B♭
God will take care of you. you.

GUIDE ME, O THOU GREAT JEHOVAH

Words by WILLIAM WILLIAMS
Verse 1 translated by PETER WILLIAMS
Verse 2, 3 translated by WILLIAM WILLIAMS
Music by JOHN HUGHES

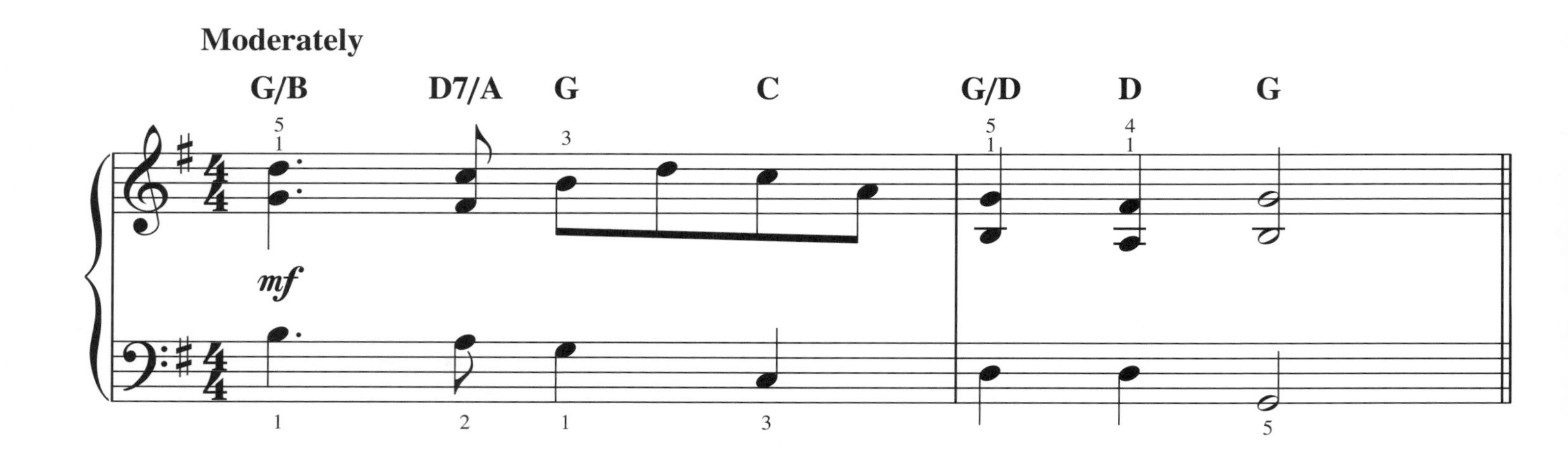

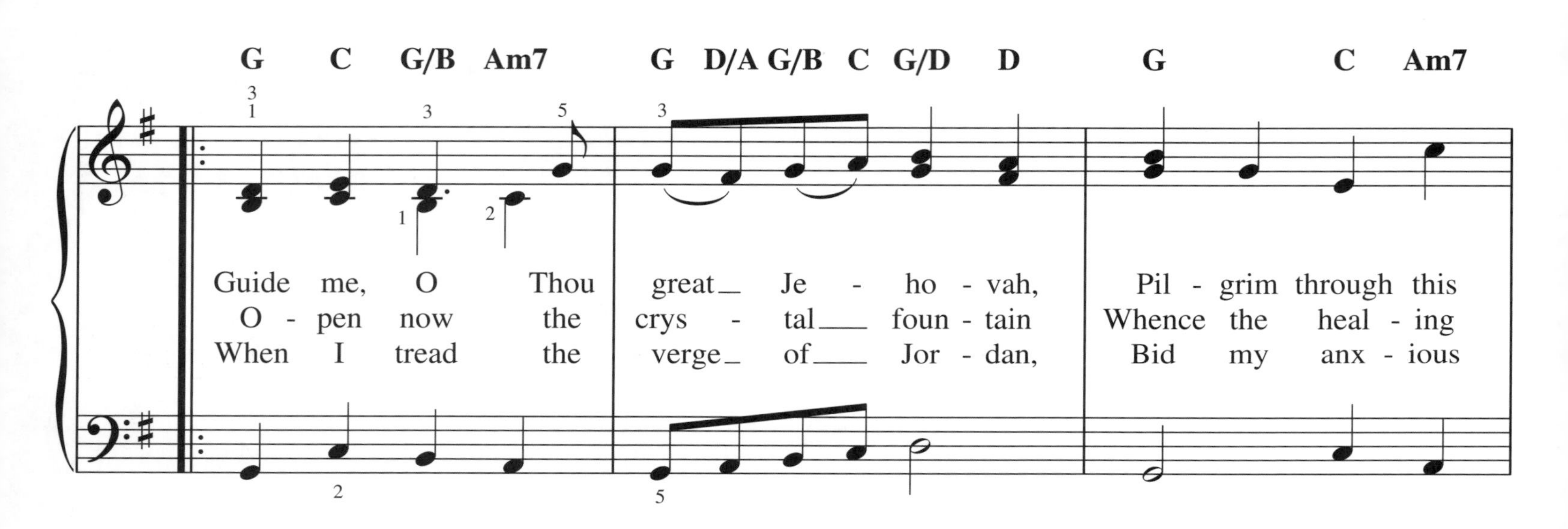

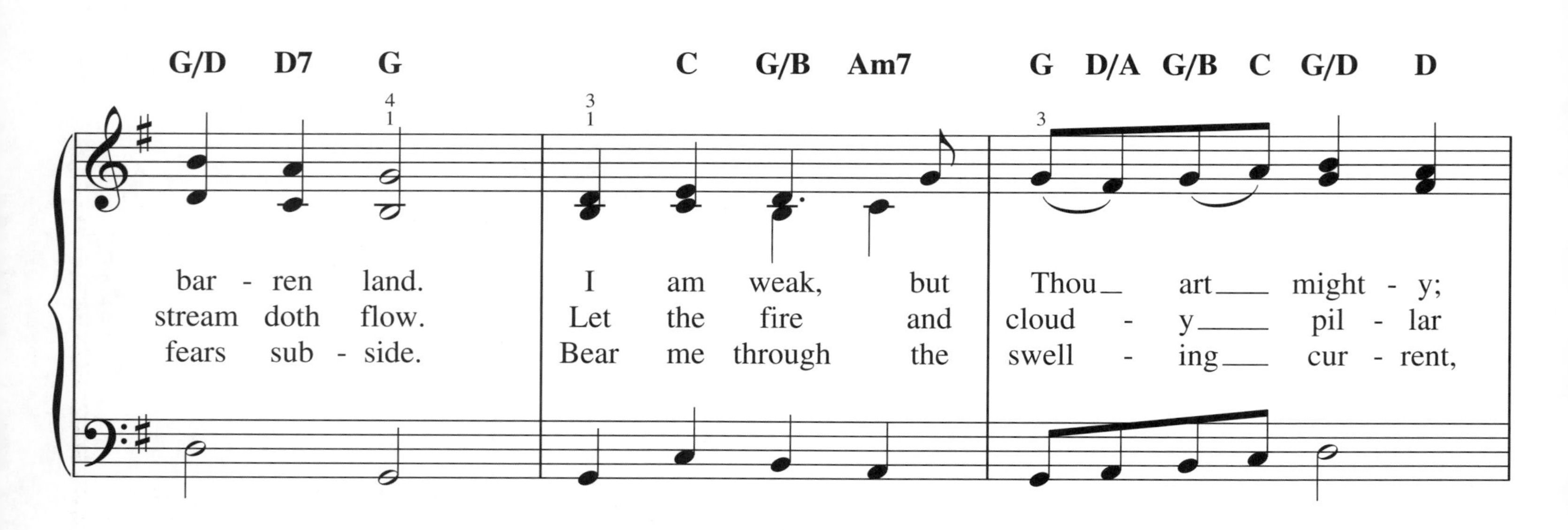

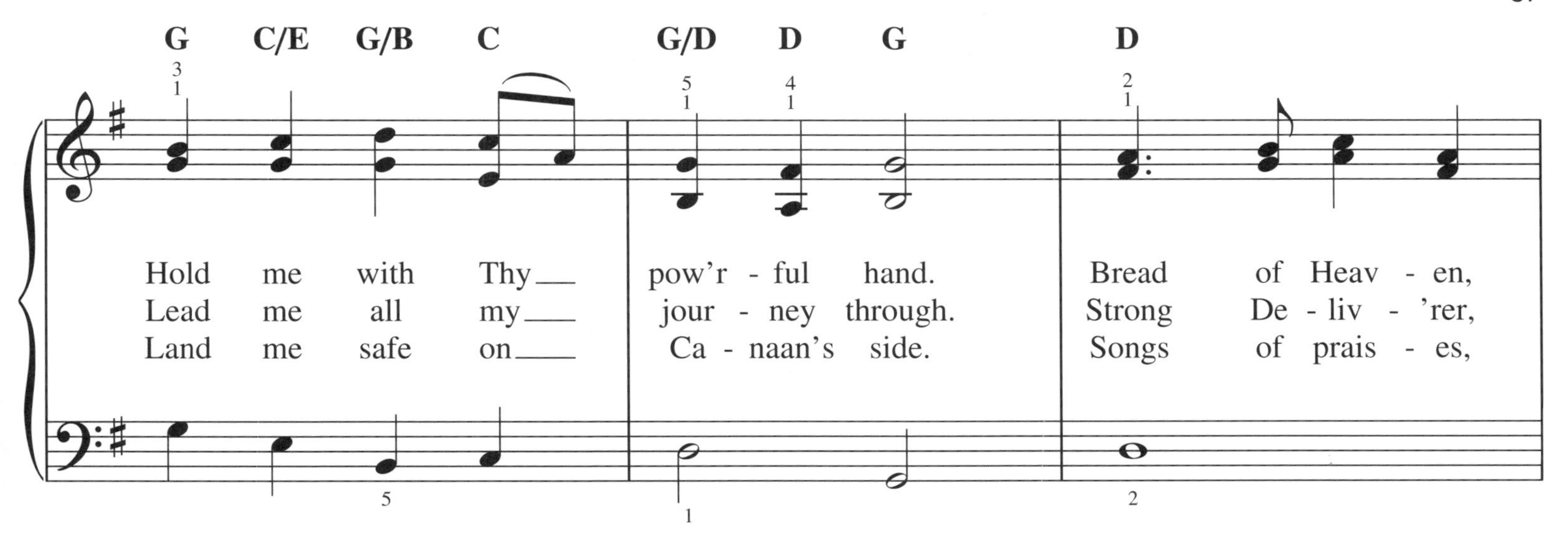
G C/E G/B C G/D D G D
Hold me with Thy pow'r - ful hand. Bread of Heav - en,
Lead me all my jour - ney through. Strong De - liv - 'rer,
Land me safe on Ca - naan's side. Songs of prais - es,

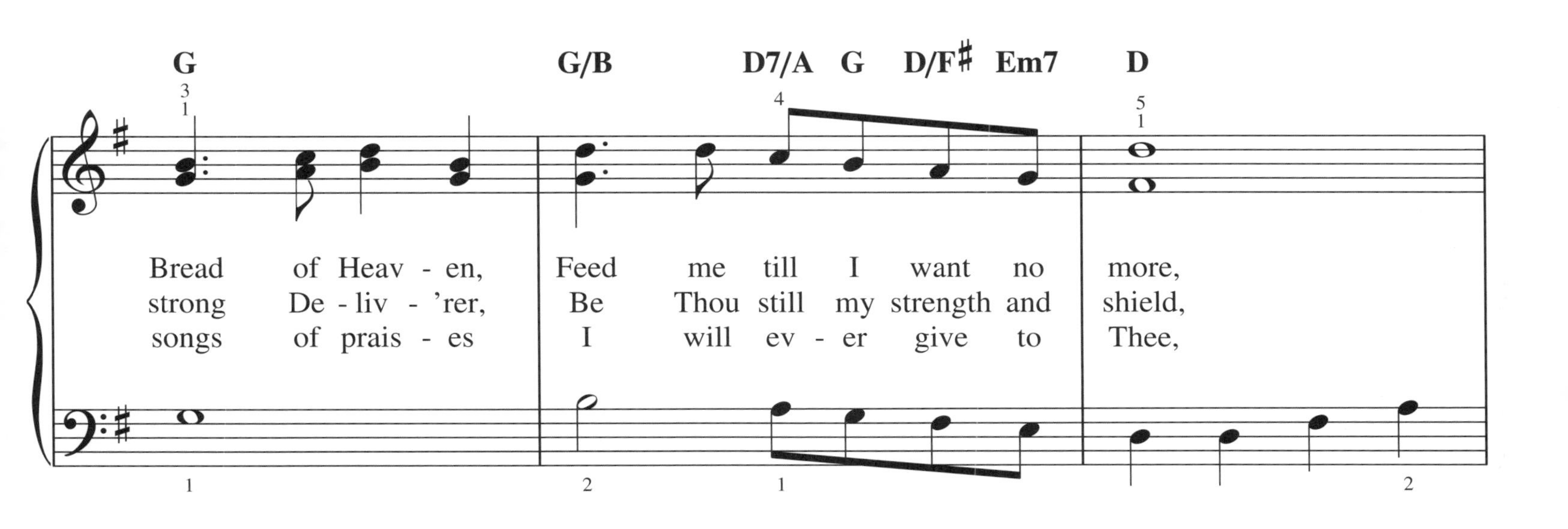
G G/B D7/A G D/F♯ Em7 D
Bread of Heav - en, Feed me till I want no more,
strong De - liv - 'rer, Be Thou still my strength and shield,
songs of prais - es I will ev - er give to Thee,

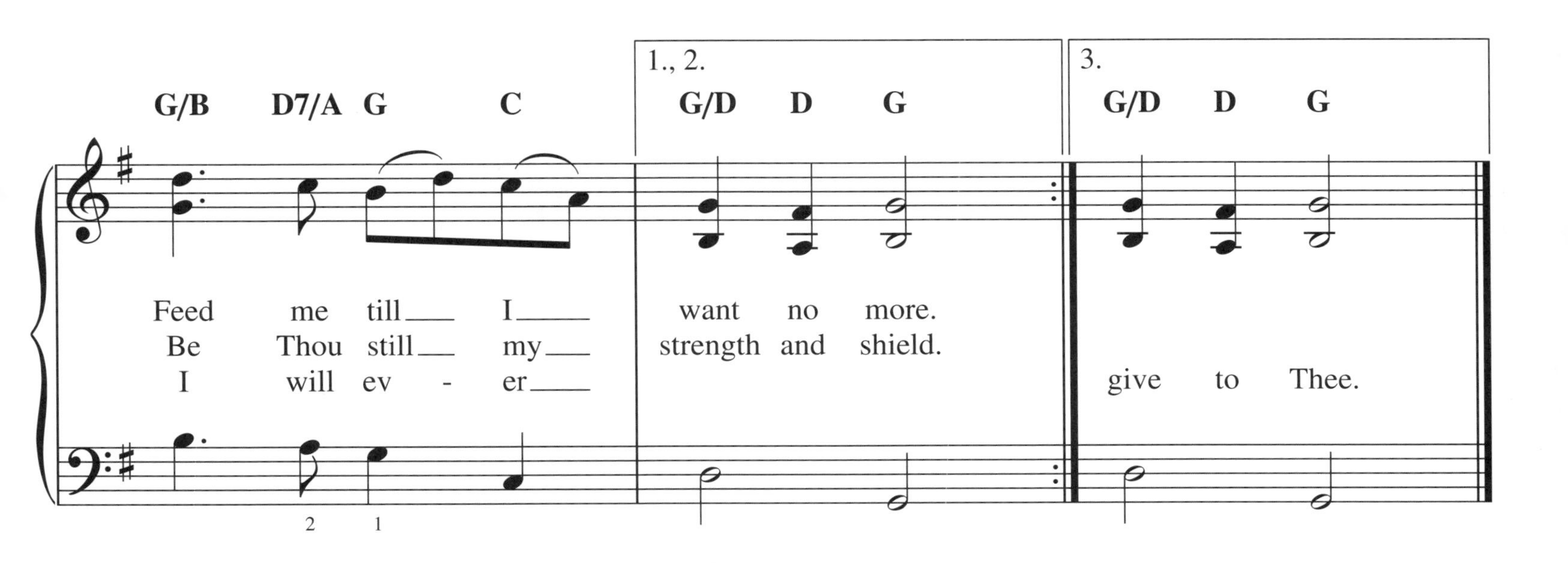
1., 2.
3.
G/B D7/A G C G/D D G G/D D G
Feed me till I want no more.
Be Thou still my strength and shield.
I will ev - er give to Thee.

HE LEADETH ME

Words by JOSEPH H. GILMORE
Music by WILLIAM B. BRADBURY

HEAVENLY SUNLIGHT

Words by HENRY J. ZELLEY
Music by GEORGE HARRISON COOK

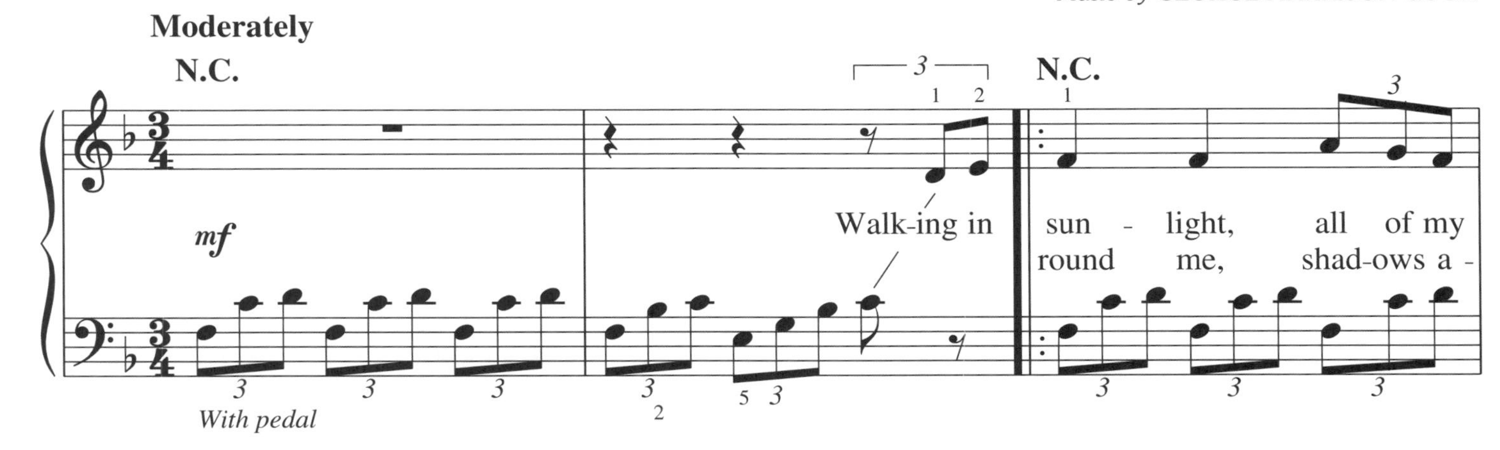

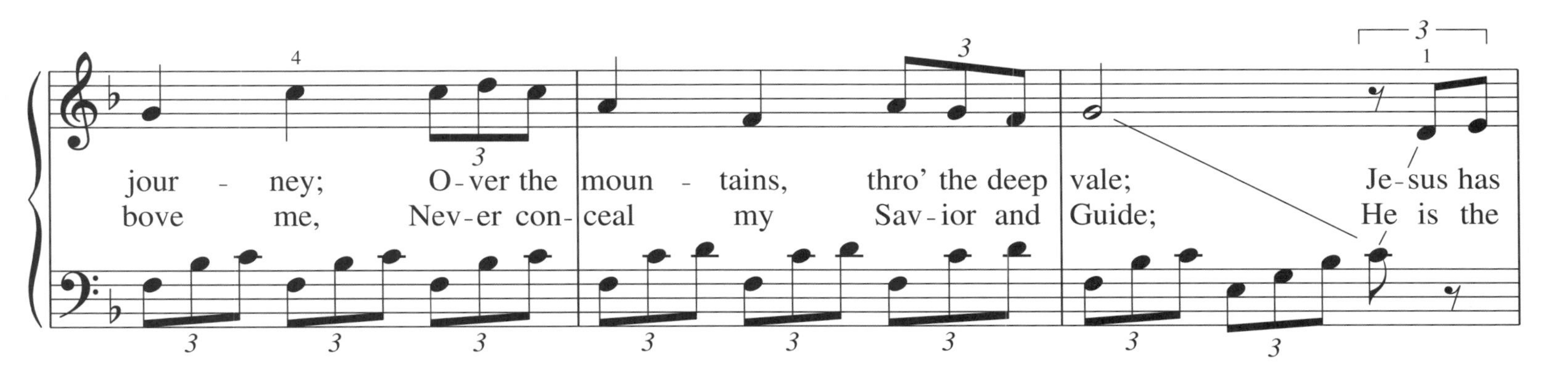

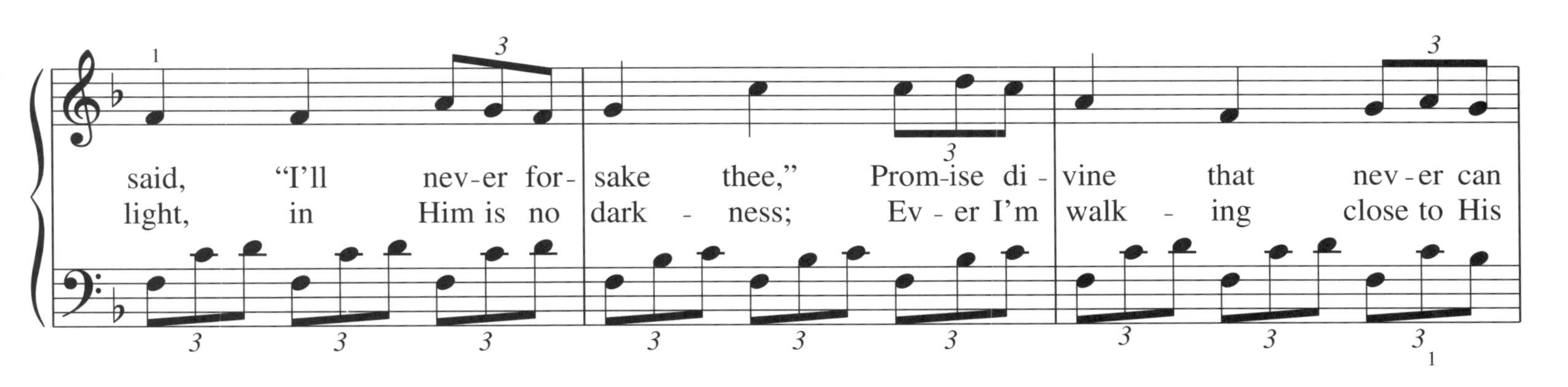

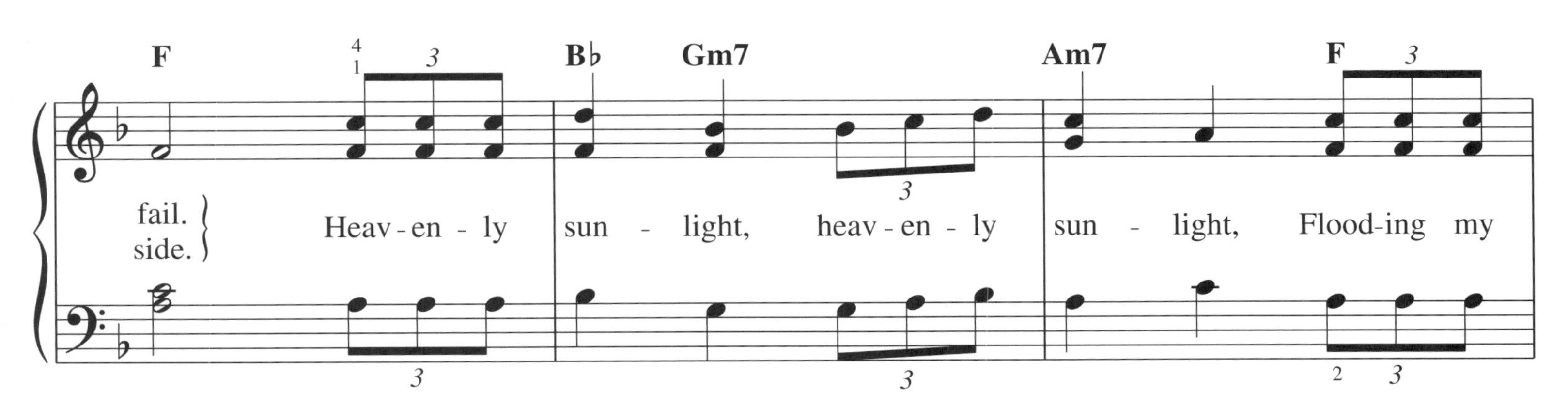

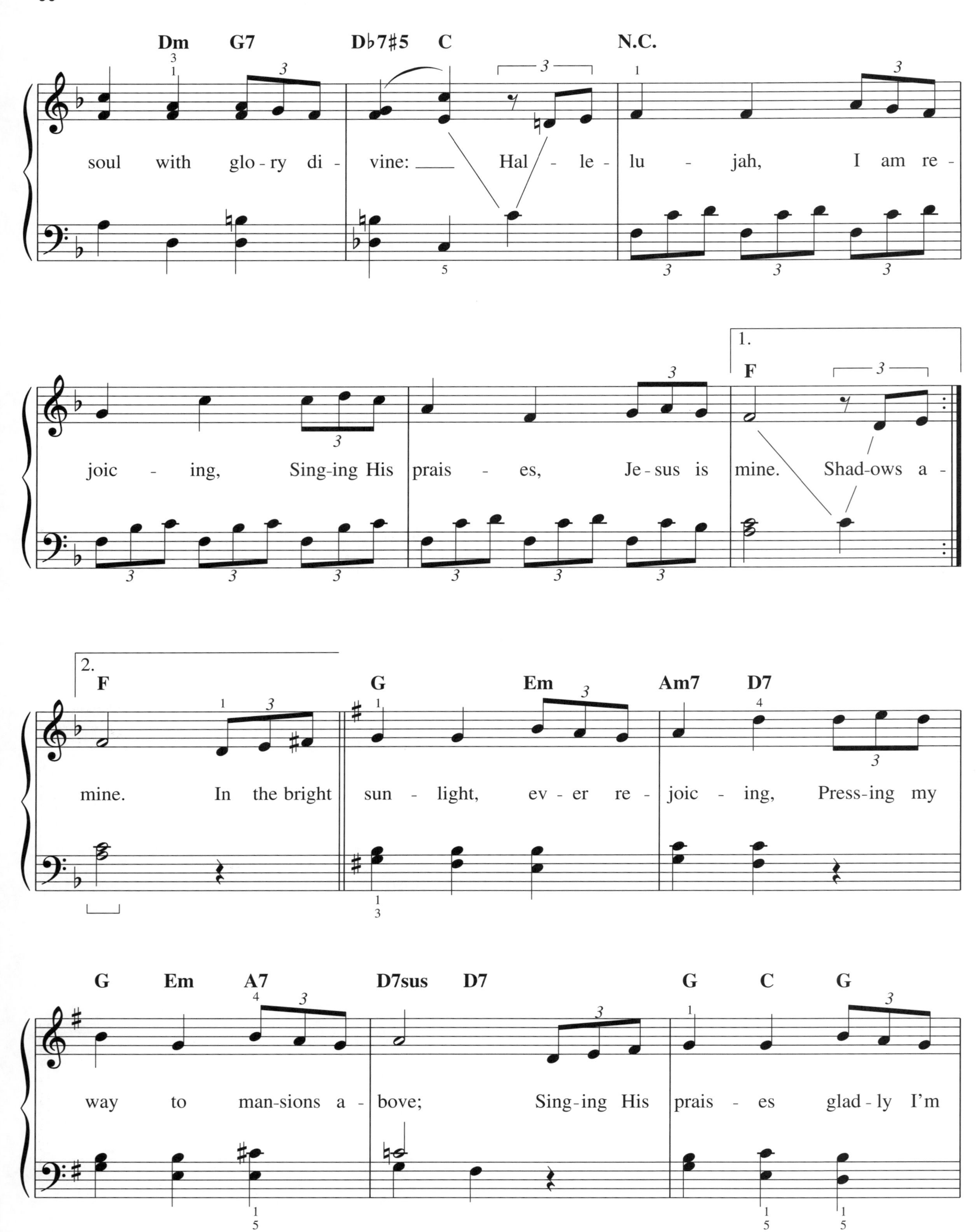

Dm G7 D♭7♯5 C N.C.
soul with glo - ry di - vine: Hal - le - lu - jah, I am re -
joic - ing, Sing-ing His prais - es, Je - sus is
1.
F
mine. Shad-ows a -
2.
F G Em Am7 D7
mine. In the bright sun - light, ev - er re - joic - ing, Press-ing my
G Em A7 D7sus D7 G C G
way to man-sions a - bove; Sing-ing His prais - es glad - ly I'm

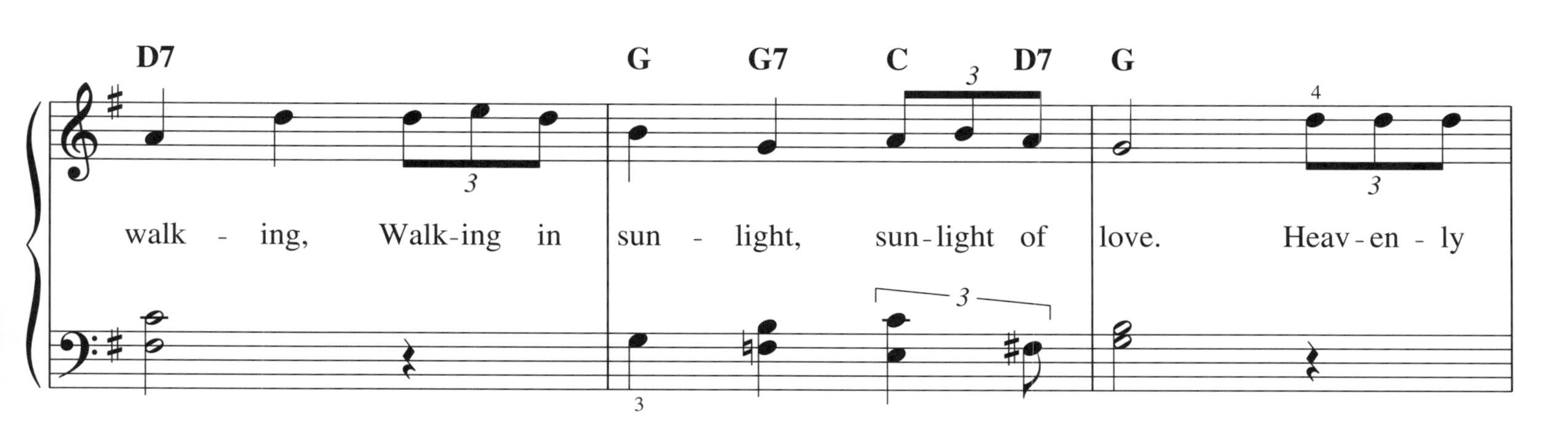
D7 G G7 C D7 G
walk - ing, Walk-ing in sun - light, sun-light of love. Heav-en - ly

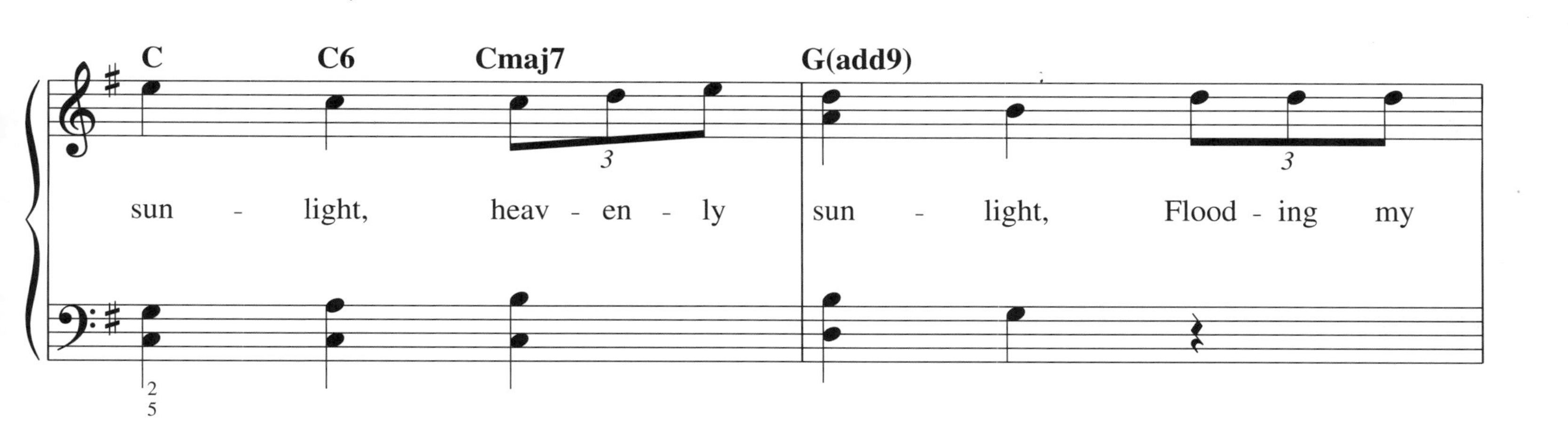
C C6 Cmaj7 G(add9)
sun - light, heav - en - ly sun - light, Flood - ing my

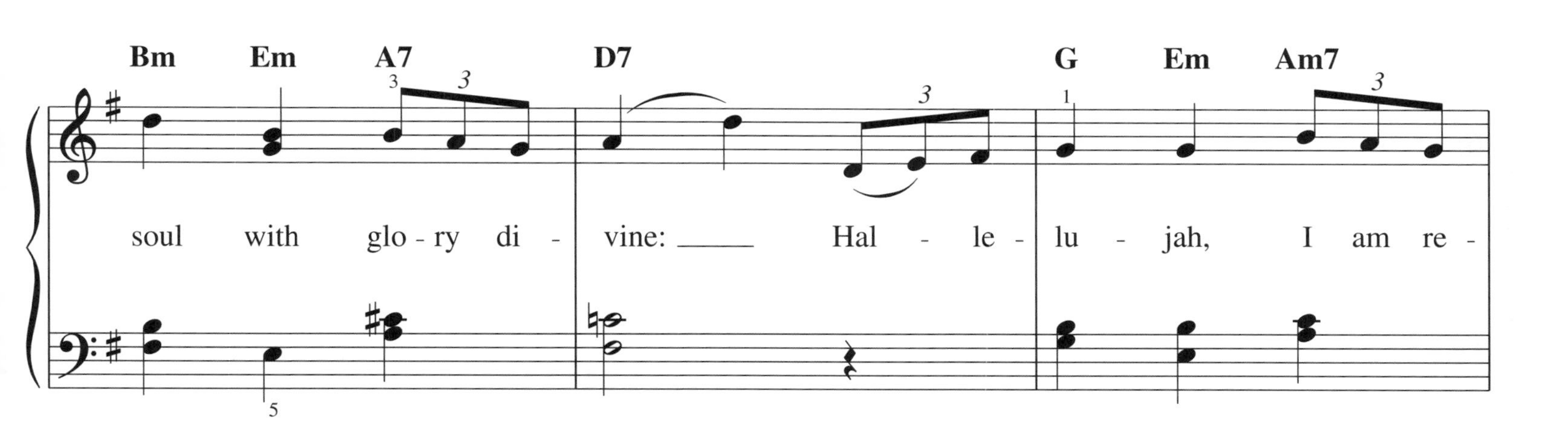
Bm Em A7 D7 G Em Am7
soul with glo - ry di - vine: Hal - le - lu - jah, I am re -

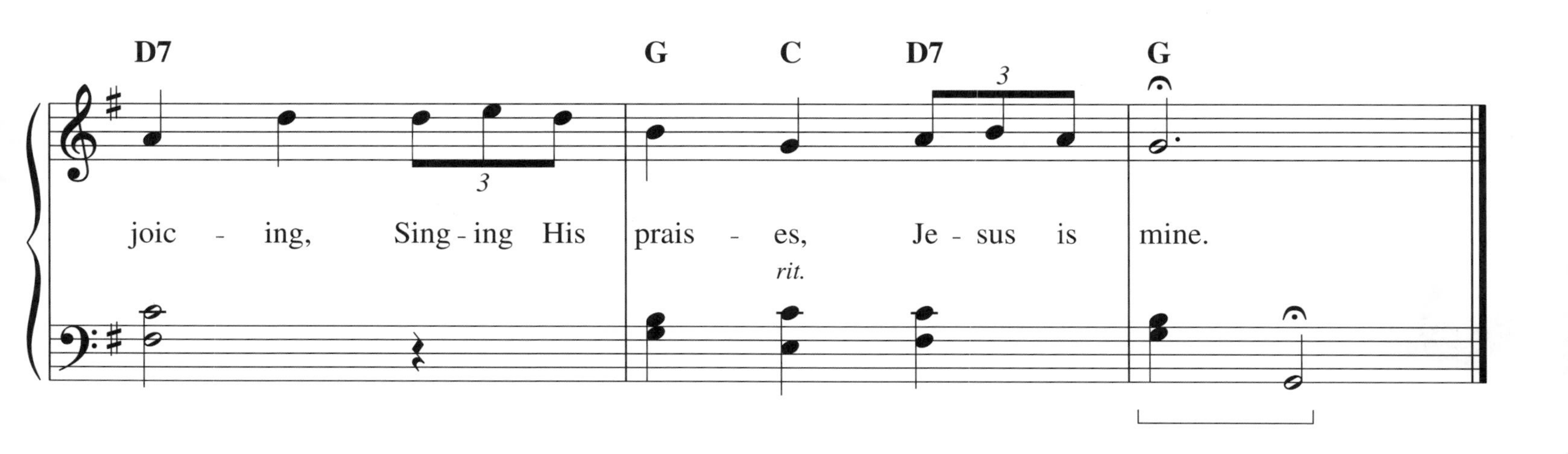
D7 G C D7 G
joic - ing, Sing - ing His prais - es, Je - sus is mine.
rit.

HIGHER GROUND

Words by JOHNSON OATMAN, JR.
Music by CHARLES H. GABRIEL

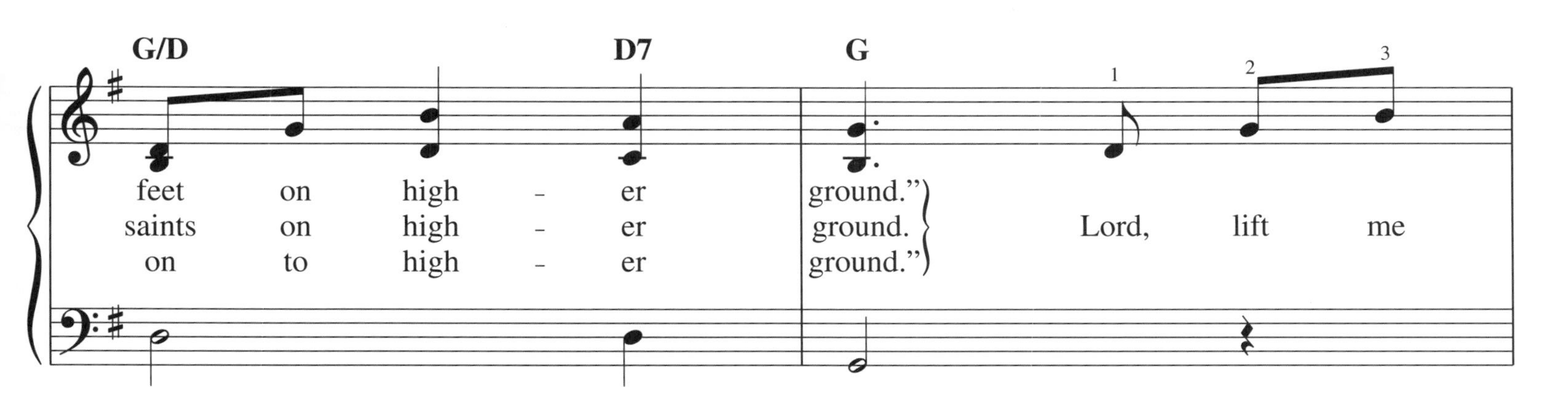
G/D
D7
G
feet on high - er ground."
saints on high - er ground.
on to high - er ground."
Lord, lift me

D7
up and let me stand, by faith, on heav - en's ta - ble -

G
C
land; a high - er plane than I have found. Lord, plant my

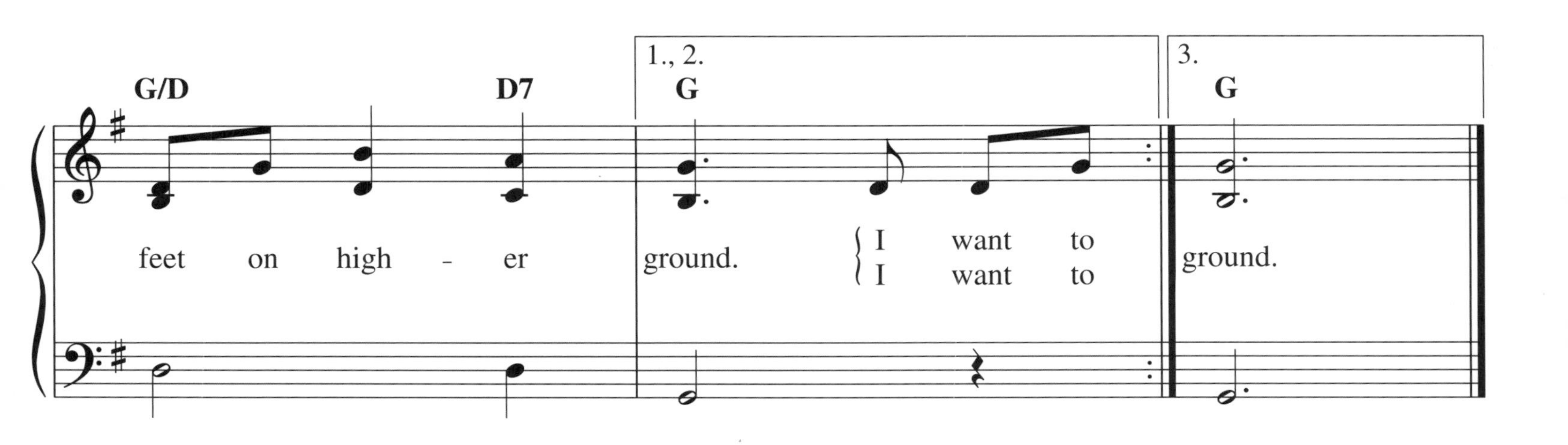
G/D
D7
1., 2.
G
3.
G
feet on high - er ground.
I want to
I want to
ground.

HOLY, HOLY, HOLY

Text by REGINALD HEBER
Music by JOHN B. DYKES

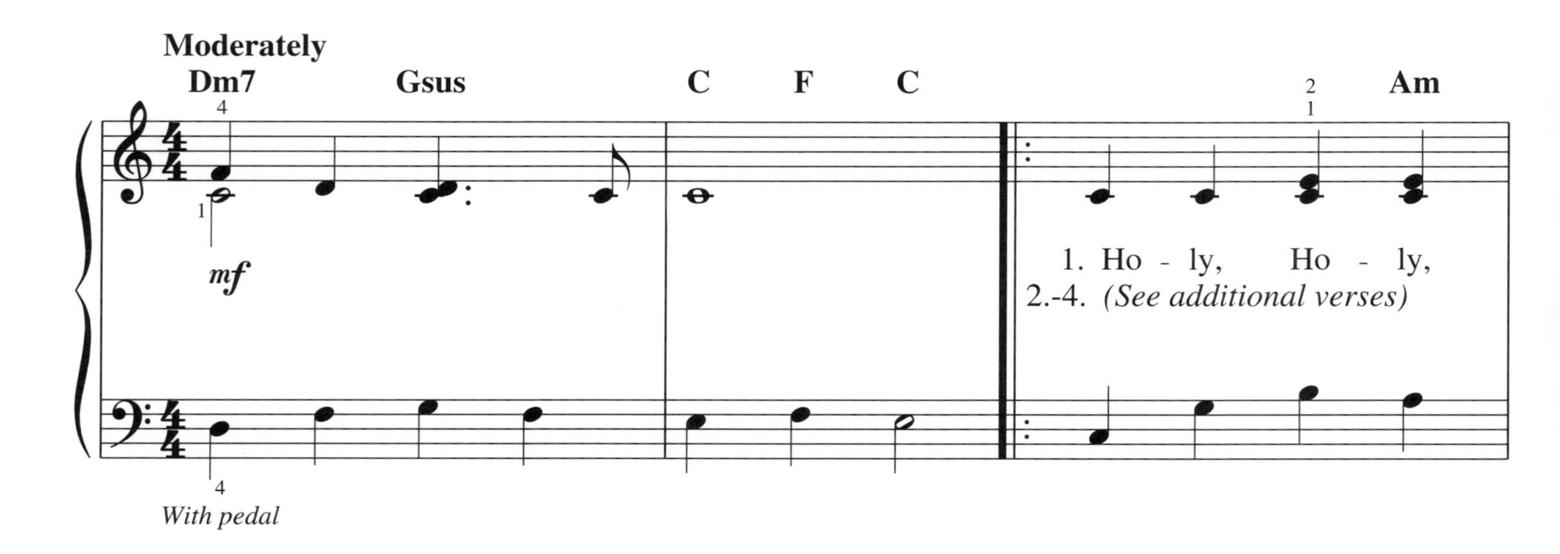

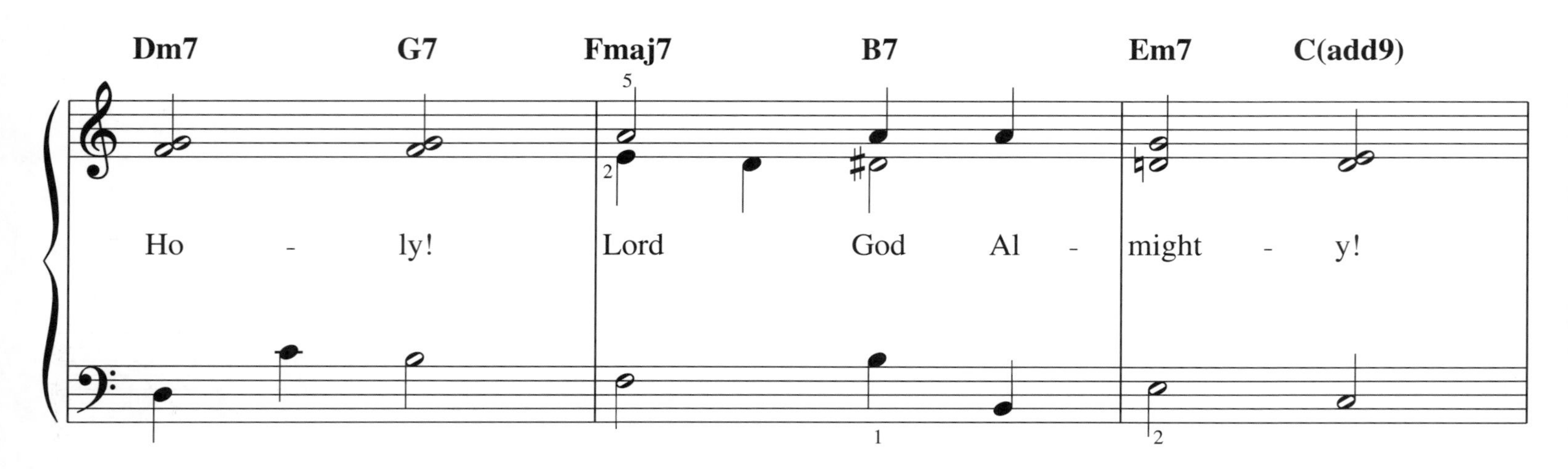

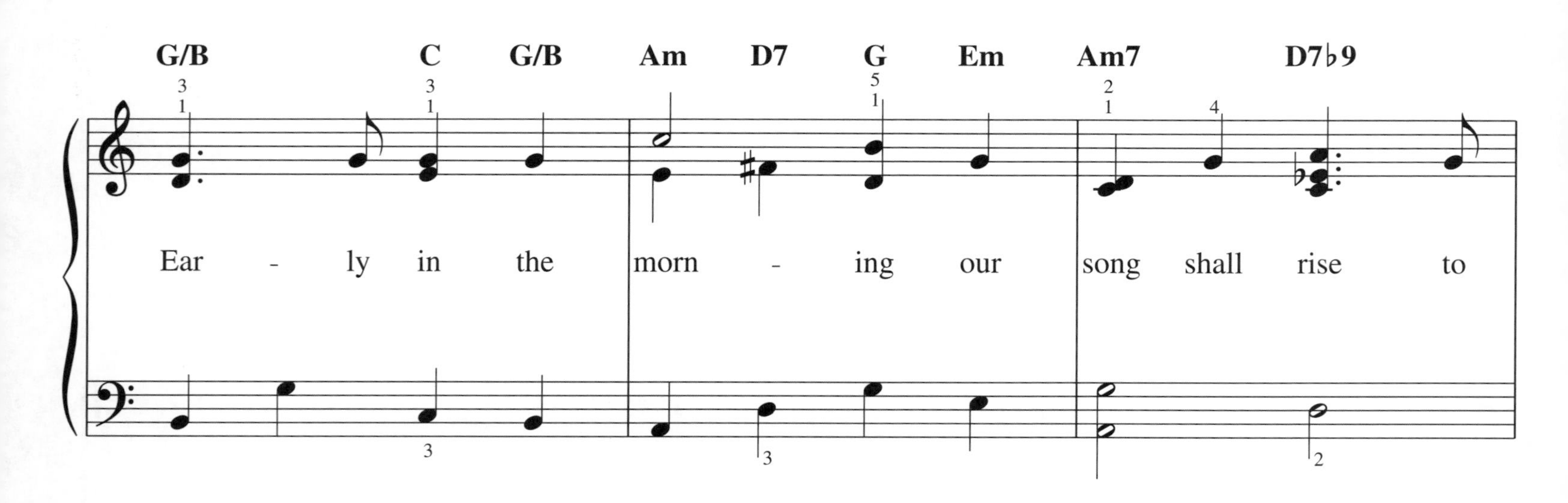

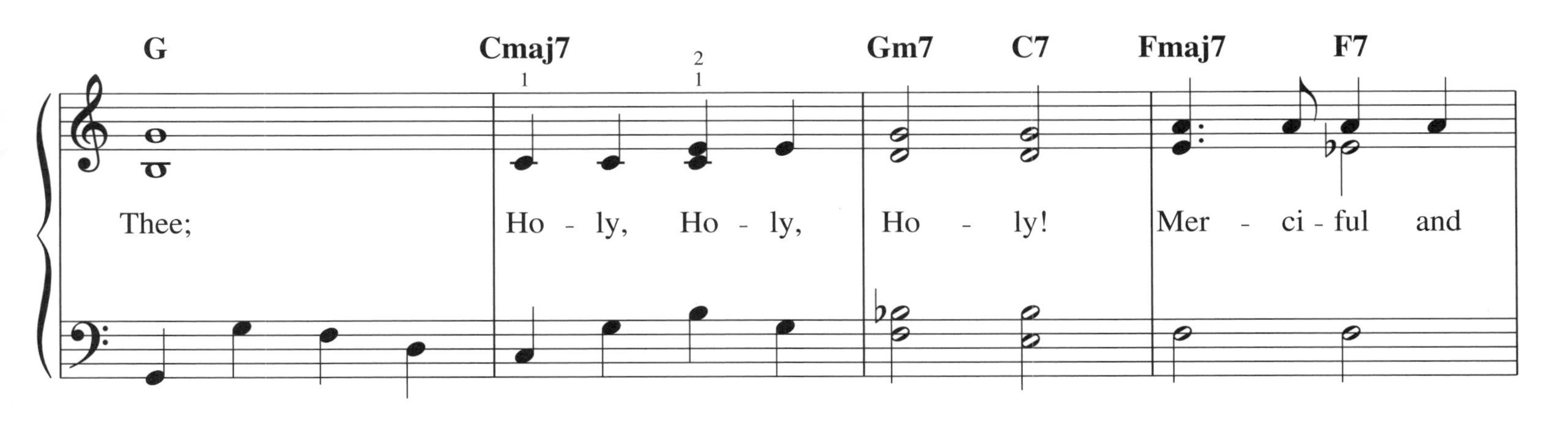

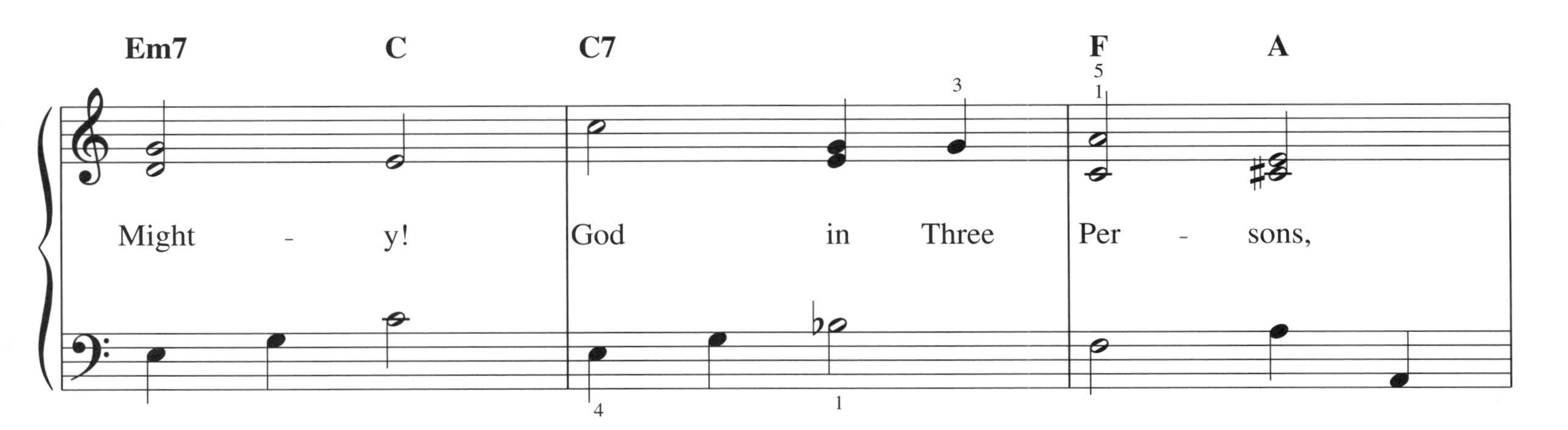

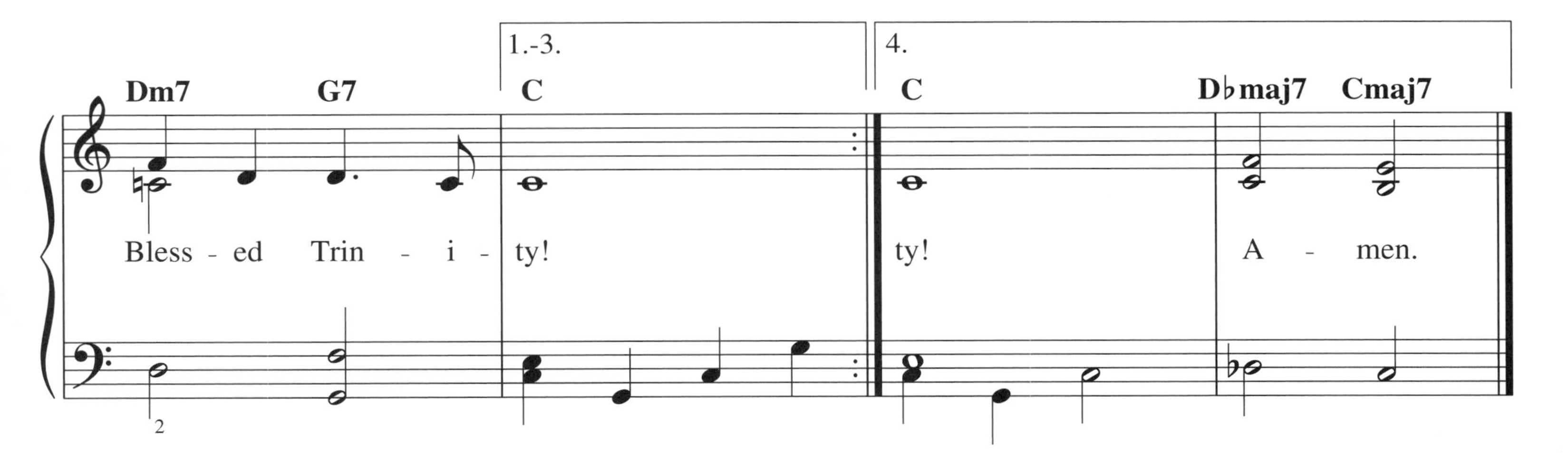

Additional Verses

2. Holy, Holy, Holy! All the saints adore Thee,
   Casting down their golden crowns around the glassy sea;
   Cherubim and seraphim falling down before Thee,
   Who wert, and art, and evermore shalt be.

3. Holy, Holy, Holy! Though the darkness hide Thee,
   Though the eye of sinful man Thy glory may not see,
   Only Thou art holy; there is none beside Thee,
   Perfect in power, in love, and purity.

4. Holy, Holy, Holy! Lord God Almighty!
   All Thy works shall praise Thy Name, in earth and sky and sea;
   Holy, Holy, Holy! Merciful and Mighty!
   God in Three Persons, blessed Trinity! Amen.

HOSANNA, LOUD HOSANNA

Words by JENETTE THRELFALL, based on Matthew 21:1-11
Music taken from *Gesangbuch der Herzogl*

Moderately

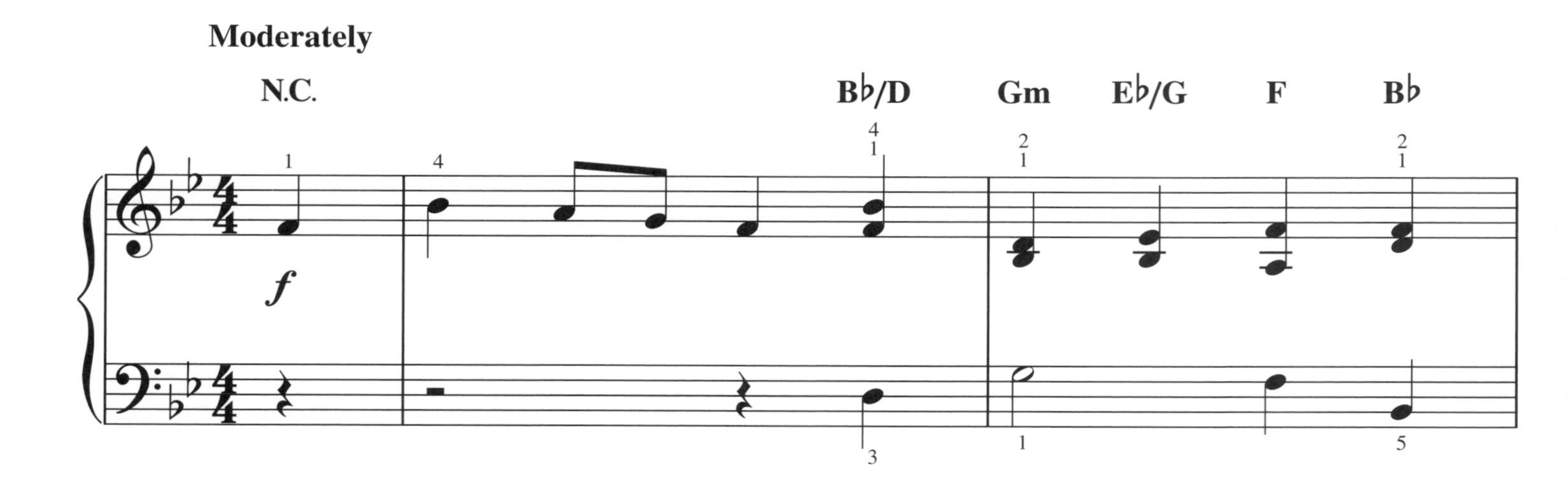

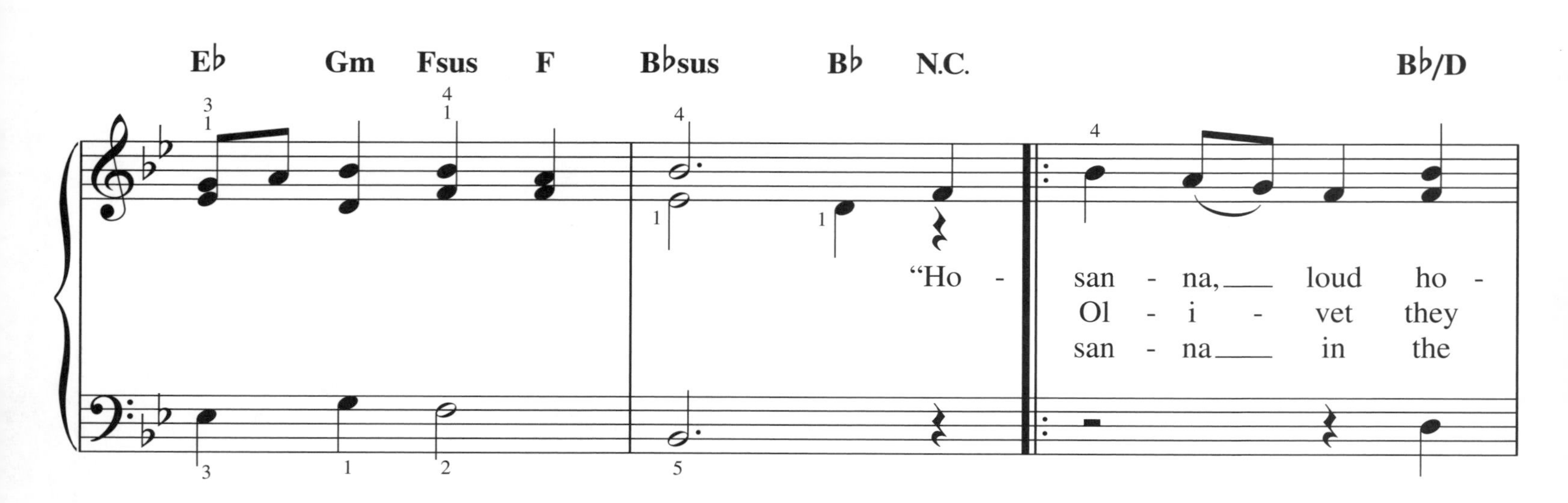

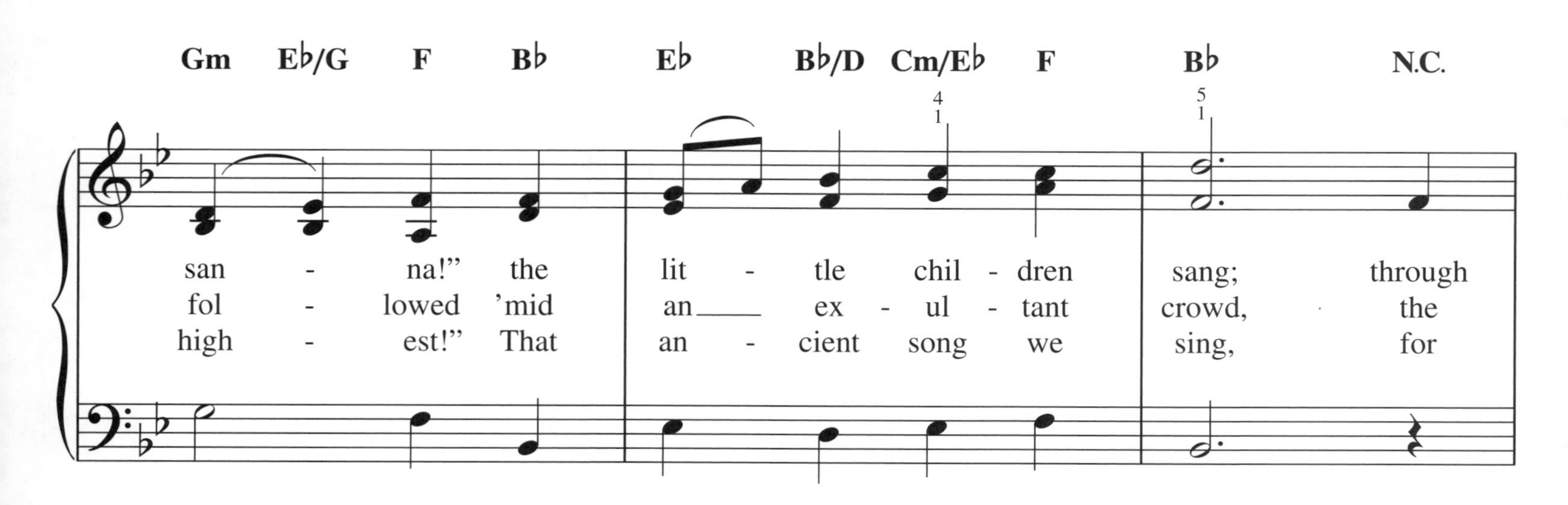

Bb/D Gm Eb/G F Bb Eb Gm Fsus F
pil - lared court and tem - ple the love - ly an - them
vic - tor palm branch wav - ing and chant - ing clear and
Christ is our Re - deem - er, the Lord of heav'n, our
Bb F/A Bb Eb F
rang. To Je - sus, who had blessed them close
loud. The Lord of men and an - gels rode
King. O may we ev - er praise Him with
Bb F/A Bb Eb Fsus F N.C. Bb/D
fold - ed to His breast, the chil - dren sang their
on in low - ly state, nor scorned that lit - tle
heart and life and voice, and in His bliss - ful
Gm Eb/G F Bb Eb Gm Fsus F
1., 2.
Bb
3.
Bb
prais - es, the sim - plest and the best. From
chil - dren should on His bid - ding wait. "Ho -
pres - ence e - ter - nal - ly re - joice.

HOW FIRM A FOUNDATION

Words from JOHN RIPPON's *A Selection of Hymns*
Early American Melody

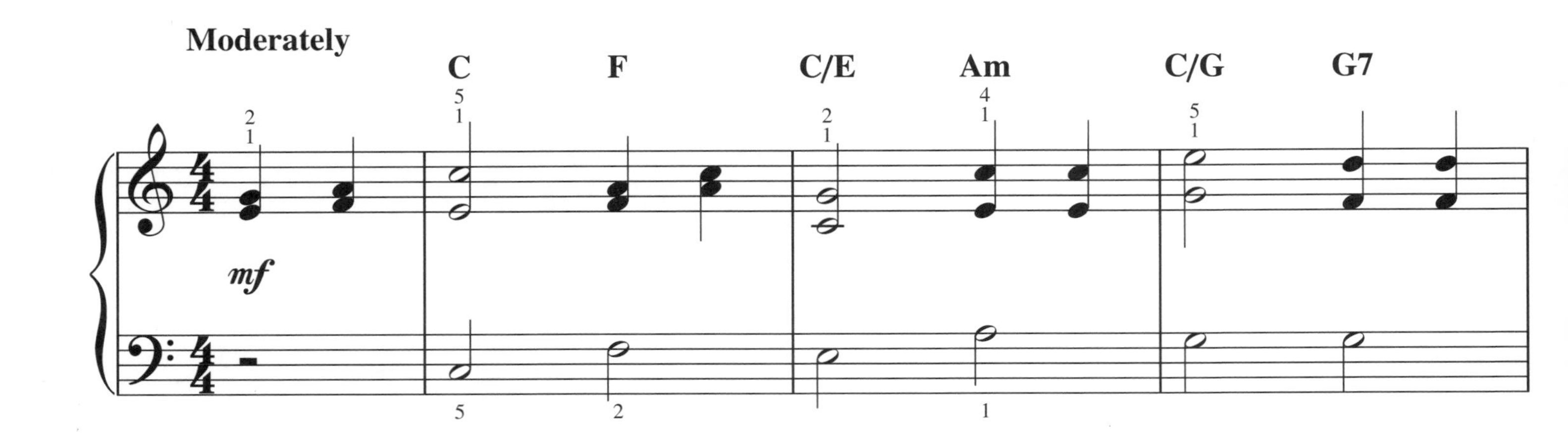

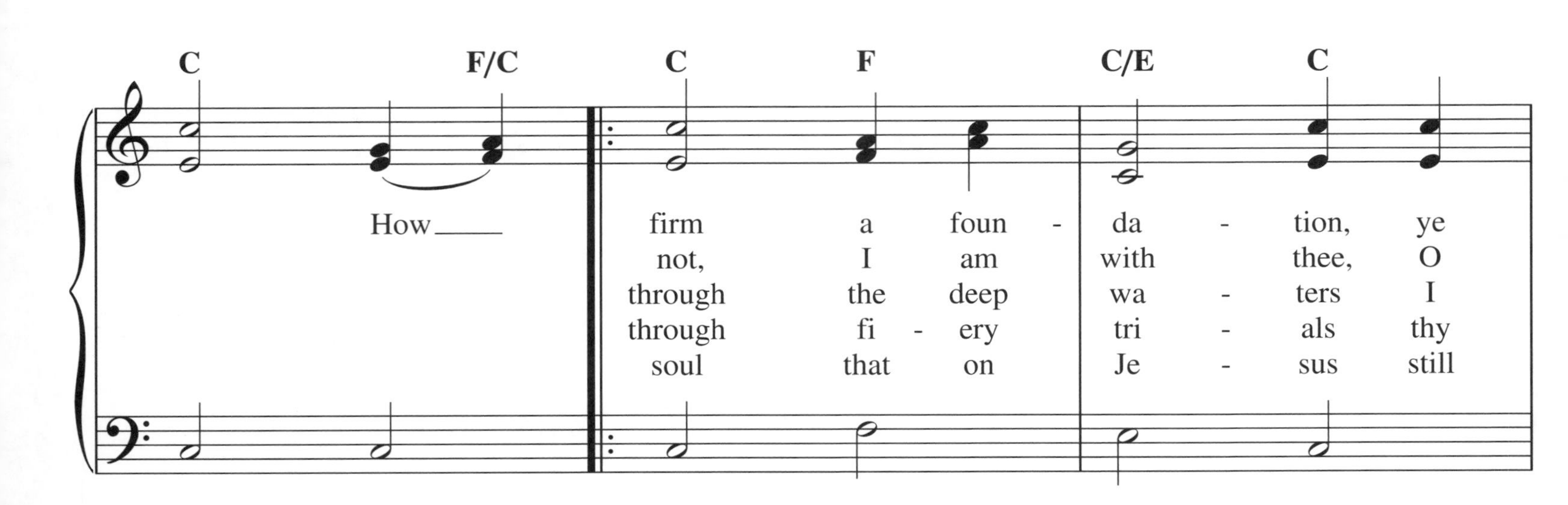

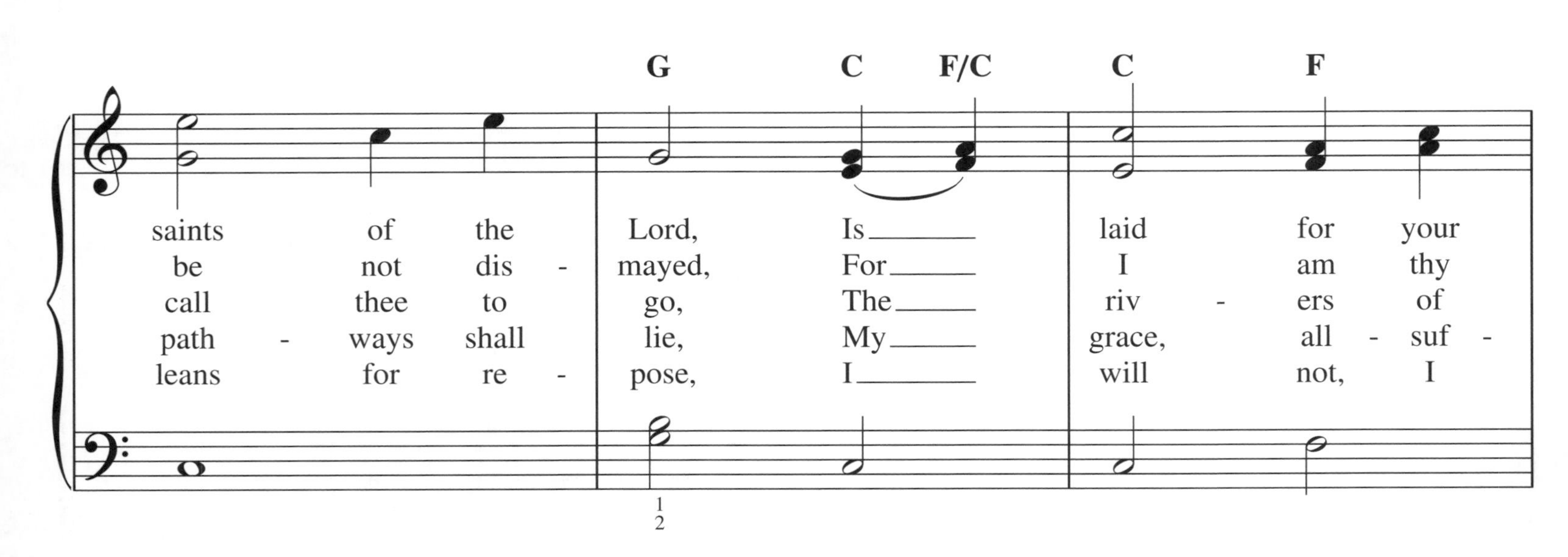

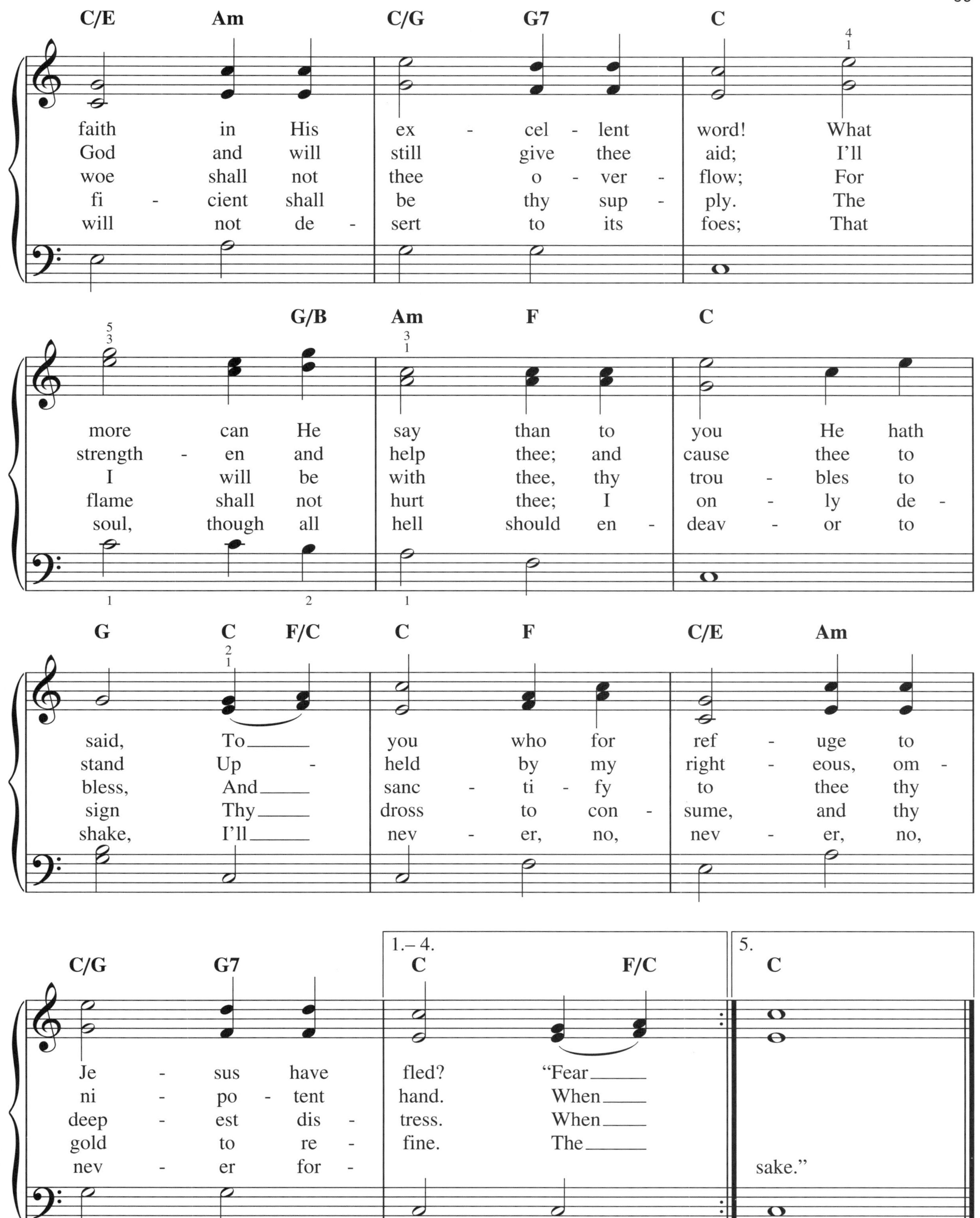
C/E Am C/G G7 C
faith in His ex - cel - lent word! What
God and will still give thee aid; I'll
woe shall not thee o - ver - flow; For
fi - cient shall be thy sup - ply. The
will not de - sert to its foes; That
G/B Am F C
more can He say than to you He hath
strength - en and help thee; and cause thee to
I will be with thee, thy trou - bles to
flame shall not hurt thee; I on - ly de -
soul, though all hell should en - deav - or to
G C F/C C F C/E Am
said, To you who for ref - uge to
stand Up - held by my right - eous, om -
bless, And sanc - ti - fy to thee thy
sign Thy dross to con - sume, and thy
shake, I'll nev - er, no, nev - er, no,
C/G G7
1.– 4. C F/C
5. C
Je - sus have fled? "Fear
ni - po - tent hand. When
deep - est dis - tress. When
gold to re - fine. The
nev - er for - sake."

I AM THINE, O LORD

Words by FANNY J. CROSBY
Music by WILLIAM H. DOANE

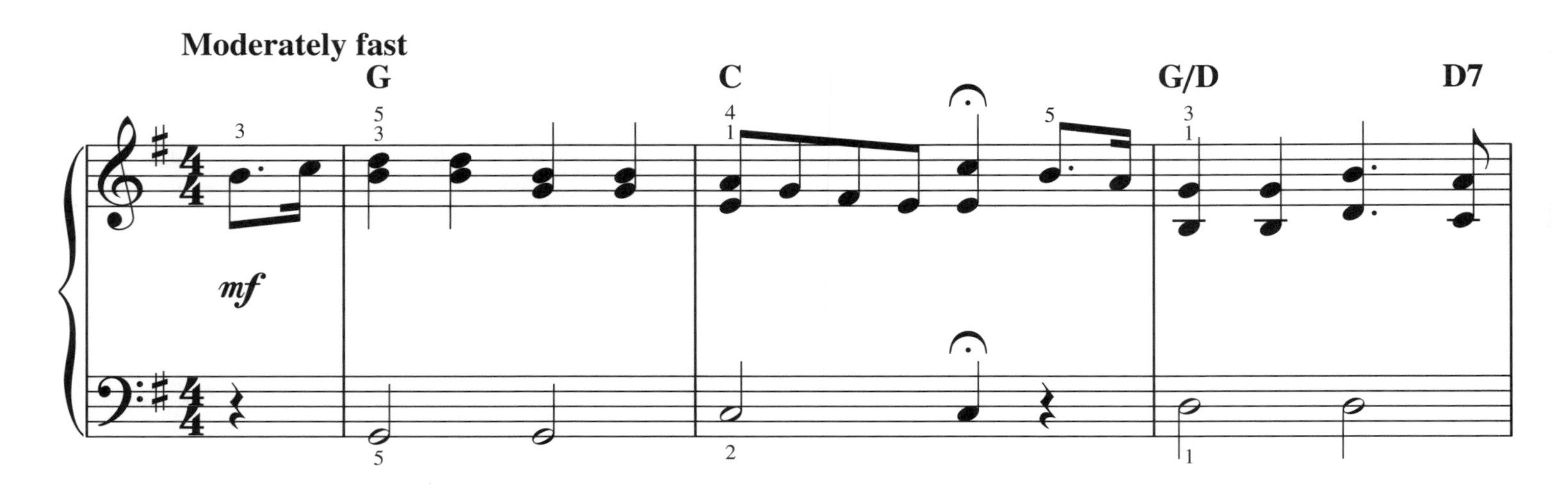

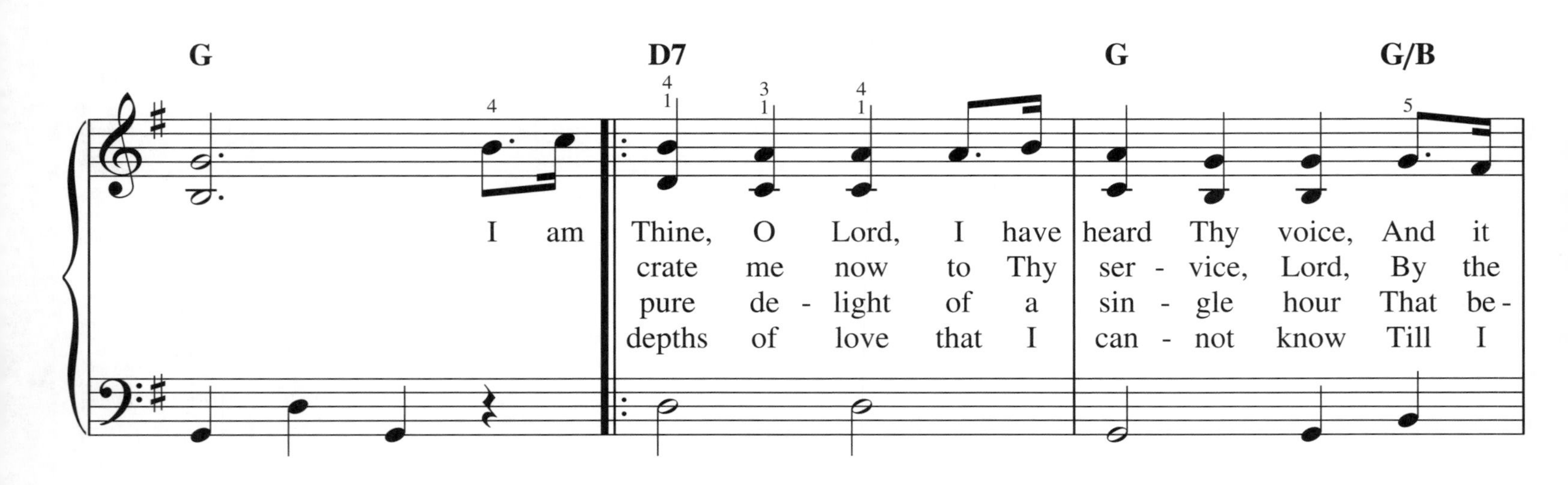

G C Am D D7 G
arms of faith And be clos - er drawn to Thee.
stead - fast hope, And my will be lost in Thine.
Thee, my God, I com - mune as friend with friend!
may not reach Till I rest in peace with Thee.
Draw me
C G G/B C G/B Am G
near - er, near - er, bless - ed Lord, To the cross where Thou hast
D G D/A G/B G7/B C
died; Draw me near - er, near - er, near - er, bless - ed Lord, To Thy
G/D D7
1.–3. G
4. G
pre - cious, bleed - ing side.
Con - se -
O the
There are
side.

I HAVE DECIDED TO FOLLOW JESUS

Folk Melody from India
Arranged by AUILA READ

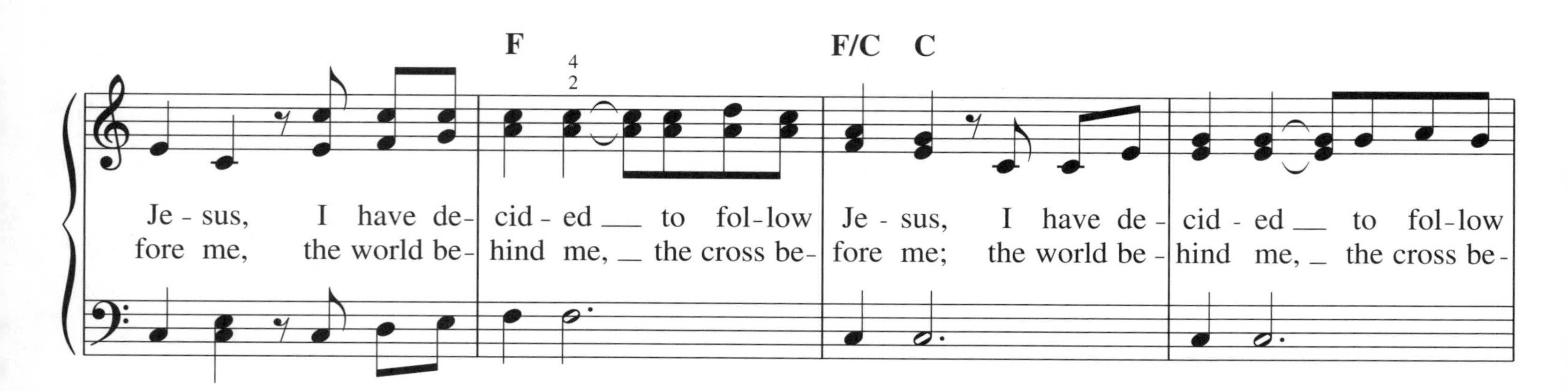

Additional Verses

3. Though none go with me, still I will follow, *etc.*

4. Will you decide now to follow Jesus? *etc.*

I NEED THEE EVERY HOUR

Words by ANNIE S. HAWKS
Music by ROBERT LOWRY

I LOVE TO TELL THE STORY

Words by A. CATHERINE HANKEY
Music by WILLIAM G. FISCHER

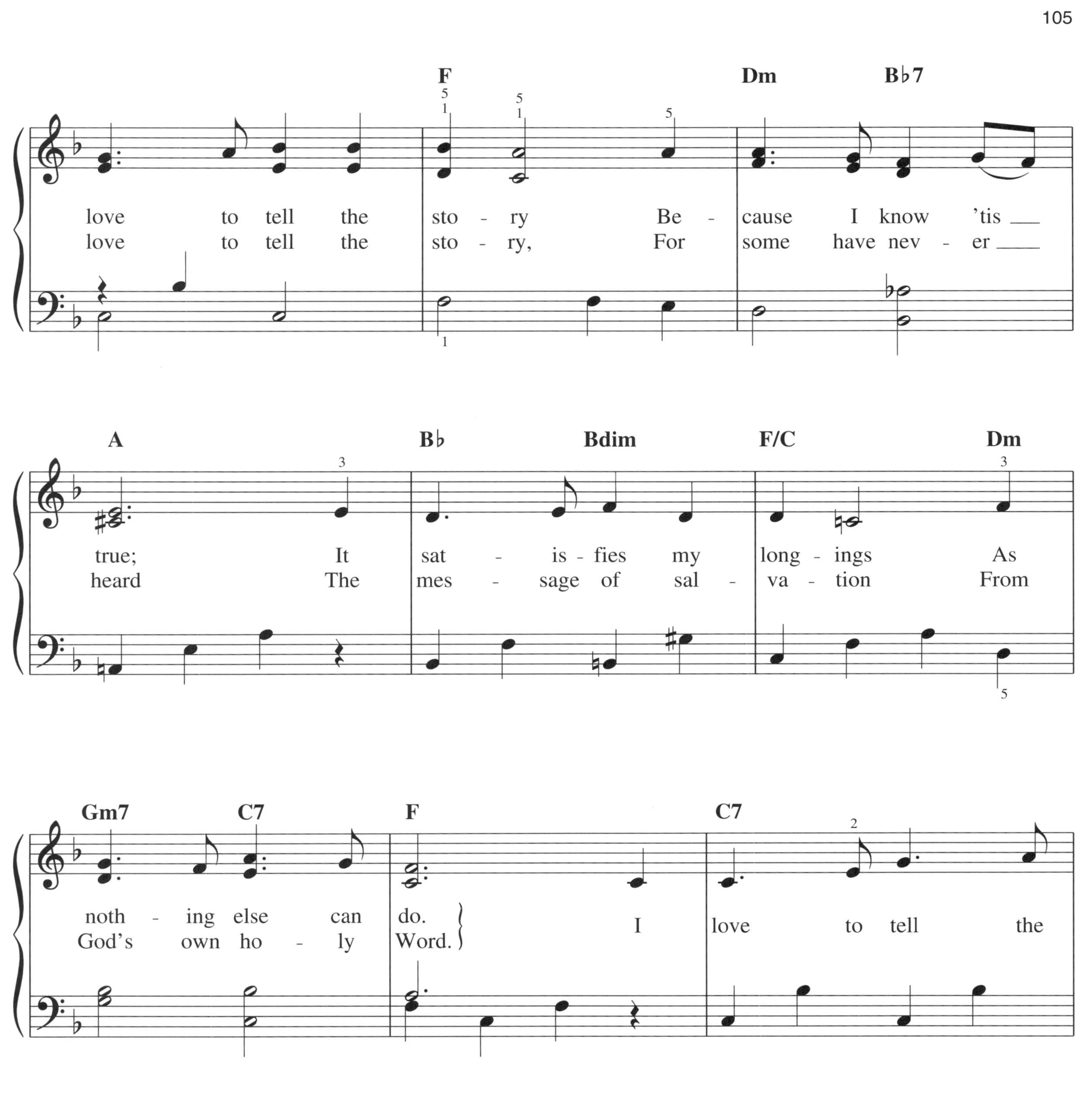
F Dm B♭7
love to tell the sto - ry Be - cause I know 'tis
love to tell the sto - ry, For some have nev - er
A B♭ Bdim F/C Dm
true; It sat - is - fies my long - ings As
heard The mes - sage of sal - va - tion From
Gm7 C7 F C7
noth - ing else can do.
God's own ho - ly Word.
I love to tell the

F F7 B♭ E♭7 F
sto - ry, 'Twill be my theme in glo - ry to

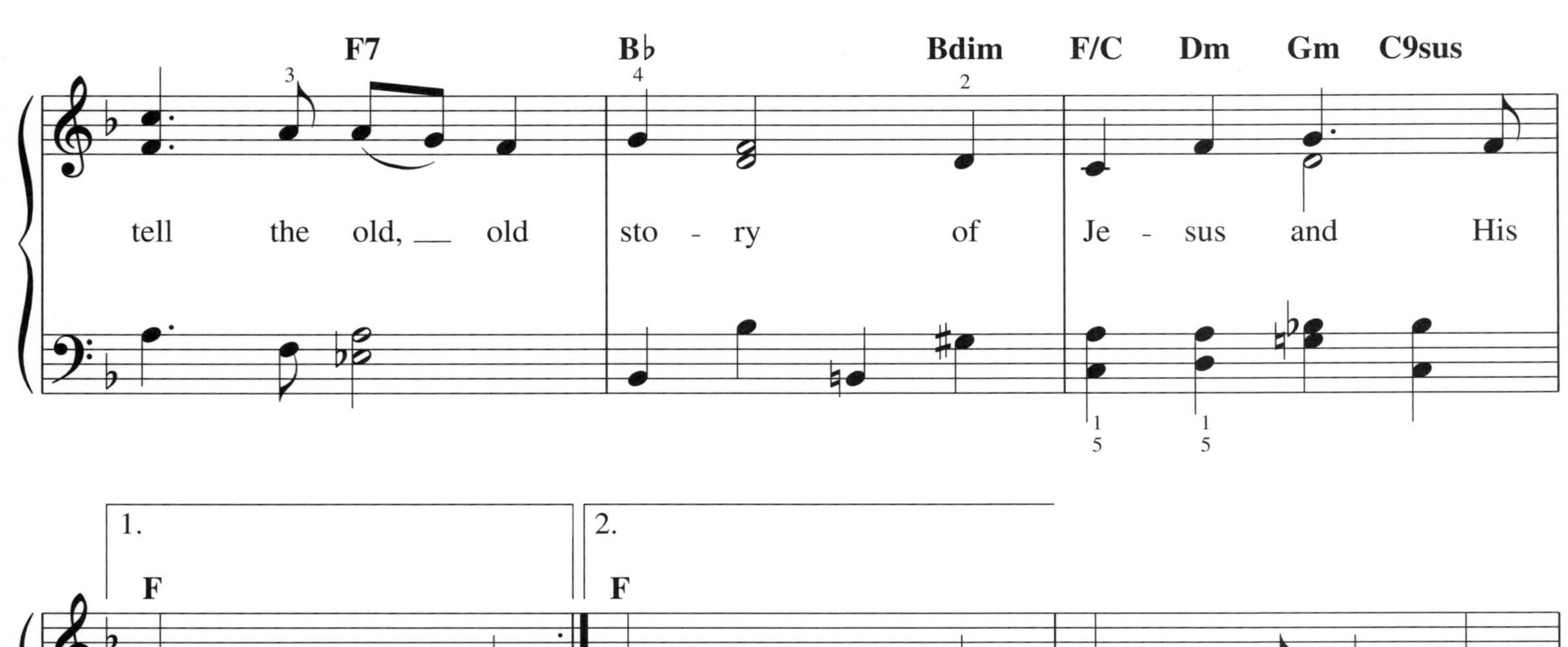
F7
B♭
Bdim
F/C
Dm
Gm
C9sus
tell the old, _ old sto - ry of Je - sus and His

1.
2.
F
F
love. I love. I love to tell the

B♭
F/A
sto - ry; For those who know _ it best Seem

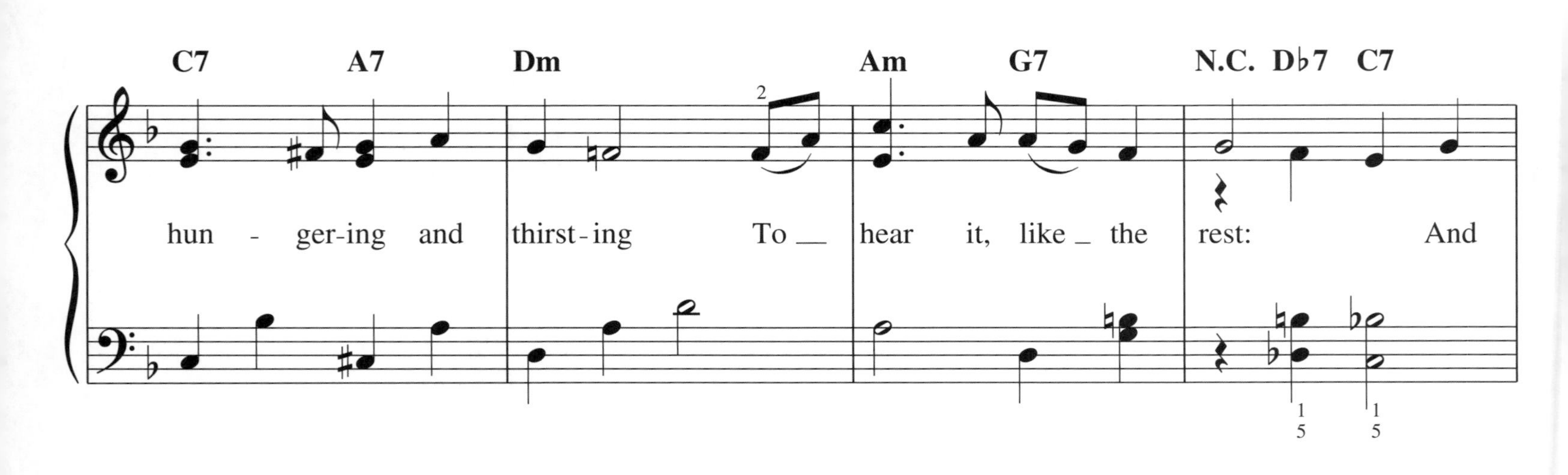
C7
A7
Dm
Am
G7
N.C.
D♭7
C7
hun - ger-ing and thirst-ing To _ hear it, like _ the rest: And

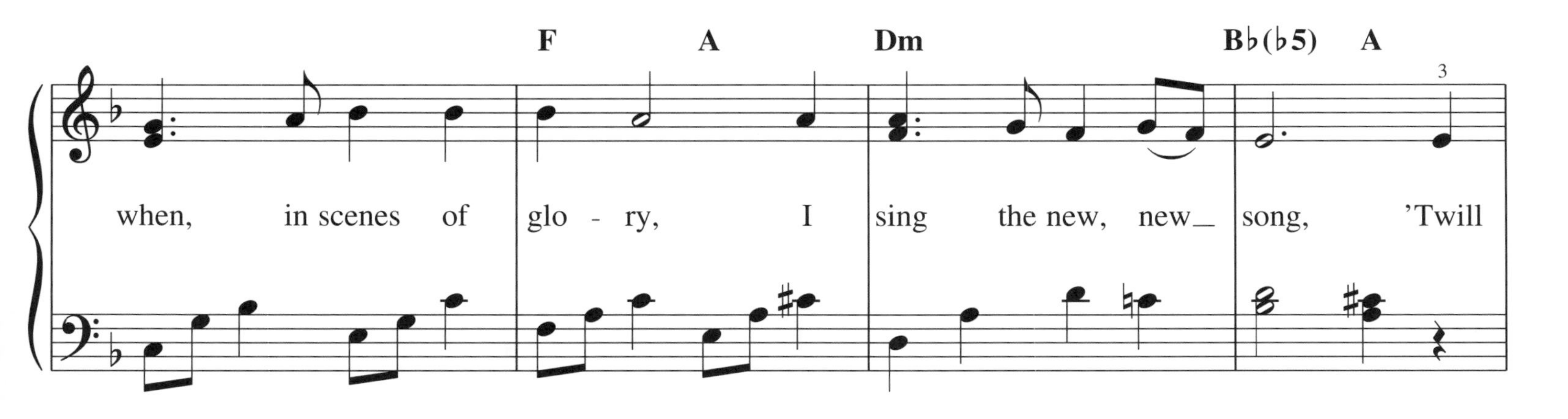
F A Dm B♭(♭5) A
when, in scenes of glo - ry, I sing the new, new_ song, 'Twill

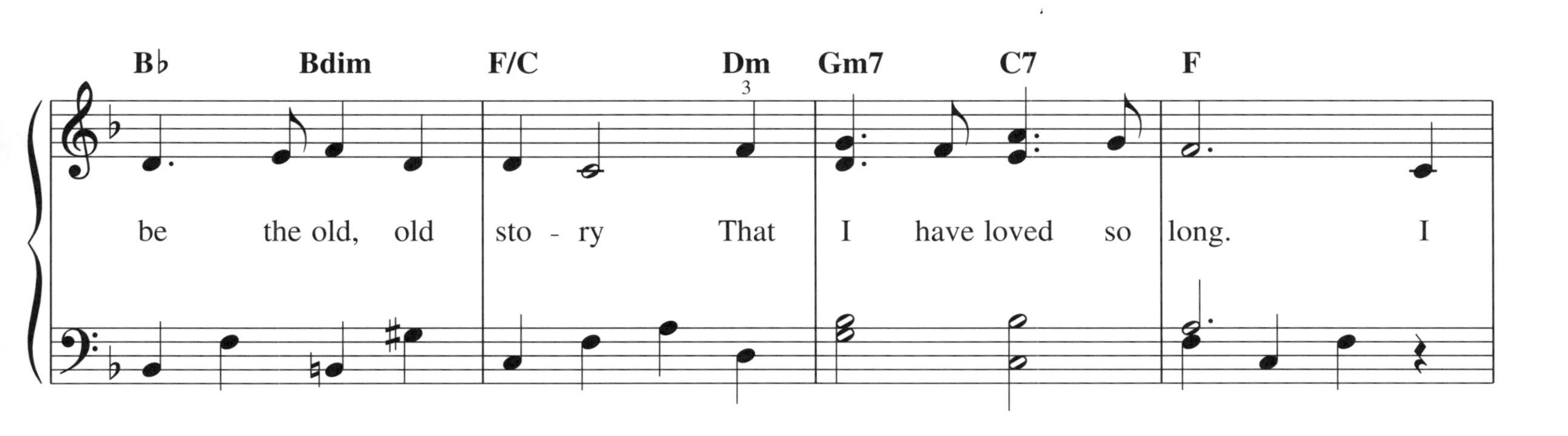
B♭ Bdim F/C Dm Gm7 C7 F
be the old, old sto - ry That I have loved so long. I

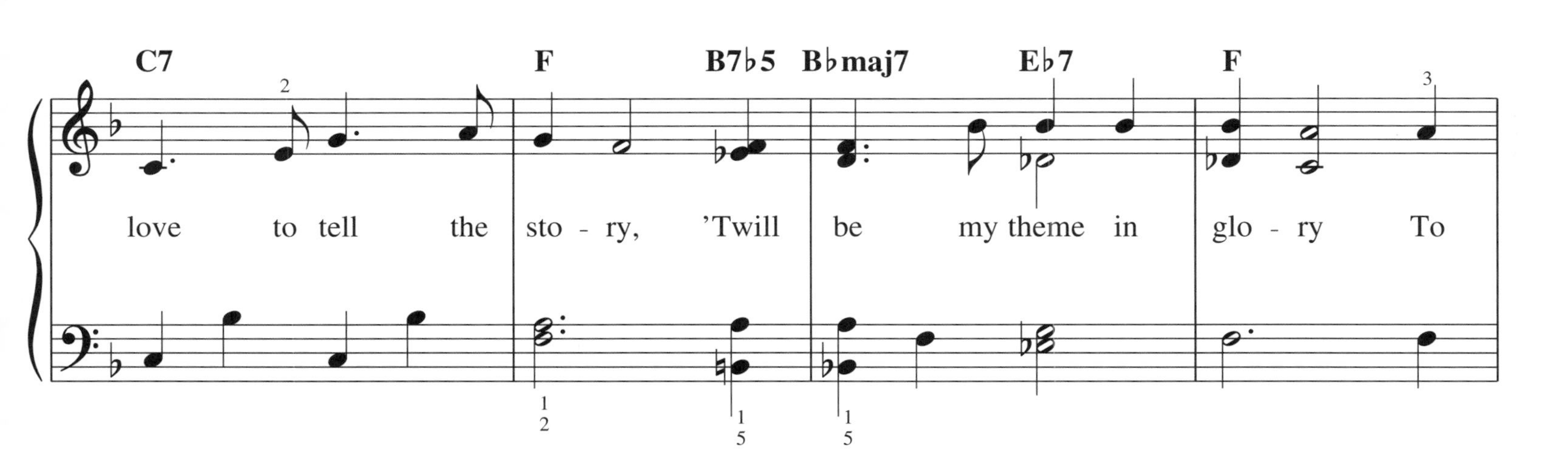
C7 F B7♭5 B♭maj7 E♭7 F
love to tell the sto - ry, 'Twill be my theme in glo - ry To

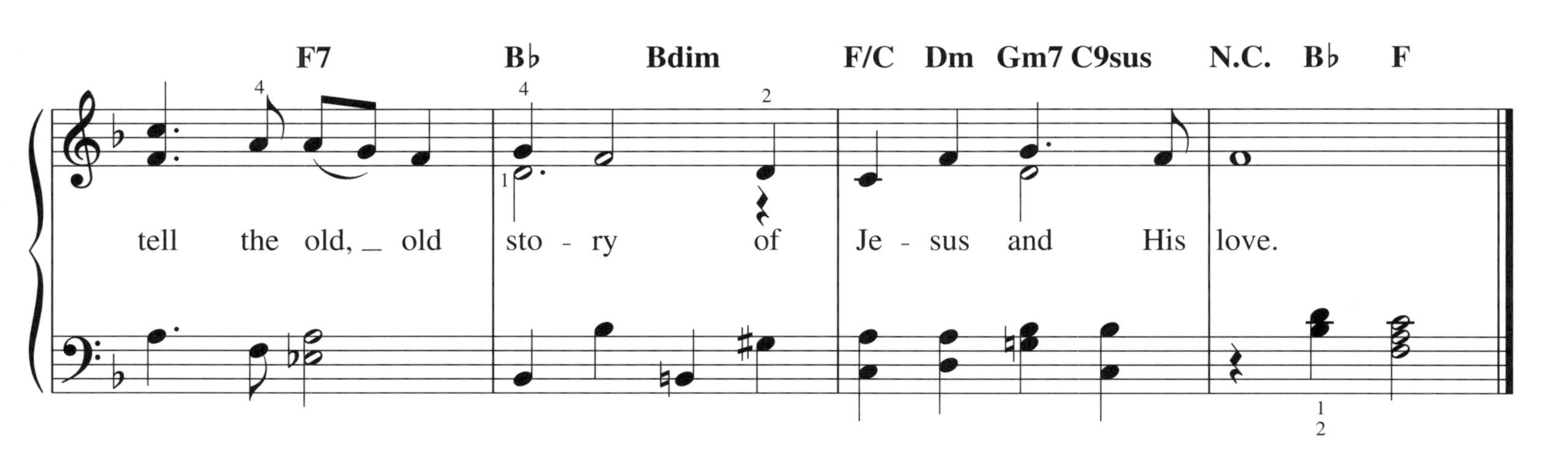
F7 B♭ Bdim F/C Dm Gm7 C9sus N.C. B♭ F
tell the old,_ old sto - ry of Je - sus and His love.

I SING THE MIGHTY POWER OF GOD

Words by ISAAC WATTS
Music from *Gesangbuch der Herzogl*

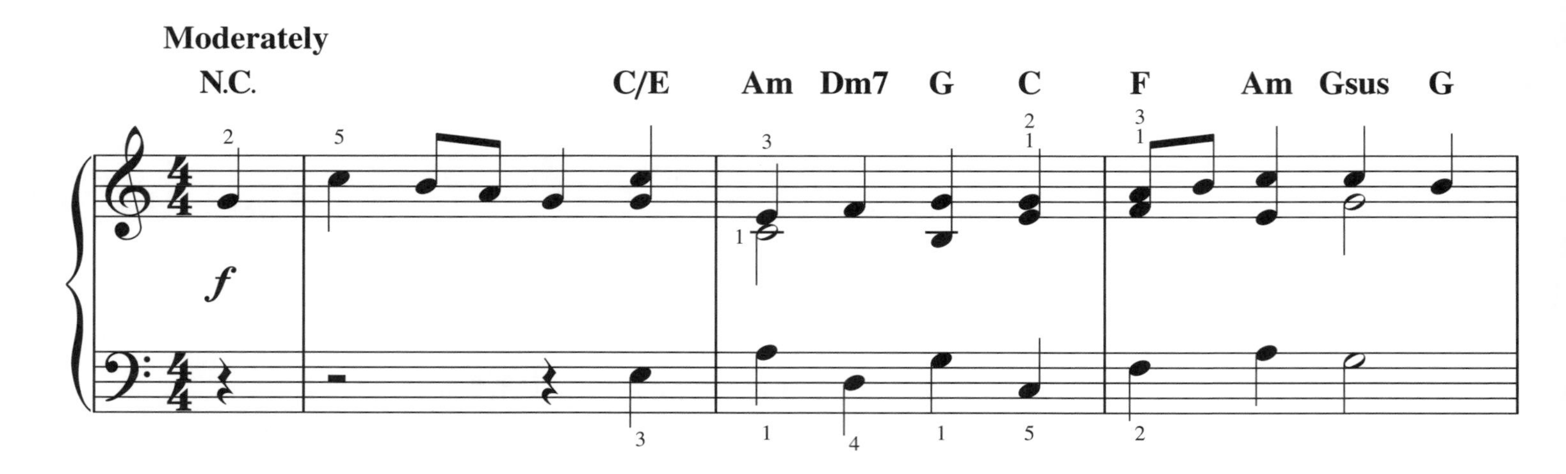

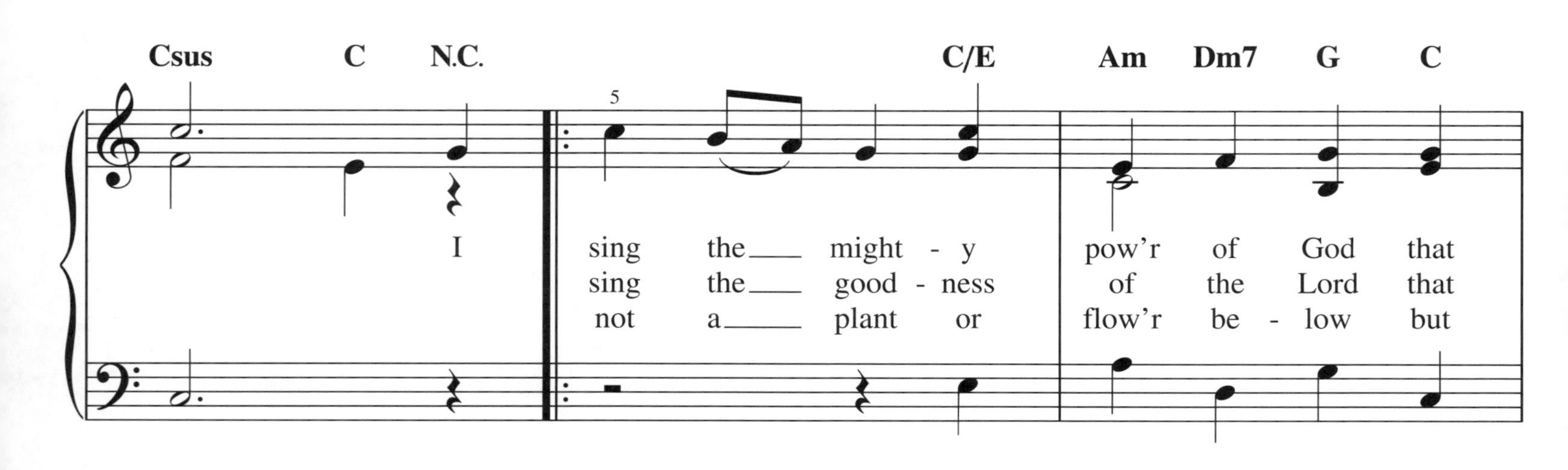

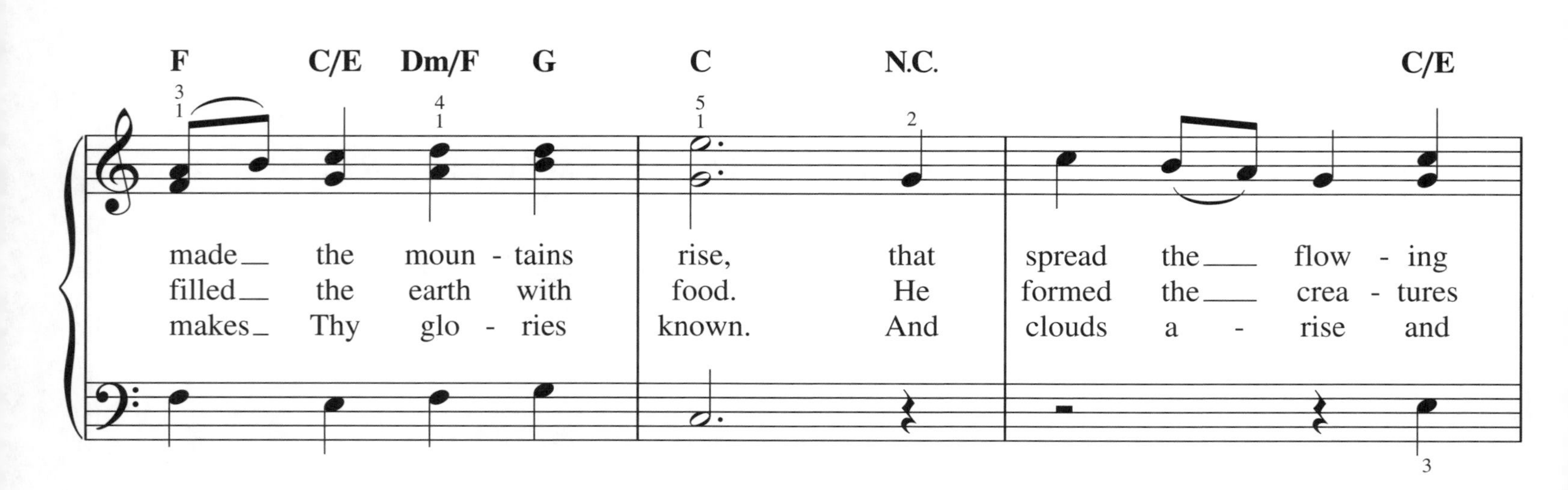

Am Dm7 G C F Am Gsus G C
seas a - broad and built the loft - y skies. I
with His word and then pro - nounced them good. Lord,
tem - pests blow by or - der from Thy throne. While
G/B C F G C G/B C F
sing the wis - dom that or - dained the sun to rule the
how Thy won - ders are dis - played wher - e’er I turn my
all that bor - rows life from Thee is ev - er in Thy
Gsus G N.C. C/E Am Dm7 G C
day. The moon shines full at His com - mand, and
eye, if I sur - vey the ground I tread, or
care, and ev - ’ry - where that man can be, Thou,
1., 2.
3.
F Am Gsus G Csus N.C. Csus C
all the stars o - bey. I
gaze up - on the sky! There’s
God, art pres - ent there.

I STAND AMAZED IN THE PRESENCE

(My Savior's Love)

Words and Music by
CHARLES H. GABRIEL

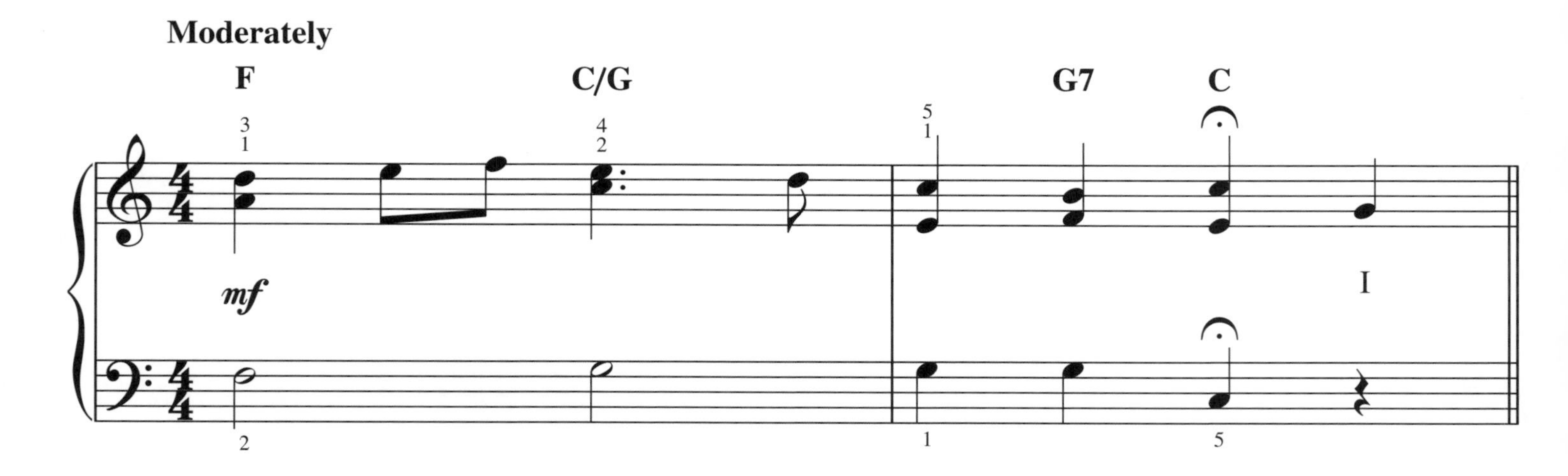

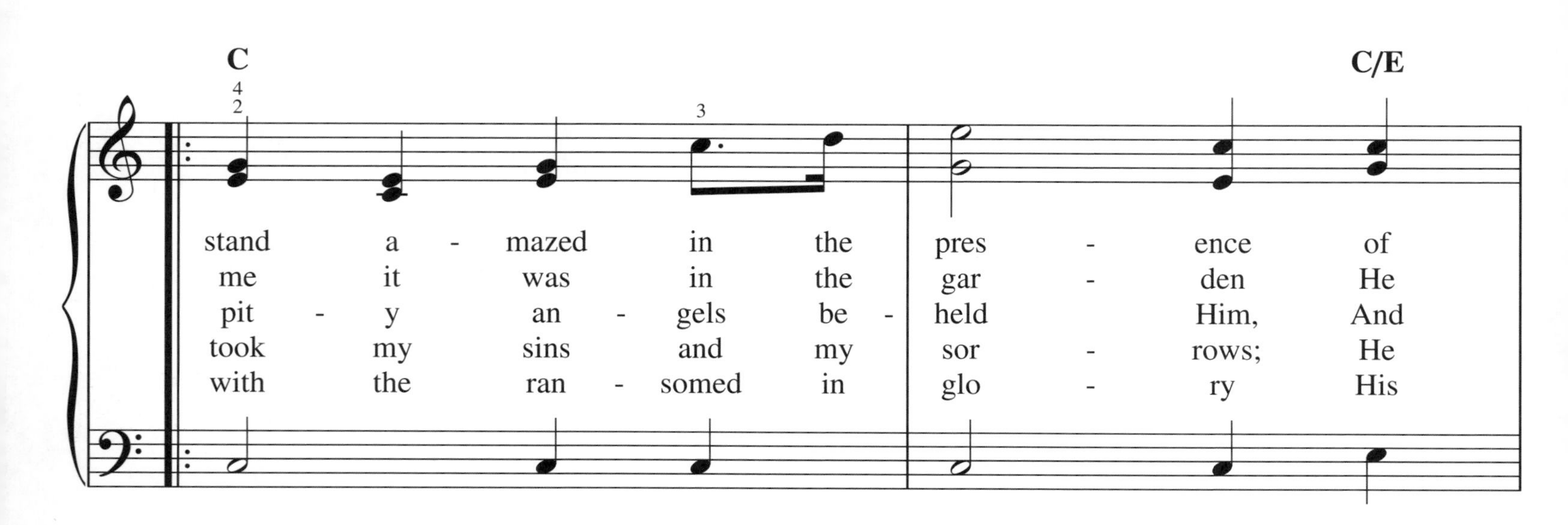

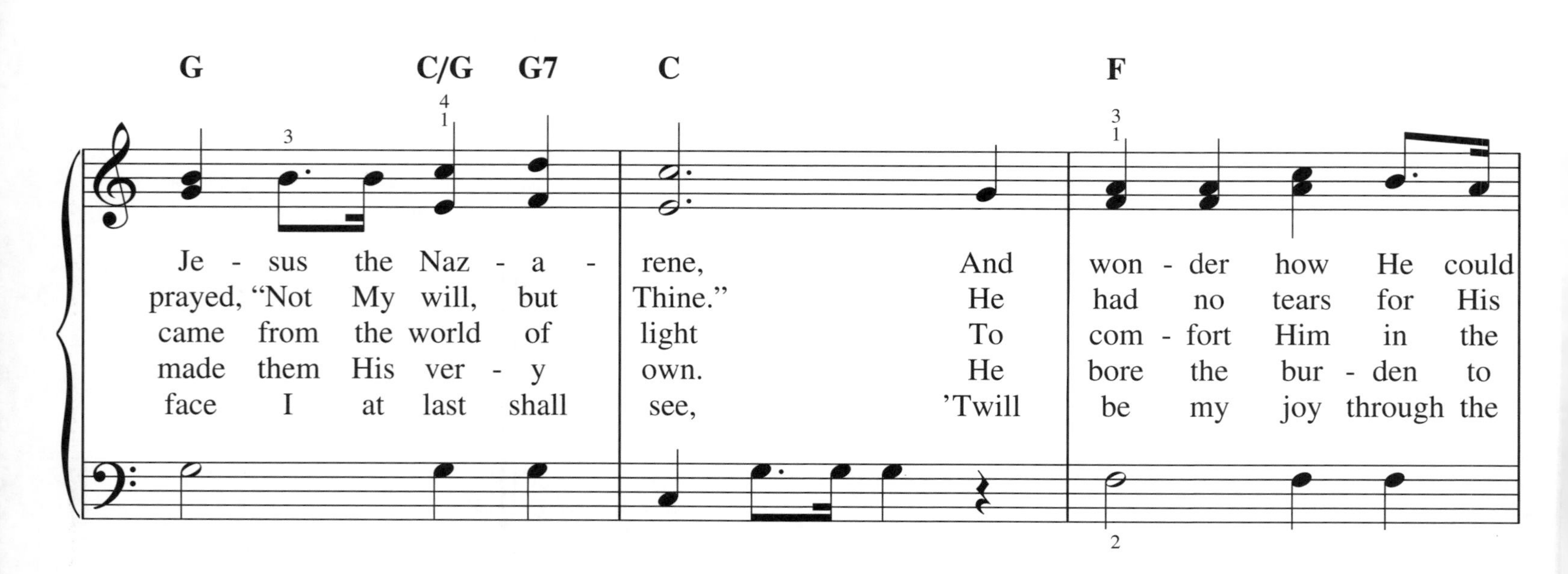

C C/E Dm/F C/G G7 C F/C C
love me, A sin - ner, con - demned, un - clean.
own griefs, But sweat - drops of blood for mine.
sor - rows He bore for my soul that night.
Cal - v'ry And suf - fered and died a - lone.
ag - es To sing of His love for me.
How mar - vel - ous! How won - der - ful! And my song shall
G
C/G G C
ev - er be: How mar - vel - ous! How won - der - ful
F C/G
1.– 4. G7 C
5. G7 C
is my Sav - ior's love for me! For In He When
love for me!

I SURRENDER ALL

Words by J.W. VAN DEVENTER
Music by W.S. WEEDEN

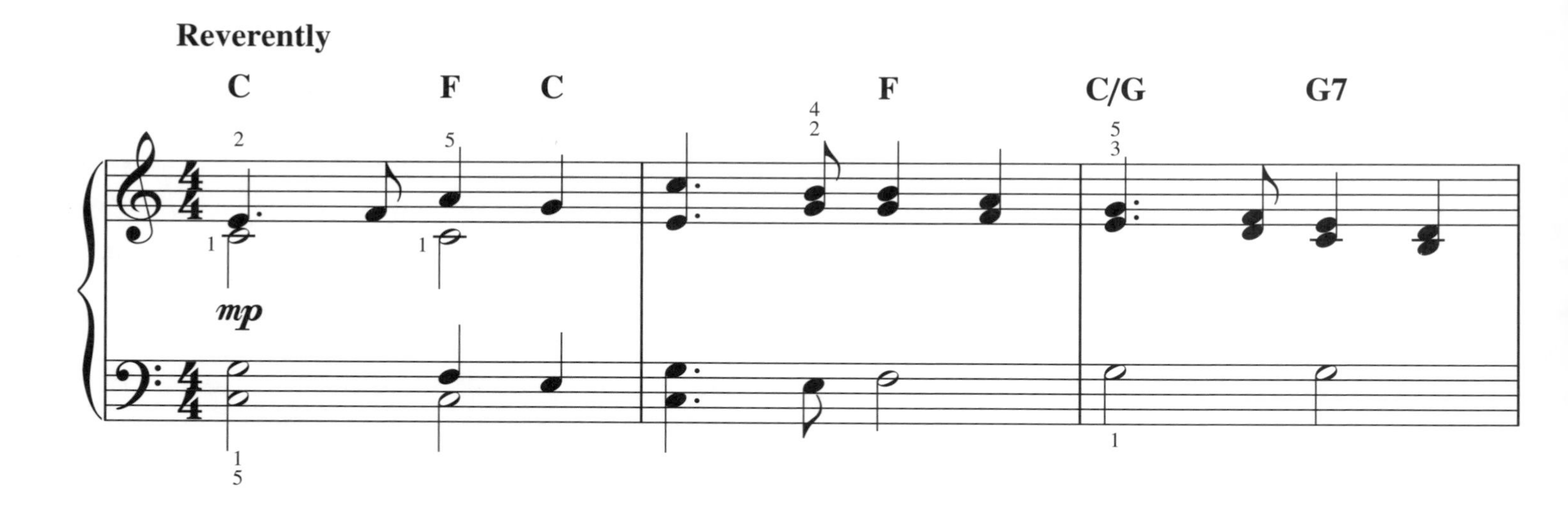

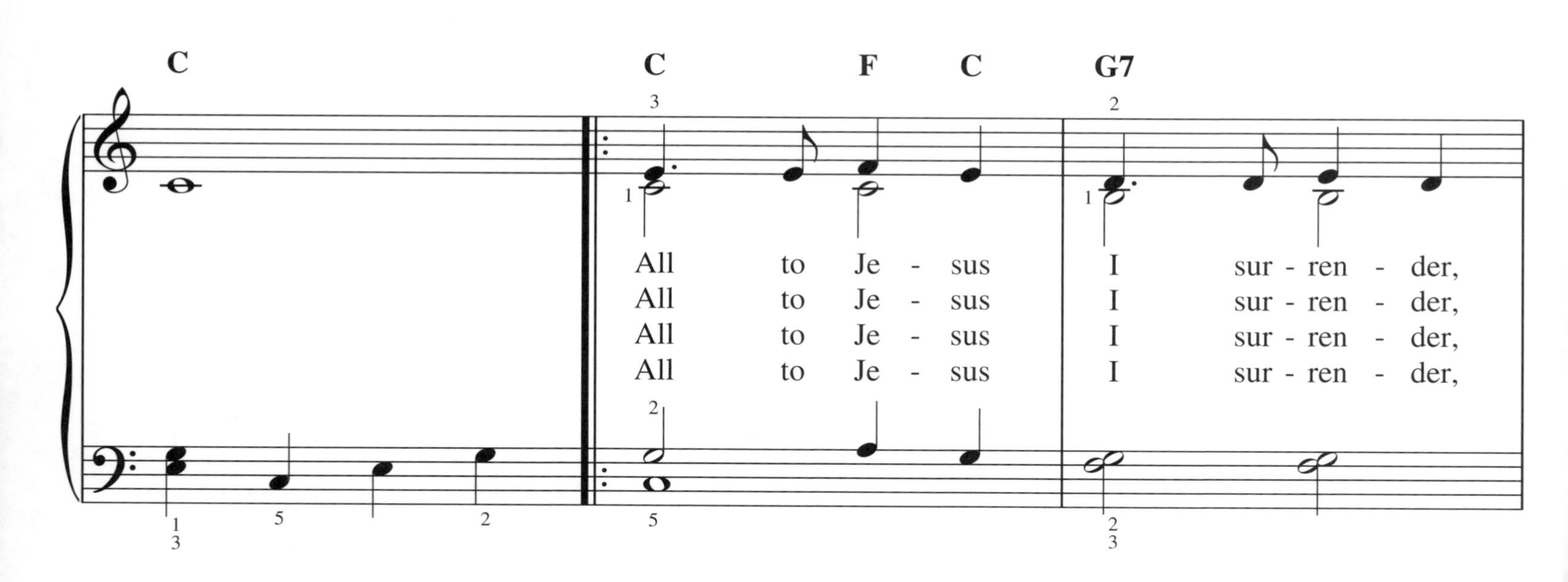

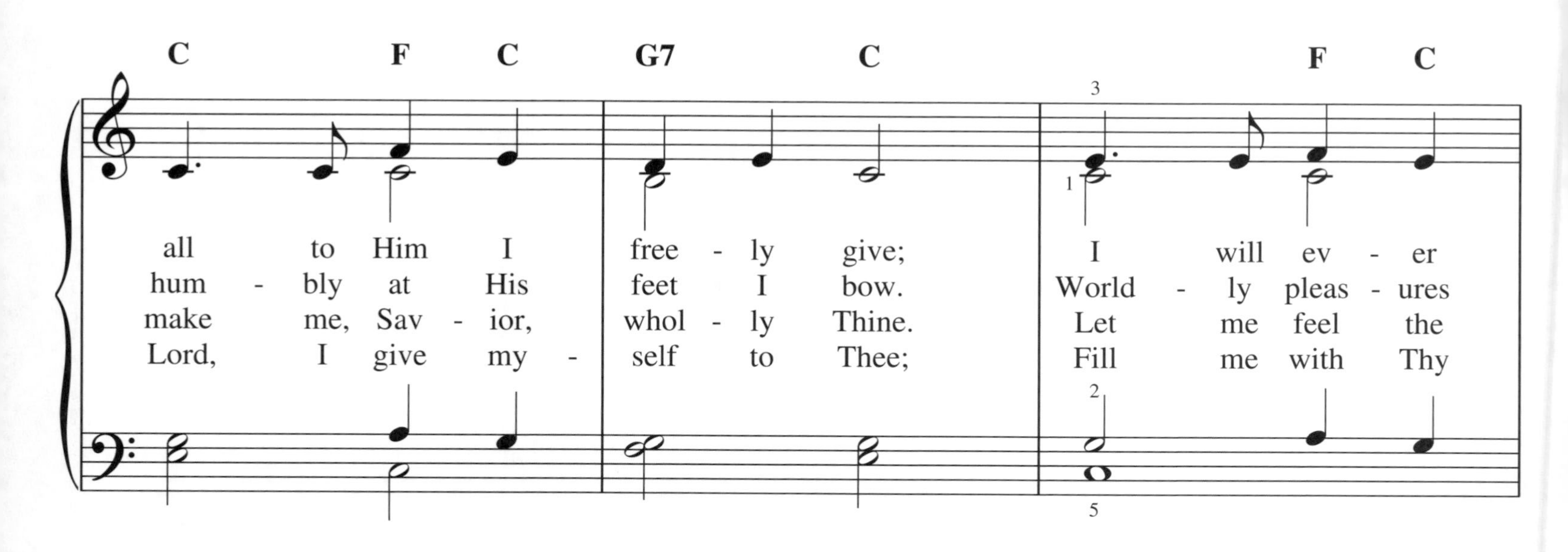

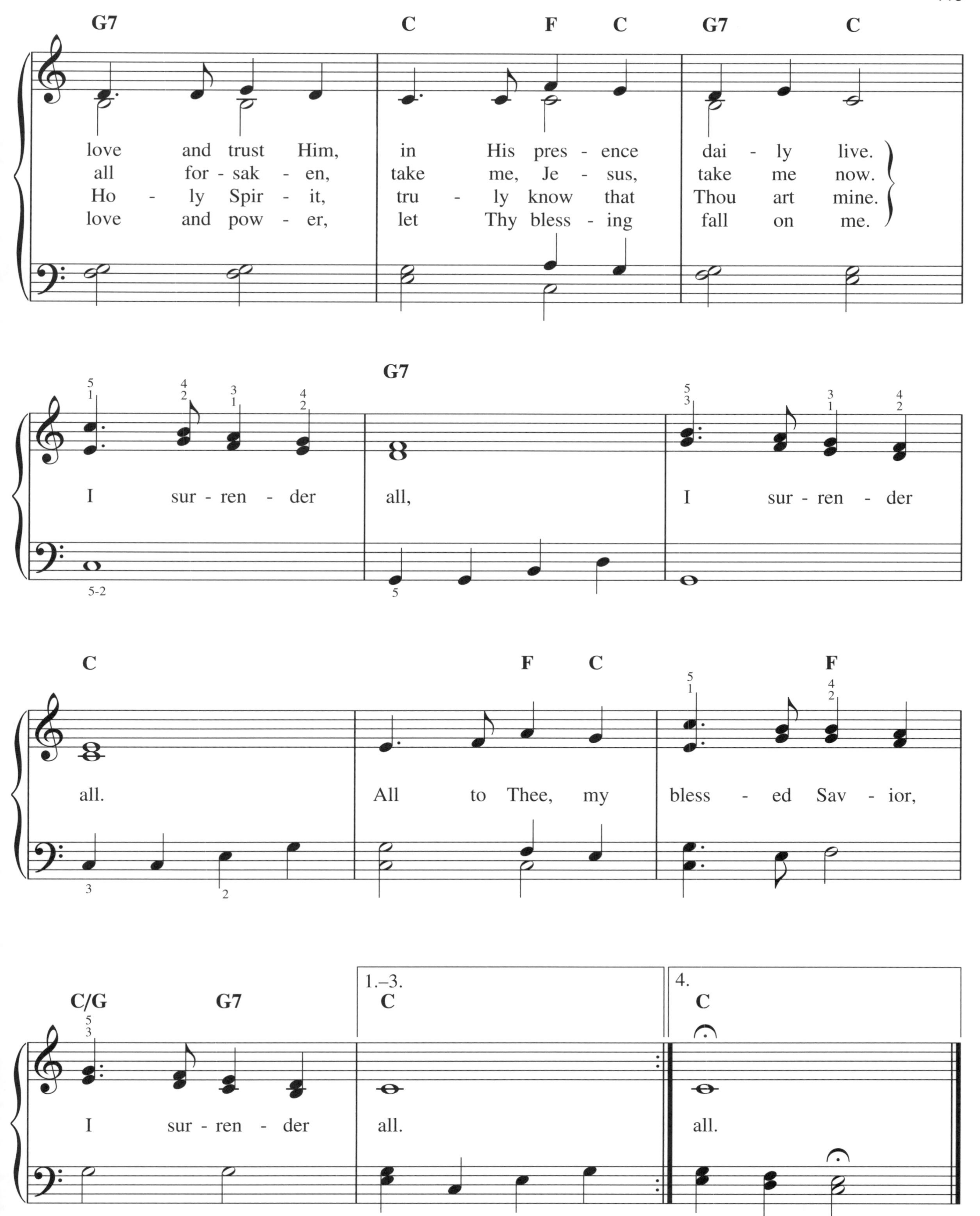
G7 C F C G7 C
love and trust Him, in His pres - ence dai - ly live.
all for - sak - en, take me, Je - sus, take me now.
Ho - ly Spir - it, tru - ly know that Thou art mine.
love and pow - er, let Thy bless - ing fall on me.
G7
I sur - ren - der all, I sur - ren - der
C F C F
all. All to Thee, my bless - ed Sav - ior,
C/G G7 1.–3. C 4. C
I sur - ren - der all. all.

I'VE FOUND A FRIEND, O SUCH A FRIEND!

Words by JAMES G. SMALL
Music by GEORGE C. STEBBINS

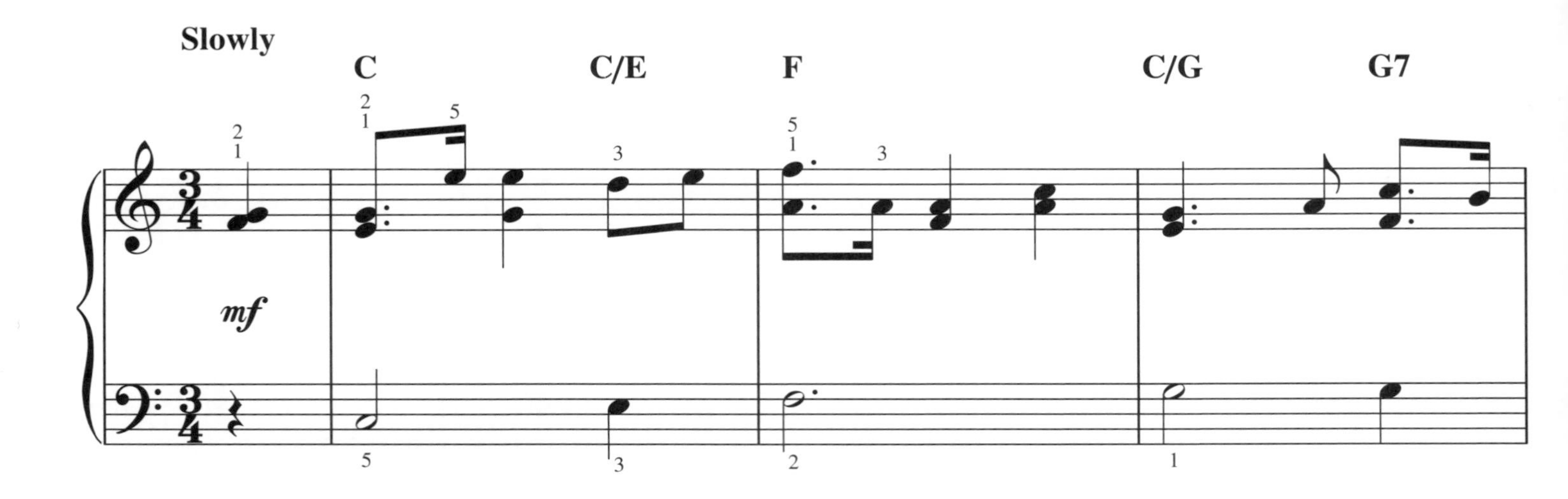

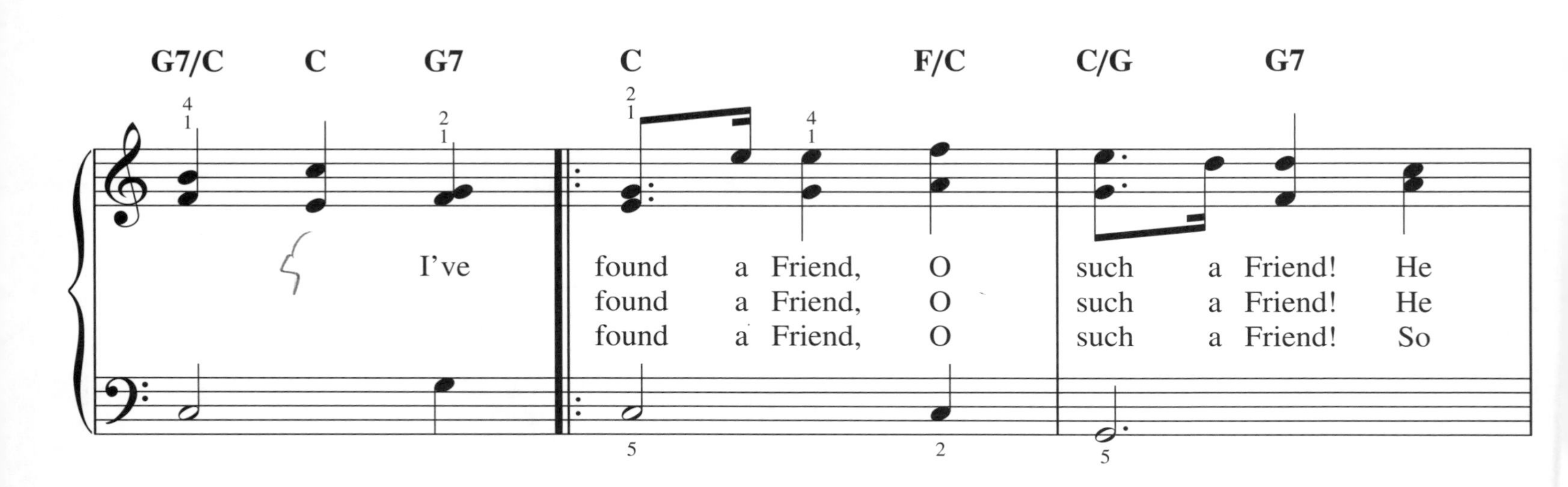

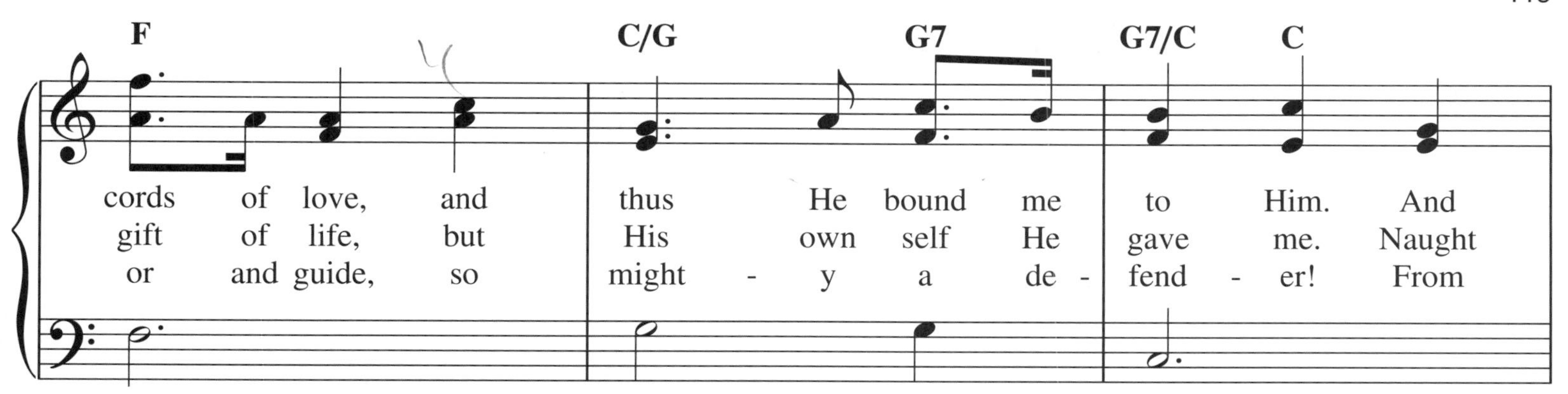
F C/G G7 G7/C C
cords of love, and thus He bound me to Him. And
gift of life, but His own self He gave me. Naught
or and guide, so might - y a de - fend - er! From

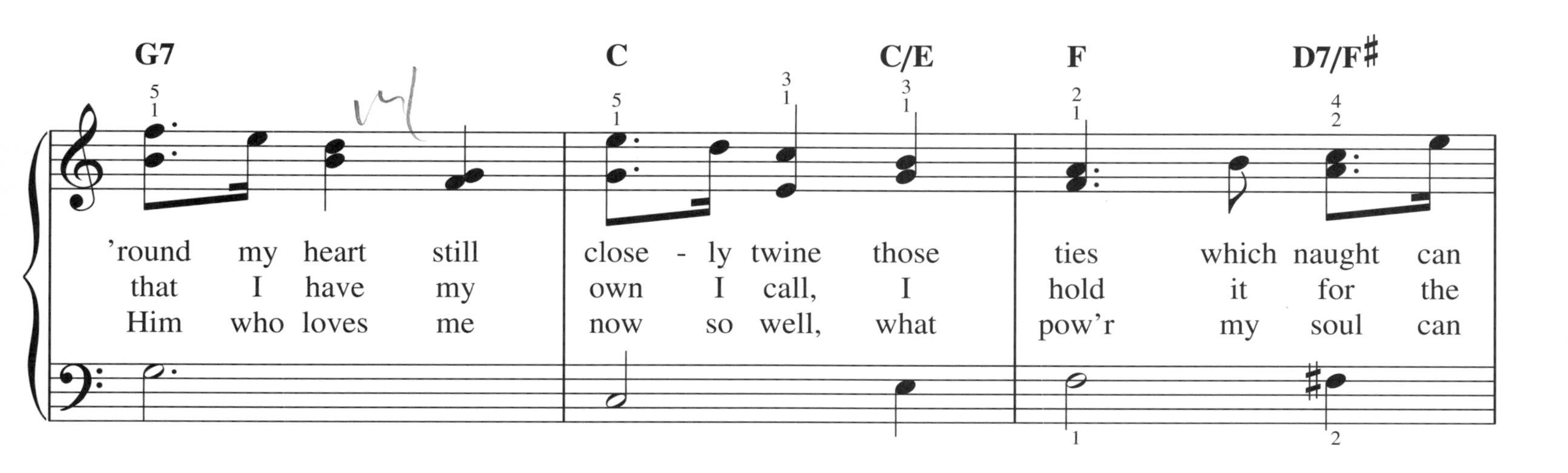
G7 C C/E F D7/F♯
'round my heart still close - ly twine those ties which naught can
that I have my own I call, I hold it for the
Him who loves me now so well, what pow'r my soul can

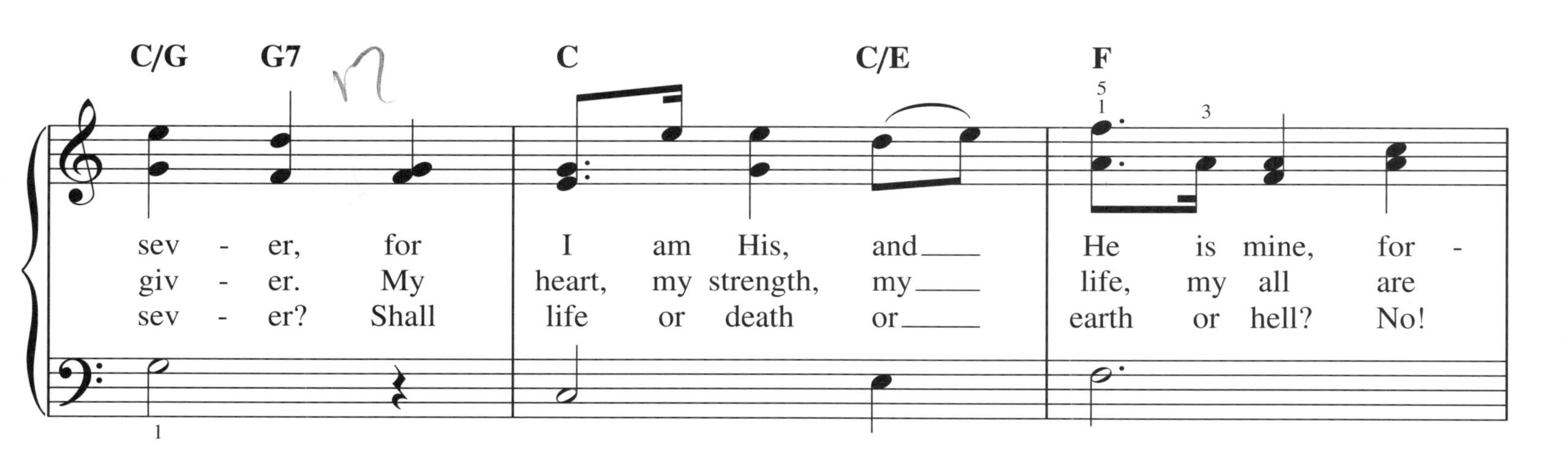
C/G G7 C C/E F
sev - er, for I am His, and He is mine, for -
giv - er. My heart, my strength, my life, my all are
sev - er? Shall life or death or earth or hell? No!

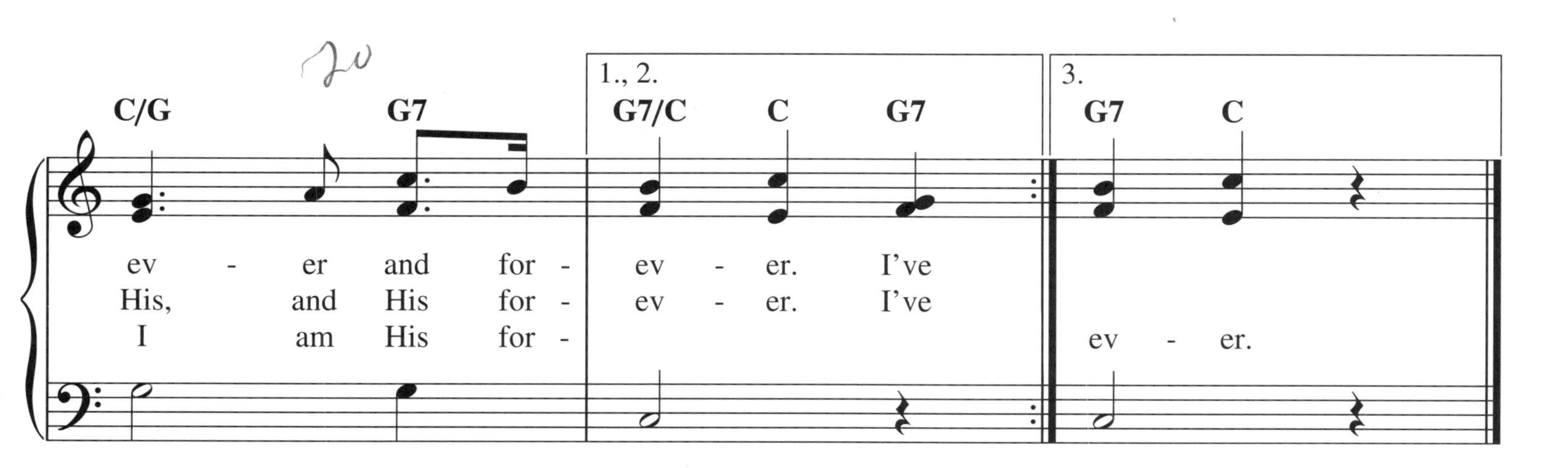
1., 2.
3.
C/G G7 G7/C C G7 G7 C
ev - er and for - ev - er. I've
His, and His for - ev - er. I've
I am His for - ev - er.

IN THE CROSS OF CHRIST I GLORY

Words by JOHN BOWRING
Music by ITHAMAR CONKEY

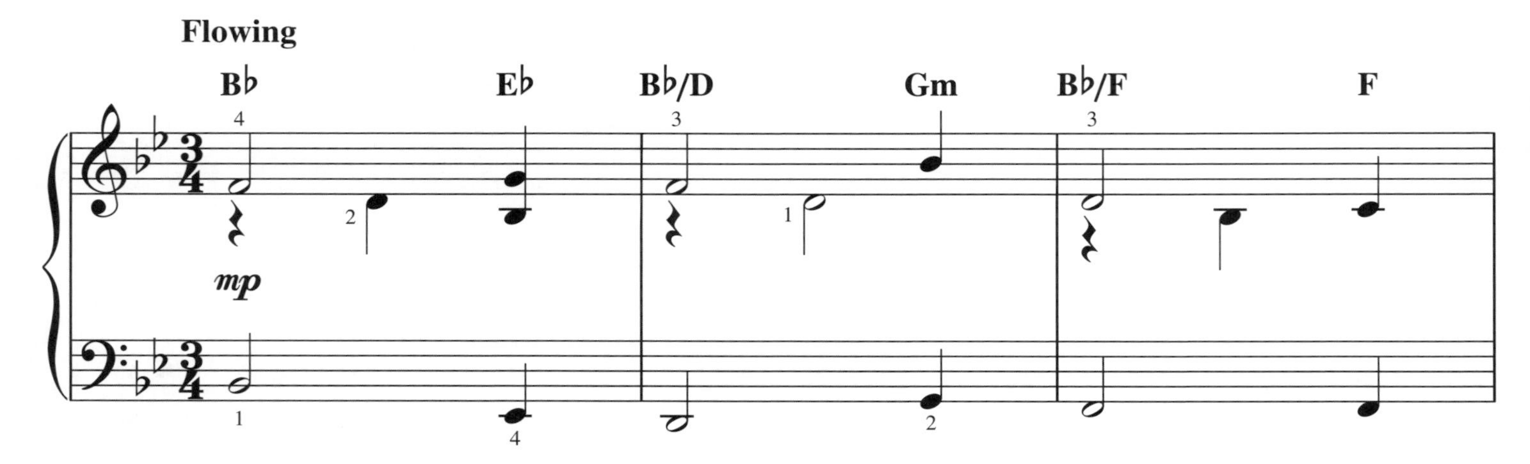

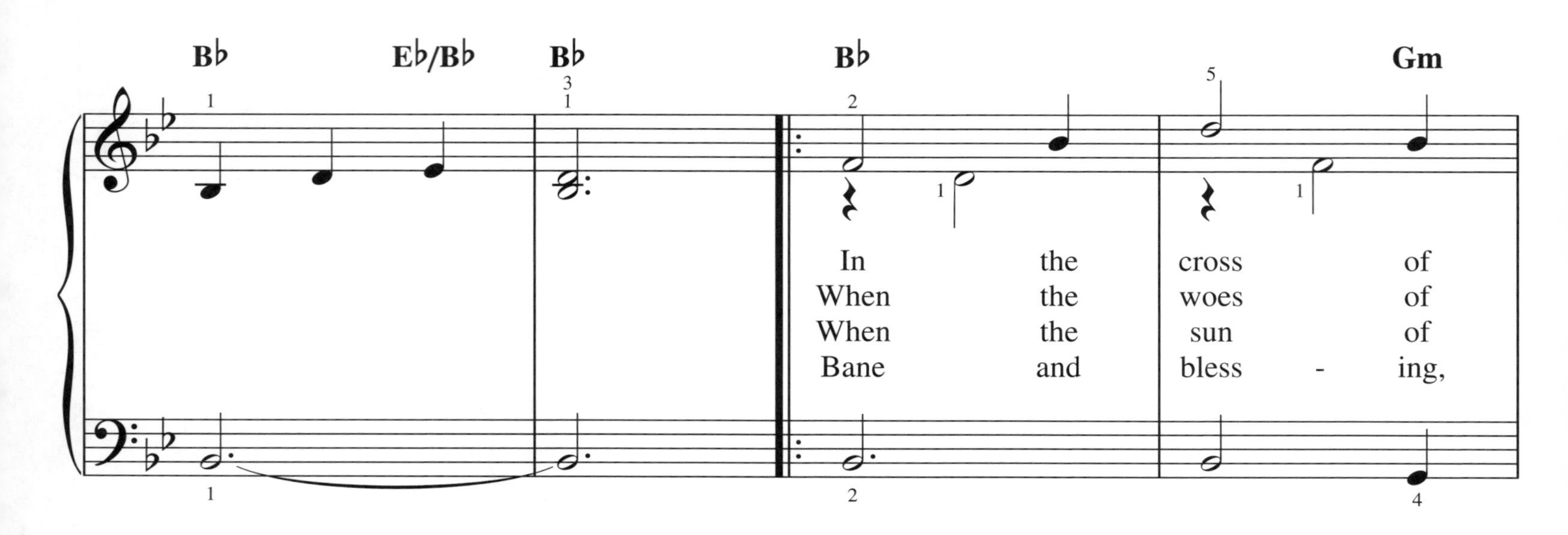

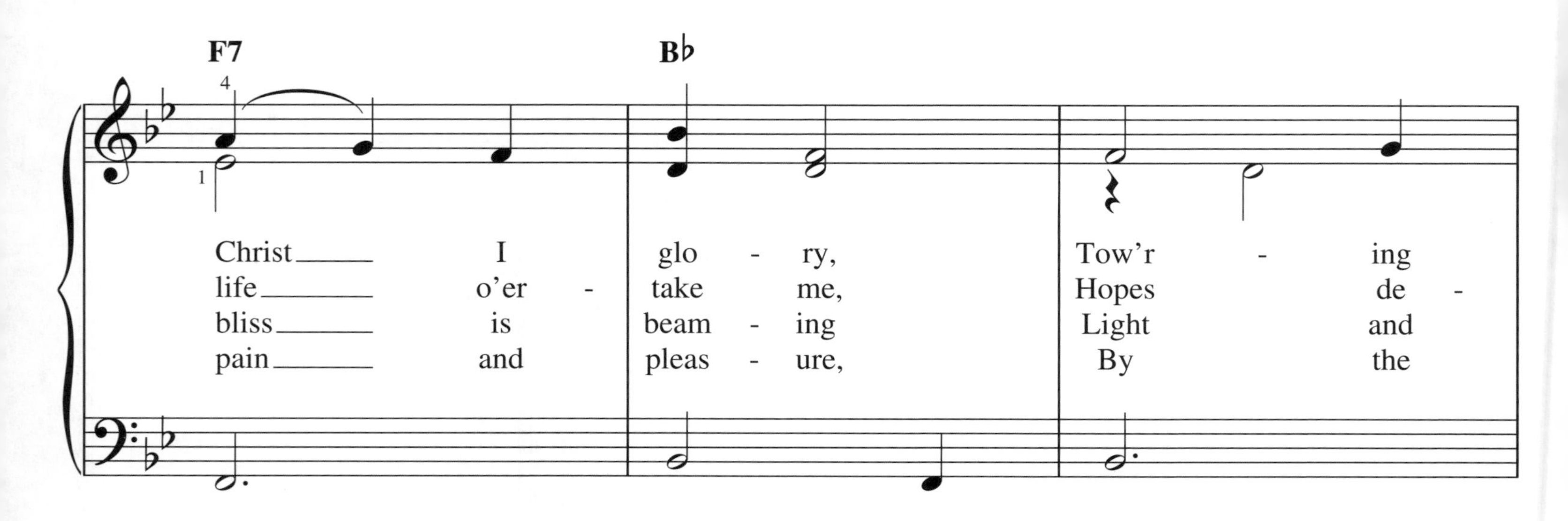

Gm Gm/C C7 F F/A
o'er the wrecks of time.
ceive and fears an - noy,
love up - on my way.
cross are sanc - ti - fied,
B♭ Gm F7
All the light of sa - cred
Nev - er shall the cross for -
From the cross the ra - diance
Peace is there that knows no
B♭ B♭/D E♭ B♭/D Gm
sto - ry Gath - ers round its
sake me; Lo, it glows with
stream - ing Adds more lus - ter
meas - ure, Joys that through all
1.–3. 4.
B♭/F F B♭ E♭/B♭ B♭ B♭ E♭/B♭ B♭
head sub - lime.
peace and joy.
to the day.
time a - bide.

IN THE GARDEN

Words and Music by
C. AUSTIN MILES

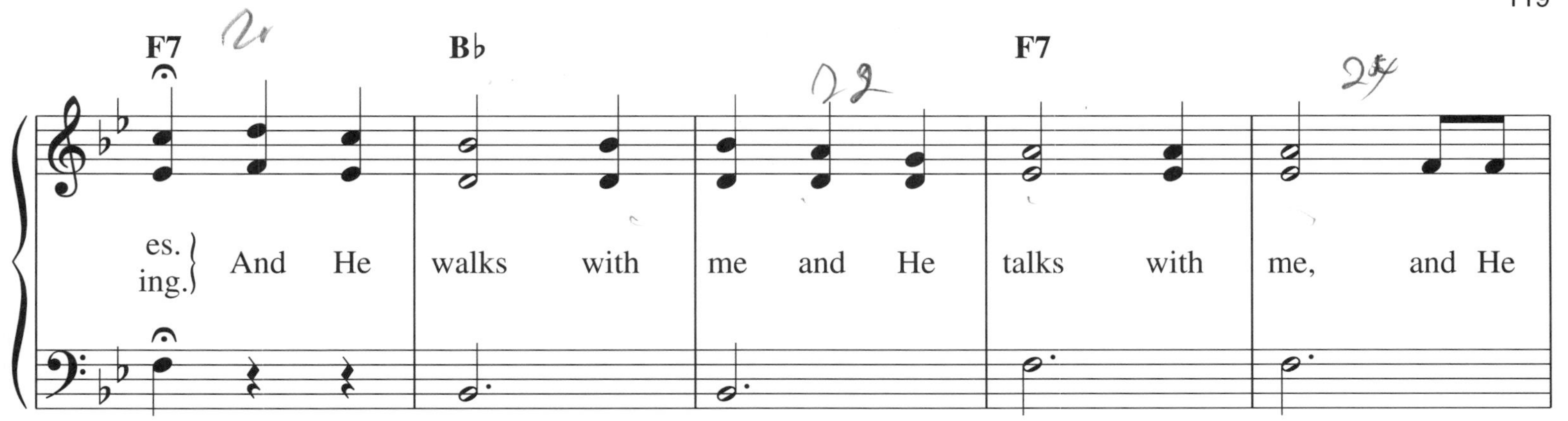
F7
B♭
F7
es. And He walks with me and He talks with me, and He
ing.

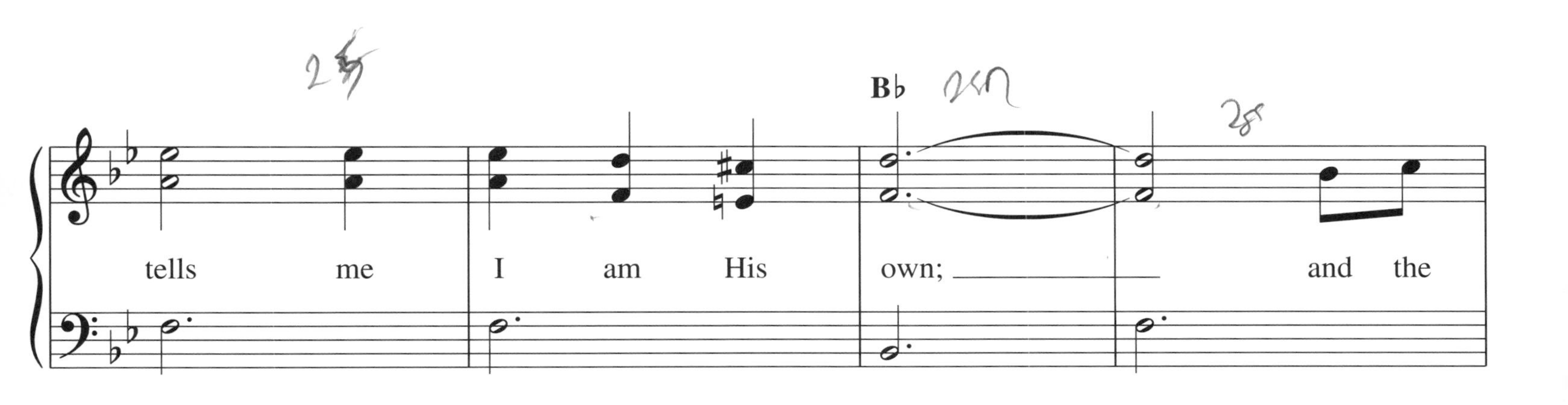
B♭
tells me I am His own; and the

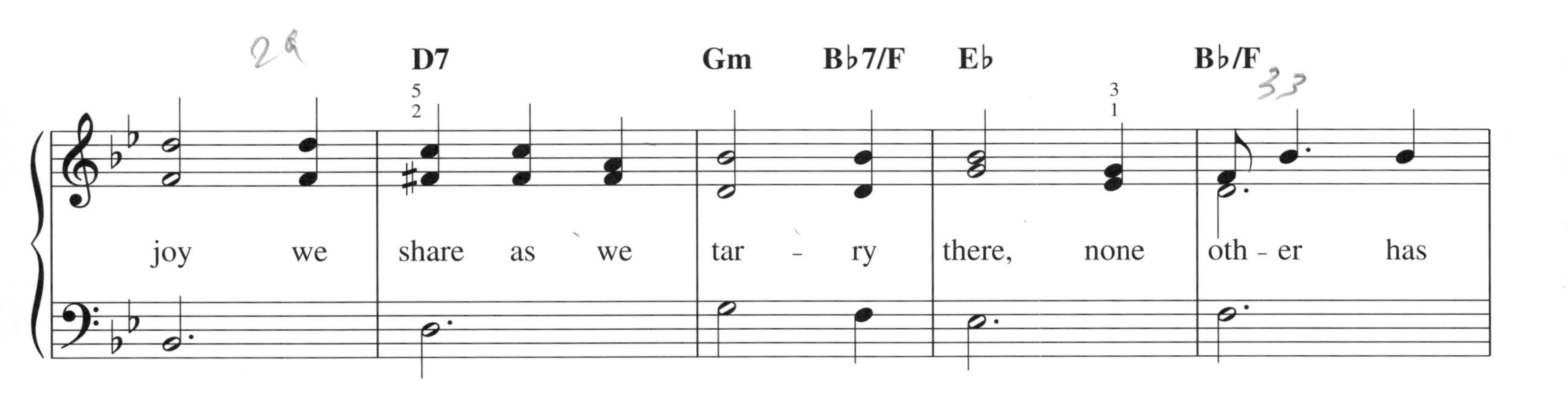
D7
Gm
B♭7/F
E♭
B♭/F
joy we share as we tar - ry there, none oth - er has

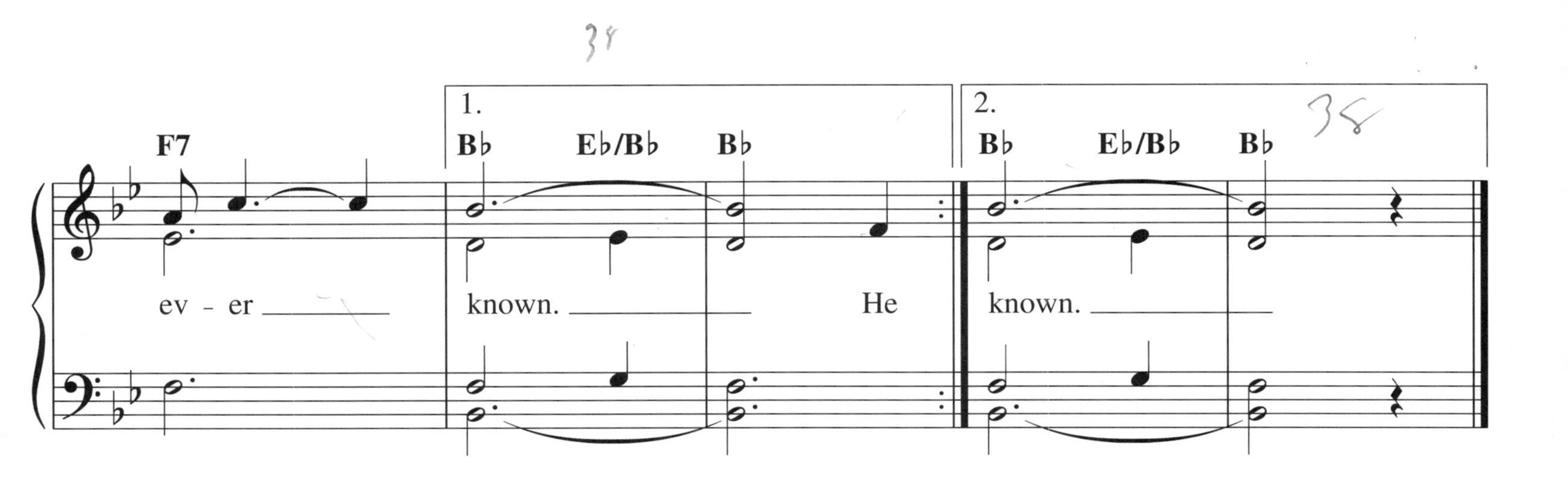
F7
1.
B♭
E♭/B♭
B♭
2.
B♭
E♭/B♭
B♭
ev - er known. He known.

IN THE HOUR OF TRIAL

Words by JAMES MONTGOMERY
Altered by FRANCES A. HUTTON
Music by SPENCER LANE

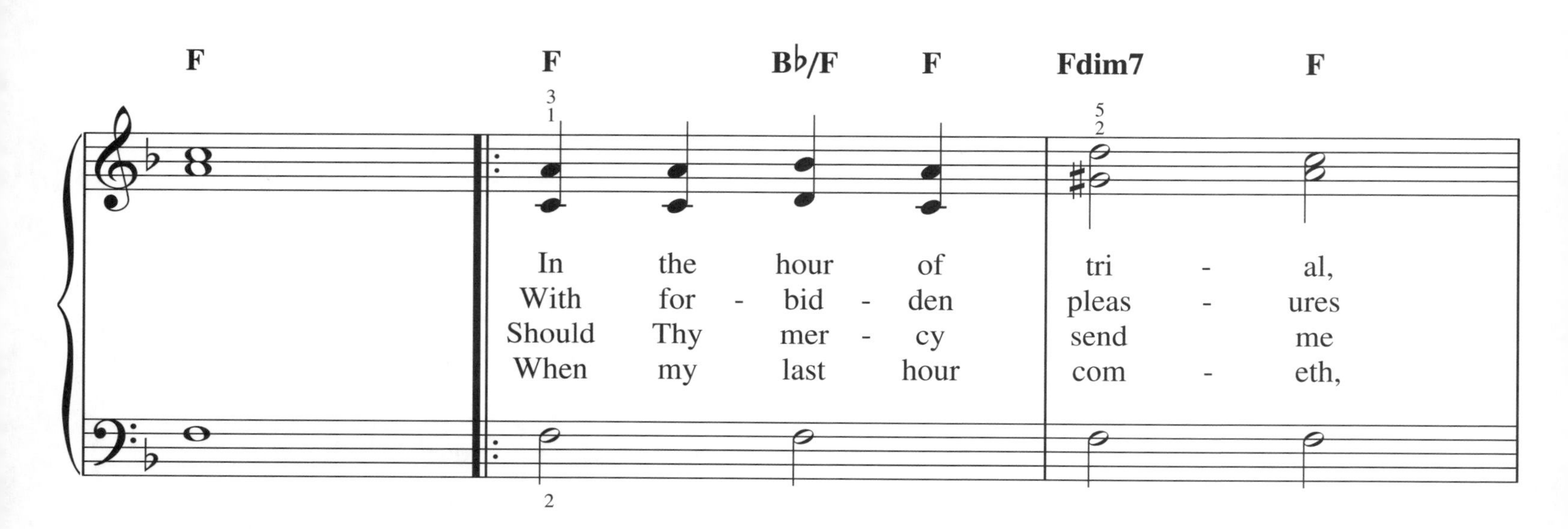

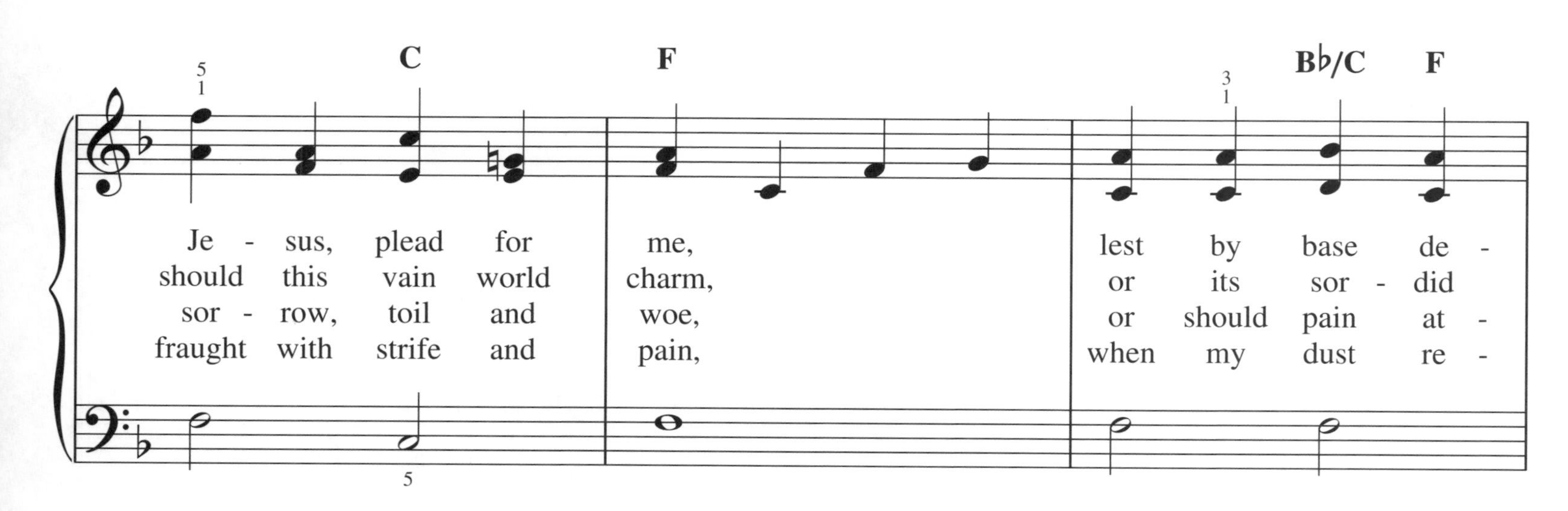

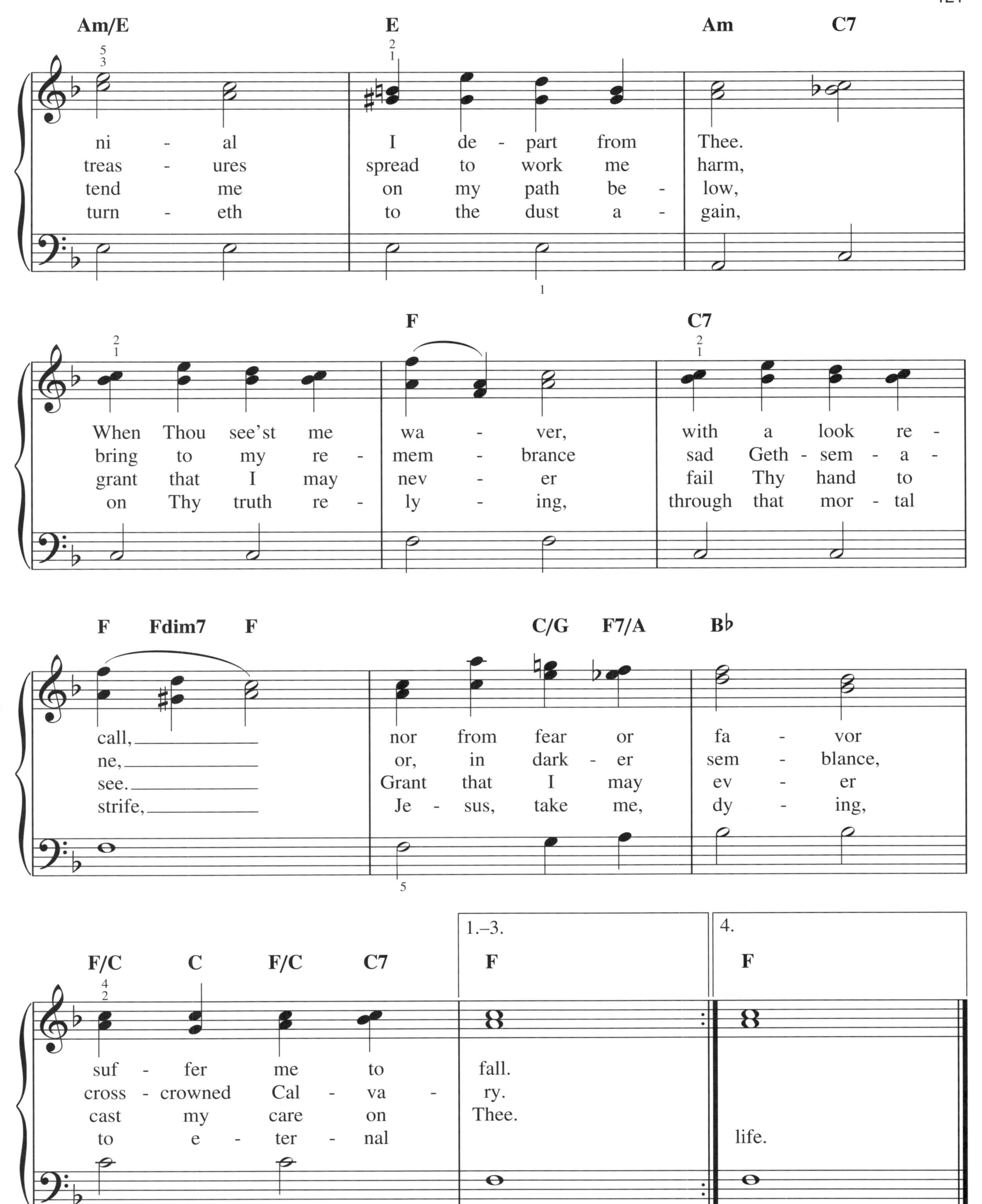
Am/E
E
Am
C7
ni - al
I de - part from
Thee.
treas - ures
spread to work me
harm,
tend me
on my path be -
low,
turn - eth
to the dust a -
gain,
F
C7
When Thou see'st me
wa - ver,
with a look re -
bring to my re -
mem - brance
sad Geth - sem - a -
grant that I may
nev - er
fail Thy hand to
on Thy truth re -
ly - ing,
through that mor - tal
F
Fdim7
F
C/G
F7/A
B♭
call,
nor from fear or
fa - vor
ne,
or, in dark - er
sem - blance,
see.
Grant that I may
ev - er
strife,
Je - sus, take me,
dy - ing,
1.–3.
4.
F/C
C
F/C
C7
F
F
suf - fer me to
fall.
cross - crowned Cal - va -
ry.
cast my care on
Thee.
to e - ter - nal
life.

IT IS WELL WITH MY SOUL

Words by HORATIO G. SPAFFORD
Music by PHILIP P. BLISS

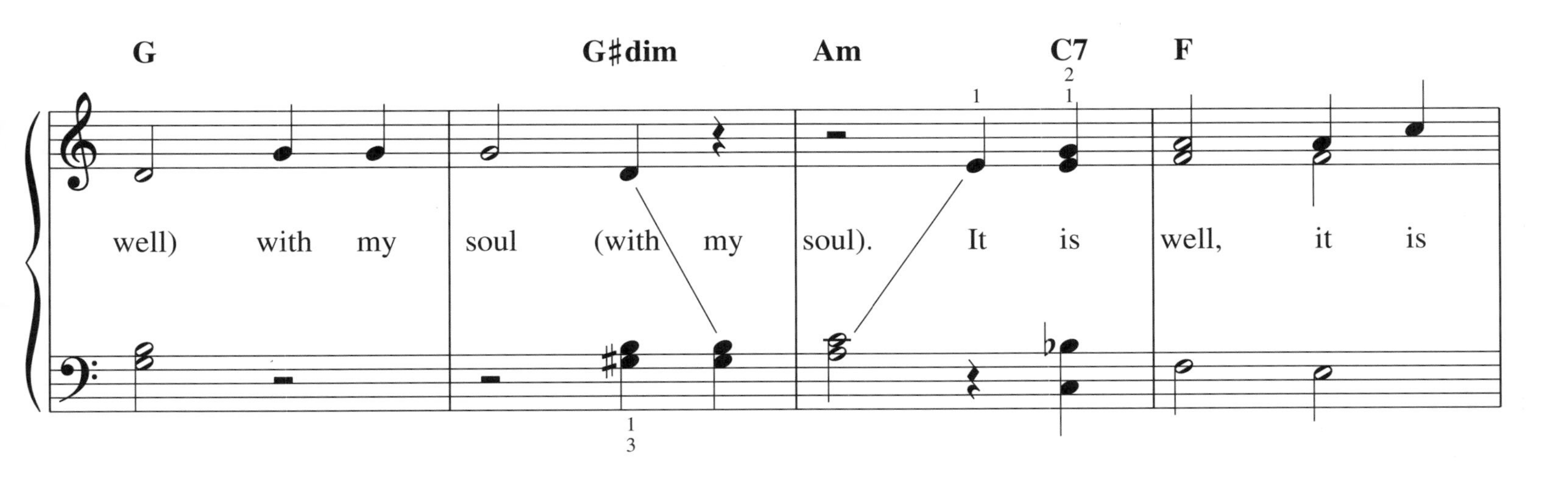

Additional Verses

3. My sin, oh, the bliss of this glorious thought:
   My sin, not in part, but the whole,
   Is nailed to the cross, and I bear it no more;
   Praise the Lord, praise the Lord, O my soul!
   Chorus

4. And, Lord, haste the day when the faith shall be sight,
   The clouds be rolled back as a scroll,
   The trumpet shall sound, and the Lord shall descend;
   Even so, it is well with my soul.
   Chorus

JESUS CALLS US O'ER THE TUMULT

Words by CECIL FRANCES ALEXANDER
Music by WILLIAM H. JUDE

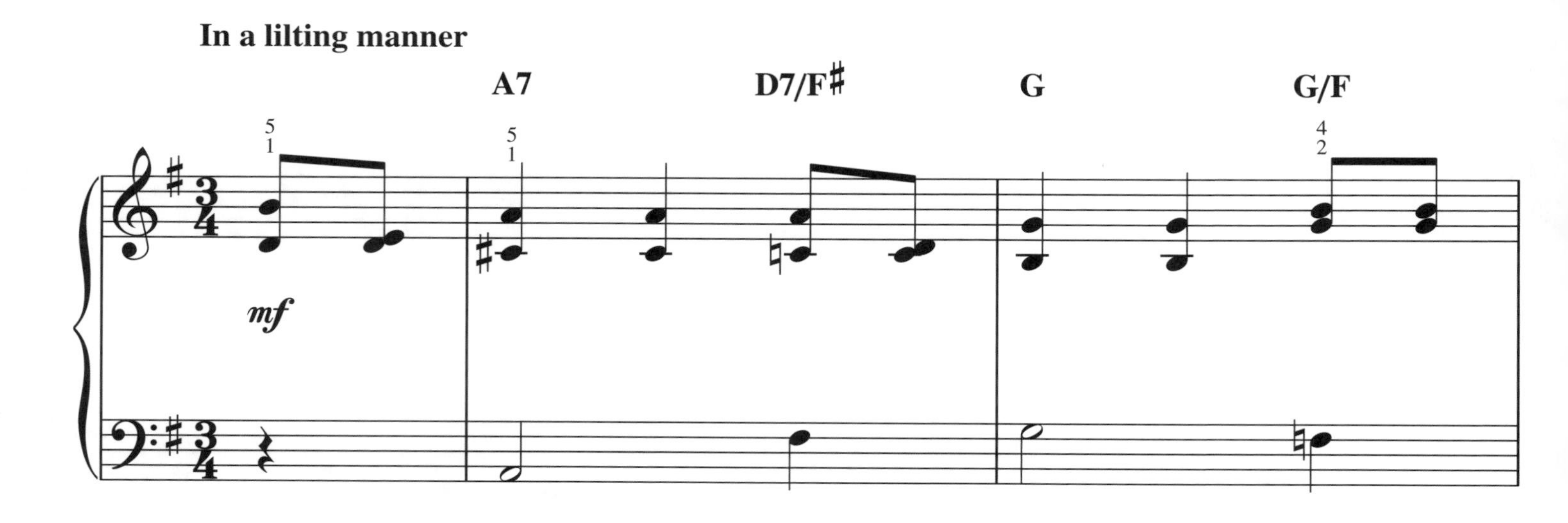

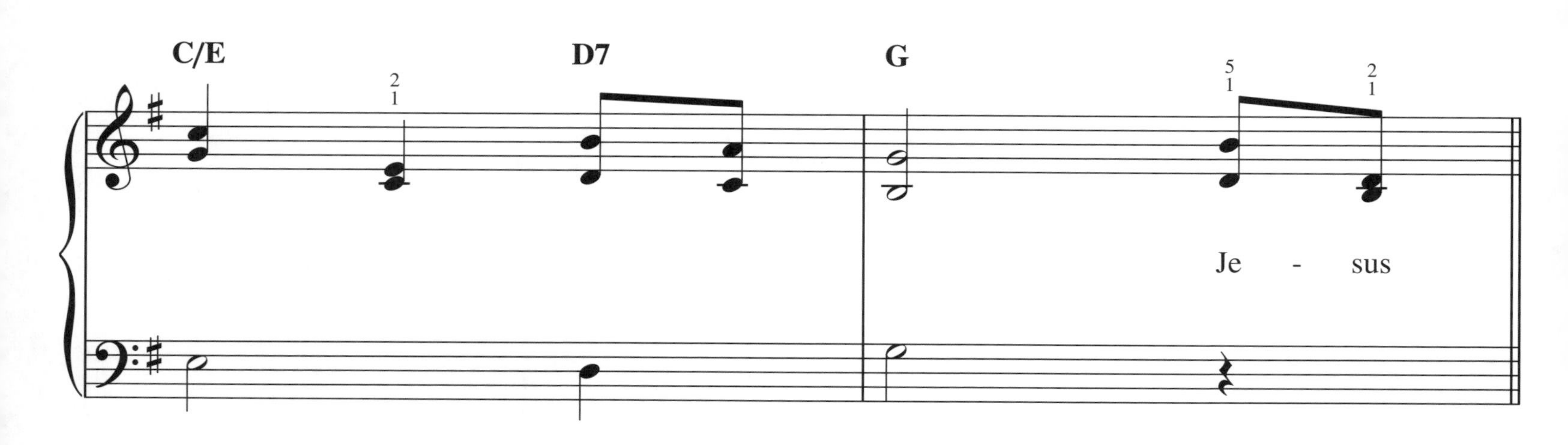

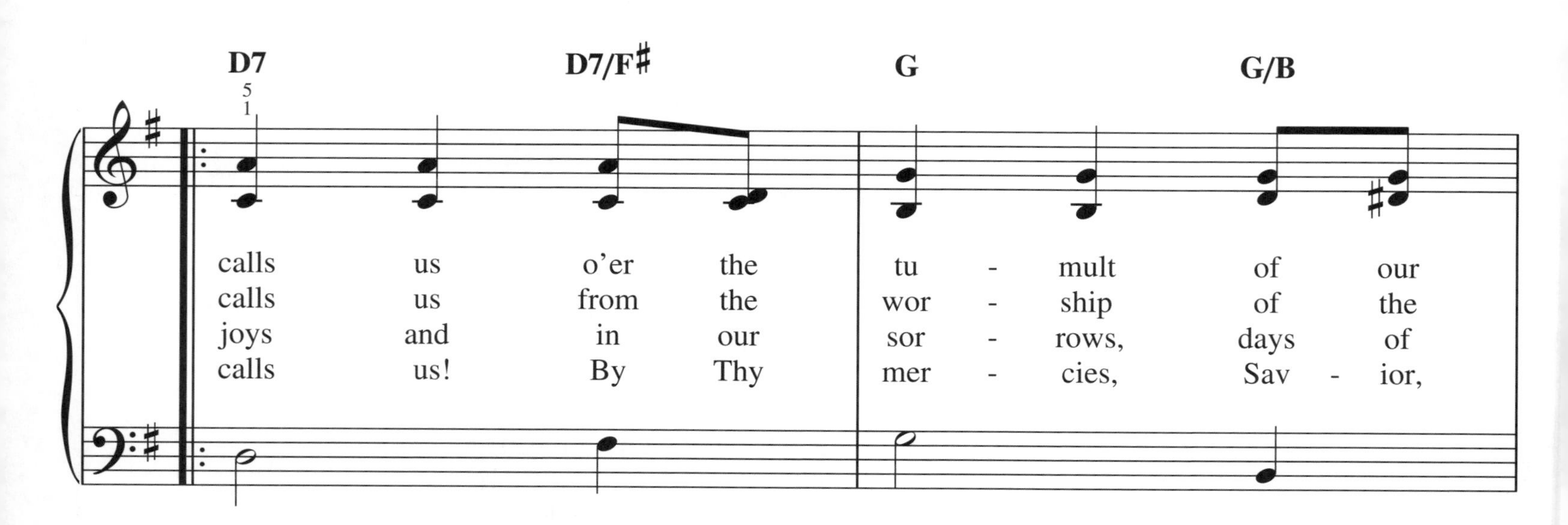

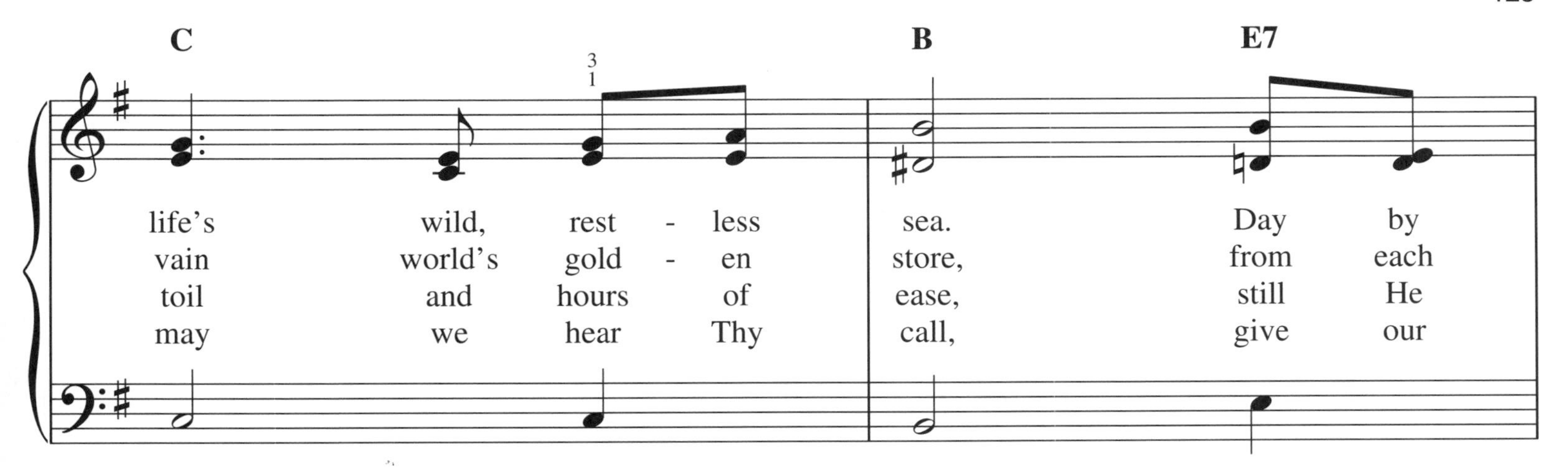
C
3
1
B
E7
life's wild, rest - less sea. Day by
vain world's gold - en store, from each
toil and hours of ease, still He
may we hear Thy call, give our

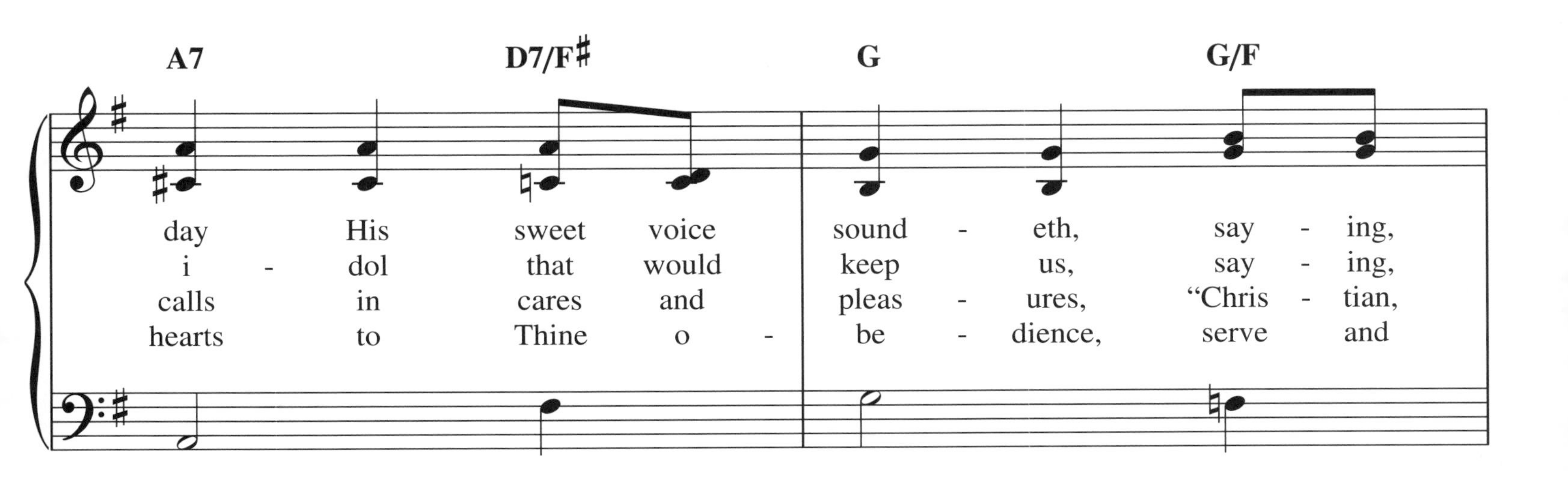
A7
D7/F♯
G
G/F
day His sweet voice sound - eth, say - ing,
i - dol that would keep us, say - ing,
calls in cares and pleas - ures, "Chris - tian,
hearts to Thine o - be - dience, serve and

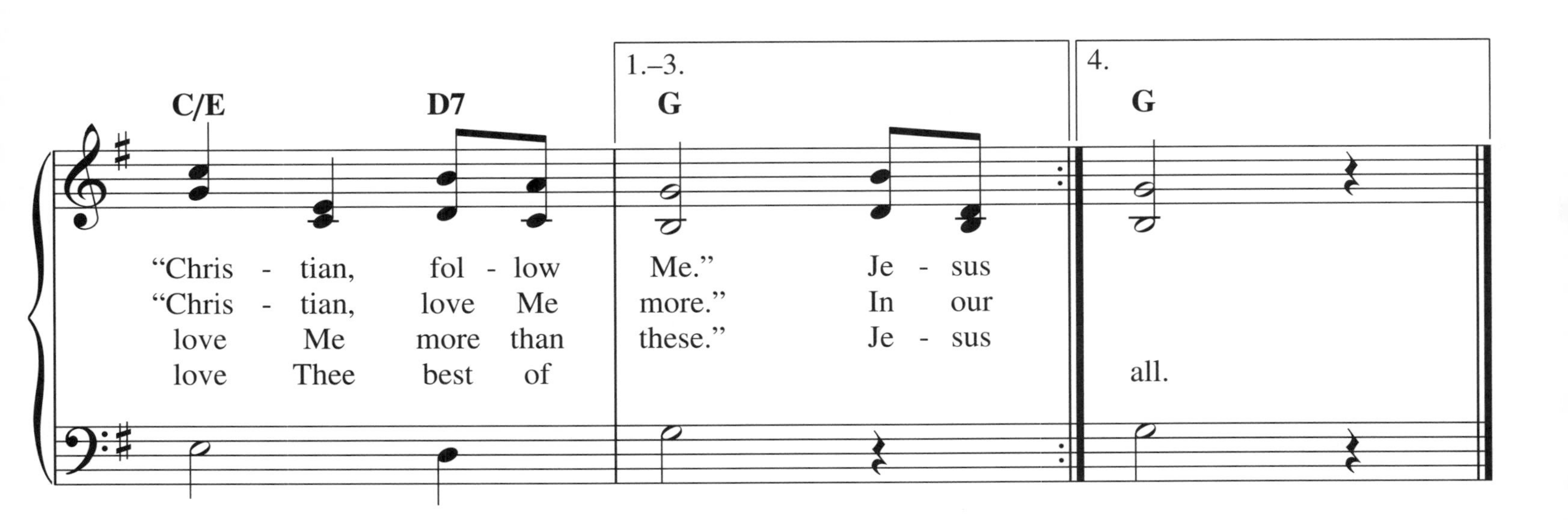
C/E
D7
1.–3.
G
4.
G
"Chris - tian, fol - low Me." Je - sus
"Chris - tian, love Me more." In our
love Me more than these." Je - sus
love Thee best of all.

JESUS, KEEP ME NEAR THE CROSS

Words by FANNY J. CROSBY
Music by WILLIAM H. DOANE

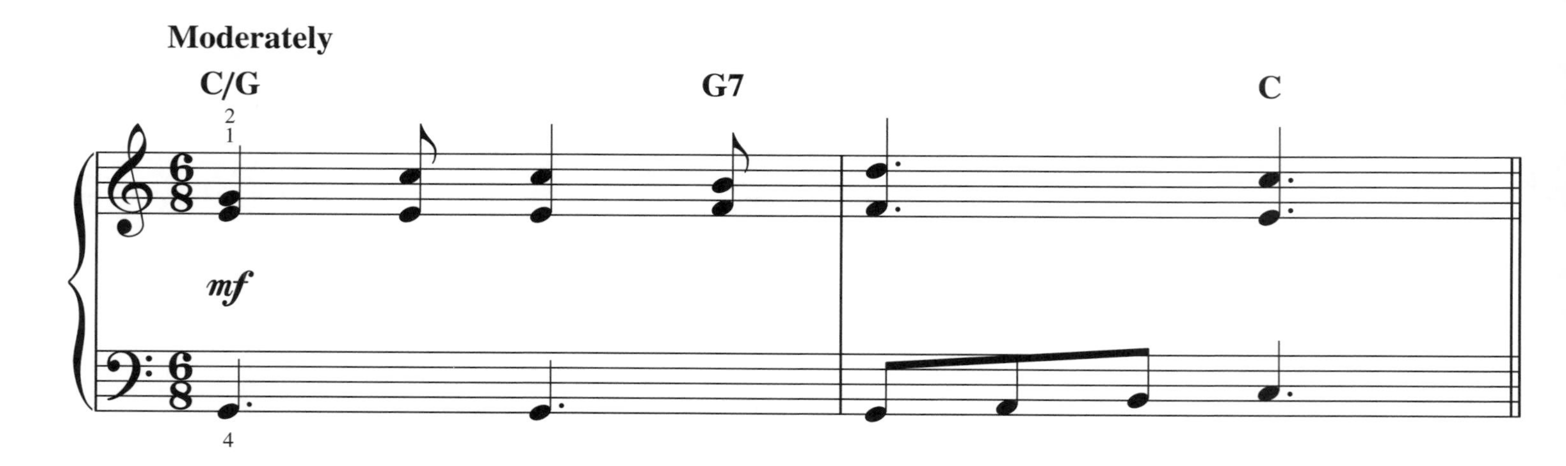

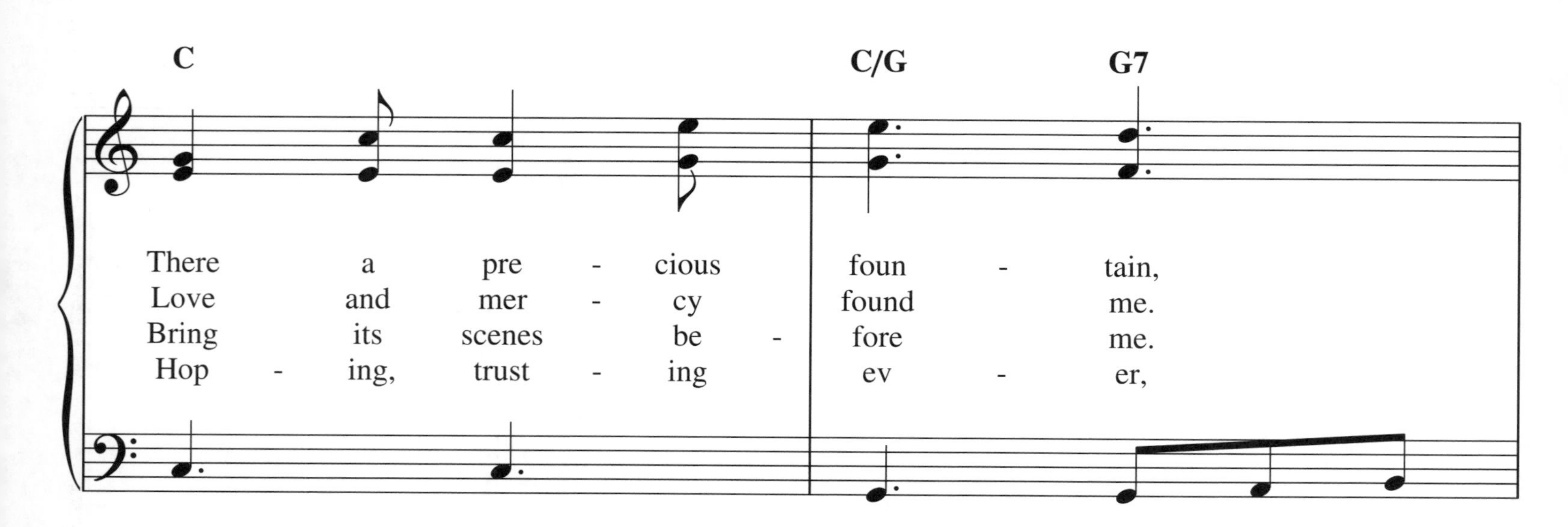

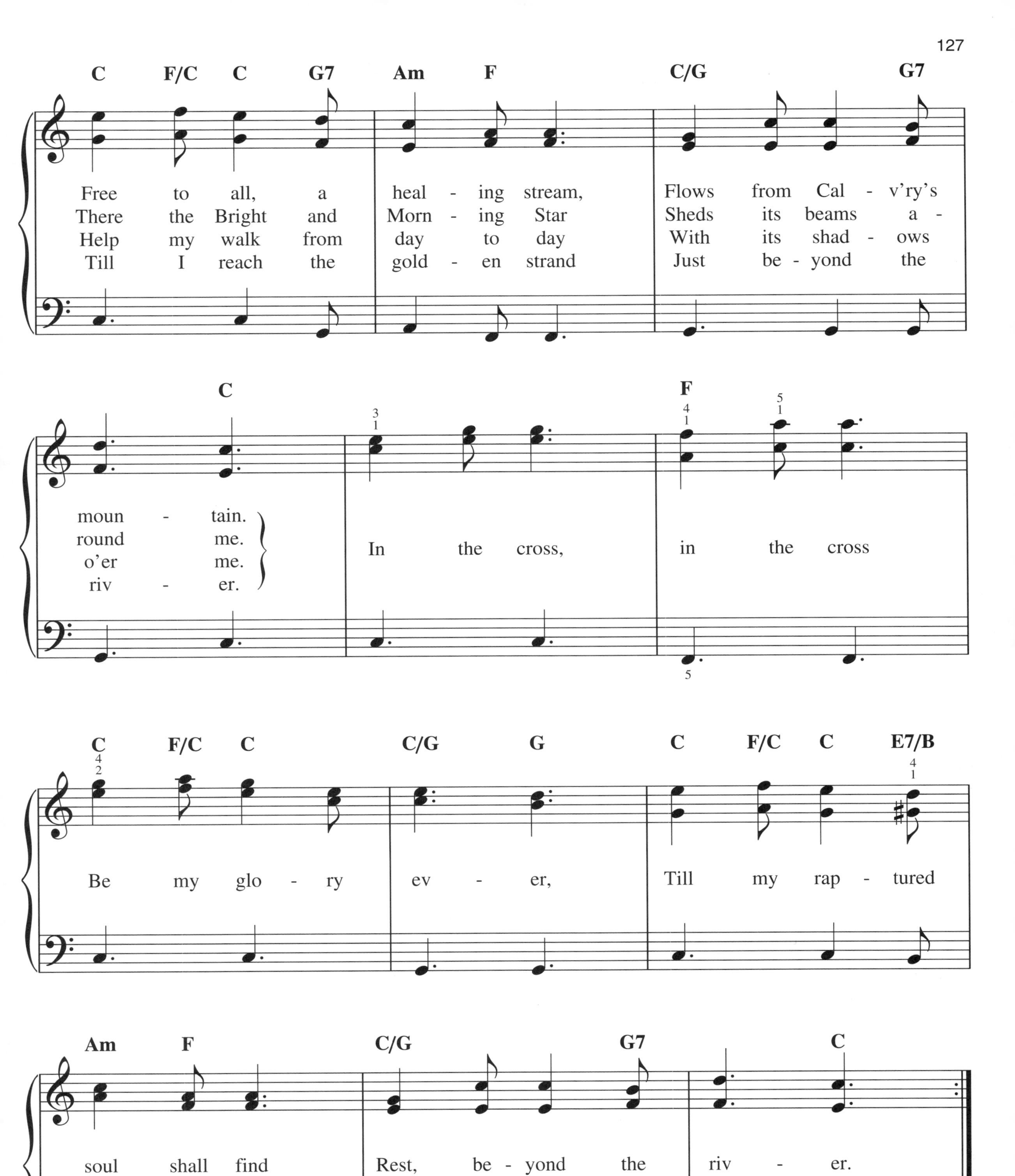
C F/C C G7 Am F C/G G7
Free to all, a heal - ing stream, Flows from Cal - v'ry's
There the Bright and Morn - ing Star Sheds its beams a -
Help my walk from day to day With its shad - ows
Till I reach the gold - en strand Just be - yond the
C F
moun - tain.
round me.
o'er me.
riv - er.
In the cross, in the cross
C F/C C C/G G C F/C C E7/B
Be my glo - ry ev - er, Till my rap - tured
Am F C/G G7 C
soul shall find Rest, be - yond the riv - er.

JESUS, LOVER OF MY SOUL

Words by CHARLES WESLEY
Music by SIMEON B. MARSH

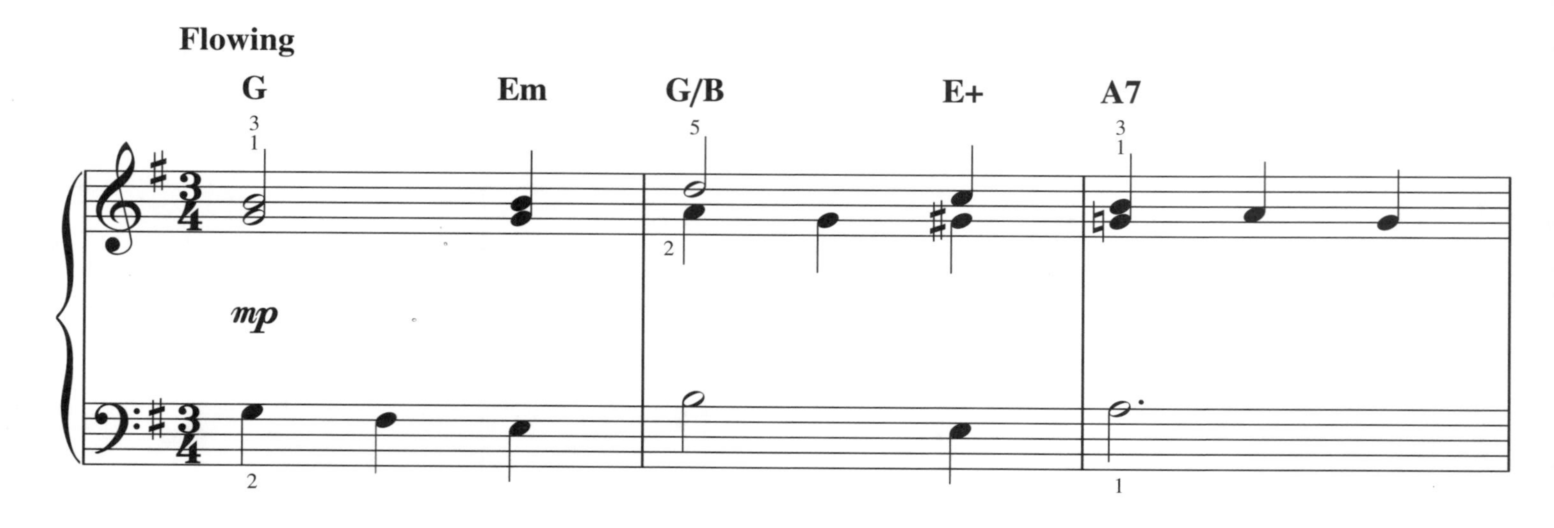

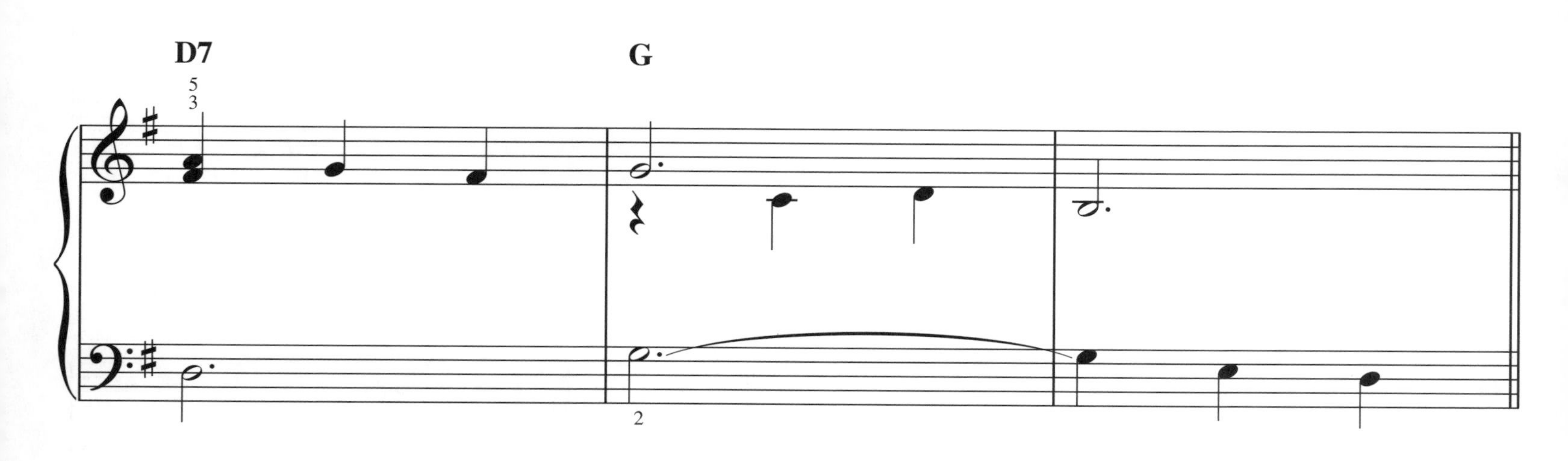

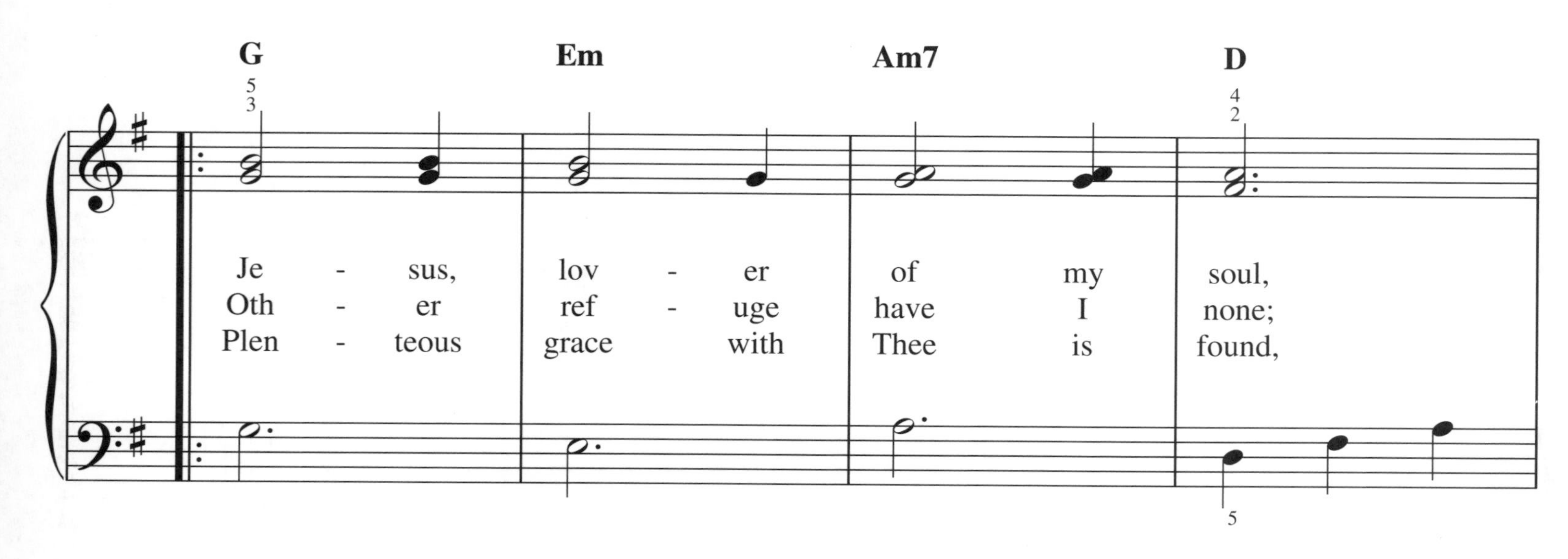

G
G/F
E7
A7
D7
Let me to Thy bos - om
Hangs my help - less soul on
Grace to cov - er all my
G
Em
fly.
Thee;
sin;
While the near - er
Leave, ah, leave me
Let the heal - ing
Am7
D
G
G/F
E7
wa - ters roll,
not a - lone,
streams a - bound;
While the tem - pest
Still sup - port and
Make and keep me
A7
D7
G
still is high;
com - fort me!
pure with - in!

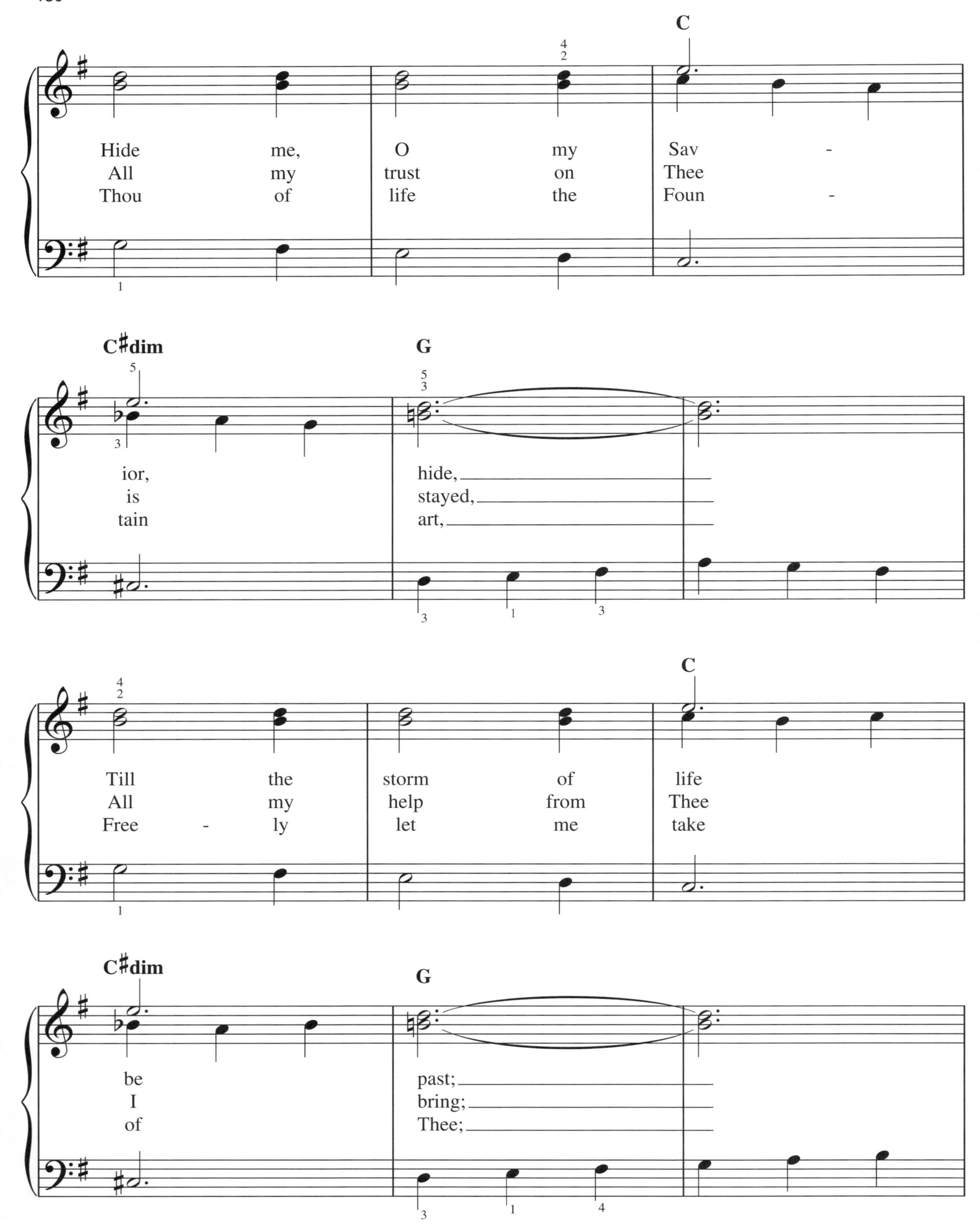
C
Hide me, O my Sav - ior, hide,
All my trust on Thee is stayed,
Thou of life the Foun - tain art,
C♯dim
G
Till the storm of life be past;
All my help from Thee I bring;
Free - ly let me take of Thee;

Em
Am7
Safe in - to the ha - ven
Cov - er my de - fense - less
Spring Thou up with - in my
D
G
G/F
E7
guide; Oh, re - ceive my
head With the shad - ow
heart! Rise to all e -
A7
D
1., 2.
G
soul at last!
of Thy wing!
ter - ni -
3.
G
ty!

JESUS PAID IT ALL

Words by ELVINA M. HALL
Music by JOHN T. GRAPE

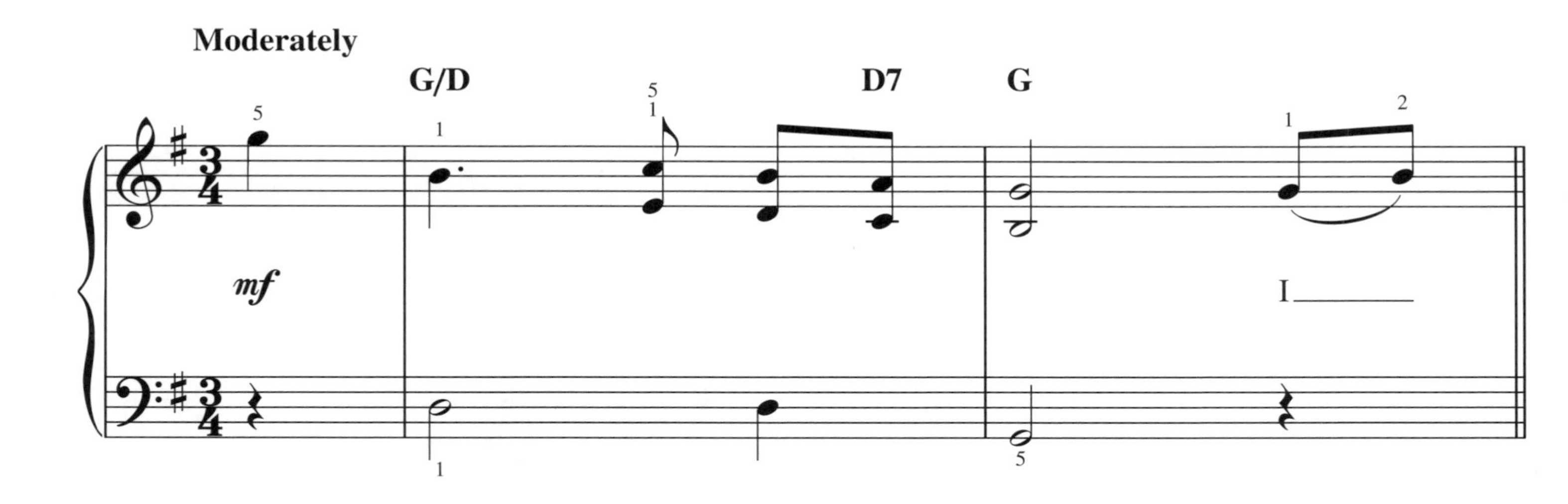

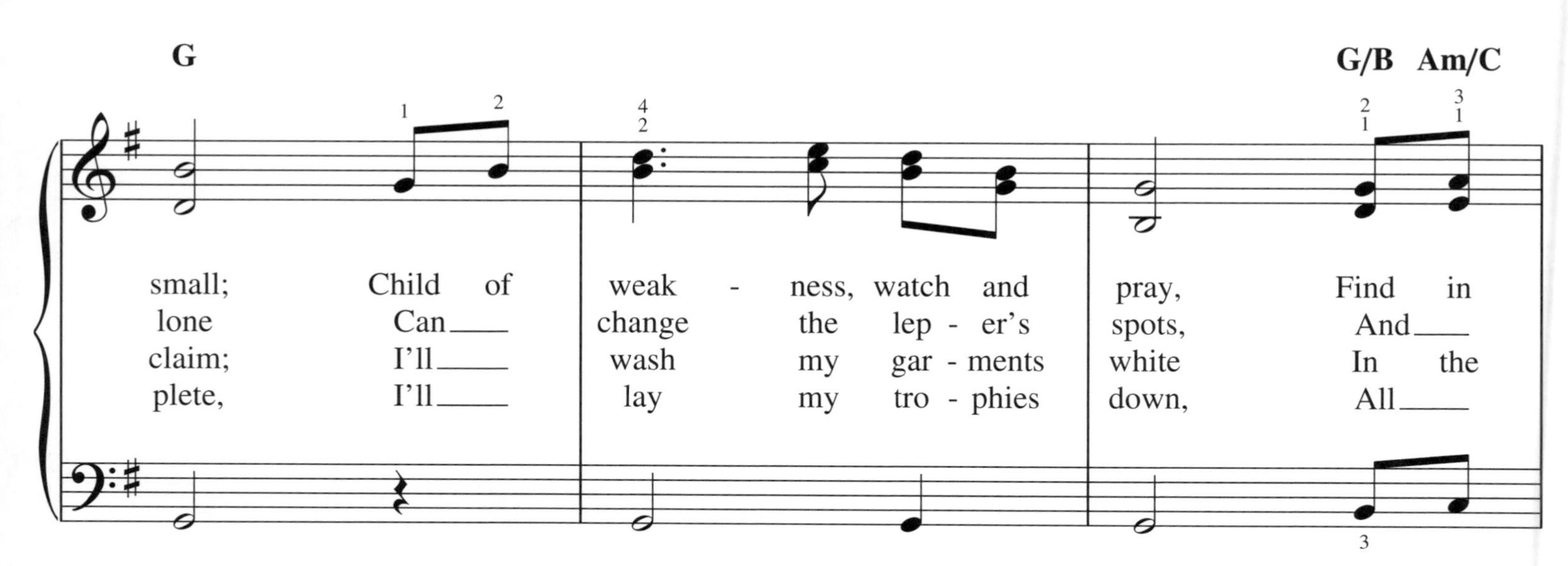

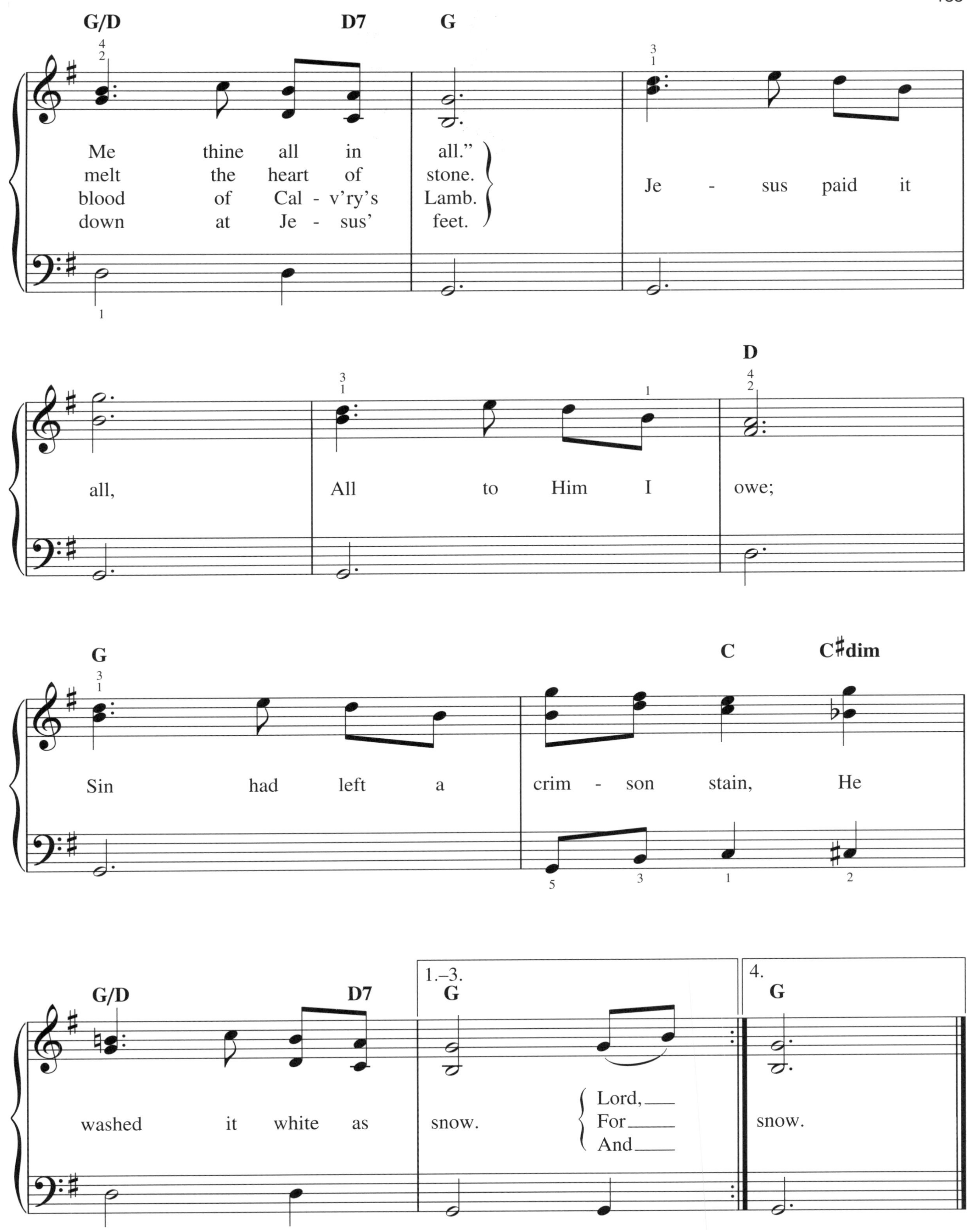
G/D D7 G
Me thine all in all."
melt the heart of stone.
blood of Cal - v'ry's Lamb.
down at Je - sus' feet.
Je - sus paid it
all,
All to Him I
D
owe;
G
Sin had left a
C C♯dim
crim - son stain, He
G/D D7
washed it white as
1.–3.
G
snow.
Lord,
For
And
4.
G
snow.

JESUS SHALL REIGN

Words by ISAAC WATTS
Music by JOHN HATTON

Stately

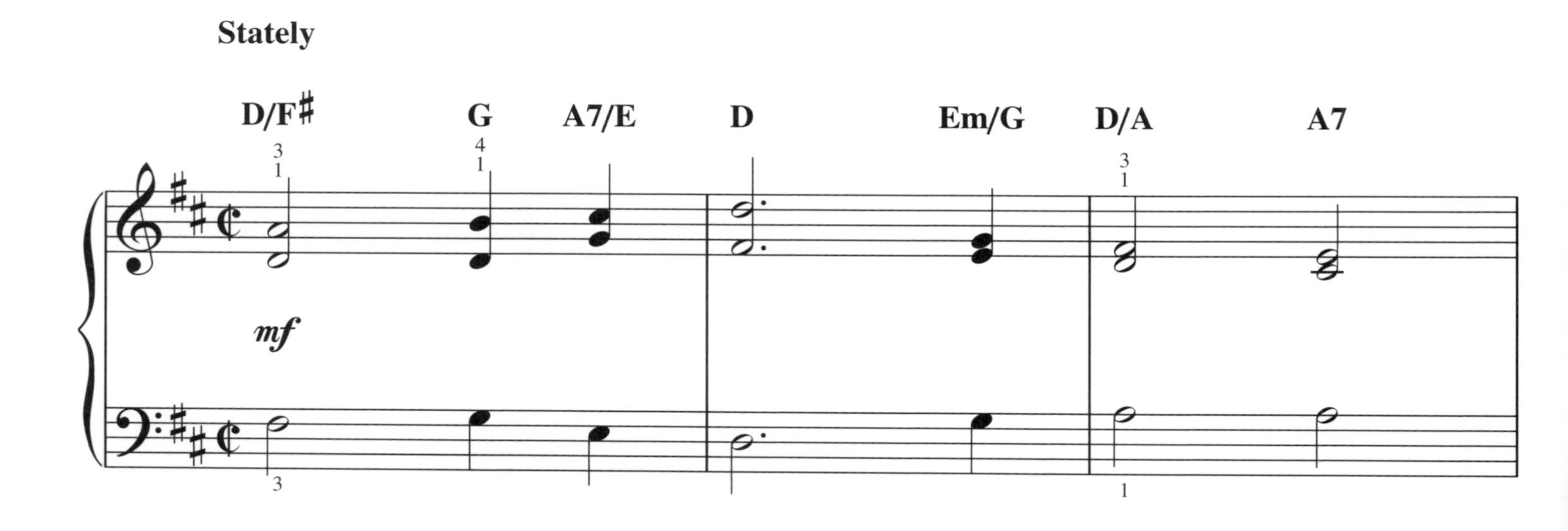

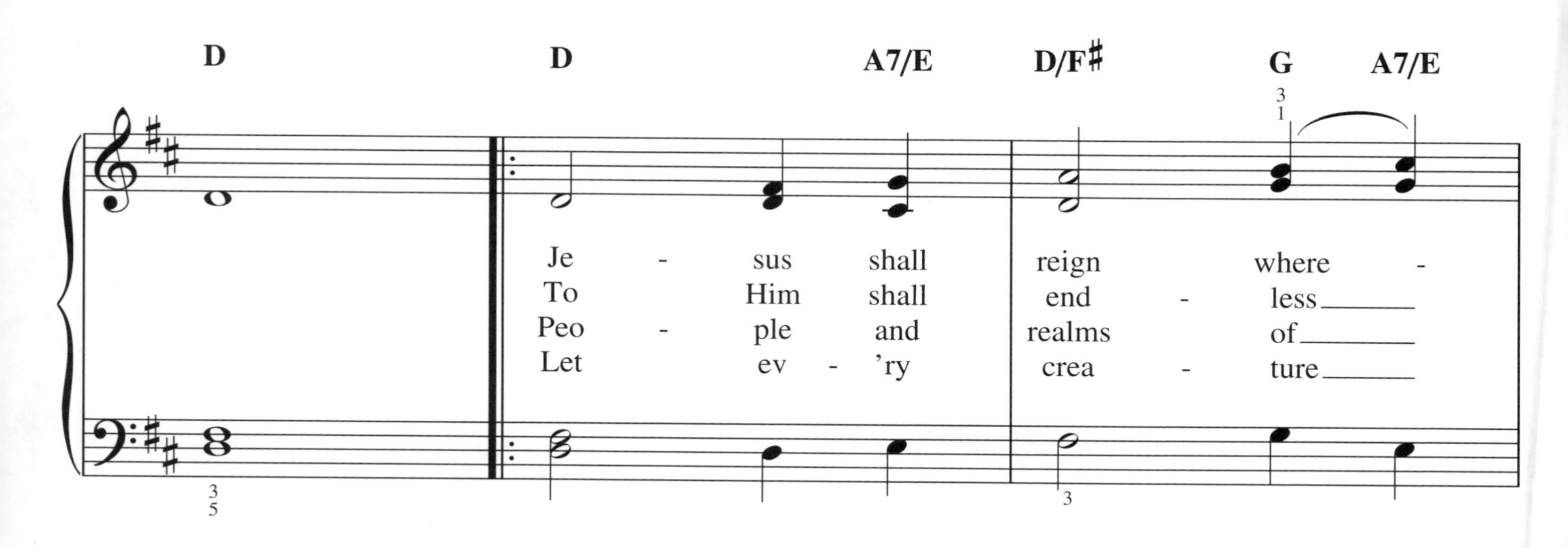

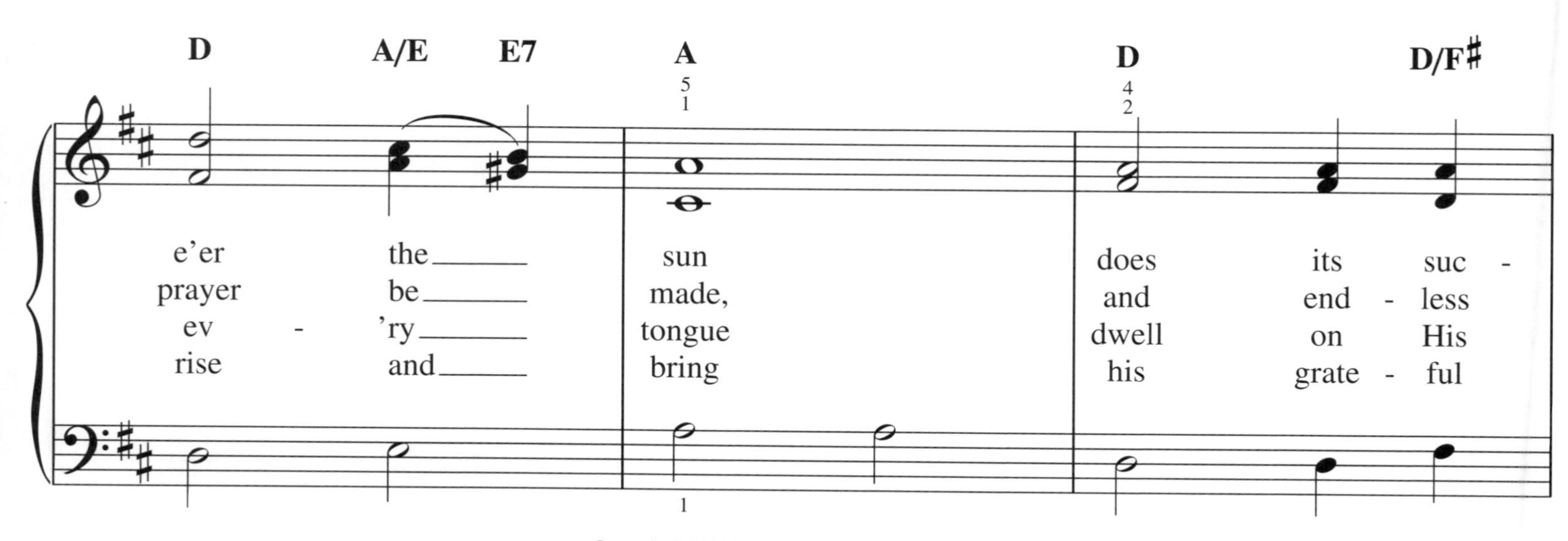

G D/F♯ Em D A
ces - sive jour - neys run.
praises - es crown His head.
love with sweet - est song.
hon - ors to our King.
D A7 D D/F♯ G D/F♯ A7/E D
His king - dom spread from shore to
His name like sweet per - fume shall
And in - fant voic - es shall pro -
An - gels de - scend with songs a -
A D/F♯ G A7/E D Em/G
shore, till moons shall wax and
rise with ev - 'ry morn - ing
claim their ear - ly bless - ings
gain, and earth re - peat the
D/A A7 1.–3. D 4. D
wane no more.
sac - ri - fice.
on His name.
loud "A - men!"

JESUS, THE VERY THOUGHT OF THEE

Words attributed to BERNARD OF CLAIRVAUX
Translated by EDWARD CASWALL
Music by JOHN BACCHUS DYKES

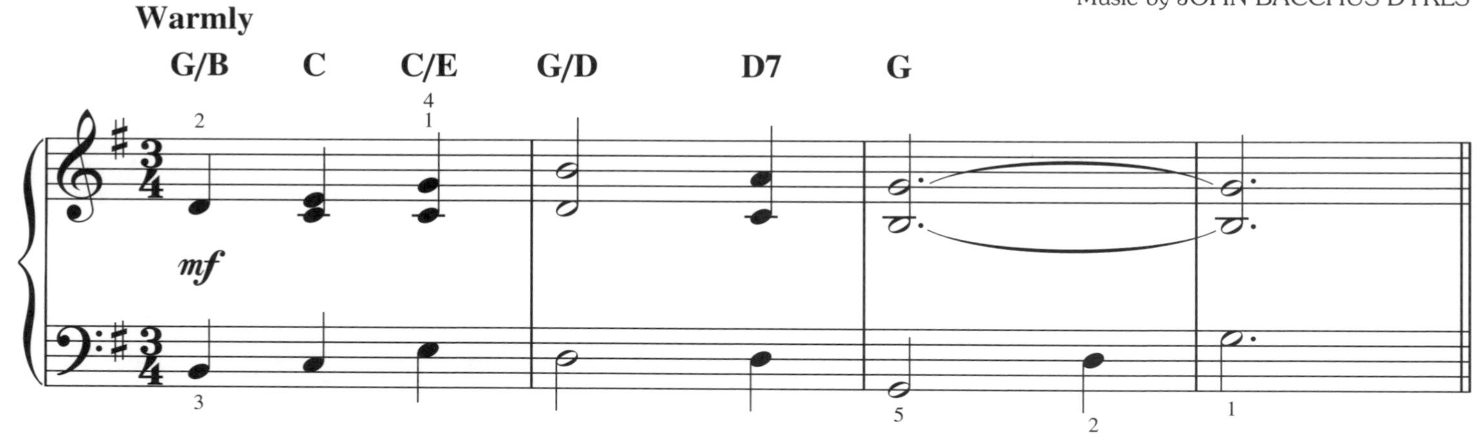

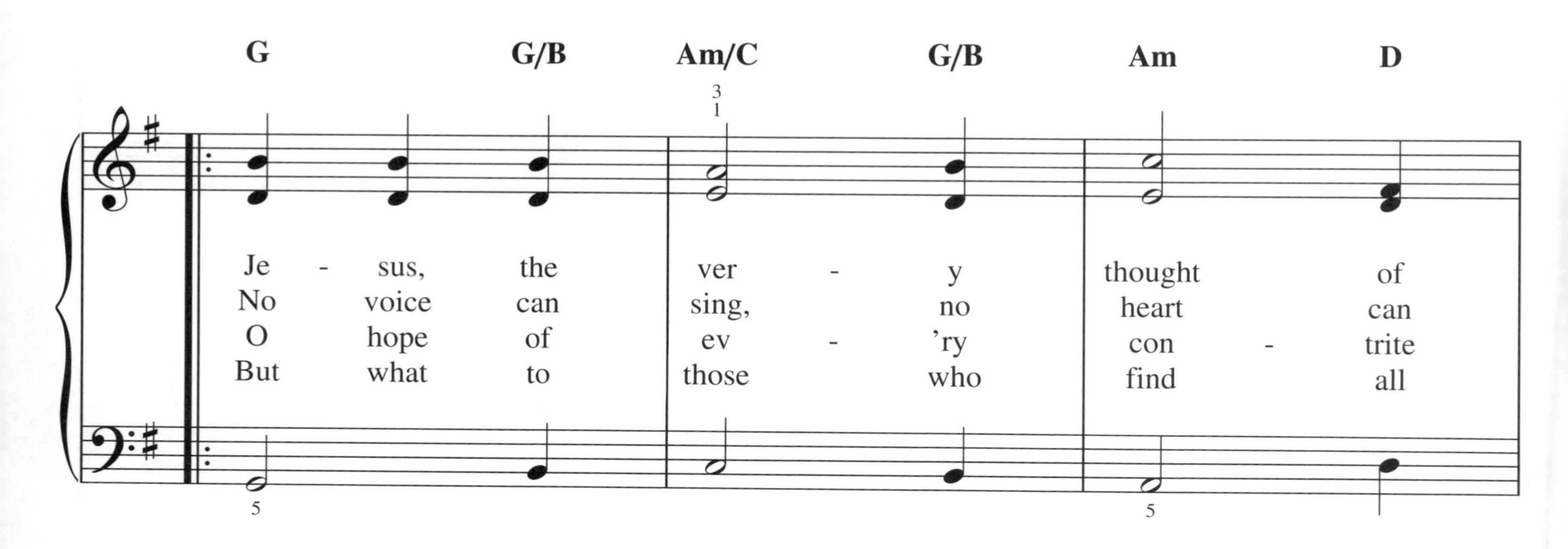

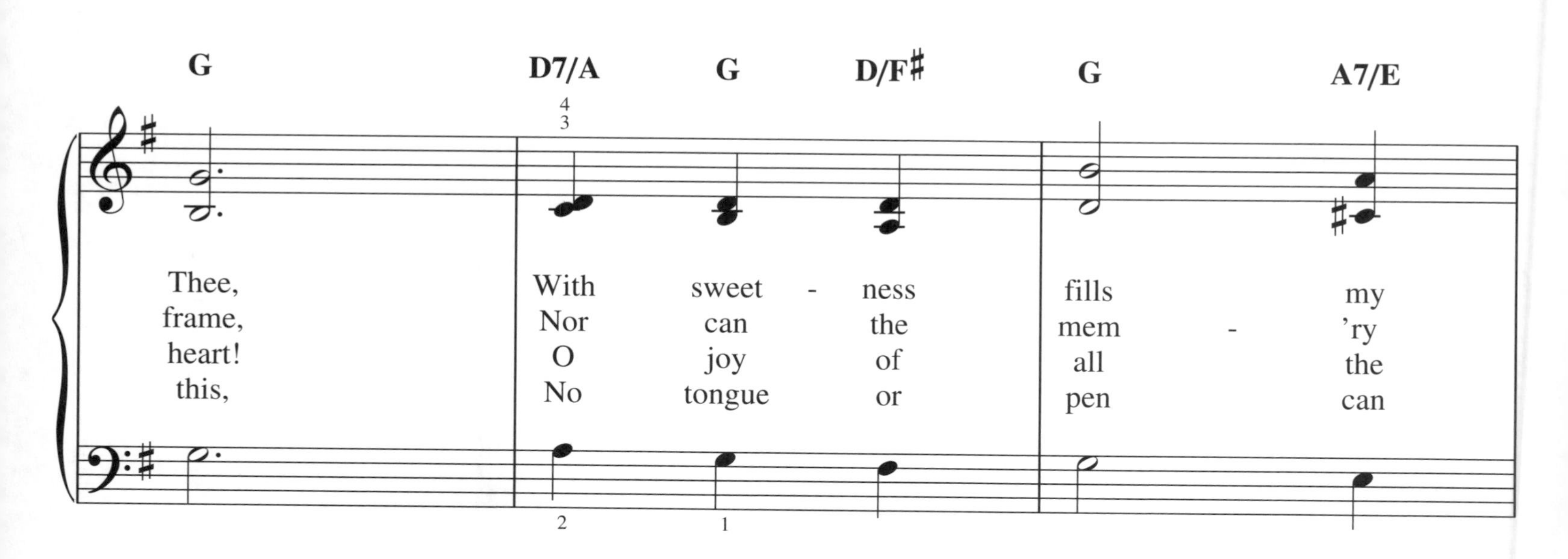

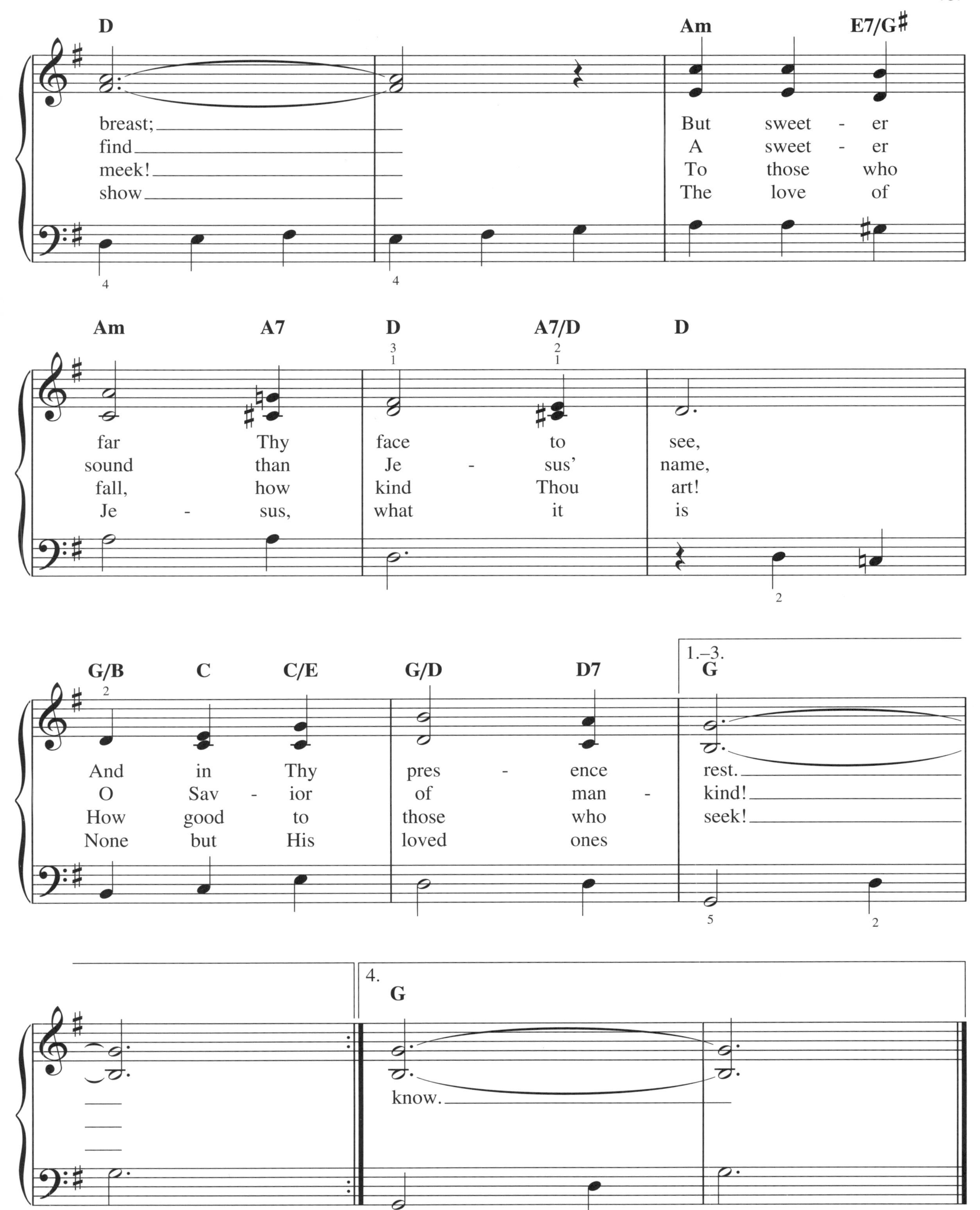
D
Am
E7/G♯
breast;
find
meek!
show
But sweet - er
A sweet - er
To those who
The love of
Am
A7
D
A7/D
D
far Thy face to see,
sound than Je - sus' name,
fall, how kind Thou art!
Je - sus, what it is
G/B
C
C/E
G/D
D7
1.–3.
G
And in Thy pres - ence rest.
O Sav - ior of man - kind!
How good to those who seek!
None but His loved ones
4.
G
know.

JESUS WALKED THIS LONESOME VALLEY

Traditional Spiritual

Moderately slow

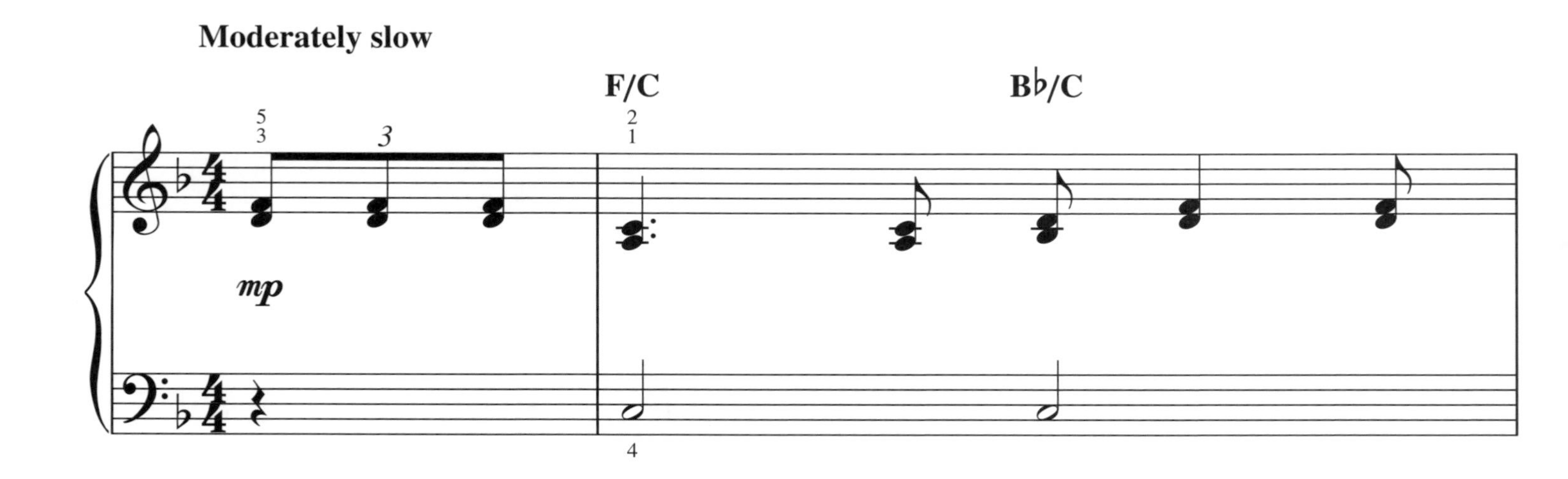

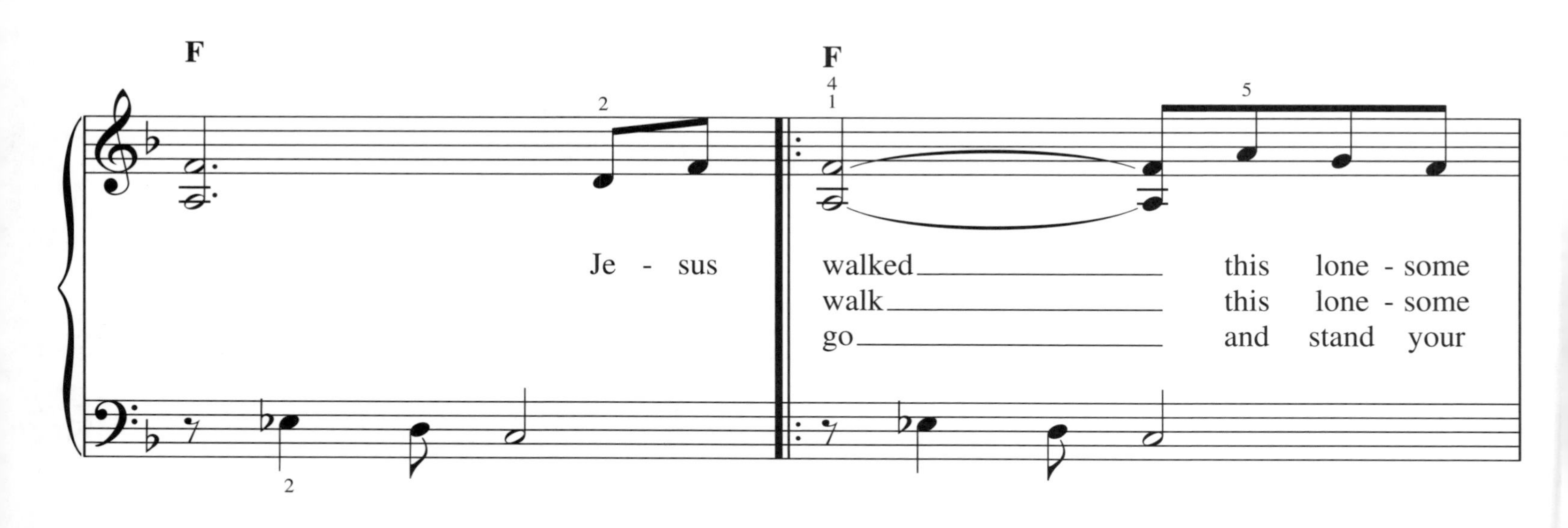

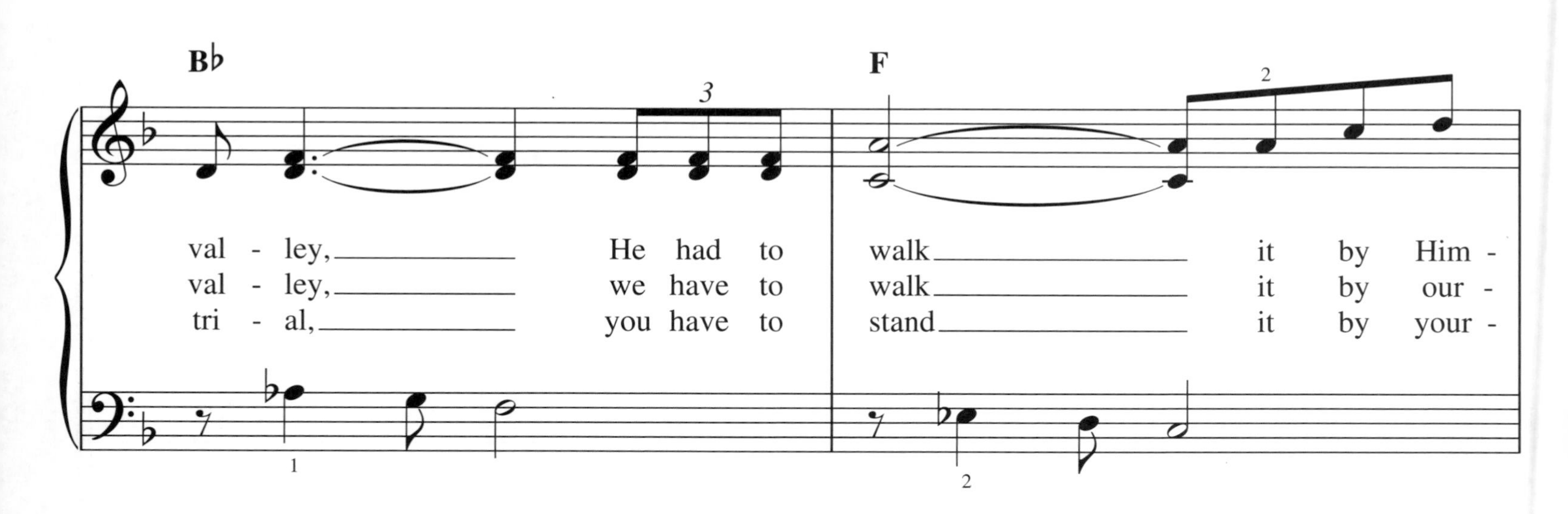

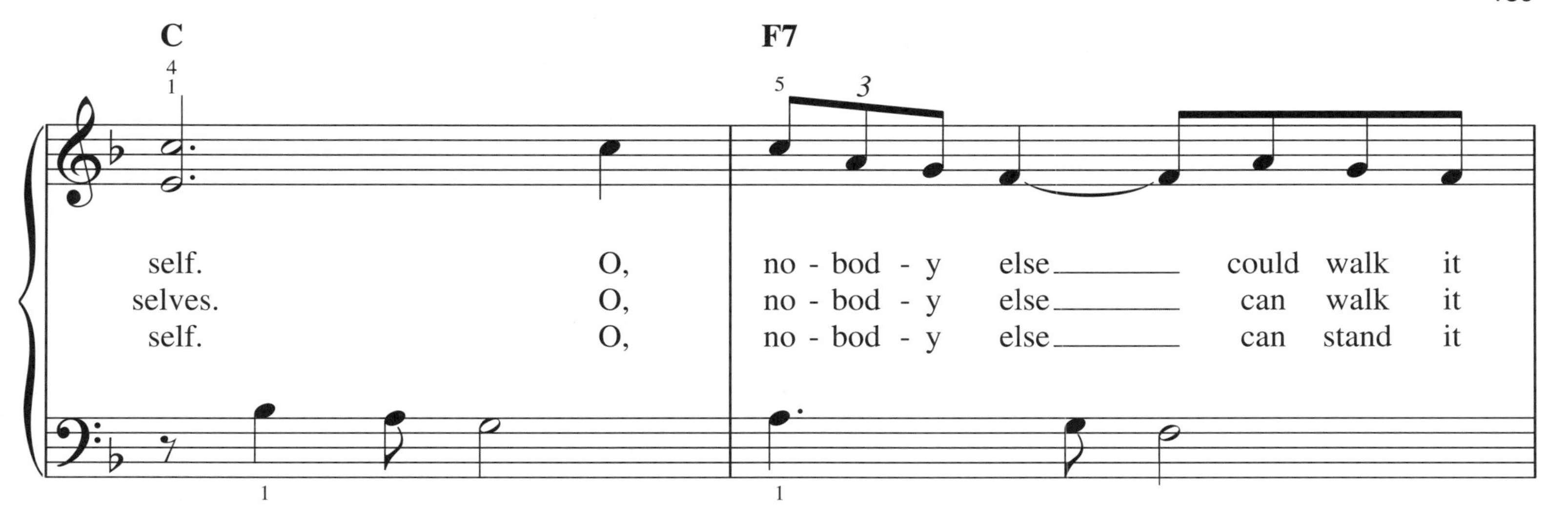
C
F7
self.
O,
no - bod - y else could walk it
selves.
O,
no - bod - y else can walk it
self.
O,
no - bod - y else can stand it

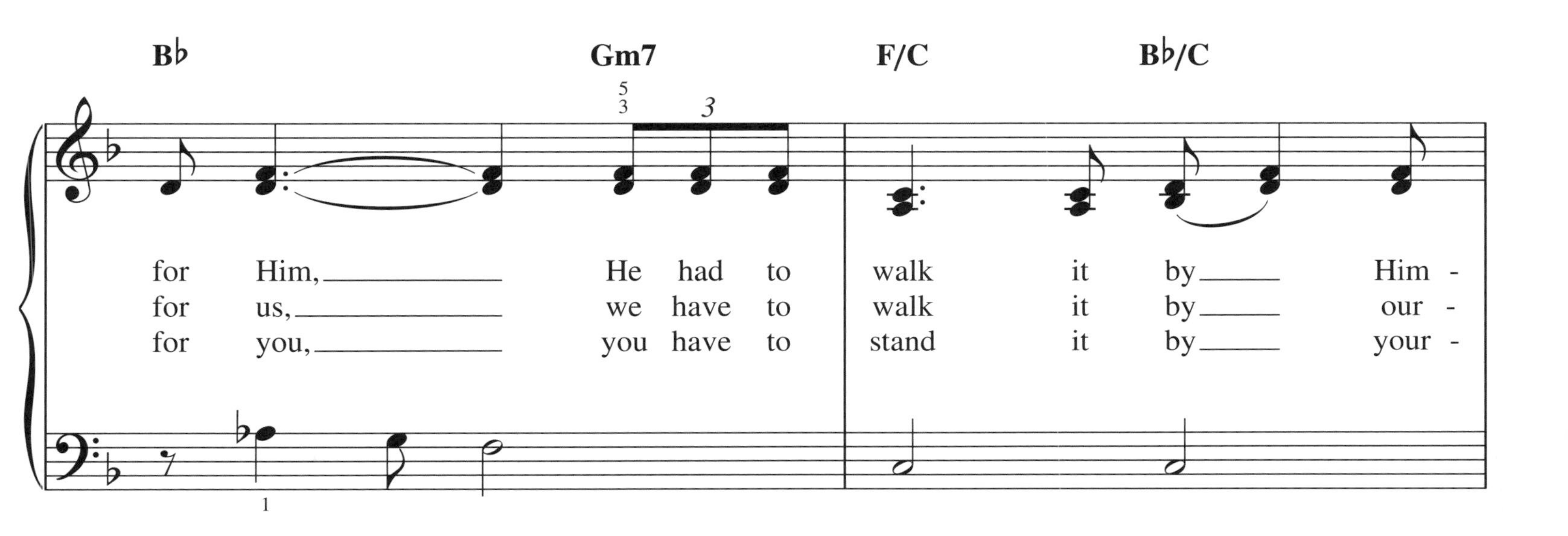
B♭
Gm7
F/C
B♭/C
for Him, He had to walk it by Him -
for us, we have to walk it by our -
for you, you have to stand it by your -

1., 2.
3.
F
F
self. We must
selves. You must
self.

JOYFUL, JOYFUL, WE ADORE THEE

Words by HENRY VAN DYKE
Music by LUDWIG VAN BEETHOVEN,
melody from *Ninth Symphony*
Adapted by EDWARD HODGES

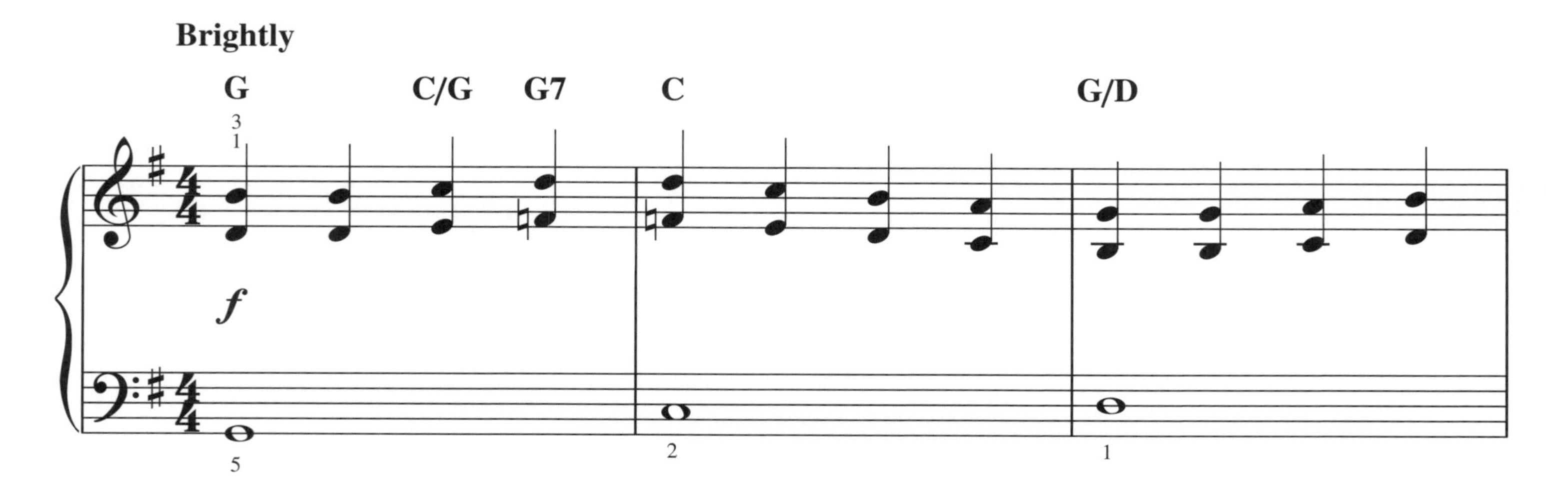

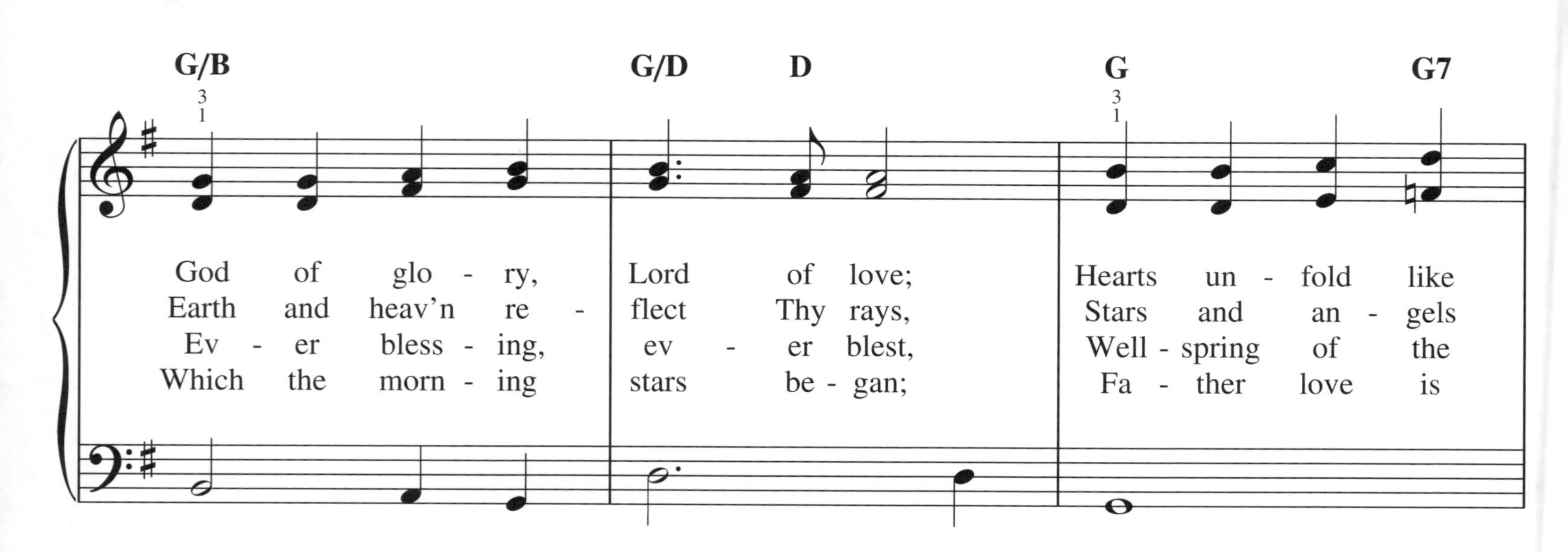

C G/D D7 G
flow'rs be - fore Thee, O - p'ning to the sun a - bove.
sing a - round Thee, Cen - ter of un - bro - ken praise.
joy of liv - ing, O - cean depth of hap - py rest!
reign - ing o'er us, Broth - er love binds man to man.
D G/D D G/D D B/D#
Melt the clouds of sin and sad - ness, Drive the dark of
Field and for - est, vale and moun - tain, Flow - 'ry mead - ow,
Thou our Fa - ther, Christ our Broth - er; All who live in
Ev - er sing - ing, march we on - ward, Vic - tors in the
Em A D G C/G G7 C
doubt a - way; Giv - er of im - mor - tal glad - ness,
flash - ing sea, Chant - ing bird and flow - ing foun - tain
love are Thine. Teach us how to love each oth - er,
midst of strife; Joy - ful mu - sic leads us sun - ward
G/D 1.–3. D7 G 4. D7 G
Fill us with the light of day.
Call us to re - joice in Thee.
Lift us to the joy di - vine.
In the tri - umph song of life.

JUST AS I AM

Words by CHARLOTTE ELLIOTT
Music by WILLIAM B. BRADBURY

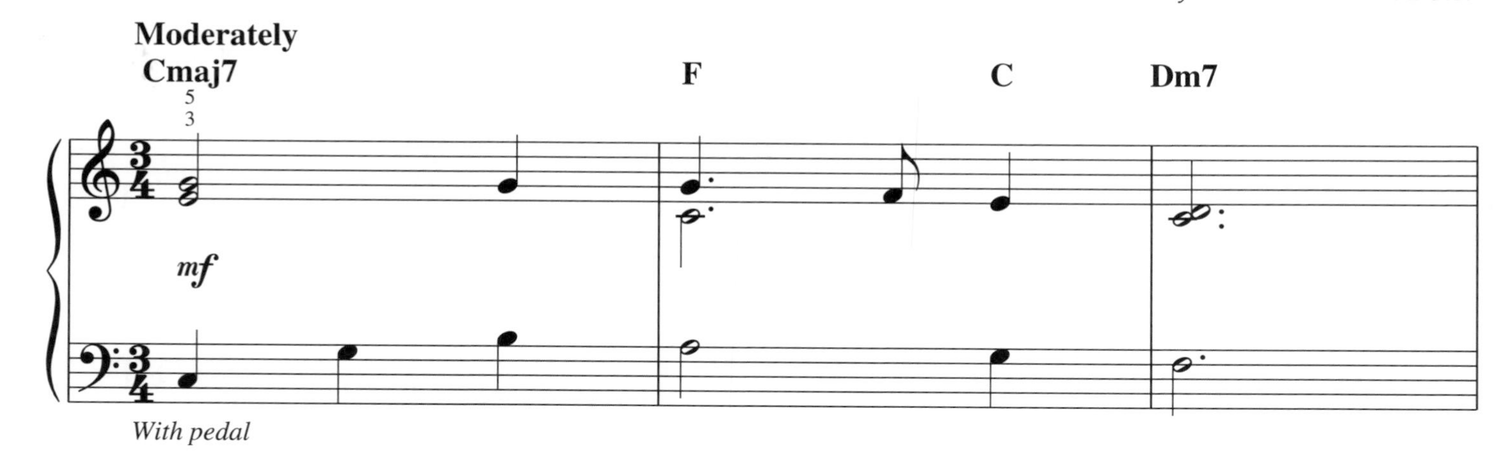

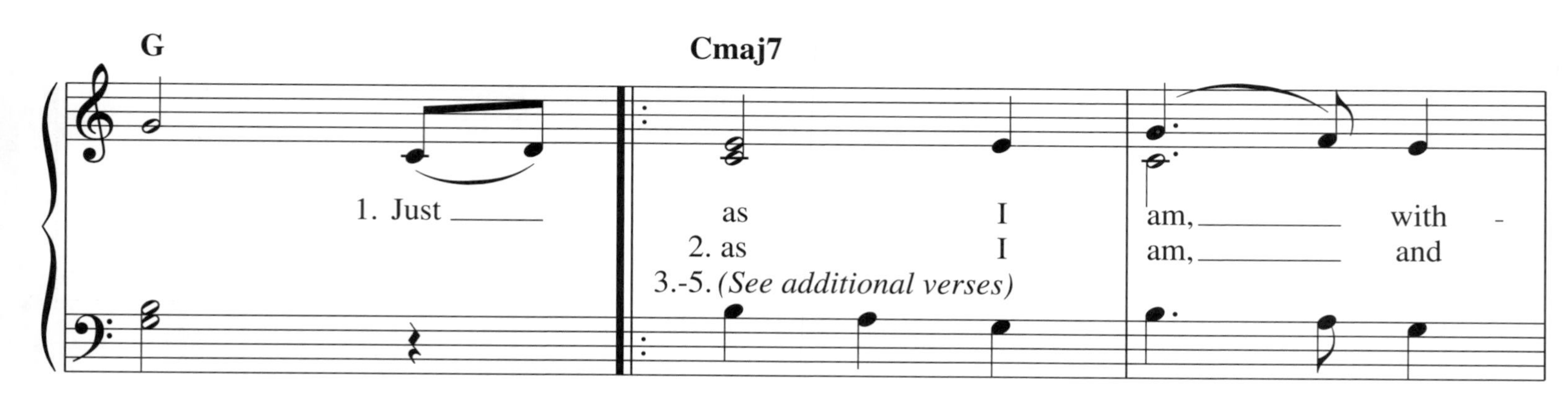

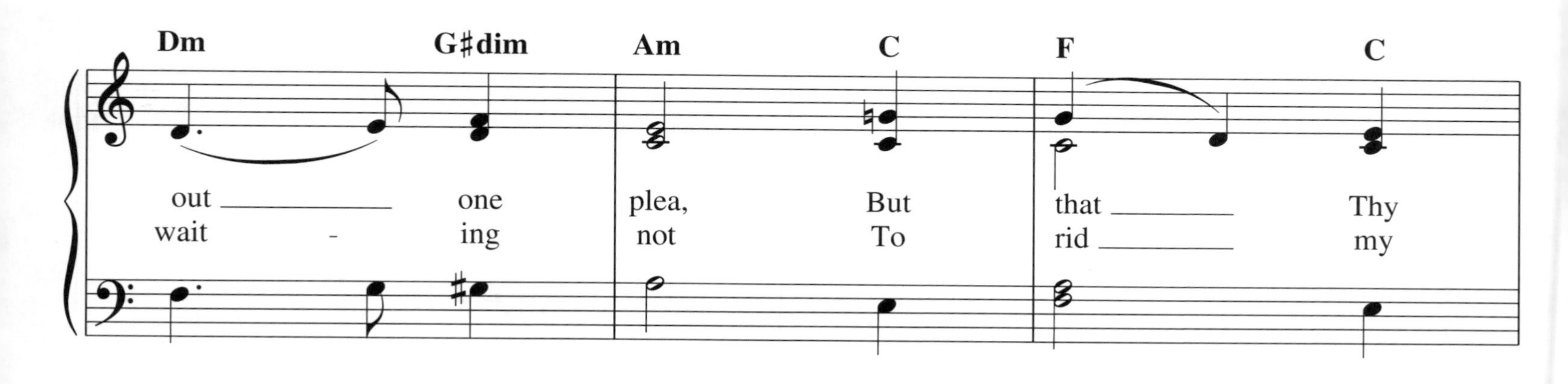

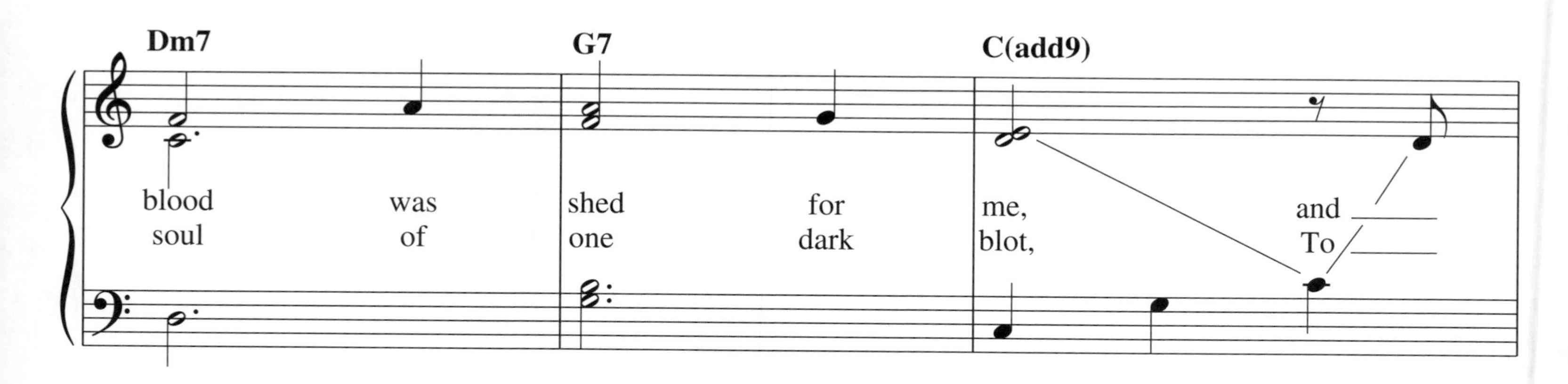

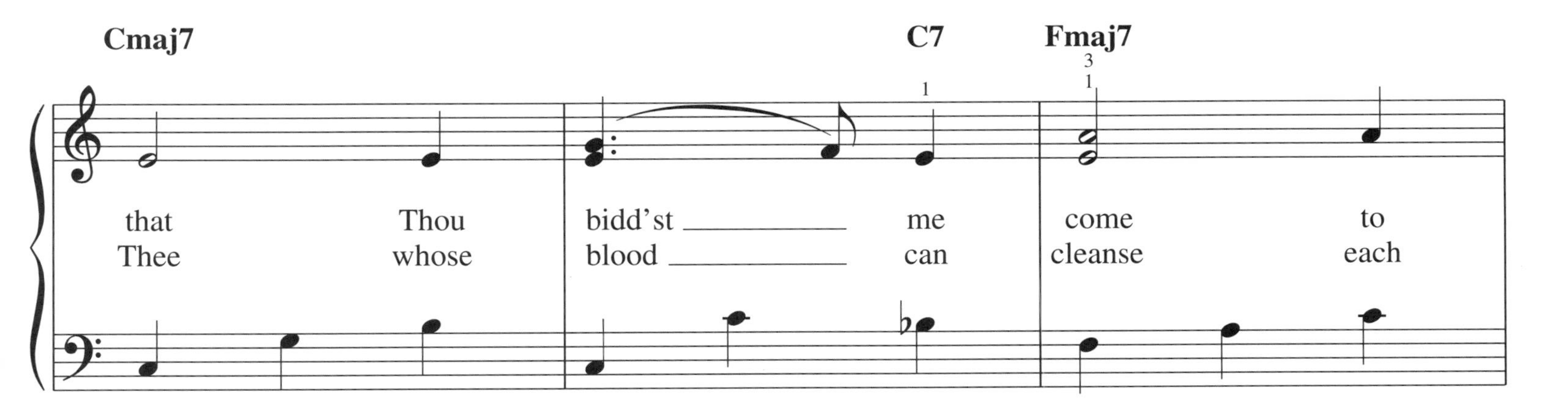
Cmaj7
C7
Fmaj7
that Thou bidd'st me come to
Thee whose blood can cleanse each

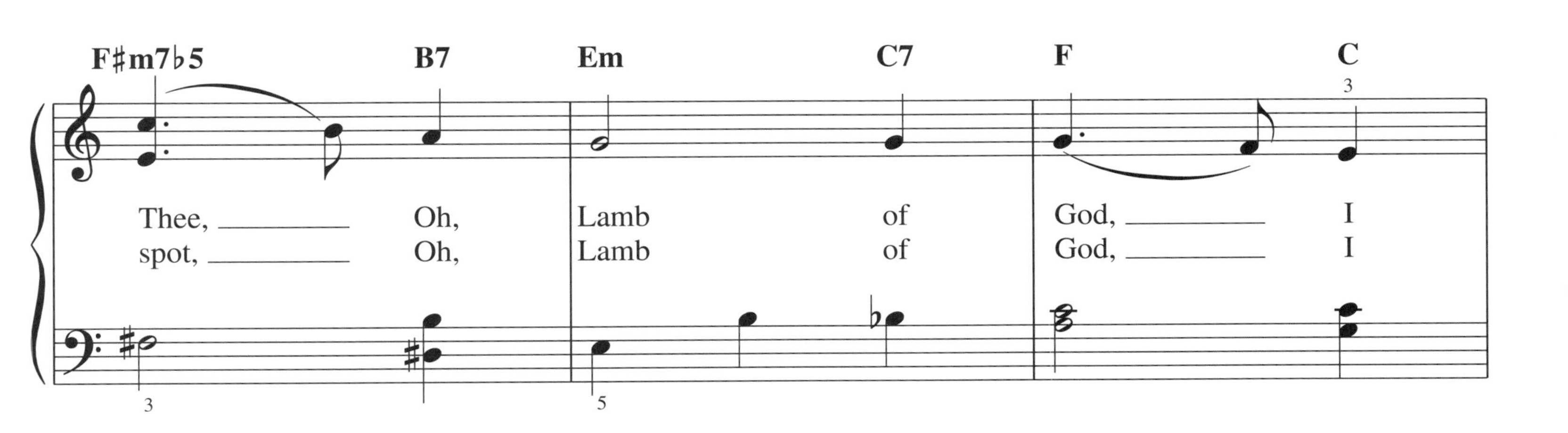
F♯m7♭5
B7
Em
C7
F
C
Thee, Oh, Lamb of God, I
spot, Oh, Lamb of God, I

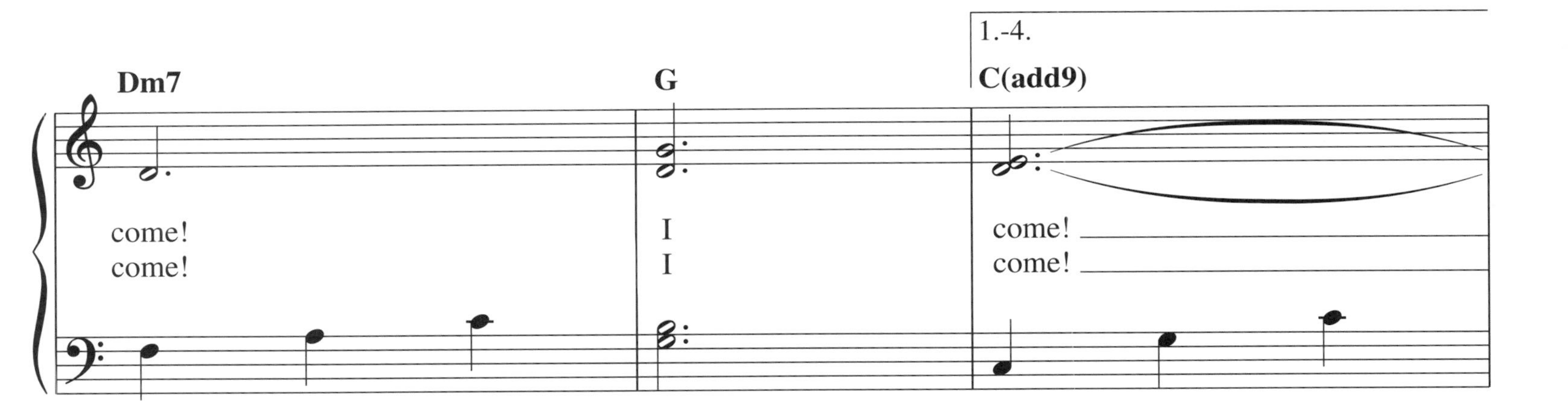
1.-4.
Dm7
G
C(add9)
come! I come!
come! I come!

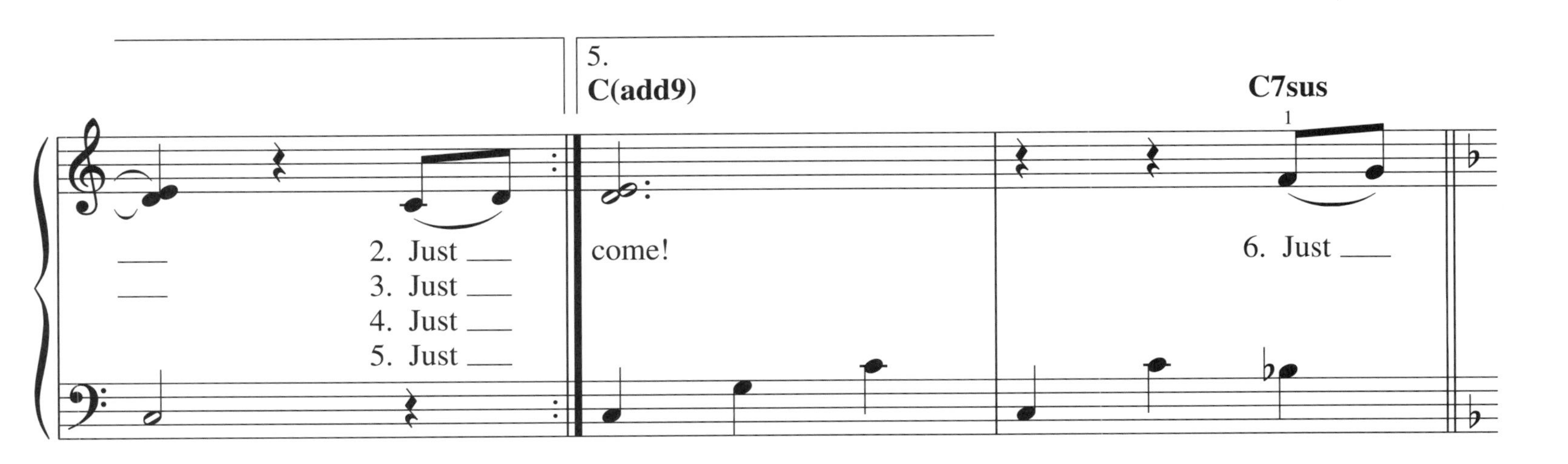
5.
C(add9)
C7sus
2. Just
3. Just
4. Just
5. Just
come!
6. Just

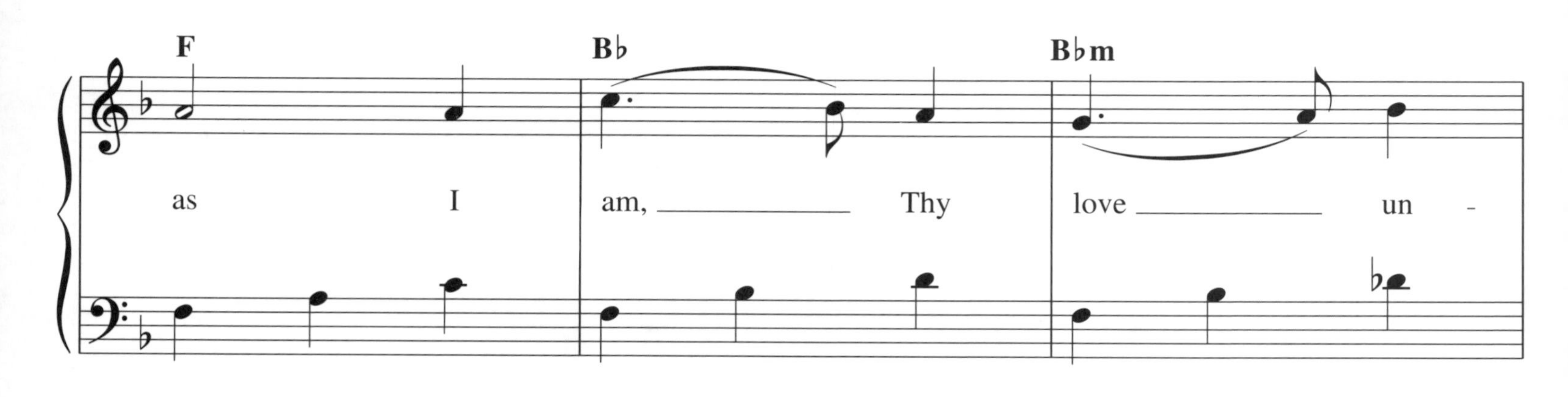
F
B♭
B♭m
as I am, Thy love un -

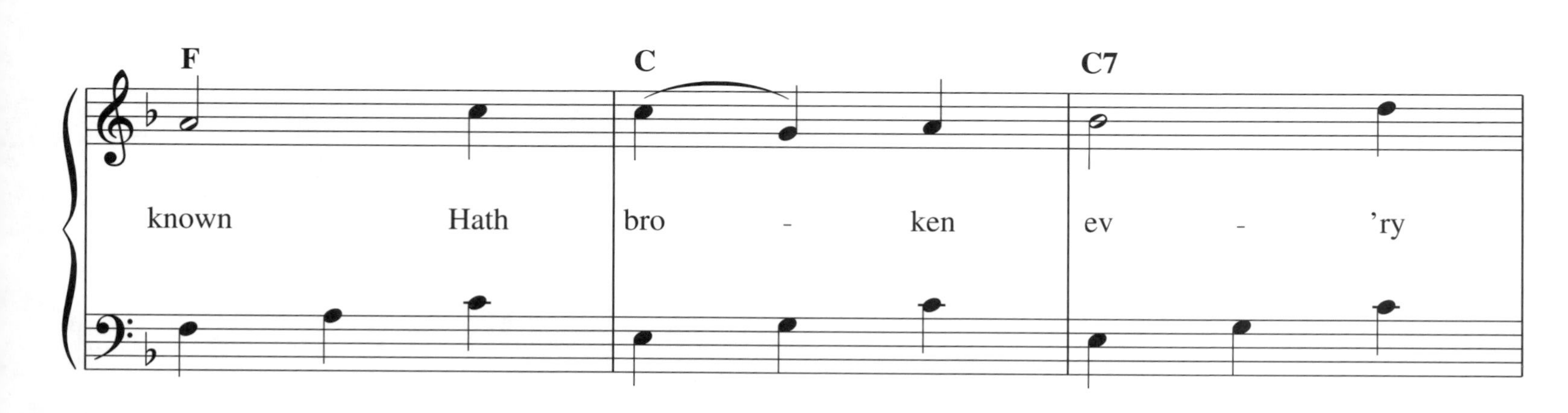
F
C
C7
known Hath bro - ken ev - 'ry

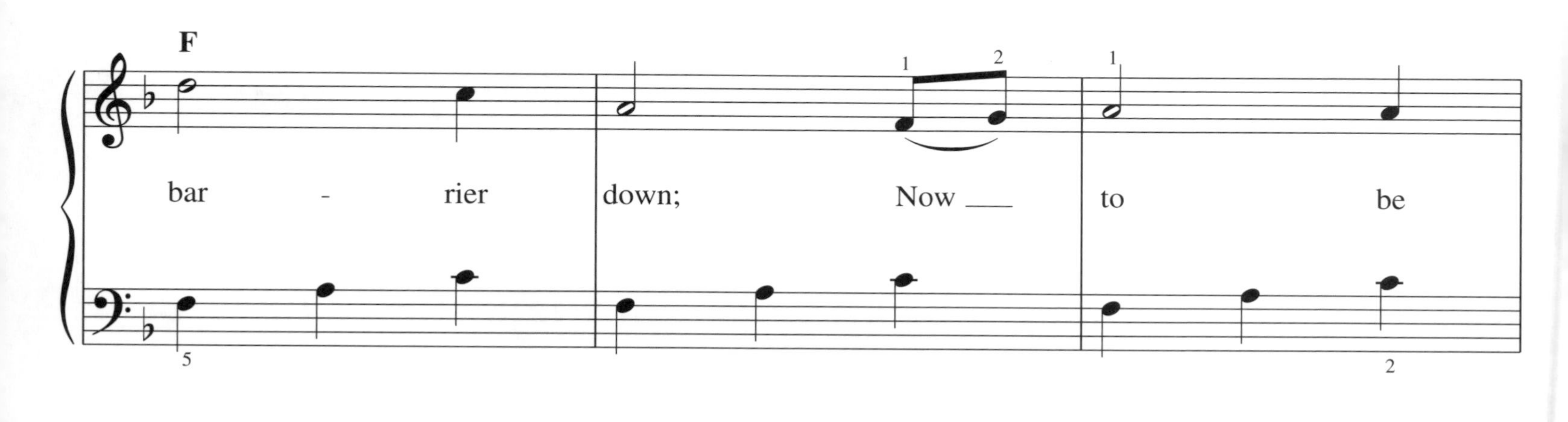
F
bar - rier down; Now to be

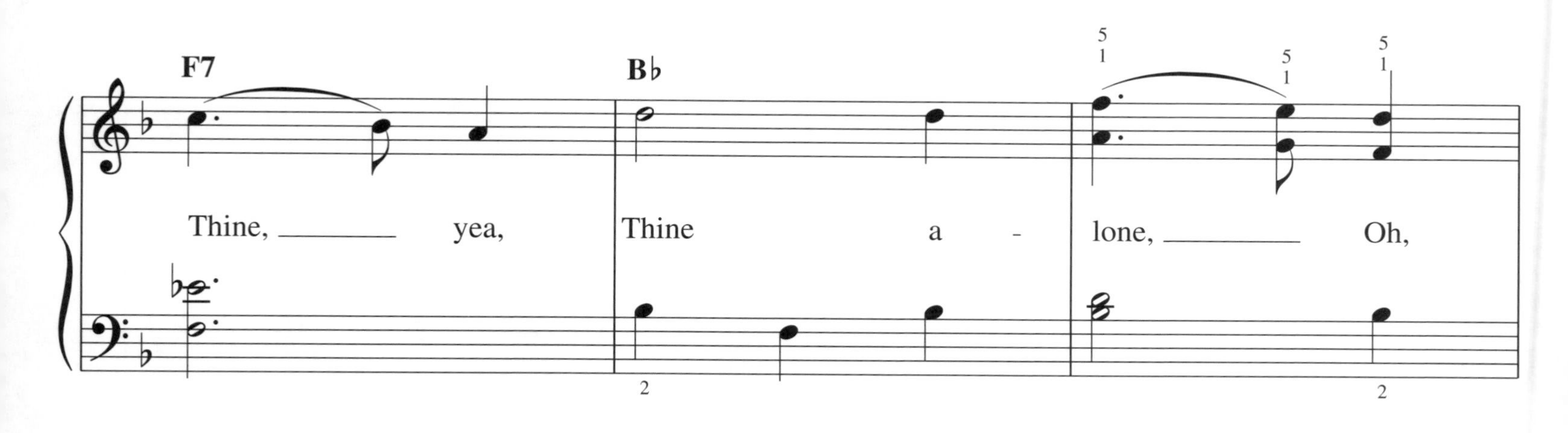
F7
B♭
Thine, yea, Thine a - lone, Oh,

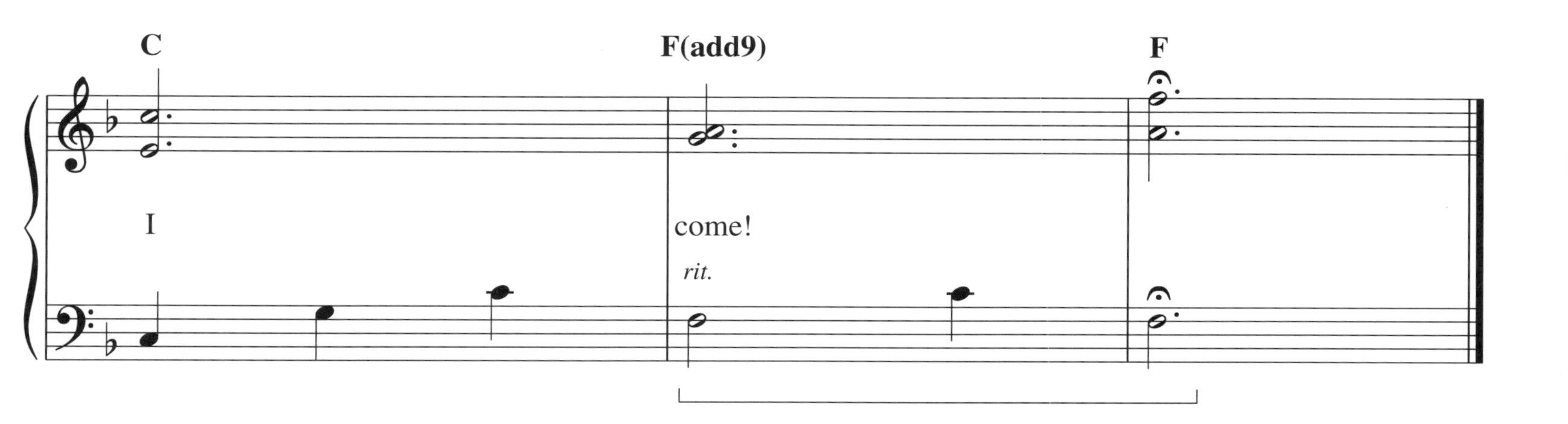

Additional Verses

3. Just as I am, tho' tossed about
   With many a conflict, many a doubt,
   Fightings within and fears without,
   Oh, Lamb of God, I come! I come!

4. Just as I am, poor, wretched, blind;
   Sight, riches, healing of the mind,
   Yea, all I need in Thee to find,
   Oh, Lamb of God, I come! I come!

5. Just as I am, Thou wilt receive,
   Wilt welcome, pardon, cleanse, relieve,
   Because Thy promise I believe,
   Oh, Lamb of God, I come! I come!

THE KING OF LOVE MY SHEPHERD IS

Words by HENRY BAKER
Traditional Irish Melody

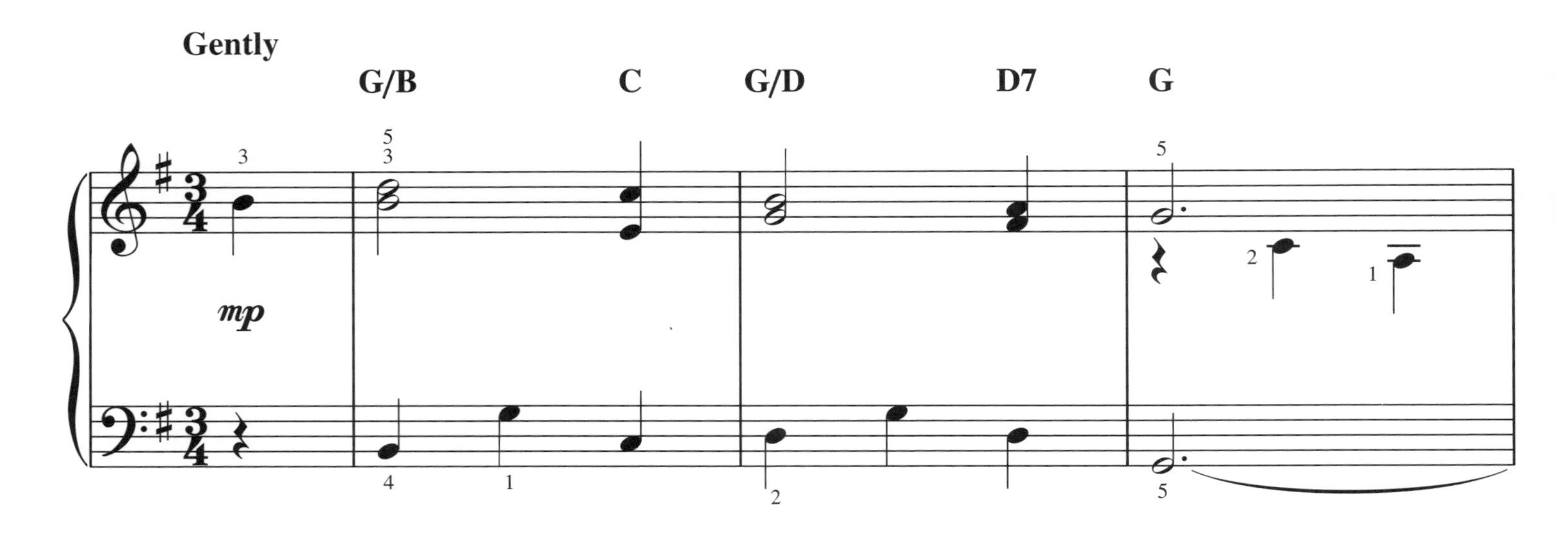

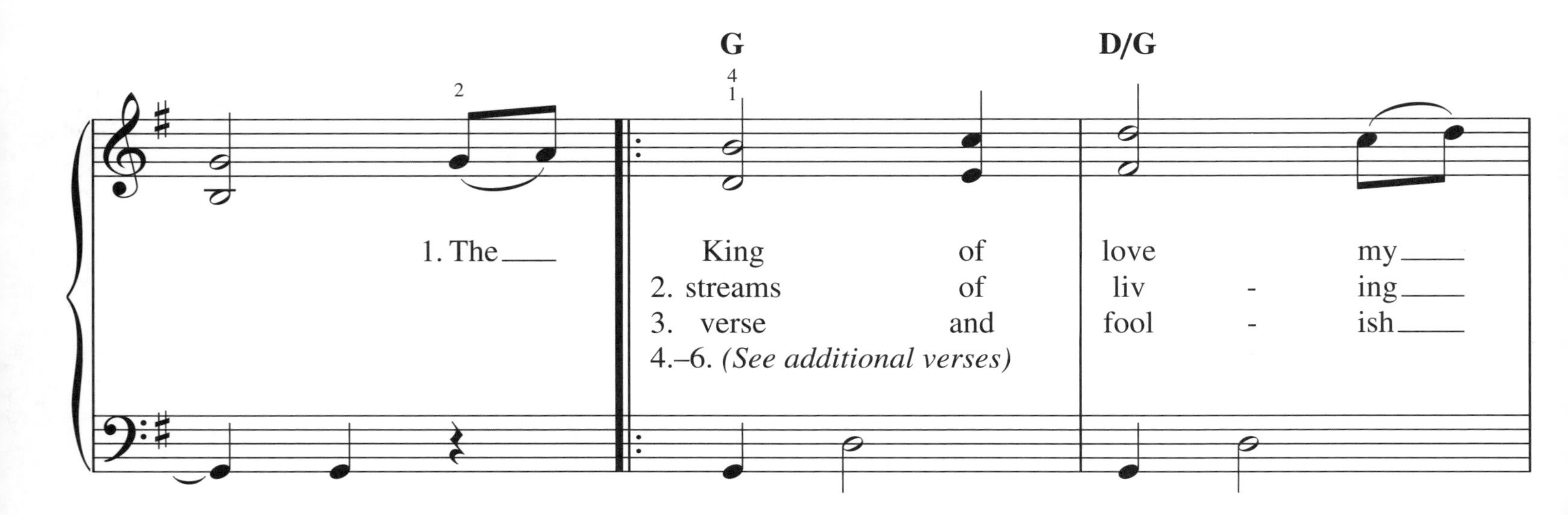

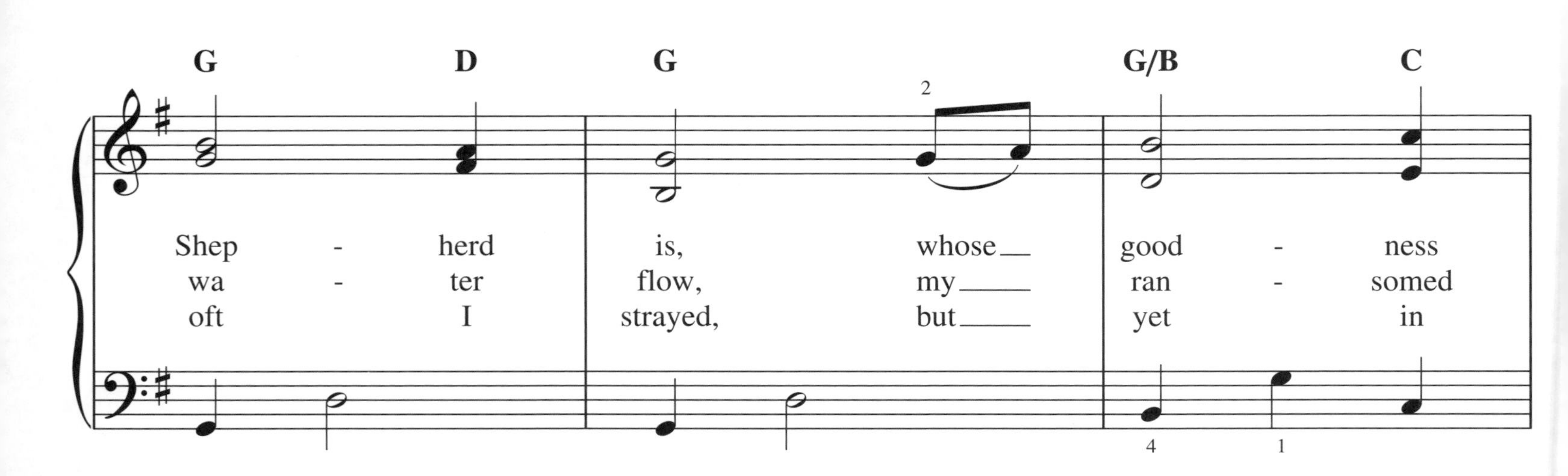

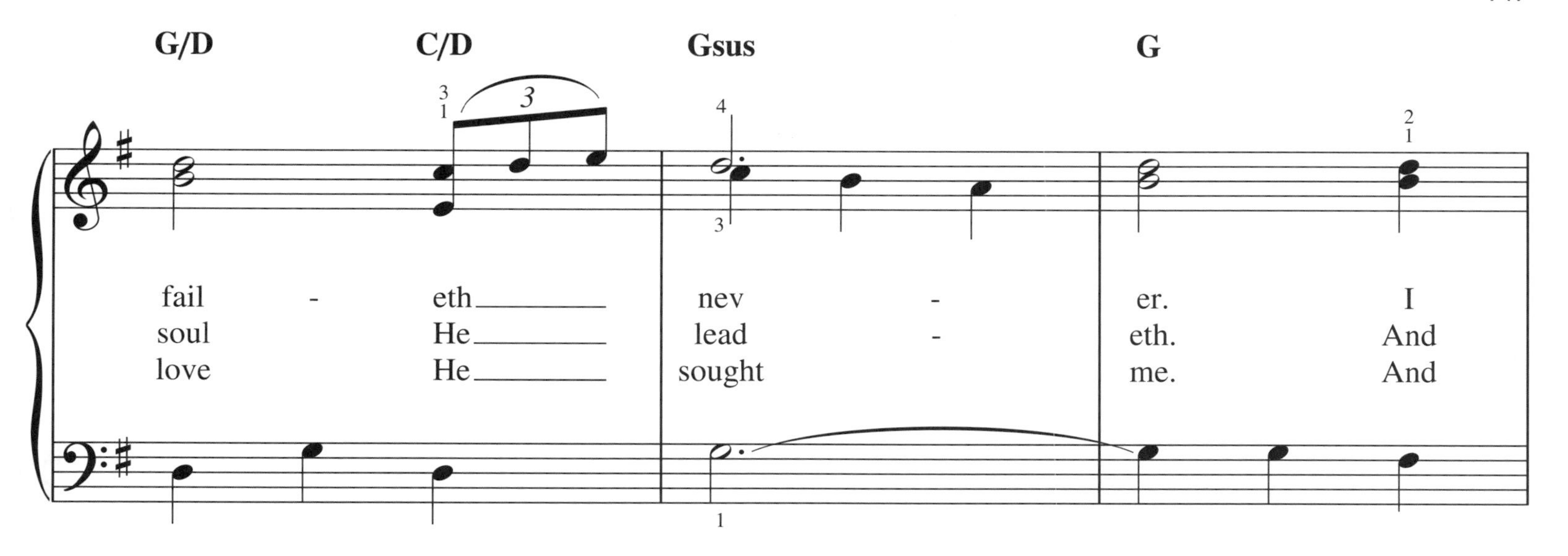
G/D
C/D
Gsus
G
fail - eth nev - er. I
soul He lead - eth. And
love He sought me. And

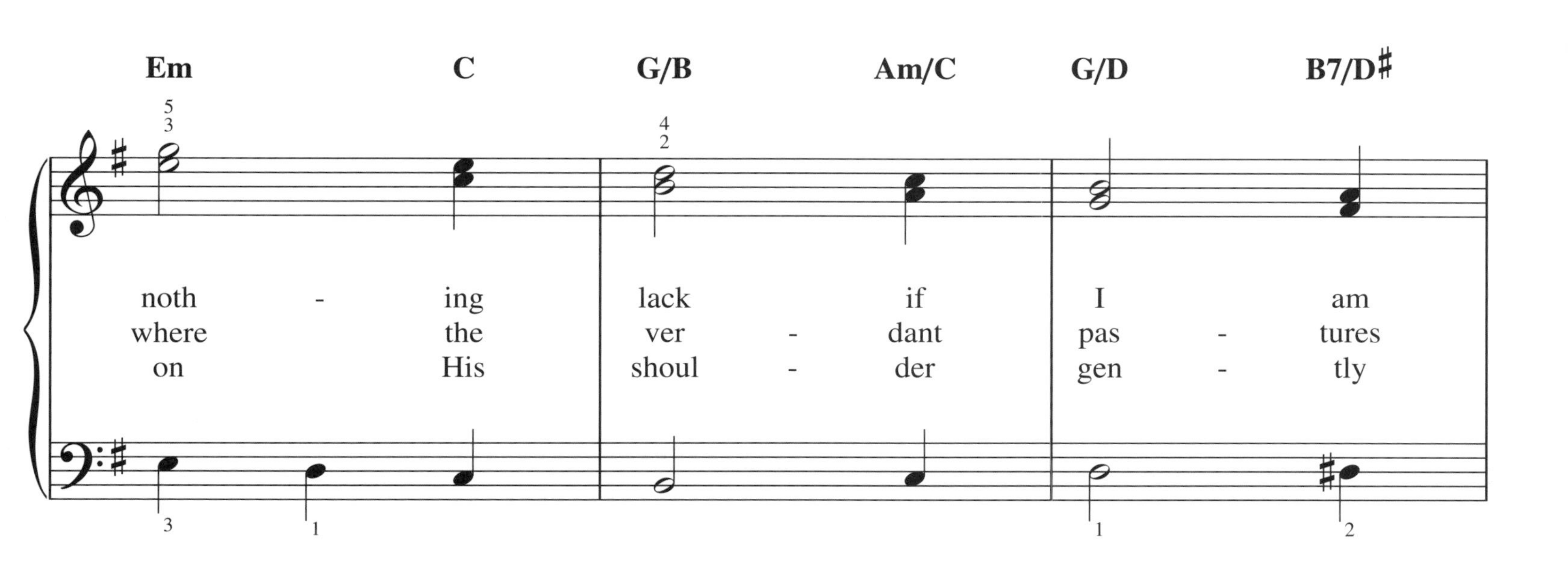
Em
C
G/B
Am/C
G/D
B7/D#
noth - ing lack if I am
where the ver - dant pas - tures
on His shoul - der gen - tly

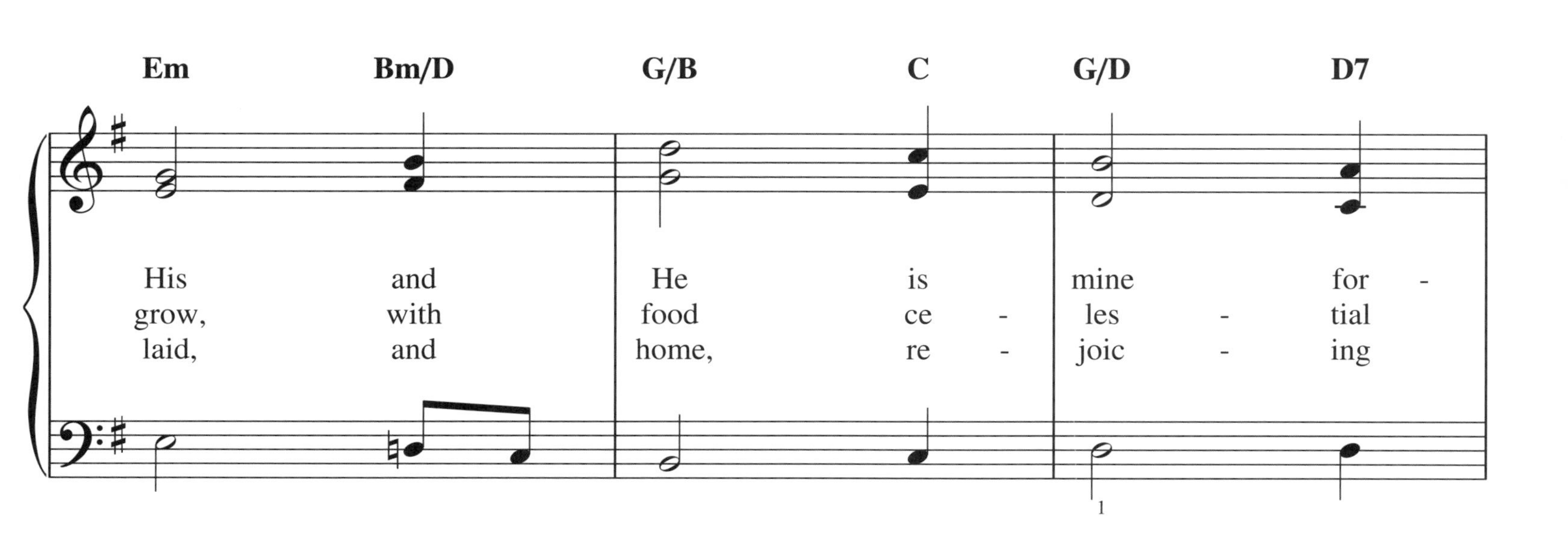
Em
Bm/D
G/B
C
G/D
D7
His and He is mine for -
grow, with food ce - les - tial
laid, and home, re - joic - ing

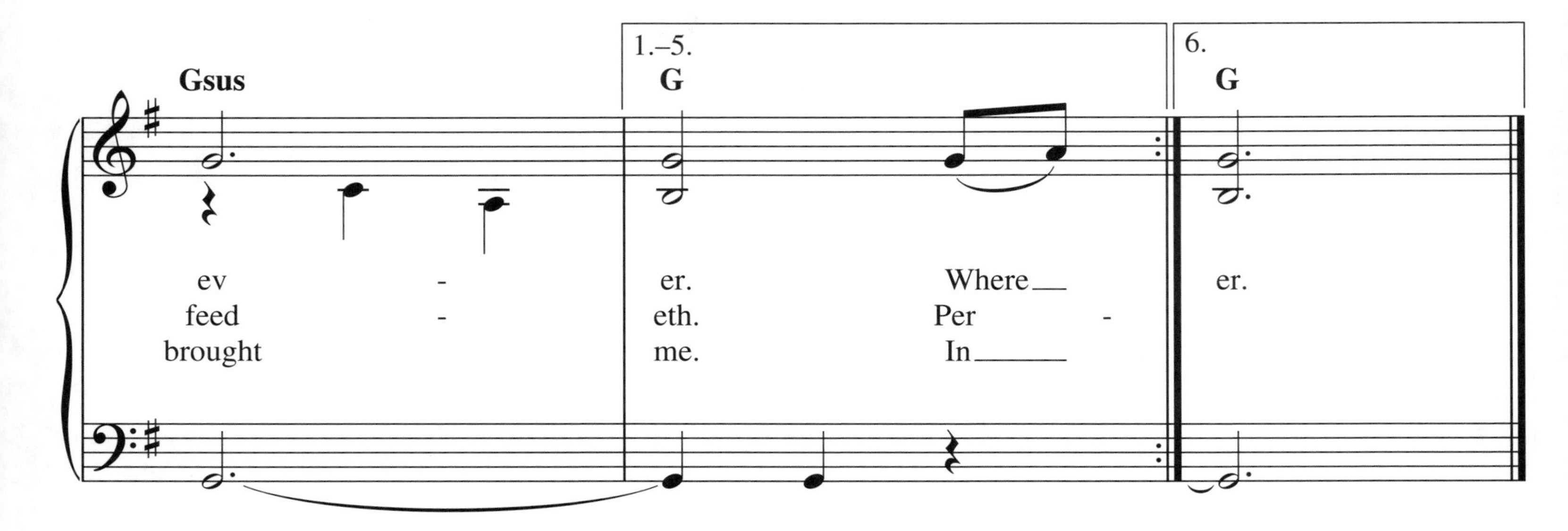

Additional Verses

4. In death's dark vale I fear no ill
   With Thee, dear Lord beside me.
   Thy rod and staff my comfort still,
   Thy cross before to guide me.

5. Thou spreadst a table in my sight,
   Thine unction grace bestoweth.
   And O what transport of delight
   From Thy pure chalice floweth!

6. And so through all the length of days
   Thy goodness faileth never.
   Good Shepherd may I sing Thy praise
   Within Thy house forever.

LEAD ON, O KING ETERNAL

Words by ERNEST W. SHURTLEFF
Music by HENRY T. SMART

LEANING ON THE EVERLASTING ARMS

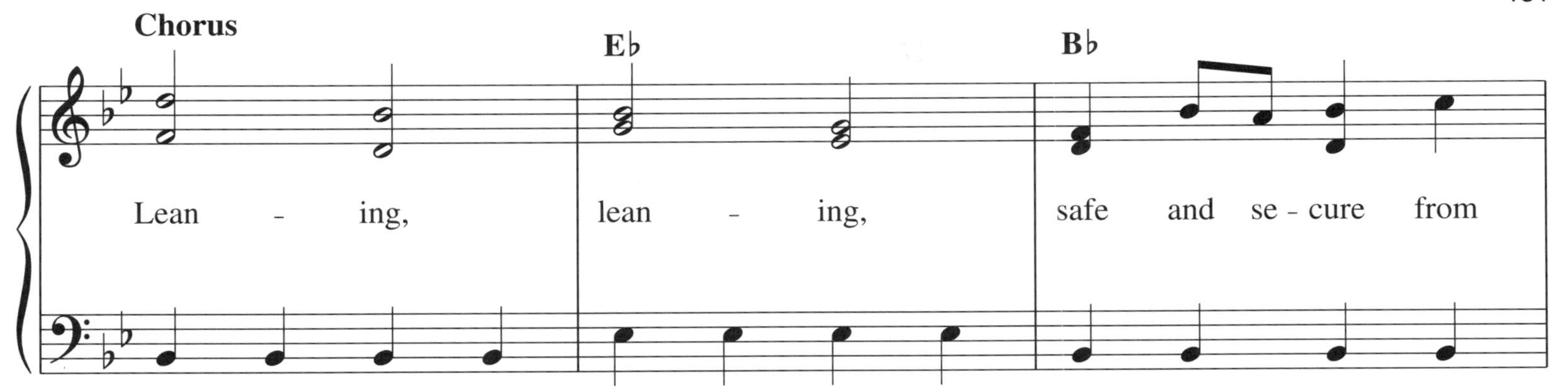

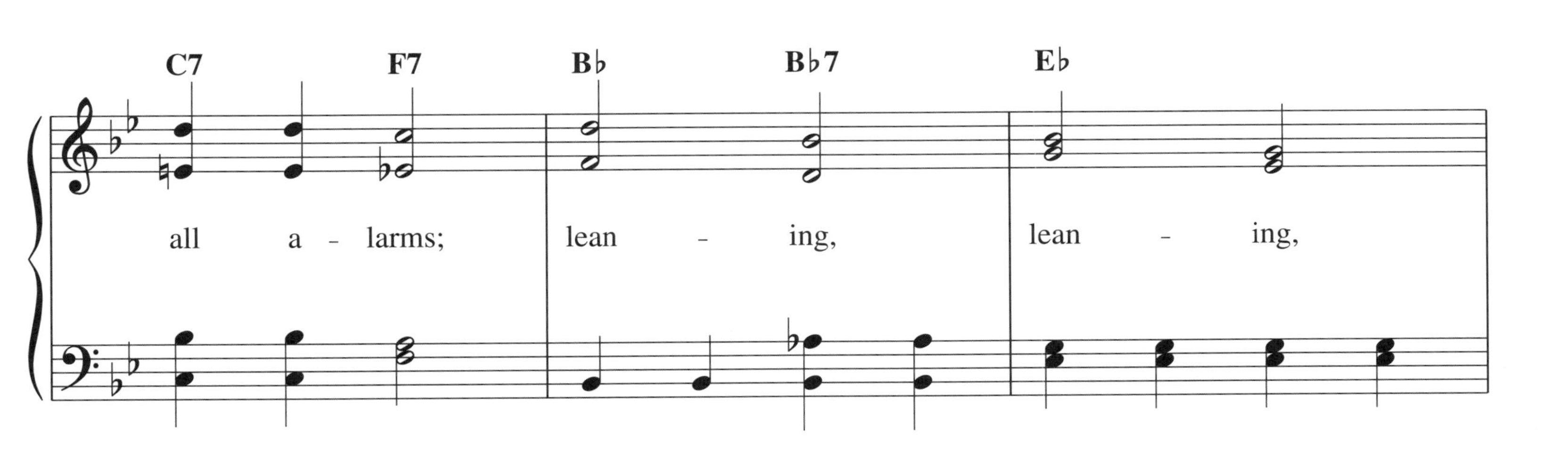

Additional Verse

3. What have I to dread, what have I to fear,
   Leaning on the everlasting arms?
   I have blessed peace with my Lord so near,
   Leaning on the everlasting arms.
   Chorus

LET ALL MORTAL FLESH KEEP SILENCE

Words from the *Liturgy of St. James*
Translated by GERARD MOULTRIE
17th Century French Carol

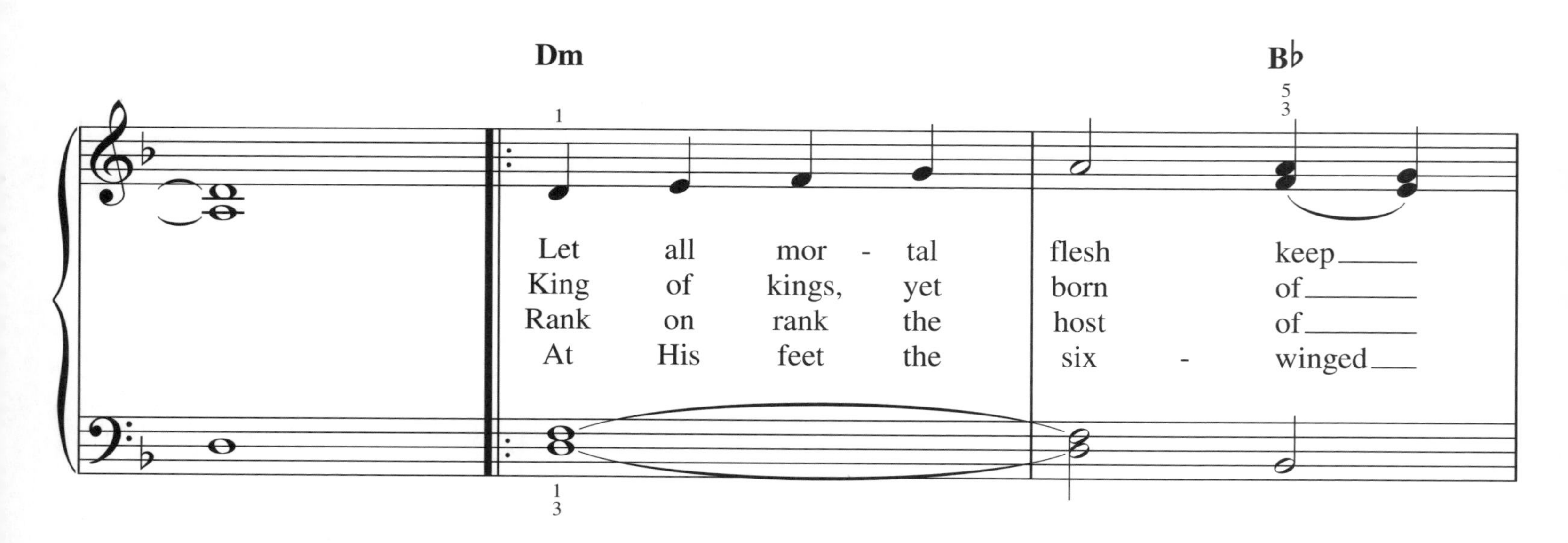

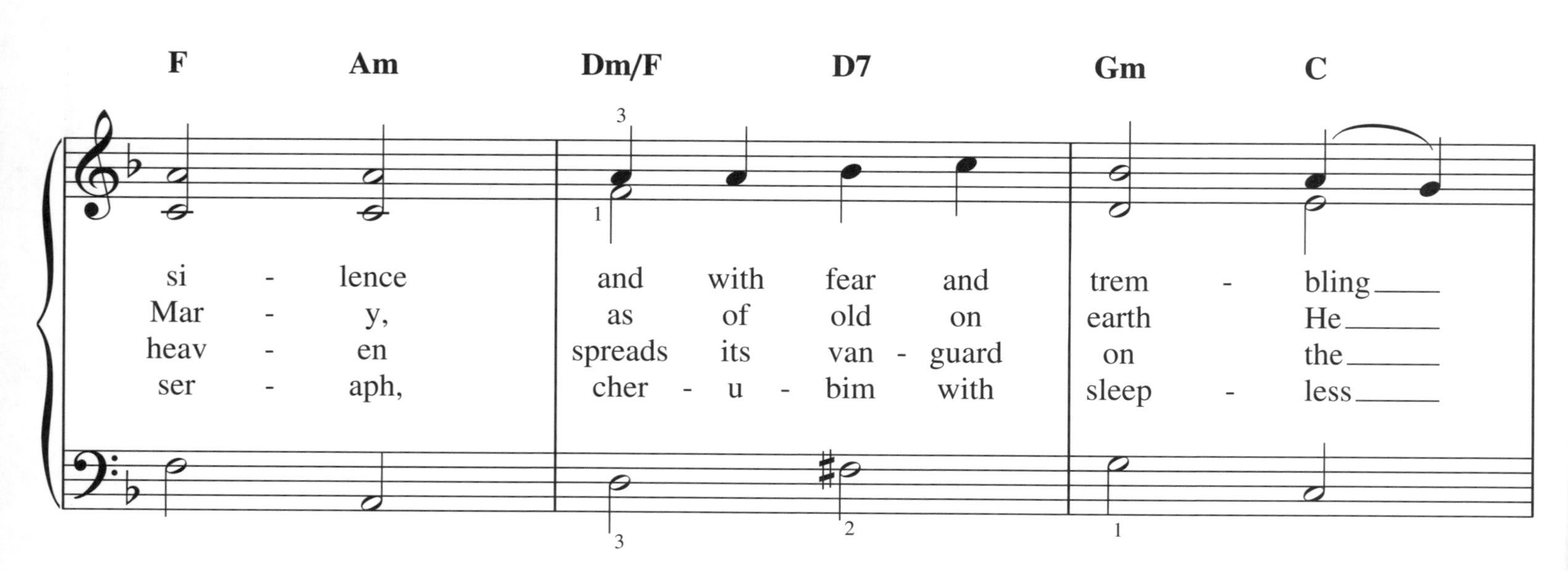

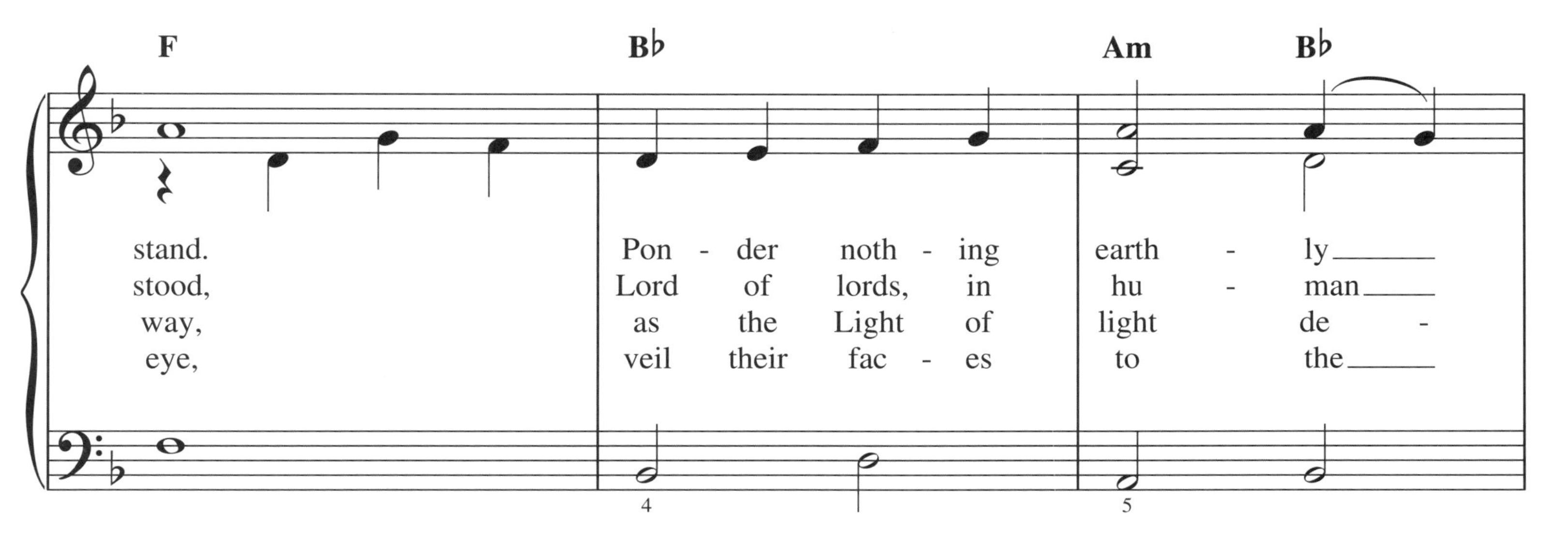
F
B♭
Am
B♭
stand. Pon - der noth - ing earth - ly
stood, Lord of lords, in hu - man
way, as the Light of light de -
eye, veil their fac - es to the
4
5

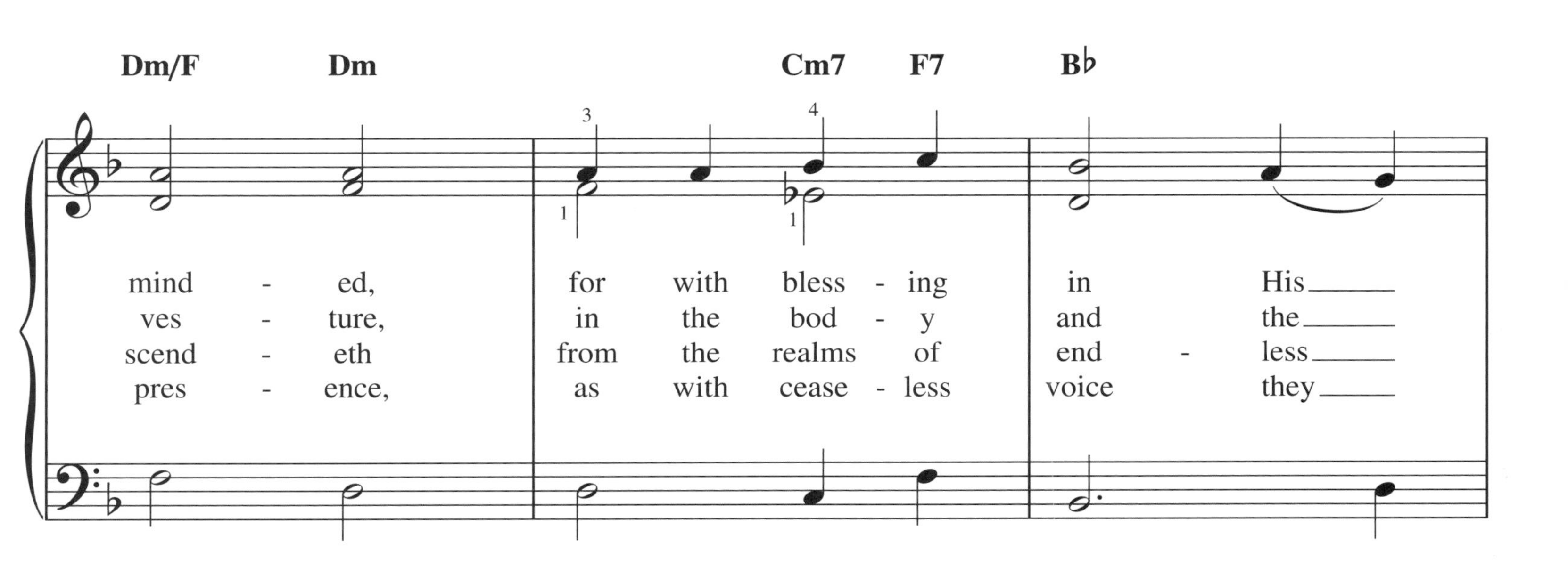
Dm/F
Dm
Cm7
F7
B♭
3
4
1
1
mind - ed, for with bless - ing in His
ves - ture, in the bod - y and the
scend - eth from the realms of end - less
pres - ence, as with cease - less voice they

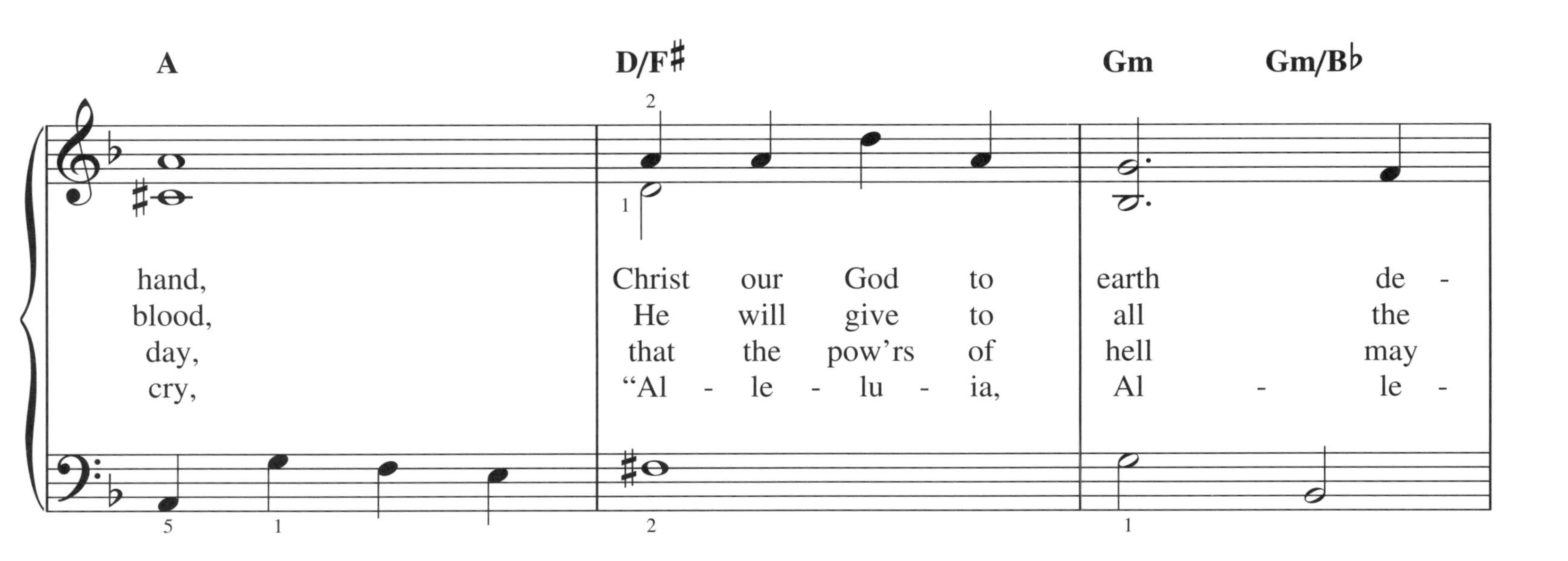
A
D/F♯
Gm
Gm/B♭
2
1
hand, Christ our God to earth de -
blood, He will give to all the
day, that the pow'rs of hell may
cry, "Al - le - lu - ia, Al - le -
5
1
2
1

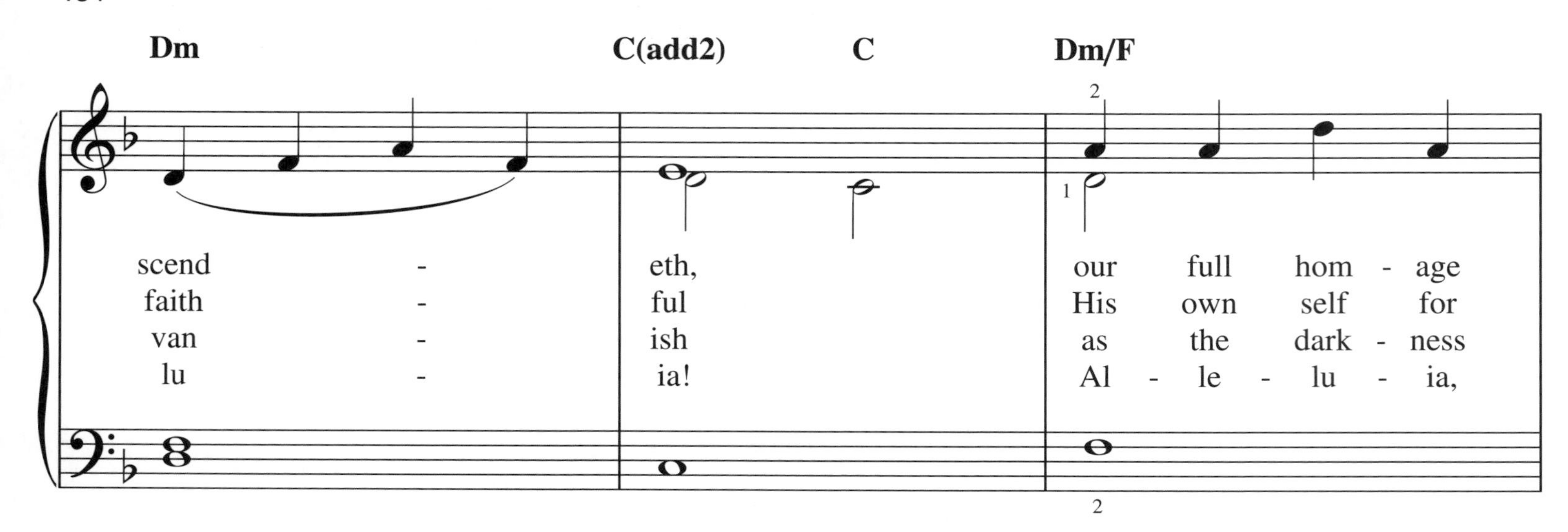
Dm
C(add2)
C
Dm/F
scend - eth, our full hom - age
faith - ful His own self for
van - ish as the dark - ness
lu - ia! Al - le - lu - ia,

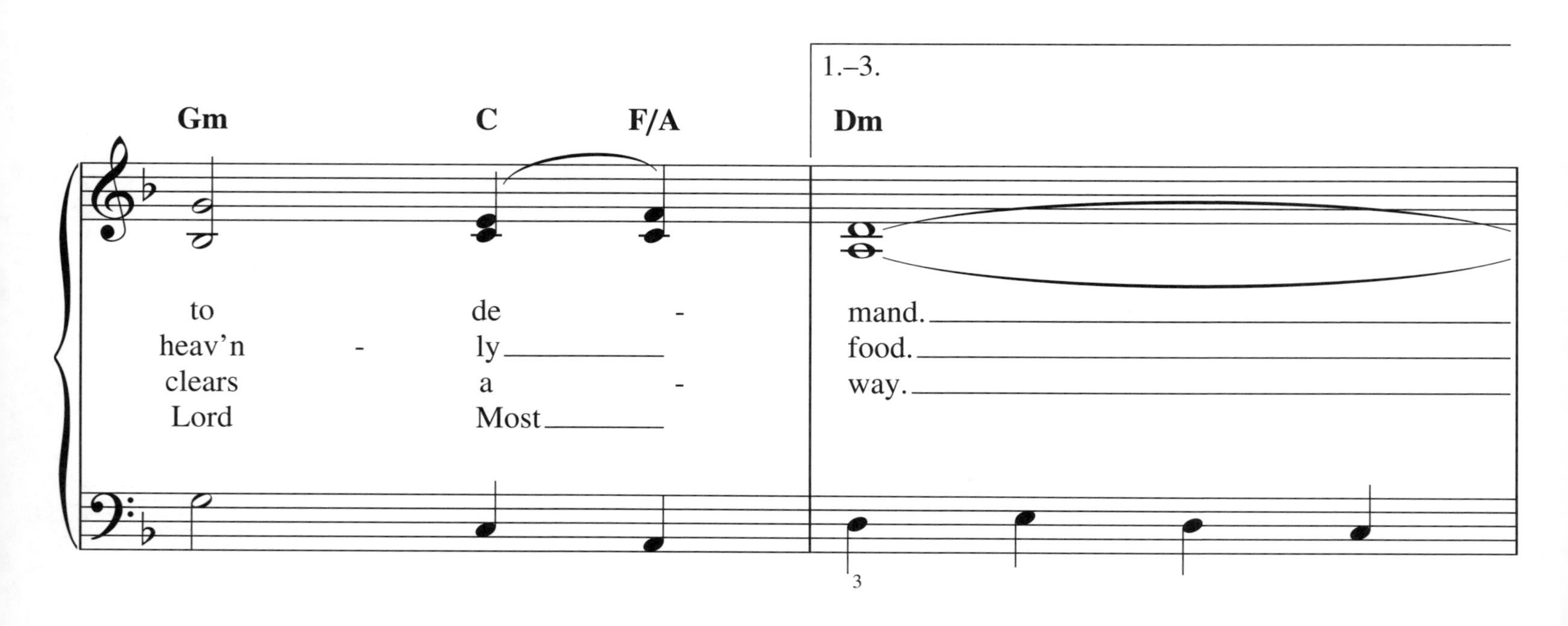
1.–3.
Gm
C
F/A
Dm
to de - mand.
heav'n - ly food.
clears a - way.
Lord Most

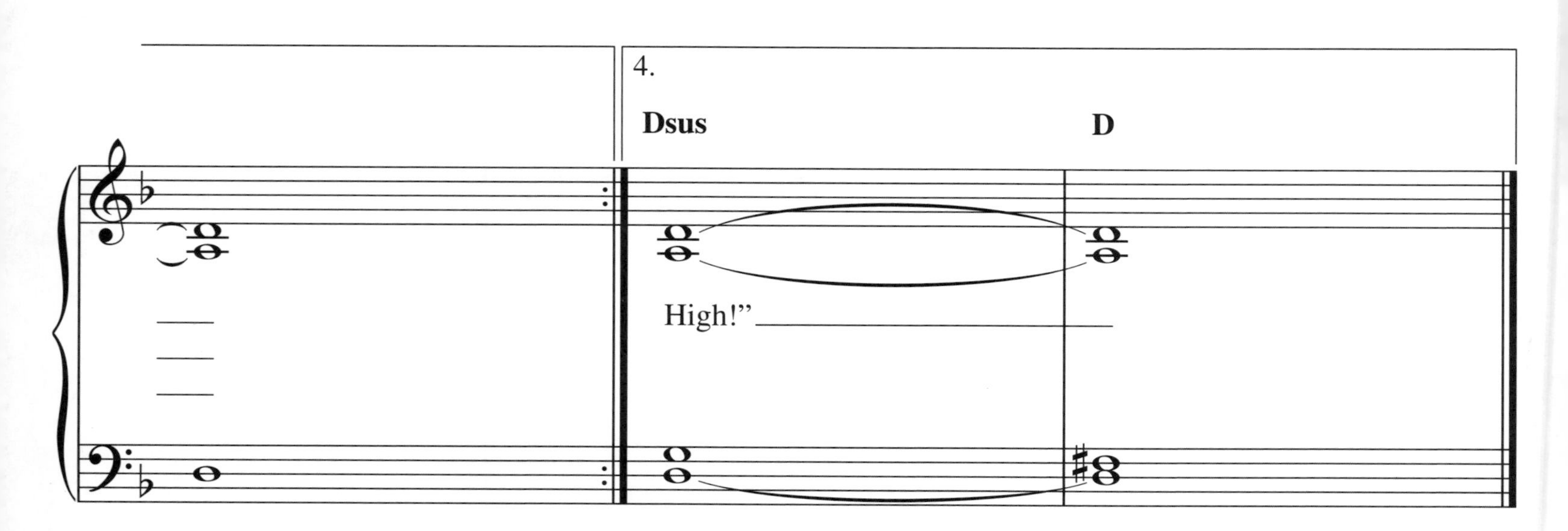
4.
Dsus
D
High!"

LET US BREAK BREAD TOGETHER

Traditional Spiritual

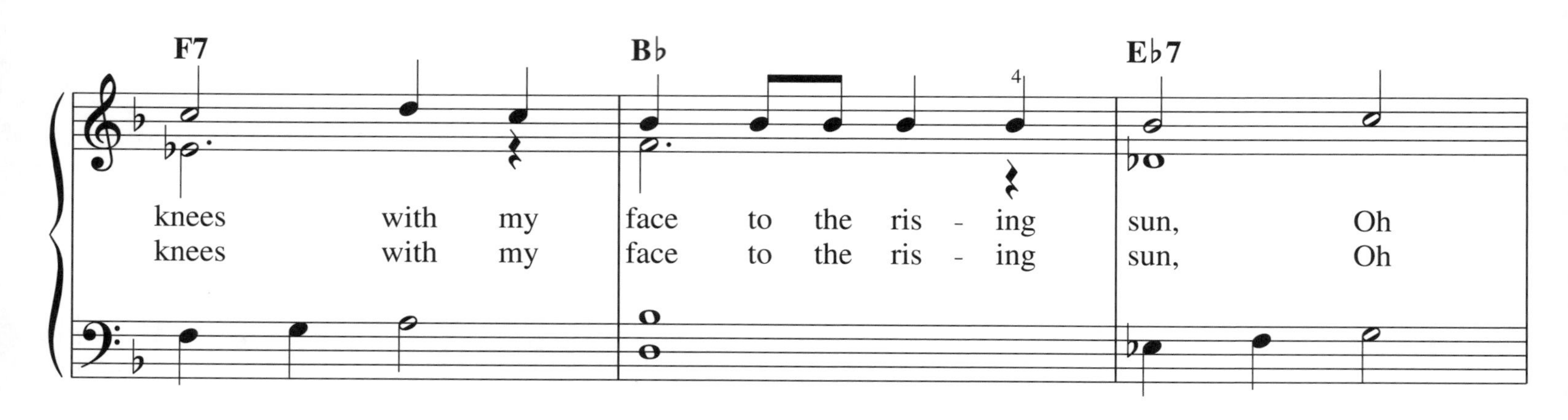
F7
B♭
E♭7
knees with my face to the ris - ing sun, Oh
knees with my face to the ris - ing sun, Oh

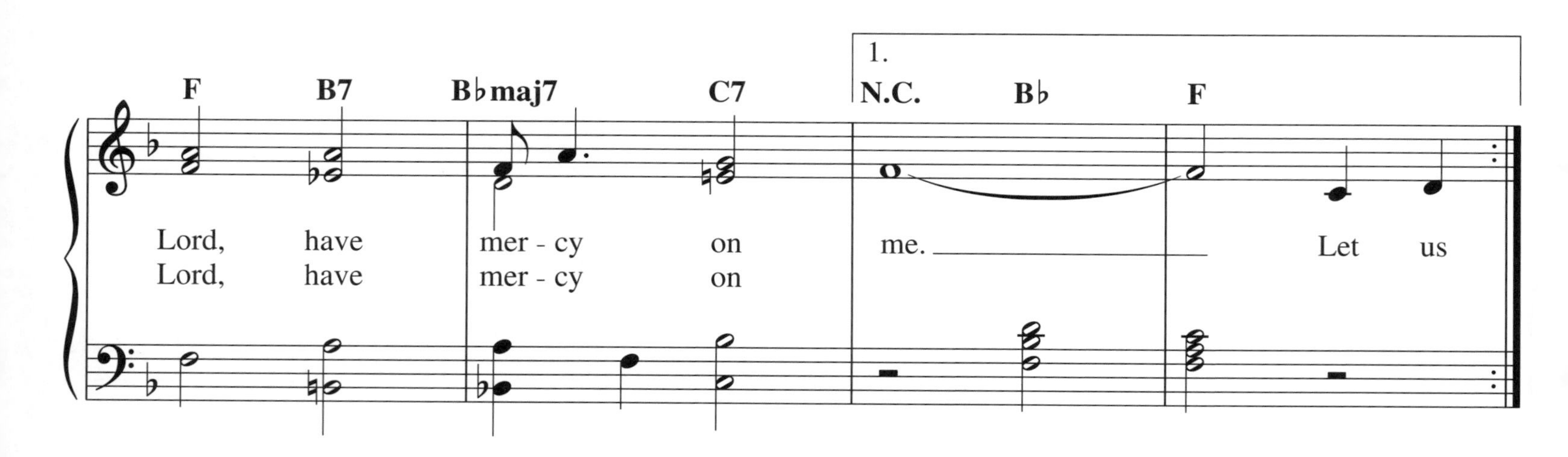
1.
F
B7
B♭maj7
C7
N.C.
B♭
F
Lord, have mer - cy on me. Let us
Lord, have mer - cy on

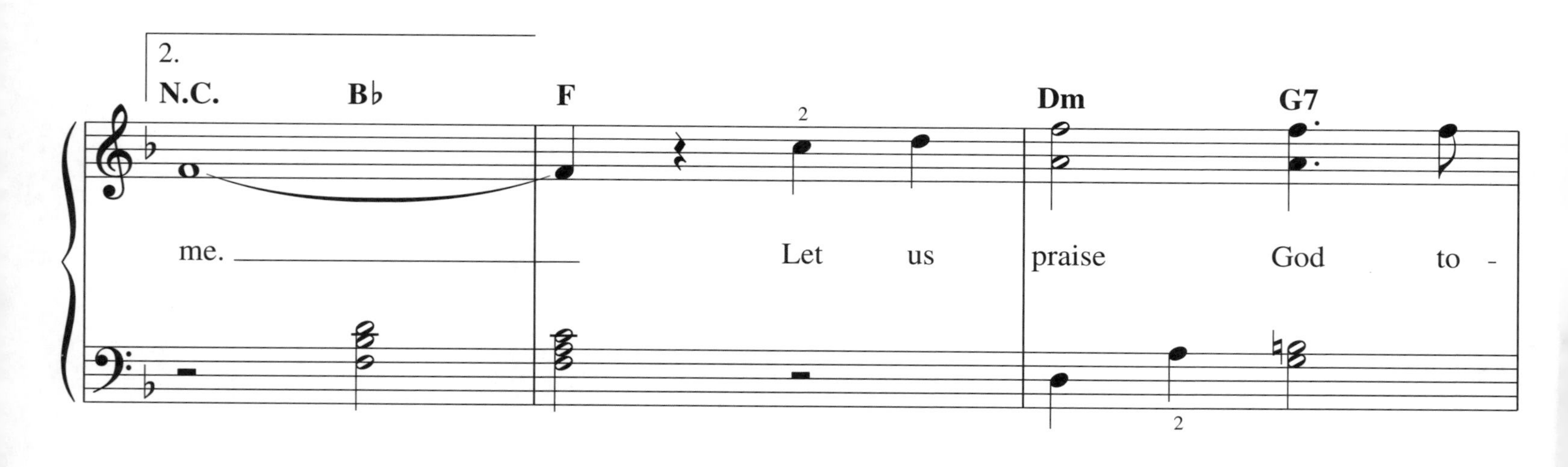
2.
N.C.
B♭
F
Dm
G7
me. Let us praise God to -

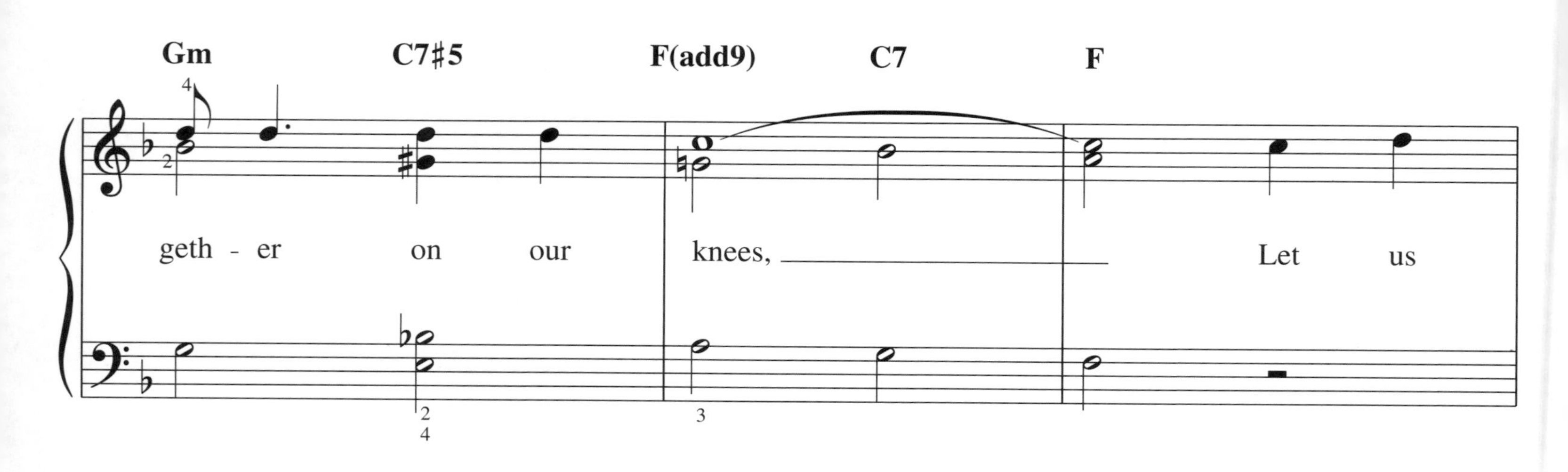
Gm
C7♯5
F(add9)
C7
F
geth - er on our knees, Let us

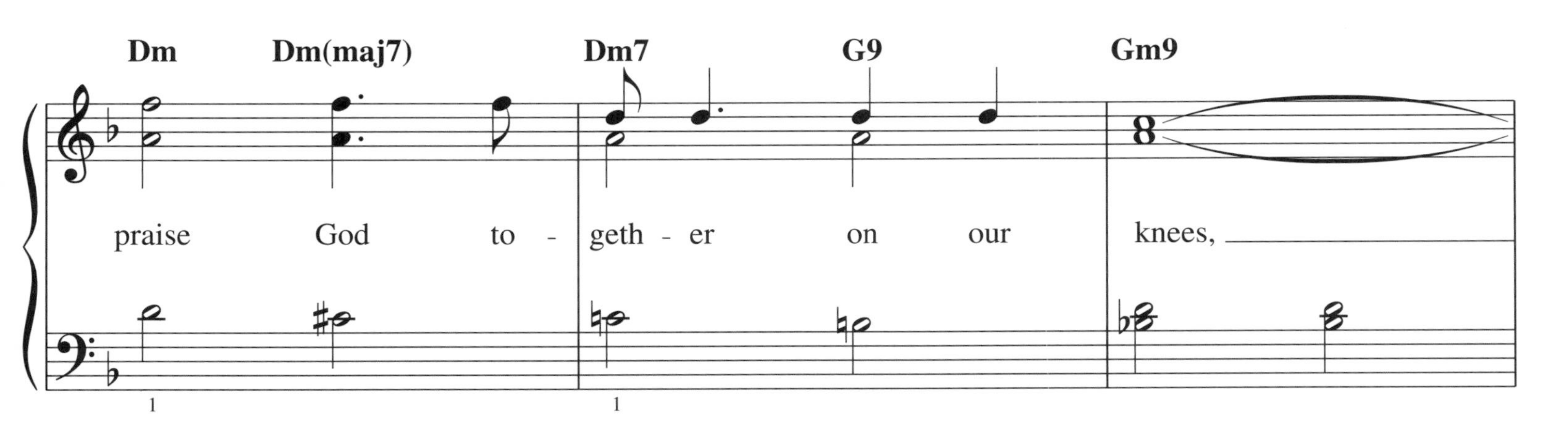
Dm
Dm(maj7)
Dm7
G9
Gm9
praise God to - geth - er on our knees,

C7
N.C.
F
E+
Cm/E♭
D7
Oh, When I fall on my knees with my

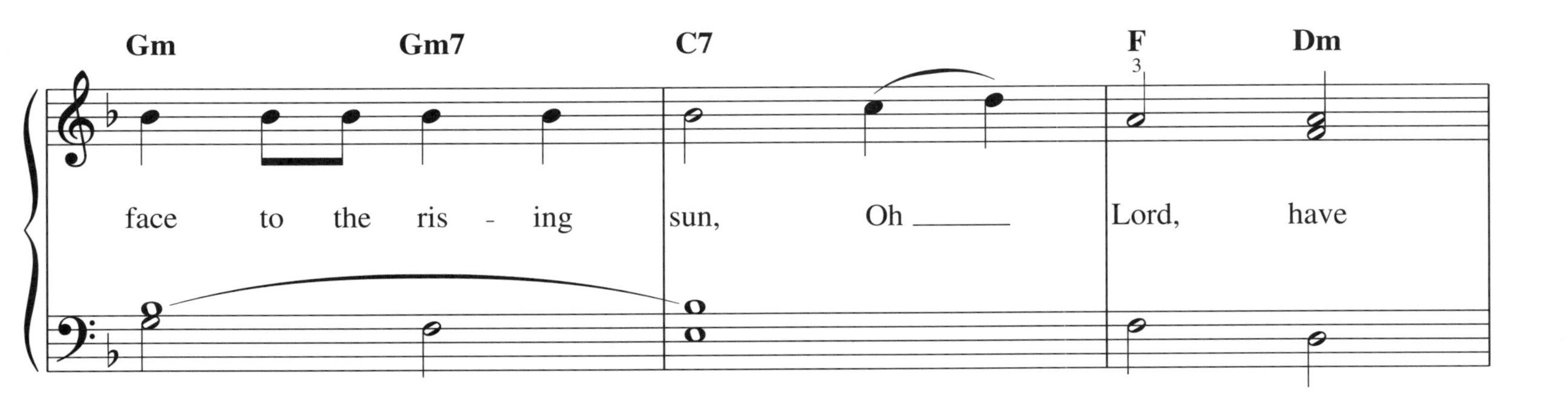
Gm
Gm7
C7
F
Dm
face to the ris - ing sun, Oh Lord, have

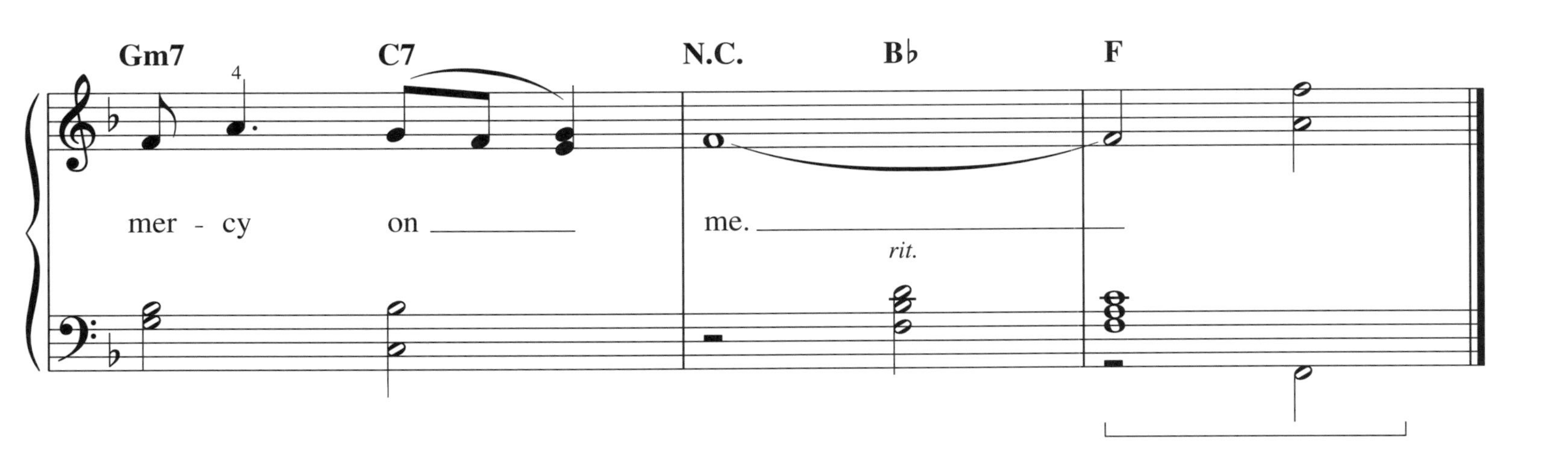
Gm7
C7
N.C.
B♭
F
mer - cy on me.
rit.

A MIGHTY FORTRESS IS OUR GOD

Words and Music by MARTIN LUTHER
Translated by FREDERICK H. HEDGE
Based on Psalm 46

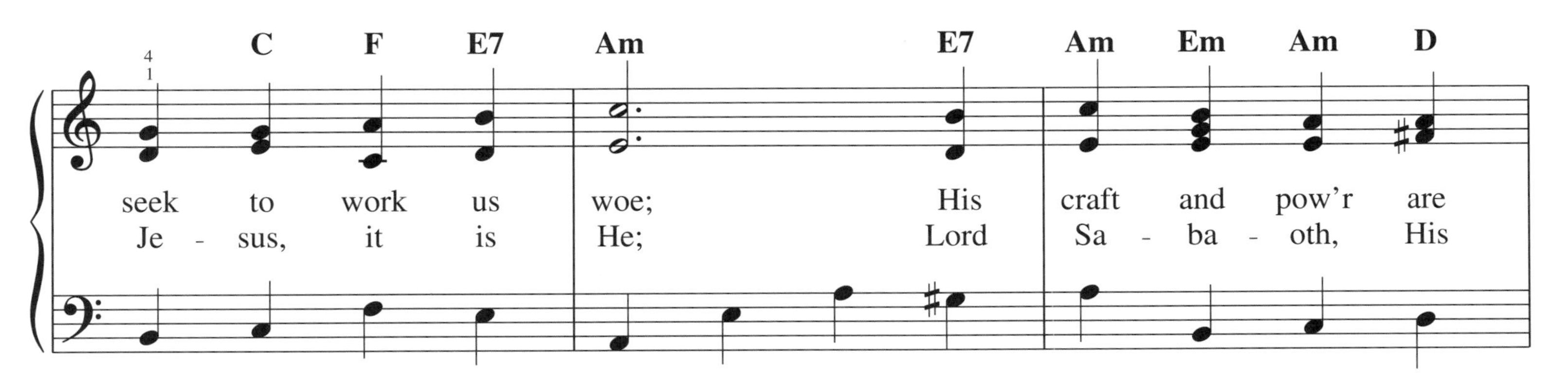

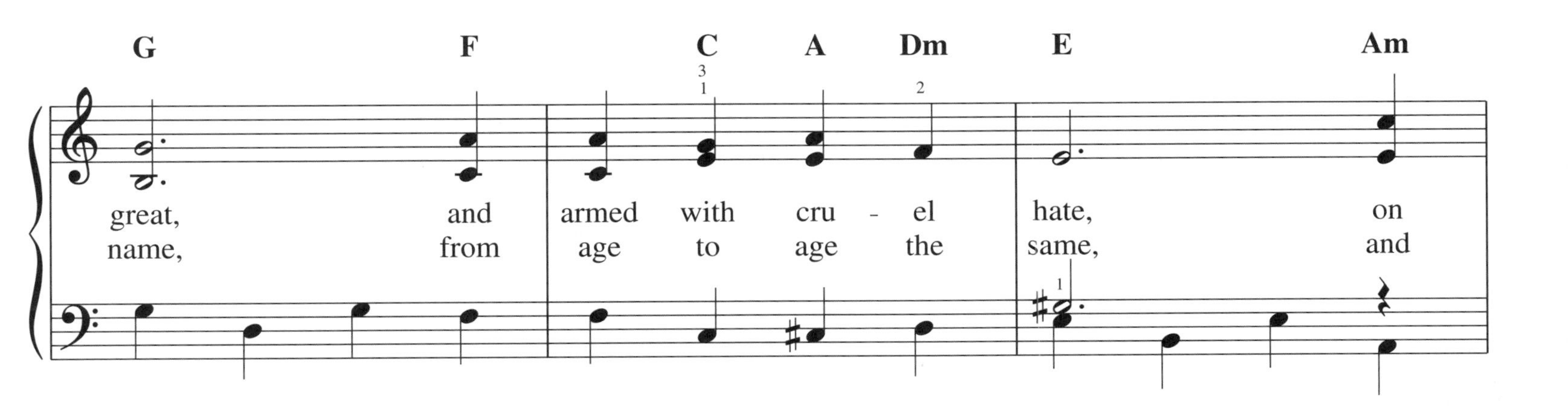

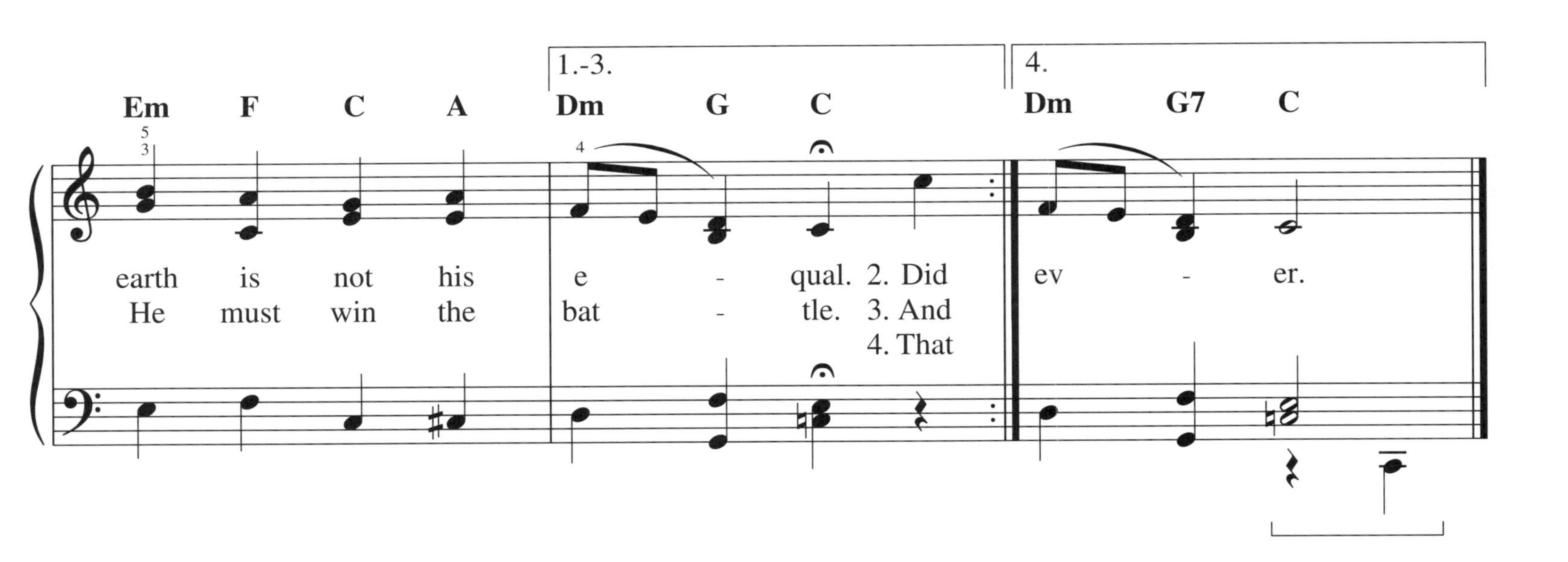

Additional Verses

3. And though this world, with devils filled,
Should threaten to undo us,
We will not fear, for God hath willed
His truth to triumph through us.
The Prince of Darkness grim,
We tremble not for him;
His rage we can endure,
For lo, his doom is sure;
One little word shall fell him.

4. That word above all earthly powers,
No thanks to them, abideth.
The Spirit and the gifts are ours,
Through Him who with us sideth.
Let goods and kindred go,
This mortal life also.
The body they may kill;
God's truth abideth still;
His kingdom is forever.

MORE LOVE TO THEE

Words by ELIZABETH PAYSON PRENTISS
Music by WILLIAM H. DOANE

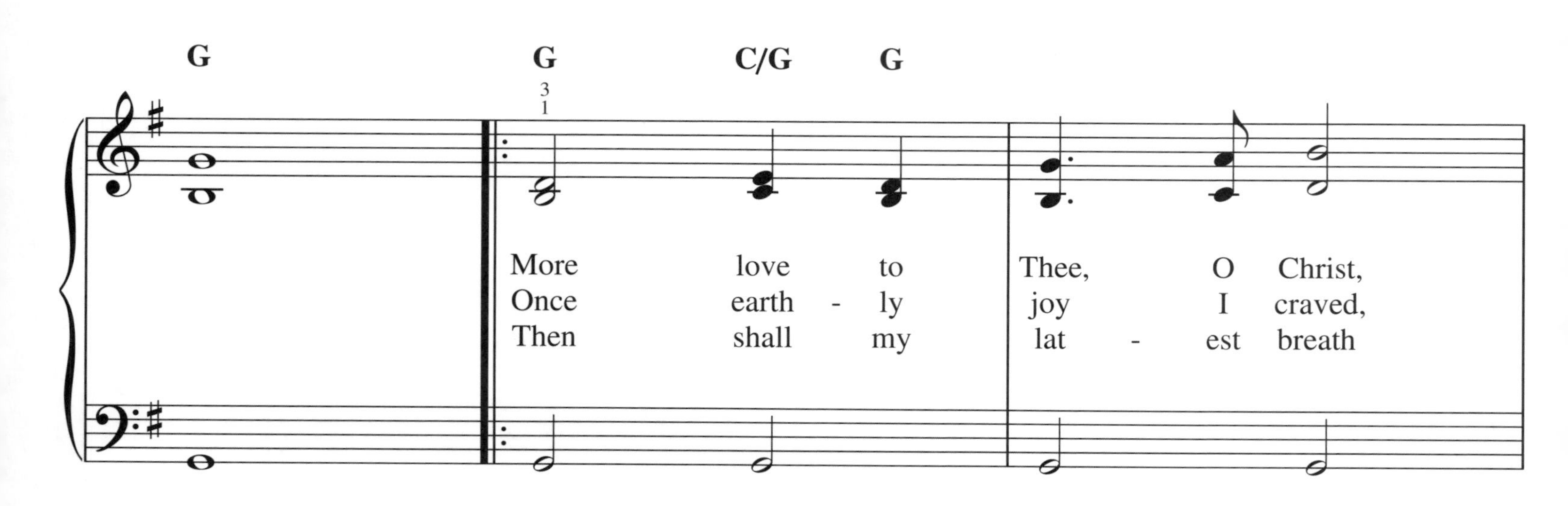

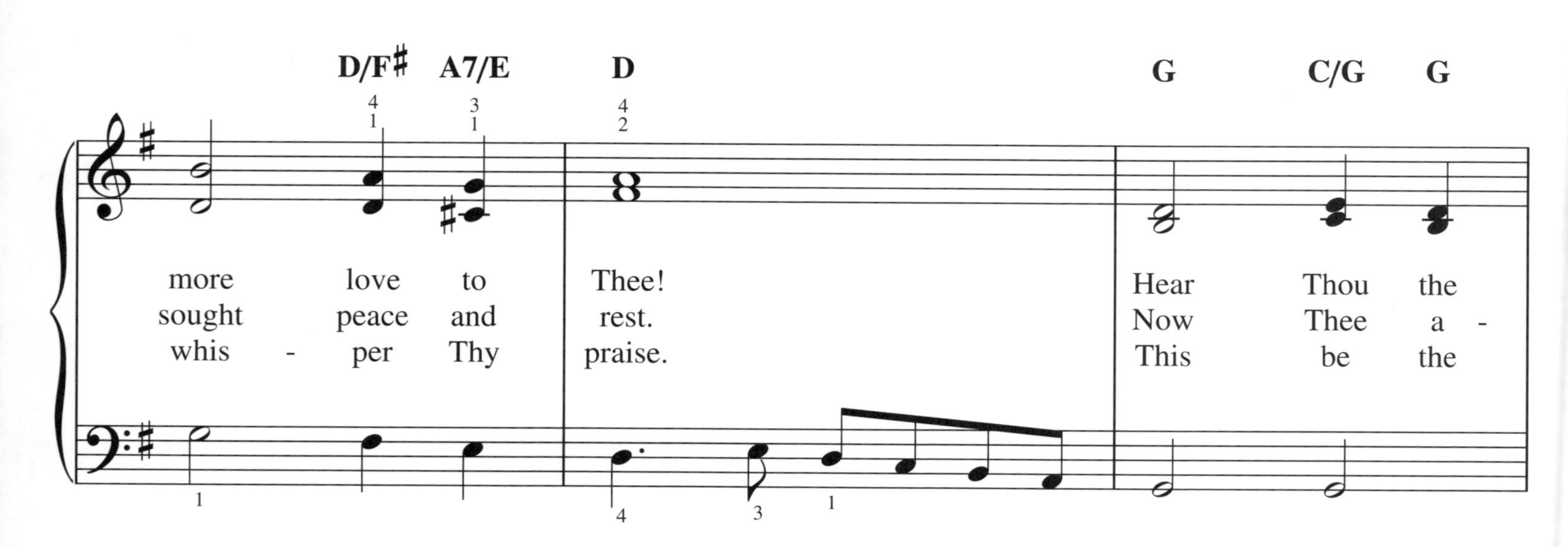

Am/C G/D D7 G
prayer I make on bend - ed knee.
lone I seek; give what is best.
part - ing cry my heart shall raise.
C C/G G D
This is my ear - nest plea:
This all my prayer shall be:
This still my prayer shall be:
More love, O
G C G/B
Christ to Thee, more love to Thee,
Am/C G/D D7
1., 2.
G
3.
Gsus G
more love to Thee!
Thee!

MUST JESUS BEAR THE CROSS ALONE

Words by THOMAS SHEPHERD
Music by GEORGE N. ALLEN

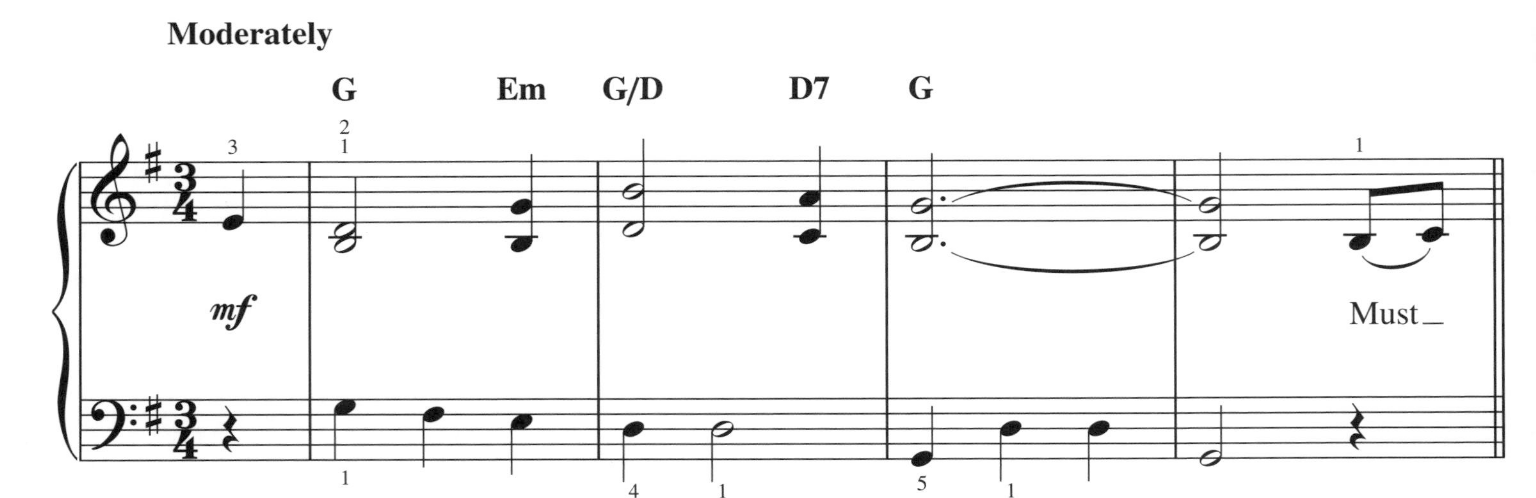

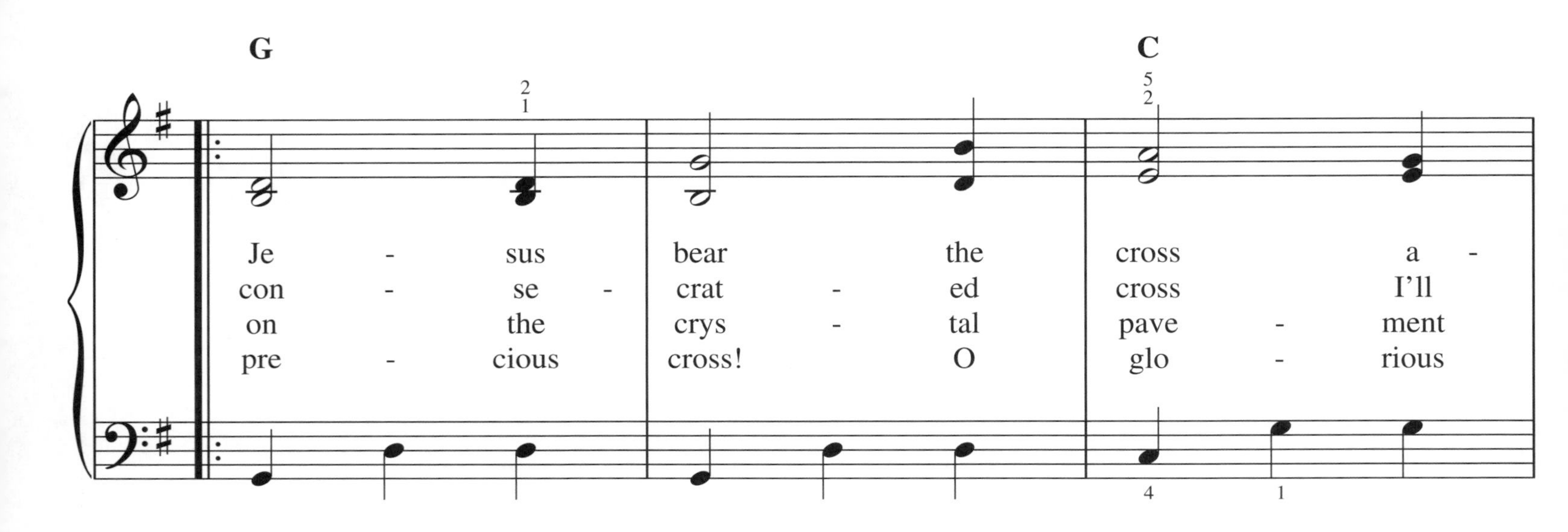

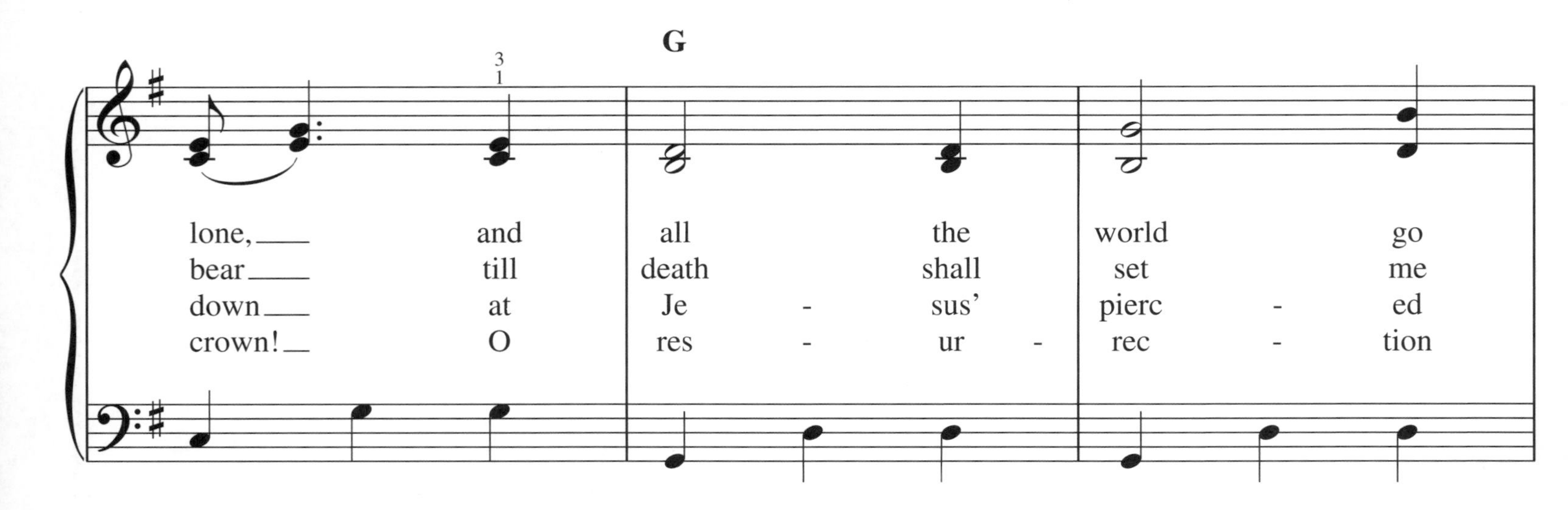

D
G
free? No, there's a
free, and then go
feet, joy - ful I'll
day! Ye an - gels,
C
cross for ev - 'ry - one, and
home, my crown to wear, for
cast my gold - en crown and
from the stars come down and
G Em G/D D7
1.–3.
G
there's a cross for me.
there's a crown for me.
His dear name re - peat.
bear my soul a -
The
Up -
O
4.
G
way.

MY FAITH LOOKS UP TO THEE

Words by RAY PALMER
Music by LOWELL MASON

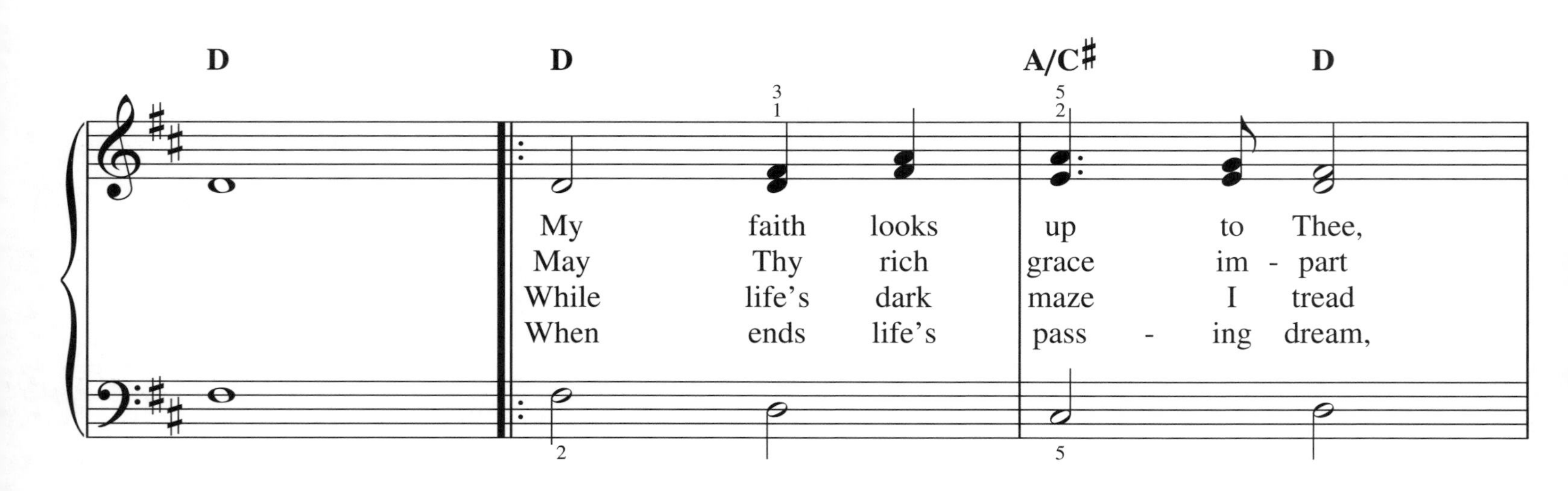

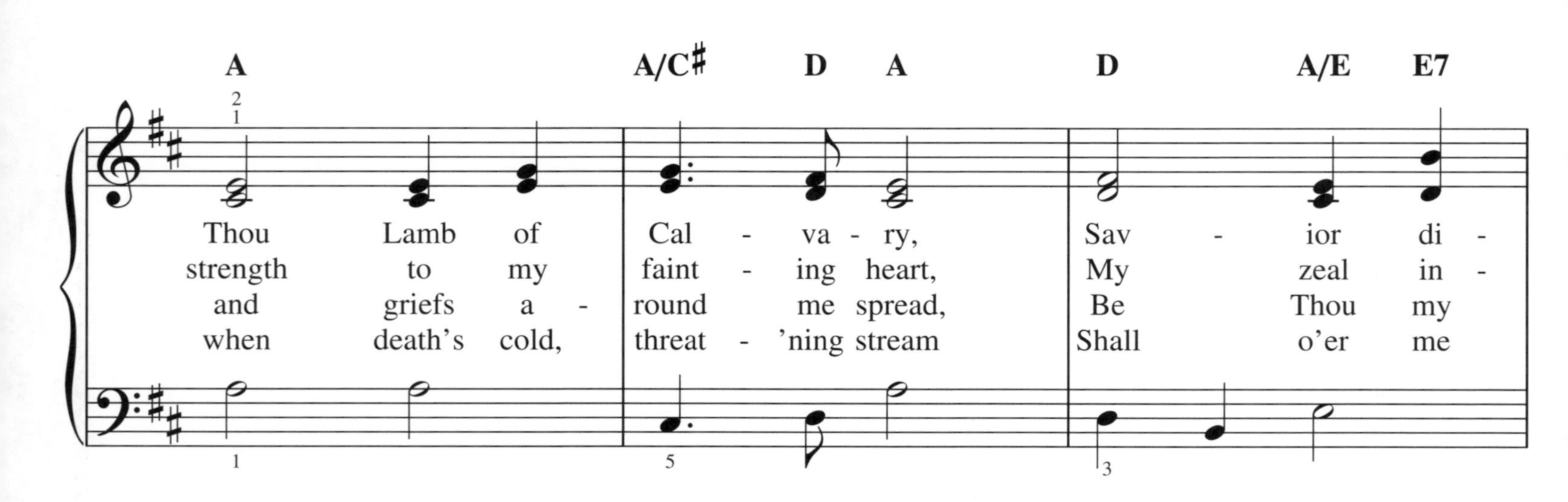

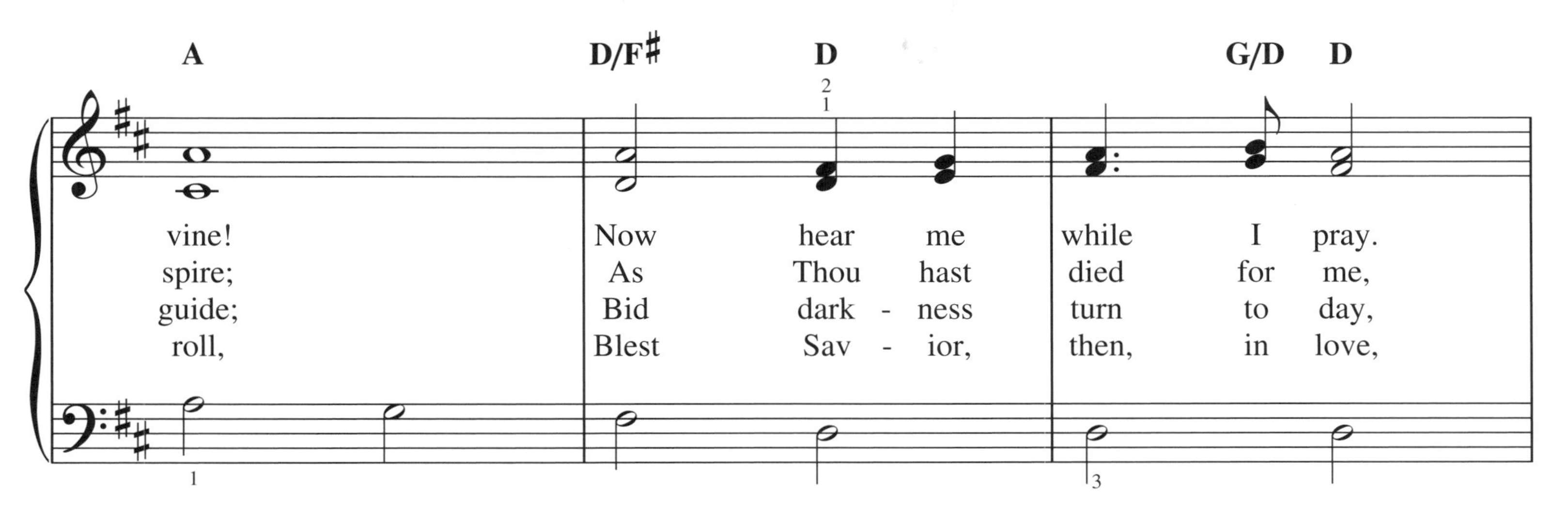
A D/F♯ D G/D D
vine! Now hear me while I pray.
spire; As Thou hast died for me,
guide; Bid dark - ness turn to day,
roll, Blest Sav - ior, then, in love,

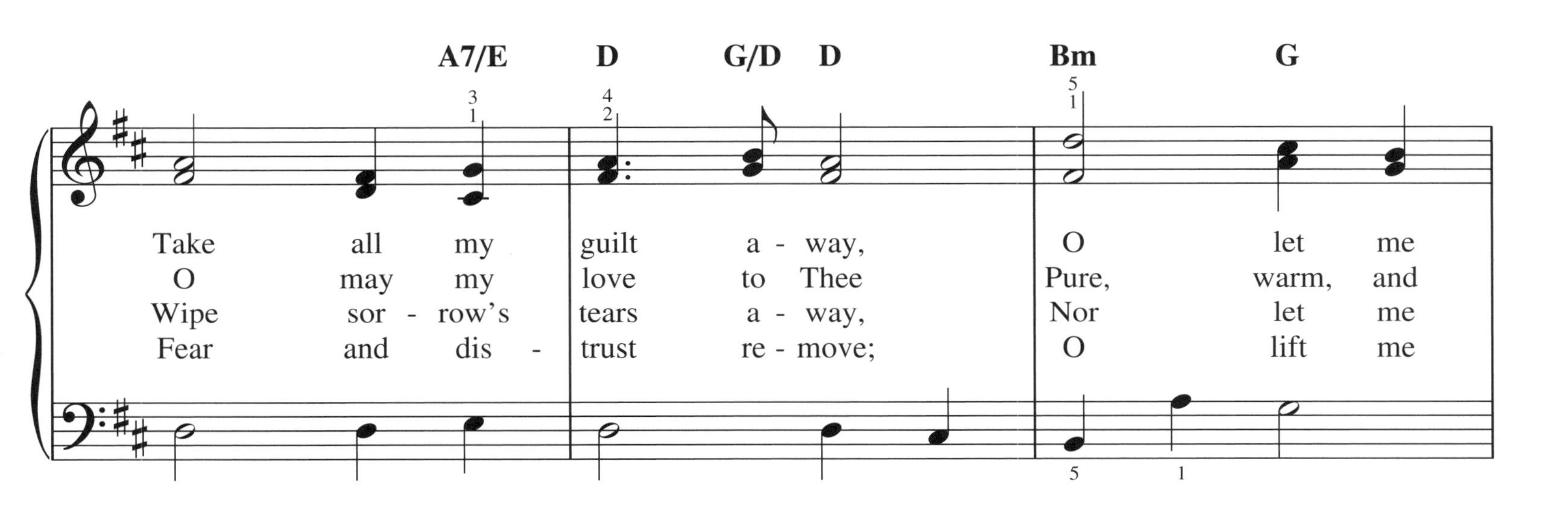
A7/E D G/D D Bm G
Take all my guilt a - way, O let me
O may my love to Thee Pure, warm, and
Wipe sor - row's tears a - way, Nor let me
Fear and dis - trust re - move; O lift me

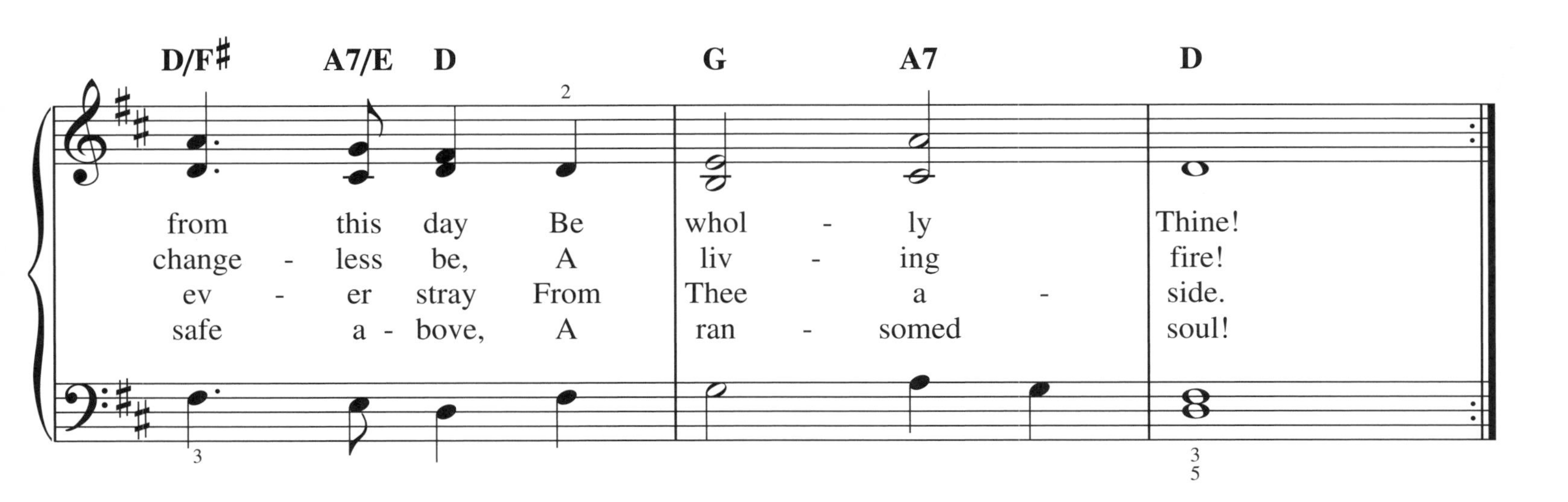
D/F♯ A7/E D G A7 D
from this day Be whol - ly Thine!
change - less be, A liv - ing fire!
ev - er stray From Thee a - side.
safe a - bove, A ran - somed soul!

MY JESUS, I LOVE THEE

Words by WILLIAM R. FEATHERSTONE
Music by ADONIRAM J. GORDON

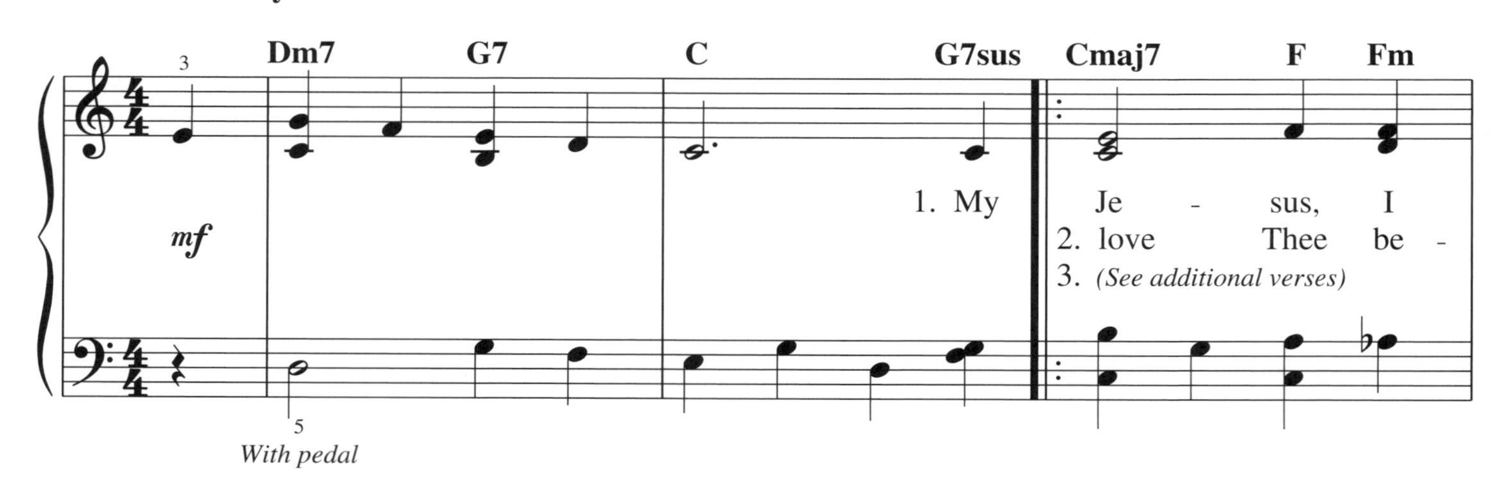

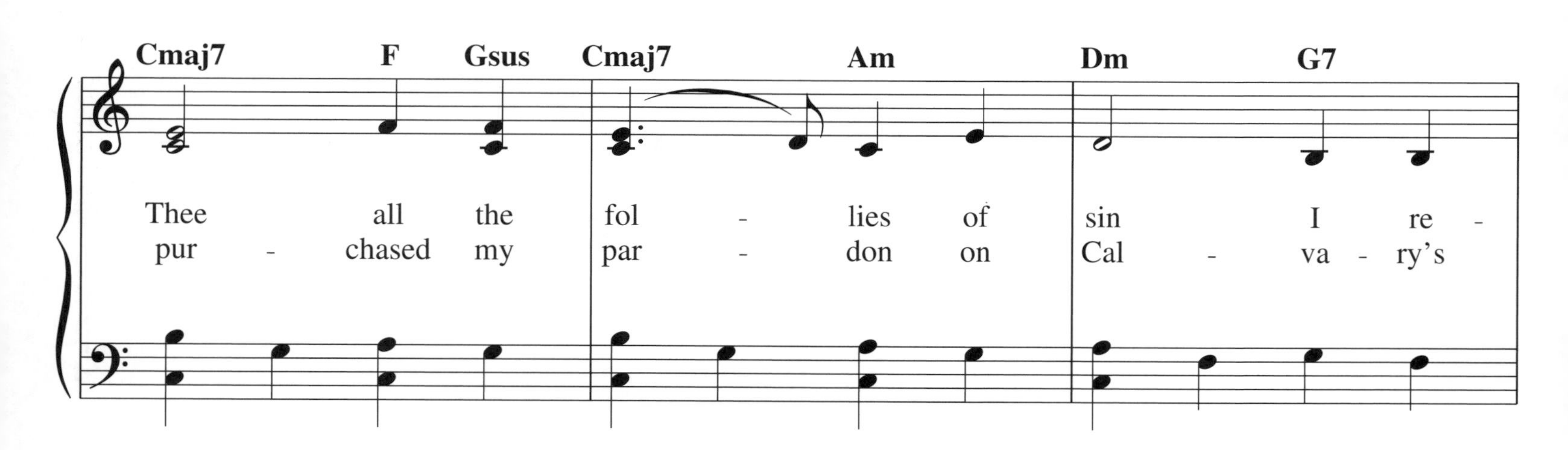

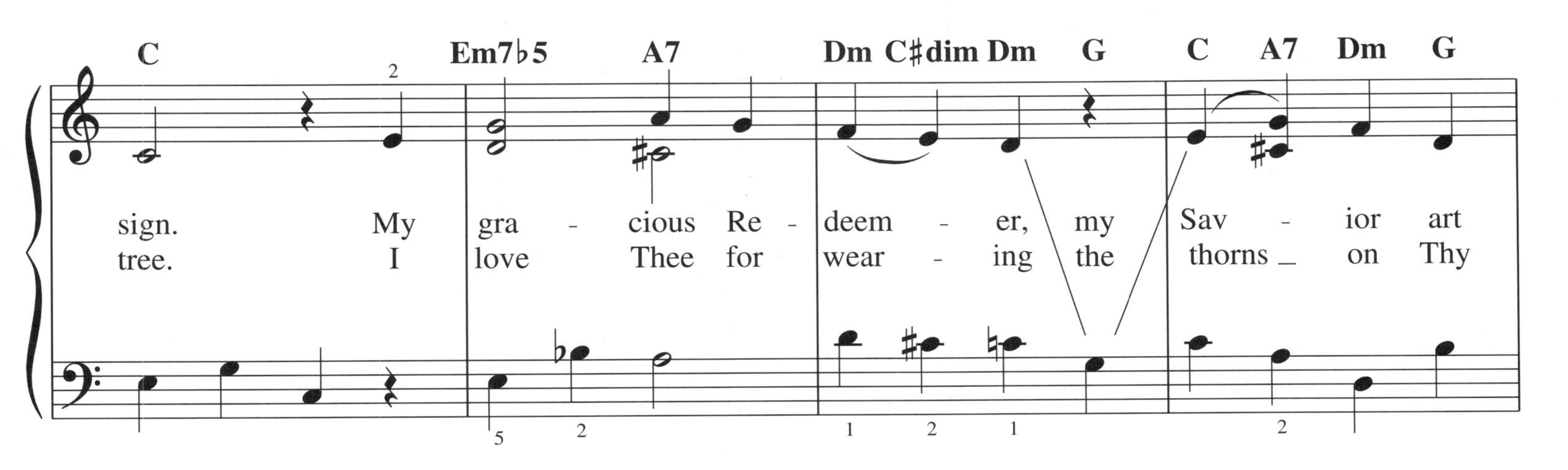

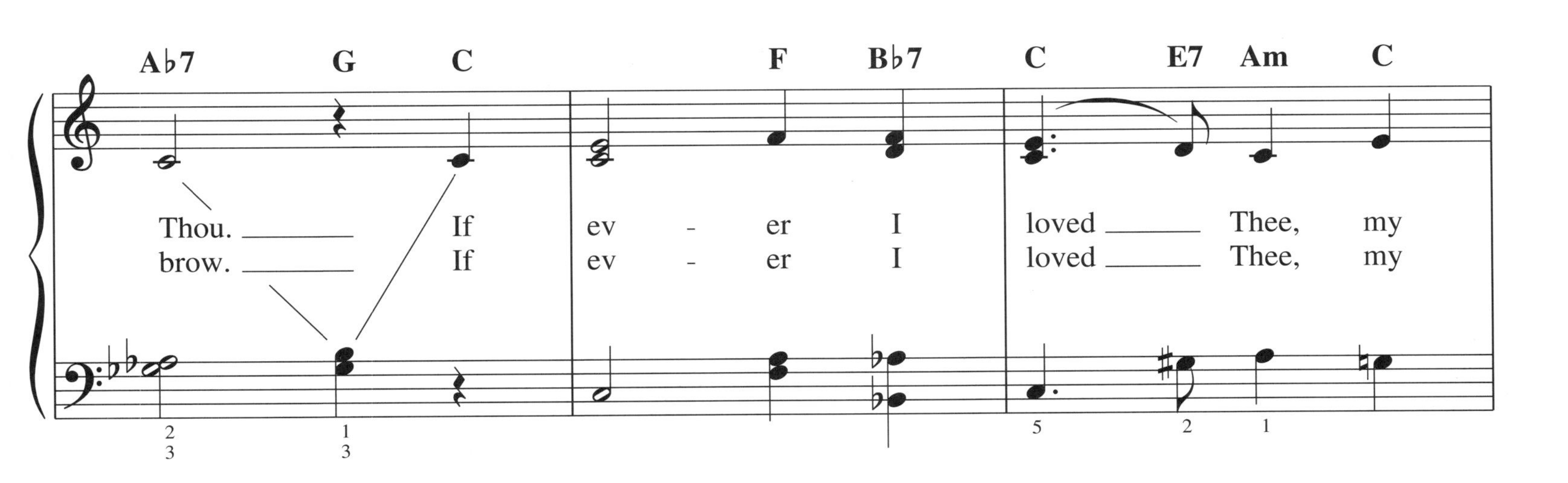

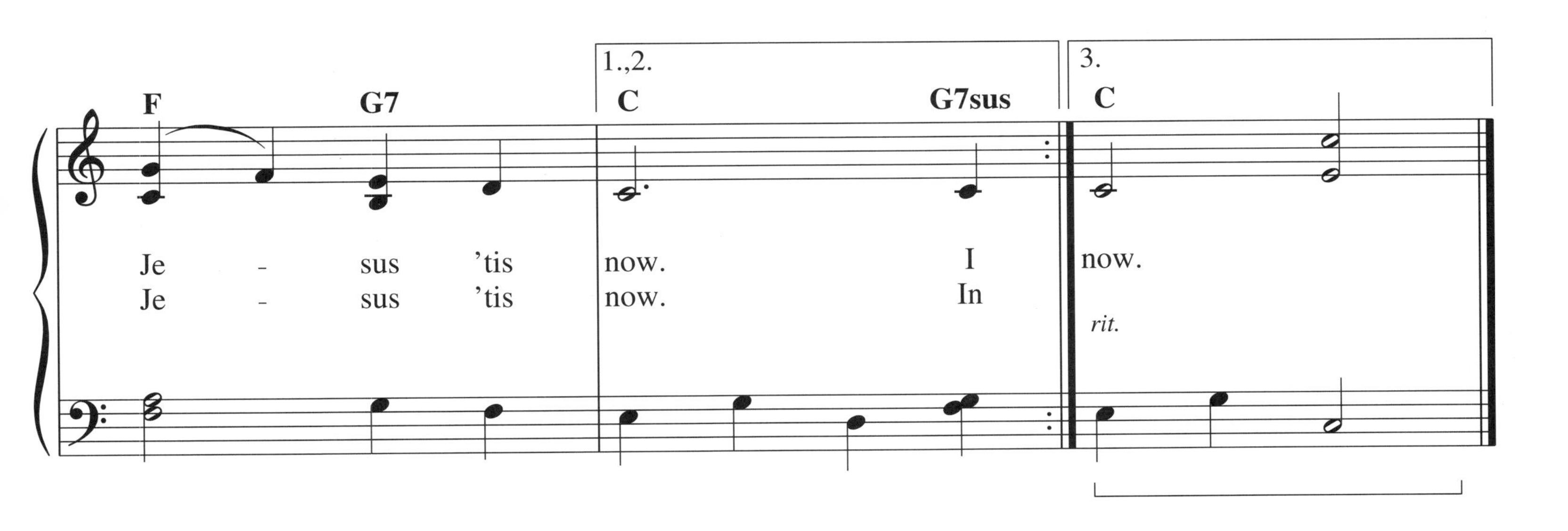

Additional Verses

3. In mansions of glory and endless delight,
   I'll ever adore Thee in heaven so bright.
   I'll sing with the glittering crown on my brow.
   If ever I loved Thee, my Jesus 'tis now.

NEAREER, MY GOD, TO THEE

Words by SARAH F. ADAMS
Based on Genesis 28:10-22
Music by LOWELL MASON

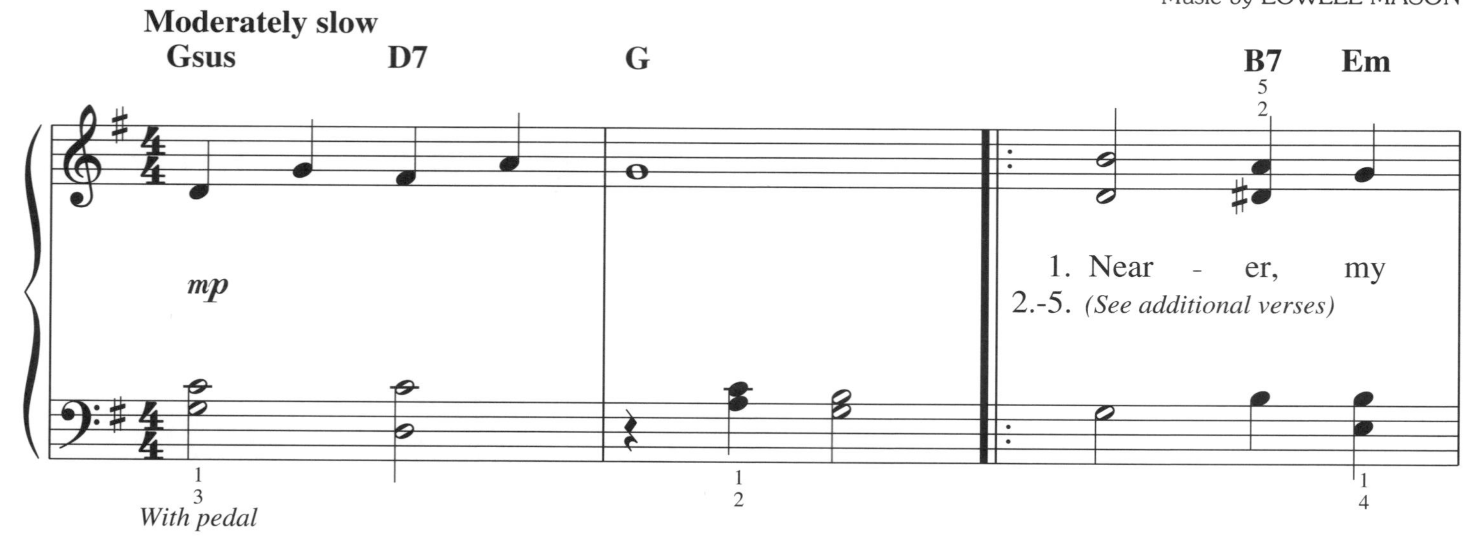

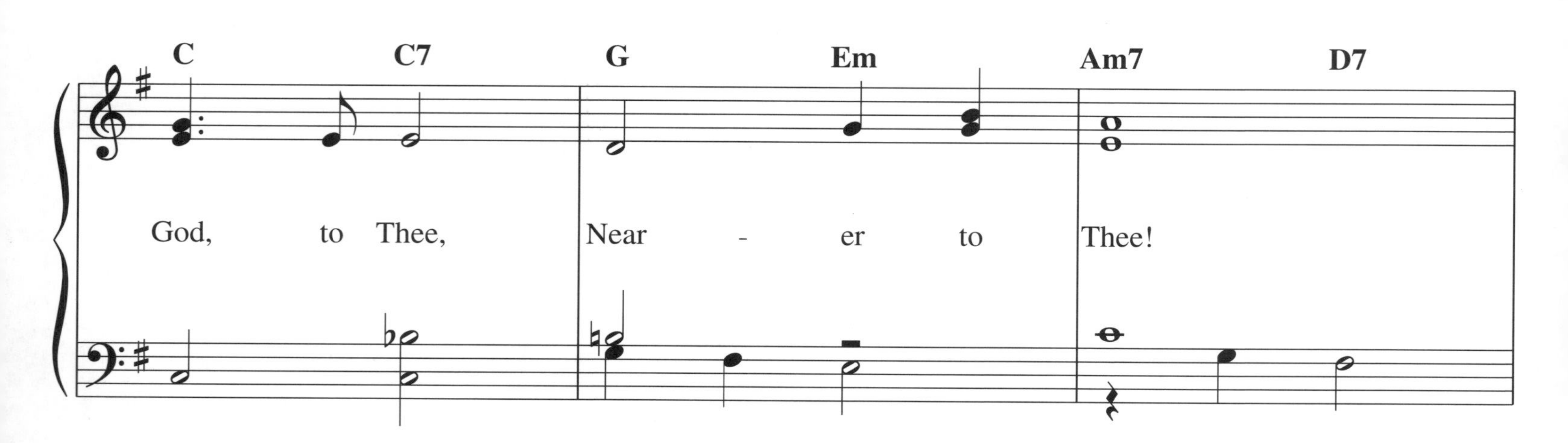

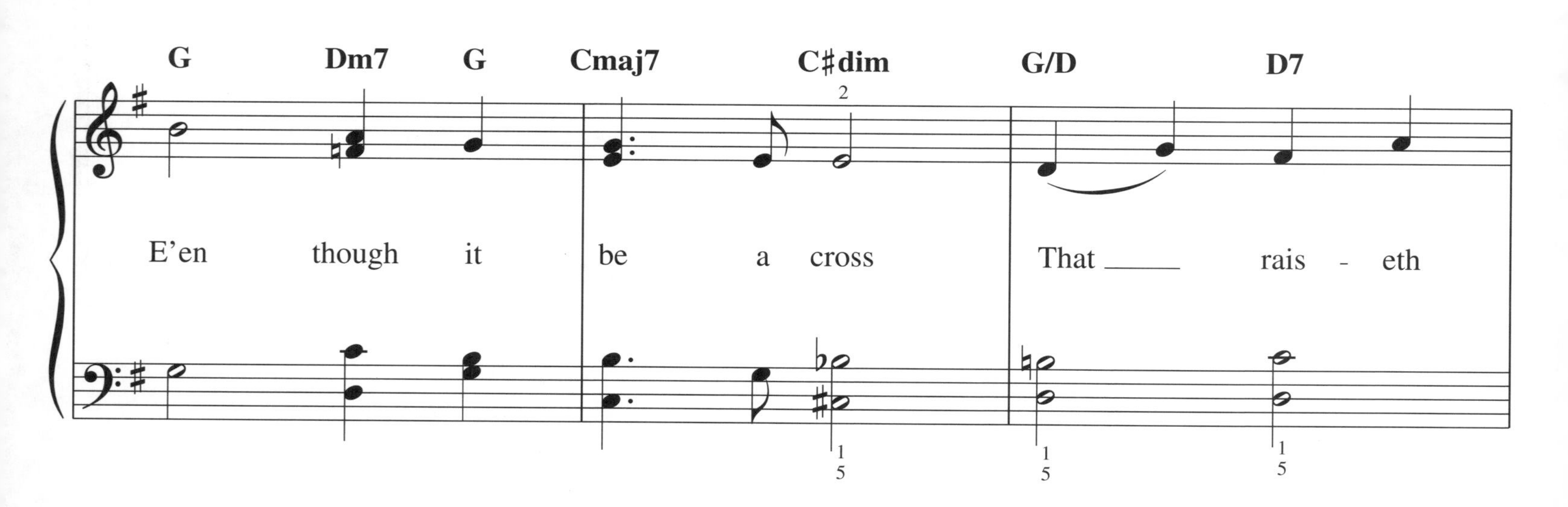

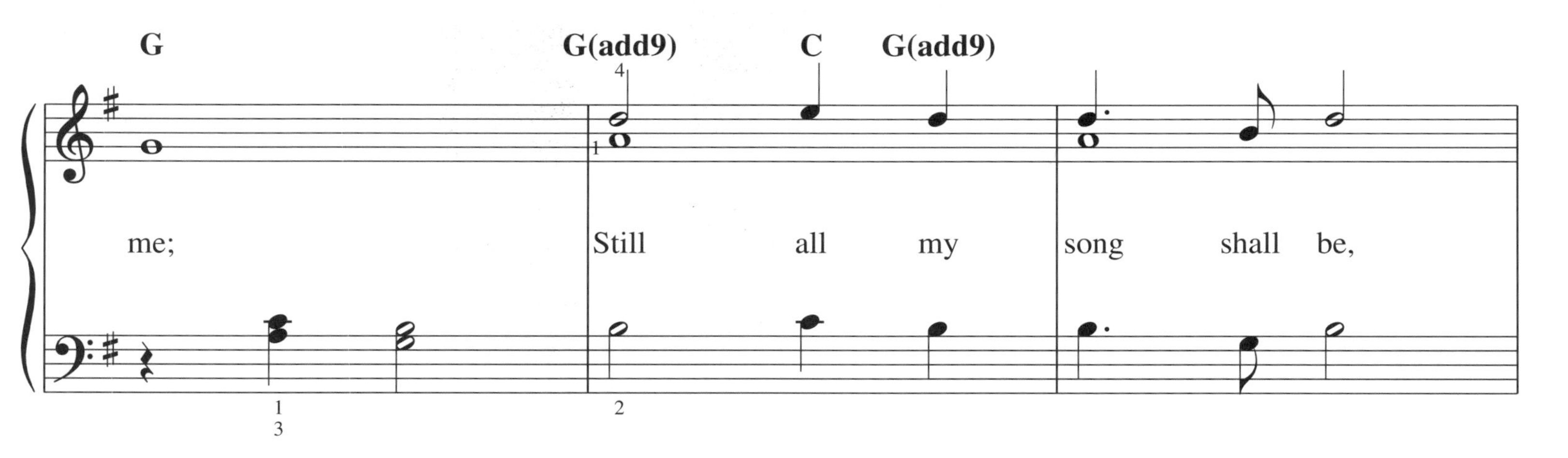

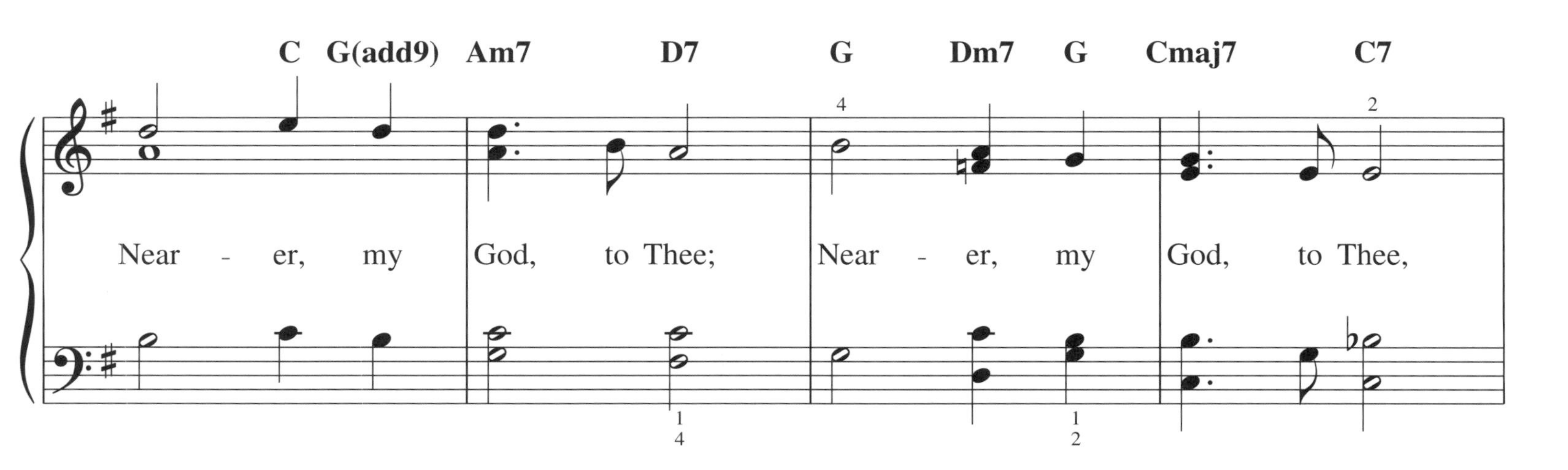

Additional Verses

2. Though like the wanderer,
The sun gone down,
Darkness be over me,
My rest a stone;
Yet in my dreams I'd be
Nearer, my God, to Thee!

3. There let the way appear
Steps unto heaven:
All that Thou sendest me
In mercy given:
Angels to beckon me
Nearer, my God, to Thee!

4. Then, with my waking thoughts
Bright with Thy praise
Out of my stony griefs
Bethel I'll raise;
So by my woes to be
Nearer, my God, to Thee!

5. Or if on joyful wing
Cleaving the sky,
Sun, moon, and stars forgot,
Upward I fly;
Still all my song shall be,
Nearer, my God, to Thee! Amen.

NOW THANK WE ALL OUR GOD

German Words by MARTIN RINKART
English Translation by CATHERINE WINKWORTH
Music by JOHANN CRÜGER

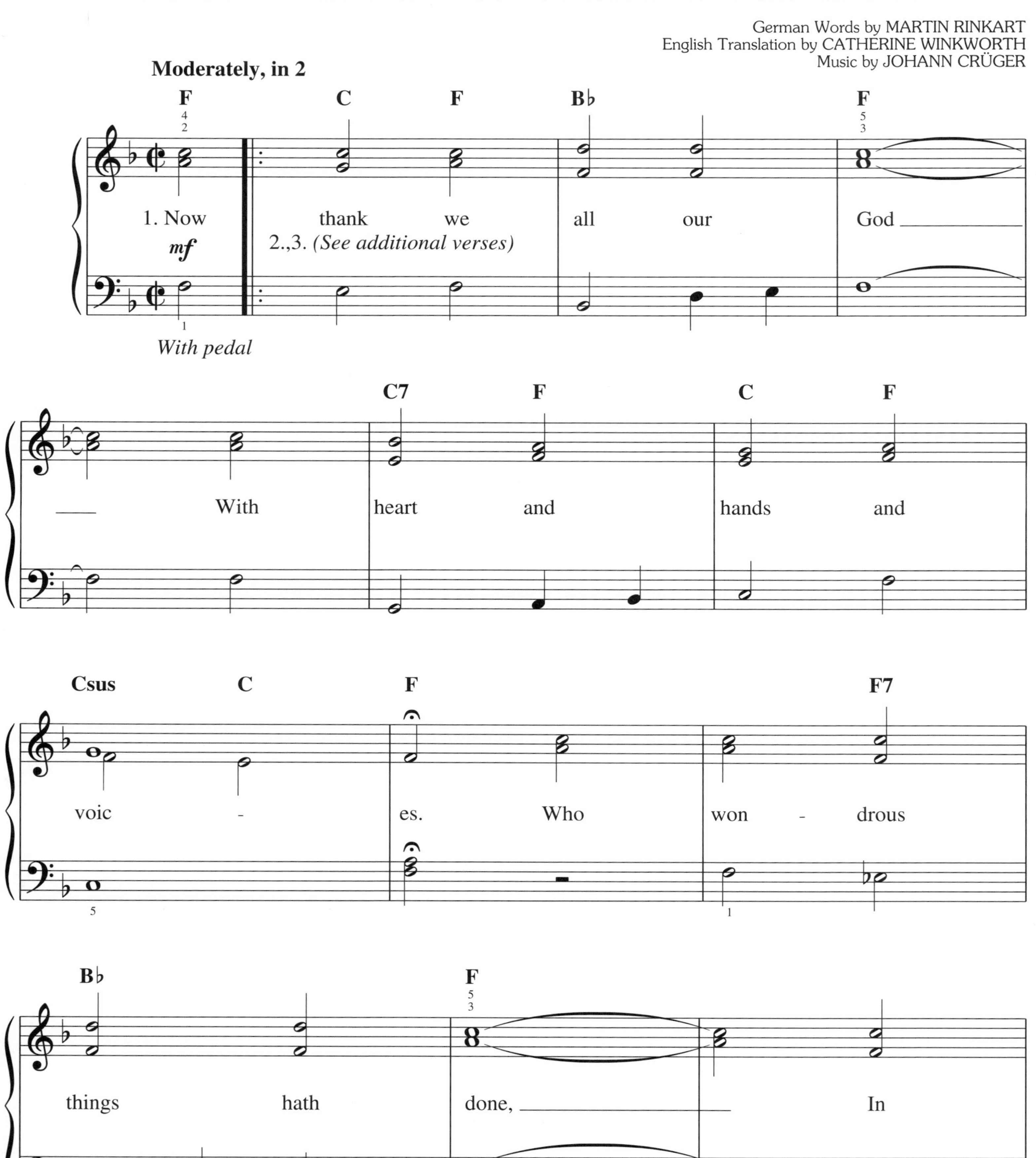

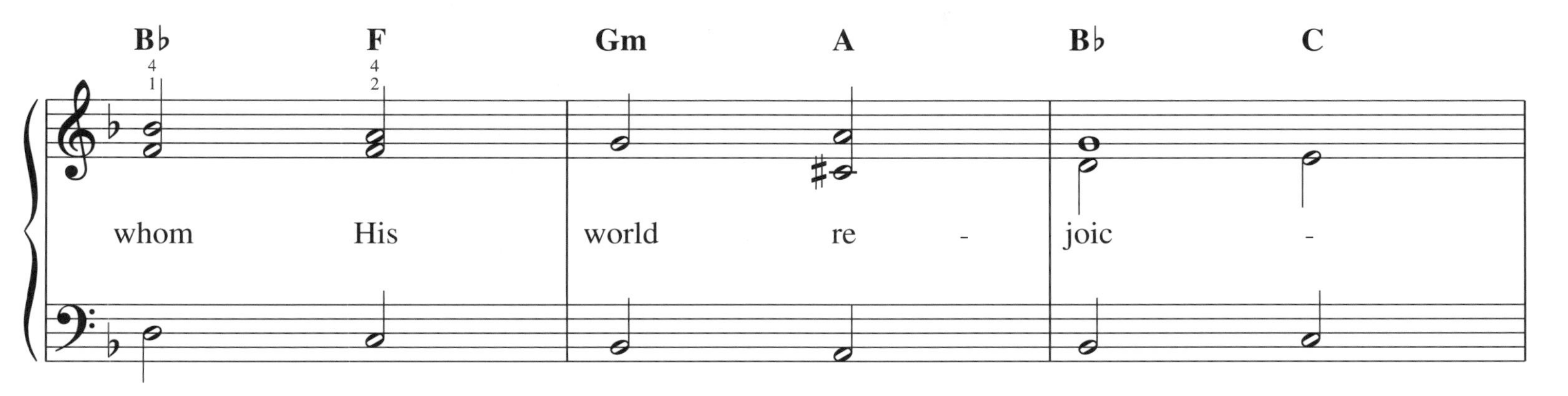
B♭
F
Gm
A
B♭
C
whom His world re - joic -

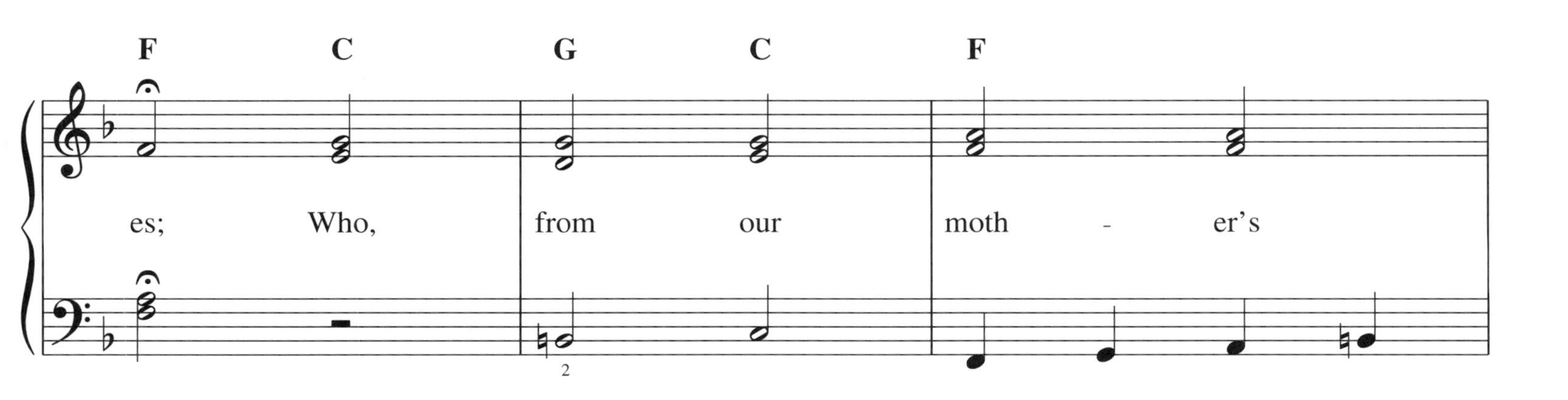
F
C
G
C
F
es; Who, from our moth - er's

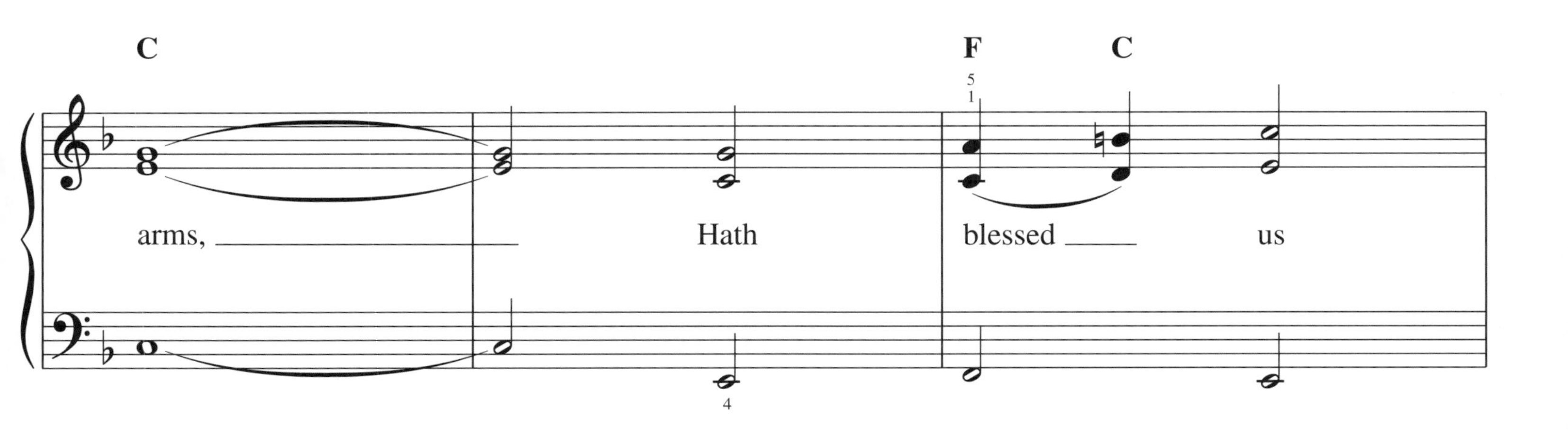
C
F
C
arms, Hath blessed us

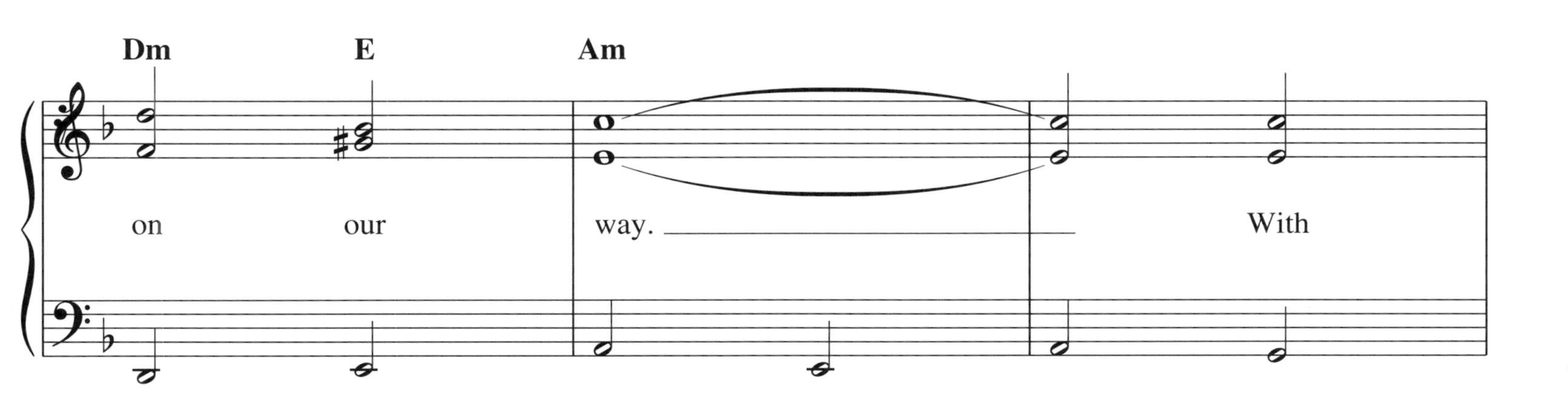
Dm
E
Am
on our way. With

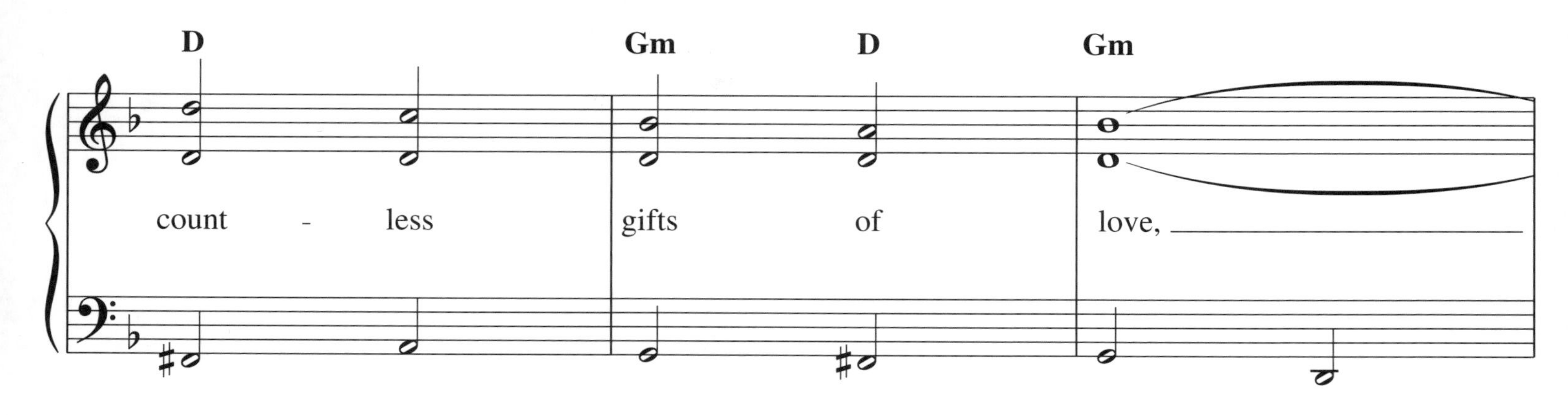

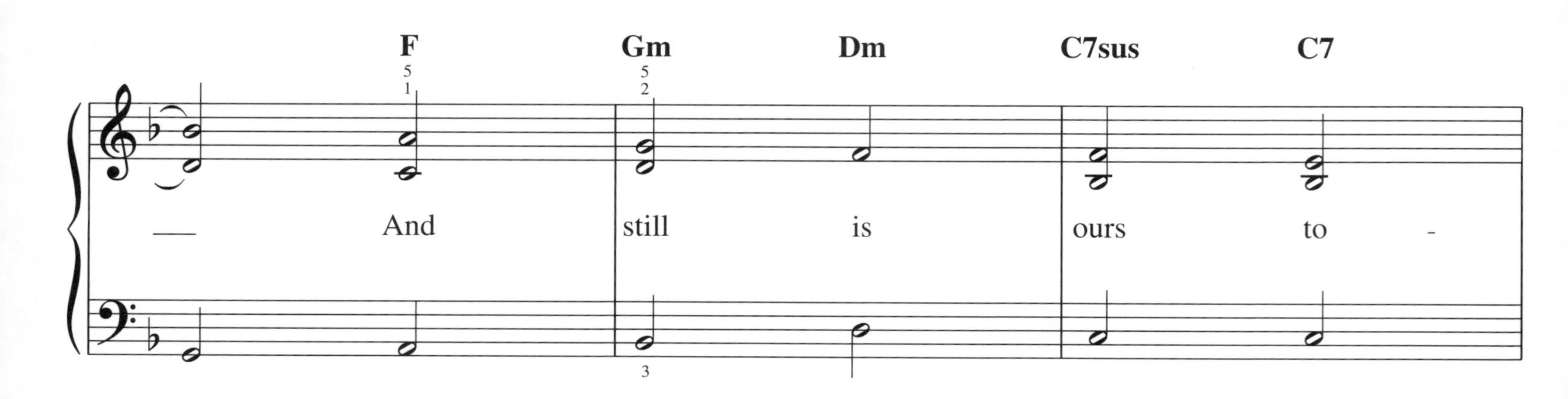

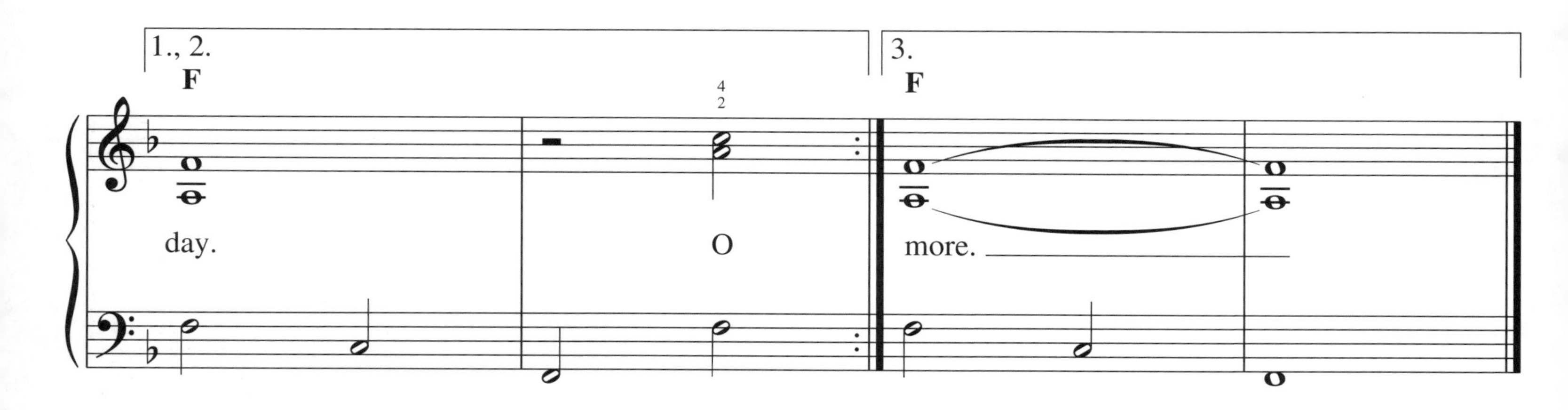

Additional Verses

2. (O) may this bounteous God through all our life be near us,
With ever joyful hearts and blessed peace to cheer us;
And keep us in His grace, and guide us when perplexed,
And free us from all ills, in this world and the next.

3. (All) praise and thanks to God the Father now be given,
The Son and Him who reigns with them in highest heaven;
The one eternal God, whom earth and heav'n adore;
For thus it was, is now, and shall be evermore.

O FOR A THOUSAND TONGUES TO SING

O GOD, OUR HELP IN AGES PAST

Words by ISAAC WATTS
Paraphrased from Psalm 90:1-5
Music by WILLIAM CROFT

THE OLD RUGGED CROSS

Words and Music by
REV. GEORGE BENNARD

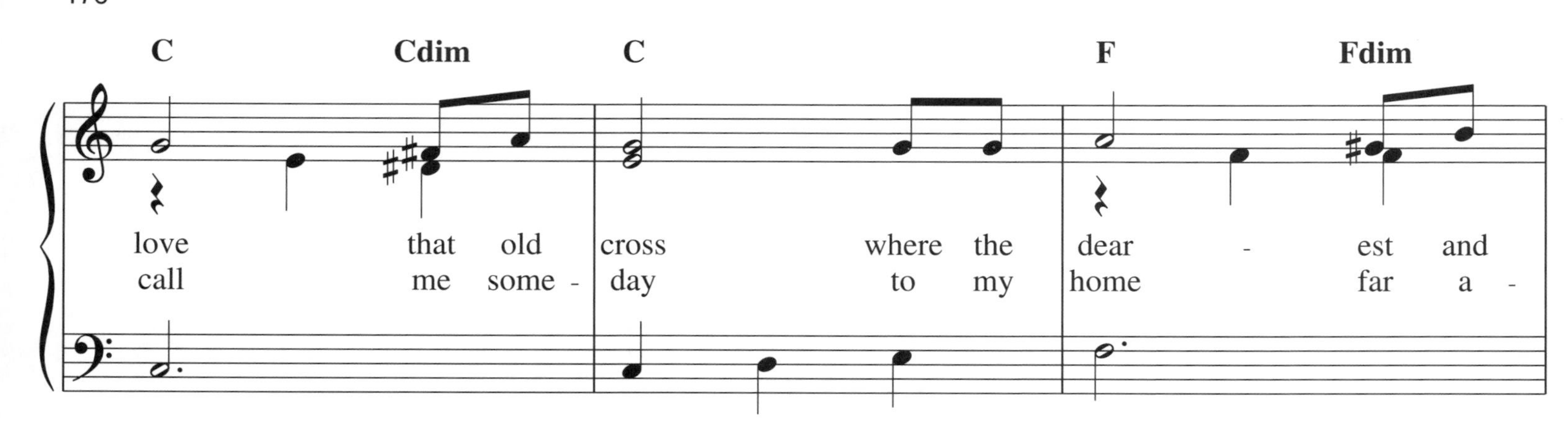
C
Cdim
C
F
Fdim
love that old cross where the dear - est and
call me some - day to my home far a -

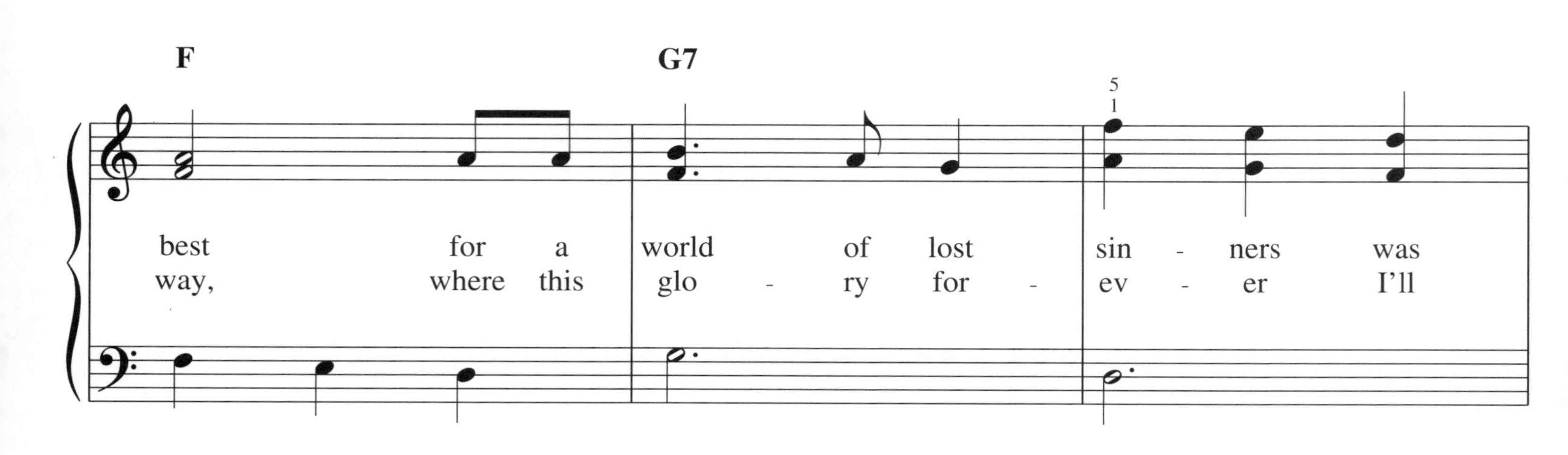
F
G7
best for a world of lost sin - ners was
way, where this glo - ry for - ev - er I'll

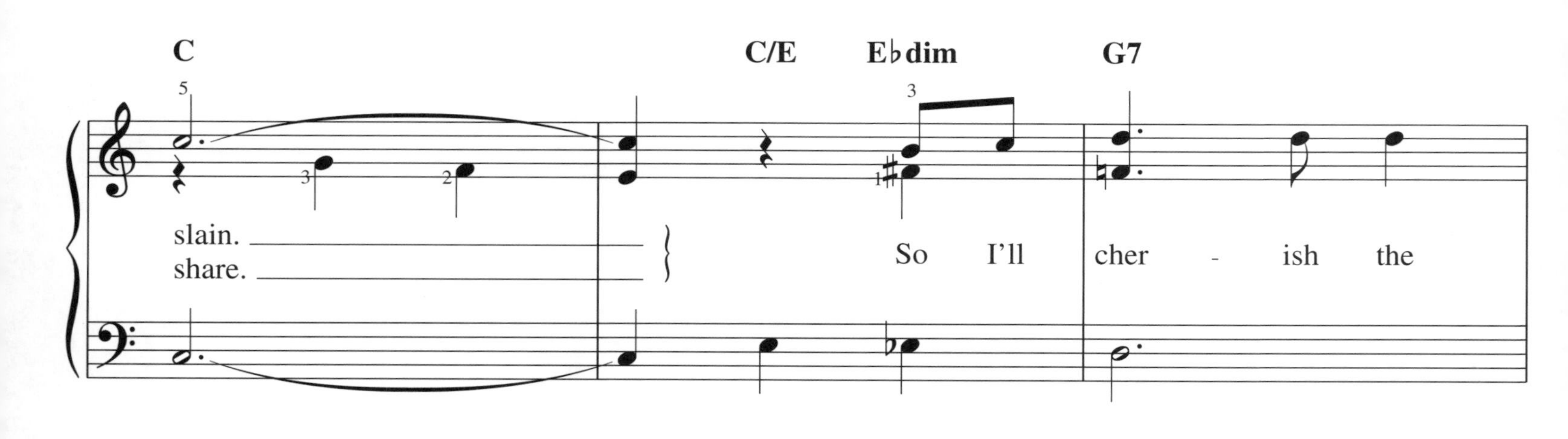
C
C/E
E♭dim
G7
slain.
share.
So I'll cher - ish the

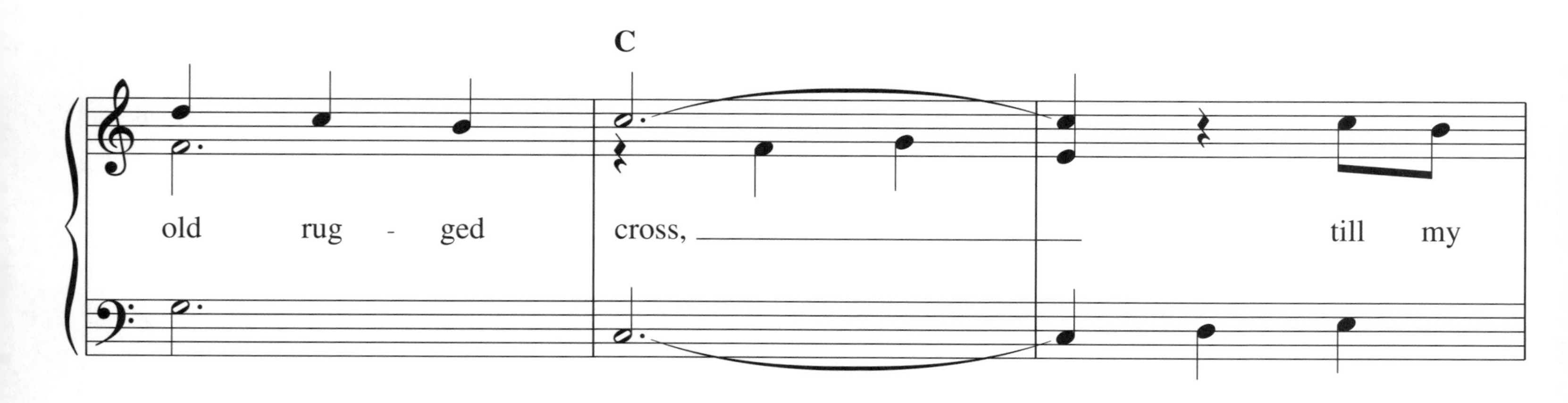
C
old rug - ged cross, till my

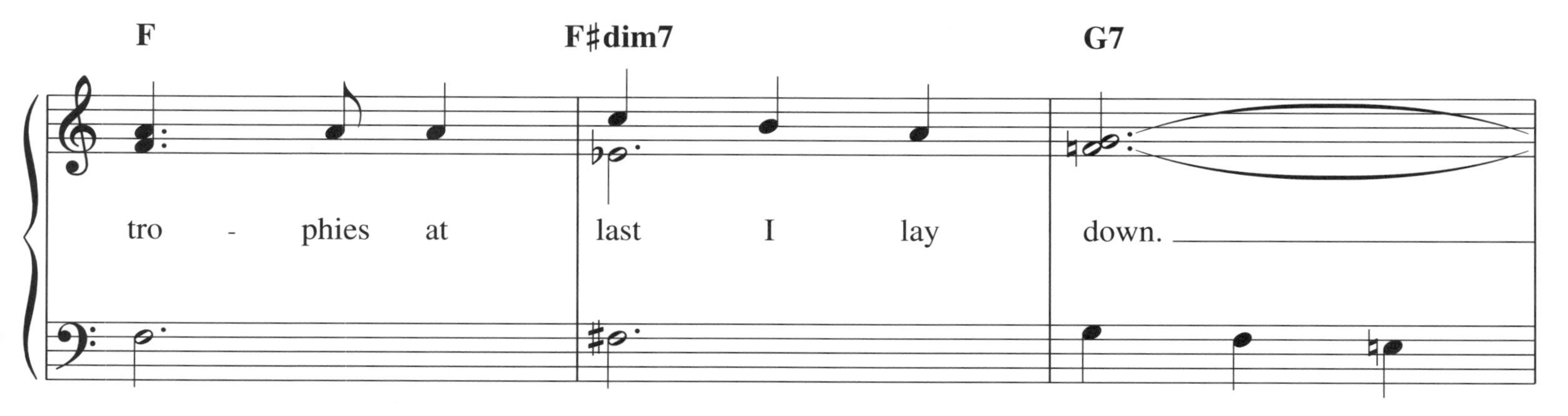
F
F♯dim7
G7
tro - phies at
last I lay
down.

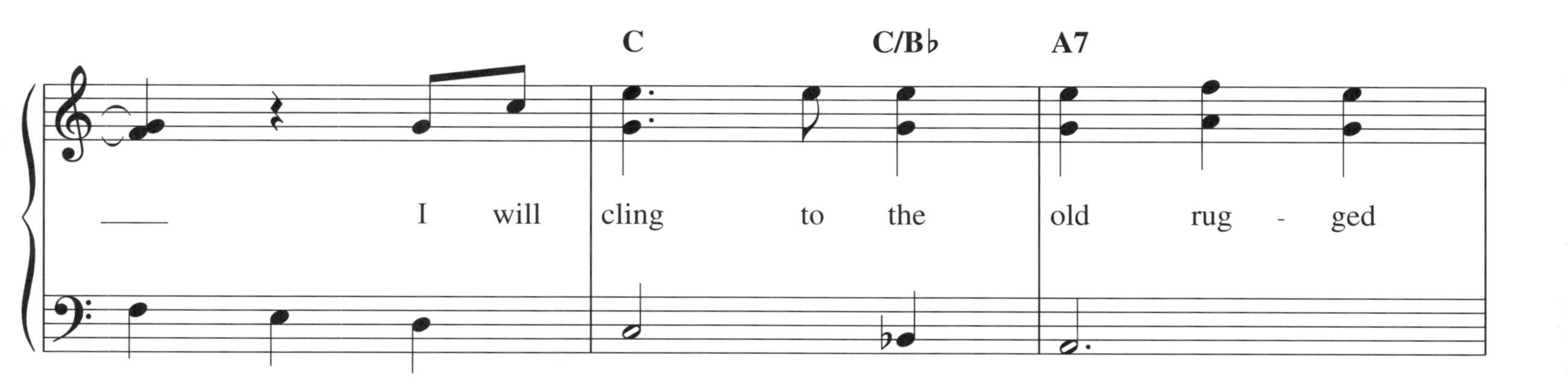
C
C/B♭
A7
I will
cling to the
old rug - ged

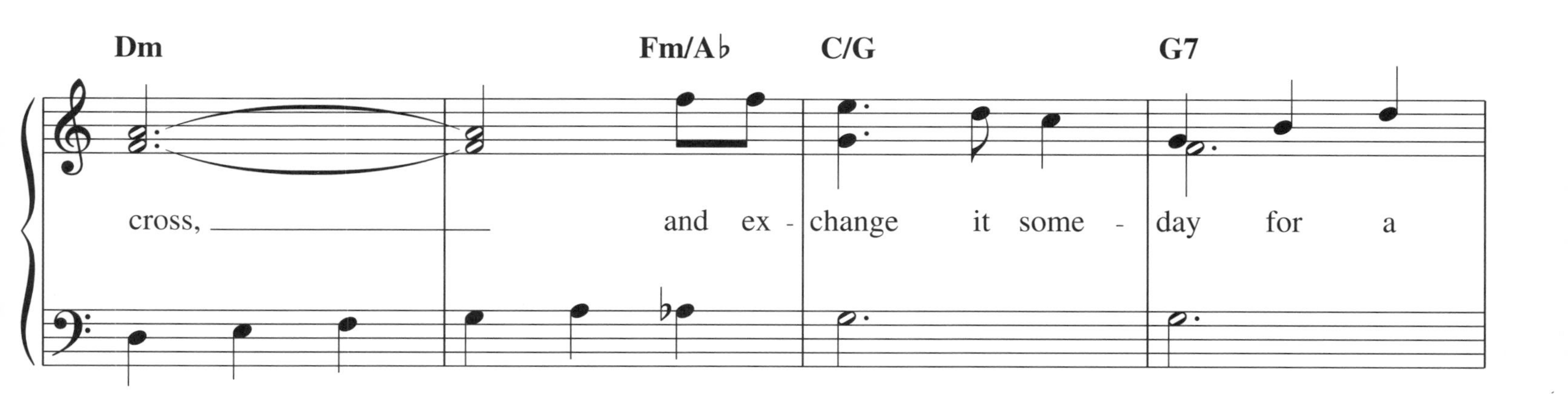
Dm
Fm/A♭
C/G
G7
cross,
and ex -
change it some -
day for a

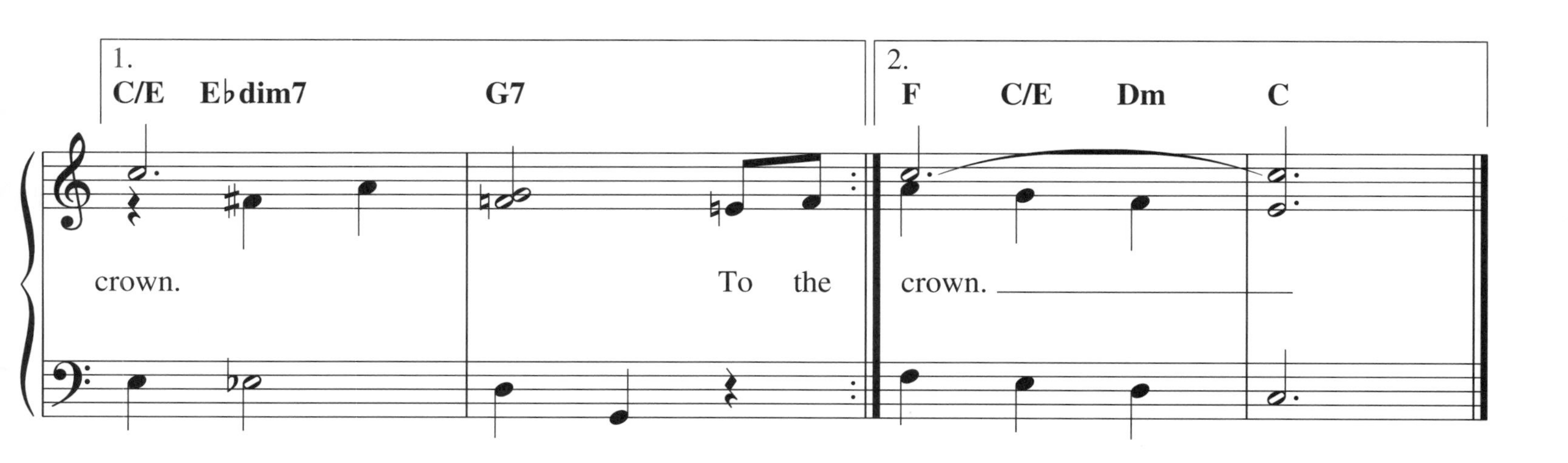
1.
C/E
E♭dim7
G7
crown.
To the
2.
F
C/E
Dm
C
crown.

O LOVE THAT WILT NOT LET ME GO

Words by GEORGE MATHESON
Music by ALBERT LISTER PEACE

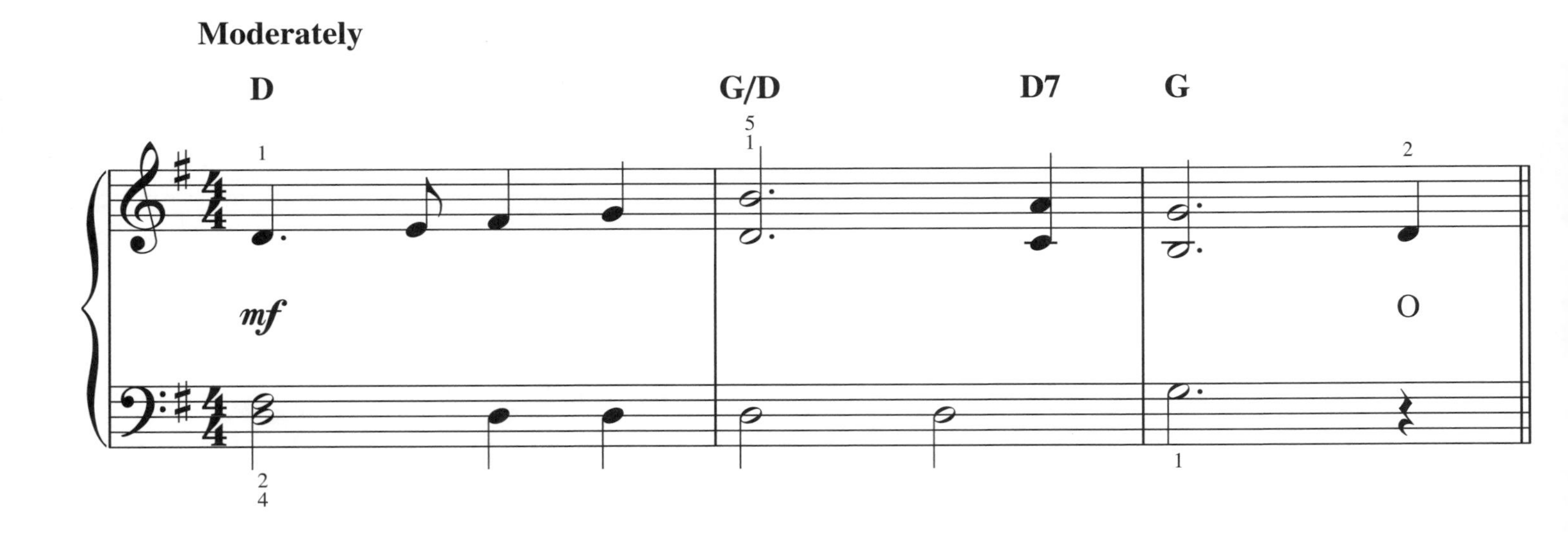

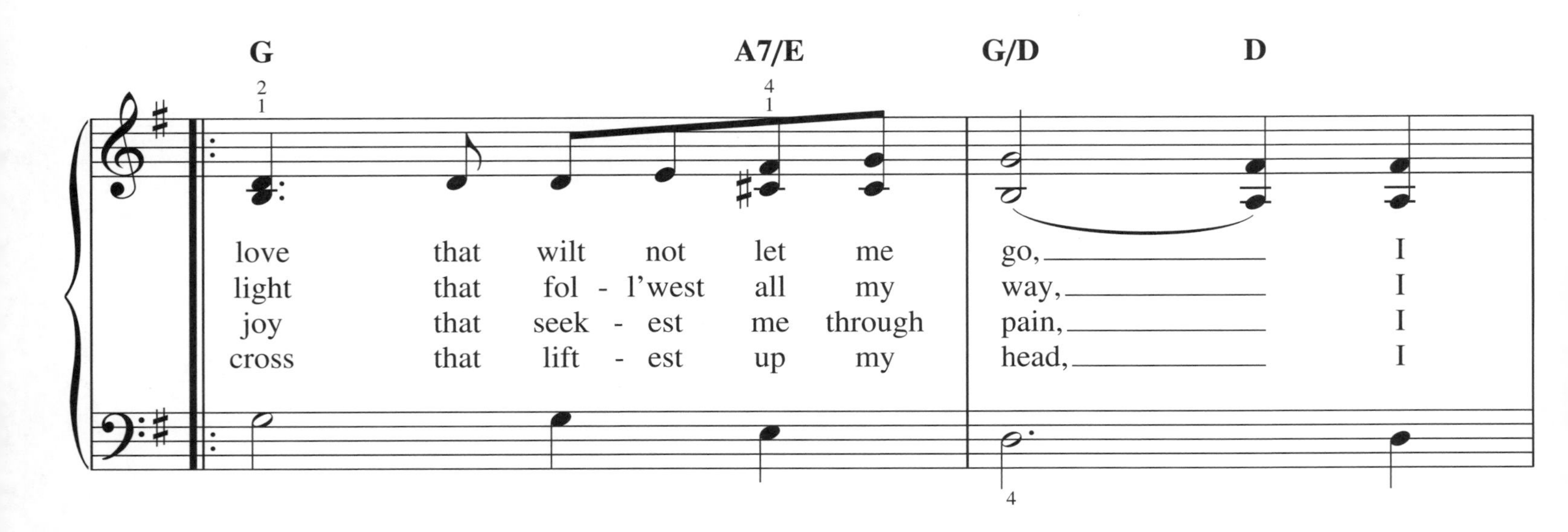

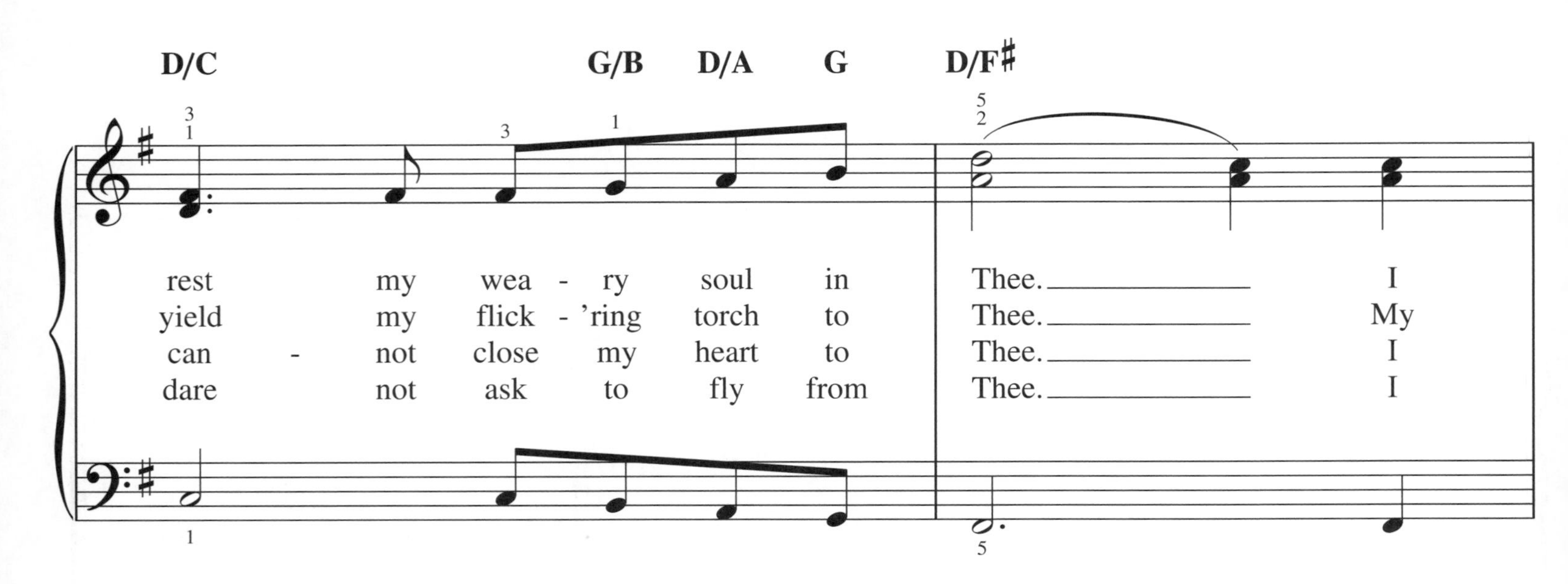

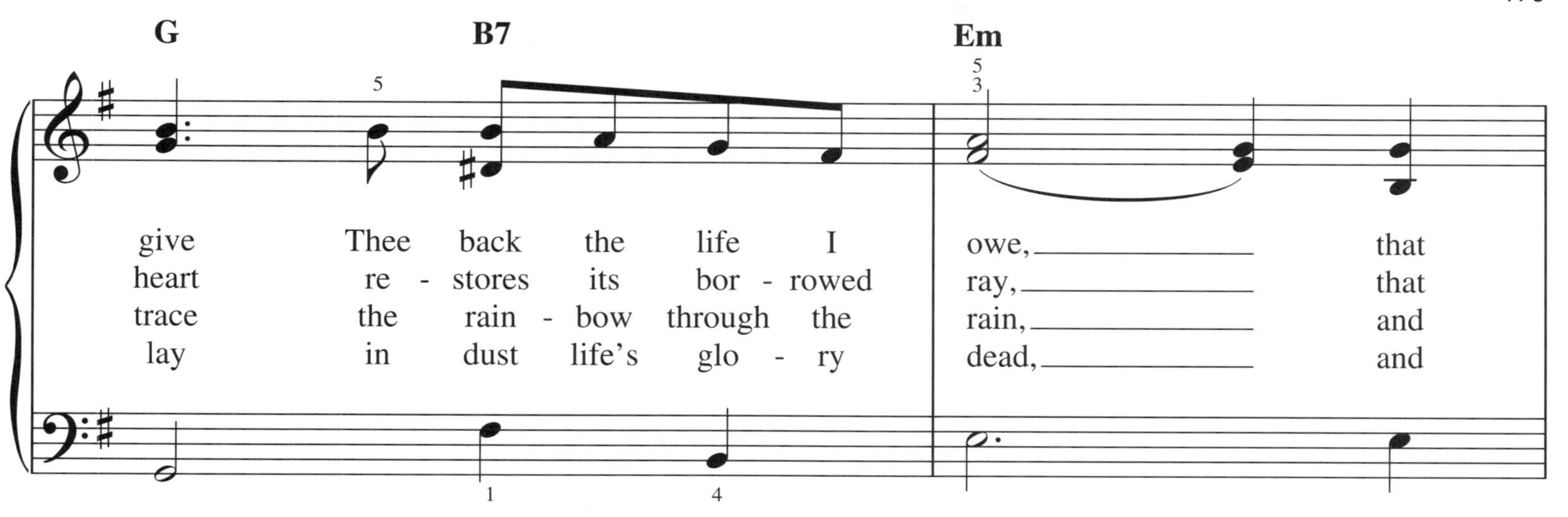
G
B7
Em
give Thee back the life I owe, that
heart re - stores its bor - rowed ray, that
trace the rain - bow through the rain, and
lay in dust life's glo - ry dead, and

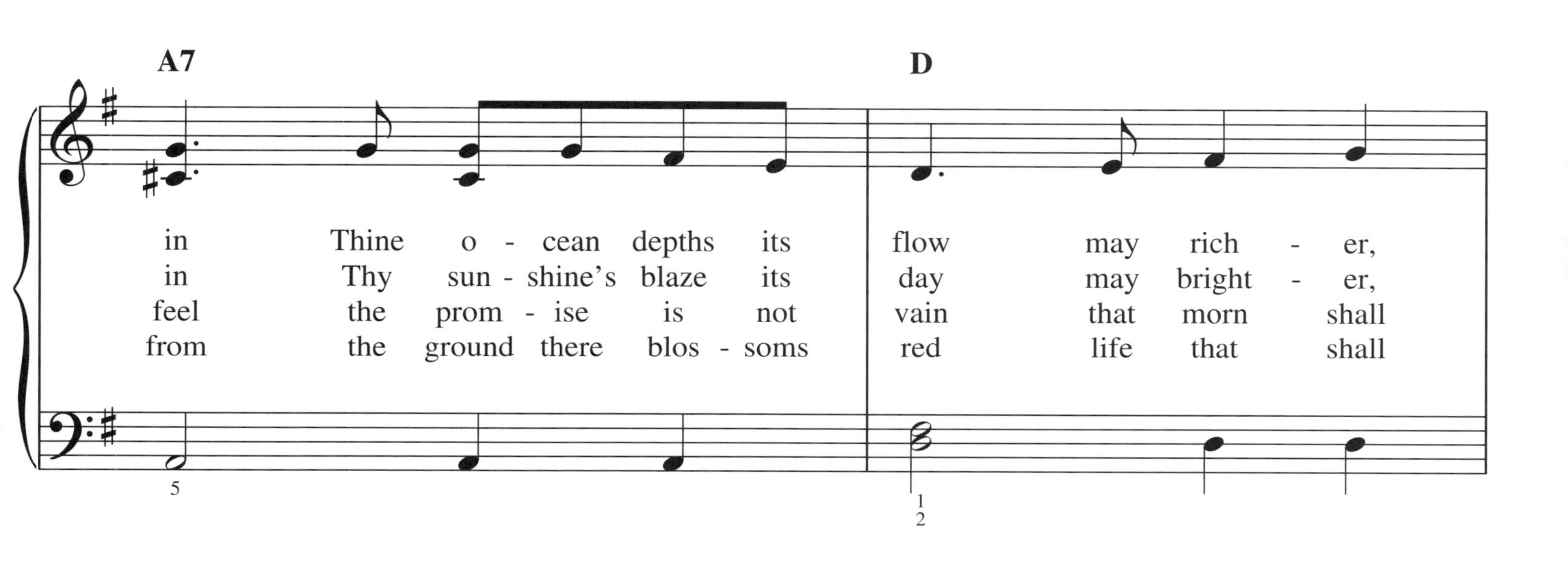
A7
D
in Thine o - cean depths its flow may rich - er,
in Thy sun - shine's blaze its day may bright - er,
feel the prom - ise is not vain that morn shall
from the ground there blos - soms red life that shall

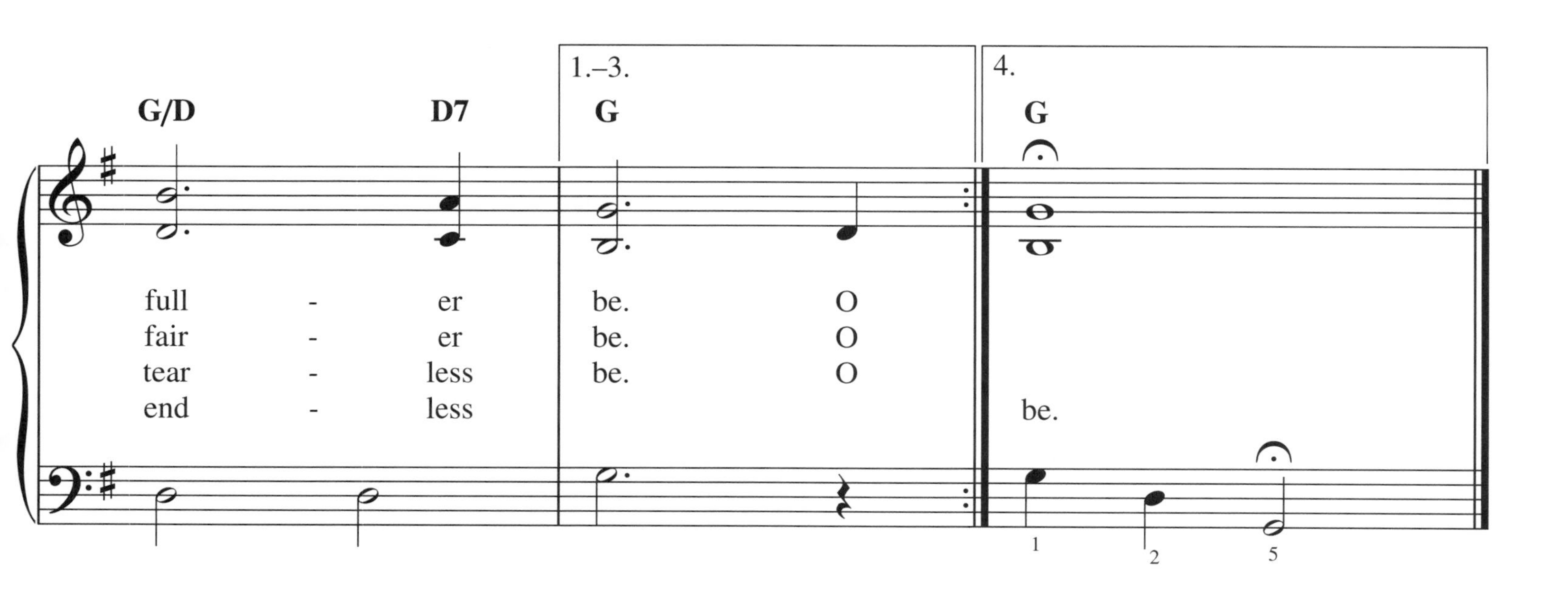
1.–3.
4.
G/D
D7
G
G
full - er be. O
fair - er be. O
tear - less be. O
end - less be.

O MASTER, LET ME WALK WITH THEE

Words by WASHINGTON GLADDEN
Music by H. PERCY SMITH

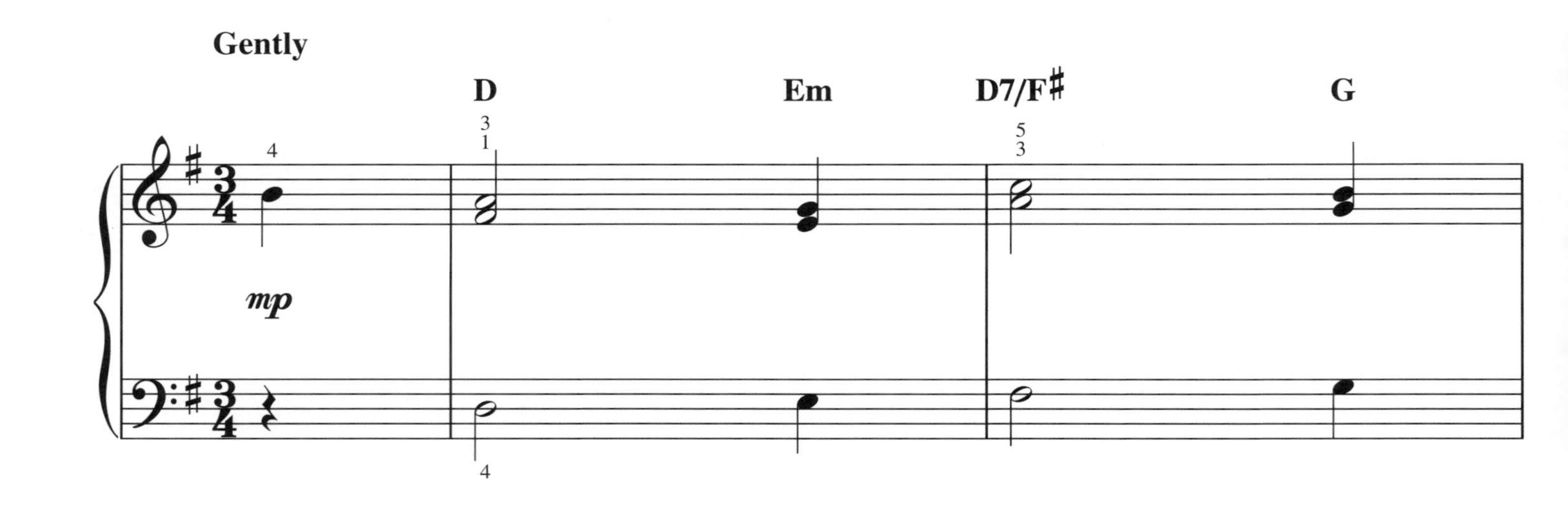

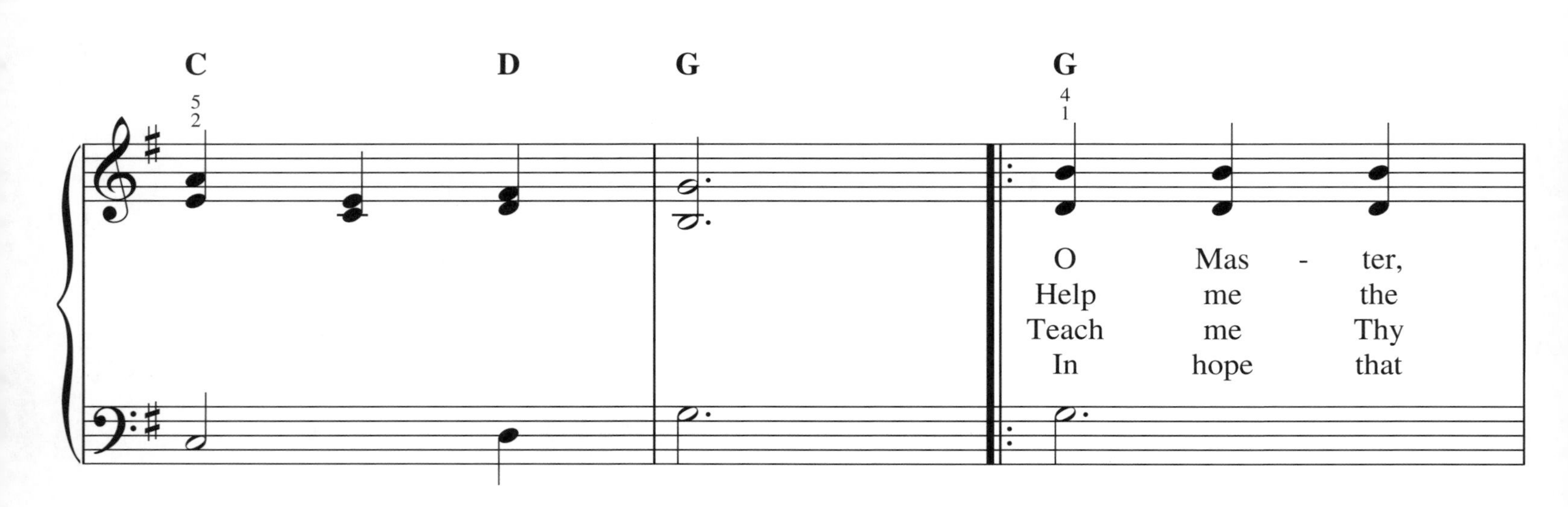

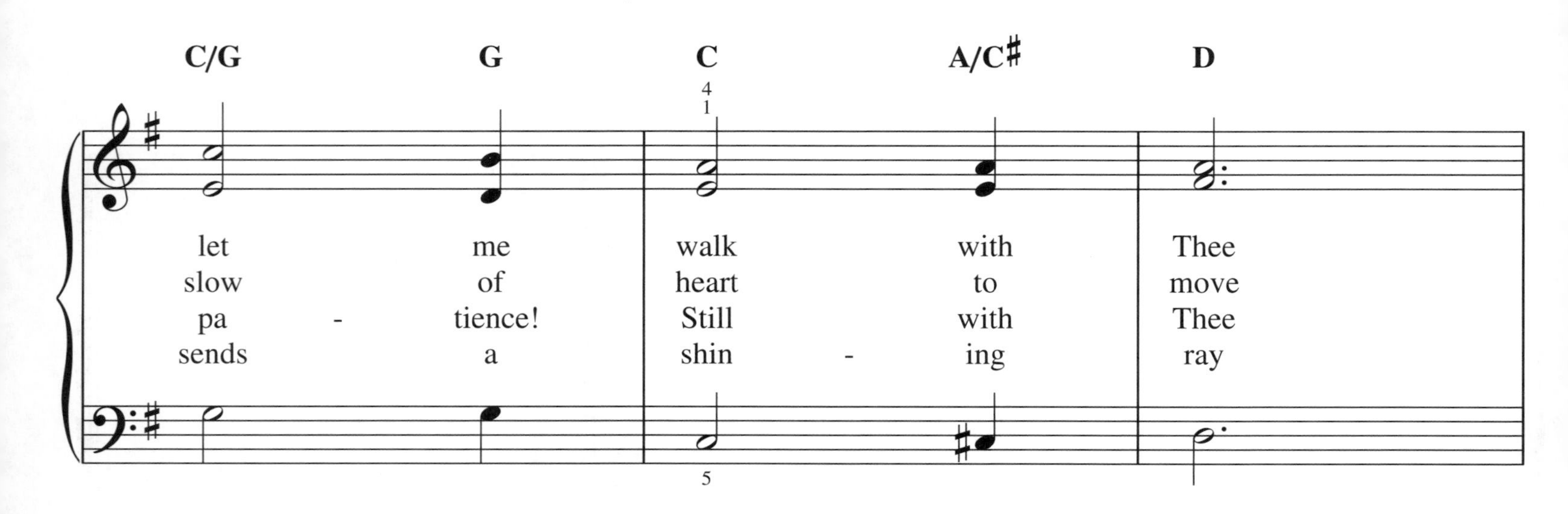

Em7 D7/F♯ G Em7 A7
In low - ly paths of serv - ice
By some clear win - ning word of
In clos - er, dear - er com - pa -
Far down the fu - ture's broad - 'ning
D D/C G/B
free; Tell me Thy se - cret,
love. Teach me the way - ward
ny, In work that keeps faith
way, In peace that on - ly
C G/B Dsus D G D Em
help me bear The strain of
feet to stay, And guide them
sweet and strong, In trust that
Thou can'st give, With Thee, O
D7/F♯ G C D G
toil, the fret of care.
in the home - ward way.
tri - umphs o - ver wrong.
Mas - ter, let me live.

O WORSHIP THE KING

Words by ROBERT GRANT
Music attributed to JOHANN MICHAEL HAYDN
Arranged by WILLIAM GARDINER

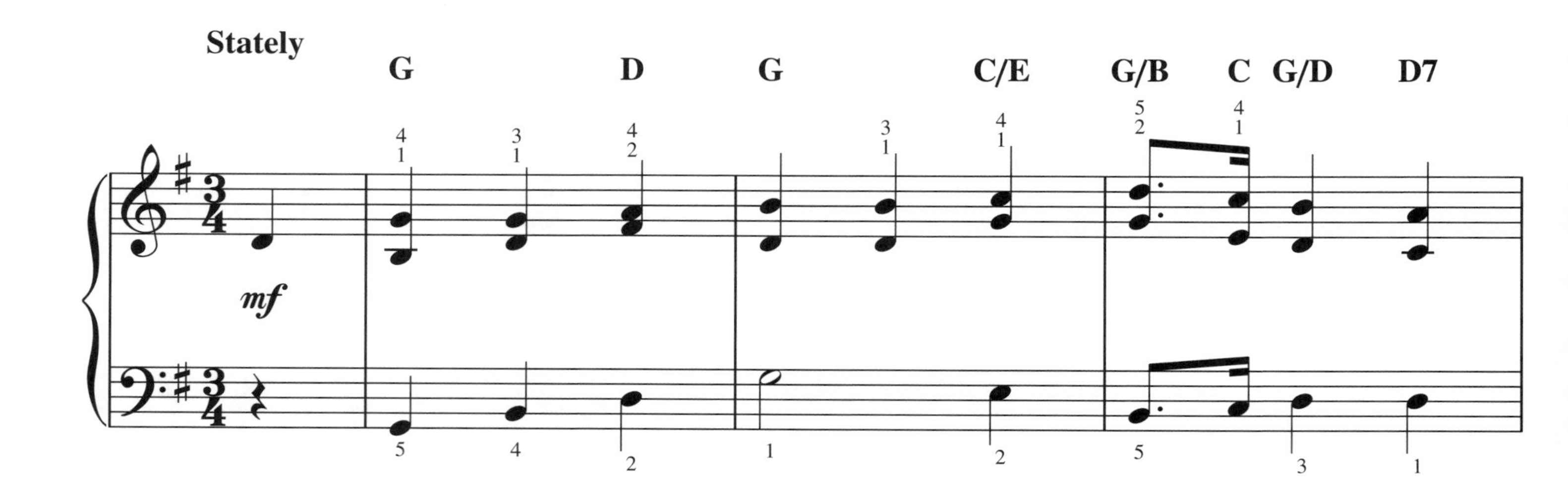

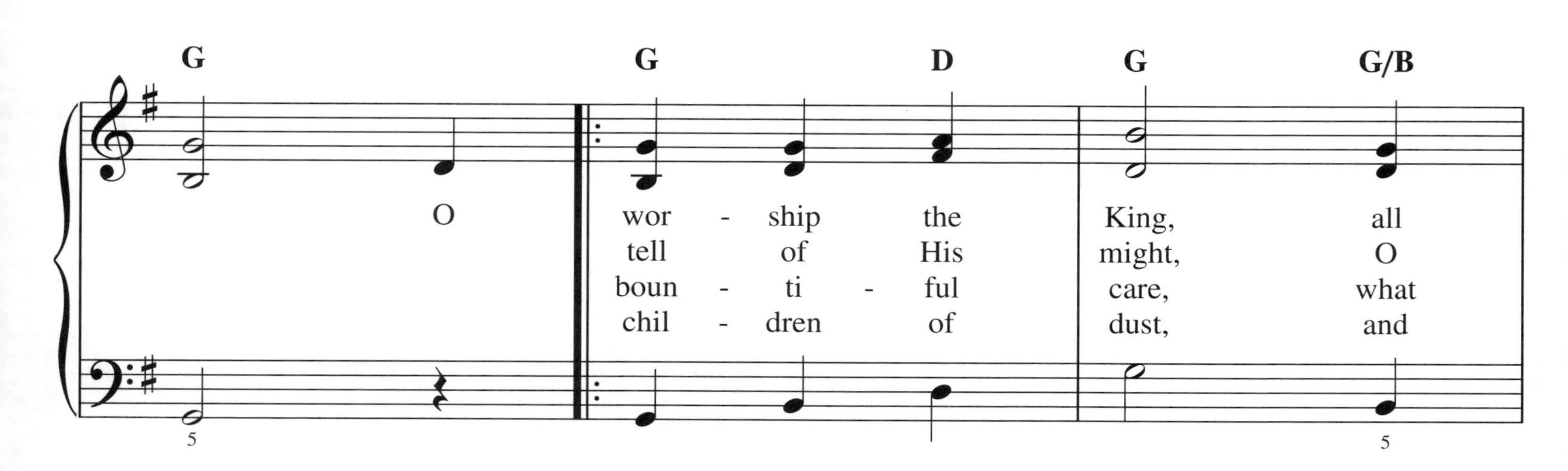

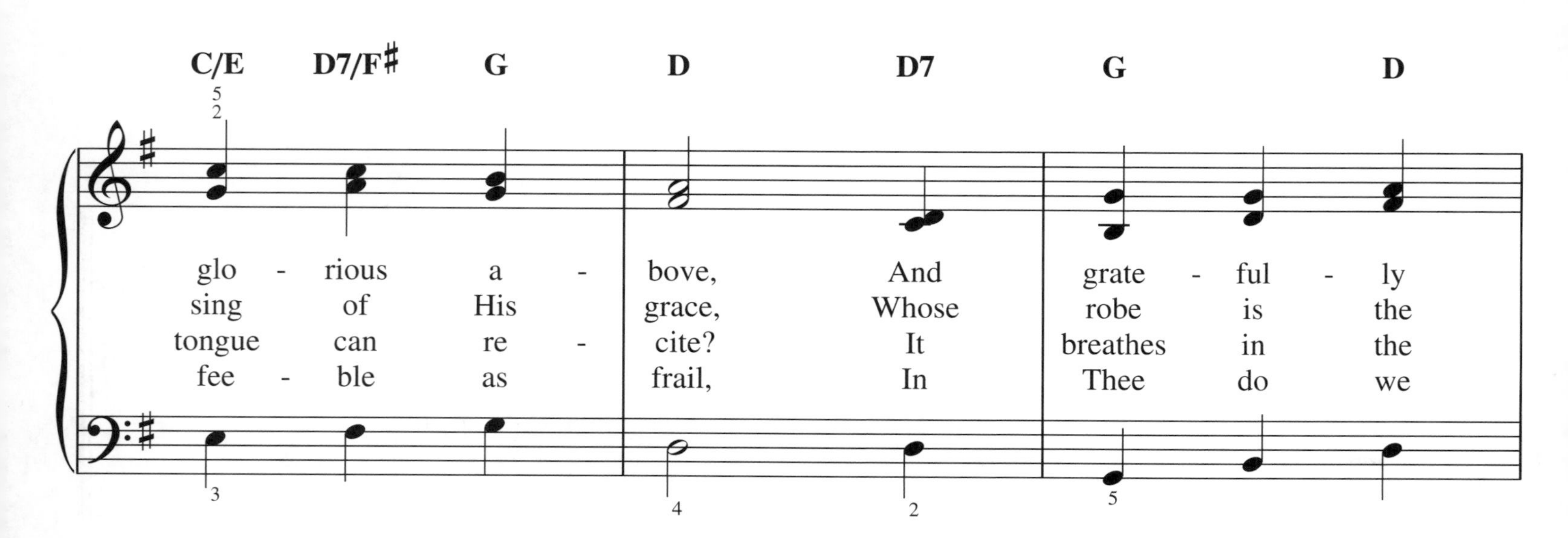

G C/E G/B C G/D D7 G D
sing His won - der - ful love. Our
light, whose can - o - py space. His
air, it shines in the light. It
trust, nor find Thee to fail. Thy
A7/D D7 G/D D G/D
Shield and De - fend - er, the An - cient of
char - iots of wrath the deep thun - der - clouds
streams from the hills, it de - scends to the
mer - cies how ten - der, how firm to the
D7 G D G C/E
Days, Pa - vil - ioned in splen - dor, and
form, And dark is His path on the
plain, And sweet - ly dis - tills in the
end! Our Mak - er, De - fend - er, Re -
G/B C G/D D7
gird - ed with
wings of the
dew and the
deem - er and
1.–3.
G
praise. O
storm. Thy
rain. Frail
4.
G
Friend!

ONLY BELIEVE

Words and Music by
PAUL RADER

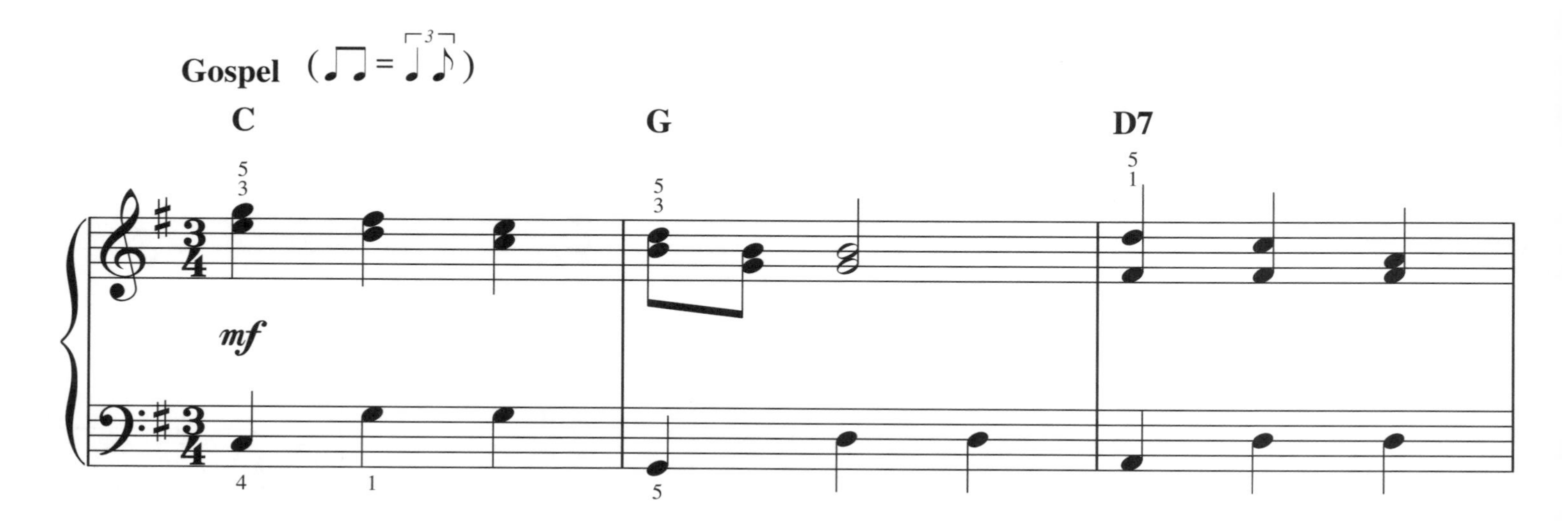

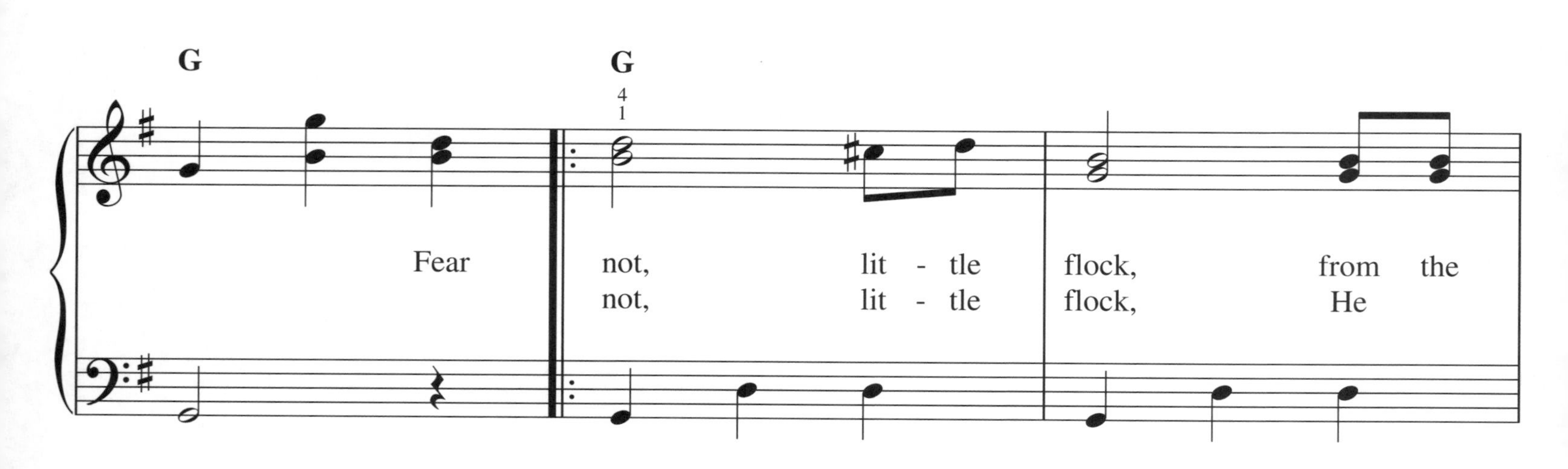

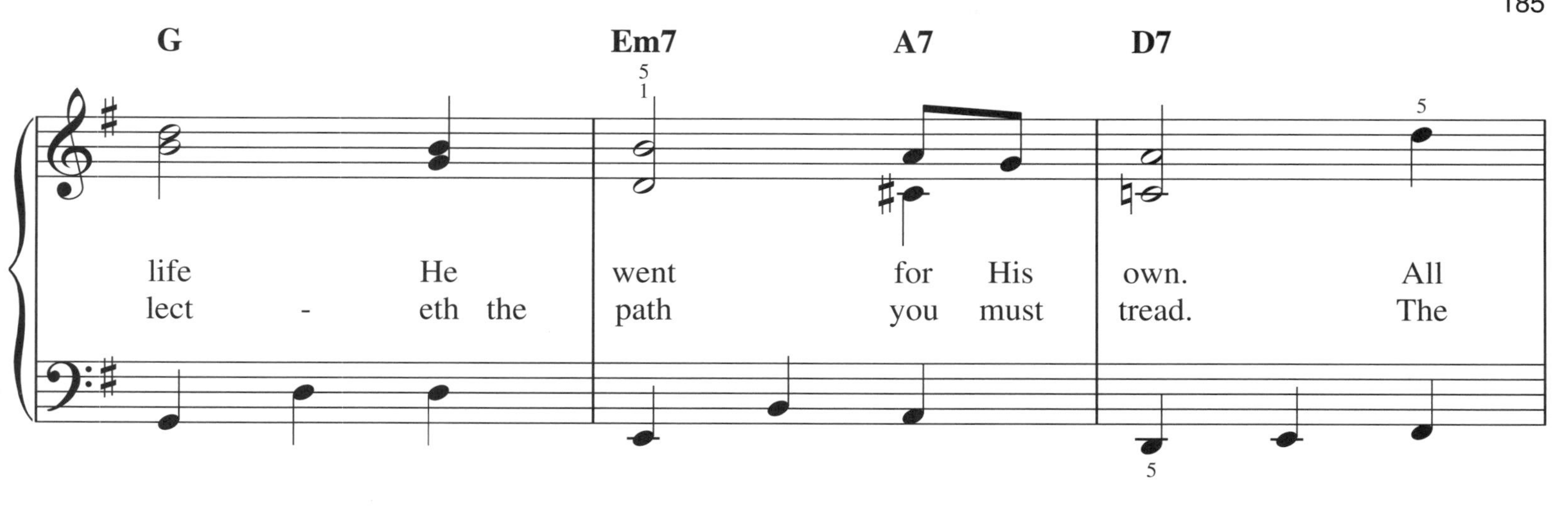
G
Em7
A7
D7
life He went for His own. All
lect - eth the path you must tread. The

G
G7
F/A
G7/B
pow - er in earth, all pow - er a -
wa - ters of Ma - rah He'll sweet - en for

C
G
C
bove, is giv - en to Him for the
thee; He drank all the bit - ter in

G/D
D7
G
D
G
flock of His love.
Geth - se - ma - ne.
On - ly be -

C
G
lieve, on - ly be - lieve. All things are

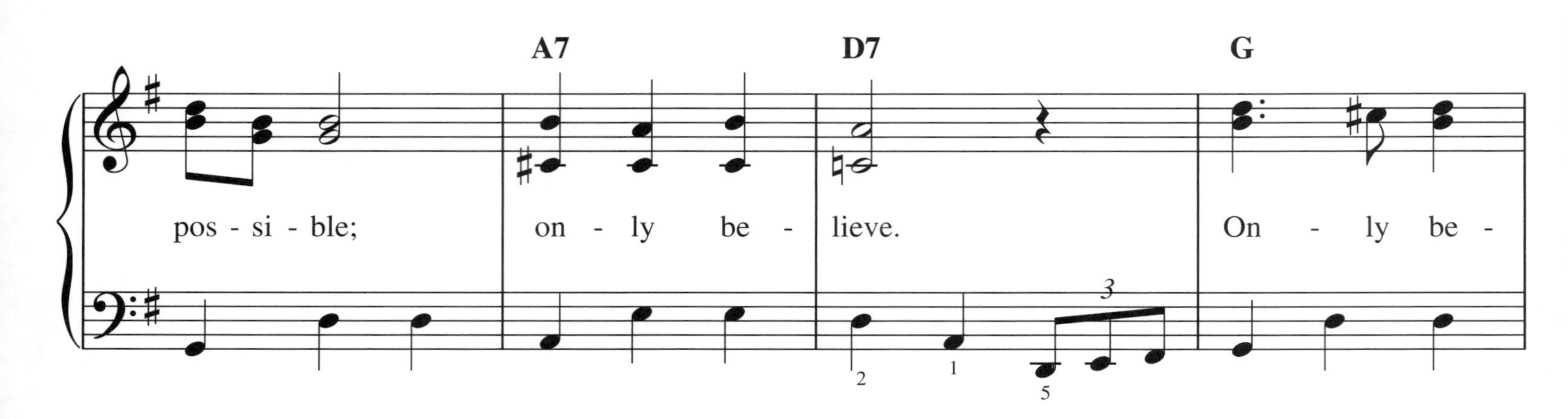
A7
D7
G
pos - si - ble; on - ly be - lieve. On - ly be -

C
C♯dim7
lieve, on - ly be - lieve. All things are

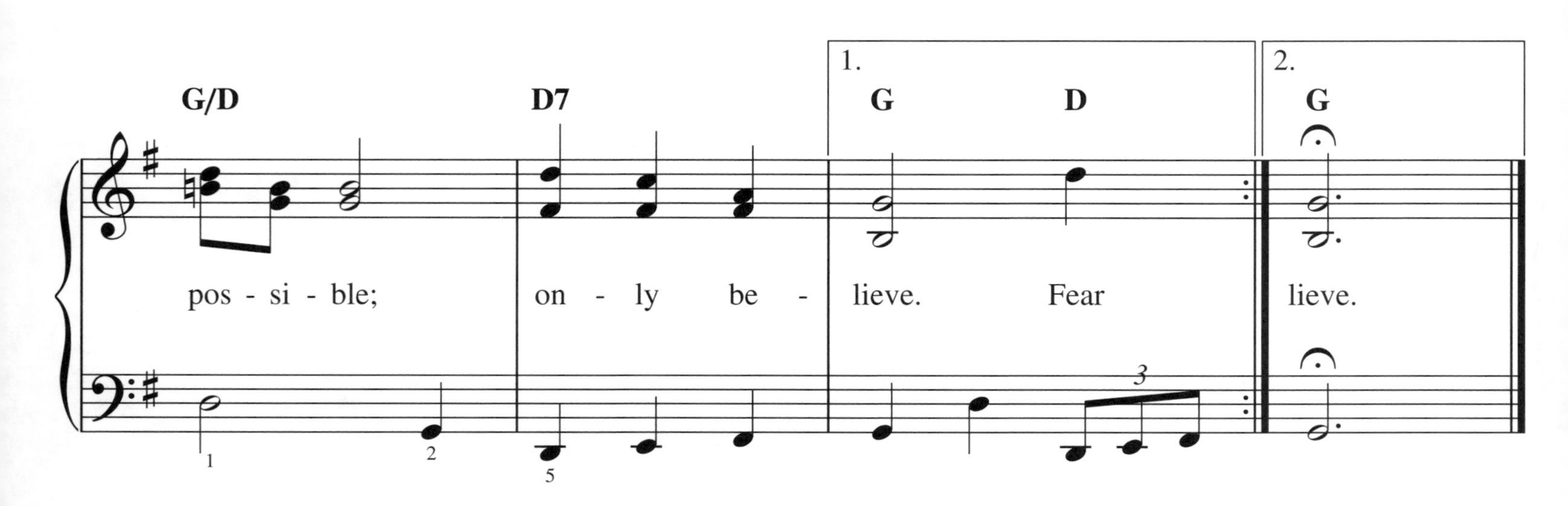
G/D
D7
1.
G
D
2.
G
pos - si - ble; on - ly be - lieve. Fear lieve.

OPEN MY EYES, THAT I MAY SEE

Words and Music by
CLARA H. SCOTT

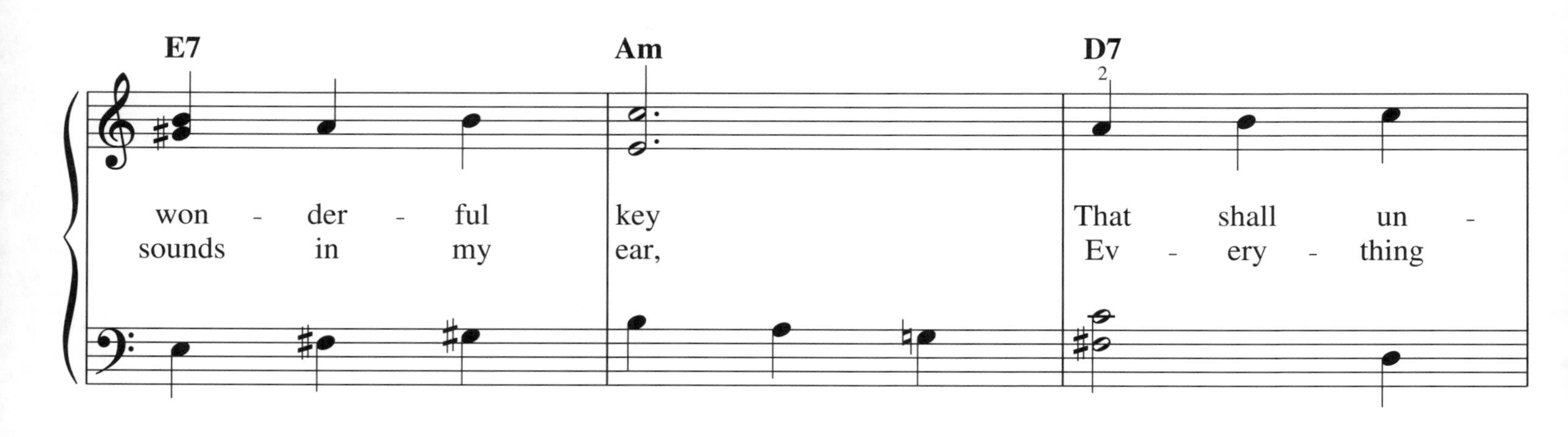
E7
Am
D7
2
won - der - ful
key
That shall un -
sounds in my
ear,
Ev - ery - thing

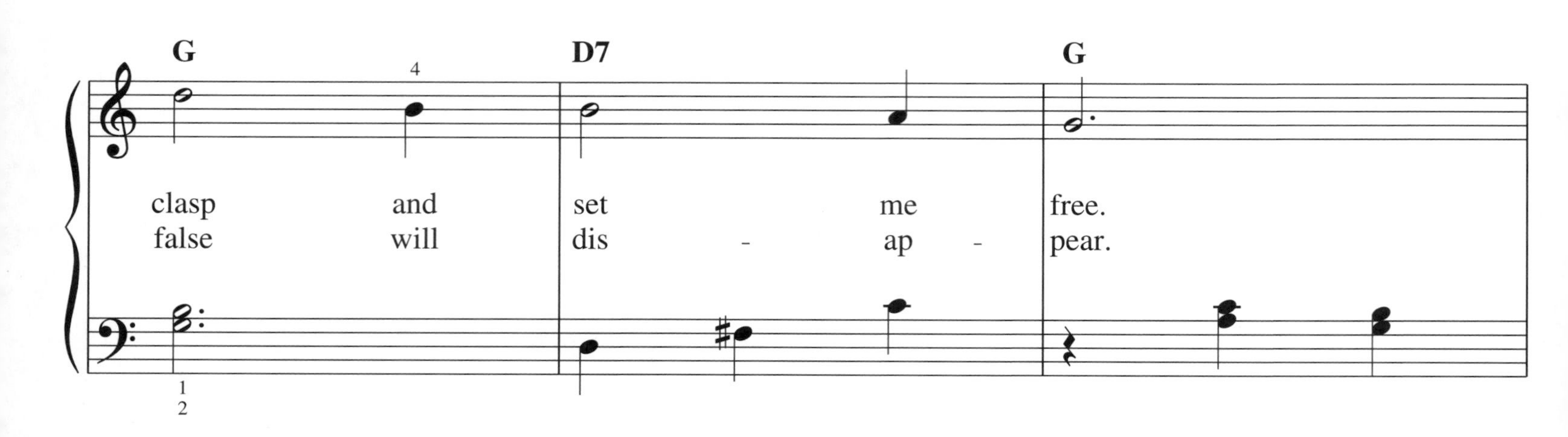
G
4
D7
G
clasp and
set me
free.
false will
dis - ap -
pear.
1
2

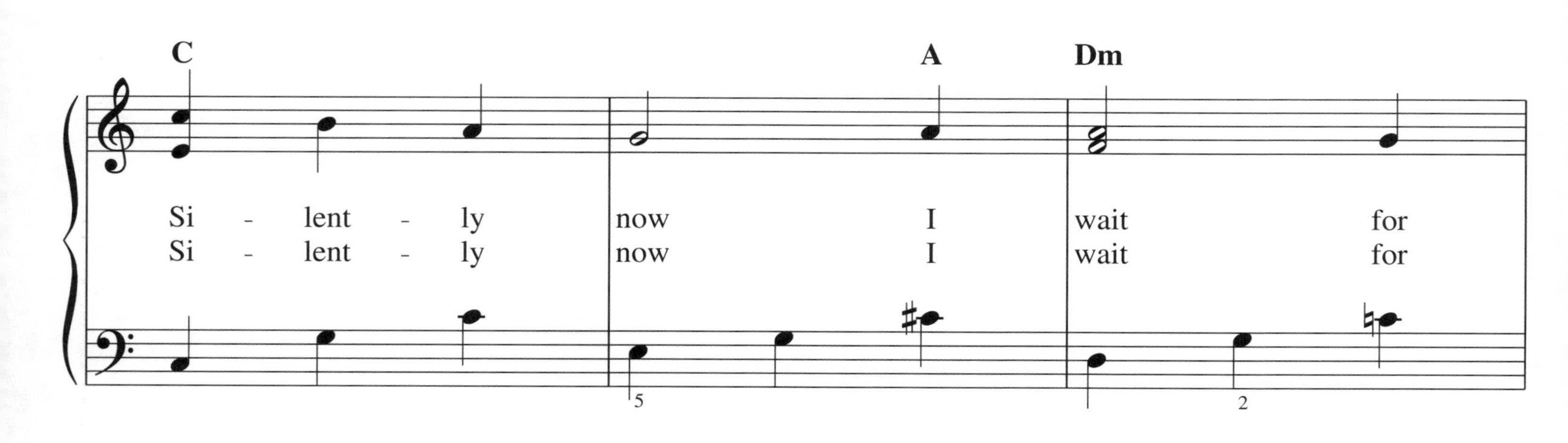
C
A
Dm
Si - lent - ly
now I
wait for
Si - lent - ly
now I
wait for
5
2

G7sus
G
Thee,
Read - y, my
God, Thy
Thee,
Read - y, my
God, Thy

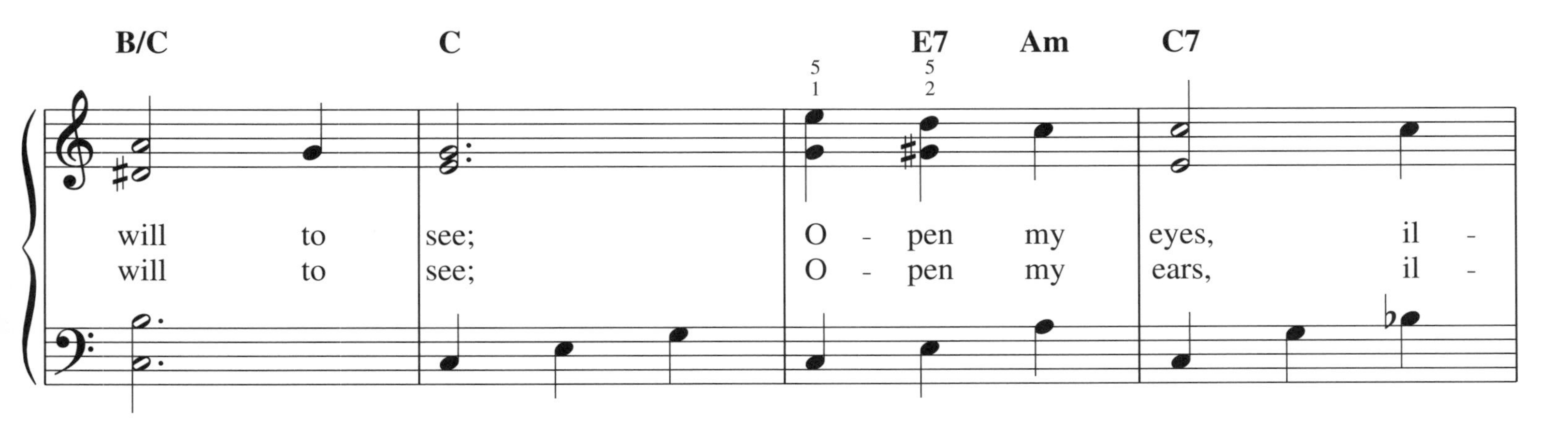

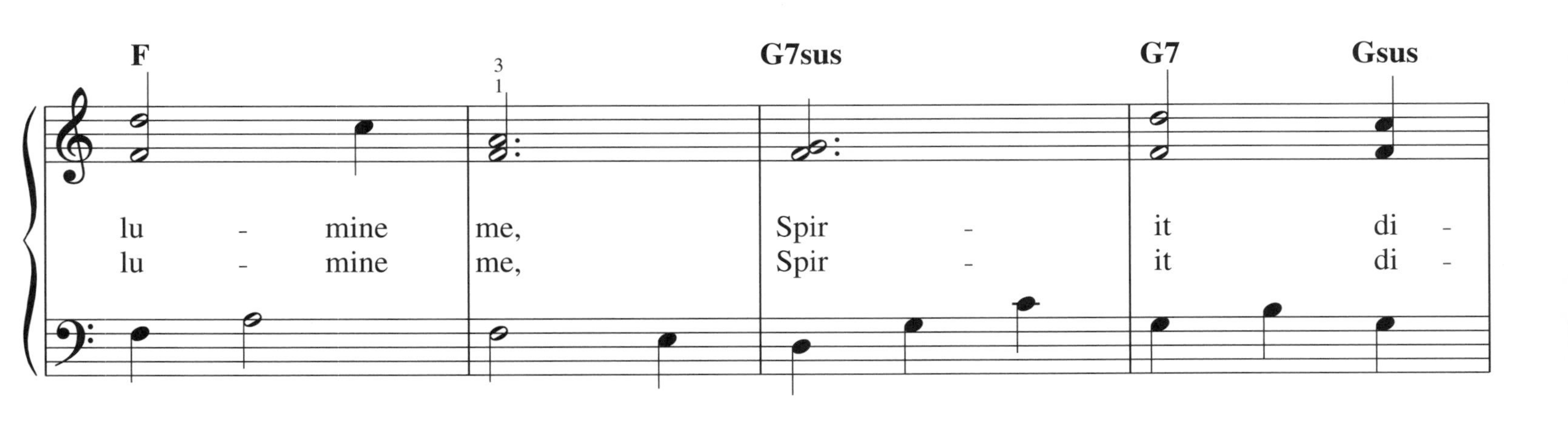

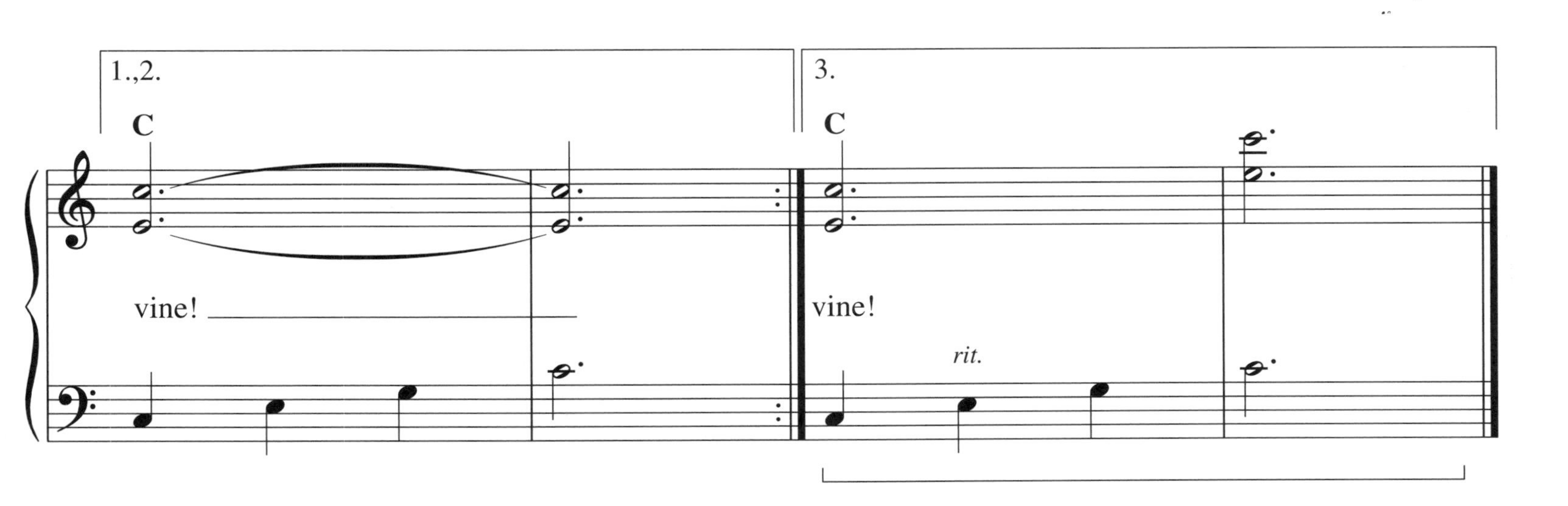

Additional Verse

3. Open my mouth and let me bear
   Gladly the warm truth everywhere;
   Open my heart and let me prepare
   Love with Thy children thus to share.
   Silently now I wait for Thee,
   Ready, my God, Thy will to see;
   Open my heart, illumine me,
   Spirit divine!

ONWARD, CHRISTIAN SOLDIERS

Words by SABINE BARING-GOULD
Music by ARTHUR S. SULLIVAN

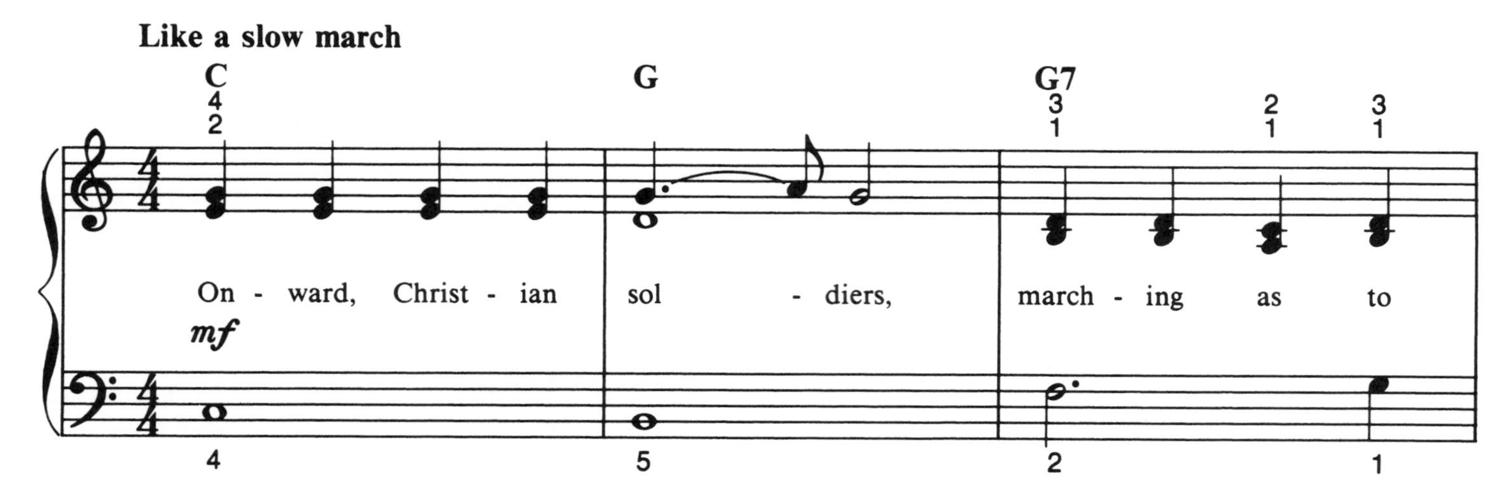

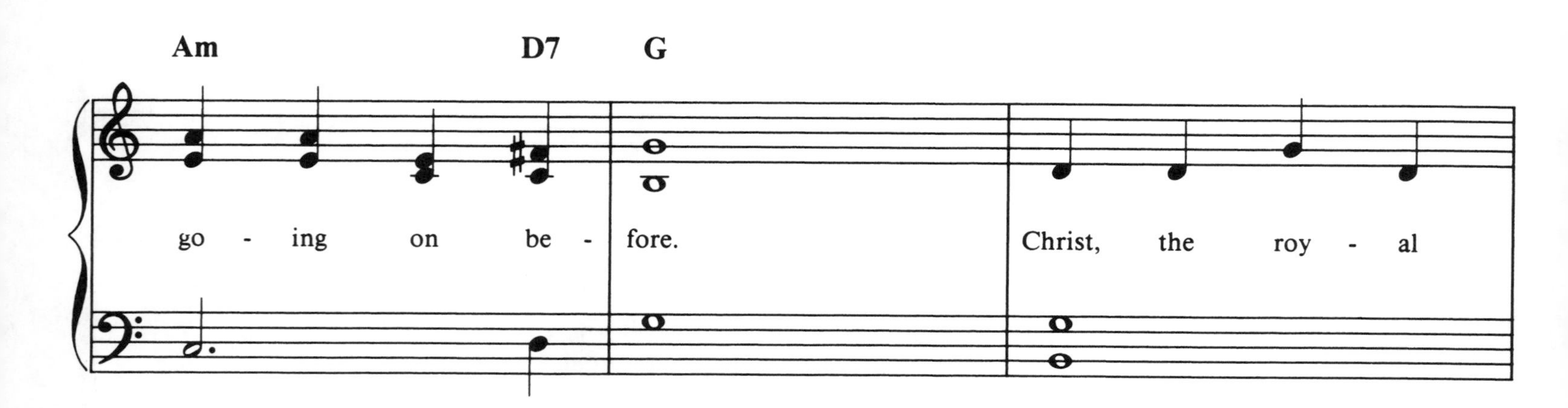

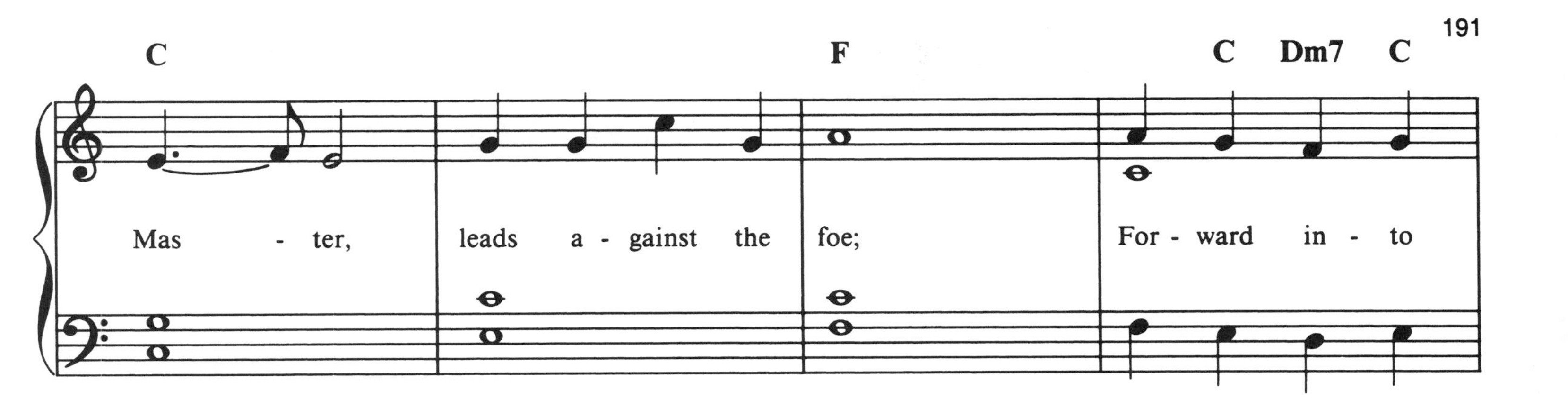
C
F
C Dm7 C
Mas - ter, leads a - gainst the foe; For - ward in - to

F C Dm7 C F C Dm7 C G
bat - tle, see His ban - ners go!

C
G7
C
On - ward, Christ - ian sol - diers, march - ing as to war,
f

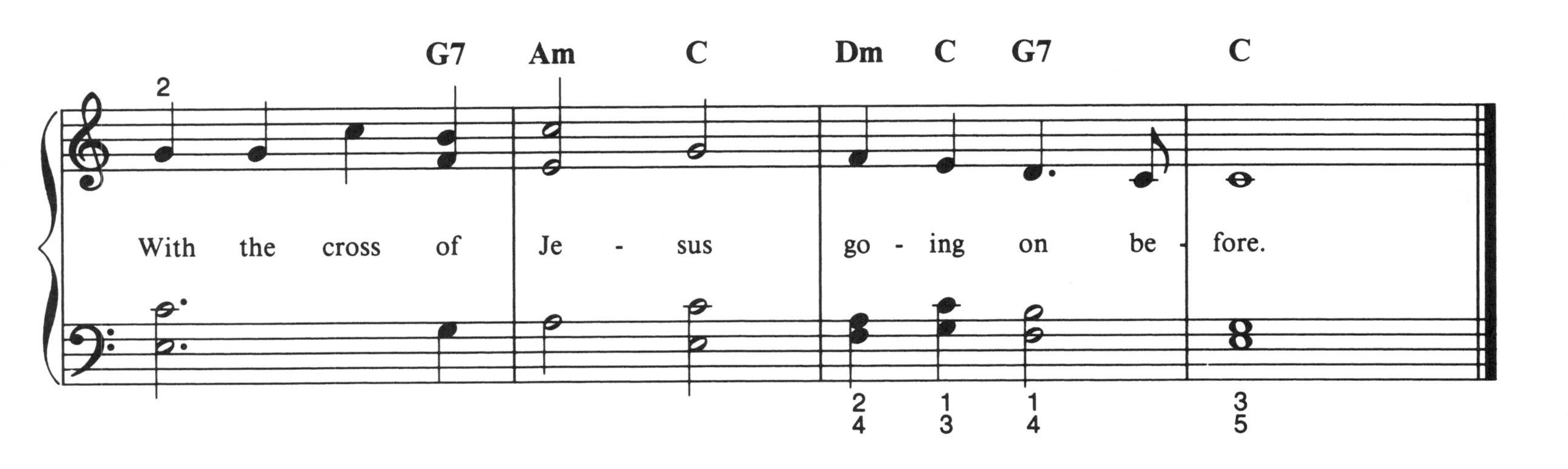
G7 Am C Dm C G7 C
With the cross of Je - sus go - ing on be - fore.

PRAISE THE LORD! YE HEAVENS, ADORE HIM

Words from *Founding Hospital Collection*
V.3 by EDWARD OSLER
Music by FRANZ JOSEPH HAYDN

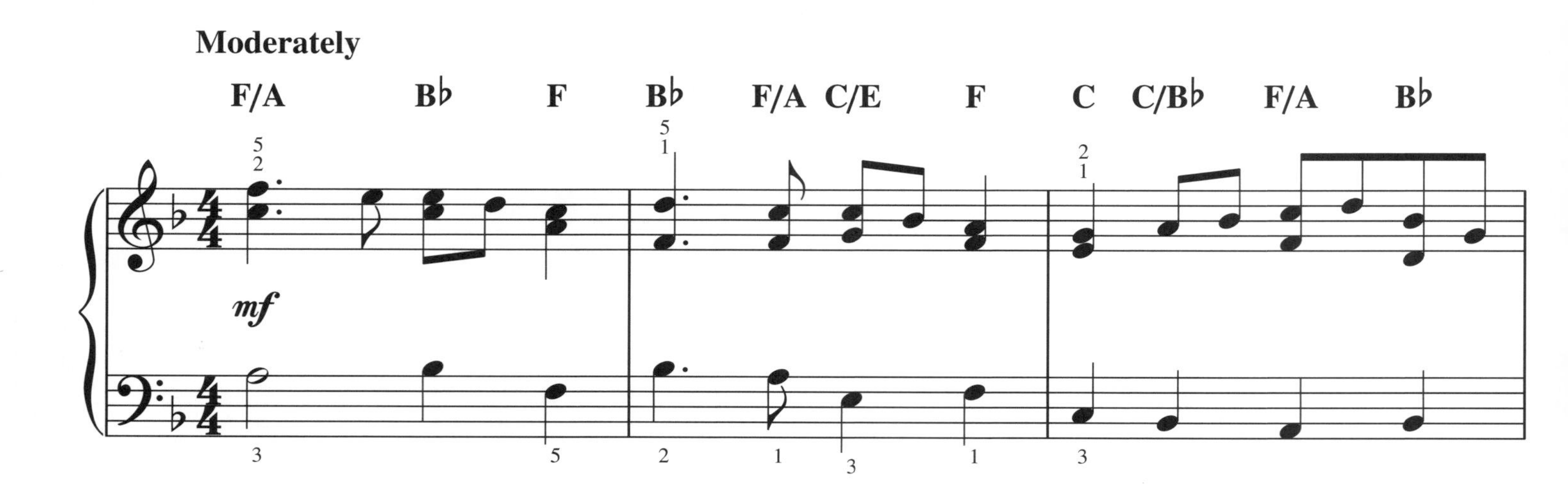

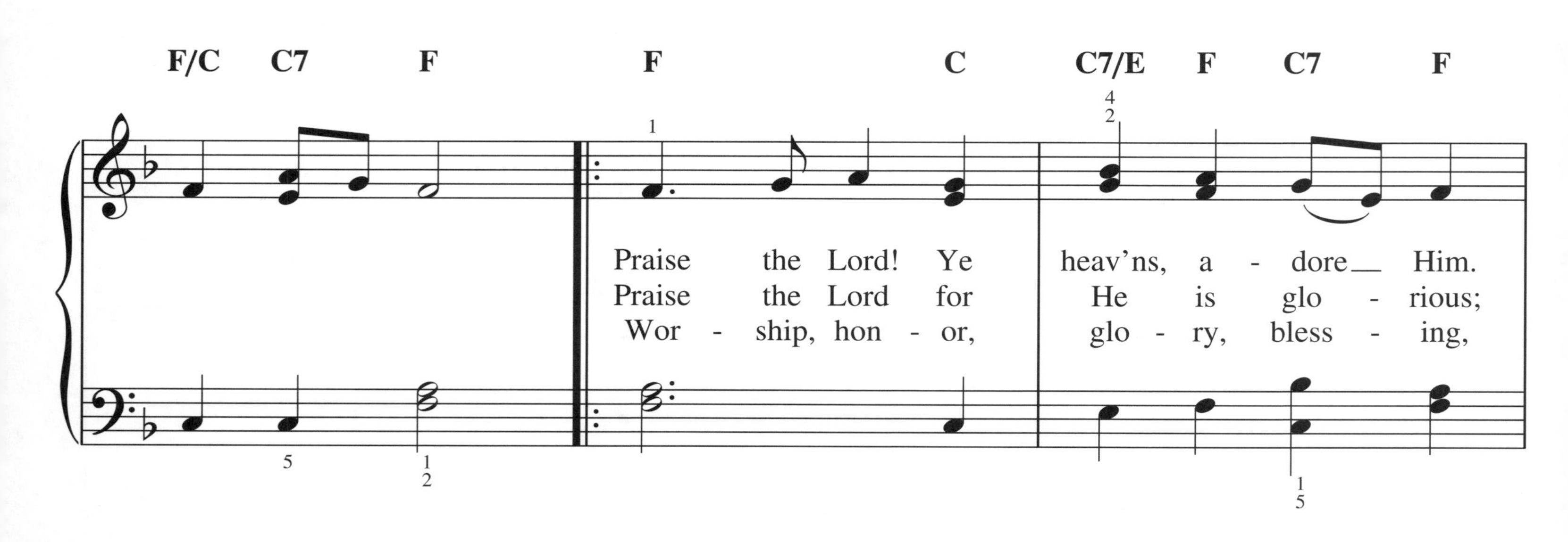

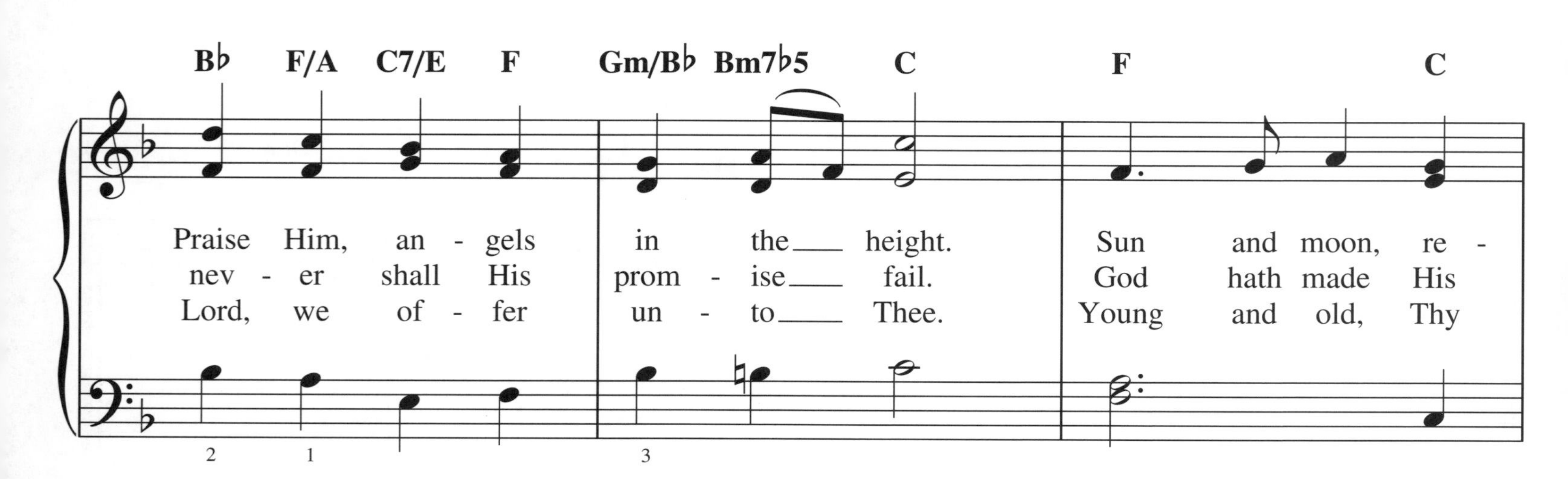

C7/E F C7 F Bb F/A C7/E F Gm/Bb Bm7b5 C
joice be - fore Him. Praise Him, all ye stars of light.
saints vic - to - rious; sin and death shall not pre - vail.
praise ex - press - ing, in glad hom - age bend the knee.
F/C C C7/E F C F/A C7 Dm
Praise the Lord for He hath spo - ken; worlds His might - y
Praise the God of our sal - va - tion! Hosts on high, His
All the saints in heav'n a - dore Thee; we would bow be -
G7 C F/A Bb F Bb F/A C/E F
voice o - beyed. Laws which nev - er shall be bro - ken
pow'r pro - claim. Heav'n and earth and all cre - a - tion,
fore Thy throne. As Thine an - gels serve be - fore Thee,
C C/Bb F/A Bb
for their guid - ance He hath made.
laud and mag - ni - fy His name.
so on earth Thy will be done.
1., 2.
F/C C7 F
3.
F/C C7 F

PRECIOUS MEMORIES

Words and Music by
J.B.F. WRIGHT

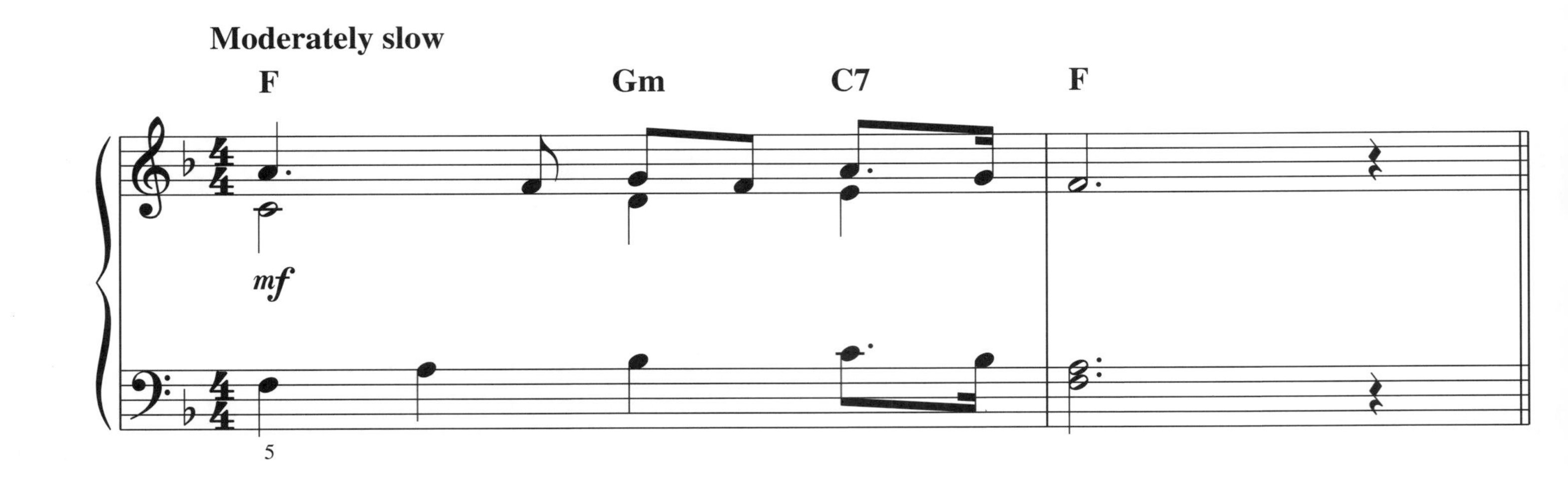

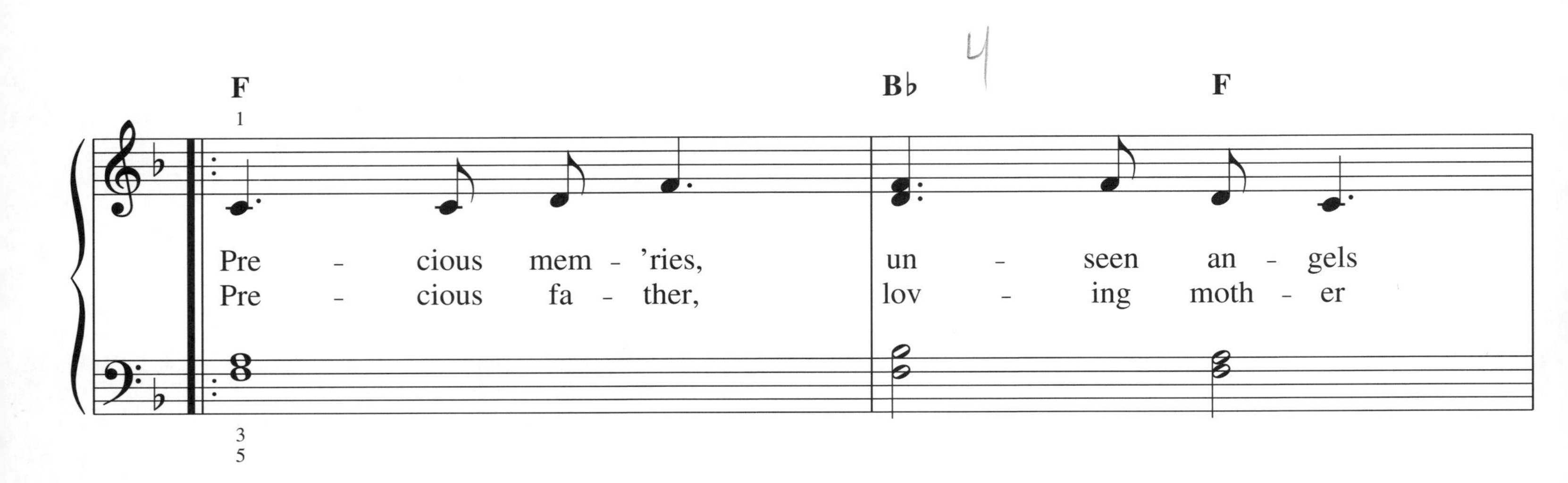

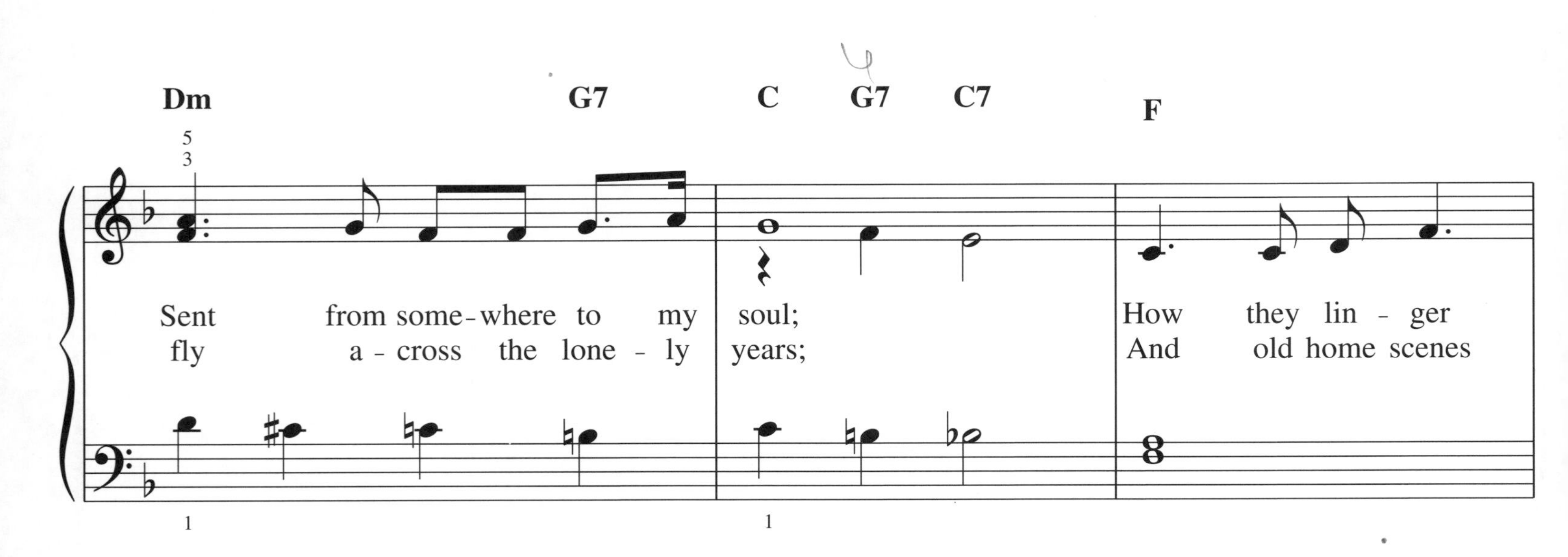

B♭
F
Gm
C7
F
ev - er near me
of my child - hood
And the sa - cred past un - fold.
In fond mem - o - ry ap - pears.
F+
B♭
B♭m
Pre - cious mem - 'ries, how they lin - ger, How they ev - er flood my
F
G7
B♭
F
soul; In the still - ness of the mid - night
Gm
C7
1.
F
2.
F
pre - cious sa - cred scenes un - fold.
fold.

REJOICE, THE LORD IS KING

Words by CHARLES WESLEY
Music by JOHN DARWALL

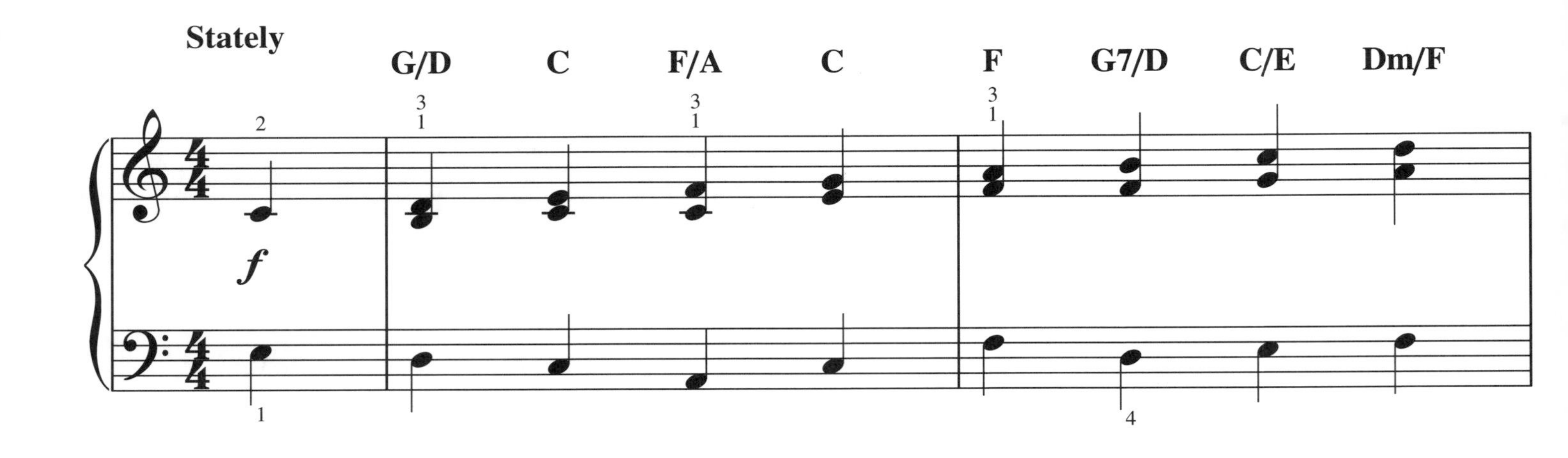

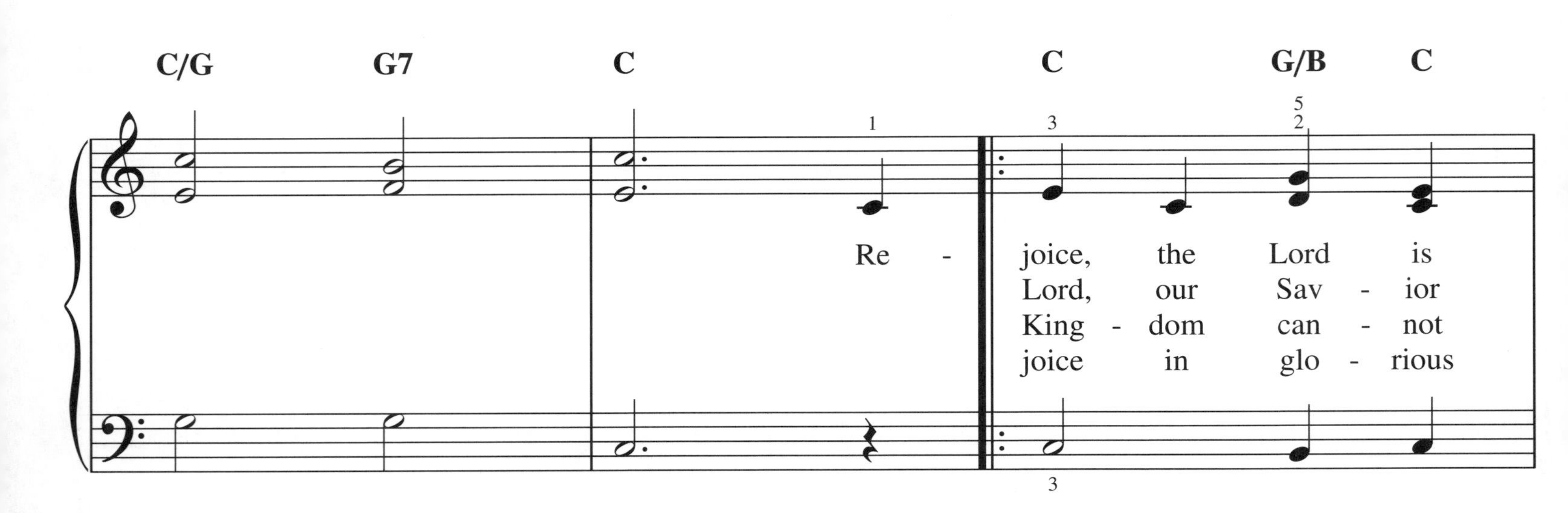

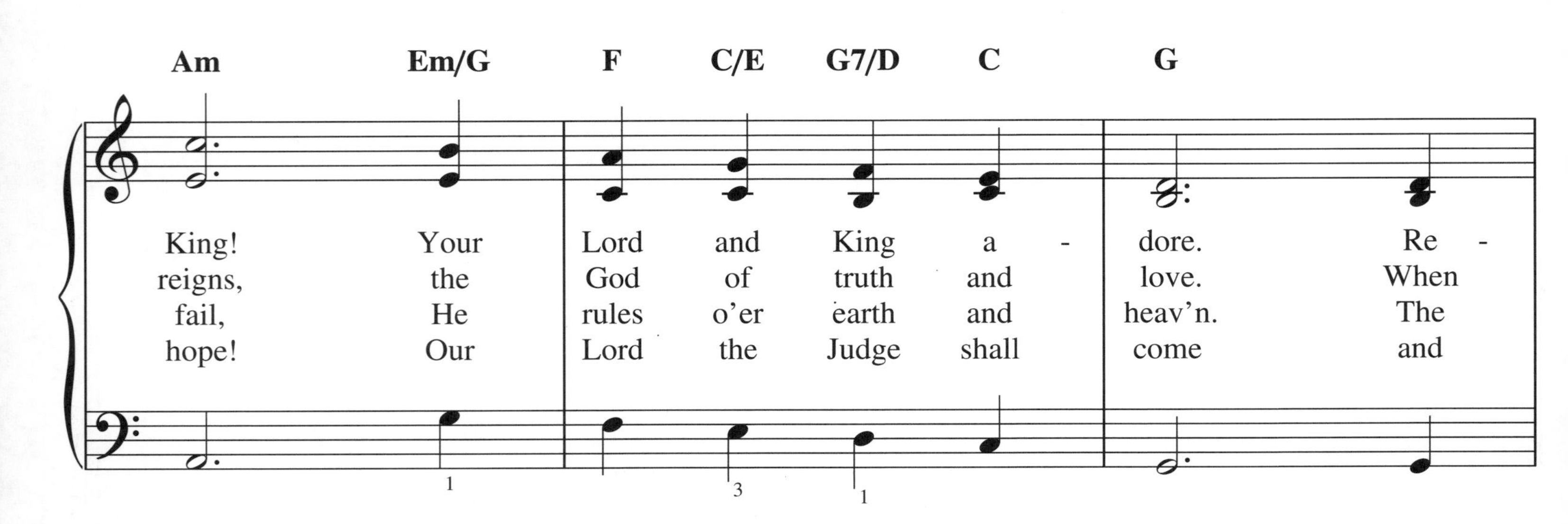

C Am G/B D D/C G/B C
joice, give thanks and sing and tri - umph
He had purged our stains, He took His
keys of death and hell are to our
take His ser - vants up to their e -
G/D D7 G C F G7/D
ev - er - more.
seat a - bove.
Je - sus giv'n.
ter - nal home.
Lift up your
C C/E G/D C F/A C F G7/D C/E Dm/F
heart, lift up your voice! Re - joice, a - gain I
C/G G7 1.–3. C 4. C
say, re - joice!
The
His
Re -
joice!

REJOICE, YE PURE IN HEART

Words by EDWARD HAYES PLUMPTRE
Music by ARTHUR HENRY MESSITER

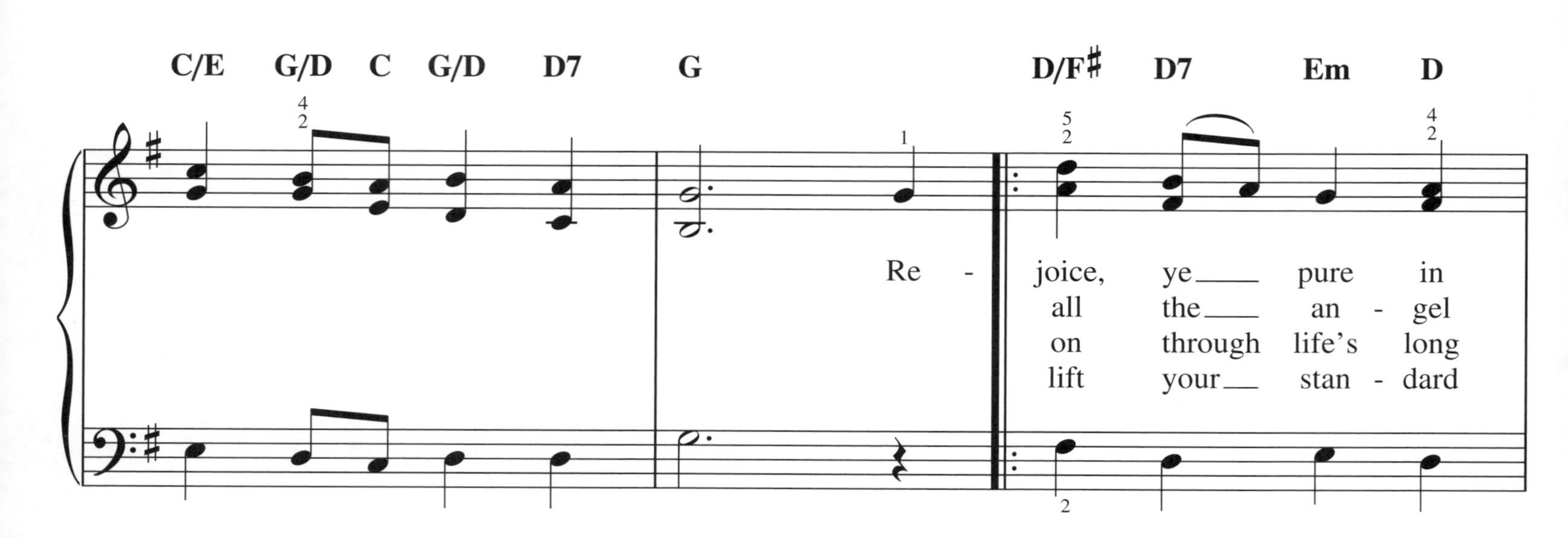

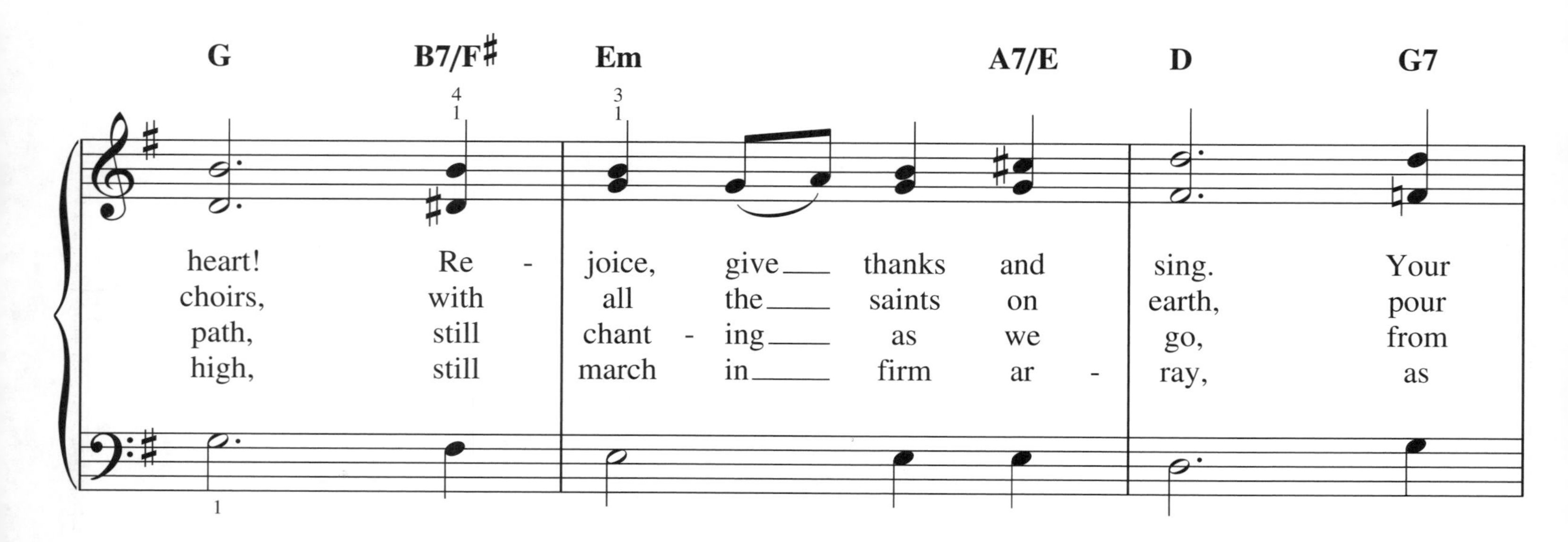

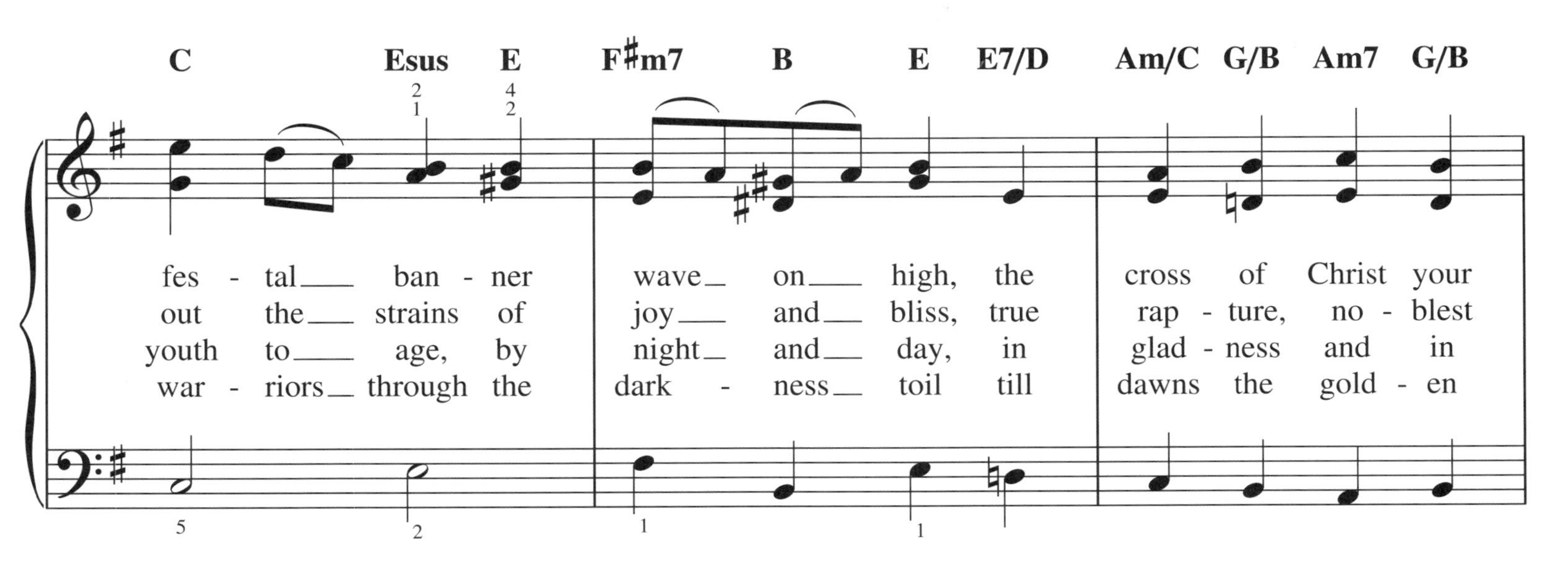
C Esus E F♯m7 B E E7/D Am/C G/B Am7 G/B
fes - tal ban - ner wave on high, the cross of Christ your
out the strains of joy and bliss, true rap - ture, no - blest
youth to age, by night and day, in glad - ness and in
war - riors through the dark - ness toil till dawns the gold - en

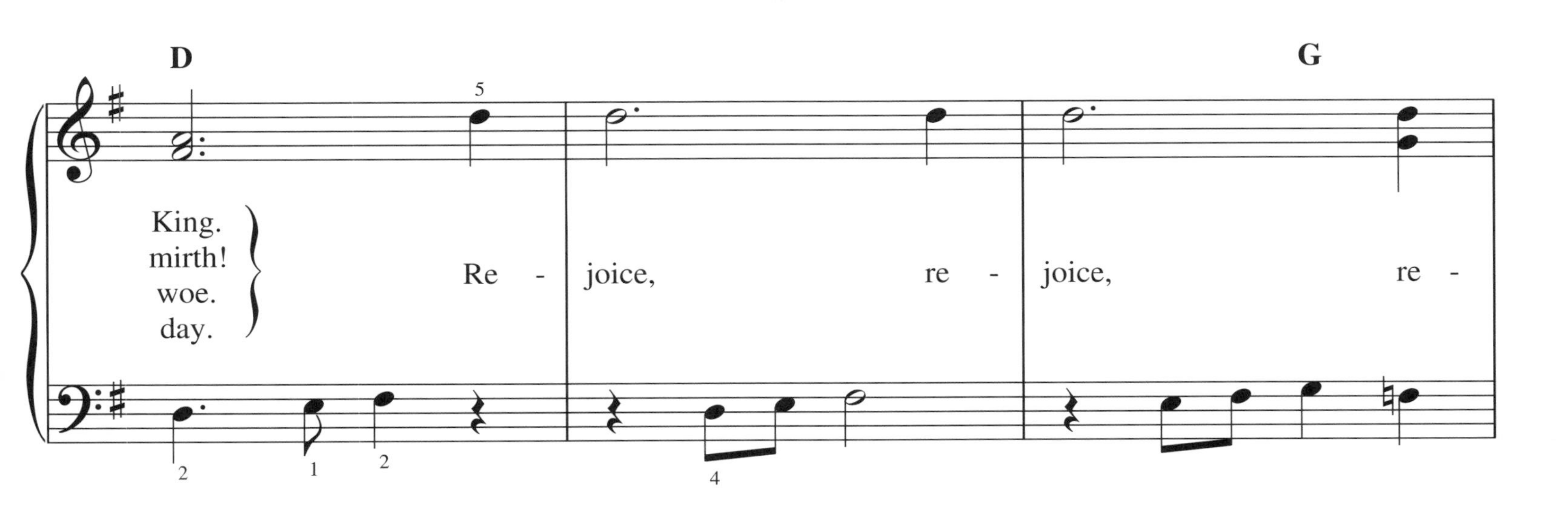
D G
King.
mirth!
woe.
day.
Re - joice, re - joice, re -

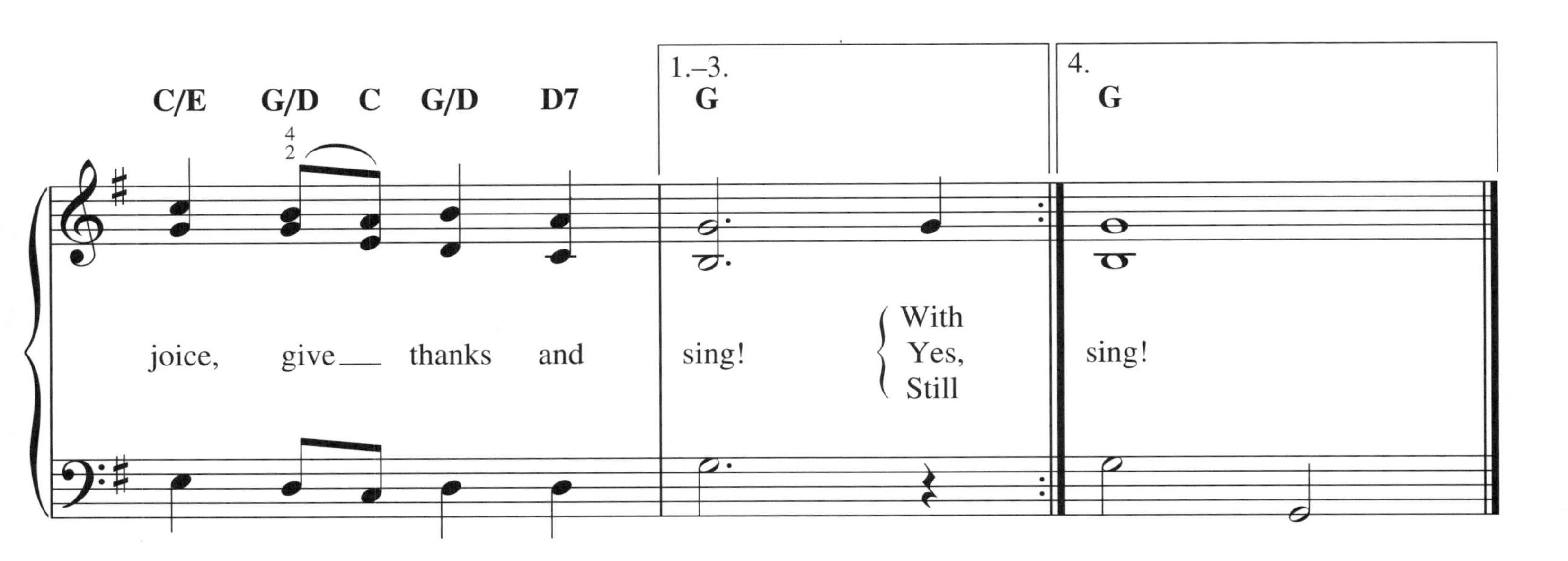
1.–3. 4.
C/E G/D C G/D D7 G G
joice, give thanks and sing!
With
Yes,
Still
sing!

ROCK OF AGES

Words by AUGUSTUS M. TOPLADY
v.1,2,4 altered by THOMAS COTTERILL
Music by THOMAS HASTINGS

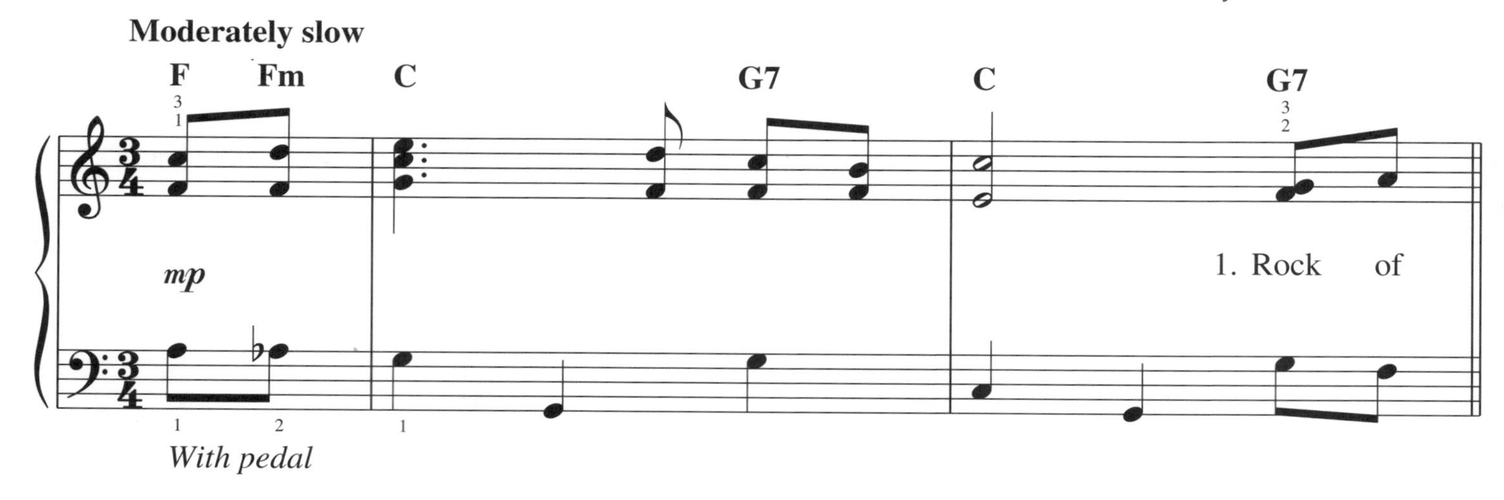

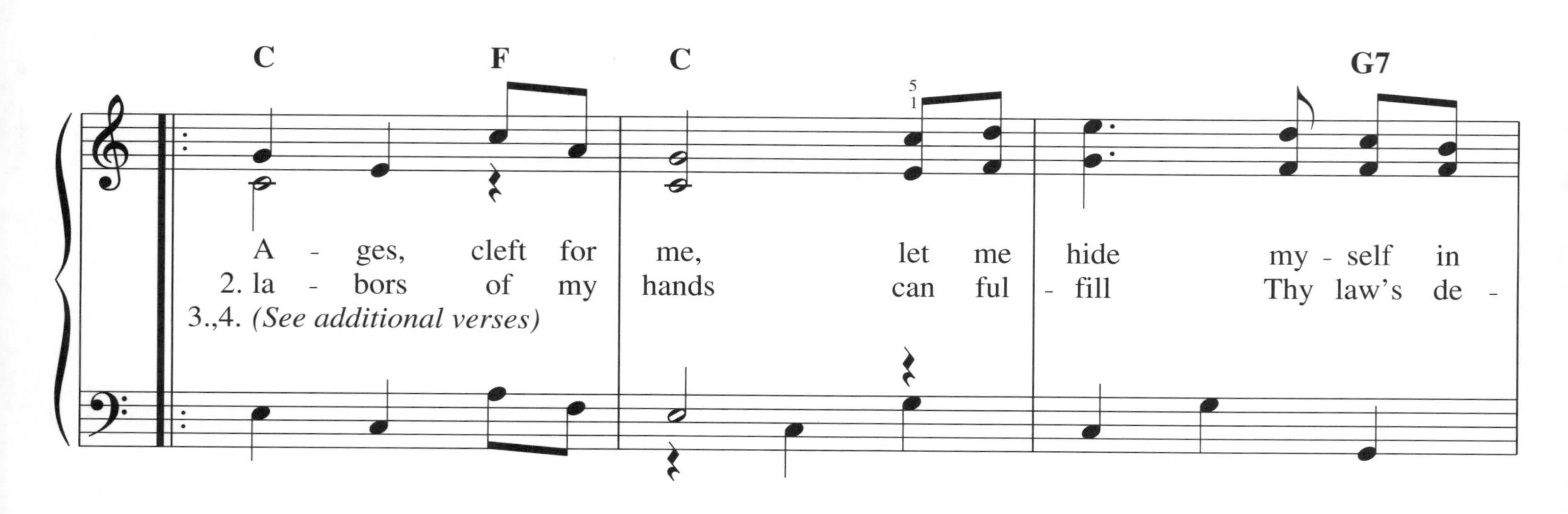

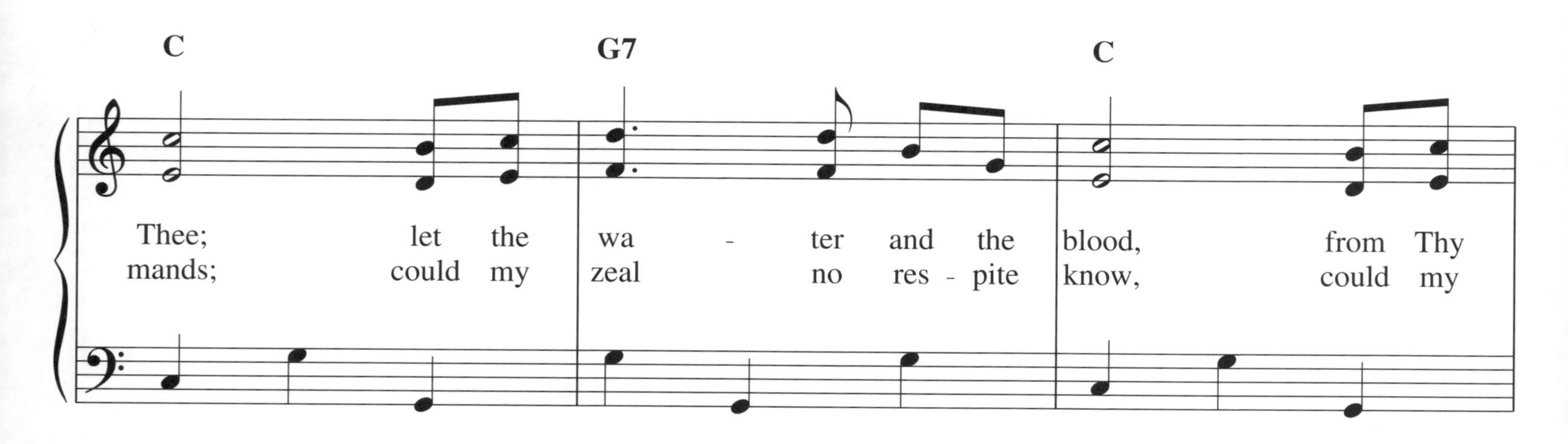

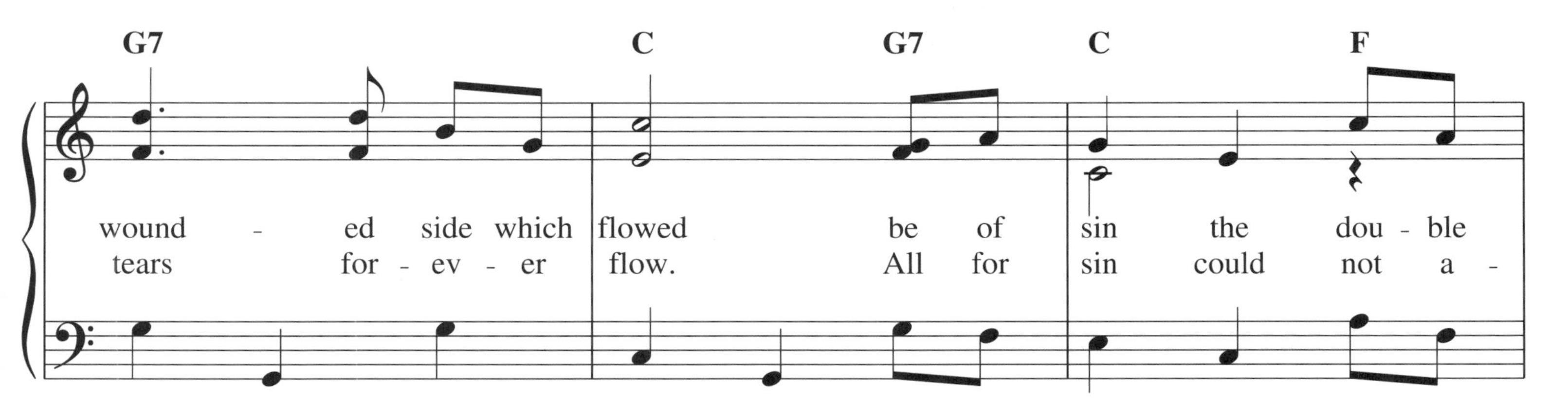

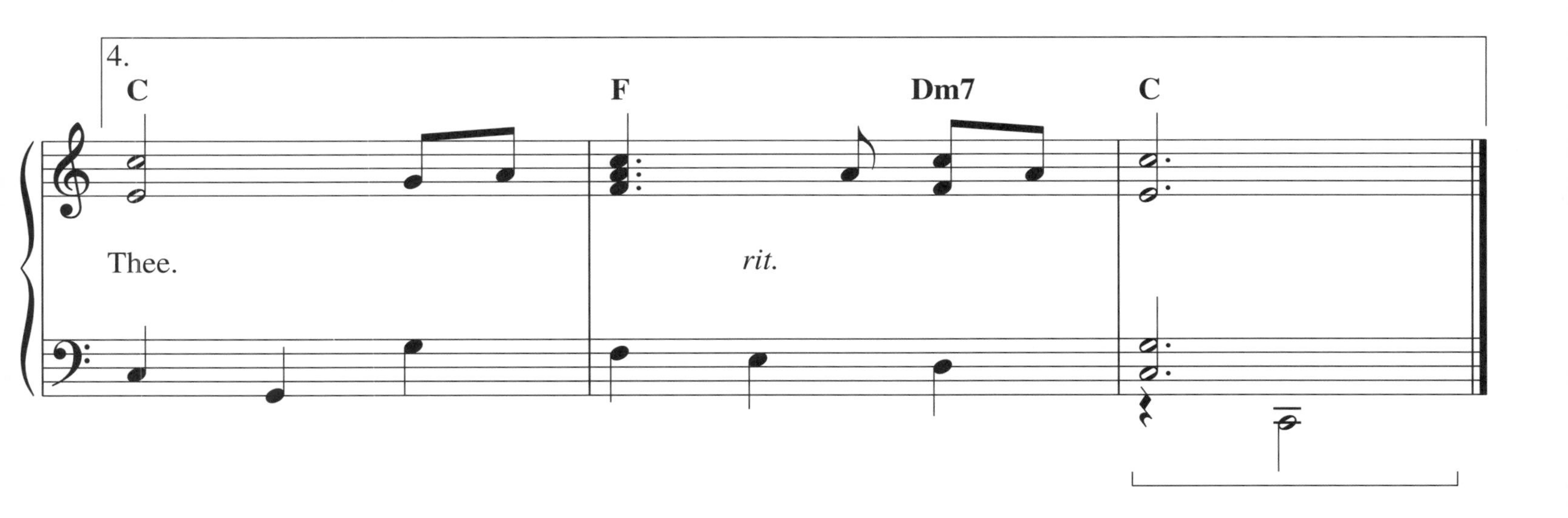

Additional Verses

3. Nothing in my hand I bring,
Simply to the cross I cling;
Naked, come to Thee for dress;
Helpless, look to Thee for grace.
Foul, I to the fountain fly;
Wash me, Savior, or I die.

4. While I draw this fleeting breath,
When mine eyes shall close in death,
When I soar to worlds unknown,
See Thee on Thy judgment throne,
Rock of Ages, cleft for me,
Let me hide myself in Thee.

SAVIOR, LIKE A SHEPHERD LEAD US

Words from *Hymns For The Young*
Attributed to DOROTHY A. THRUPP
Music by WILLIAM B. BRADBURY

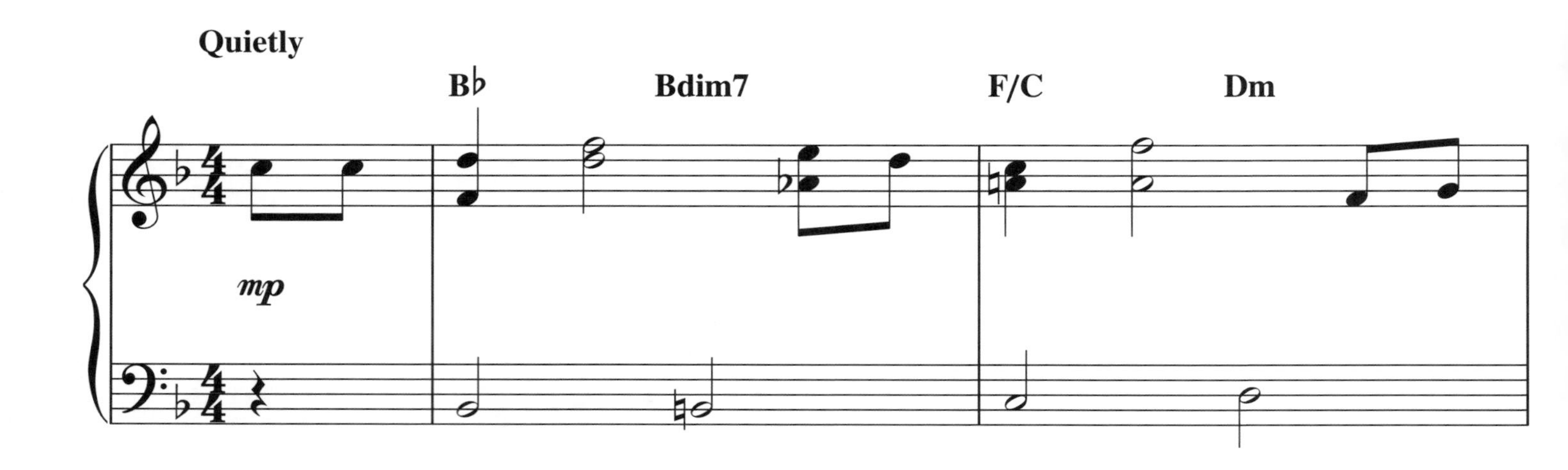

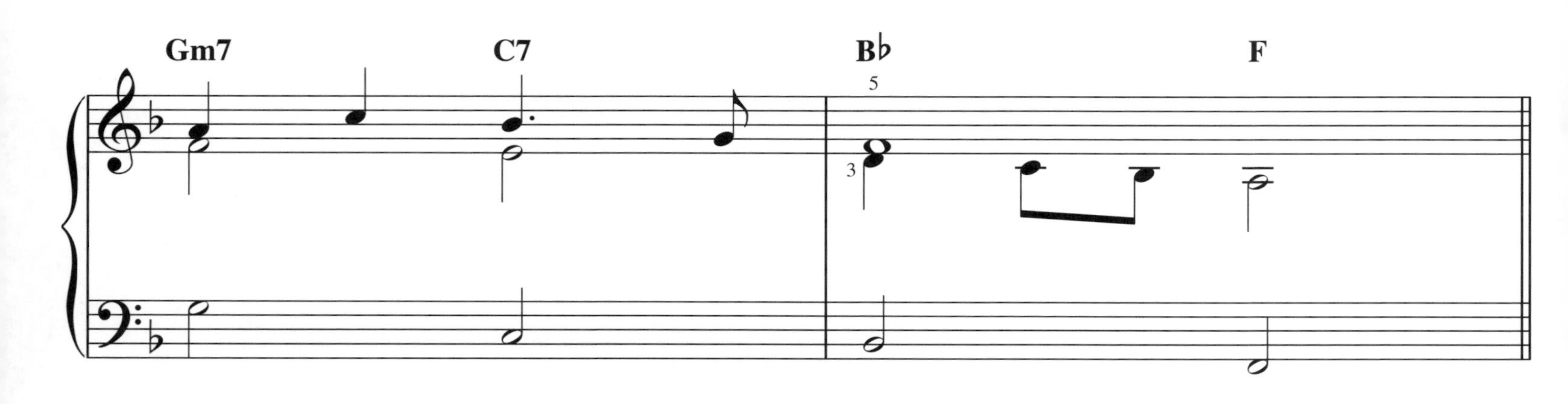

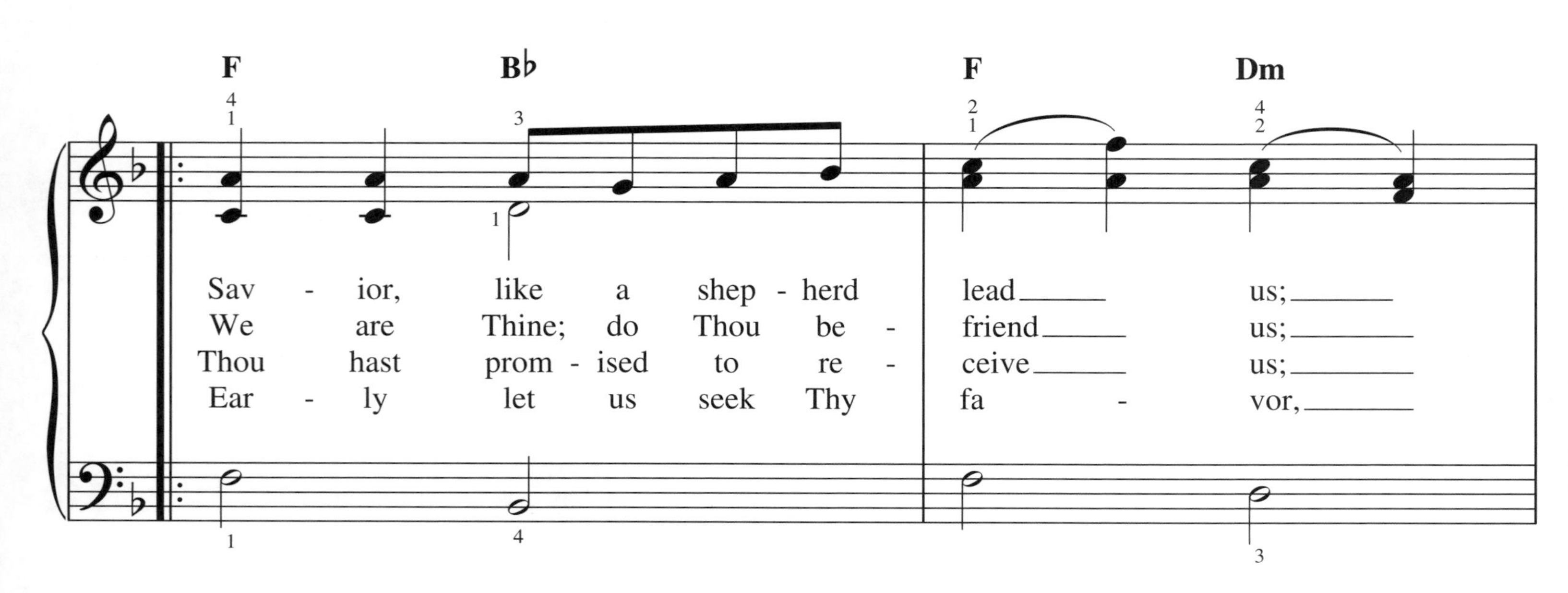

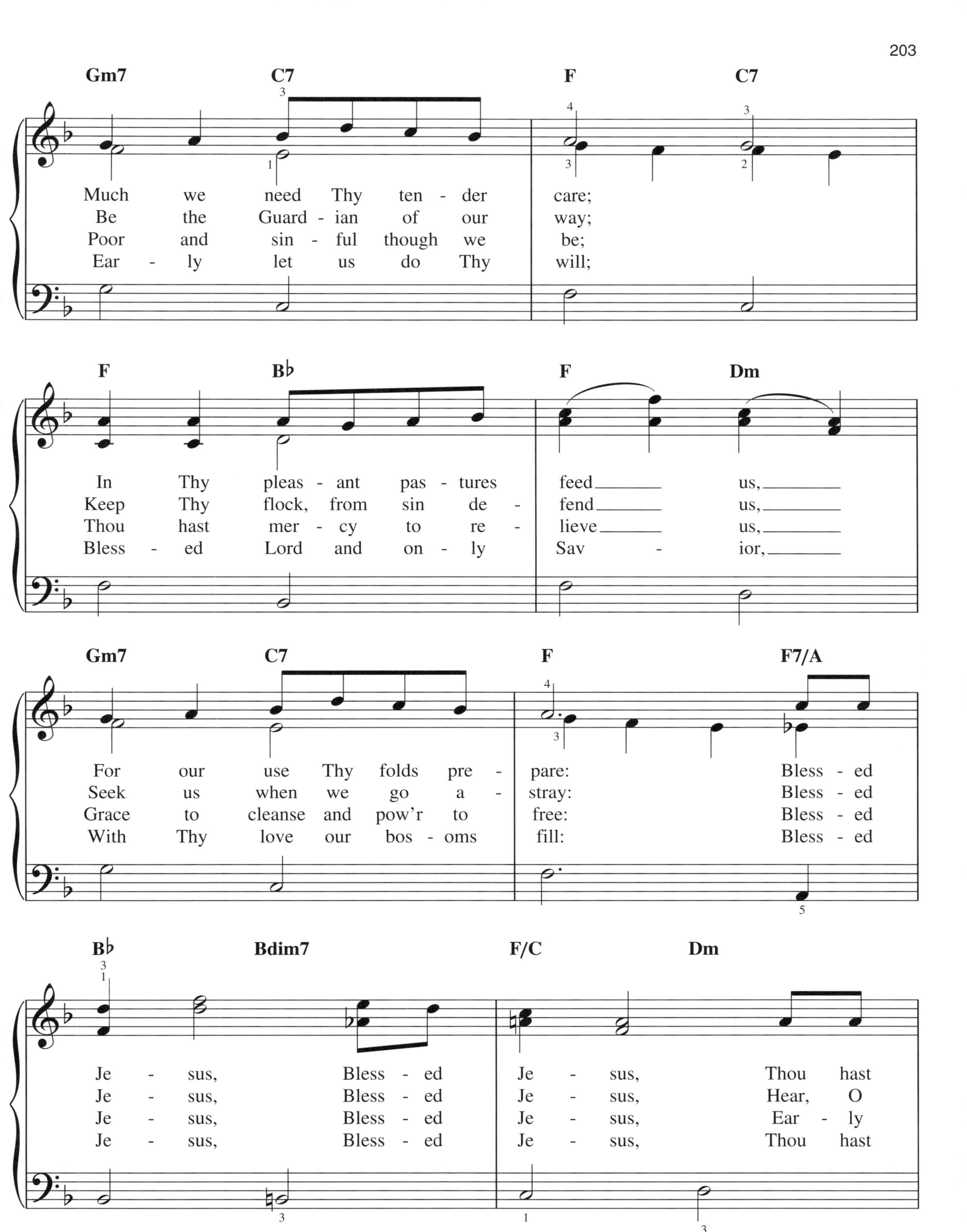
Gm7 C7 F C7
Much we need Thy ten - der care;
Be the Guard - ian of our way;
Poor and sin - ful though we be;
Ear - ly let us do Thy will;
F B♭ F Dm
In Thy pleas - ant pas - tures feed us,
Keep Thy flock, from sin de - fend us,
Thou hast mer - cy to re - lieve us,
Bless - ed Lord and on - ly Sav - ior,
Gm7 C7 F F7/A
For our use Thy folds pre - pare: Bless - ed
Seek us when we go a - stray: Bless - ed
Grace to cleanse and pow'r to free: Bless - ed
With Thy love our bos - oms fill: Bless - ed
B♭ Bdim7 F/C Dm
Je - sus, Bless - ed Je - sus, Thou hast
Je - sus, Bless - ed Je - sus, Hear, O
Je - sus, Bless - ed Je - sus, Ear - ly
Je - sus, Bless - ed Je - sus, Thou hast

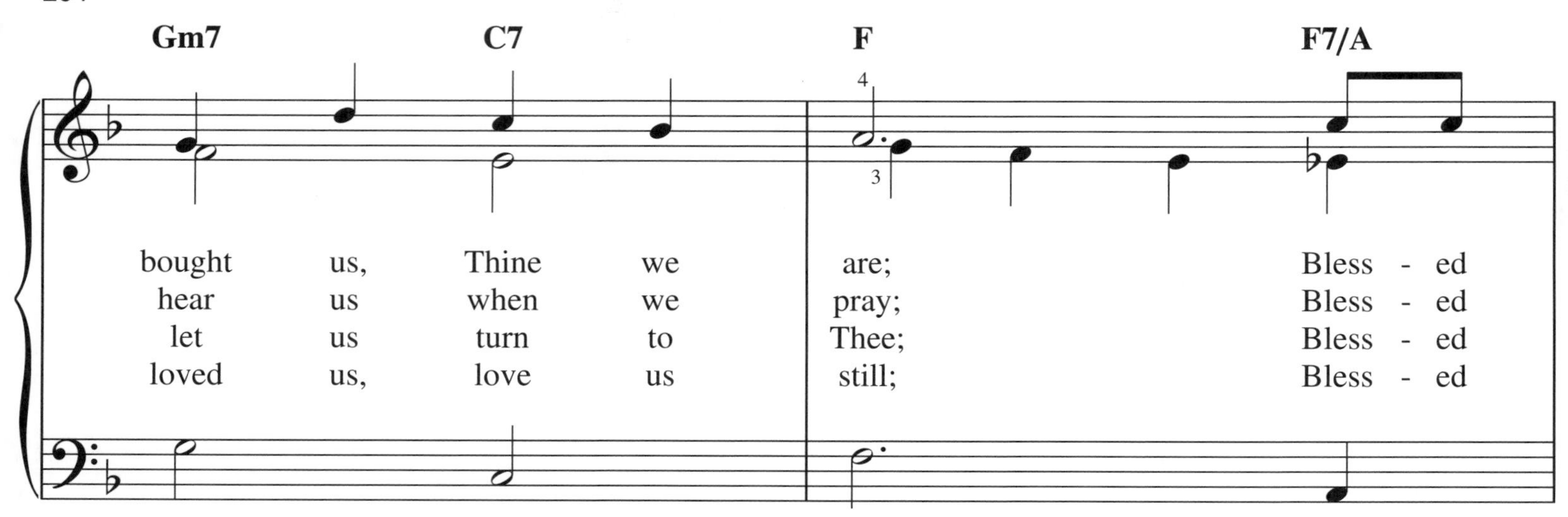
Gm7
C7
F
F7/A
bought us, Thine we are; Bless - ed
hear us when we pray; Bless - ed
let us turn to Thee; Bless - ed
loved us, love us still; Bless - ed

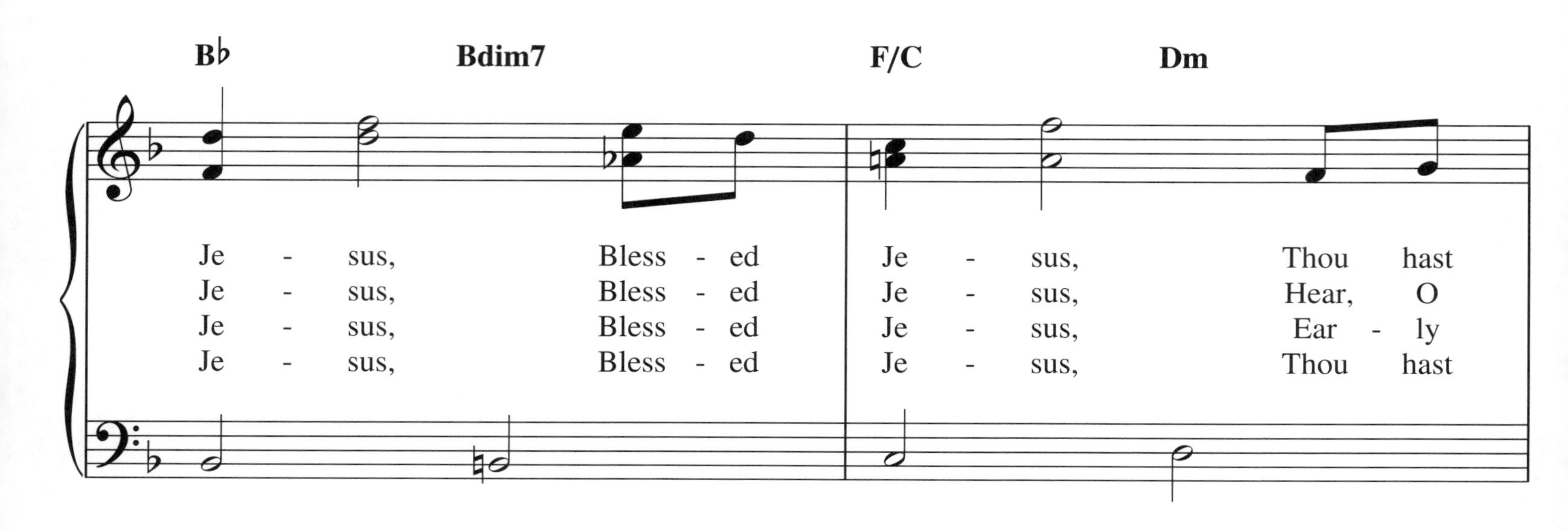
B♭
Bdim7
F/C
Dm
Je - sus, Bless - ed Je - sus, Thou hast
Je - sus, Bless - ed Je - sus, Hear, O
Je - sus, Bless - ed Je - sus, Ear - ly
Je - sus, Bless - ed Je - sus, Thou hast

Gm7
C7
1.–3.
B♭
F
C7
4.
B♭
F
bought us, Thine we are.
hear us when we pray.
let us turn to Thee.
loved us, love us still.

SOFTLY AND TENDERLY

Words and Music by
WILL L. THOMPSON

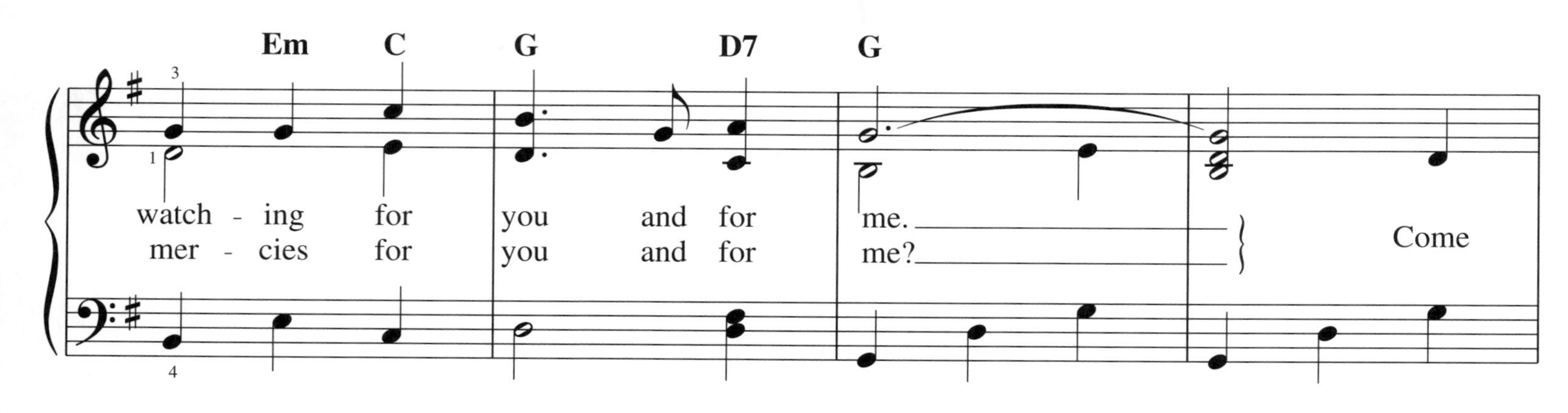
Em C G D7 G
watch - ing for you and for me.
mer - cies for you and for me?
Come

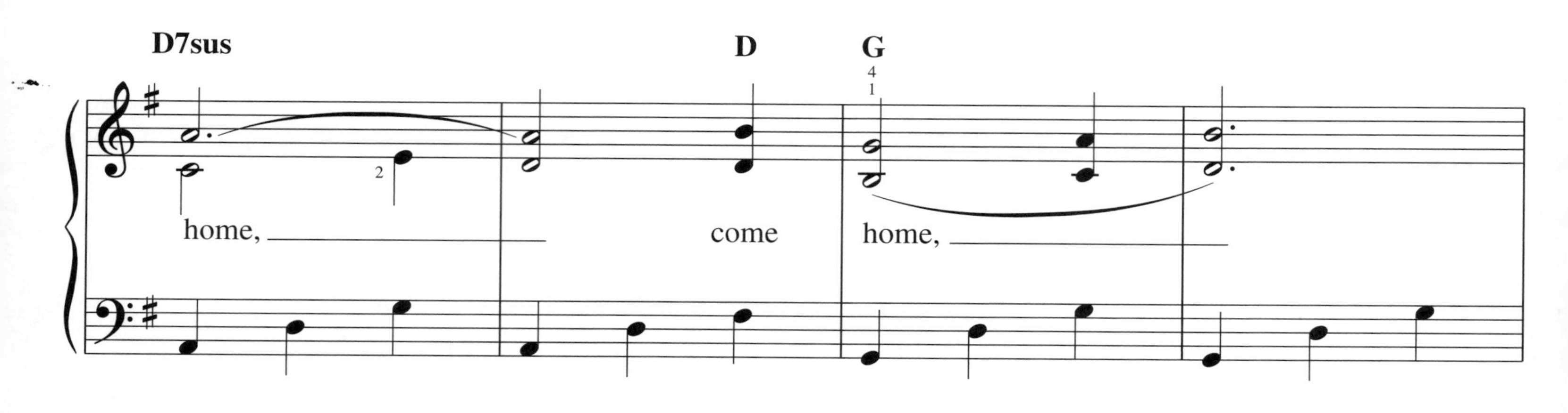
D7sus D G
home, come home,

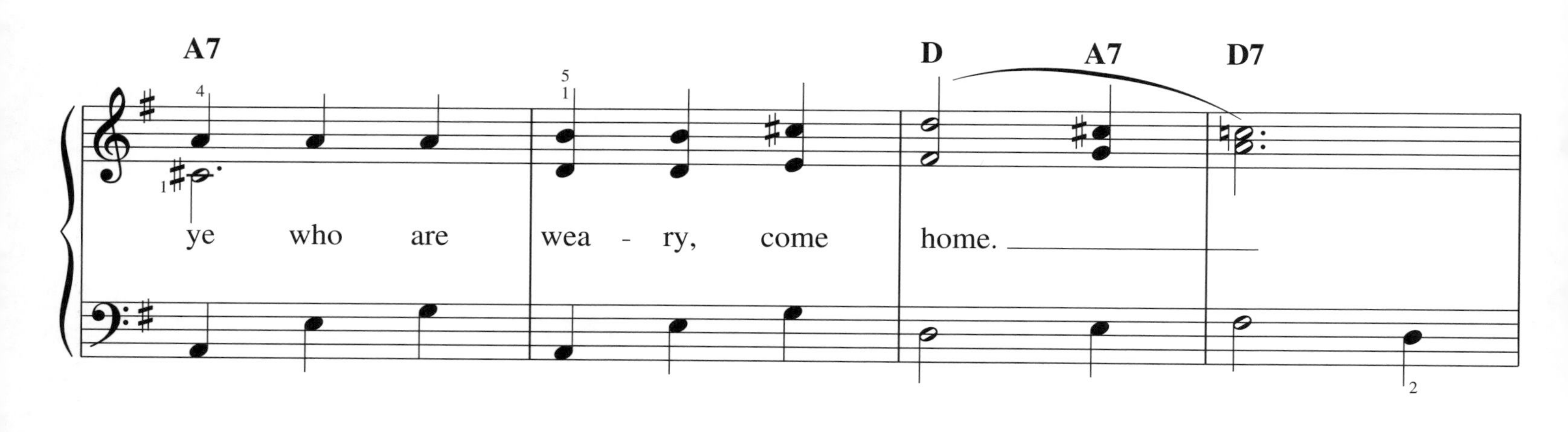
A7 D A7 D7
ye who are wea - ry, come home.

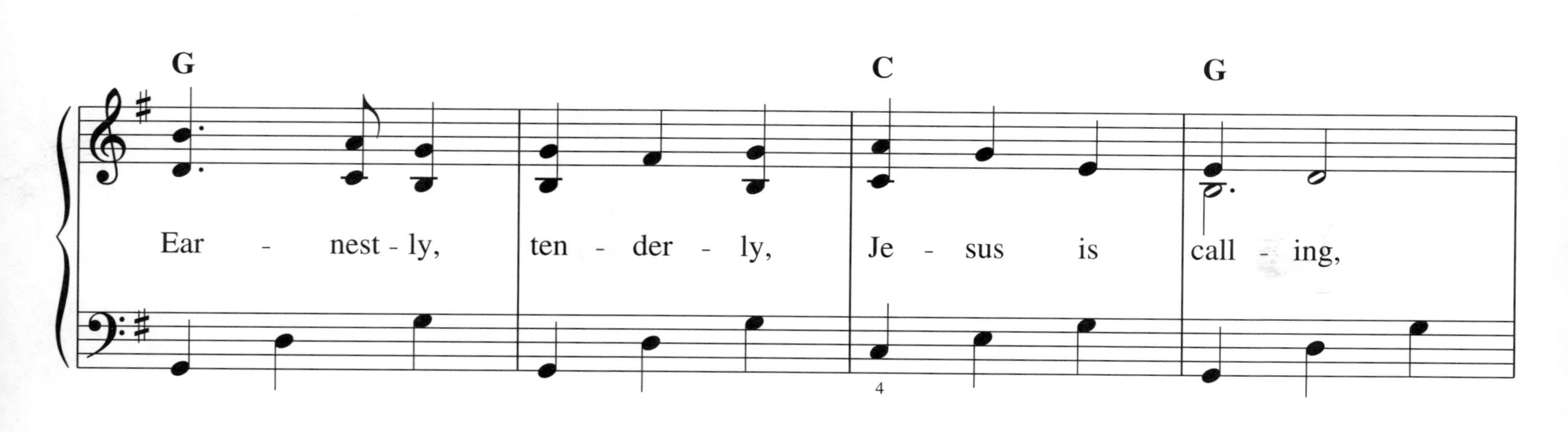
G C G
Ear - nest - ly, ten - der - ly, Je - sus is call - ing,

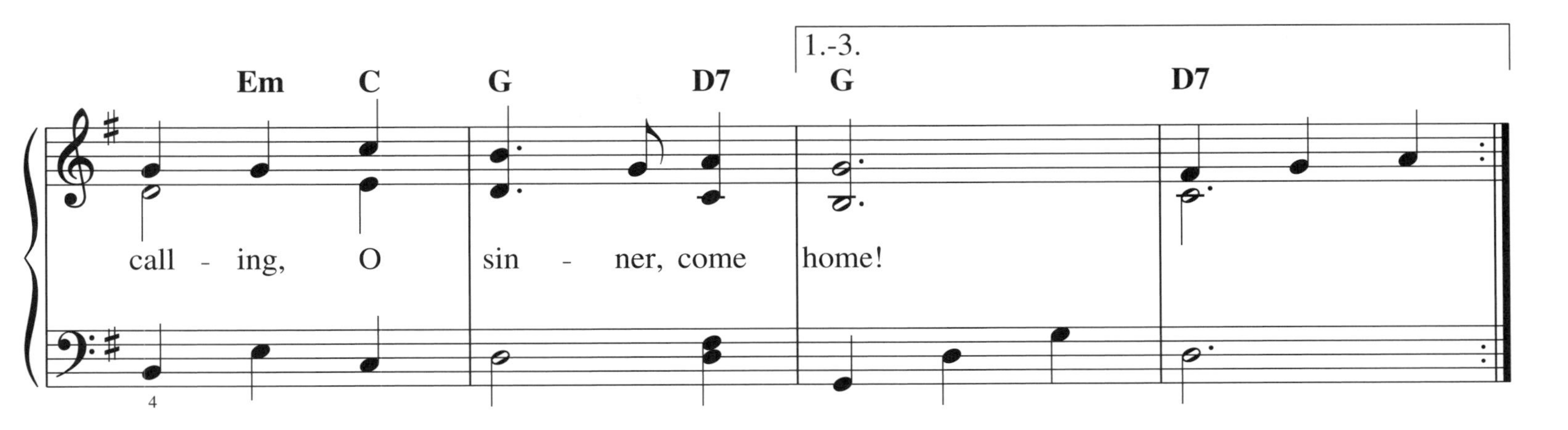

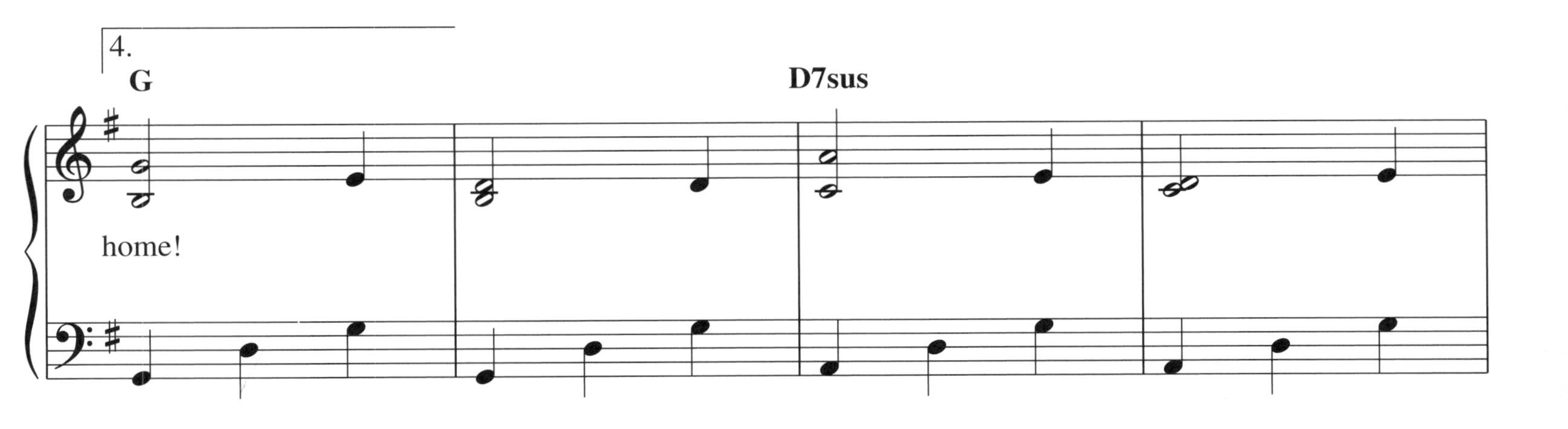

Additional Verses

3. Oh! for the wonderful love He has promised,
   Promised for you and for me.
   Tho' we have sinned, He has mercy and pardon,
   Pardon for you and for me.

4. Time is now fleeting, the moments are passing,
   Passing for you and for me.
   Shadows are gathering, death beds are coming,
   Coming for you and for me.

SPIRIT OF GOD, DESCEND UPON MY HEART

Words by GEORGE CROLY
Music by FREDERICK COOK ATKINSON

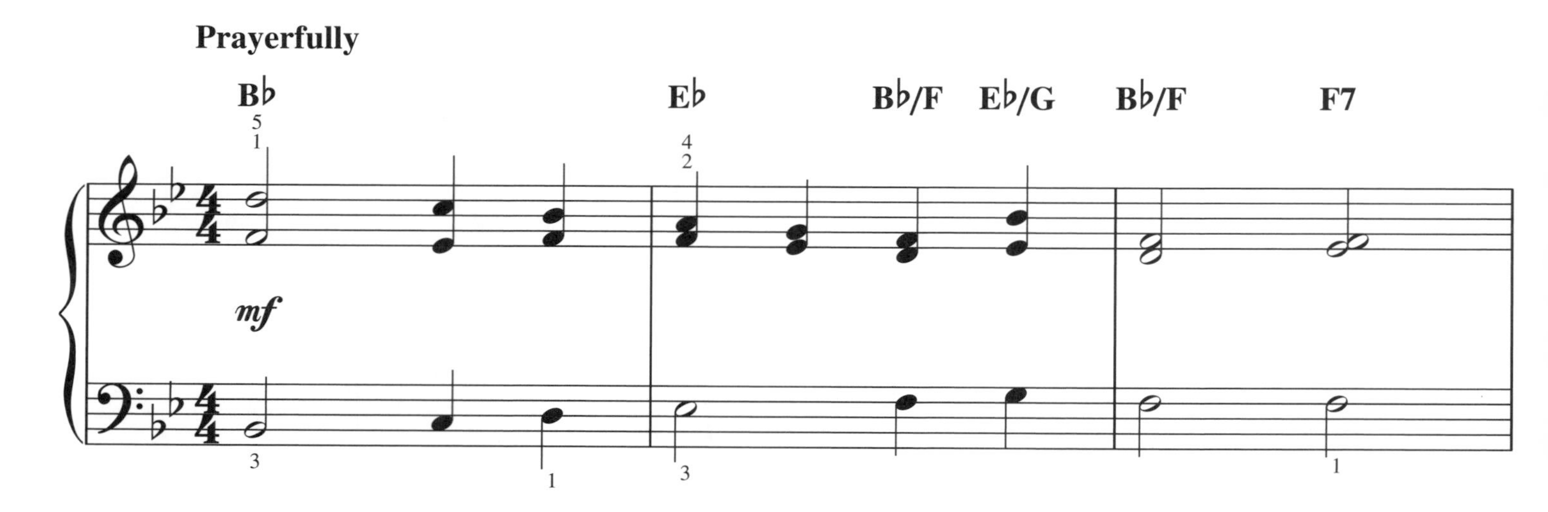

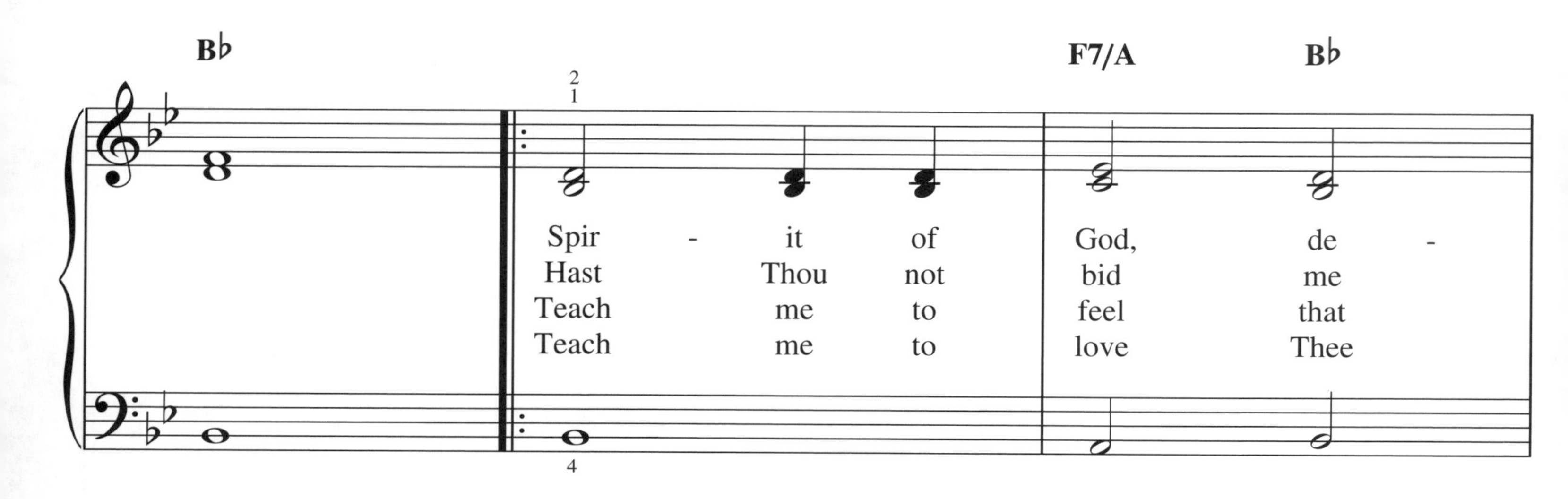

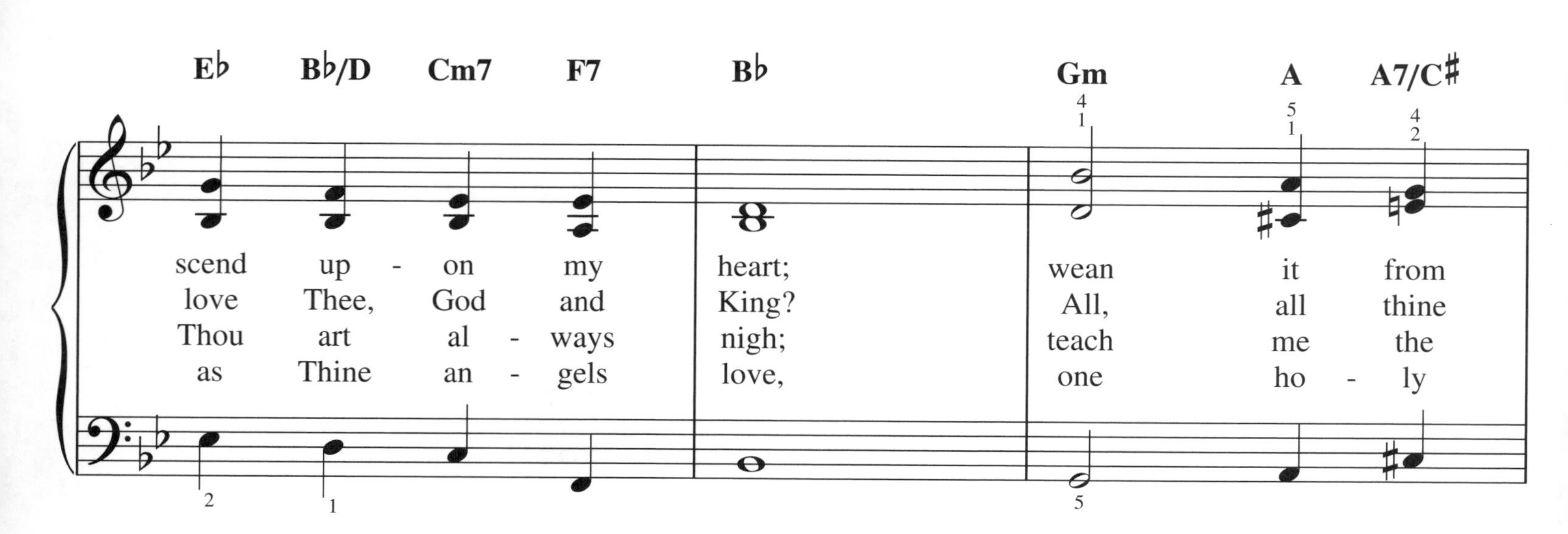

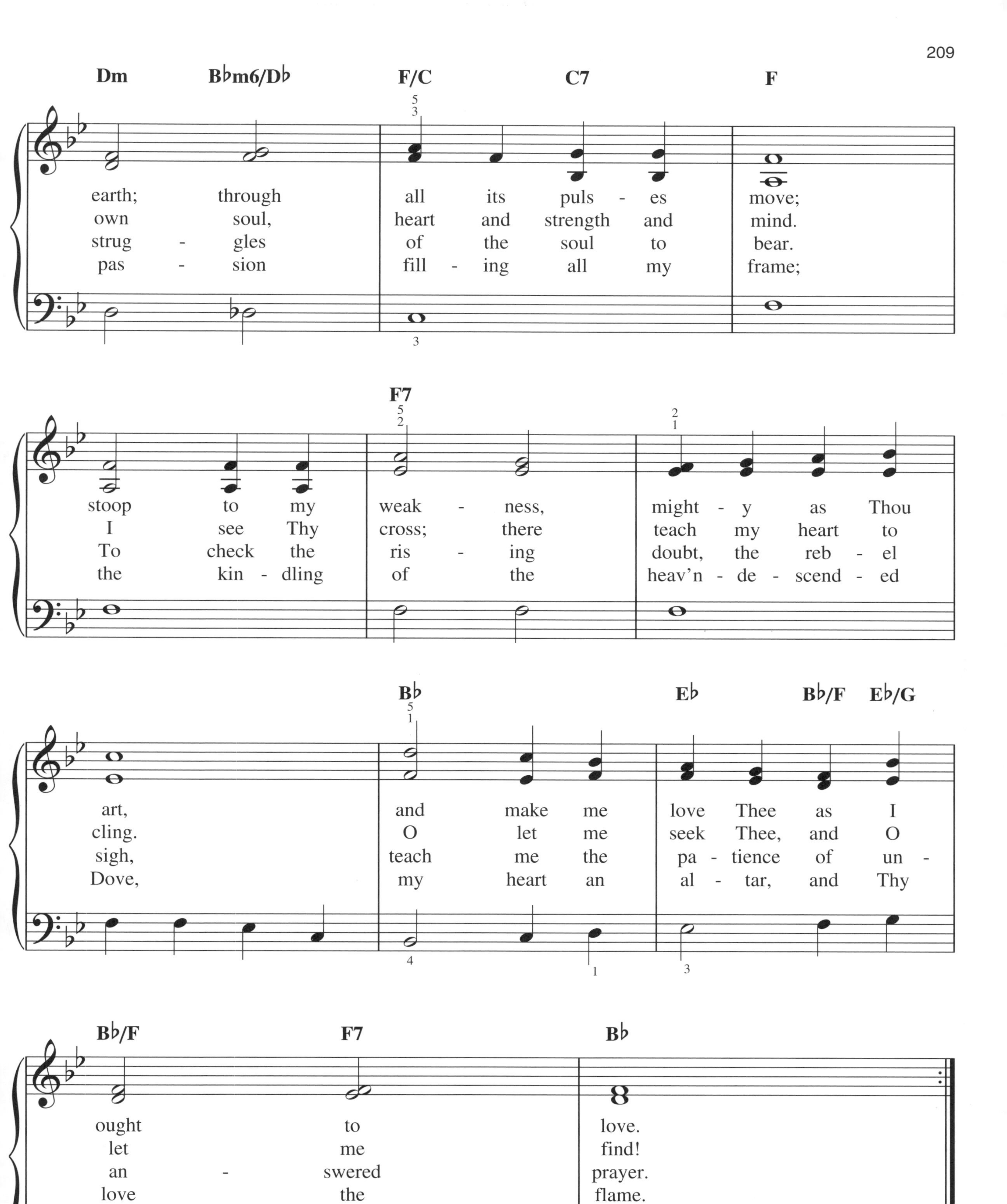
Dm Bbm6/Db F/C C7 F
earth; through all its puls - es move;
own soul, heart and strength and mind.
strug - gles of the soul to bear.
pas - sion fill - ing all my frame;
F7
stoop to my weak - ness, might - y as Thou
I see Thy cross; there teach my heart to
To check the ris - ing doubt, the reb - el
the kin - dling of the heav'n - de - scend - ed
Bb Eb Bb/F Eb/G
art, and make me love Thee as I
cling. O let me seek Thee, and O
sigh, teach me the pa - tience of un -
Dove, my heart an al - tar, and Thy
Bb/F F7 Bb
ought to love.
let me find!
an - swered prayer.
love the flame.

STAND UP AND BLESS THE LORD

Words by JAMES MONTGOMERY
Music by CHARLES LOCKHART

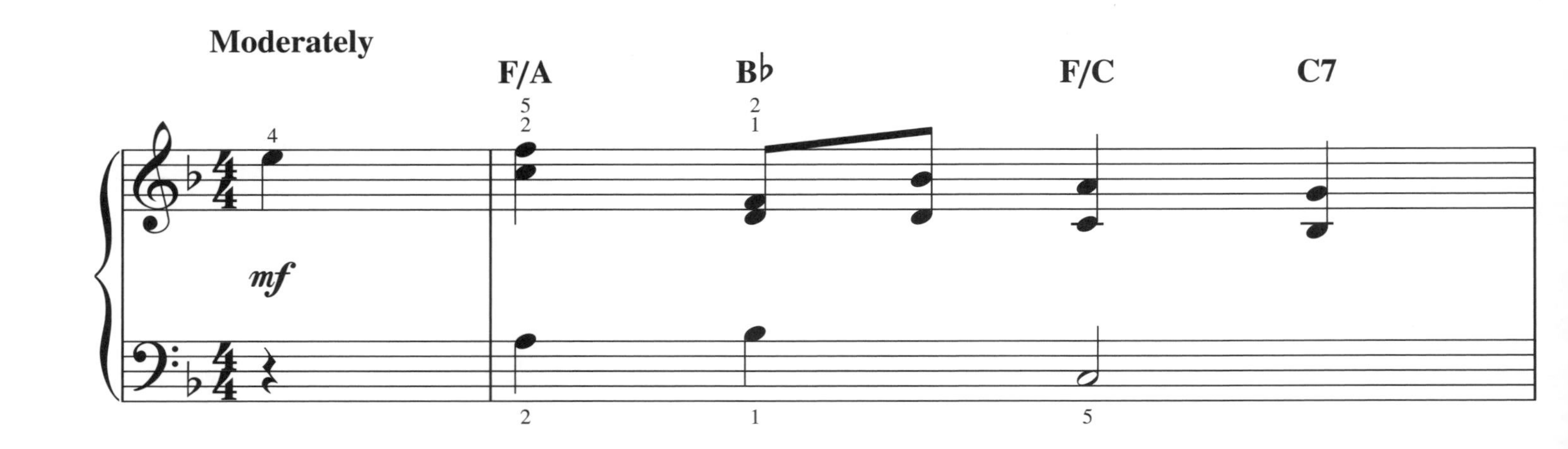

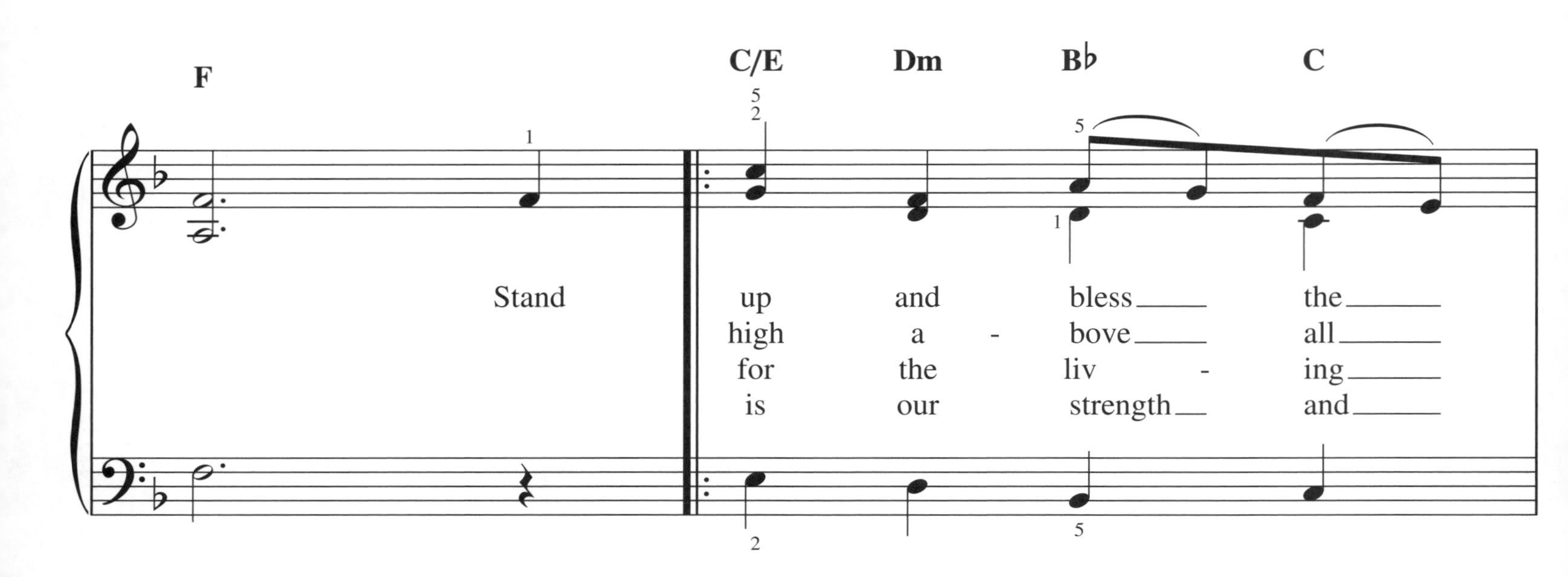

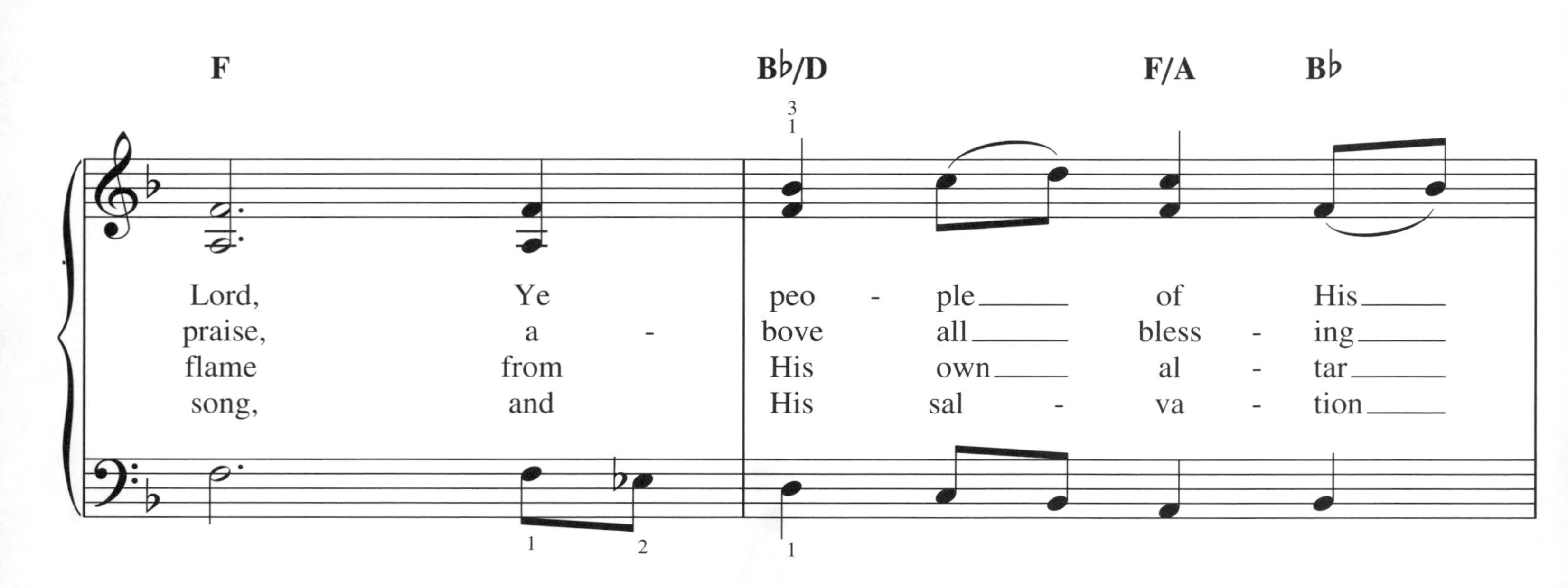

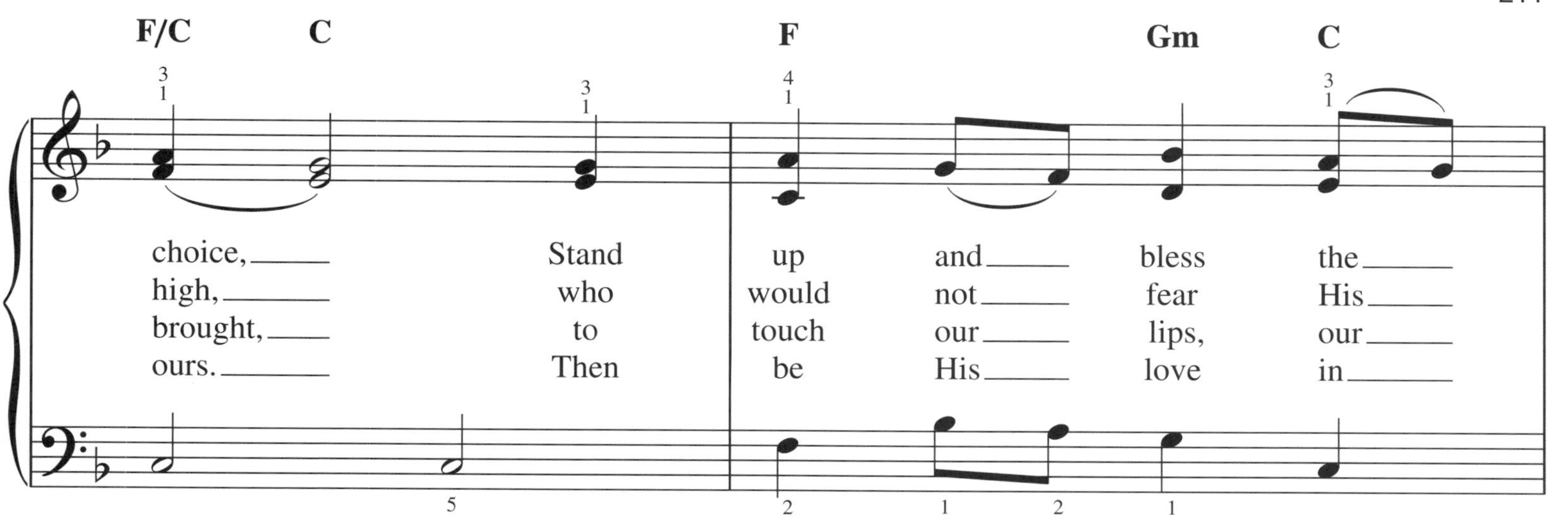
F/C C F Gm C
choice, Stand up and bless the
high, who would not fear His
brought, to touch our lips, our
ours. Then be His love in

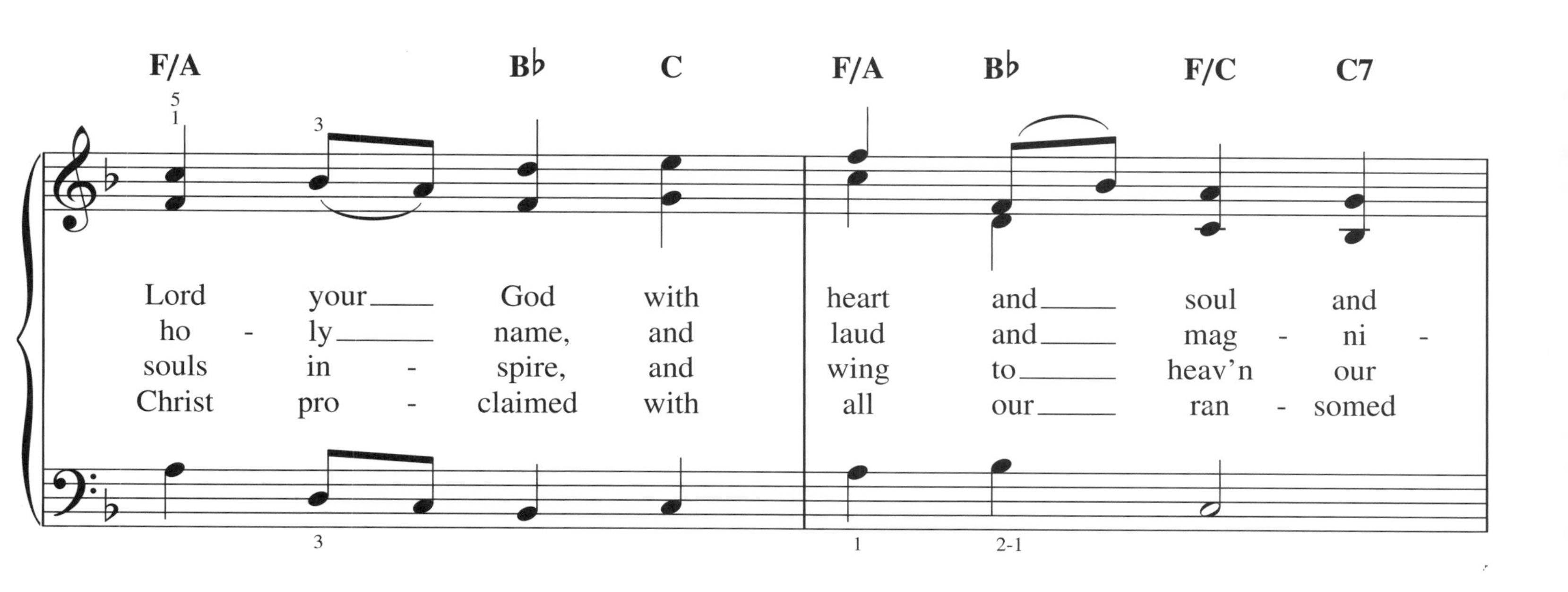
F/A B♭ C F/A B♭ F/C C7
Lord your God with heart and soul and
ho - ly name, and laud and mag - ni -
souls in - spire, and wing to heav'n our
Christ pro - claimed with all our ran - somed

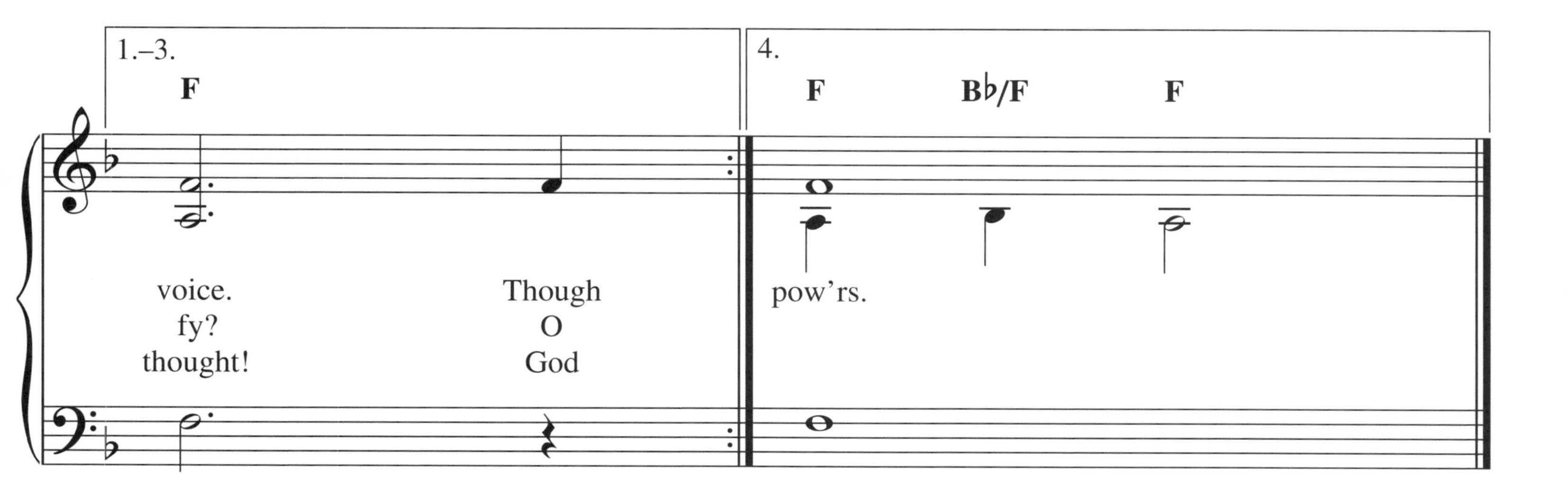
1.–3.
F
voice. Though
fy? O
thought! God
4.
F B♭/F F
pow'rs.

STAND UP, STAND UP FOR JESUS

Words by GEORGE DUFFIELD, JR.
Music by GEORGE J. WEBB

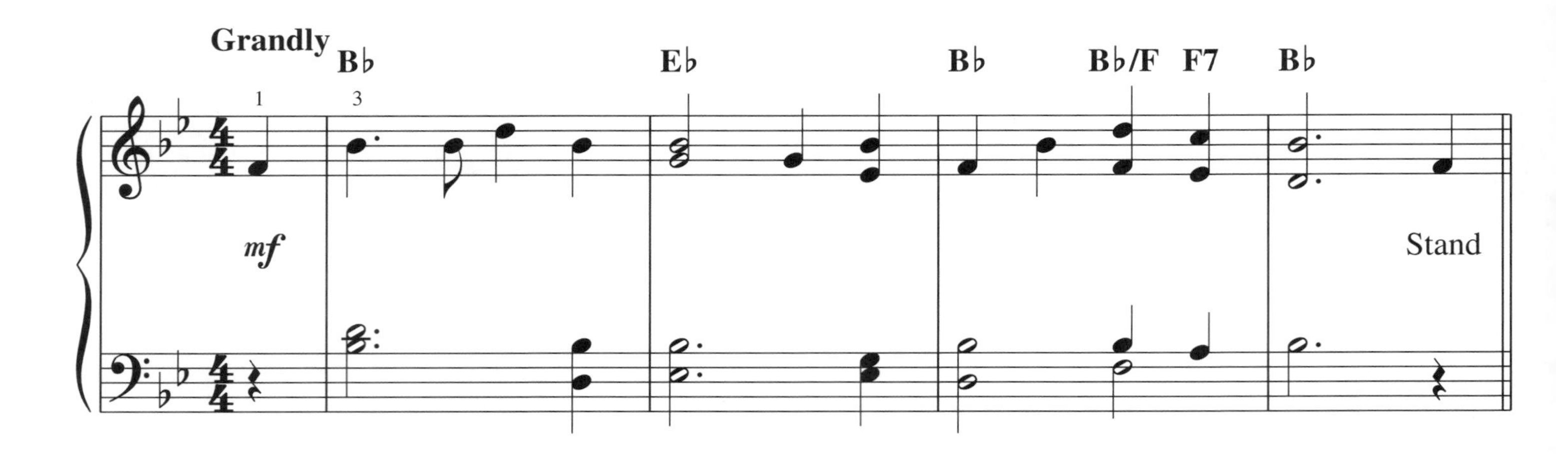

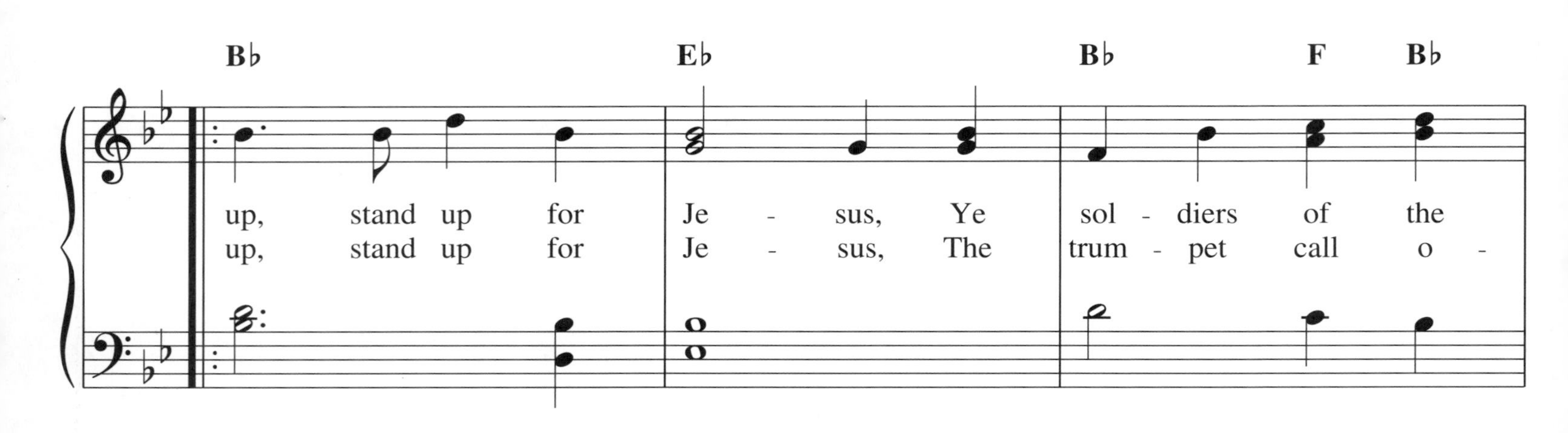

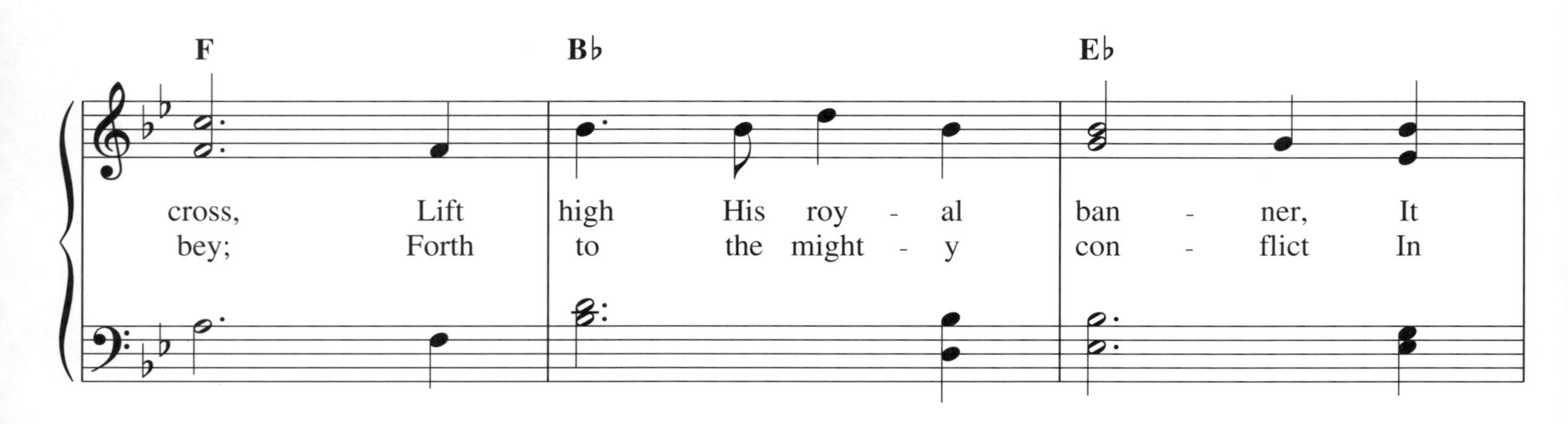

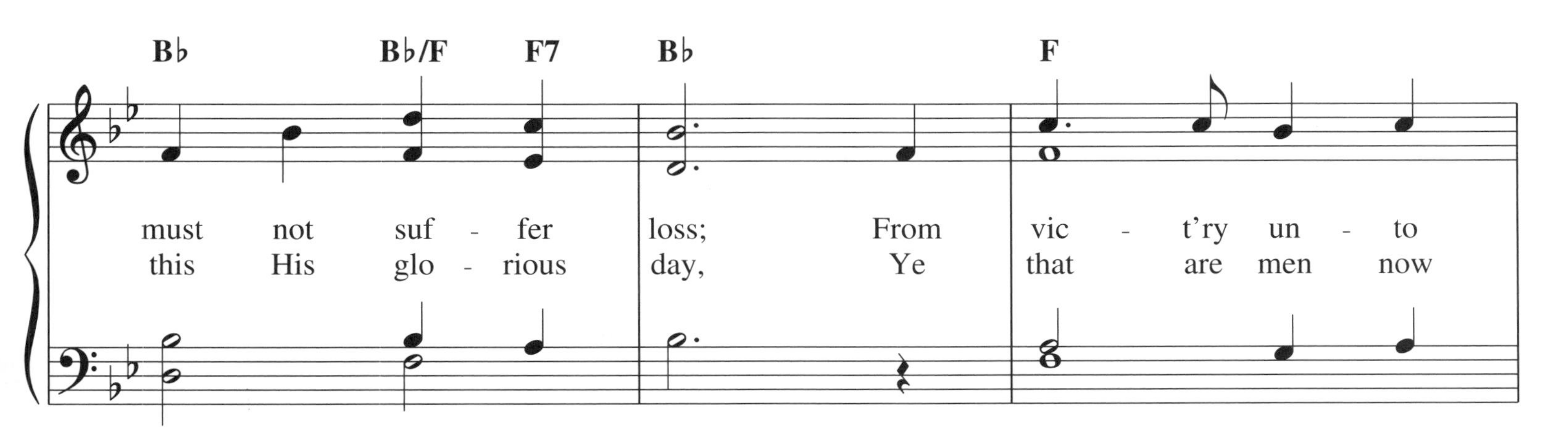

B♭ B♭/F F7 B♭ F
must not suf - fer loss; From vic - t'ry un - to
this His glo - rious day, Ye that are men now

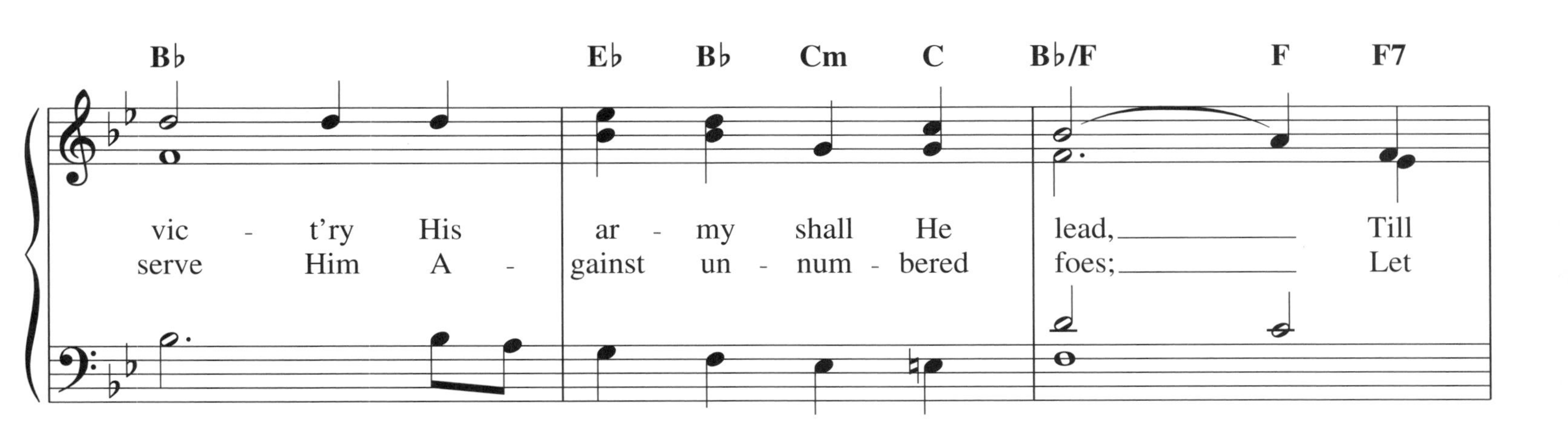

B♭ E♭ B♭ Cm C B♭/F F F7
vic - t'ry His ar - my shall He lead, Till
serve Him A - gainst un - num - bered foes; Let

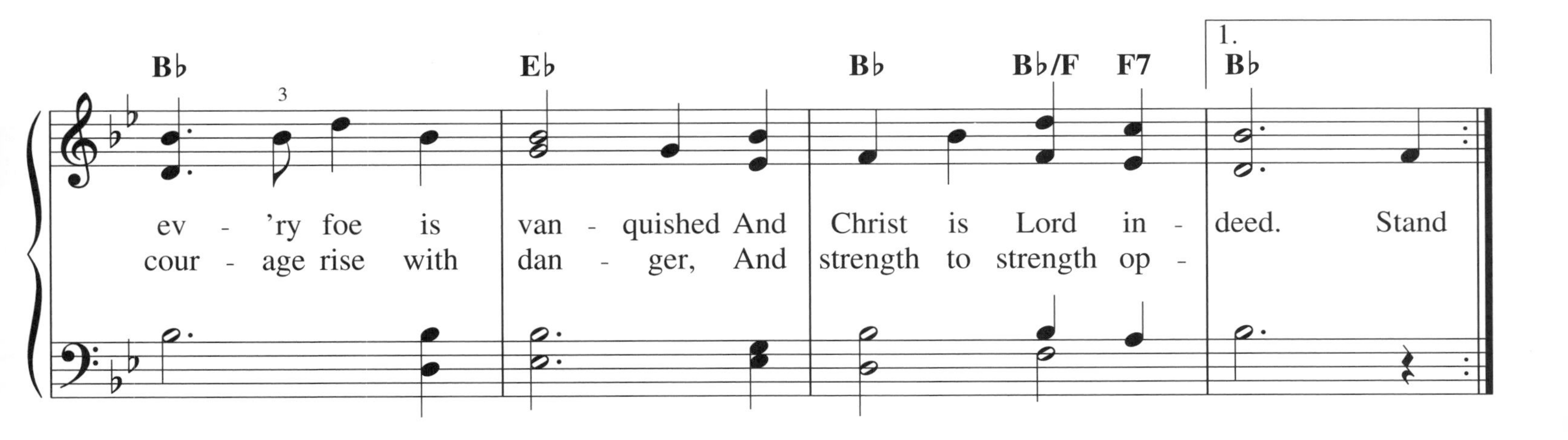

B♭ E♭ B♭ B♭/F F7 1. B♭
ev - 'ry foe is van - quished And Christ is Lord in - deed. Stand
cour - age rise with dan - ger, And strength to strength op -

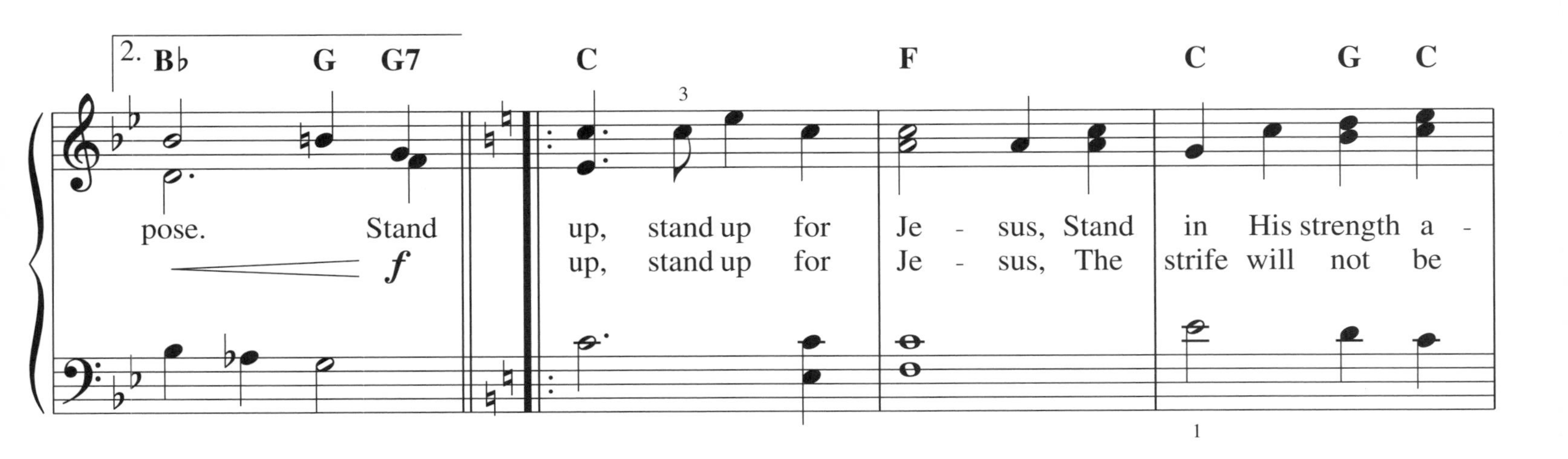

2. B♭ G G7 C F C G C
pose. Stand up, stand up for Je - sus, Stand in His strength a -
f
up, stand up for Je - sus, The strife will not be

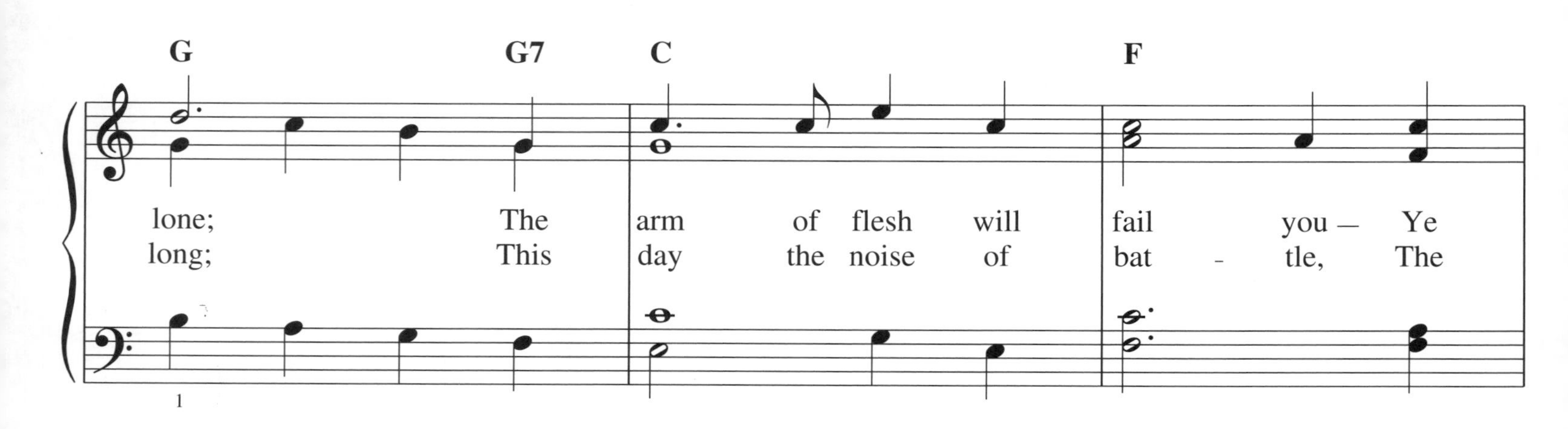
G G7 C F
lone; The arm of flesh will fail you — Ye
long; This day the noise of bat - tle, The

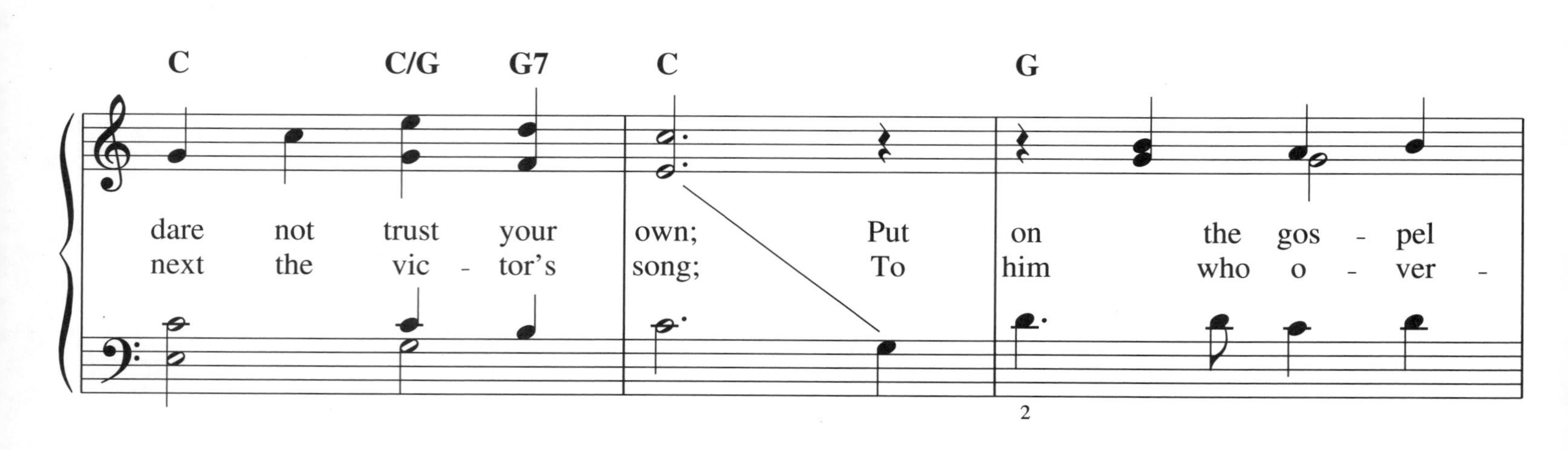
C C/G G7 C G
dare not trust your own; Put on the gos - pel
next the vic - tor's song; To him who o - ver -

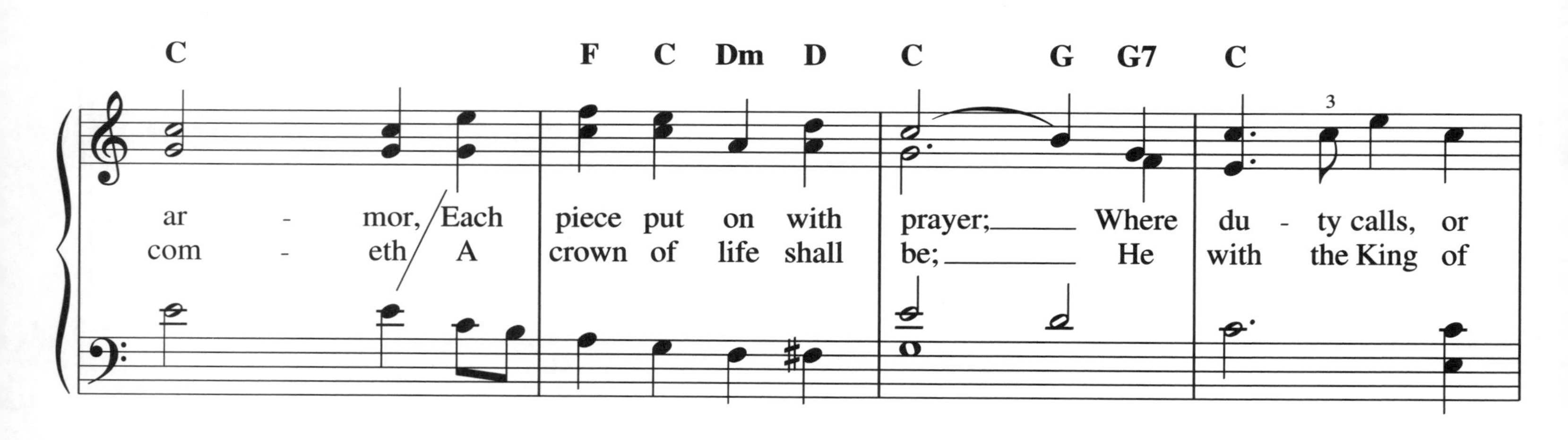
C F C Dm D C G G7 C
ar - mor, Each piece put on with prayer; Where du - ty calls, or
com - eth A crown of life shall be; He with the King of

F C C/G G7 1. C 2. F/C C
dan - ger, Be nev - er want - ing there. Stand
glo - ry Shall reign e - ter - nal - ly.

TELL ME THE STORY OF JESUS

Words by FANNY J. CROSBY
Music by JOHN R. SWENEY

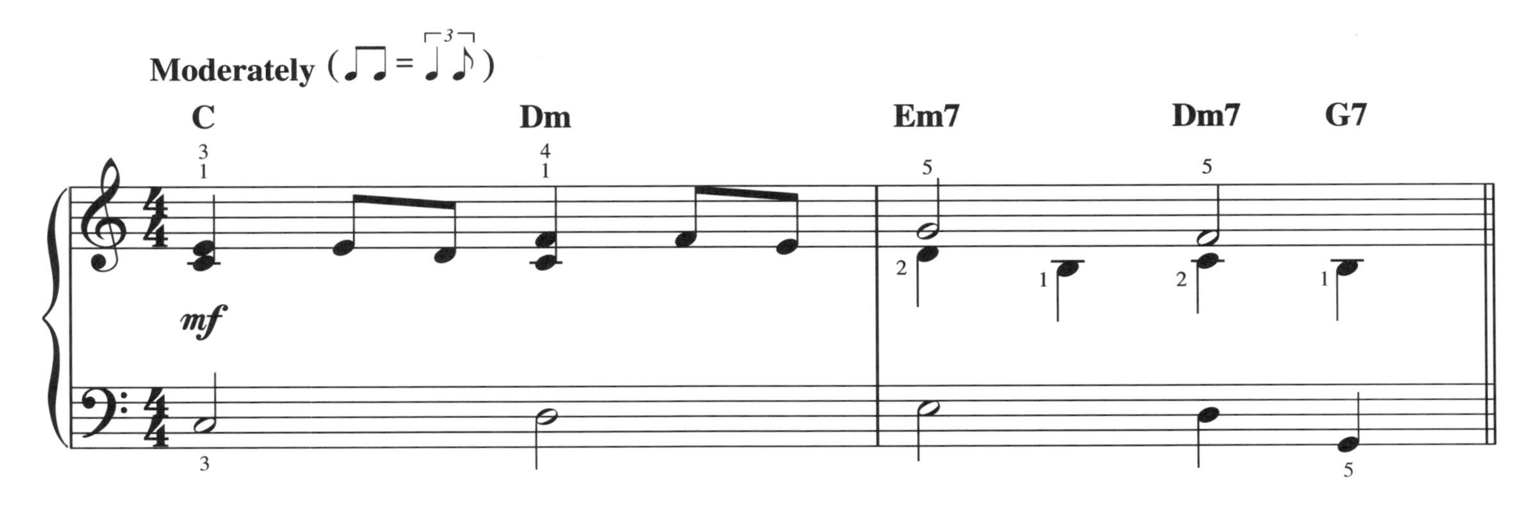

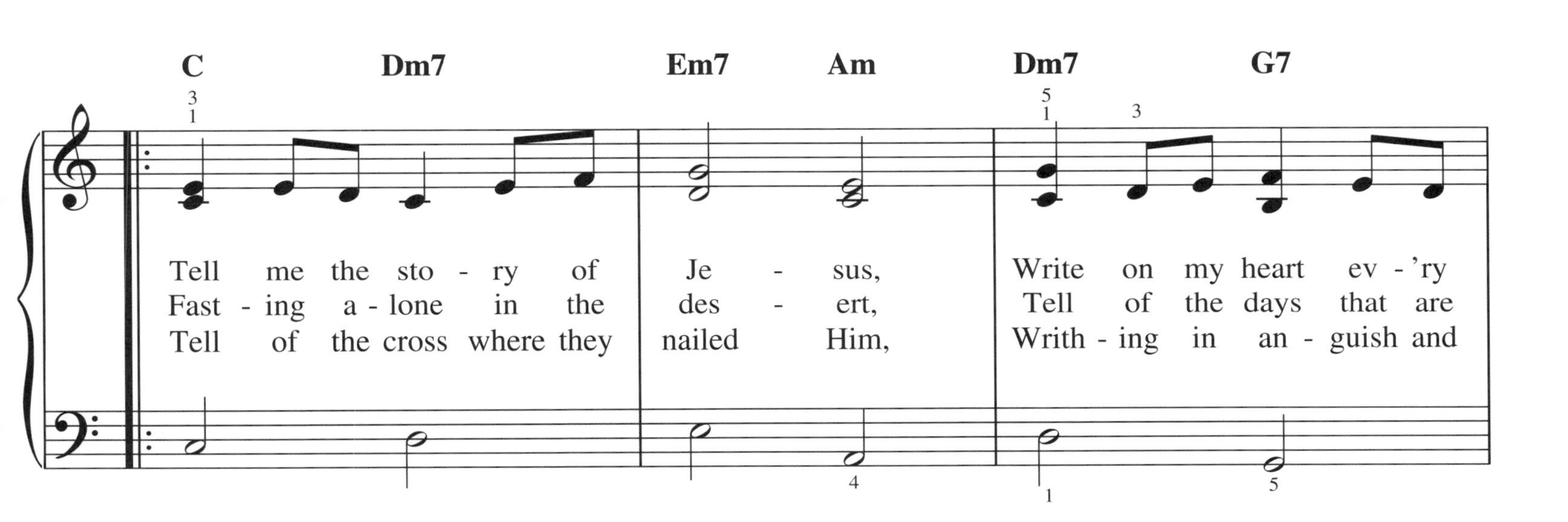

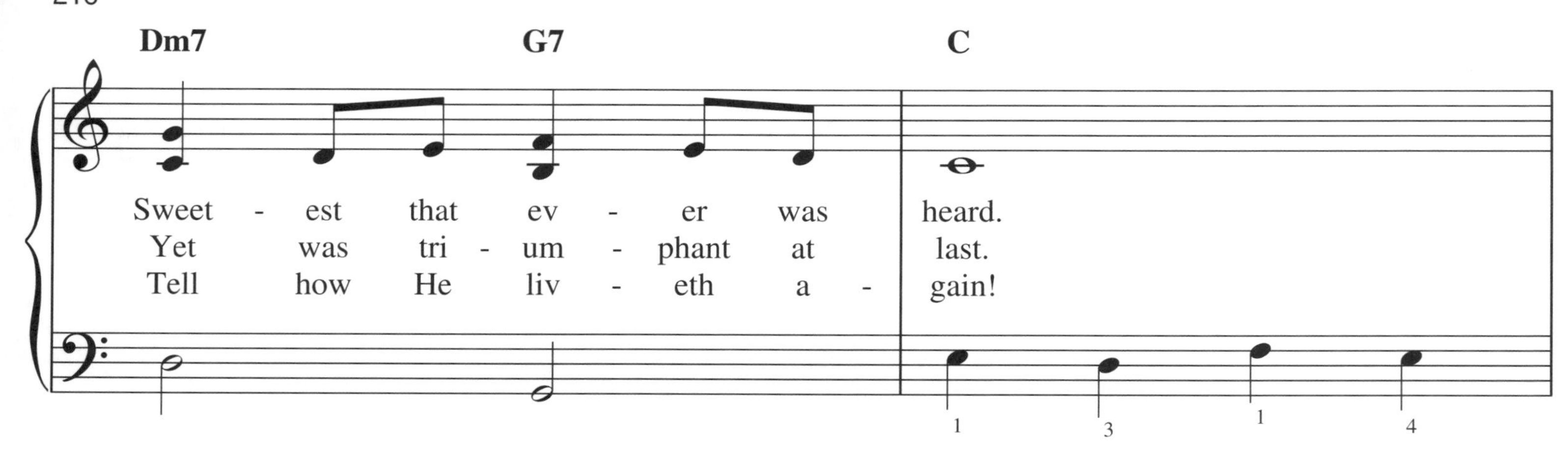
Dm7
G7
C
Sweet - est that ev - er was heard.
Yet was tri - um - phant at last.
Tell how He liv - eth a - gain!

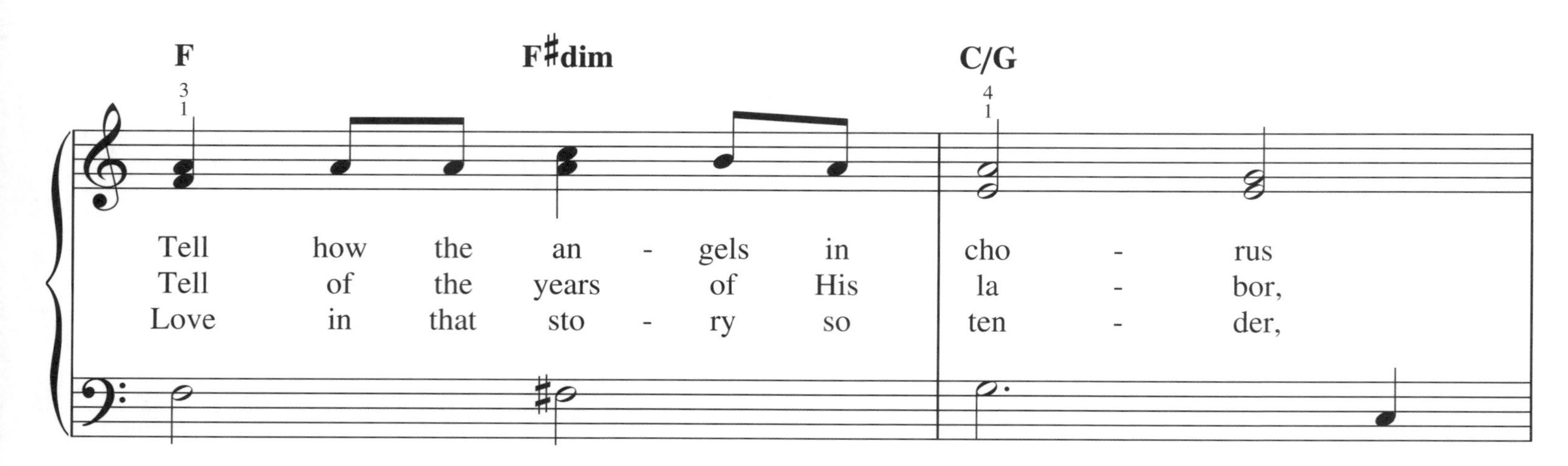
F
F♯dim
C/G
Tell how the an - gels in cho - rus
Tell of the years of His la - bor,
Love in that sto - ry so ten - der,

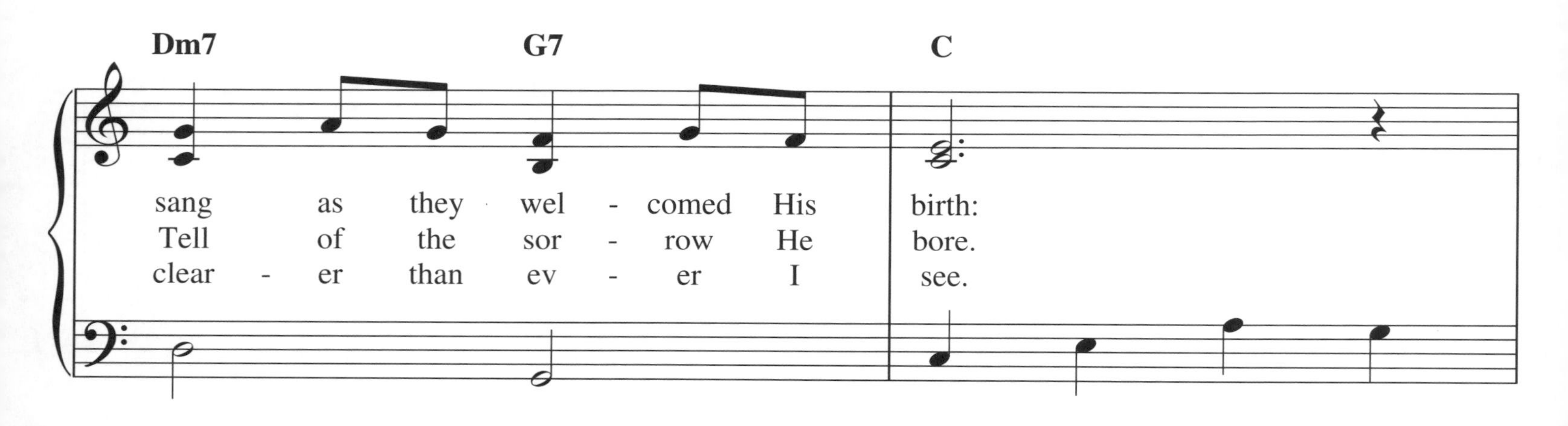
Dm7
G7
C
sang as they wel - comed His birth:
Tell of the sor - row He bore.
clear - er than ev - er I see.

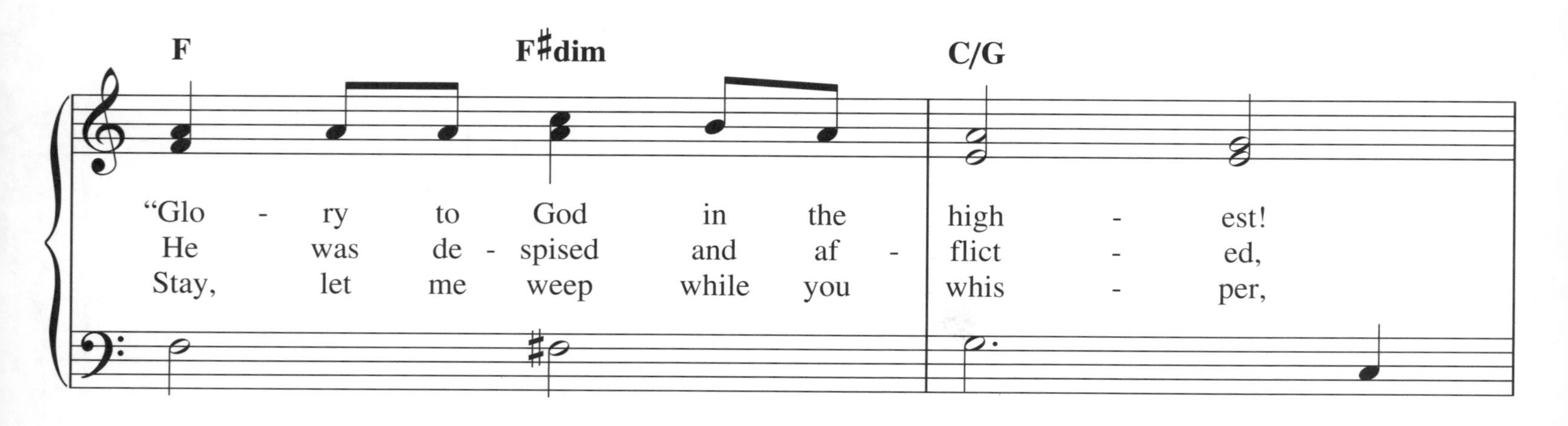
F
F♯dim
C/G
"Glo - ry to God in the high - est!
He was de - spised and af - flict - ed,
Stay, let me weep while you whis - per,

G/D
D7
G7
Peace and good tid - ings to earth."
Home - less, re - ject - ed and poor.
"Love paid the ran - som for me."
C
Dm
Em7
Am
Dm7
G7
Tell me the sto - ry of Je - sus;
Write on my heart ev - 'ry

C
Dm7
Em7
Am
word.
Tell me the sto - ry most pre - cious,

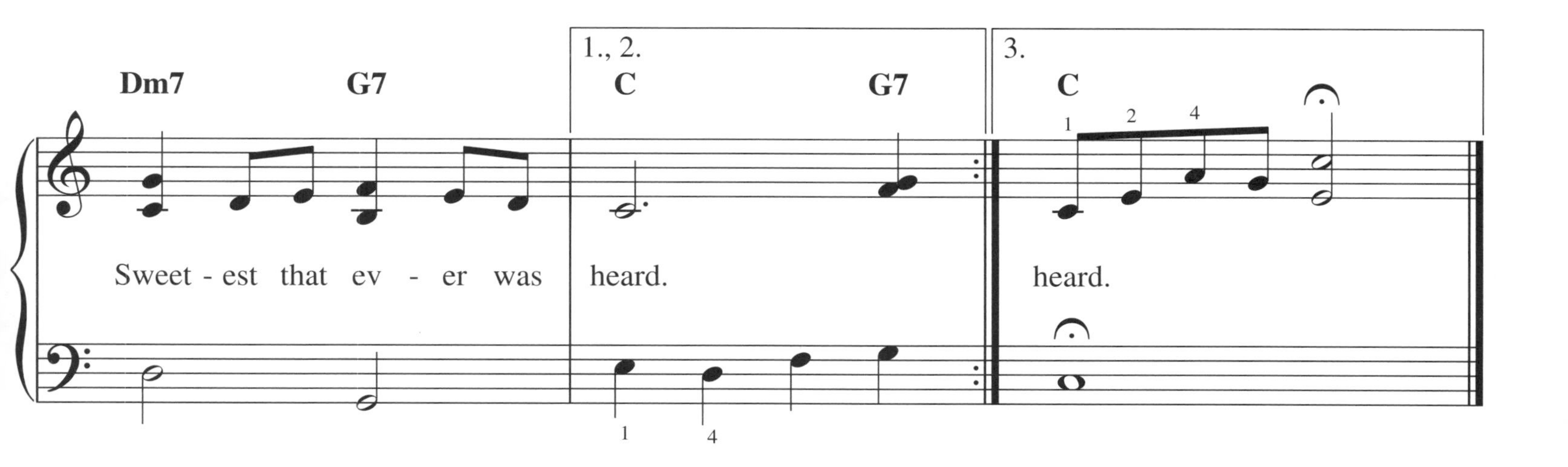
Dm7
G7
1., 2.
C
G7
3.
C
Sweet - est that ev - er was heard.
heard.

TAKE TIME TO BE HOLY

Words by WILLIAM D. LONGSTAFF
Music by GEORGE C. STEBBINS

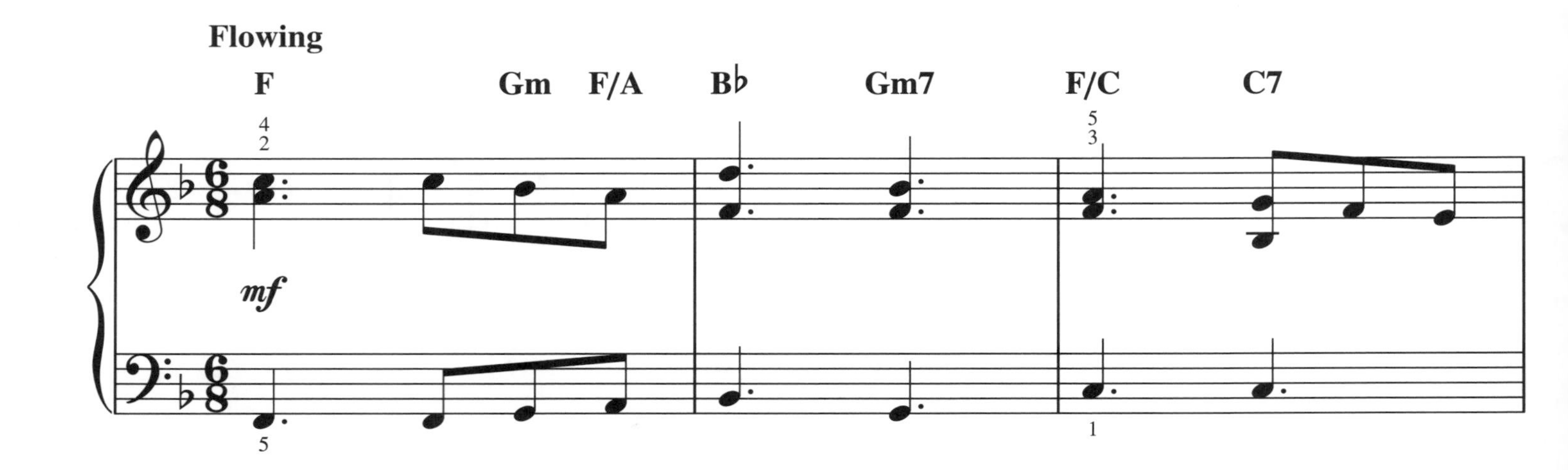

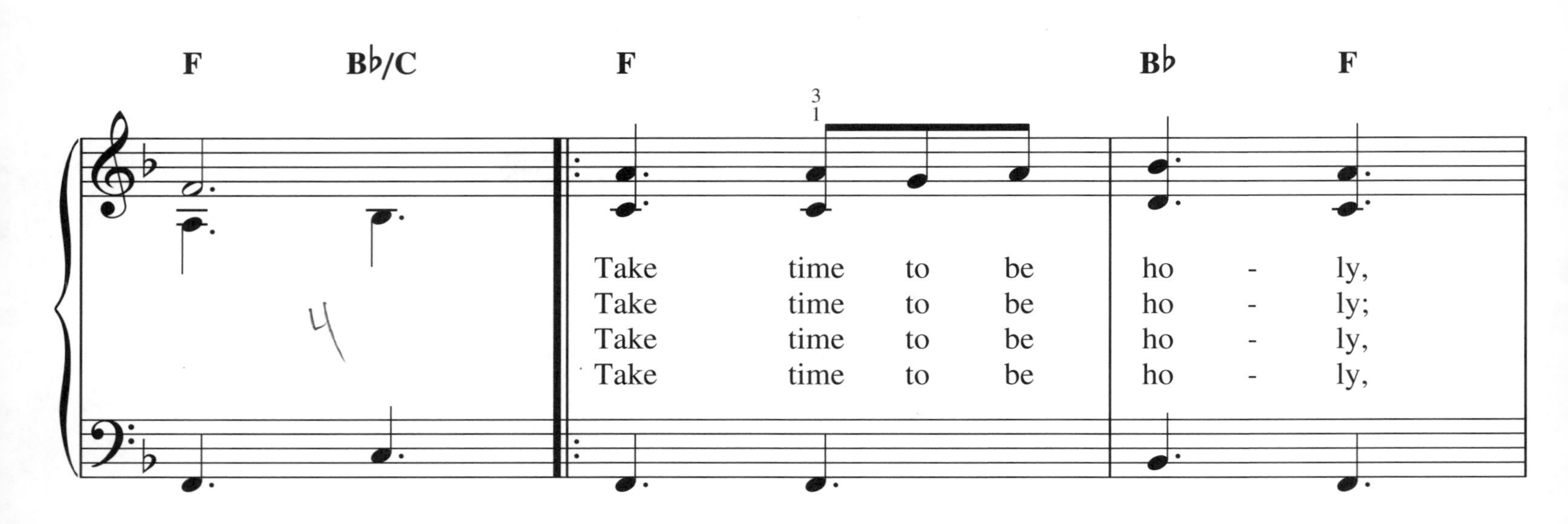

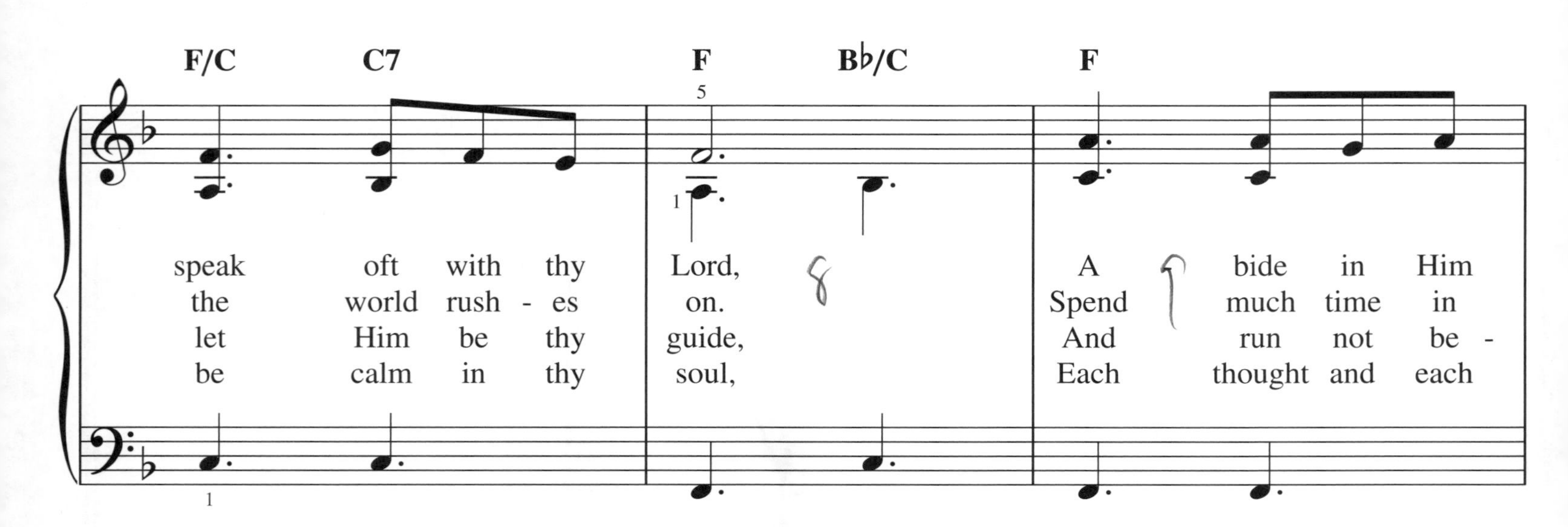

Bb F Gsus G C
al - ways and feed on His Word.
se - cret with Je - sus a - lone.
fore Him, what - ev - er be - tide.
mo - tive be - neath His con - trol.
C7 F C7
Make friends of God's chil - dren, help those who are
By look - ing to Je - sus, like Him thou shalt
In joy or in sor - row, still fol - low thy
Thus led by His Spir - it to foun - tains of
F F/A F Gm F/A Bb Gm
weak, For - get - ting in noth - ing
be; Thy friends in thy con - duct
Lord; And, look - ing to Je - sus,
love, Thou soon shalt be fit - ted
F/C C7 1.–3. F Bb/C 4. F
His bless - ing to seek.
His like - ness shall see.
still trust in His Word.
for serv - ice a - bove.

TELL ME THE STORIES OF JESUS

Words by WILLIAM H. PARKER
Music by FREDERIC A. CHALLINOR

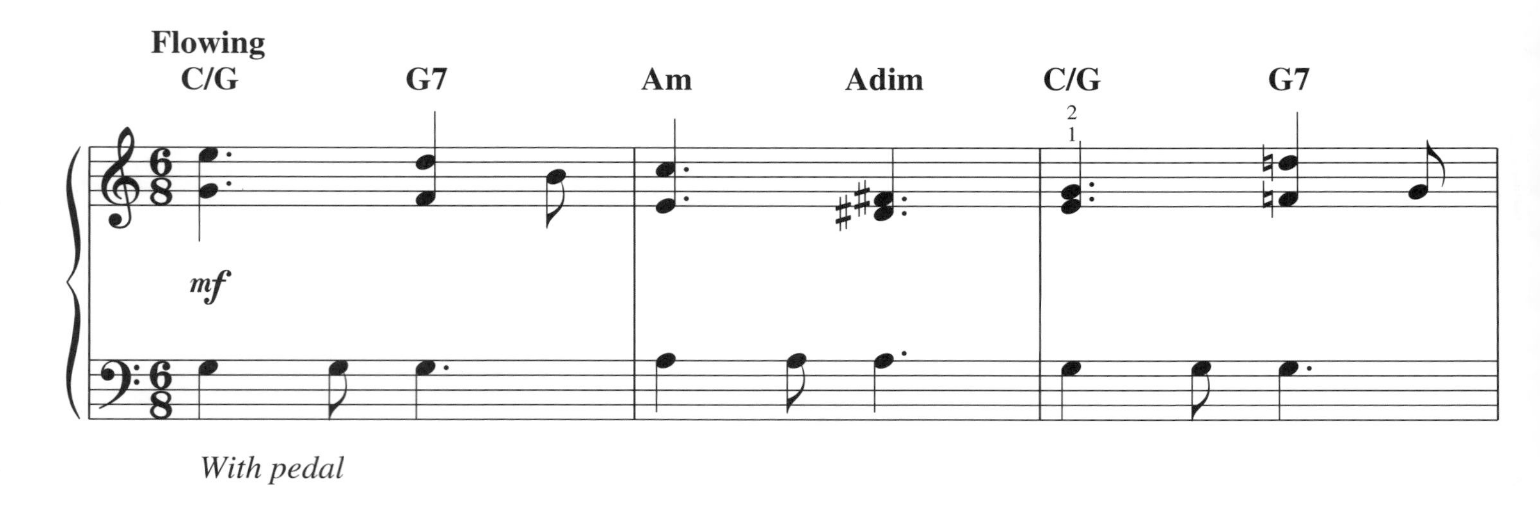

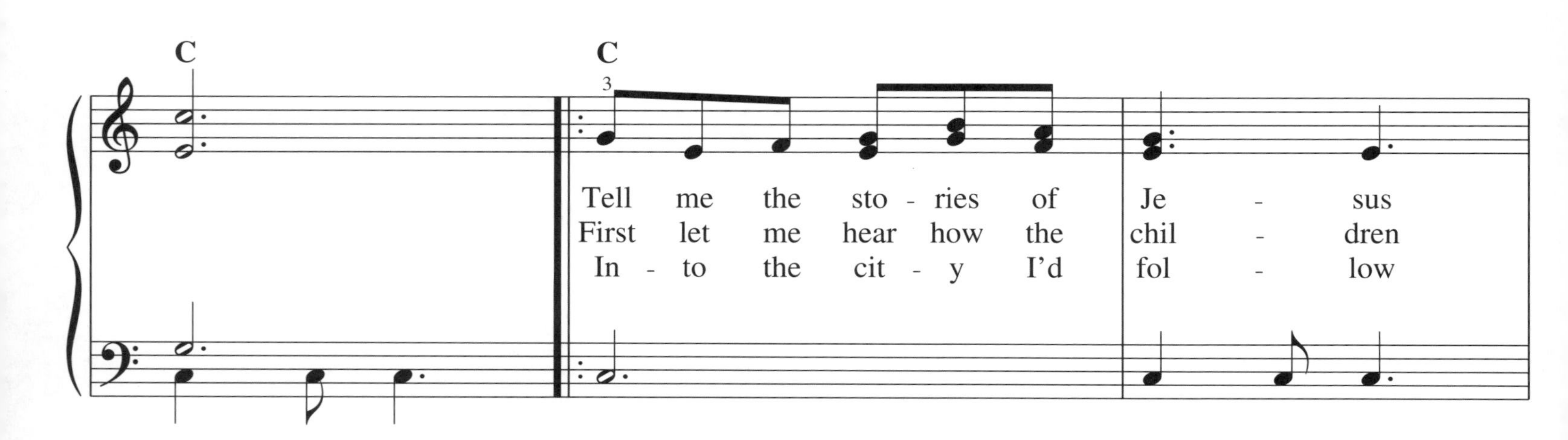

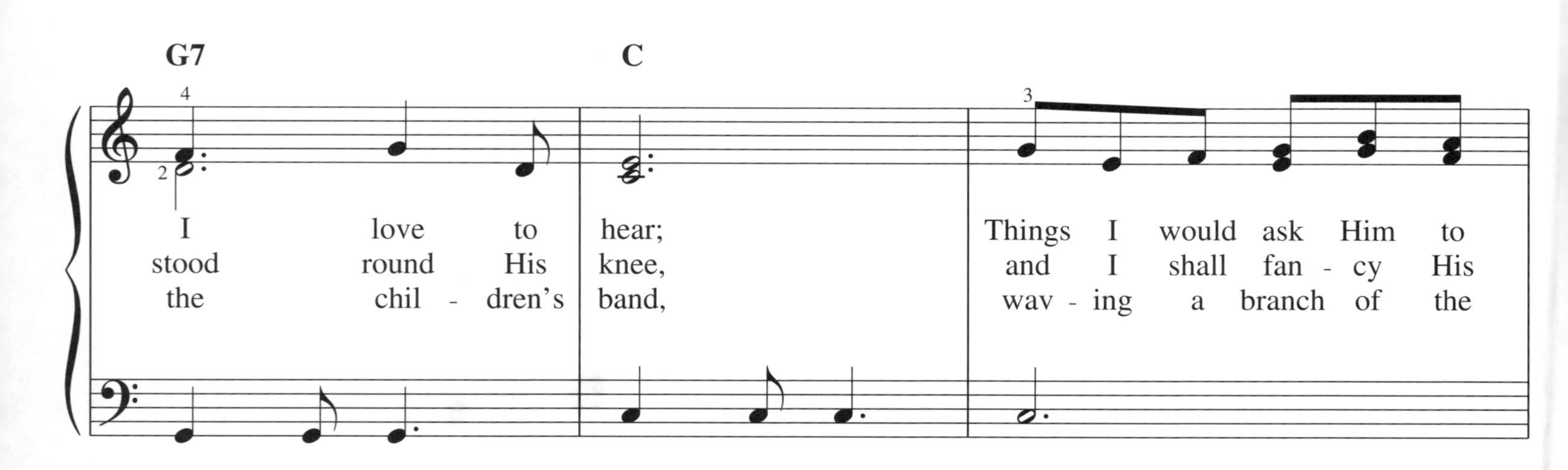

G/D
D7
G
tell me if He were here;
bless - ing rest - ing on me;
palm tree high in my hand;
G7
C
C7
Scenes by the way - side, tales of the
words full of kind - ness, deeds full of
one of His her - alds, Yes, I would
A/C♯
Dm
C/G
G7
Am
Adim
sea, sto - ries of Je - sus,
grace, all in the love - light
sing loud - est ho - san - nas,
C/G
G7
C
tell them to me.
of Je - sus' face.
"Je - sus is King!"

THERE IS A FOUNTAIN

Words by WILLIAM COWPER
Traditional American Melody
Arranged by LOWELL MASON

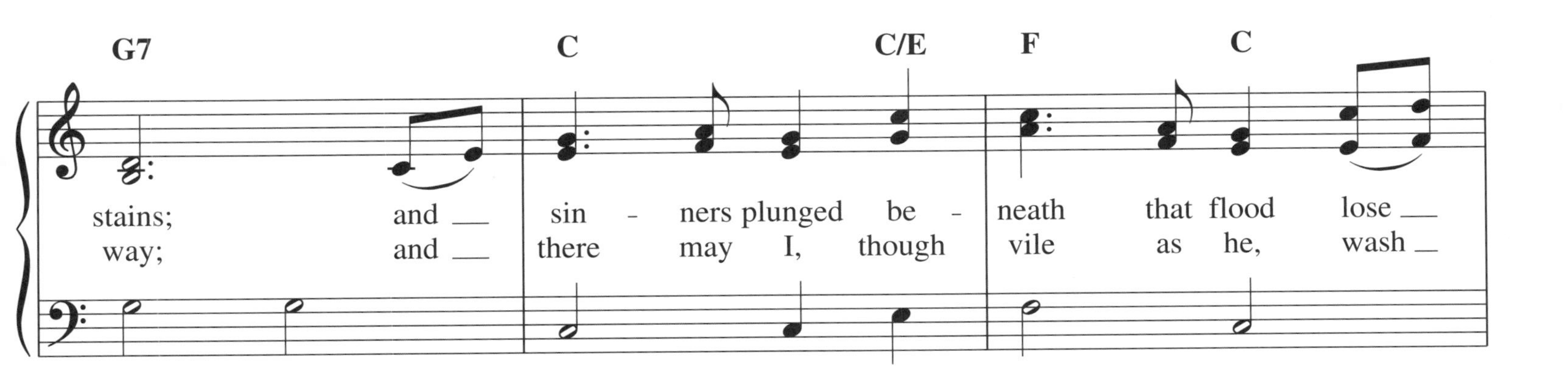

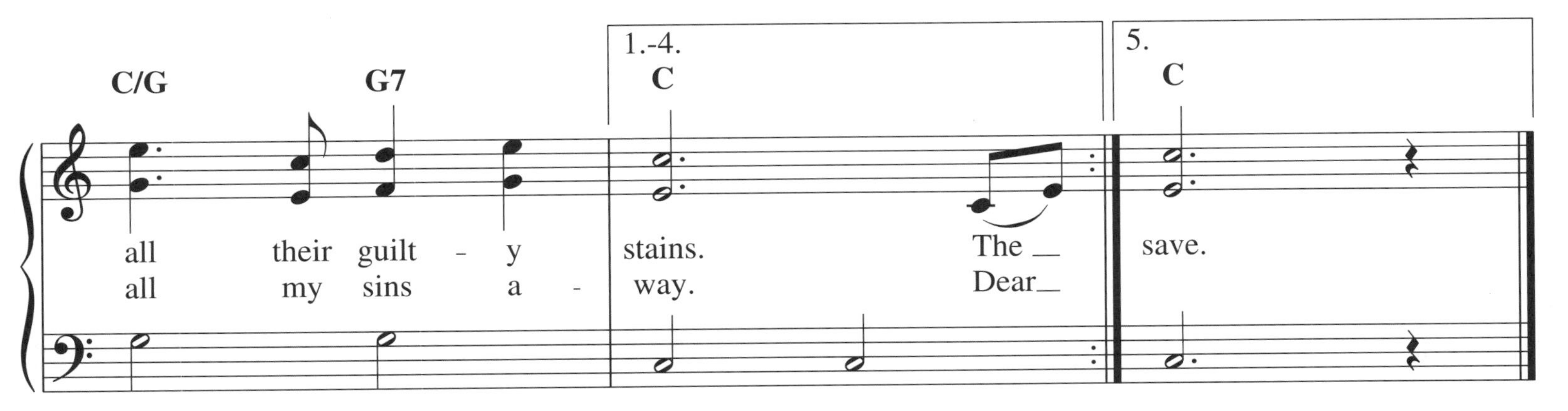

Additional Verses

3. Dear dying Lamb, Thy precious blood
Shall never lose its pow'r,
Till all the ransomed Church of God
Be saved to sin no more:
Be saved to sin no more,
Be saved to sin no more.
Till all the ransomed Church of God
Be saved to sin no more.

4. E'er since, by faith, I saw the stream
Thy flowing wounds supply,
Redeeming love has been my theme
And shall be till I die:
And shall be till I die,
And shall be till I die.
Redeeming love has been my theme
And shall be till I die.

5. When this poor lisping, stamm'ring tongue
Lies silent in the grave,
Then in a nobler, sweeter song
I'll sing Thy pow'r to save;
I'll sing Thy pow'r to save,
I'll sing Thy pow'r to save.
Then in a nobler, sweeter song
I'll sing Thy pow'r to save.

THERE IS POWER IN THE BLOOD

Words and Music by
LEWIS E. JONES

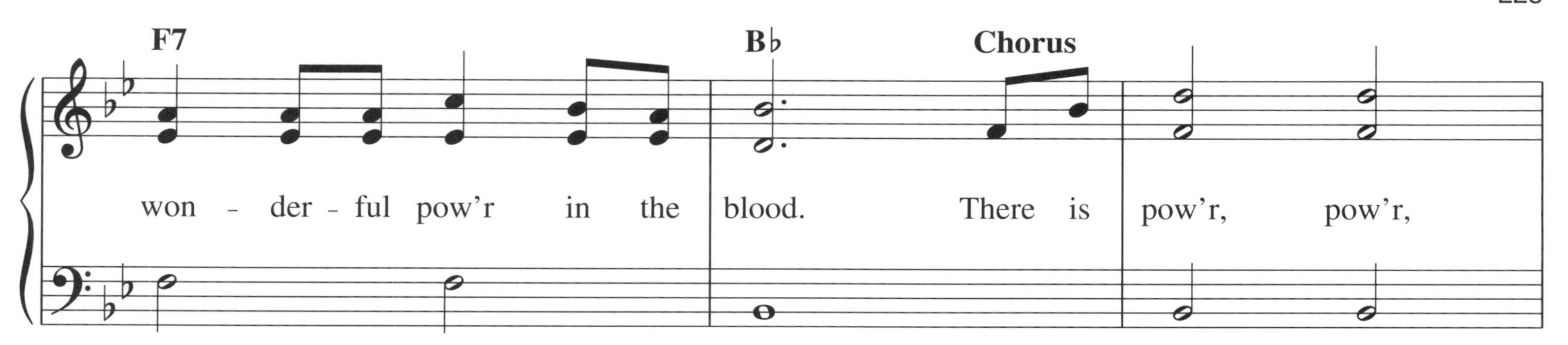

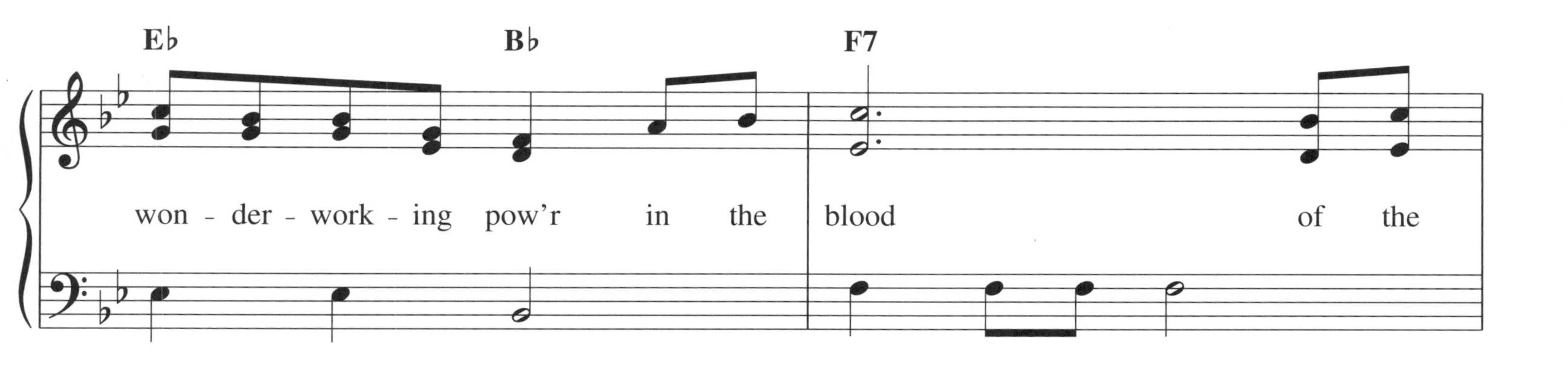

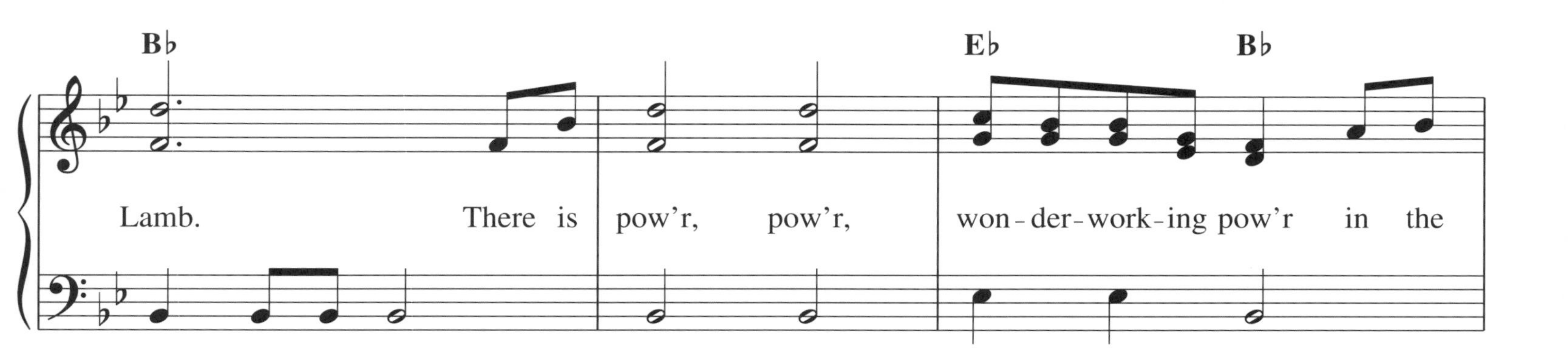

Additional Verses

3. Would you be whiter, much whiter than snow?
   There's pow'r in the blood, pow'r in the blood;
   Sin-stains are lost in its live-giving flow.
   There's wonderful pow'r in the blood.
   Chorus

4. Would you do service for Jesus your King?
   There's pow'r in the blood, pow'r in the blood;
   Would you live daily His praises to sing?
   There's wonderful pow'r in the blood.
   Chorus

THINE IS THE GLORY

Words by EDMOND LOUIS BUDRY
Music by GEORGE FRIDERIC HANDEL

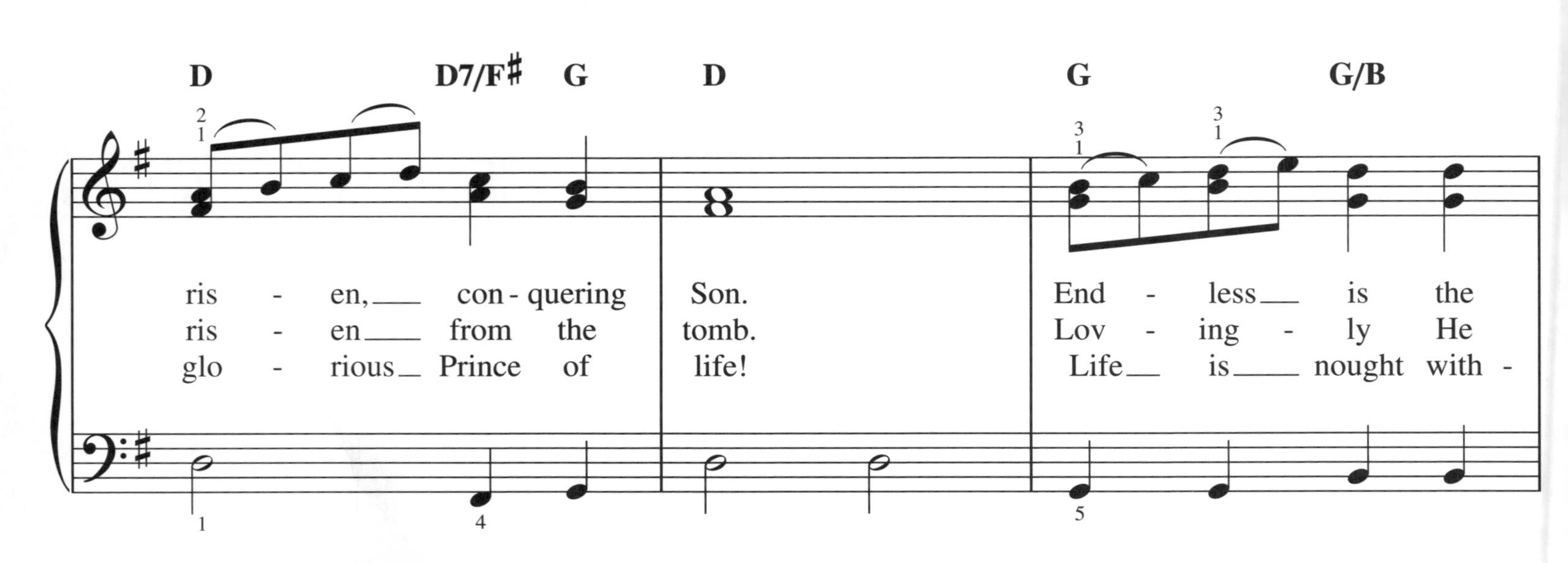

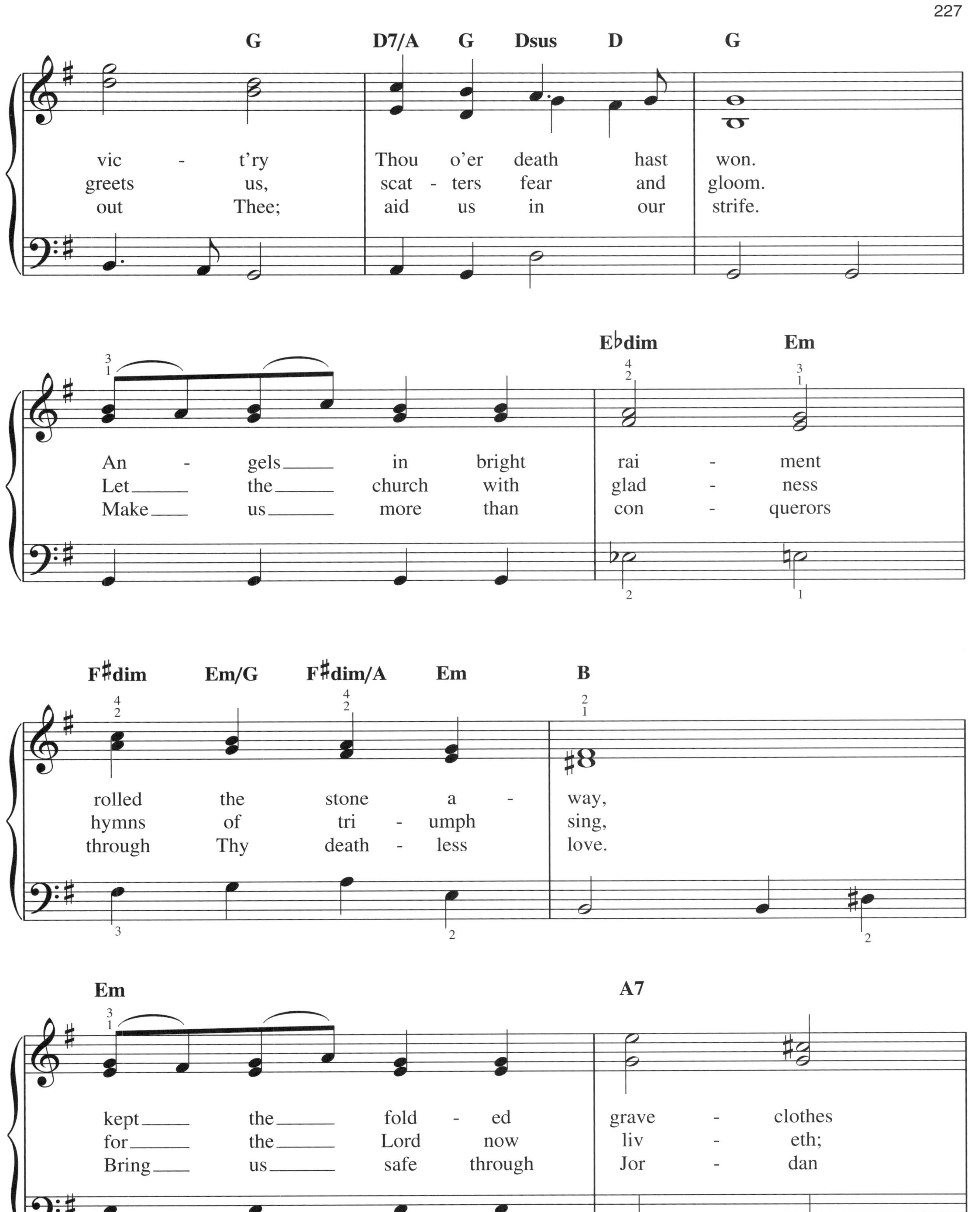
G D7/A G Dsus D G
vic - t'ry Thou o'er death hast won.
greets us, scat - ters fear and gloom.
out Thee; aid us in our strife.
E♭dim Em
An - gels in bright rai - ment
Let the church with glad - ness
Make us more than con - querors
F♯dim Em/G F♯dim/A Em B
rolled the stone a - way,
hymns of tri - umph sing,
through Thy death - less love.
Em A7
kept the fold - ed grave - clothes
for the Lord now liv - eth;
Bring us safe through Jor - dan

Bm
G
A7
D
G
G/B
D7/A
where Thy bod - y lay.
death hath lost its sting.
to Thy home a - bove.
Thine is the
G
G/B
D
D7/F♯
G
D
glo - ry,
ris - en, con - quering
Son.
G
G/B
G
End - less is the
vic - t'ry
D7/A
G
Dsus
D
1., 2.
G
3.
Gsus
G
Thou o'er death hast
won.
won.

TRUST AND OBEY

Words by JOHN H. SAMMIS
Music by DANIEL B. TOWNER

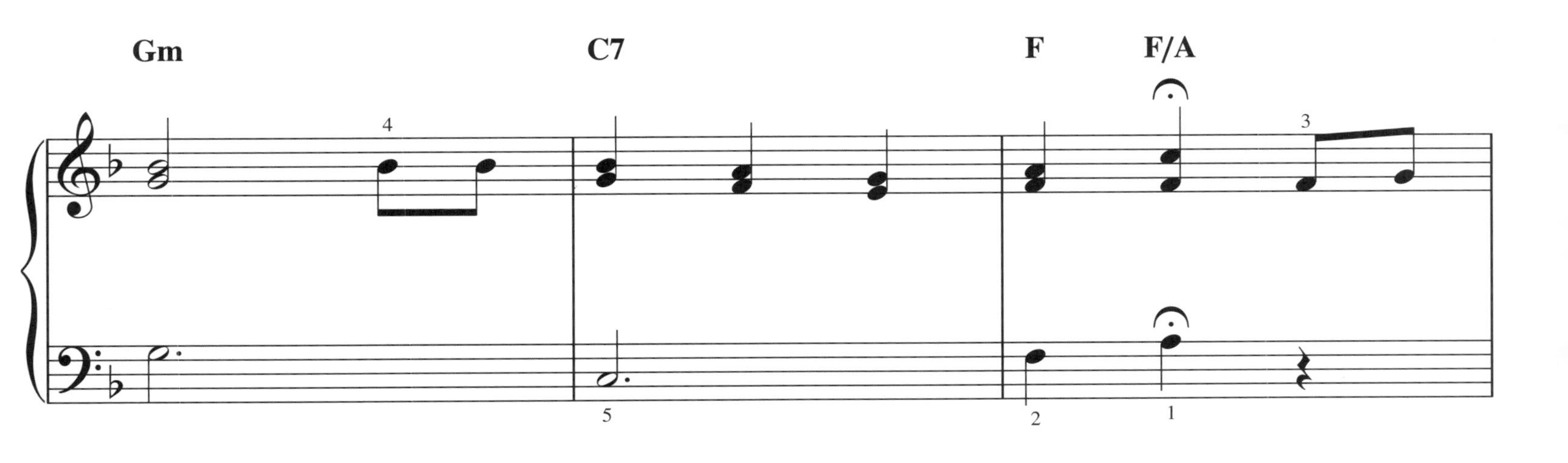

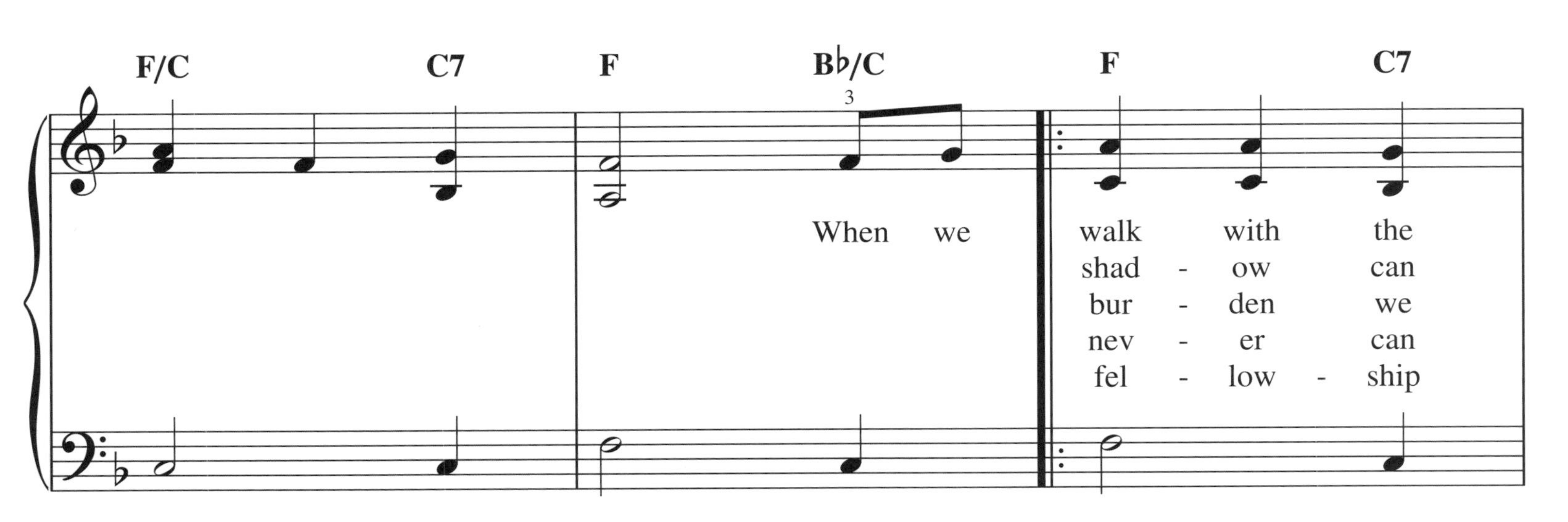

F C C7/E F
Lord in the light of His Word, what a
rise, not a cloud in the skies, but His
bear, not a sor - row we share, but our
prove the de - lights of His love un - til
sweet we will sit at His feet, or we'll
B♭ F C
glo - ry He sheds on our way! While we
smile quick - ly drives it a - way. Not a
toil He doth rich - ly re - pay. Not a
all on the al - tar we lay, for the
walk by His side in the way. What He
F C7 F C C7/E
do His good will, He a - bides with us
doubt nor a fear, not a sigh nor a
grief nor a loss, not a frown nor a
fa - vor He shows and the joy He be -
says we will do, where He sends we will
F B♭
still, and with all who will
tear can a - bide while we
cross, but is blest if we
stows are for them who will
go; nev - er fear, on - ly

F/C
C7
F
trust and o - bey.
trust and o - bey.
trust and o - bey.
trust and o - bey.
trust and o - bey.
C
C/E
F
D
D7/F♯
Trust and o - bey, for there's no oth - er
Gm
C7
F
F/A
way to be hap - py in Je - sus, but to
F/C
C7
1.– 4.
F
B♭/C
5.
F
trust and o - bey.
Not a
Not a
But we
Then in
bey.

THIS IS MY FATHER'S WORLD

Words by MALTBIE D. BABCOCK
Music by FRANKLIN L. SHEPPARD

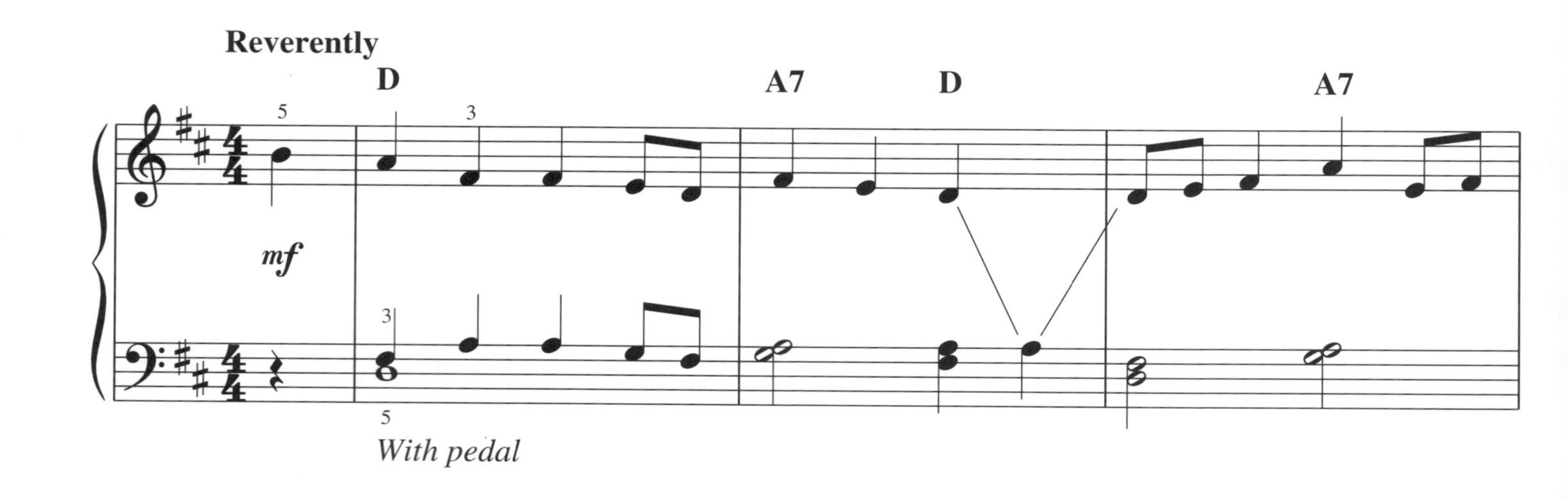

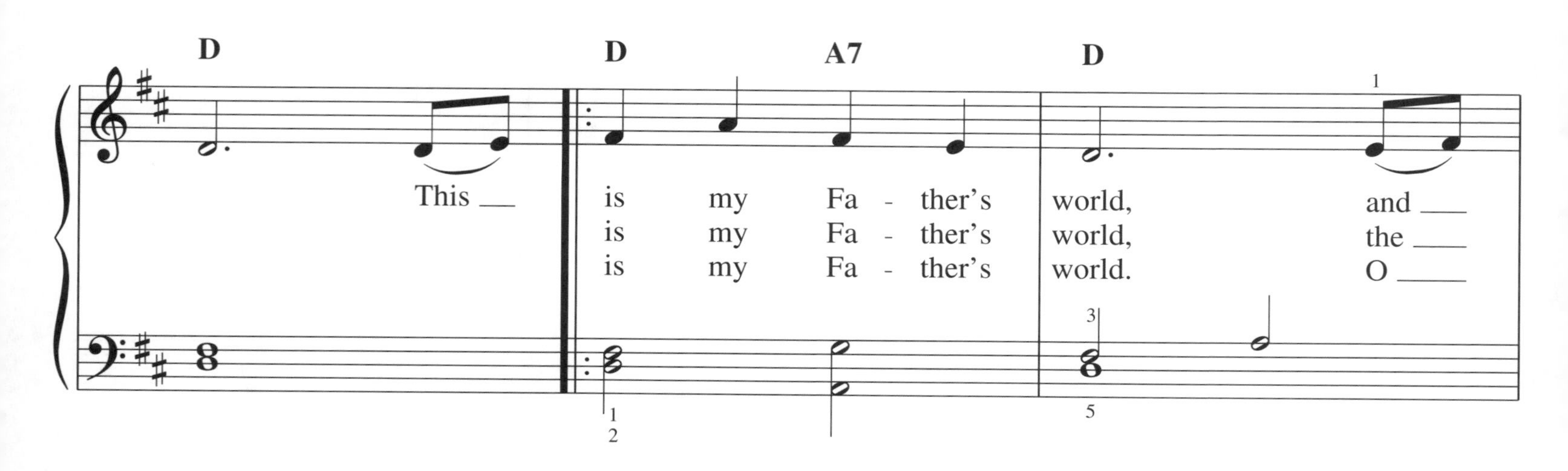

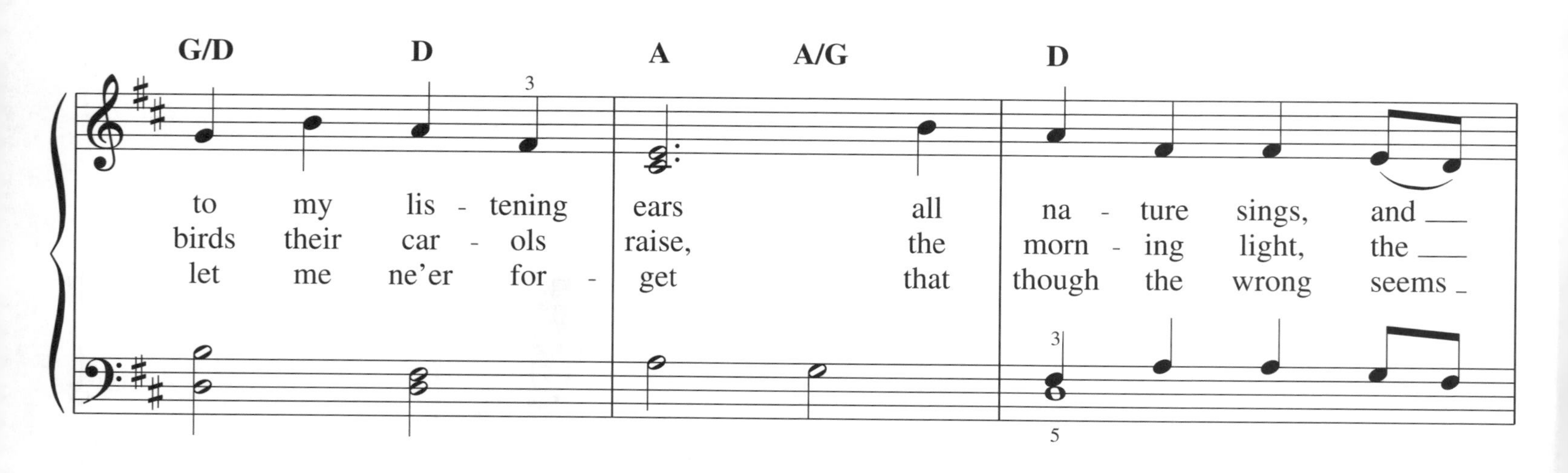

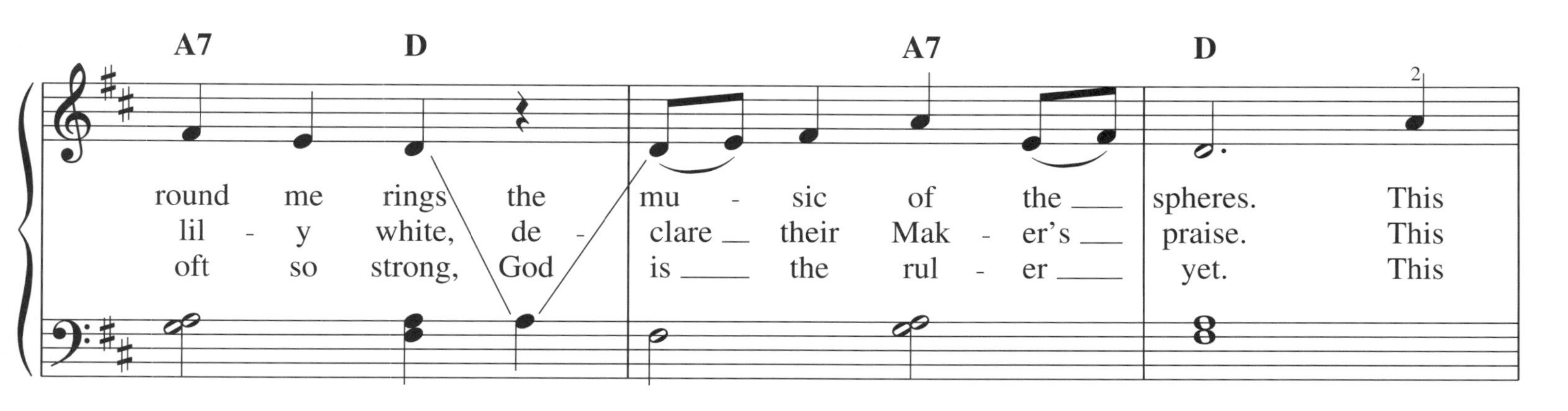
A7 D A7 D
round me rings the mu - sic of the spheres. This
lil - y white, de - clare their Mak - er's praise. This
oft so strong, God is the rul - er yet. This

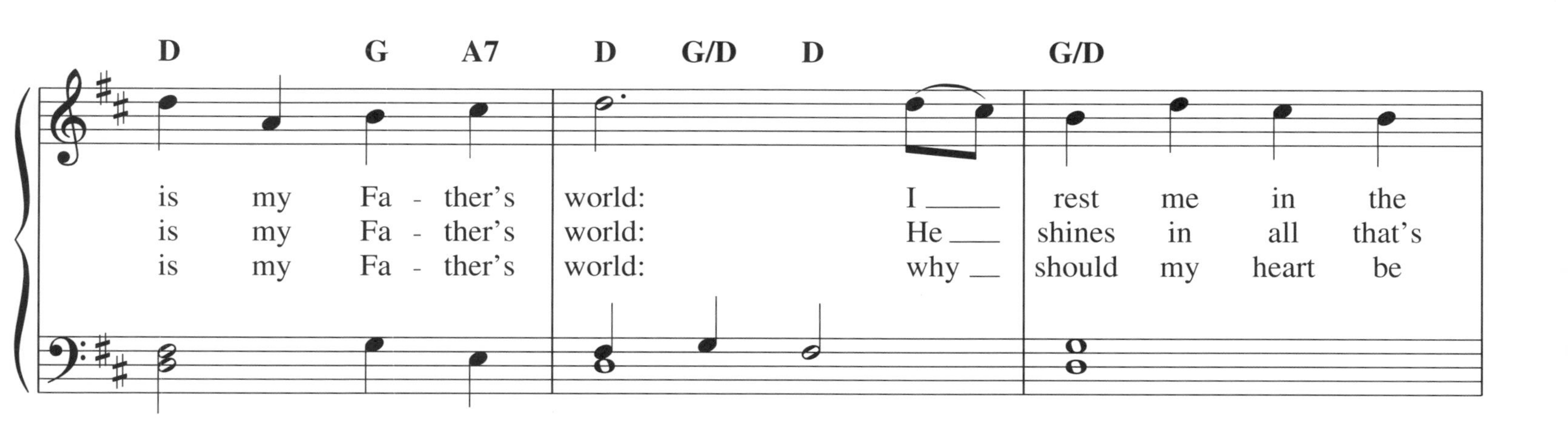
D G A7 D G/D D G/D
is my Fa - ther's world: I rest me in the
is my Fa - ther's world: He shines in all that's
is my Fa - ther's world: why should my heart be

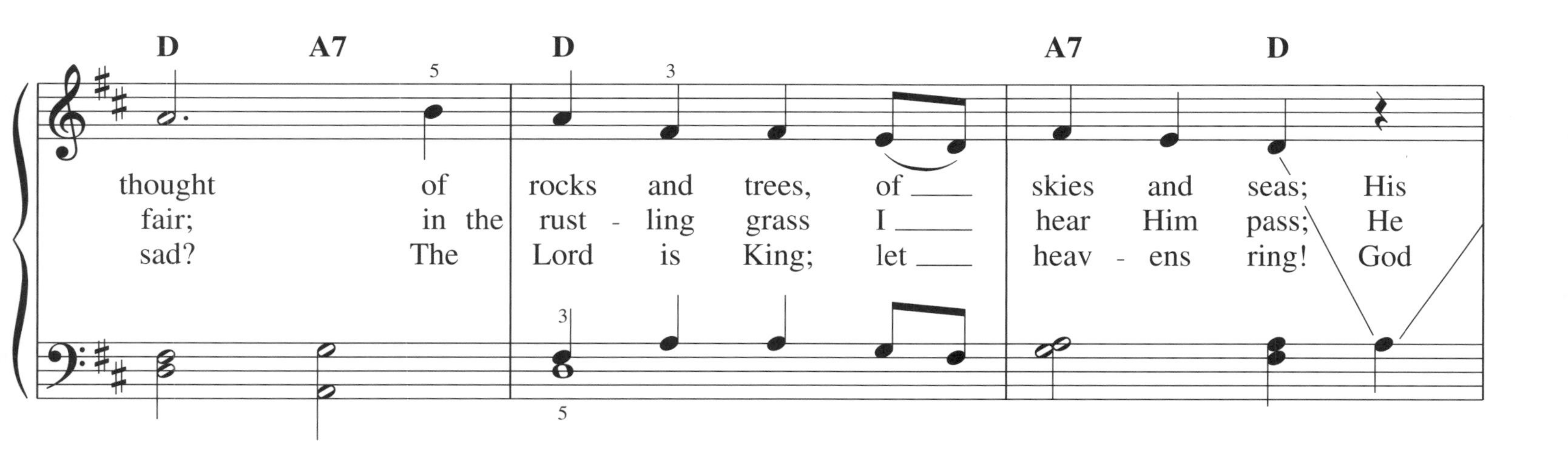
D A7 D A7 D
thought of rocks and trees, of skies and seas; His
fair; in the rust - ling grass I hear Him pass; He
sad? The Lord is King; let heav - ens ring! God

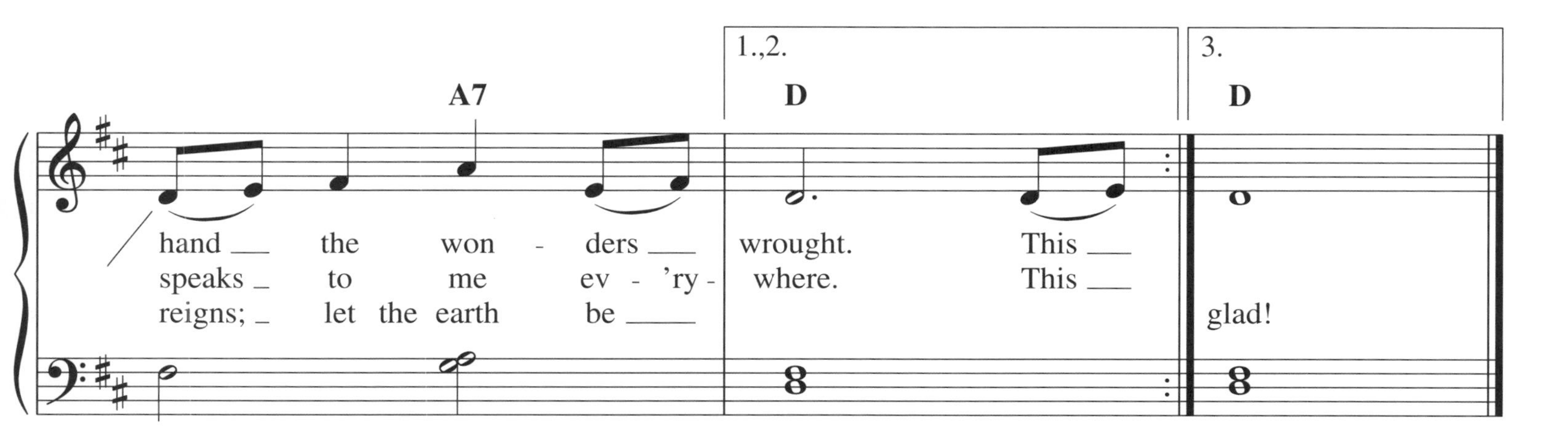
1.,2. 3.
A7 D D
hand the won - ders wrought. This
speaks to me ev - 'ry - where. This
reigns; let the earth be glad!

WE ARE CLIMBING JACOB'S LADDER

Traditional Spiritual

Soulfully

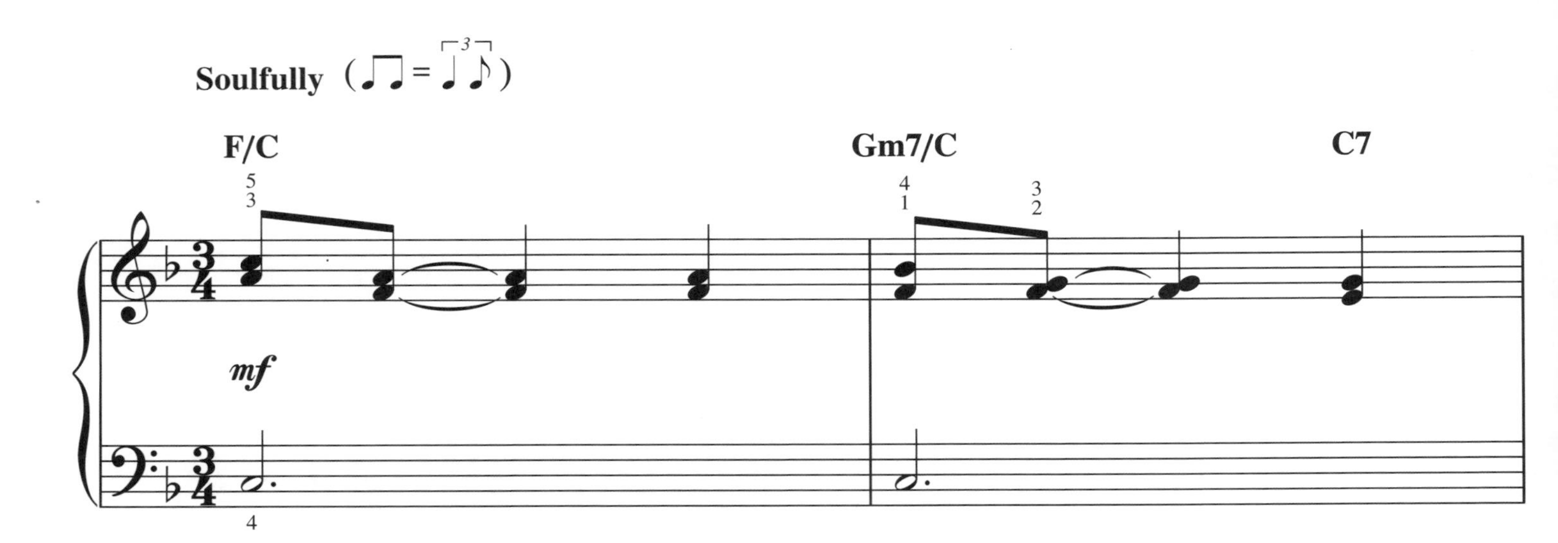

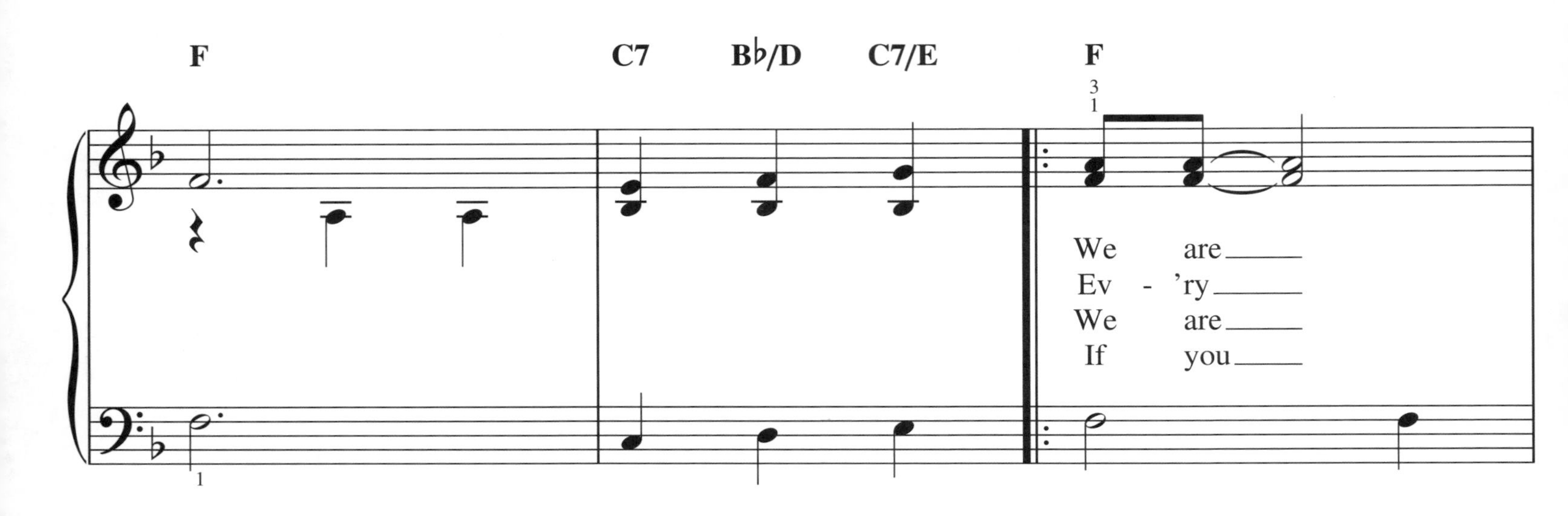

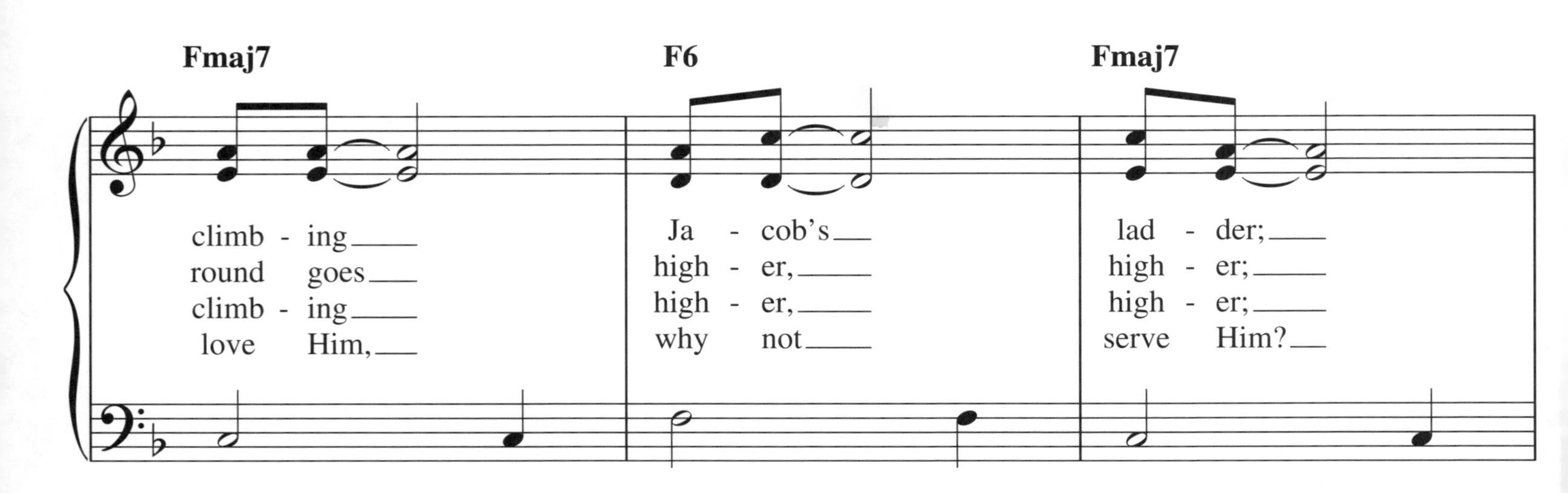

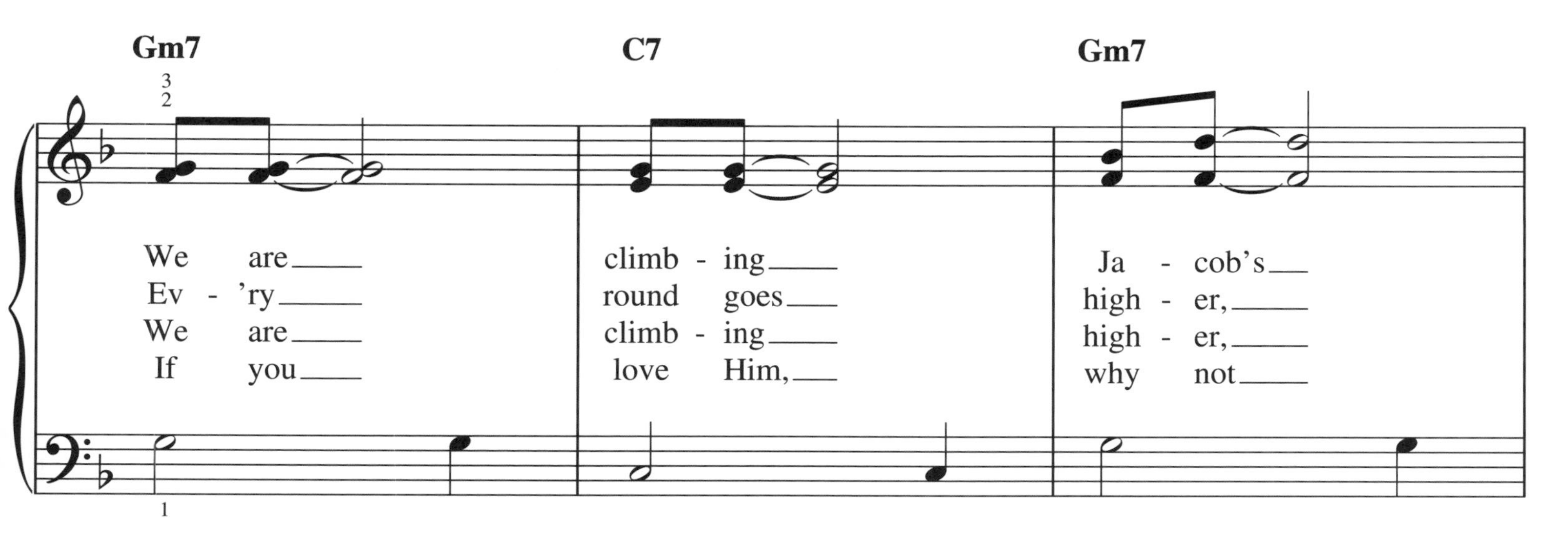
Gm7
C7
Gm7
We are
Ev - 'ry
We are
If you
climb - ing
round goes
climb - ing
love Him,
Ja - cob's
high - er,
high - er,
why not

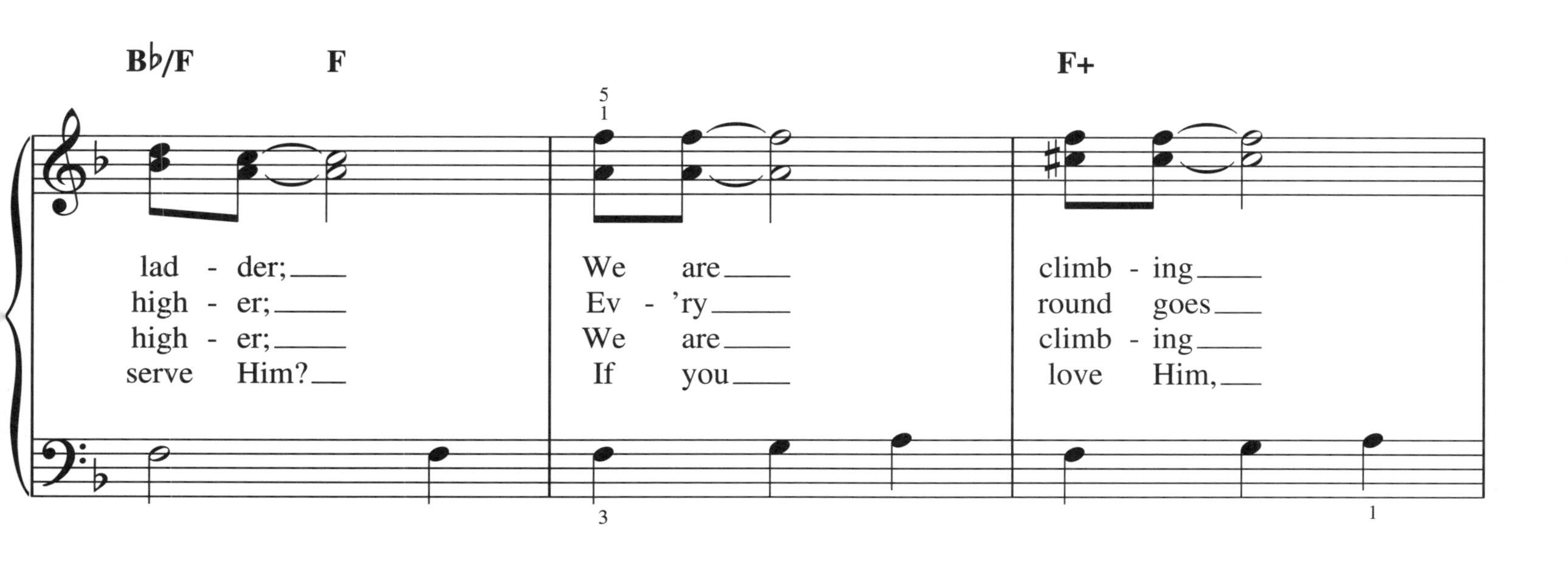
B♭/F
F
F+
lad - der;
high - er;
high - er;
serve Him?
We are
Ev - 'ry
We are
If you
climb - ing
round goes
climb - ing
love Him,

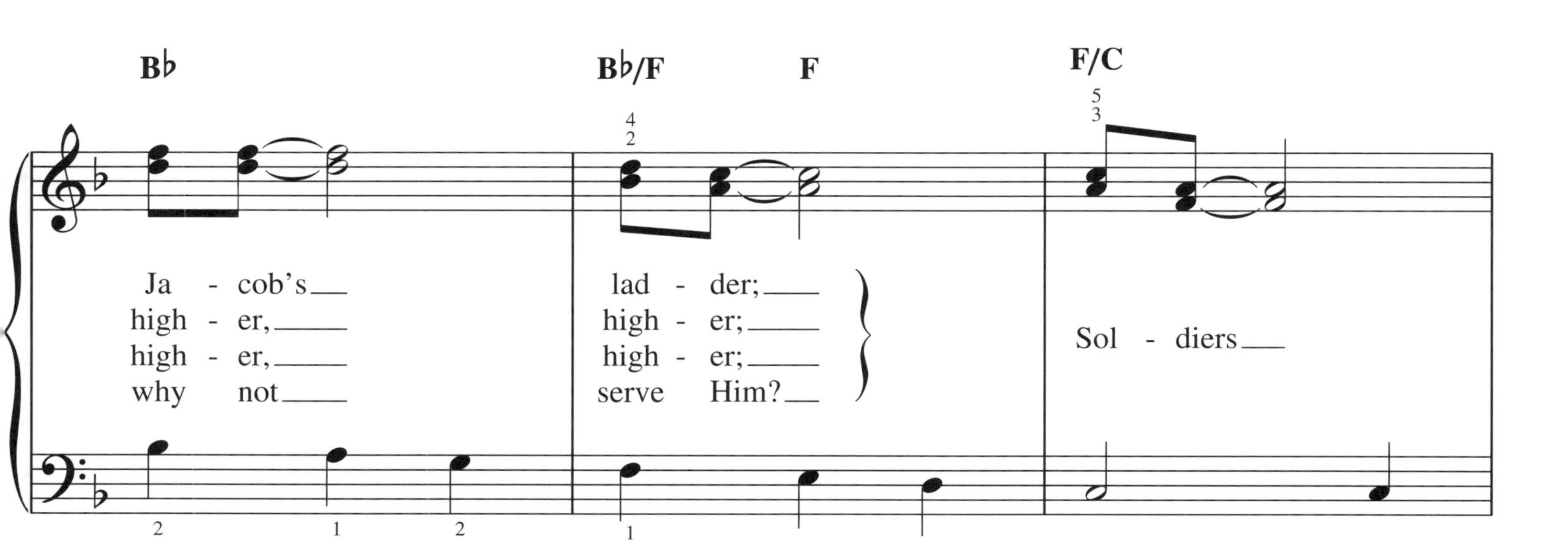
B♭
B♭/F
F
F/C
Ja - cob's
high - er,
high - er,
why not
lad - der;
high - er;
high - er;
serve Him?
Sol - diers

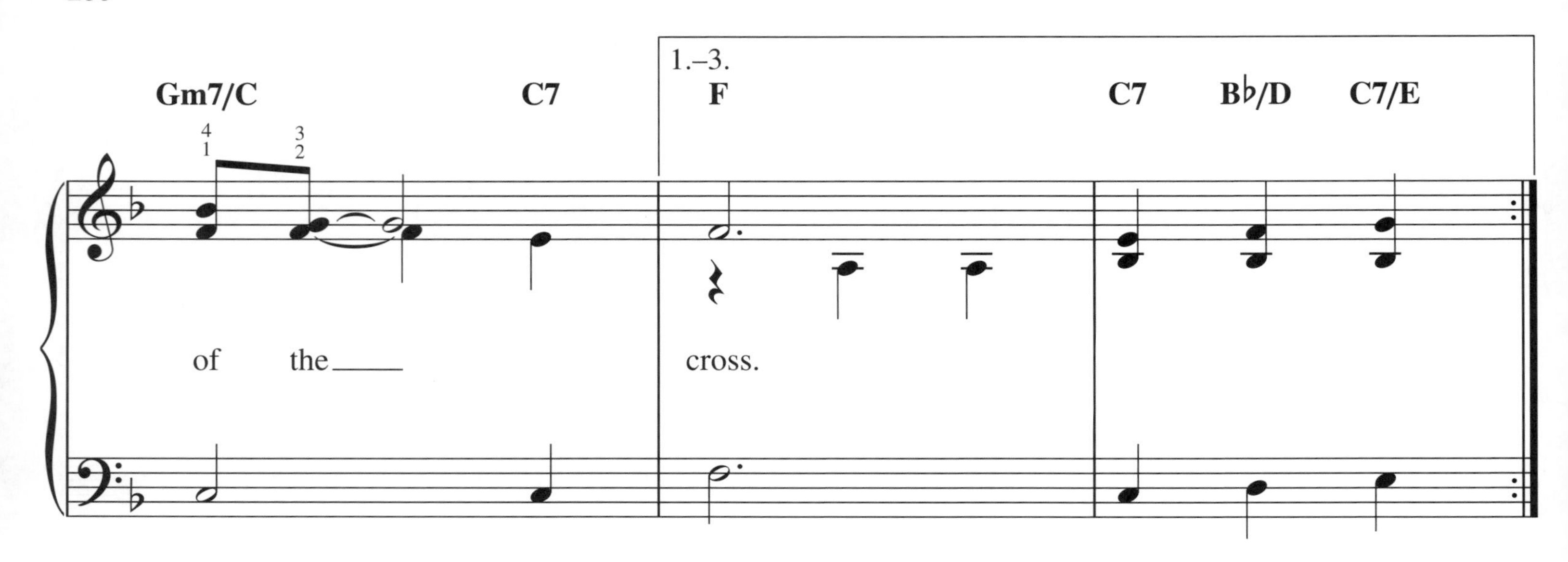
Gm7/C
C7
1.–3.
F
C7
B♭/D
C7/E
of the
cross.

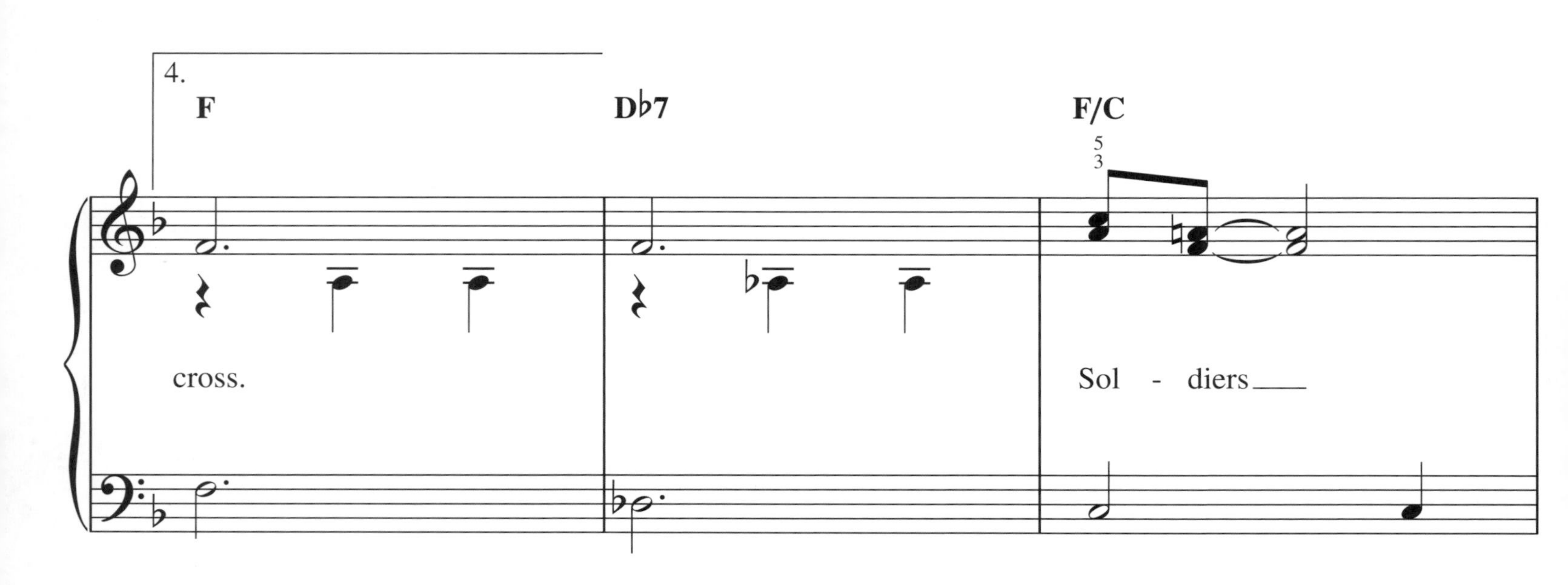
4.
F
D♭7
F/C
cross.
Sol - diers

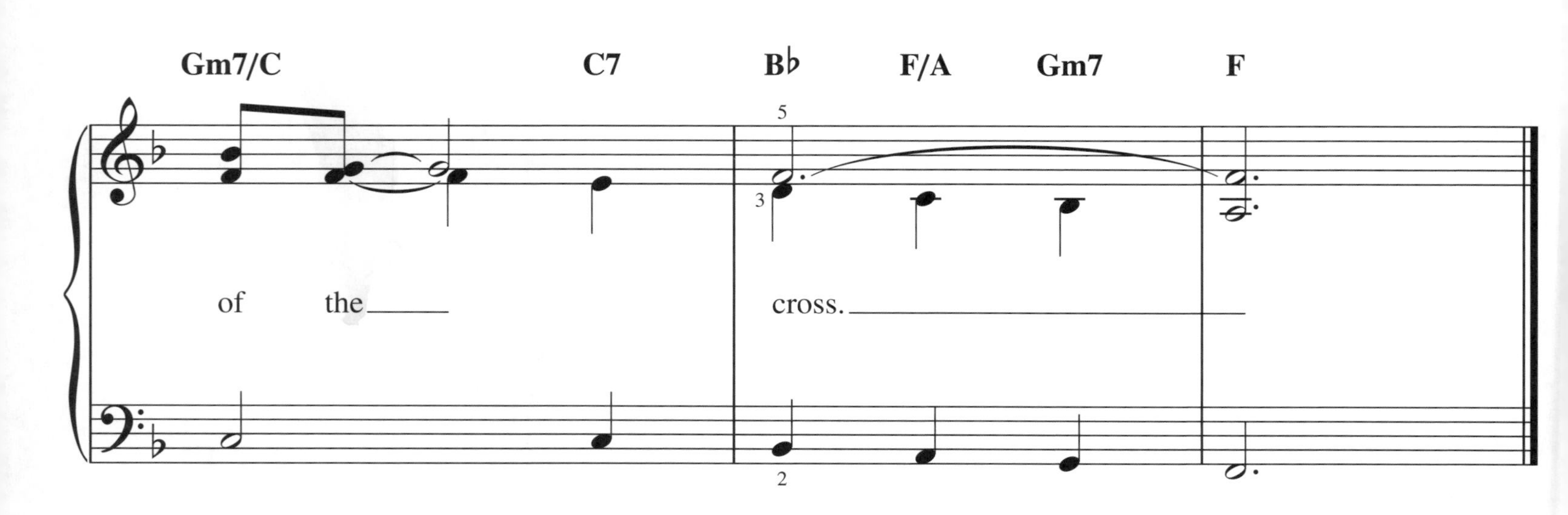
Gm7/C
C7
B♭
F/A
Gm7
F
of the
cross.

WE GATHER TOGETHER

Words from *Nederlandtsch Gedenckclanck*
Translated by THEODORE BAKER
Netherlands Folk Melody
Arranged by EDWARD KREMSER

WE PLOW THE FIELDS AND SCATTER

Words by MATTHIAS CLAUDIUS
Translated by JANE M. CAMPBELL
Music by JOHANN A.P. SCHULTZ

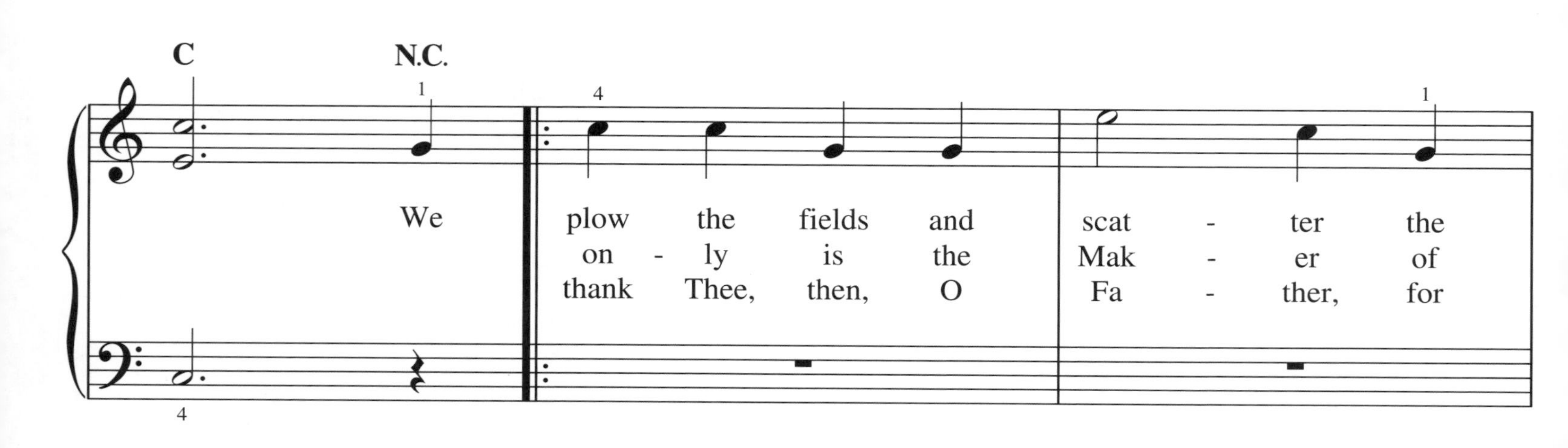

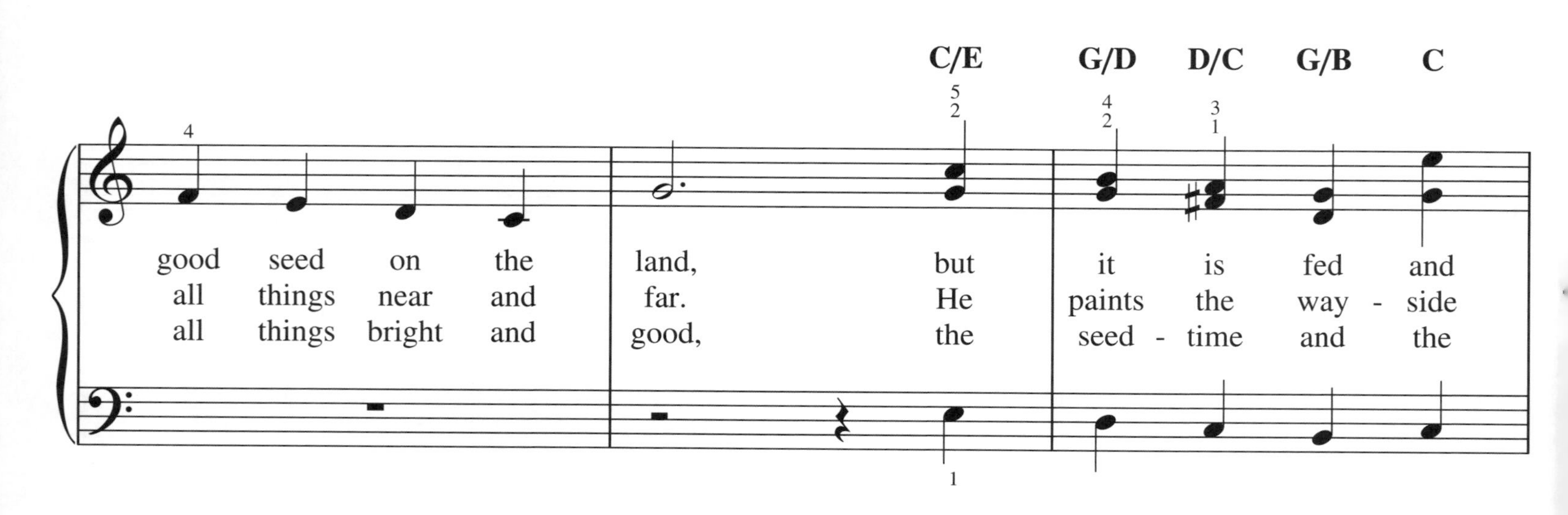

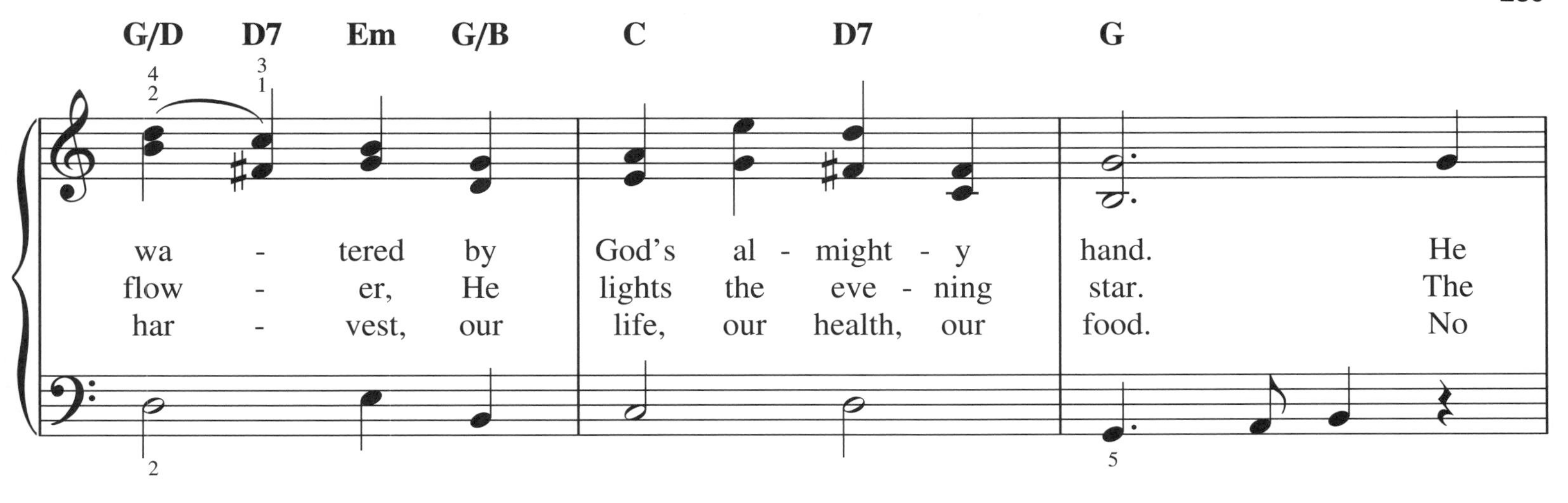
G/D D7 Em G/B C D7 G
wa - tered by God's al - might - y hand. He
flow - er, He lights the eve - ning star. The
har - vest, our life, our health, our food. No

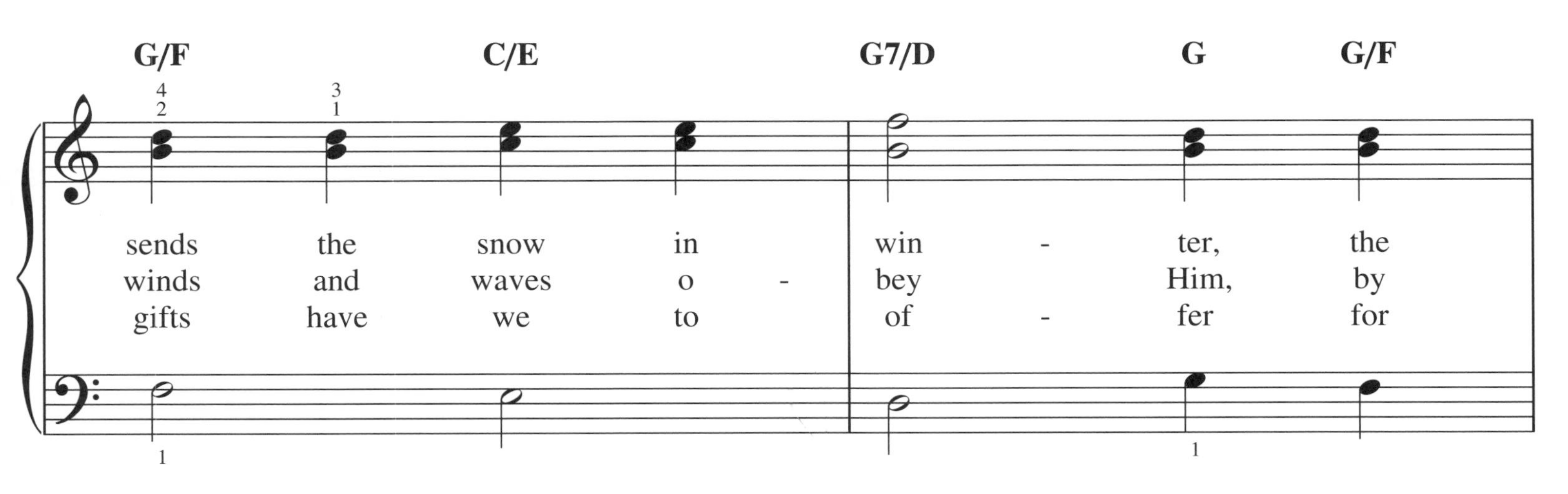
G/F C/E G7/D G G/F
sends the snow in win - ter, the
winds and waves o - bey Him, by
gifts have we to of - fer for

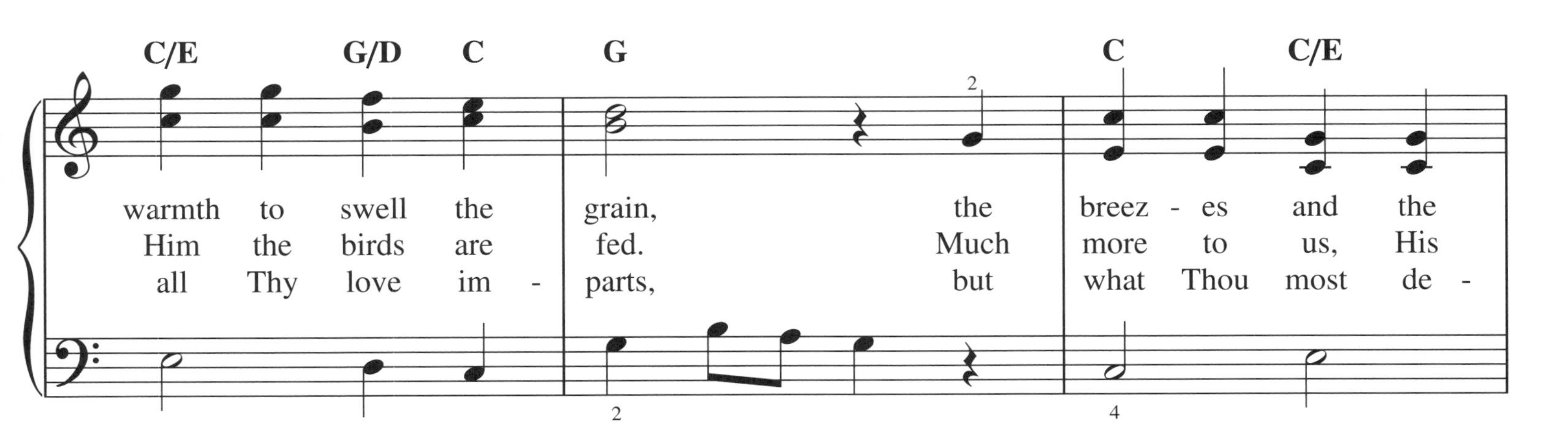
C/E G/D C G C C/E
warmth to swell the grain, the breez - es and the
Him the birds are fed. Much more to us, His
all Thy love im - parts, but what Thou most de -

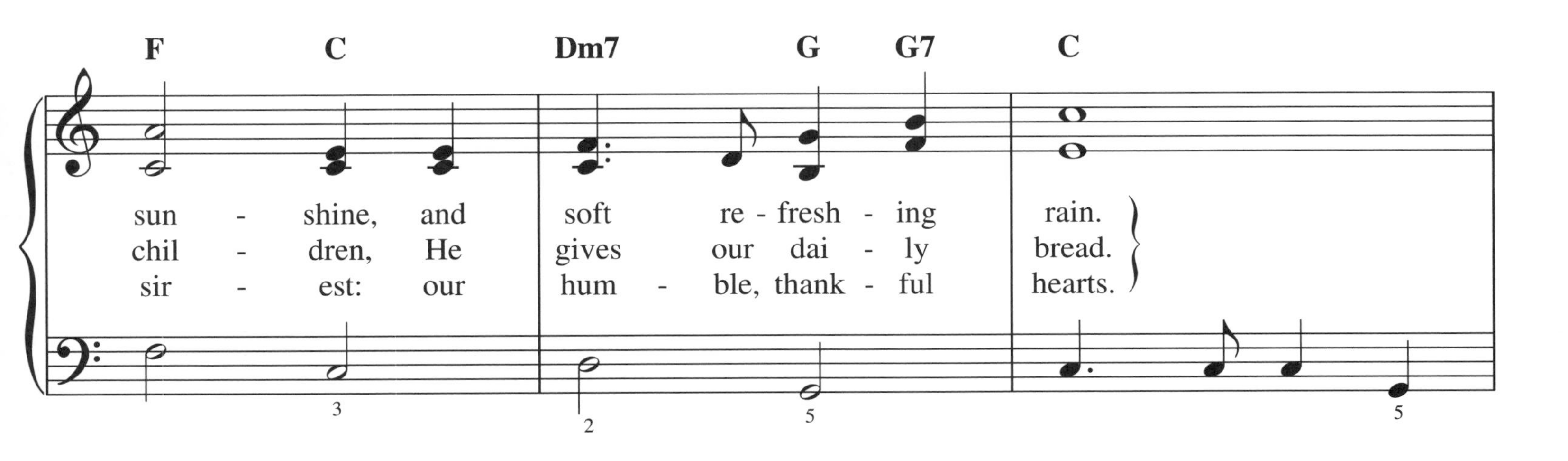
F C Dm7 G G7 C
sun - shine, and soft re - fresh - ing rain.
chil - dren, He gives our dai - ly bread.
sir - est: our hum - ble, thank - ful hearts.

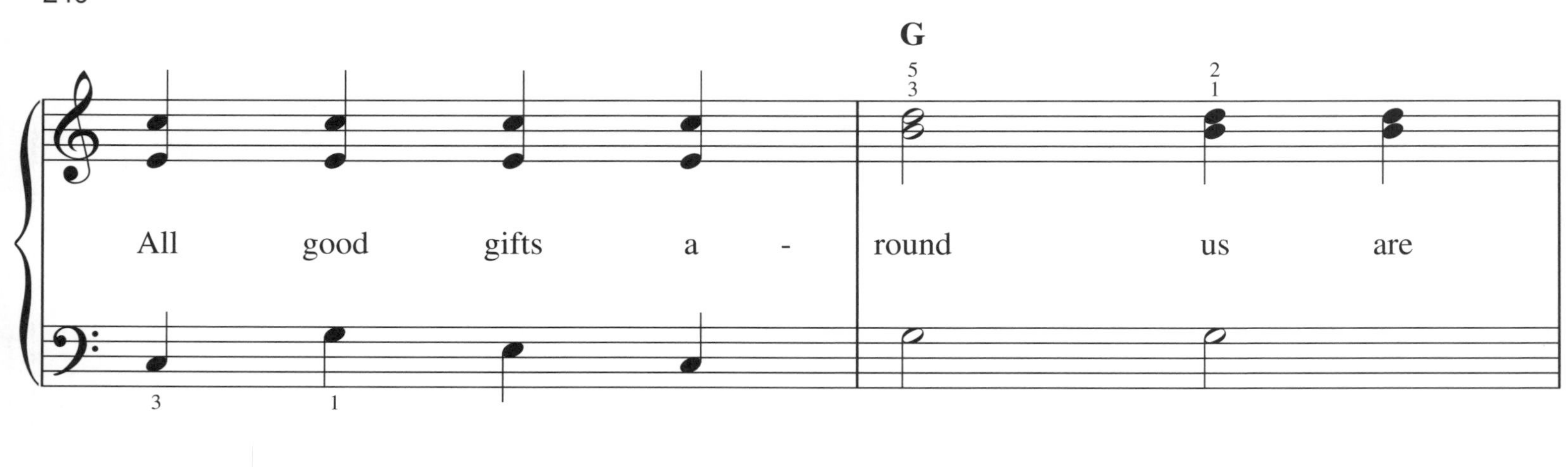
G
5
3
2
1
All good gifts a - round us are
3
1

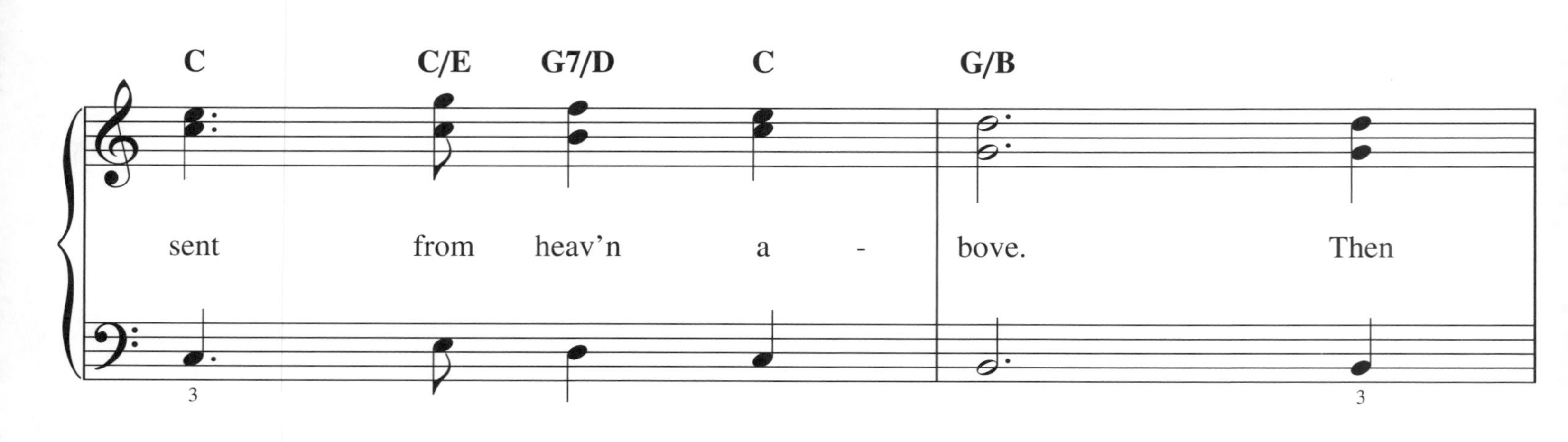
C C/E G7/D C G/B
sent from heav'n a - bove. Then
3
3

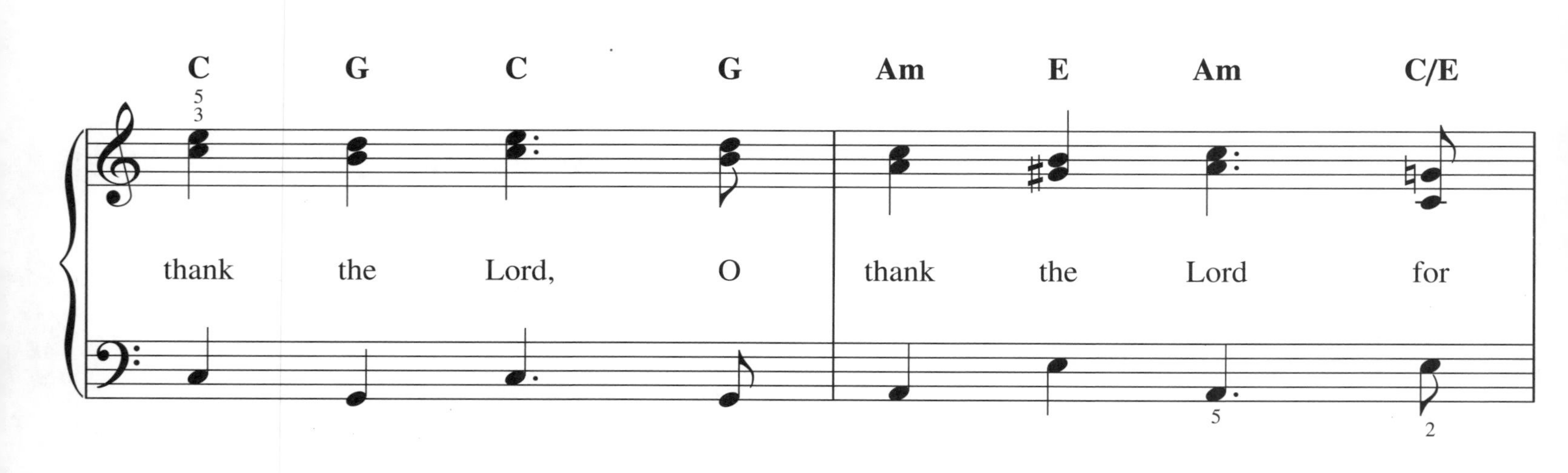
C G C G Am E Am C/E
5
3
thank the Lord, O thank the Lord for
5
2

1., 2.
3.
F Dm C/G G C N.C. C
all His love. He
We
love.
1

WHEN I SURVEY THE WONDROUS CROSS

Words by ISAAC WATTS
Music arranged by LOWELL MASON
Based on Plainsong

WE WOULD SEE JESUS

Words by ANNA B. WARNER
Music by FRANKLIN E. BELDEN

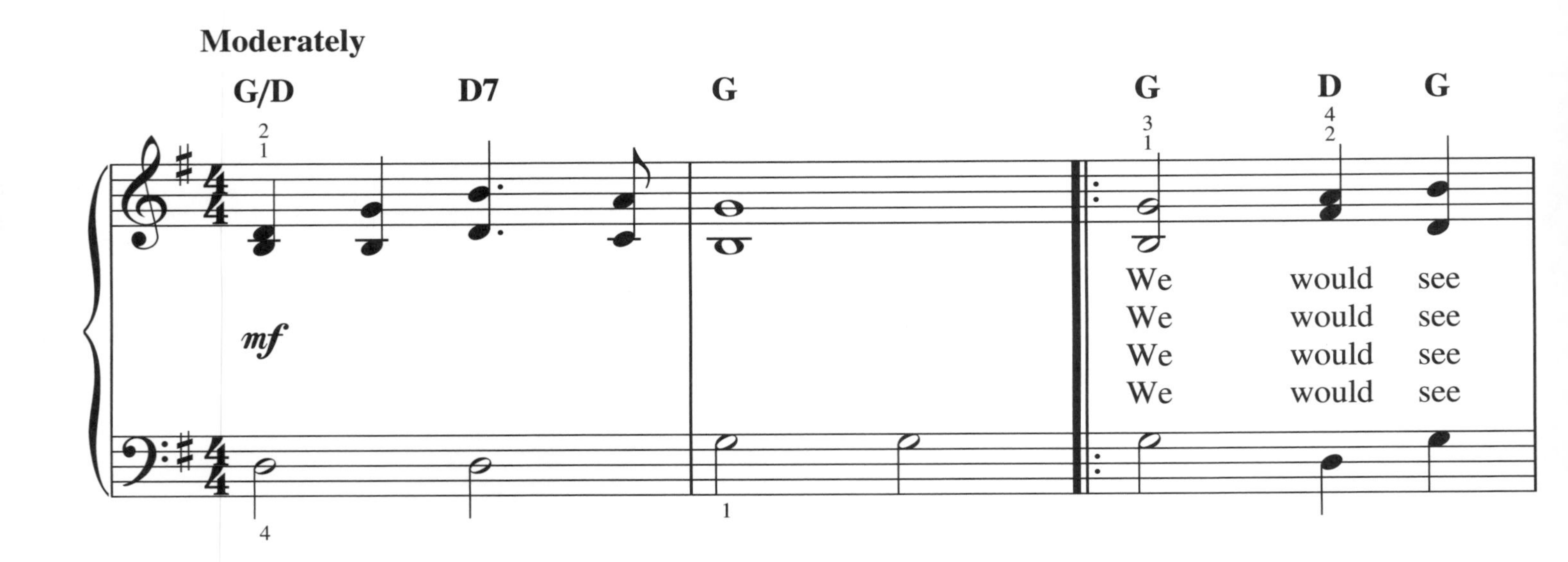

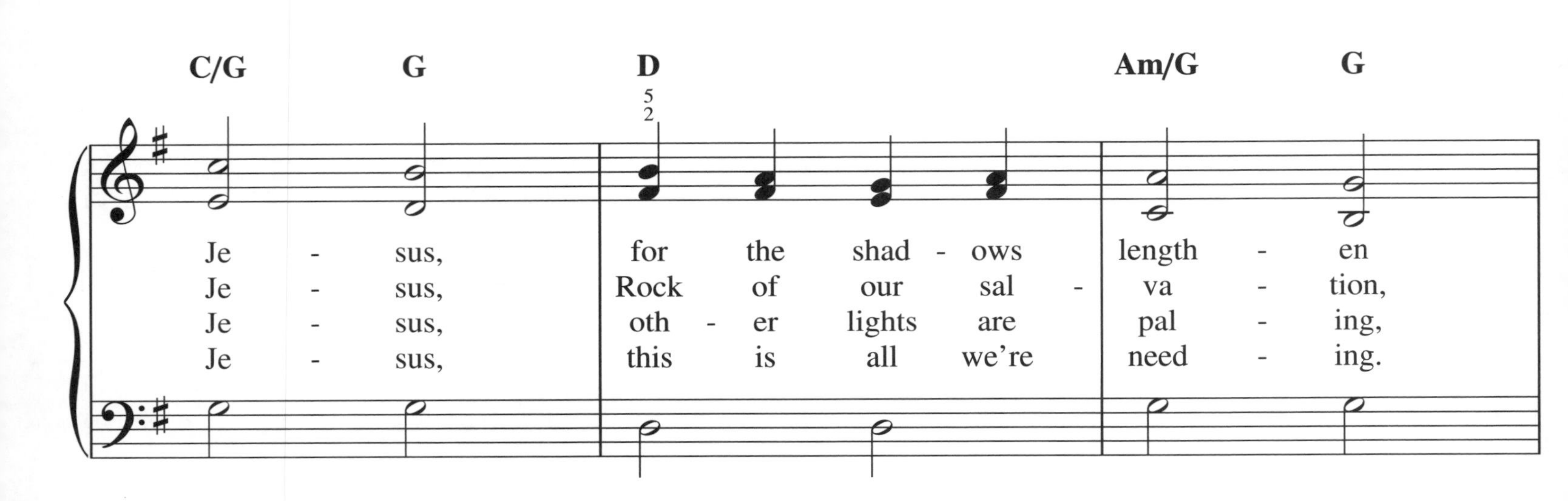

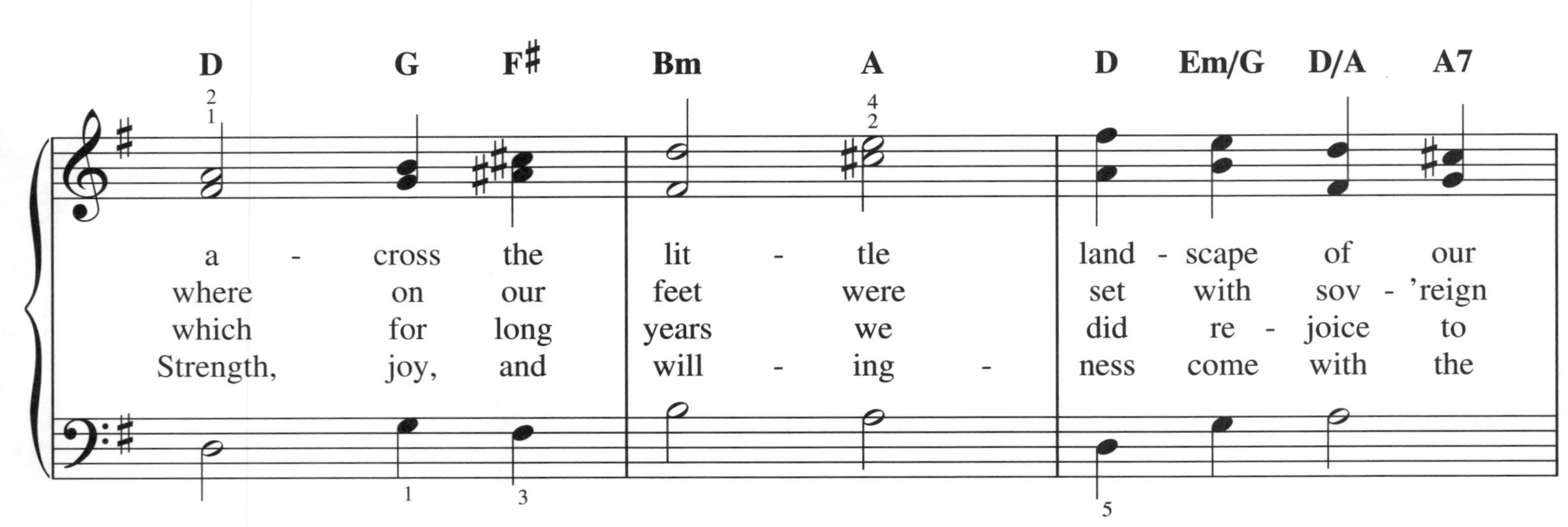

D
G/D
D7
life.
grace.
see.
sight.
We would see Je - sus,
Not life, nor death, with
The bless - ings of this
We would see Je - sus,
G
our weak faith to strength - en,
all their ag - i - ta - tion,
sin - ful world are fail - ing;
dy - ing, ris - en, plead - ing,
Em
G7/D
C
for the last con - flict
can thence re - move us,
we would not mourn them
soon to re - turn and
G/D
D7
1.–3.
G
4.
G
in this mor - tal strife.
gaz - ing on His face.
in ex - change for Thee.
end this mor - tal night!

WERE YOU THERE?

Traditional Spiritual

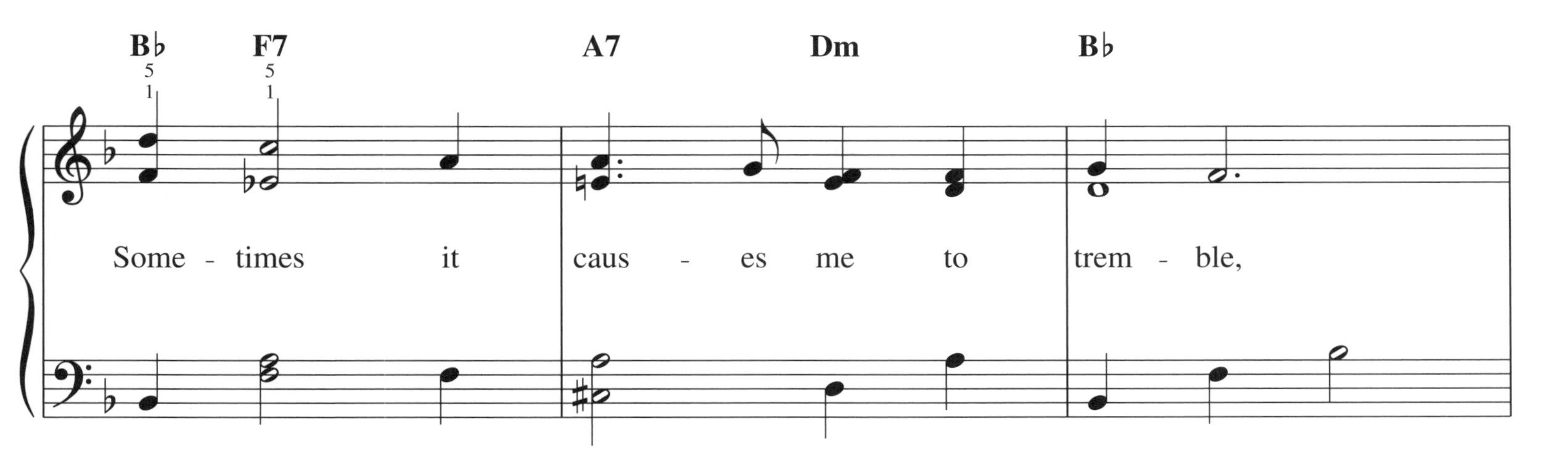

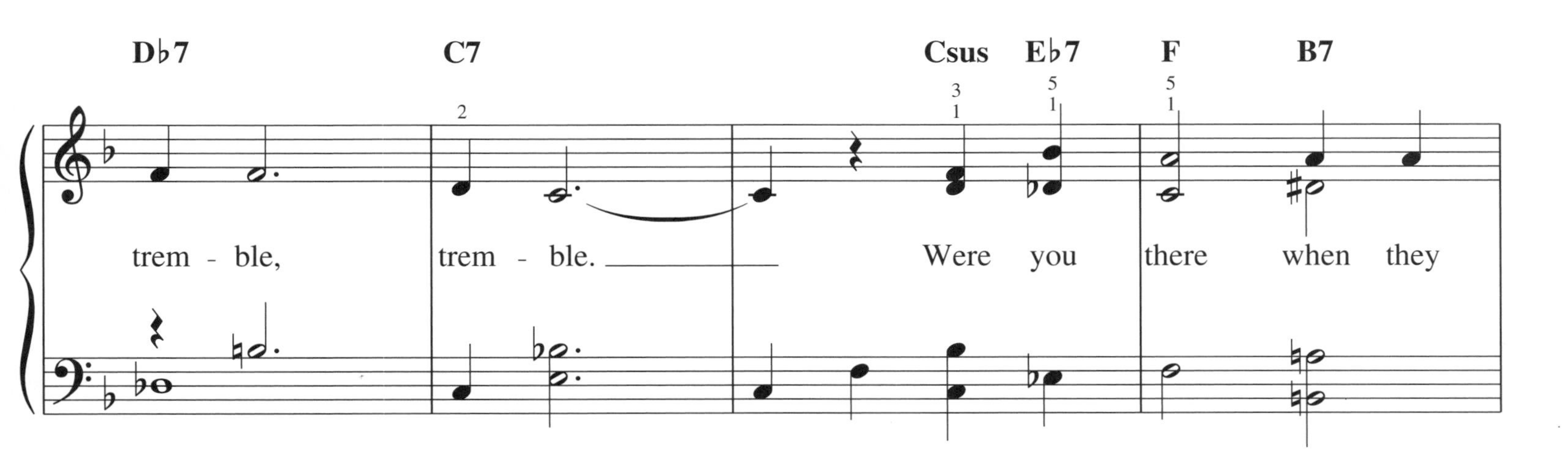

Additional Verses

2. Were you there when they nailed Him to the tree?
   Were you there when they nailed Him to the tree?
   Oh! Sometimes it causes me to tremble, tremble, tremble.
   Were you there when they nailed Him to the tree?

3. Were you there when they laid Him in the tomb?
   Were you there when they laid Him in the tomb?
   Oh! Sometimes it causes me to tremble, tremble, tremble.
   Were you there when they laid Him in the tomb?

WHAT A FRIEND WE HAVE IN JESUS

Words by JOSEPH M. SCRIVEN
Music by CHARLES C. CONVERSE

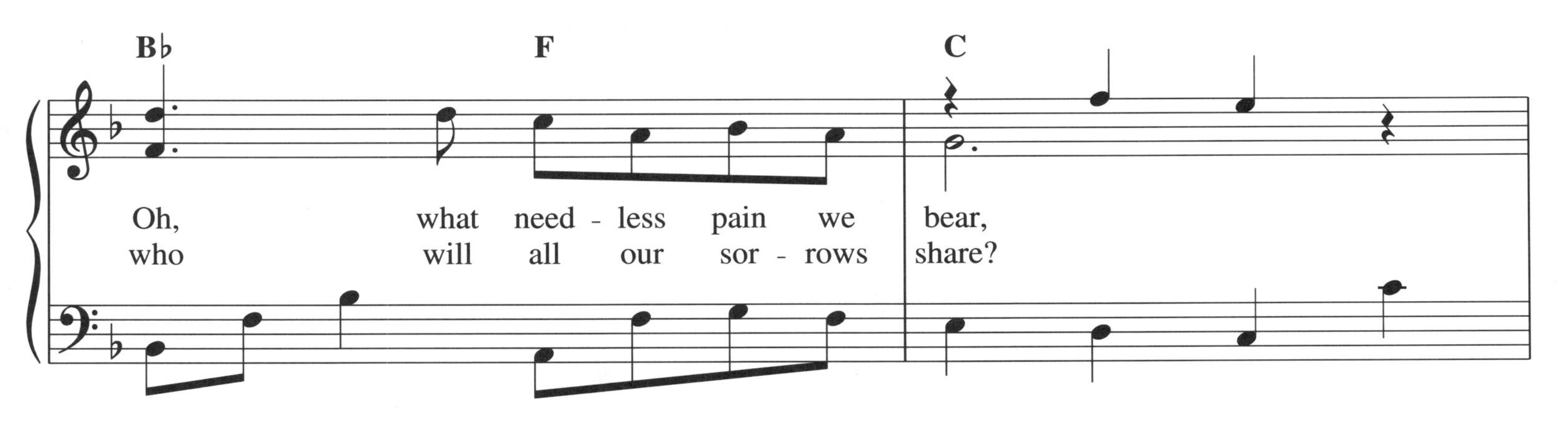

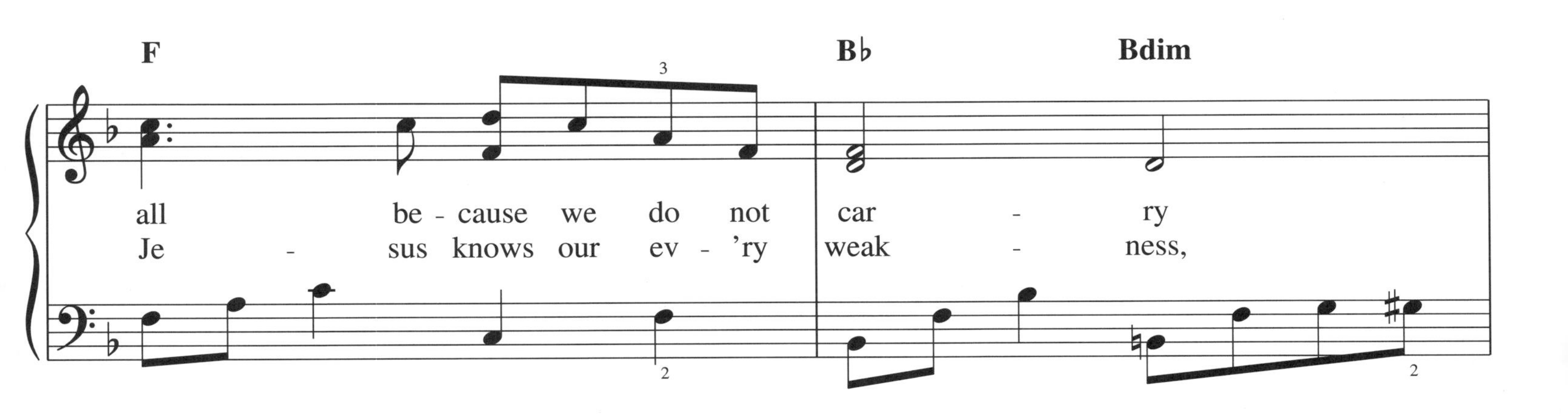

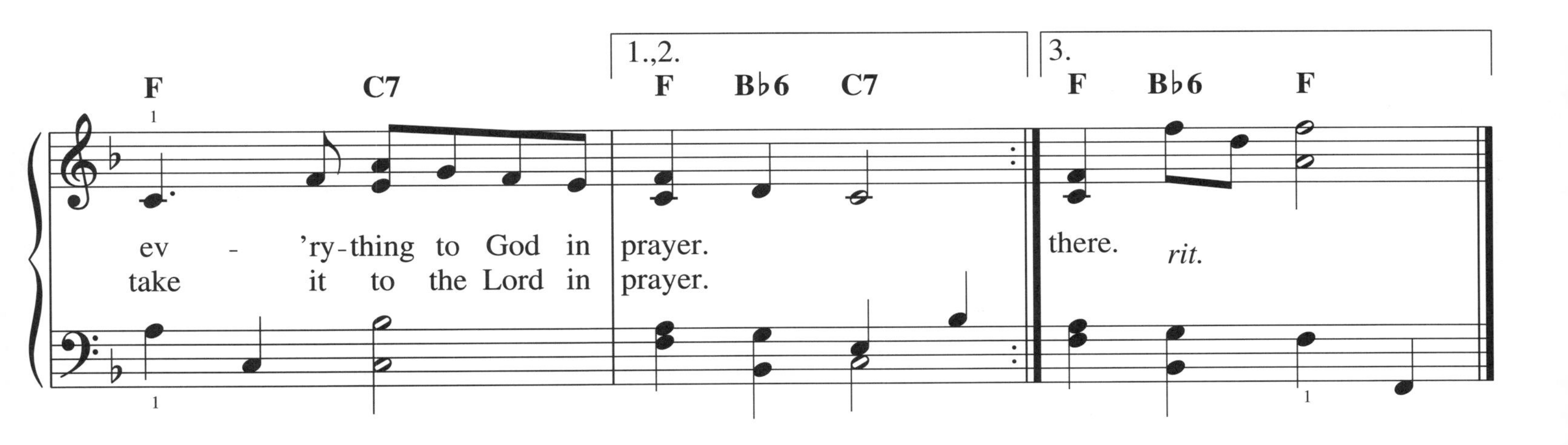

Additional Verse

3. Are we weak and heavy-laden,
   Cumbered with a load of care?
   Precious Savior, still our refuge:
   Take it to the Lord in prayer.
   Do thy friends despise, forsake thee?
   Take it to the Lord in prayer:
   In His arms He'll take and shield thee,
   Thou wilt find a solace there.

WHEN I CAN READ MY TITLE CLEAR

Words by ISAAC WATTS
Traditional American Melody
attributed to JOSEPH C. LOWRY

Moderately

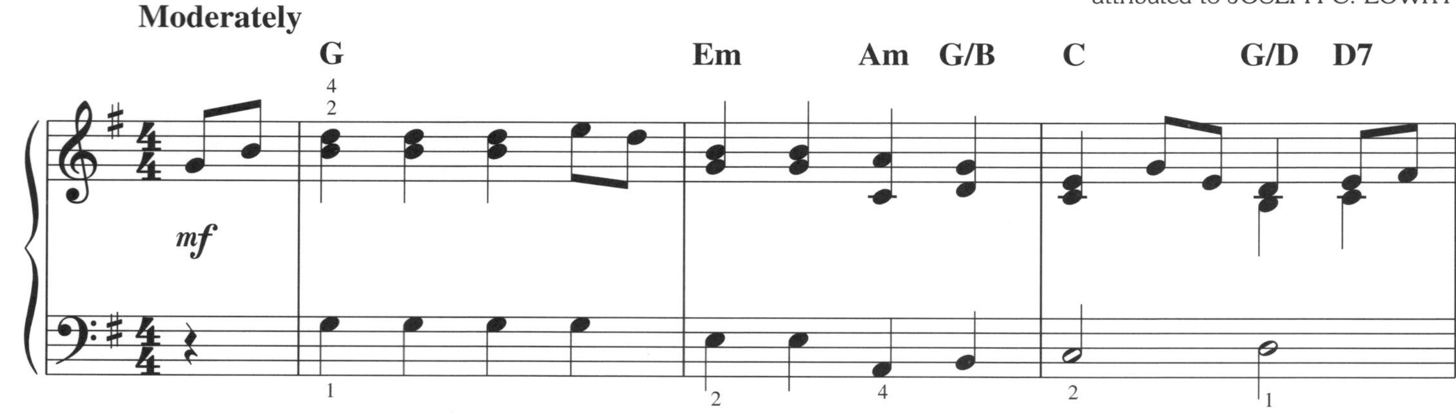

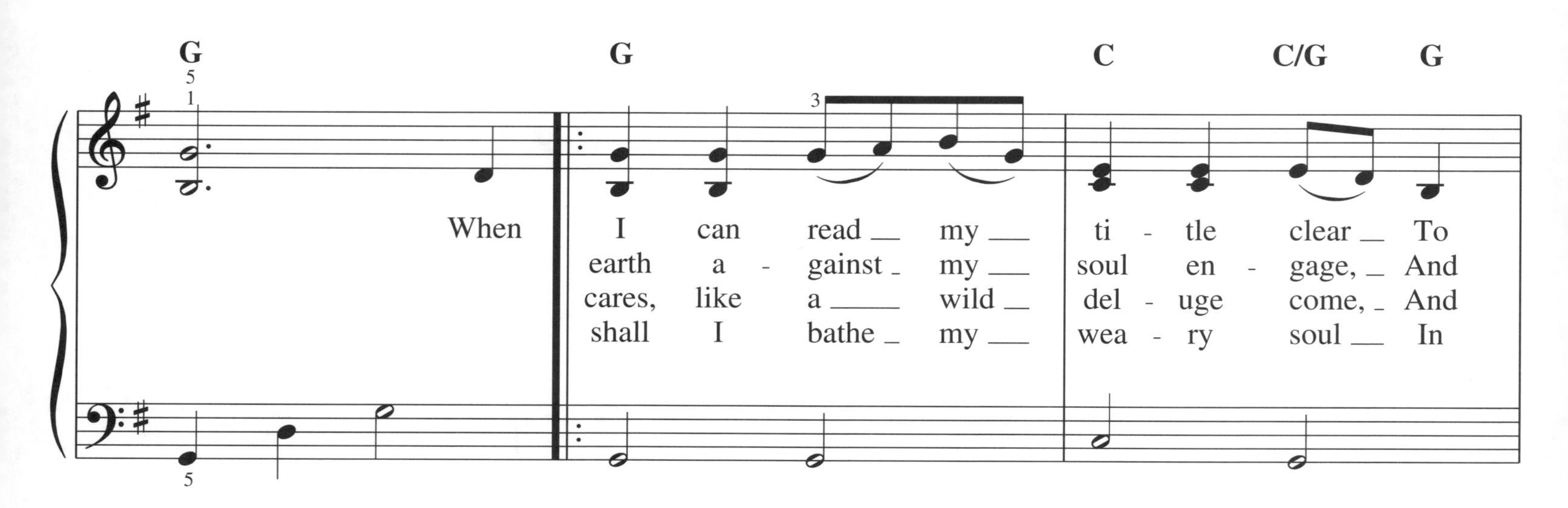

Em Am G/B C G/D D7 G
ev - 'ry fear, And wipe my weep - ing eyes; And
Sa - tan's rage, And face a frown - ing world; And
reach my home, My God, my heav'n, my all; My
trou - ble roll A - cross my peace - ful breast; A -
C C/G
wipe my weep - ing eyes, And wipe my weep - ing
face a frown - ing world, And face a frown - ing
God, my heav'n, my all, My God, my heav'n, my
cross my peace - ful breast, A - cross my peace - ful
G/D D G Em Am G/B
eyes, I'll bid fare - well to ev - 'ry fear, And
world, Then I can smile at Sa - tan's rage, And
all, May I but safe - ly reach my home, My
breast, And not a wave of trou - ble roll A -
1.-3. 4.
C G/D D7 G C G/B Am7 G
wipe my weep - ing eyes. Should
face a frown - ing world. Let
God, my heav'n, my all. There
cross my peace - ful breast.

WHEN MORNING GILDS THE SKIES

Words from *Katholisches Gesangbuch*
Translated by EDWARD CASWALL
Music by JOSEPH BARNBY

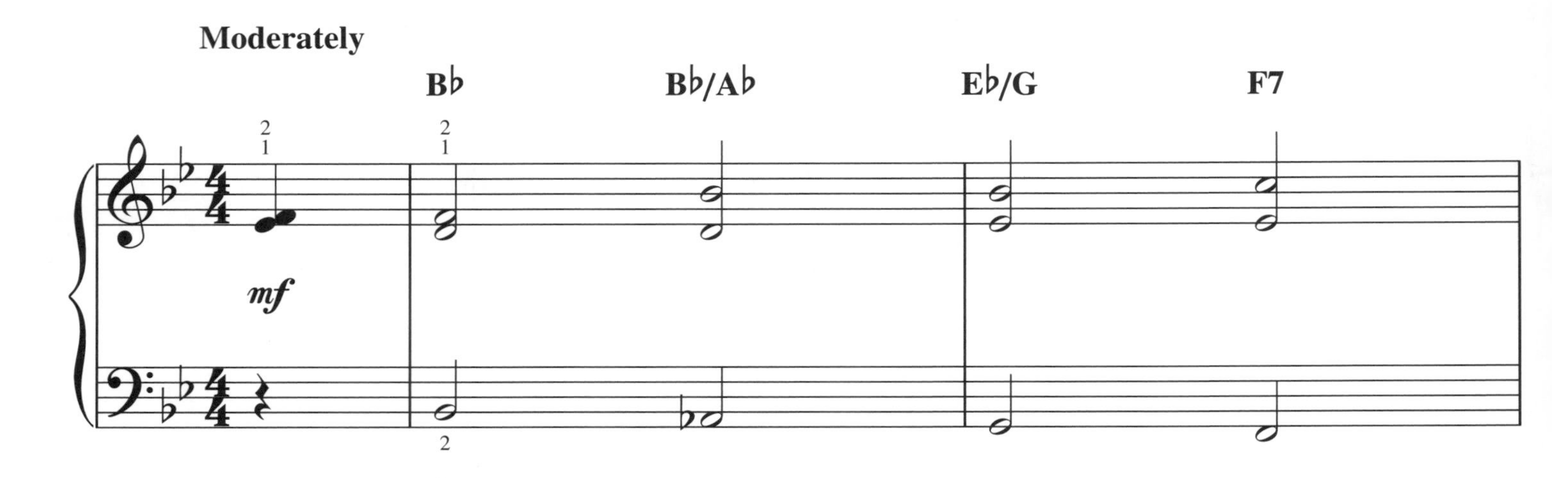

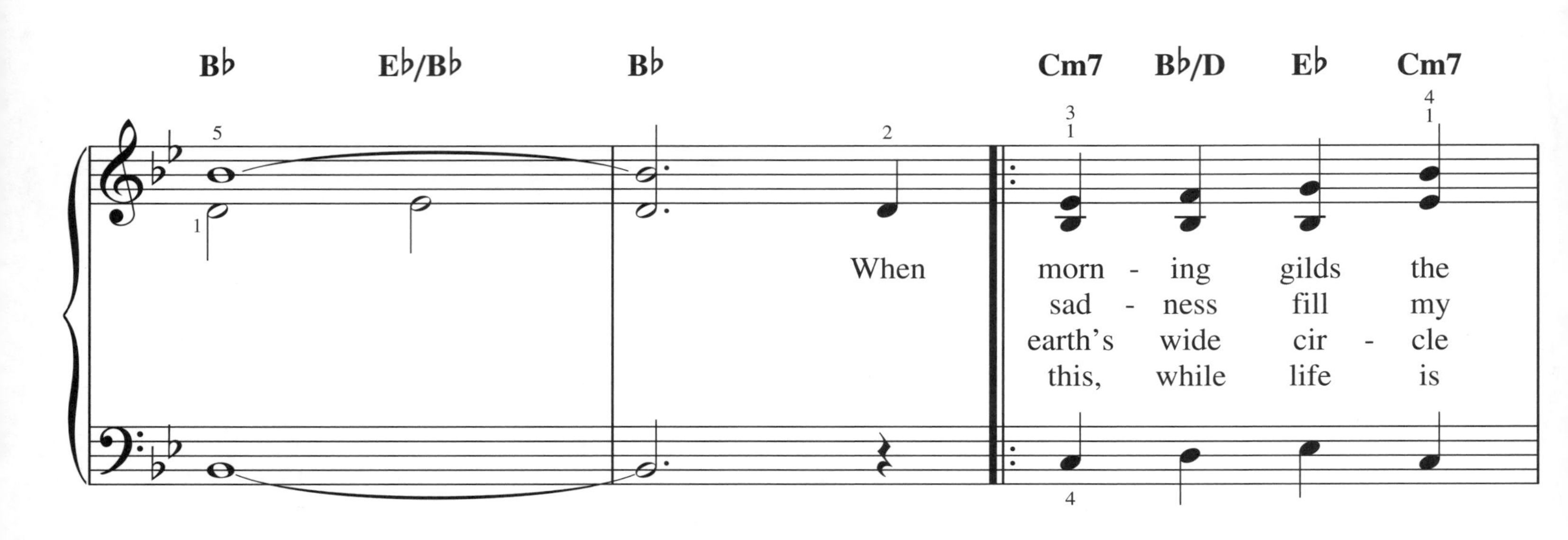

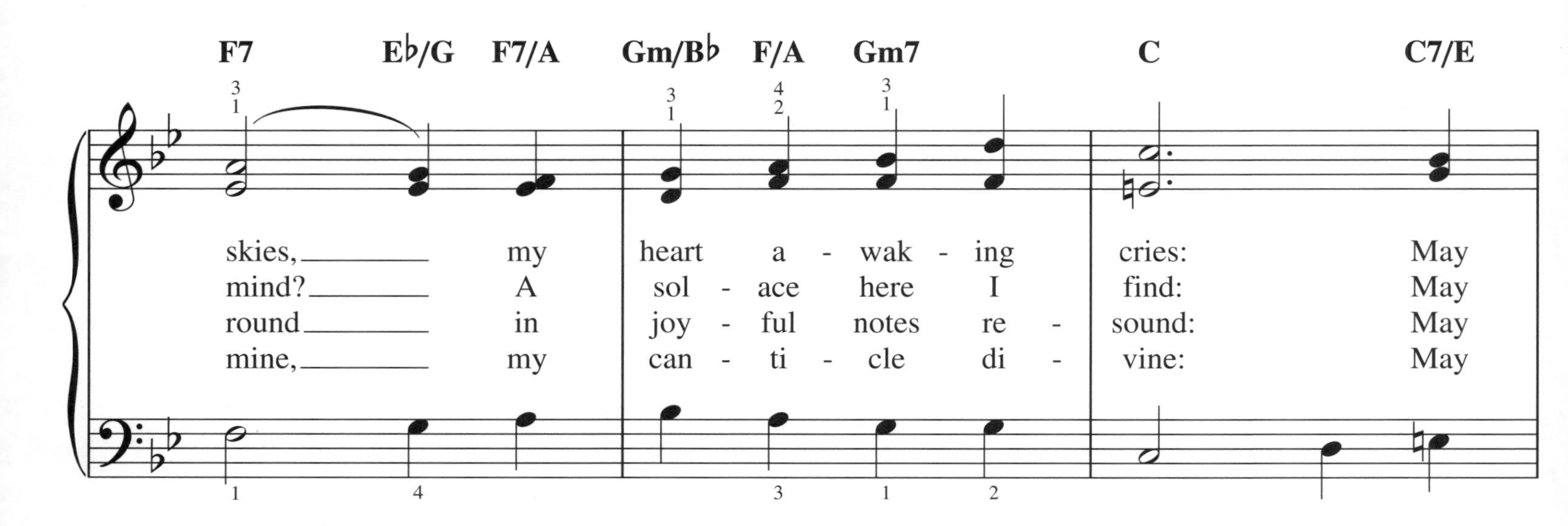

F Bb C7 F F/Eb Bb/D F7/C Eb/Bb
Je - sus Christ be praised! A - like at work and
Je - sus Christ be praised! Or fades my earth - ly
Je - sus Christ be praised! Let air and sea and
Je - sus Christ be praised! Be this th'e - ter - nal
F7 F/Eb Bb/D Am/C C7 F F7/C
prayer, to Je - sus I re - pair: May
bliss? My com - fort still is this: May
sky from depth to height re - ply: May
song through all the ag - es long: May
Bb Bb/Ab Eb/G F7 1.–3. Bb Eb/Bb
Je - sus Christ be praised!
Je - sus Christ be praised!
Je - sus Christ be praised!
Je - sus Christ be
Bb
Does
Let
Be
4. Bb Eb/Bb Bb
praised!

WORK, FOR THE NIGHT IS COMING

Words by ANNIE L. COGHILL
Music by LOWELL MASON

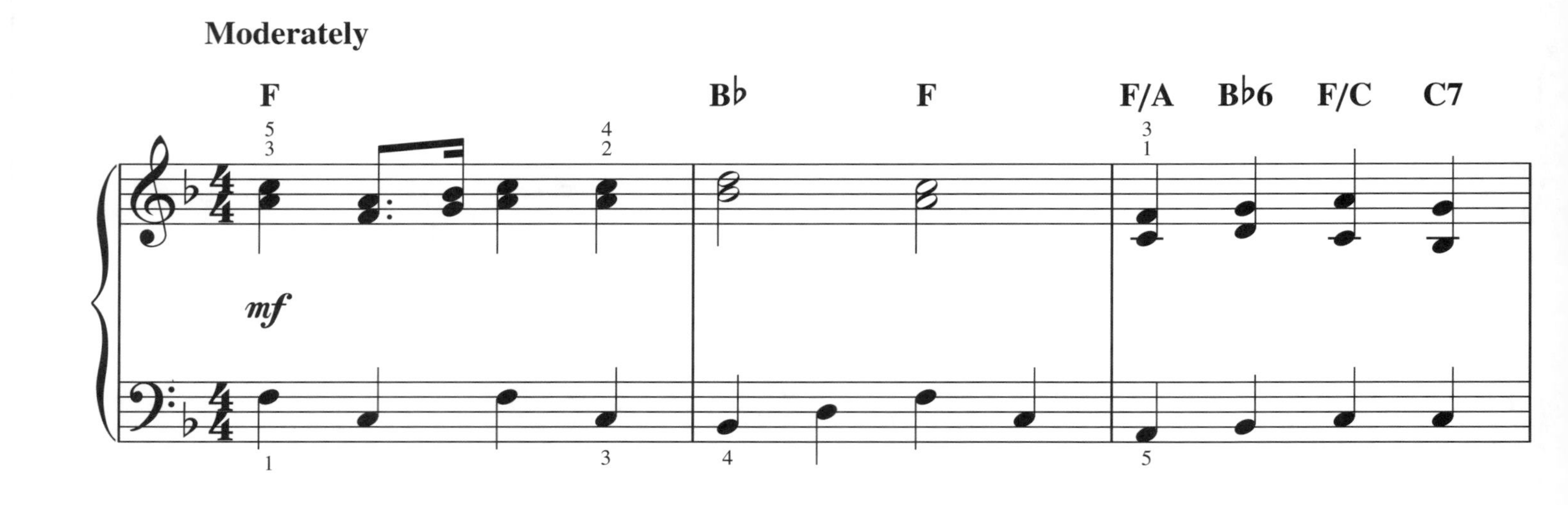

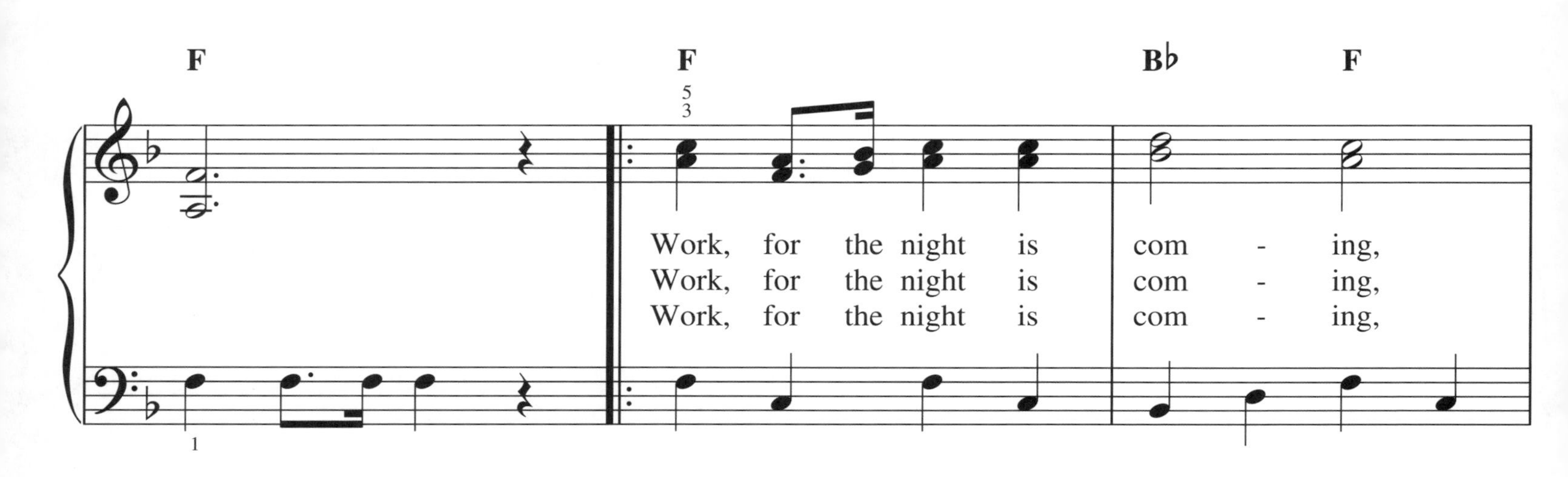

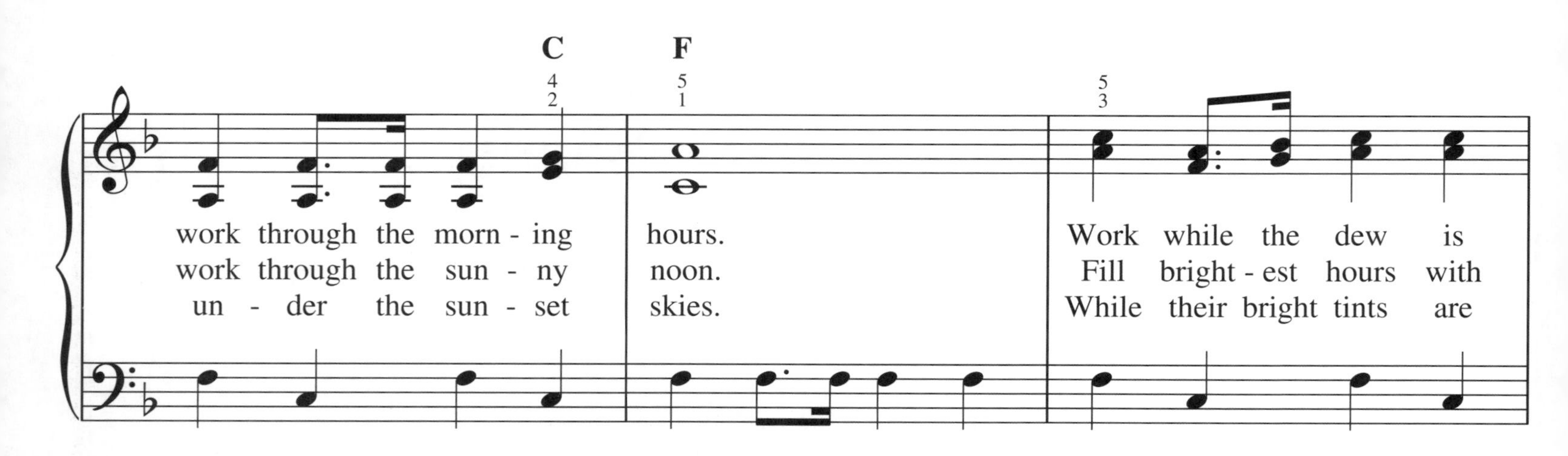

B♭ F F/A B♭6 F/C C7 F
4
spar - kling, work 'mid spring - ing flowers.
la - bor; rest comes sure and soon.
glow - ing, work, for day - light flies.
C F G7
2
1
3
1
Work when the day grows bright - er, work in the glow - ing
Give ev - 'ry fly - ing min - ute some - thing to keep in
Work till the last beam fad - eth, fad - eth to shine no
2
1
C F B♭ F
4
2
sun. Work, for the night is com - ing,
store. Work, for the night is com - ing,
more. Work while the night is dark - 'ning,
F/A B♭6 F/C C7
1., 2.
F
3.
F
when man's work is done.
when man works no more.
when man's work is o'er.

WONDROUS LOVE

Southern American Folk Hymn

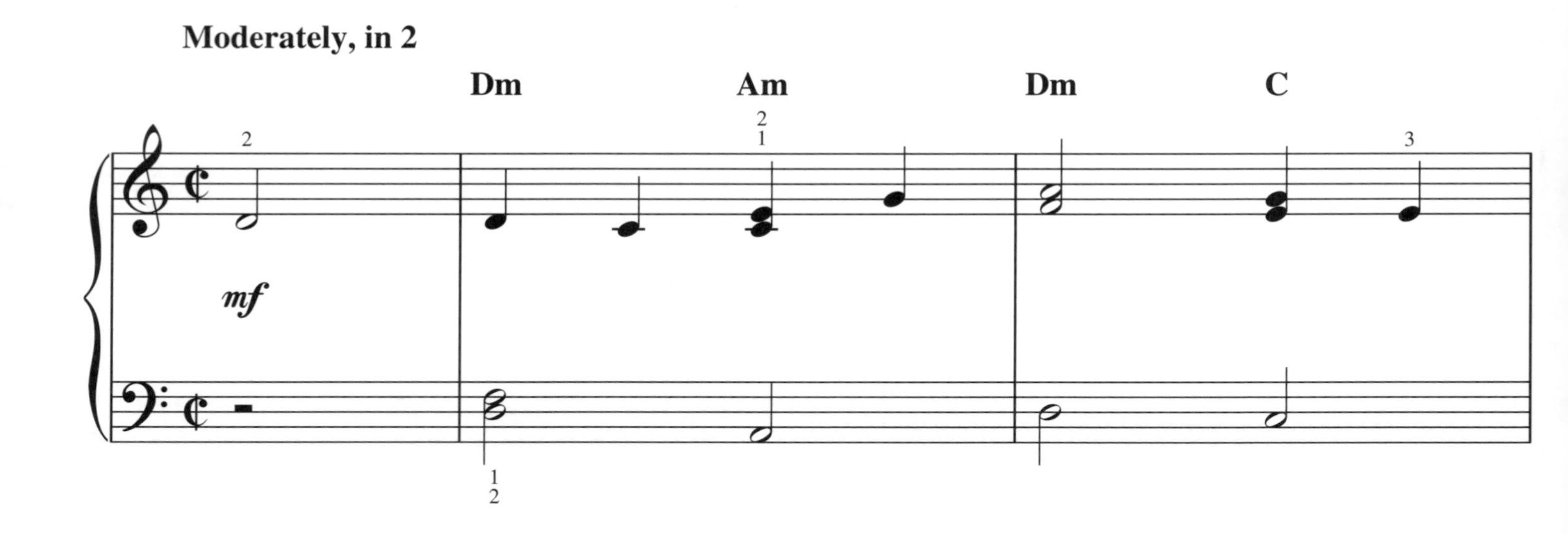

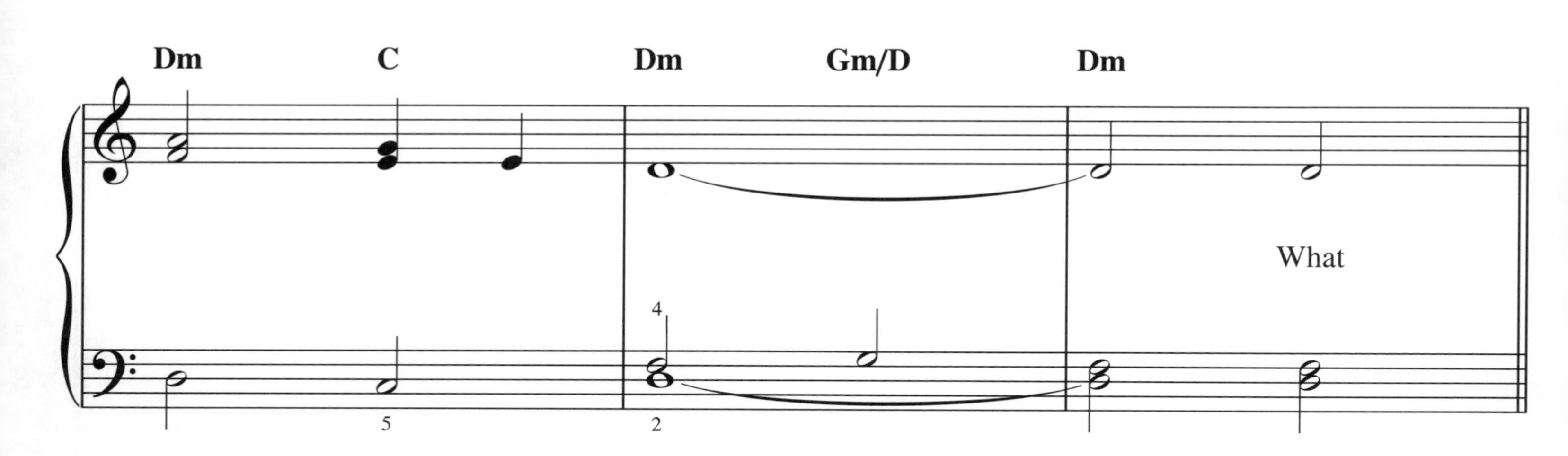

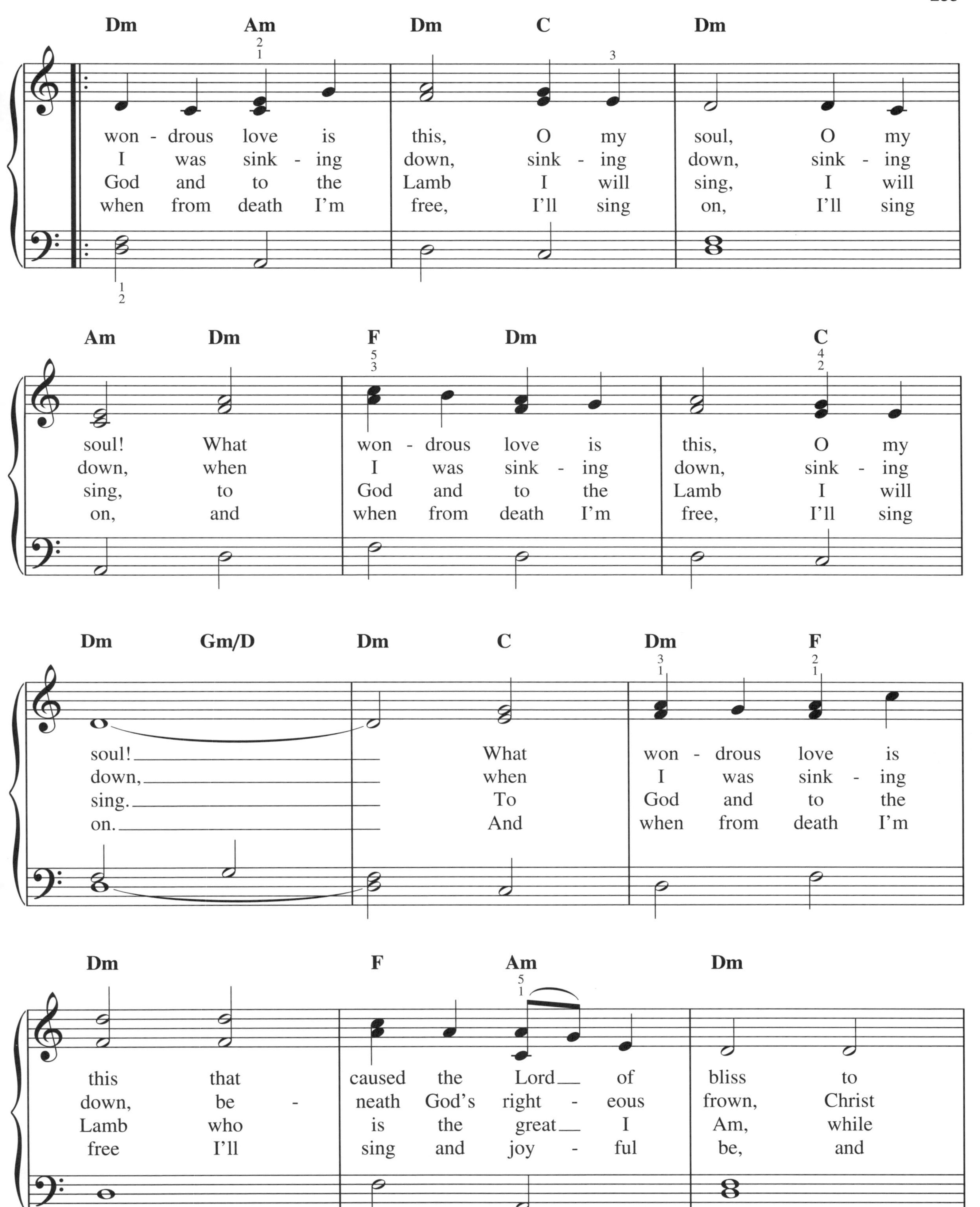
Dm Am Dm C Dm
won - drous love is this, O my soul, O my
I was sink - ing down, sink - ing down, sink - ing
God and to the Lamb I will sing, I will
when from death I'm free, I'll sing on, I'll sing
Am Dm F Dm C
soul! What won - drous love is this, O my
down, when I was sink - ing down, sink - ing
sing, to God and to the Lamb I will
on, and when from death I'm free, I'll sing
Dm Gm/D Dm C Dm F
soul! What won - drous love is
down, when I was sink - ing
sing. To God and to the
on. And when from death I'm
Dm F Am Dm
this that caused the Lord of bliss to
down, be - neath God's right - eous frown, Christ
Lamb who is the great I Am, while
free I'll sing and joy - ful be, and

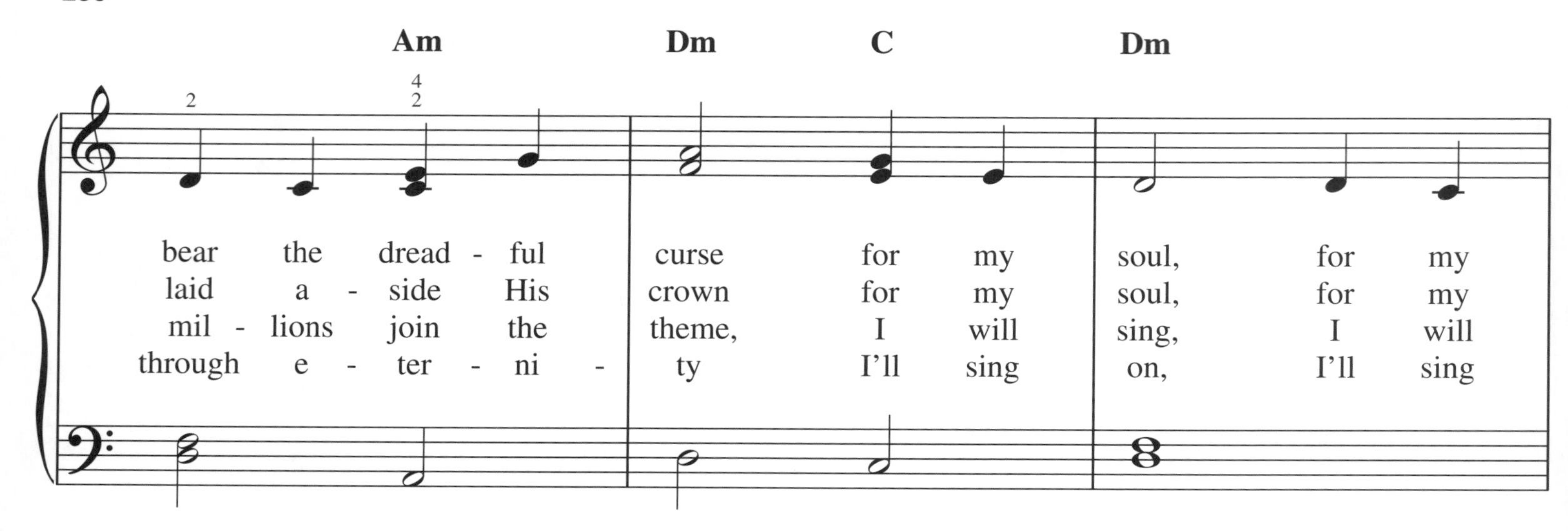
Am
Dm
C
Dm
bear the dread - ful curse for my soul, for my
laid a - side His crown for my soul, for my
mil - lions join the theme, I will sing, I will
through e - ter - ni - ty I'll sing on, I'll sing

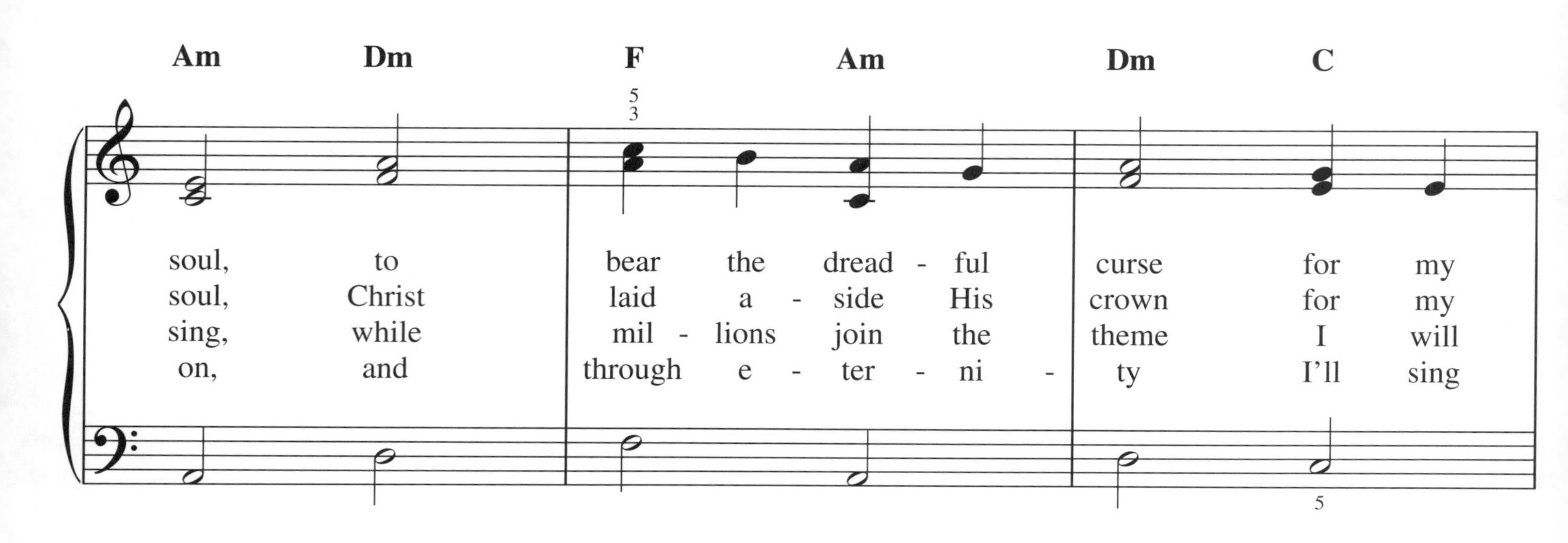
Am
Dm
F
Am
Dm
C
soul, to bear the dread - ful curse for my
soul, Christ laid a - side His crown for my
sing, while mil - lions join the theme I will
on, and through e - ter - ni - ty I'll sing

1.–3.
4.
Dm
Gm/D
Dm
Dm
Gm/D
Dm
soul. When
soul. To
sing. And
on.